Genre, Gen~~re~~ and World Cinema

19

Genre, Gender, Race, and World Cinema

Edited by Julie F. Codell

Blackwell
Publishing

Editorial material and organization © 2007 by Julie F. Codell

BLACKWELL PUBLISHING
350 Main Street, Malden, MA 02148-5020, USA
9600 Garsington Road, Oxford OX4 2DQ, UK
550 Swanston Street, Carlton, Victoria 3053, Australia

The right of Julie F. Codell to be identified as the Author of the Editorial
Material in this Work has been asserted in accordance with the UK Copyright,
Designs, and Patents Act 1988.

First published 2007 by Blackwell Publishing Ltd

1   2007

Library of Congress Cataloging-in-Publication Data

Genre, gender, race, and world cinema / edited by Julie F. Codell.
      p. cm.
   Includes bibliographical references and index.
   ISBN-13: 978-1-4051-3232-9 (hardcover : alk. paper)
   ISBN-10: 1-4051-3232-9 (hardcover : alk. paper)
   ISBN-13: 978-1-4051-3233-6 (pbk. : alk. paper)
   ISBN-10: 1-4051-3233-7 (pbk. : alk. paper)
   1. Motion pictures—Social aspects.   2. Identity (Psychology) in
motion pictures.   I. Codell, Julie F.

PN1995.9.S6G39 2007
792.02'8—dc22
                                                                  2006014907

A catalogue record for this title is available from the British Library.

Set in 10/13pt Galliard
by Graphicraft Limited, Hong Kong
Printed and bound in Singapore
by Markano Print Media Pte Ltd

The publisher's policy is to use permanent paper from mills that operate
a sustainable forestry policy, and which has been manufactured from pulp
processed using acid-free and elementary chlorine-free practices. Furthermore,
the publisher ensures that the text paper and cover board used have met
acceptable environmental accreditation standards.

For further information on
Blackwell Publishing, visit our website:
www.blackwellpublishing.com

Contents

Preface

This volume is intended for students who have had at least one introductory film course. The book's general introduction, which helps bridge the introductory level and upper division or specialized courses, describes the four topics of genre, gender, race and world cinema and their overarching themes of identities, audience reception, and the cultural and social contents of film. Contributing further to this intermediary stage, the introductions to each section: (a) map themes and histories related to each of the four topics; (b) raise theoretical issues specific to each topic to introduce theory to students; and (c) cite many relevant films to offer filmographies for this course level and for students' subsequent film studies. These filmographies permit instructors to augment the films discussed in the readings and add or substitute films appropriate to their students' backgrounds and needs from those cited in section introductions.

The selected readings: (a) focus on films readily available for class viewing; (b) introduce topical concepts; and (c) create intertextual relations among readings and films, when, for example, a topic or film is the subject of several selected readings. In creating these relations, this book hopes to make comprehensible the complex nature of identities in film. Audiences and filmmakers project, create and imagine identities out of many constituents that are learned, unstable and defined by society (race, gender, class, nation, region, age and ethnicity). Most people deploy multiple identities to fit different situations. Films play a major role in shaping, interpreting and mirroring these not-always-compatible identities. Film genres are composed of narrative and visual conventions that are nonetheless always subject to revisions and modifications. In their familiarity and modifications, genres offer psychological, cultural and sociological models of identities for individuals, groups and entire societies.

These are complicated topics whose intersections are even more complicated. The book's introductions, readings and film selections are intended to facilitate understanding of these intersections and ways of discussing them in the classroom. Each section builds on earlier sections; gender, race and national identity are not mutually exclusive or discrete topics. Many parallel issues cut across all four topics: if a "hero" in a Western is female or of color, instead of the conventional white male hero, or when the Western is viewed in Asian or African countries, the genre is markedly transformed and re-interpreted, opening up avenues for investigating genres and cultural identities together. In this way, the book hopes to expand students' understanding of films in relation to larger concepts – how social changes and cultural relations modify genres, how films help viewers imagine *and* experience their own and others' identities, how representation is greater than simply the sum of narrative and images, and how theory opens up questions rather than resolving them neatly. The book's intentions are to help students expand formal analyses, presumably the bulk of their introductory course(s), into analyses of interrelations among the four interlocking topics and toward a cultural studies approach.

All books mentioned in the introductions are listed in the bibliographies. References to films in the introductions include dates and references to books include page numbers. Most of the readings are reprinted in their entirety, but a few are abbreviated, marked by ellipses for short omitted sections and brackets for longer omitted sections. All texts appear in their original punctuation, spelling, and style.

General Introduction: Film and Identities

There are numerous anthologies of essays on film, and many intended for classroom use. Some contain "classical" essays by theorists (e.g. André Bazin, Christian Metz, Laura Mulvey). Others address specific genres, or films from a particular historical period or country, or special topics like masculinity or Orientalism. And there are several anthologies intended for introductory undergraduate courses on film.

This reader offers a different approach to ease students into sophisticated analyses of films through contemporary issues. It is intended to serve the curriculum level between introductory courses on film history and upper division courses that incorporate film theory. This anthology focuses on four topics connected to the overarching topic of identity – genre, gender, race, and world cinema. These topics introduce theory in an "embodied" way, through issues that are palpable to students. The topic of identity embraces other topics of audience reception, stereotyping in film, technical practices, production, consumption, and critical theory. Identity is also an accessible and appealing topic for undergraduates as they move toward upper level or graduate courses. These four topics are also *practices*, and as practices they offer critiques of classical film theories and Eurocentric film histories, which often constitute the body of material in many introductory courses.

This book's purpose makes it useful not only to students majoring in film, but also to students whose primary disciplines include literature, history, art history, race, ethnic and gender studies, and cultural studies. The selected essays provide flexibility for classroom viewing of many films available throughout the world. Organized thematically, rather than historically or geographically, this reader aims to encourage class discussion through several kinds of essays – some of which can be applied to a variety of recent films, and some of which provide exemplary analyses of particular films to encourage students to engage in a critical discourse at an early stage of their education. Students can begin to understand not only how to read films (representation) but also how to explore them in larger cultural contexts that address reception issues (historical events, critical public reception, political and social circumstances, world cultures, etc.). Too often students have difficulty shaping research and topical papers, having had little experience of studying in depth. This book is intended to explore a few topics in greater depth than offered by a survey-type text used for introductory courses.

Readings introduce various critical theories, including post-structuralism, cultural studies, postcolonial critiques, theories of identity and society, and psychoanalytic analysis, and are drawn from a combination of single-authored books, anthologies, and journals. Readings were chosen to expand film studies into wider cultural terrains and contexts of history, politics, economics, and social conditions. These critical streams dislodge "naturalized" assumptions about culture, identity, and the "other." Films suggested for study in this volume include films directed by women and people of color and from many countries.

Although these four areas of genre, gender, race, and world cinema are not new, in the past 20 years each of these topics has been radically changed in meaning and function (genre, gender) or has emerged as a major focus (race, world cinema). Genre, for example, once considered easily identifiable and fixed, has become problematized by new or mixed genres (e.g. the "racial family" film), radical transformations of conventional genres (Westerns used and parodied in many countries), and the trans-genre of independent films and non-Hollywood/non-Eurocentric films. Gender, once defined by feminists, has been transformed by studies of masculinity and queer theory. Filmmakers, as well as audiences, now come from worldwide identities of gender, race, geography, nationality, ethnicity, and class, with overlapping identities (e.g. Black women, diasporic ethnic communities) that are often conflicted for individuals and for social groups. While Third Cinema is rooted in 1960s political radicalism among Latin American filmmakers, its definition and categorization have significantly changed with the critical mass of Asian, African, and indigenous films now made, produced, available, and accumulated over the past 20 years, making "world cinema" a more appropriate and inclusive phrase.

These four areas share a focus and reflection on identity. Identities' once-presumed biological "naturalness" has given way under post-structuralist analyses that have recognized identities as transient, political, social, and historical, subject to cultural changes and historical circumstances, and not natural or transcendent in any way. Identities of nations, ethnicities, genders, and races can no longer be definitively categorized or classified as monolithic. Identities are bricolaged, shifting, fashioned to fit social norms, self-fashioned, performative, contradictory, and inconsistent, and in every presumed category there is a range of identities, some of which contradict others – not all people in a nation or ethnic or racial group think alike or agree on social or cultural issues, for example. For this reason, some essays in this volume address overlapping topics: for example, the gendering of male melodrama crosses and disturbs the genre of melodrama, usually associated with an appeal to a female audience. Furthermore, globalization has created its own set of issues, as film has become a site of contention between global transnational or transcultural content, and the persistent authority of local cultures with their range of identities and intended audiences.

The reception of film is a crucial element of what constitutes film as a culture industry, and it is an issue that binds the four topics of this anthology. Essays in this anthology explore film's power to reflect, shape, and disturb audiences' assumptions through innovative voices and dialogues from new populations now making films. Topics of reception and identity have gained prominence, and even urgency, partly from an inverted global distribution – no longer simply the distribution of American/Hollywood and European films to the rest of the world, but the spread of non-Eurocentric films into the USA and Europe from Asia, Africa, and Latin America, and films produced by indigenous peoples not primarily identified with any nation state. A global culture has emerged everywhere due to diasporic mobility and to the mobility of virtual culture to every corner of the globe.

Distribution embraces technological changes, especially digitalization, as well as changing venues for viewing films (e.g. on computers or TV at home through video or DVD, rather than in theaters). Seeing a movie at home does not connect us to the larger social community with whom we could share a film in a theater, resonating and connecting our responses to those of others beyond our immediate family or friends. On the other hand, home viewing may increase our intimacy with a film, permit us to see a film again and again, and alter our film viewing behaviors (we don't have to be so quiet at home and can interrupt or stop and pause our viewing periodically).

Finally, genre, the first topic, also becomes an overarching theme, as sections on gender, race, and world cinema demonstrate repeatedly that genres are never fixed categories but are always subject to changes, reinterpretations, and cultural variations and mutations. Genre is "a multivalent term multiply and variously valorized by diverse user groups" (Altman, 1999, p. 214), and these groups are the subjects of parts II, III, and IV of this book. This means that receptions, readings, and interpretations of any genre or film may include acceptance, revision, or resistance of a genre's formula and retrofit that formula into new historical, cultural, racial, and gendered ideals and needs.

Pedagogically, this volume is designed to treat these topics in such a way that instructors and students can choose from many relevant films for each section, within loose parameters, in order to provoke discussion. Essays in each section survey new approaches, criticisms and multiple views of the four topics. Some sections have two essays on a single film to help students broaden their notions of analysis and interpretation. Theoretical issues are embedded in the essays in order that theory can help to open up new problems and trouble their solutions, demonstrating to students an accessible and useful function of theory – to raise questions about filmic representation and to offer complex, unresolved, and even conflicting answers and interpretations. Suggested readings at the end of the book are designed not to be comprehensive, but to suggest additional approaches to the area and some historical background instructors may want students to examine. Films selected are largely from the 1990s to the present, but the main criterion for choice of essays is the importance of a recent film in relation to the topic. Finally, parts III and IV, on race and world cinema, respectively, have longer bibliographies than the first two parts, because the topics embrace a wider scope of possible examples whose complexity, and the differences among them, must be underscored. It is important to provide a sufficient number of essays to keep students from reducing differences to a monolithic "other" and to make students aware that people of color in America and Europe and people from countries outside the "West" are highly differentiated from one another as well as from the West and from whiteness, which cannot and must no longer be the presumed standards or criteria for analysis or measures of subjectivities.

I would like to thank my friend and colleague Dana Arnold who first suggested my putting this book together and whose suggestions in its early stages were very helpful and illuminating. My editor Jayne Fargnoli offered probing critiques and scintillating conversations about films. Ken Provencher of Blackwell Publishing was very helpful in answering my questions and offering suggestions during the writing, editing, and publication processes. I want to thank my Arizona State University colleague Peter Lehman for sharing his profound film expertise with me, for his insightful comments on early drafts, and for our many talks about films and about teaching films, and the anonymous readers for their valuable criticisms and suggestions at several stages of my writing and essay selections.

I dedicate this book to my mother who encouraged my lifelong love of the movies and to Ethan and Ted, my favorite movie fans.

Reference

Altman, Rick (1999) *Film/Genre*. London: British Film Institute.

Part I
Genres:
Ever-changing Hybrids

Introduction

Genre is perhaps the most often invoked and used concept in film studies and scholarship. Many film books are devoted to one genre or another (e.g. film noir, the Western, science fiction), some originating in film practice, and some borrowed and modified from literature. Rick Altman's now classic 1984 essay "A semantic/syntactic approach to film genre" (reprinted several times and modified and republished in 1999) maps a useful set of categories and ways of defining genre using linguistic terms. One is the semantic approach, in which a genre is defined by its common traits (e.g. stock characters, settings), which make up a kind of grammar of "building blocks" that remain relatively stable over time once a genre becomes developed and prominent. The semantic approach casts a wide net, so that a genre may include films with a different number of building blocks, but this approach does not attempt to explain the content or meaning of these films. The other approach, which Altman calls a syntactic approach, is one in which the genre is defined by a "constitutive relationship between undesignated and variable place-holders," by which he means the structures or central problems/dilemmas/themes in which the semantic elements are arranged (Altman, 1999, p. 219). The syntactic approach embraces a narrower field, but explains meanings and structures, and suggests that genres change, as languages change, through use and the impact of historical and social conditions.

Altman considers these two approaches complementary, though many critics prefer one or the other. In his synthesis of these approaches, he offers a way to understand genre as socially shifting, subject to historical conditions such as changing audience tastes and experiences. He also helps to explain why some genres persist, while others peak at a particular period in time, or others never seem to reach a level of critical mass of films to form a generic category. One example Altman (1999, p. 222) gives is the musical. This genre's syntax changes from expressions of sorrow in the late 1920s to expressions of joy and social integration into community in the 1930s, despite enough identifiable grammatical elements to fit these changes into a single genre. And, of course, new genres are always emerging.

The application of semiotics, introduced into film studies by Christian Metz, parallels film to language. Altman emphasizes attention to changing historical conditions under which films are made and viewed to underscore a function of genre as communicative, a complex, many-sided dialogue (or multilogue) between filmmakers and audiences. Audience reception is part of the definitions of genres. Through viewing experiences, audiences learn what to expect when they watch a Western or film noir or science fiction film. Those expectations are part of film viewing pleasure and are also generic features that can be used, modified, and parodied by filmmakers (think of John Ford's parody of Westerns, and self-parody, in *The Man who Shot Liberty Valance*, 1962; or the playful parody of musicals in *Pennies from Heaven*, 1981) to excite, thrill, challenge, or sometimes, unintentionally, disappoint audiences. Genre binds viewers to films as part of viewers' own past film experiences. Genres are conventions, and viewers learn them as a shorthand of information that permits later films in a genre to play with the conventions or abbreviate them, knowing that audiences are familiar with those conventions. Having seen hundreds of Westerns, audiences no longer need extensive visual cues for such features as the final gun battle or "showdown."

As Thomas Schatz notes, "Like language and myth, the film genre as a textual system represents a set of rules of construction that are utilized to accomplish a specific communicative function" (Schatz, 1995, p. 96). Schatz considers the effects of the commercial commodification of Hollywood studios' production methods on Hollywood's mythic expression. Whereas myths tend to be stable over time or change slowly, commercial demands on Hollywood films force a constant state of change and cultural preoccupations that tend to destabilize mythic representations.

Furthermore, genres have become so "naturalized" that we often fail to consider why certain films taken together (Westerns, musical, noir), despite their different intentions or historical production modes, share generic features, while other films, however successful, never spawn genres or fit into any. Altman's synthesis helps us understand how films within a genre can change beyond the genre's presumed defining features or can change a genre by using generic elements in new syntactic ways.

Altman, however, recently has revised his own theories to introduce practice or the pragmatic factor into his earlier theory. He insists now that the study of genre be guided by an approach that recognizes that every film has multiple users; that different users have different readings/interpretations; that users have relationships among them, as well as between them and the cultural and social circumstances in which they live; that multiple, often conflicting, uses and interpretations have an effect on production, genre categories that are never fixed, and the reception and experiences of watching, hearing, and socially discussing a film within the contexts of any viewers' other film and other broader cultural experiences (Altman, 1999, p. 214). Throughout this book, the ways in which genres morph and mutate through the viewing practices of audiences around the globe and the cultural and economic production practices of studios and filmmakers endorse Altman's recent modifications of this linguist approach.

Genres can proliferate. Linda Williams suggests the category of body genres, including a wide range of films usually defined within other categories, some new and some old (slasher films, tear jerkers, pornography, horror films). Her body genre films all share a low cultural status, the spectacle of the female body, female victimization, and a bodily effect or response from the spectator (fear, tears, desire). Williams's suggestion reminds us that, just as in the application of genres in literary or art historical studies, the concept of genre in film studies is a convenience that helps us make some sense of heterogeneous films over time and helps us integrate films with social and historical conditions. How genres emerge, change, mutate, or die over time is a matter of importance in understanding how films function in a society at a historical moment or among diverse social groups in society (race, gender, class, nation).

As Williams's suggestions indicate, films' relationships to other films depend on criteria of such topics as content, style, and audience experience. Altman's approach emphasizes that films as genres are *intertextual* – they dialogue with other films and sometimes with literary sources from which films may be derived. They are also *discursive*. Discourse is a set of language and image-based knowledge that becomes institutionalized, expressing social and political relations, not "facts." As discursive, films are open to interpretations and reactions from audiences, including audiences born generations after the film was made. Films' meanings, then, can be expanded through new interpretations and historical viewing contexts, as Williams demonstrates by reshuffling horror and mystery genres into a new category of body genre. To reshuffle, she applied feminist theories on cultural representations of the human body to horror and mystery genres to find shared features that had been hidden or invisible in the parameters of those older genres.

One major issue is genres' changing, including their birth, death, and modifications. While the Western seems uniquely American, its format and structure were imitated in many UK films on the British Empire that borrowed Westerns' battle scenes, racial stereotypes, presumed historical "truth," and justifications for domination, while modifying the genre to fit the subject of the British Empire in India or in Africa. Some films seem to escape generic definition or blur generic distinctions with features that have been defined as postmodern – blending high and popular cultures, mixing author/director's views with audience views, refusing to follow a generic pattern or to stick to one, and often using this mixing to parody a genre while also heightening its generic identity. Genre parodies raise issues about how genres construct identities of gender, race, and nation in films.

As viewers we often expect what is called the institutional mode of representation associated with the classic Hollywood film: characters appear to be "realistic" and develop or progress in the film; the narrative is linear and its dramatic highpoints are clear, and continuities of time and space are maintained, often through techniques such as the establishing shot and shot reverse shot. Avant-garde filmmakers challenge the institutional mode of genre's presumed fixed or stable state. Some films use lighting, plot, setting, character development, and interactions to unhinge the expectation of a linear "development" and instead to mix past, present, and future time frames, confuse "reality" with "fantasy" or dreams, and raise issues of narrative credibility and narrator identity.

To explore this kind of narrative challenge to genre, I would suggest several recent films that employ a schizophrenic character or structure. While movies that apply this schizophrenic structuring may not mature into a persistent genre, they have become more prevalent over the past several years (*The Big Lebowski*, 1998; *Sixth Sense*, 1999; *Being John Malkovich*, 1999; *Fight Club*, 1999; *Memento*, 2000; *A Beautiful Mind*, 2001 (which also intersects with the biopic genre), *Identity*, 2003 (which intersects with the horror genre), and, perhaps, *The Usual Suspects*, 1995). Some of these films have been associated with certain directors (e.g. David Lynch's *Mulholland Drive*, 2001, and *Lost Highway*, 1997). Many of these films are categorized as a combination of mystery, thriller, and horror. These films are not narratives of mental states that can be carried out in the linear narrative and institutional mode (*Frances*, 1982; *Rain Man*, 1988). Instead the mental states in these films *become* the narrative within the film itself. An examination of some of these films will give students a chance to determine whether they are a genre and to explore on their own how a genre is defined and grows from historical and social circumstances, as outlined by Carl Boggs and Tom Pollard in their essay on postmodern cinema.

In part I, as in the other parts of this book, the issue of technology cuts across many film subjects and issues. Digitalization has profoundly transformed genres, usually expanding in scale their visual settings or content (landscape, battle scenes), temporal parameters (combining images across time or history, a digital time travel), or narrative elements (like symbolism), as well as blurring distinctions between real images (real people acting in real time on a real set) and digitized images, as these two kinds of images are often seamlessly integrated. As John Hess and Patricia R. Zimmerman note, in *Titanic*, for example, "invisible digital effects that replicate the verisimilitude of history" appear to recapitulate traditional realism through a seamlessness between camera and digitalization. This raises the issue of whether *Titanic* is really even a movie, or "a laboratory for computer imaging systems to institute virtually total control over commercial imagery manufacturing as it shifts from production to post-production" (Hess and Zimmerman, 1999, p. 158). Even more, this shift makes film migrate from a reference to the real (as film traditionally functioned) to "a virtual index of transnational capital's phantasm of total control over production of the fantastic," in a "phantom realism" (Hess and Zimmerman, 1999, p. 158), raising political transnational issues that anticipate issues examined in part IV of this book. Whether digitalization changes or enhances or creates genres is an important consideration, but Hess and Zimmerman raise the issue of whether digitalization goes beyond this to utterly transform film itself as radically as the introduction of sound did, and in this transformation to transmit, as film always had, its own set of political, economic, and interpretive content and conformities. Are these changes simply further postmodern developments or has digital technology reached a critical mass in film to create a new medium and new systems of production and distribution?

Part I includes Altman's latest comments on genre from his book *Film/Genre* and several essays on the ways genre intersects with political and social conditions and changes. Laura Kipnis's essay explains how technical matters of shooting and editing construct a genre, and all argue that genres and especially the mixing or blurring of divisions among genres function to question assumptions about complex issues of gender, national identity, and fantasy.

Most of the selected essays analyze "problematic" issues in genre, directors, and films that resist simple categorization or offer new kinds of genres that reflect current political and social conditions. This problematizing approach mixes syntactic and semantic by employing both and by exploring how films challenge categories and create new genres. The essay by Boggs and Pollard, a difficult one and perhaps one that should be read last in this part, offers a new category of genre, "postmodern cinema," which anticipates issues throughout the rest of the book and links genre to global issues of politics, social hierarchies, and economics. This essay offers a wide genre category embracing films by Woody Allen, Oliver Stone, Robert Altman, Quentin Tarantino, the Coen Brothers, Mike Figgis, and John Waters. This grouping blends popular filmmakers (Stone), independents (Coens, Tarantino), and the rampantly outrageous (Waters), combining directors whose films do not fall into clear genre groupings. Boggs and Pollard address contemporary themes, such as anxiety and cynicism, that mark many films of the past 10–15 years, an emerging set of generic features. Their analyses apply both the syntactic and semantic models Altman describes. Williams's essay defines a new genre, the "body genre," and maps how genres can be recategorized from conventional genres (like melodrama or science fiction, in this case) into new genre categories by an innovative recognition of shared distinguishing features. Diken and Laustsen, whose essay is sociological in nature, try to understand films that do not fit easily into pre-existing genres. Acevedo-Muñoz's essay on Almodóvar, a director whose recent films present a tragic-comedic genre (unlike his earlier comedies), links Almodóvar's use of unstable generic features to historical and political circumstances of filmmaking, providing a case study of many of the broader issues in Boggs and Pollard. The genre mixing of many independent and even Hollywood films of late redefines conventional genre assumptions, as well as offering a context for the reception of genres, the pleasures of expectations fulfilled and of expectations undermined by surprises in generic structures and plots. Genre is dynamic and endlessly transforming all the time. The selected essays address the factors that transform genres and keep them unstable and intertextual.

Further Reading

Altman, Rick (1999) *Film/Genre*. London: British Film Institute.

Brown, Nick (ed.) (1998) *Refiguring American Film Genres: History and Theory*. Los Angeles: University of California Press.

Caldwell, David (1991) "Handke's and Wenders's *Wings of Desire*: Transcending Postmodernism." *The German Quarterly*, 64, 46–54.

Dixon, Wheeler Winston (ed.) (2000) *Film Genre 2000: New Critical Essays*. Albany: State University of New York Press.

Feuer, Jane (1993) *The Hollywood Musical*, 2nd edn. London: Macmillan Press.

French, Philip (2005) *Western: Aspects of a Movie Genre*. London: Carcanet Press.

Grant, Barry Keith (ed.) (2003) *Film Genre Reader III*. Austin: University of Texas Press.

Grant, Barry Keith (series ed.) *Genres in American Cinema*. Oxford: Blackwell Publishing. Includes *Crime Films* by T. Leitch, *Thrillers* by M. Rubin, *Science Fiction Films* by J. P. Telotte, *Film Musicals* by C. Creekmur, *Action Films* by

C. Holmlund, *Road Movies* by P. B. Erens, *Historical Films* by R. Burgoyne, *Melodrama* by L. Rabinovitz.

Hantke, Steffen (ed.) (2004) *Horror Film: Creating and Marketing Fear.* Oxford: University of Mississippi Press.

Hess, John and Zimmerman, Patricia R. (1999) "Transnational Digital Imaginaries." *Wide Angle,* 21(1), 149–67.

Kitses, Jim (2004) *Horizons West: Directing the Western from John Ford to Clint Eastwood,* new edn. London: British Film Institute.

Knight, Arthur (2002) *Disintegrating the Musical: Black Performance and American Musical Film.* Durham, NC: Duke University Press.

Krutnik, Frank (1991) *In a Lonely Street: Film Noir, Genre, Masculinity.* London: Routledge.

Lawson-Peebles, Robert (1996) *Approaches to the American Musical.* Exeter: University of Exeter Press.

Neale, Stephen (2000) *Genre and Hollywood.* London: Routledge.

Rabinovitz, Lauren and Grant, Barry Keith (eds) (2006) *Melodrama.* Cambridge: Cambridge University Press.

Rowe, Kathleen (1995) *The Unruly Woman: Gender and Genres of Laughter.* Austin: University of Texas Press.

Schatz, Thomas (1995) "The Structural Influence: New Directions in Film Genre Study." In Barry Keith Grant (ed.), *Film Genre Reader II.* Austin: University of Texas.

Simmon, Scott (2003) *The Invention of the Western Film.* Cambridge: Cambridge University Press.

1

Conclusion:
A Semantic/Syntactic/Pragmatic
Approach to Genre

Rick Altman

Far from postulating a uniquely internal, formal progression, I would pro-
pose that the relationship between the semantic and the syntactic constitutes
the very site of negotiation between Hollywood and its audience, and thus
between ritual and ideological uses of genre . . . most genres go through a
period of accommodation during which the public's desires are fitted to
Hollywood's priorities (and vice-versa). . . .

*   Whenever a lasting fit is obtained . . . it is because a common ground*
has been found, a region where the audience's ritual values coincide with
Hollywood's ideological ones. . . . The successful genre owes its success . . . to its
ability to carry out both functions simultaneously. It is this sleight of hand,
this strategic overdetermination, that most clearly characterizes American
film production during the studio years.

Rick Altman, 'A Semantic/Syntactic Approach to
Film Genre' (1984, pp. 13–15)

Some years ago I published an article proposing 'A Semantic/Syntactic Approach
to Film Genre'. Reproduced as an appendix to this book, that article has enjoyed
a certain success. As often happens with attempts to reduce complex phenomena
to a simple formula, however, I remained haunted by certain aspects of my neat
and manageable semantic/syntactic approach. 'Just where, for example, do we
locate the exact border between the semantic and the syntactic?' (1984, p. 15),

Rick Altman, "Conclusion: A semantic/syntactic/pragmatic approach to genre," pp. 207–15, plus
relevant bibliography from *Film/Genre* (London: BFI Publishing, 1999). © 1999 by Rick Altman.
Reprinted by permission of the author.

I asked towards the end of the article. I might also have given voice to some more obvious and even more difficult questions: Of all the possible semantic and syntactic elements in a given film, how do we know to which ones we should attend? Don't different spectators notice different elements? Doesn't that change anything? I would have undoubtedly had ready answers at the time, but I now recognize that many of those answers would have been fundamentally circular in nature. The genre tells us what to notice, I would have said, and some spectators know the genre better than others.

Thus defended, the semantic/syntactic approach may serve analytical purposes admirably, offering a satisfying descriptive vocabulary useful for interpreting individual texts and relating them to existing generic groupings. When it comes to a broader theoretical and historical understanding, however, such a defence definitely falls short. Even though the article made a valiant and perhaps at times successful effort to account for genre history, it ignored the threat that divergent perceptions represent not only for the overall semantic/syntactic theory, but even for its descriptive adequacy. Assuming stable recognition of semantic and syntactic factors across an unstable population, I underemphasized the fact that genres look different to different audiences, and that disparate viewers may perceive quite disparate semantic and syntactic elements in the same film. This blindness in turn kept me from fully investigating the possibility that genres might serve diverse groups diversely.

Because I was seeking a clear, supple, relevant terminology that could be shared by all spectators, my perspective was ironically limited *by the very nature of my project*. In search of the transparent and the objective, I couldn't possibly see that every terminology is to some extent tied to a particular use. Just as Todorov's project is compromised by his willingness to base a theory on someone else's definition and delimitation of swans, and Wittgenstein's entire enterprise is undermined by a decision to predicate his theory on the unexamined category of games, so I found my work compromised by the unspoken assumption that terminology can be neutral. So pleased was I to have figured out why the same texts are regularly treated by ritual and ideological critics in radically opposed ways that I failed to recognize in this opposition the key to the whole problem. While the article acknowledged a genre's ability simultaneously to satisfy differing needs, which I attributed to two collective singulars (the 'audience' and 'Hollywood'), I never awakened to the fact that genres may have multiple conflicting audiences, that Hollywood itself harbours many divergent interests, and that these multiple genre practitioners use genres and generic terminology in differing and potentially contradictory ways.

I continue to believe that genres embody precisely those moments/situations/structures that are capable of simultaneously benefiting multiple users. But this ability to satisfy several groups at the same time complicates the issue significantly. When we look at established genres all we can see is the coincidence, alignment and reinforcement so characteristic of successful genres. This is why it has been important in this book to look at patterns of generic change – genre origins, genre redefinition and genre repurposing – along with the more traditional topics of generic stability and structure.

My attempt to forge an objective terminology suffered from a failure to recognize the discursive nature of genres. I take some solace in reporting that I had good company in this particular doghouse. From Aristotle to Wittgenstein and from Frye to Fowler (but with the notable exception of recent forays by Rosmarin and Beebee), most genre theories have been less than fully sensitive to generic discursivity. As I have suggested in the present book, genres now appear to me not just discursive but, because they are mechanisms for co-ordinating diverse users, multi-discursive. Instead of utilizing a single master language, as most previous genre theoreticians would have it, a genre may appropriately be considered multi-coded. Each genre is simultaneously defined by multiple codes, corresponding to the multiple groups who, by helping to define the genre, may be said to 'speak' the genre. When the diverse groups using the genre are considered together, genres appear as regulatory schemes facilitating the integration of diverse factions into a single social fabric.

A Semantic/Syntactic/Pragmatic Approach

Though semantic/syntactic terminology may be useful in describing the effects of generic discursivity, it is not by itself sufficient to expose or explain them. That is why I have found it necessary to build the semantic/syntactic/pragmatic approach presented in this book. At this point, a few words about the notion of pragmatics are in order. A simple linguistic analogy will help explain this concept. Human sound-producing capacity is theoretically infinite in nature, yet individual languages recognize as meaningful only a small percentage of the sound variations actually produced by speakers. Linguists and other language users distinguish between meaningful and meaningless sound variation by way of a simple procedure called the commutation test. This test involves hypothetically substituting one sound for another and noting whether the change of sounds makes a difference in meaning; if the meaning changes, then the difference between the two sounds is recognized as significant and meaningful. As outlined more fully in Chapter 10, this process depends on the assumption that language is split into separate levels: only by interrogating the level of meaning can we identify significance at the level of sound variation.

Following Jurij Lotman (1977), I have suggested that this pattern can be extended beyond language to an understanding of texts (1981). Beyond the levels of phonemes and morphemes, one can discern further levels dependent on the use to which language is put in a particular text or group of texts. Applying the commutation test to a poem or a film, we can discover which linguistic units take on meaning at a textual level. In one sense, this logic is flawless; the same structures that make it possible for language to communicate meaning are redeployed to create meaning at a higher level. Just as the level of meaningful words is necessary to ground the commutation that identifies which sounds are significant, so a textual level is necessary to ground linguistic meaning. To put it more simply, you can't decide which sounds are significant without knowing which of all possible sound combinations have meaning as words; similarly, you can't know which sound groupings have meaning as words without knowing how those sound clusters are used in practice. Use grounds linguistic meaning just as linguistic meaning grounds sound significance. Attention to that use is what linguists call *pragmatic* analysis.

The logic and the simplicity of this claim, along with the apparent fixity of language, kept me from recognizing one fundamental fact about this process, however. Far from being permanently grounded at a high level by some universally accepted practice, this system involves an infinite regression where each level, instead of being permanently guaranteed by the next, is only temporarily buttressed by a level that is itself only temporarily grounded by a level that is itself . . . and so on. Rather than breeding stability and security, this system thrives on borrowed time and deferral. The long history and social usefulness of individual languages may give them a high degree of apparent stability, yet even they are never as stable and secure as our dictionaries imply. The farther we go from phonemes and morphemes towards textual uses and generic uses, the more problematic and unstable the system.

Though I may have paid too little attention to the exponentially increasing 'use indeterminacy' factor as we move from left to right along the noise/phoneme/morpheme/text/genre chain, I still maintain that textual and generic signification are created in a manner similar to linguistic meaning, by use of the same principles at a higher level. We know which sounds have phonemic value by testing (through commutation) their use in specific words or expressions; we know in turn which phoneme clusters count as meaningful words by testing through commutation their use in specific texts. We know which specific textual patterns count as meaningful only by virtue of their deployment in broader cultural institutions like genres. The meaning of each level is assured only through its use at a higher level.

It is precisely this 'use factor' that pragmatics addresses. Whether we are discussing literature or cinema (or any other meaning-making system), the base language(s) surpass their own structure and meaning as they are integrated into textual uses. This is the level that semantic/syntactic terminology serves so well. In order to understand which semantic and syntactic factors actually make meaning, however, it is necessary to subject them to a further analysis based on the uses to which they are put. Though the process appears entirely linear, with each level determined and defined by the next, that linearity is actually no more than a convenient fiction, for even the simplest language or text may have multiple users and branching uses.

If the whole story were told, at every level of analysis we would have to recognize that the next level up is not limited to a single use pattern against which the lower level can be commuted. Unsure which use pattern to take seriously, we would have to commute every potentially significant unit multiple times, in relation to each of the different higher-level uses with which it is associated. Leading to massive undecidability, this situation would destroy our ability to separate meaningful sounds from noise, words from jabberwocky, and textual structures from random patterns. Linguistic clarity would be sacrificed, along with shared cultural expectations. So undesirable is this situation that virtually all cultures have devised ways to reduce linguistic usage dispersion (and thus the effects of use indeterminacy) in order to guarantee continued clear communication. If every meaning depends on an indeterminate number of conflicting users, then no stable communication can take place; so society artificially restricts the range of acceptable uses, thus controlling the potential dispersion and infinite regression of the meaning-making series. If every meaning had to be deferred, then communication would literally be impossible; society far prefers to restrict communication (which is thus always slight miscommunication) rather than risk full freedom, which might destroy communication altogether.

Linguistic variation is relatively easy to restrain. At the level of texts and institutions, however, usage dispersion is virtually impossible to contain. This is why an understanding of broad-based representational practices like literature and cinema requires a separate pragmatics. Because semantic and syntactic elements are used in so many different ways, pragmatic analysis of genres cannot depend solely on commutation as its major analytical technique. Instead of looking primarily down the chain of meaning towards texts, morphemes and phonemes, pragmatic analysis must constantly attend to the competition among multiple users that characterizes genres. As such, pragmatic analysis necessarily abandons the linearity of the linguistic model on which it was originally based. Always assuming multiple users of various sorts – not only various spectator groups, but producers, distributors, exhibitors, cultural agencies, and many others as well – pragmatics recognizes that some familiar patterns, such as genres, owe their very existence to that multiplicity.

Reception, Opposition, Poaching

The relationship between pragmatics and reception study deserves special attention. For a long time, traditional approaches to genre study assumed that genres (a) pre-exist spectators and (b) guide audience reception. Reception study denies the latter claim but accepts the former. Because the semantic/syntactic/pragmatic approach instead treats genres as a site of struggle and co-operation among multiple users, it must deny both claims. Whereas reception study limits its attention to various individuals' or groups' processing of a text or genre, pragmatic analysis treats reading as a more complex process involving not only hegemonic complicity across user groups but also a feedback system connecting user groups. Instead of a one-way text-to-reader configuration, pragmatics thus assumes a constant (if sometimes extremely slow) cross-fertilization process whereby the interests of one group may appear in the actions of another. Thus film production and genre formation cannot be systematically and simple-mindedly located upstream from film viewing, as most reception studies would have it. Instead of raising reception to an all-powerful final position in the production/ distribution/exhibition/consumption/interpretation process (as several recent theorists have done), pragmatics recognizes reception study as an appropriate way to acknowledge the activities of specific user groups, but only in order sub-sequently to embed reception in a broader process-oriented and interactive analysis of competing user groups.

Like reception study, a semantic/syntactic/pragmatic approach refuses deter-minacy to textual structures taken alone, but in addition it acknowledges the difficulty of extracting those textual structures from the institutions and social habits that frame them and lend them the appearance of making meaning on their own. While pragmatic analysis sometimes destabilizes meaning by showing just how dependent it is on particular uses of a text or genre, at other times it succeeds in revealing the meaning-grounding institutions that make meaning seem to arise directly out of semantics and syntax. Just as it is no longer accept-able to base all genre theory on the special cases of the musical and the Western, it is unacceptable to base our understanding of textual determinacy on the case of marginal reception. Yet, as I have argued, marginal reception does have a special position in the theory of genres, like that of nations, because new struc-tures regularly grow out of spectator positions once characterized as downright eccentric.

Just as it is essential to understand the breadth of a semantic/syntactic/prag-matic approach as compared to reception study, it is important to distinguish between the systemic approach of pragmatics and the more limited (though helpful) notions offered by Stuart Hall and Michel de Certeau. Because Hall and de Certeau have concentrated heavily – especially in their most influential work – on the act of reading itself, they have often failed to address the broader problems covered by pragmatic analysis. In his article 'Encoding/Decoding' (1980), Hall has described readers as either accepting, negotiating or opposing an intended reading. For de Certeau, 'readers are travellers; they move across lands belonging to someone else, like nomads poaching their way across fields they did not write, despoiling the wealth of Egypt to enjoy it themselves' (1984, p. 174). The 'poaching nomad' metaphor proves strikingly revelatory of Hall's and de Certeau's fundamental conservatism. According to de Certeau's account, there once was a great nation named Egypt, now despoiled by a tribe of nomads. Nothing before, nothing after. But how did Egypt get to be a great nation and what happened to the nomads? De Certeau's 'snapshot' historiography occludes discussion of these questions.

Instead of describing the overall process of reading and its relationship to institutions, both Hall and de Certeau are content to enlarge a single moment of that process. How did intended readings become identifiable as such? How did some people achieve the right to encode meanings, while others are reduced to decoding? As Hall and his followers model the situation, even the most oppositional reading is still just an act of decoding, ultimately dependent on a prior act of encoding. While the connections between encoding and decoding are carefully traced, no clear path leads from decoding to subsequent encodings, from opposing to intending, from the margins of a current society to the centre of a reconfigured society. Similarly, de Certeau assumes that the map has already been drawn by others, and that no nomadic activity can ever alter it. Not even squatters, who might claim their rights and thus settle the land, readers are treated as poachers on land owned by someone else, who established claim to the land in some mythic past. But just what did happen to Joseph, Moses and their tribe of nomads?

Over the past two decades, reception study has become a growth industry. Surprisingly, however, reception-oriented theorists have failed to draw the radical conclusions of their insights. Stressing localized reception (in time as well as space) of texts produced by someone outside the reception sphere, critics have never taken seriously the ability of audiences to generate their own texts and thus to become intenders, mappers and owners in their own right. Only when we voluntarily restrict our vision to a narrow slice of history do the players appear to be Egypt and the nomads. When we take a wider view, we easily recognize that civilizations have a more complex relation to poachers and nomads. In fact, every civilization was, in an important sense, produced by the settling of nomads. But once they have settled and drawn a new map, every former band of nomads is nothing more than another Egypt now subject to the poaching of a new band of nomads. With each cycle, the nomadic poachers become property owners, and thus authors, map-makers and intenders, thereby establishing the capital that attracts still others' poaching activity.

Tales of marauding tribes on the southern reaches of the Nile may seem entirely unrelated to film genre, yet the systems operate similarly. In order to create new film cycles, producers must attach new adjectives to existing substantival genres. In so doing, producers are precisely 'poaching' on established genre territory. Yet this unauthorized, product-differentiating activity often settles into a new genre immediately subject to further nomadic raiding. Cycles and genres, nomads and civilizations, raids and institutions, poachers and owners – all are part of the ongoing remapping process that alternately energizes and fixes human perception. When cycles settle into genres, their fixity makes them perfect targets for raids by new cycles. When their wandering in the wilderness is done, nomads spawn civilizations only to be robbed and plundered by yet other wandering tribes. After their raid on existing film vocabulary, feminist film critics formed a series of successful institutions that for now protect their acquisitions but must eventually succumb to yet other raiders. Successful poachers eventually retire with their spoils to a New World where they are in turn despoiled by a new generation of poachers. Those who poached on *drama* by adding to it a nomadic *melo-* need not be surprised when a new group of nomads kidnaps the resultant *melodrama* and mates it with a wandering *family.*

Writing at a point in history when it was essential to free critics from the tyranny of textual analysis, Hall and de Certeau rightly accord to readers a degree of freedom and activity previously unavailable. To the extent that they restrict their analysis to a single category of users (readers), however, they are unable to capture the pragmatic complexity of literary and filmic systems. In their work, and that of many other critics and theoreticians writing over the last two decades, one senses a residue of the preceding text-based era. Today we have good cause to understand texts as one part of a far broader cultural enterprise. Only by shifting attention from reception practices alone to the broader – and conflicting – usage patterns of all users can we escape the residual tyranny of the text-king.

Planning and Using Cities and Texts

When production and reception are thought of as primarily mental activities, they are not always easy to imagine. Material examples offer a more satisfying way of figuring the challenge and the promise of a semantic/syntactic/pragmatic approach. City planning offers particularly clear benefits in this regard. Take the example of Brasilia, recently recounted to me by Brazilian film scholar Ismail Xavier. As designed in the 50s by city-planner Lúcio Costa and architect Oscar Niemeyer, Brazil's new inland capital was to consist of multi-class units each with all necessary services. It soon became clear, however, that this utopian vision would not succeed, since government functionaries seeking lodging close to their centrally located offices quickly drove lower-class residents out of convenient locations. That is, the carefully developed Costa/Niemeyer plan, with a clearly identified syntactic arrangement of semantic elements, was opposed by a group of poachers. Thus far, the circumstances bear out Hall's and de Certeau's approaches.

Where the pragmatic side of semantic/syntactic/pragmatic analysis shows its mettle, however, is in its geographical and chronological expansion of use analysis. It is not enough to concentrate on the functionaries' reading of this city plan. What benefits accrued to other groups through this process? Why did the lower classes move? Did they find benefits in their new location (such as reduced cost, increased space, or intensified communication within their own group)? What interest beyond easy access to the workplace did the new inhabitants have (for example, the prestige of centrality in a city lacking more traditional markers of success, such as differentiated buildings)? The original plan clearly served the well-known leftist utopian notions of the planners; what social, economic and government purposes are served by the functionaries' poaching? The original plan represented an ideal, indeed a *genre*, of city planning characteristic of many projects around the world, before and since. The subsequent re-ghettoization just as clearly introduced a revised set of relationships among the city's users, corresponding to a different genre built on partial satisfaction of the needs of multiple user groups.

The above 'geographical' expansion of pragmatic analysis to other contemporary user groups must be complemented by a 'chronological' expansion to past and future city-planning projects. Costa and Niemeyer were clearly designing not just as individuals with an imagination, but also in response to the experience of previous populations in previous spaces. That is, they themselves are the site not of a single user priority but of several contradictory priorities representing practitioners of previous city plans. Their own plan is thus 'their own plan' only to the extent that such an expression can imply co-ordination of several use desires evinced by others. Moving down the flow of time, how did Costa and Niemeyer use the experience of Brasilia in their subsequent planning? How did this experiment affect others' plans? While each architect's attempt to resolve the problems addressed by Costa and Niemeyer might be thought of as a particular individual's design, it must be recognized that subsequent planners are simply the interpreters of user desires made evident by Brasilia and other related designs. To the extent that an individual planner balances those needs in a way already made familiar by other planners, a particular genre is reinforced and renewed. As opposed to the analysis of individual texts and their reception, understanding of genres requires this geographical and chronological expansion.

Just as city planners once thought that people would automatically inhabit their city as designed, so genre theorists once believed that readers and viewers would automatically follow the lead of textual producers. In fact, there was once a time when both expectations were to a great extent correct – not because use-as-planned is built into cities or texts, but because the economic and social support structures surrounding cities and texts silently and effectively exhorted populations and audiences to play their expected role. As long as audiences and critics alike regularly took the practice of use-as-directed to imply use-as-planned, we needed to be reminded of the difference between the two. Fifteen years ago, it was important to have Roger Odin, in his initial foray into the realm of semio-pragmatics, point out that 'images never tell us how to read them' (1983, p. 68).

In 1999, however, we no longer need to be reminded that different audiences can make different meanings out of the same text. Instead, what we need is an approach that

- addresses the fact that every text has multiple users;
- considers why different users develop different readings;
- theorizes the relationship among those users; and
- actively considers the effect of multiple conflicting uses on the production, labelling, and display of films and genres alike.

In constructing a semantic/syntactic/pragmatic approach to genre, 1 have attempted to address these very goals. This has led me to propose that what we call *genre* is in fact something quite different from what has always been supposed.

Instead of a word or a category capable of clear and stable definition (the goal of previous genre theorists), genre has here been presented as a multivalent term multiply and variously valorized by diverse user groups. Successful genres of course carry with them an air of user agreement about the nature both of genres in general and of this genre in particular, thus implying that genres are the unproblematic product of user sharing. In fact, the moments of clear and stable sharing typically adduced as generic models represent special cases within a broader general situation of user competition. While genres may make meaning by regulating and co-ordinating disparate users, they always do so in an arena where users with divergent interests compete to carry out their own programmes.

As a final point, which has ramifications far too broad to have entered fully into the argument of this book, I would simply point out that what I have just claimed about genre is true of every communicative structure in every language ever devised. Though the social utility of language has forced cultures to downplay this point, every word, every meaningful gesture, every film image makes meaning only through a process of multiple commutation engendered by the multiple usefulness of the sign in question. In spite of Saussure's claim to be presenting a *Course in GENERAL Linguistics,* our theories of language have always been theories of the exception, of the socially stabilized special case. A truly general theory would have to pass – as I have here – through analysis of contradictory usage, constant repurposing and systematic miscommunication, thus surpassing the specially determinate situation we call language.

The positions presented and defended in this book offer an avenue to a renewed general theory of meaning, one that fully recognizes the importance of competition and miscomprehension to any theory of communication and comprehension. Presented here solely with relation to film genre, semantic/syntactic/pragmatic analysis may be applied to any set of texts, because it is truly based on a general theory of meaning.

References

Altman, Rick (1981) 'Intratextual Rewriting: Textuality as Language Formation', in Wendy Steiner (ed.), *The Sign in Music and Literature.* Austin: University of Texas Press.

Altman, Rick (1984) 'A Semantic/Syntactic Approach to Film Genre', *Cinema Journal,* 23(3), 6–18.

De Certeau, Michel (1984) *The Practice of Everyday Life.* Berkeley: University of California Press.

Hall, Stuart (1980) 'Encoding/Decoding', in Stuart Hall, Dorothy Hobson, Andrew Lowe, Paul Willis (eds), *Culture, Media, Language.* London: Hutchinson.

Lotman, Jurij (1977) *The Structure of the Artistic Text,* trans. Ronald Vroon. Ann Arbor: Michigan Slavic Materials.

Odin, Roger (1983) 'Pour une sémio-pragmatique du cinéma,' *Iris,* 1(1), 67–82.

2

Film Bodies: Gender, Genre, and Excess

Linda Williams

When my seven-year-old son and I go to the movies we often select from among categories of films that promise to be sensational, to give our bodies an actual physical jolt. He calls these movies "gross." My son and I agree that the fun of "gross" movies is in their display of sensations that are on the edge of respectable. Where we disagree – and where we as a culture often disagree, along lines of gender, age, or sexual orientation – is in which movies are over the edge, too "gross." To my son the good "gross" movies are those with scary monsters like Freddy Krueger (of the *Nightmare on Elm Street* series) who rip apart teenagers, especially teenage girls. These movies both fascinate and scare him; he is actually more interested in talking about than seeing them.

A second category, one that I like and my son doesn't, are sad movies that make you cry. These are gross in their focus on unseemly emotions that may remind him too acutely of his own powerlessness as a child. A third category, of both intense interest and disgust to my son (he makes the puke sign when speaking of it), he can only describe euphemistically as "the 'K' word." K is for kissing. To a seven-year-old boy it is kissing precisely which is obscene.

There is no accounting for taste, especially in the realm of the "gross." As a culture we most often invoke the term to designate excesses we wish to exclude; to say, for example, which of the Robert Mapplethorpe photos we draw the line at, but not to say what form and structure and function operate within the representations deemed excessive. Because so much attention goes to determining where to draw the line, discussions of the gross are often a highly confused

Linda Williams, "Film Bodies: Gender, Genre, and Excess," pp. 2–13 from *Film Quarterly* 44:4 (Summer 1991). © 1991 by The Regents of the University of California. Reprinted by permission of the author and The University of California Press.

hodgepodge of different categories of excess. For example, pornography is today more often deemed excessive for its violence than for its sex, while horror films are excessive in their displacement of sex onto violence. In contrast, melodramas are deemed excessive for their gender- and sex-linked pathos, for their naked displays of emotion; Ann Douglas once referred to the genre of romance fiction as "soft-core emotional porn for women" (Douglas, 1980).

Alone or in combination, heavy doses of sex, violence, and emotion are dismissed by one faction or another as having no logic or reason for existence beyond their power to excite. Gratuitous sex, gratuitous violence and terror, gratuitous emotion are frequent epithets hurled at the phenomenon of the "sensational" in pornography, horror, and melodrama. This essay explores the notion that there may be some value in thinking about the form, function, and system of seemingly gratuitous excesses in these three genres. For if, as it seems, sex, violence, and emotion are fundamental elements of the sensational effects of these three types of films, the designation "gratuitous" is itself gratuitous. My hope, therefore, is that by thinking comparatively about all three "gross" and sensational film body genres we might be able to get beyond the mere fact of sensation to explore its system and structure as well as its effect on the bodies of spectators.

Body Genres

The repetitive formulas and spectacles of film genres are often defined by their differences from the classical realist style of narrative cinema. These classical films have been characterized as efficient action-centered, goal-oriented linear narratives driven by the desire of a single protagonist, involving one or two lines of action, and leading to definitive closure. In their influential study of the Classical Hollywood Cinema, Bordwell, Thompson, and Staiger call this the Classical Hollywood style (1985).

As Rick Altman has noted in a recent article (1989), both genre study and the study of the somewhat more nebulous category of melodrama has long been hampered by assumptions about the classical nature of the dominant narrative to which melodrama and some individual genres have been opposed. Altman argues that Bordwell, Thompson, and Staiger, who locate the Classical Hollywood Style in the linear, progressive form of the Hollywood narrative, cannot accommodate "melodramatic" attributes like spectacle, episodic presentation, or dependence on coincidence except as limited exceptions or "play" within the dominant linear causality of the classical (Altman, 1989, 346).

Altman writes: "Unmotivated events, rhythmic montage, highlighted parallelism, overlong spectacles – these are the excesses in the classical narrative system that alert us to the existence of a competing logic, a second voice." (345–6) Altman, whose own work on the movie musical has necessarily relied upon analyses of seemingly "excessive" spectacles and parallel constructions, thus makes a strong case for the need to recognize the possibility that excess may itself be organized as a system (347). Yet analyses of systems of excess have been much slower to emerge in the genres whose non-linear spectacles have centered more directly upon the gross display of the human body. Pornography and horror films are two such systems of excess. Pornography is the lowest in cultural esteem, gross-out horror is next to lowest.

Melodrama, however, refers to a much broader category of films and a much larger system of excess. It would not be unreasonable, in fact, to consider all three of these genres under the extended rubric of melodrama, considered as a filmic mode of stylistic and/or emotional excess that stands in contrast to more "dominant" modes of realistic, goal-oriented narrative. In this extended sense melodrama can encompass a broad range of films marked by "lapses" in realism, by "excesses" of spectacle and displays of primal, even infantile emotions, and by narratives that seem circular and repetitive. Much of the interest of melodrama to film scholars over the last fifteen years originates in the sense that the form exceeds the normative system of much narrative cinema. I shall limit my focus here, however, to a more narrow sense of melodrama, leaving the broader category of the sensational to encompass the three genres I wish to consider. Thus, partly for purposes of contrast with pornography, the melodrama I will consider here will consist of the form that has most interested feminist critics – that of "the woman's film" or "weepie." These are films addressed to women in their tradi-tional status under patriarchy – as wives, mothers, abandoned lovers, or in their traditional status as bodily hysteria or excess, as in the frequent case of the woman "afflicted" with a deadly or debilitating disease.[1]

What are the pertinent features of bodily excess shared by these three "gross" genres? First, there is the spectacle of a body caught in the grip of intense sensation or emotion. Carol Clover, speaking primarily of horror films and pornography, has called films which privilege the sensational "body" genres (Clover, 1987, 189). I am expanding Clover's notion of low body genres to include the sensation of overwhelming pathos in the "weepie." The body spectacle is featured most sensationally in pornography's portrayal of orgasm, in horror's portrayal of violence and terror, and in melodrama's portrayal of weeping. I propose that an investigation of the visual and narrative pleasures found in the portrayal of these three types of excess could be important to a new direction in genre criticism that would take as its point of departure – rather than as an unexamined assumption – questions of gender construction, and gender address in relation to basic sexual fantasies.

Another pertinent feature shared by these body genres is the focus on what could probably best be called a form of ecstasy. While the classical meaning of the original Greek word is insanity and bewilderment, more contemporary meanings suggest components of direct or indirect sexual excitement and rapture, a rapture which informs even the pathos of melodrama.

Visually, each of these ecstatic excesses could be said to share a quality of uncontrollable convulsion or spasm – of the body "beside itself" with sexual pleasure, fear and terror, or overpowering sadness. Aurally, excess is marked by recourse not to the coded articulations of language but to inarticulate cries of pleasure in porn, screams of fear in horror, sobs of anguish in melodrama.

Looking at, and listening to, these bodily ecstasies, we can also notice something else that these genres seem to share: though quite differently gendered with respect to their targeted audiences, with pornography aimed, presumably, at active men and melodramatic weepies aimed, presumably, at passive women, and with contemporary gross-out horror aimed at adolescents careening wildly between the two masculine and feminine poles, in each of these genres the bodies of women figured on the screen have functioned traditionally as the primary *embodiments* of pleasure, fear, and pain.

In other words, even when the pleasure of viewing has traditionally been constructed for masculine spectators, as is the case in most traditional heterosexual pornography, it is the female body in the grips of an out-of-control ecstasy that has offered the most sensational sight. So the bodies of women have tended to function, ever since the eighteenth-century origins of these genres in the Marquis de Sade, Gothic fiction, and the novels of Richardson, as both the *moved* and the *moving*. It is thus through what Foucault has called the sexual saturation of the female body that audiences of all sorts have received some of their most powerful sensations (Foucault, 1978, 104).

There are, of course, other film genres which both portray and affect the sensational body – e.g., thrillers, musicals, comedies. I suggest, however, that the film genres that have had especially low cultural status – which have seemed to exist as excesses to the system of even the popular genres – are not simply those which sensationally display bodies on the screen and register effects in the bodies of spectators. Rather, what may especially mark these body genres as low is the perception that the body of the spectator is caught up in an almost involuntary mimicry of the emotion or sensation of the body on the screen along with the fact that the body displayed is female. Physical clown comedy is another "body" genre concerned with all manner of gross activities and body functions – eating shoes, slipping on banana peels. Nonetheless, it has not been deemed gratuitously excessive, probably because the reaction of the audience does not mimic the sensations experienced by the central clown. Indeed, it is almost a rule that the audience's physical reaction of laughter does not coincide with the often dead-pan reactions of the clown.

In the body genres I am isolating here, however, it seems to be the case that the success of these genres is often measured by the degree to which the audience sensation mimics what is seen on the screen. Whether this mimicry is exact, e.g., whether the spectator at the porn film actually orgasms, whether the spectator at the horror film actually shudders in fear, whether the spectator of the melodrama actually dissolves in tears, the success of these genres seems a self-evident matter of measuring bodily response. Examples of such measurement can be readily observed: in the "peter meter" capsule reviews in *Hustler* magazine, which measure the power of a porn film in degrees of erection of little cartoon penises; in horror films which measure success in terms of screams, fainting, and heart attacks in the audience (horror producer William Castle specialized in this kind of thing with such films as *The Tingler*, 1959); and in the long-standing tradition of women's films measuring their success in terms of one-, two-, or three-handkerchief movies.

What seems to bracket these particular genres from others is an apparent lack of proper esthetic distance, a sense of over-involvement in sensation and emotion. We feel manipulated by these texts – an impression that the very colloquialisms of "tear jerker" and "fear jerker" express – and to which we could add pornography's even cruder sense as texts to which some people might be inclined to "jerk off." The rhetoric of violence of the jerk suggests the extent to which viewers feel too directly, too viscerally manipulated by the text in specifically gendered ways. Mary Ann Doane, for example, writing about the most genteel of these jerkers – the maternal melodrama – equates the violence of this emotion to a kind of "textual rape" of the targeted female viewer, who is "feminized through pathos" (Doane, 1987, 95).

Feminist critics of pornography often evoke similar figures of sexual/textual violence when describing the operation of this genre. Robin Morgan's slogan "pornography is the theory, and rape is the practice" is well known (Morgan, 1980, 139). Implicit in this slogan is the notion that women are the objectified victims of pornographic representations, that the image of the sexually ecstatic woman so important to the genre is a celebration of female victimization and a prelude to female victimization in real life.

Less well known, but related, is the observation of the critic of horror films, James Twitchell, who notices that the Latin *horrere* means to bristle. He describes the way the nape hair stands on end during moments of shivering excitement. The aptly named Twitchell thus describes a kind of erection of the hair founded in the conflict between reactions of "fight and flight" (Twitchell, 1985, 10). While male victims in horror films may shudder and scream as well, it has long been a dictum of the genre that women make the best victims. "Torture the women!" was the famous advice given by Alfred Hitchcock.[2]

In the classic horror film the terror of the female victim shares the spectacle along with the monster. Fay Wray and the mechanized monster that made her scream in *King Kong* is a familiar example of the classic form. Janet Leigh in the shower in *Psycho* is a familiar example of a transition to a more sexually explicit form of the tortured and terrorized woman. And her daughter, Jamie Lee Curtis in *Halloween*, can serve as the more contemporary version of the terrorized woman victim. In both of these later films the spectacle of the monster seems to take second billing to the increasingly numerous victims slashed by the sexually disturbed but entirely human monsters.

In the woman's film a well-known classic is the long-suffering mother of the two early versions of *Stella Dallas* who sacrifices herself for her daughter's upward mobility. Contemporary film goers could recently see Bette Midler going through the same sacrifice and loss in the film *Stella*. Debra Winger in *Terms of Endearment* is another familiar example of this maternal pathos.

With the above genre stereotypes in mind we should now ask about the status of bodily excess in each of these genres. It is simply the unseemly, "gratuitous" presence of the sexually ecstatic woman, the tortured woman, the weeping woman – and the accompanying presence of the sexual fluids, the blood and the tears that flow from her body and which are presumably mimicked by spectators – that mark the excess of each type of film? How shall we think of these bodily displays in relation to one another, as a system of excess in the popular film? And finally, how excessive are they really?

The psychoanalytic system of analysis that has been so influential in film study in general and in feminist film theory and criticism has been remarkably ambivalent about the status of excess in its major tools of analysis. The categories of fetishism, voyeurism, sadism, and masochism frequently invoked to describe the pleasures of film spectatorship are by definition perversions. Perversions are usually defined as sexual excesses, specifically as excesses which are deflected away from "proper" end goals onto substitute goals or objects – fetishes instead of genitals, looking instead of touching, etc. – which seem excessive or gratuitous. Yet the perverse pleasures of film viewing are hardly gratuitous. They have been considered so basic that they have often been presented as norms. What is a film, after all, without voyeurism? Yet, at the same time, feminist critics have asked, what is the position of women within this pleasure geared to a presumably sadistic "male gaze"? (Mulvey, 1975) To what extent is she its victim? Are the orgasmic woman of pornography and the tortured woman of horror merely in the service of the sadistic male gaze? And is the weeping woman of melodrama appealing to the abnormal perversions of masochism in female viewers?

These questions point to the ambiguity of the terms of perversion used to describe the normal pleasures of film viewing. Without attempting to go into any of the complexities of this discussion here – a discussion which must ultimately relate to the status of the term perversion in theories of sexuality themselves – let me simply suggest the value of not invoking the perversions as terms of condemnation. As even the most cursory reading of Freud shows, sexuality is by definition perverse. The "aims" and "objects" of sexual desire are often obscure and inherently substitutive. Unless we are willing to see reproduction as the common goal of the sexual drive, we have to admit, as Jonathan Dollimore has put it, that we are all perverts. Dollimore's goal of retrieving the "concept of perversion as a category of cultural analysis" – as a structure intrinsic to all sexuality rather than extrinsic to it – is crucial to any attempt to understand cultural forms – such as our three body genres – in which fantasy predominates.[3]

Structures of Perversion in the "Female Body Genres"

Each of the three body genres I have isolated hinges on the spectacle of a "sexually saturated" female body, and each offers what many feminist critics would agree to be spectacles of feminine victimization. But this victimization is very different in each type of film and cannot be accounted for simply by pointing to the sadistic power and pleasure of masculine subject positions punishing or dominating feminine objects.

Many feminists have pointed to the victimization of the woman performer of pornography who must actually do the acts depicted in the film, as well as to the victimization of characters within the films (Dworkin, 1979; MacKinnon, 1987). Pornography, in this view, is fundamentally sadistic. In women's weepies, on the other hand, feminists have pointed to the spectacles of intense suffering and loss as masochistic.

In horror films, while feminists have often pointed to the women victims who suffer simulated torture and mutilation as victims of sadism (Williams, 1983), more recent feminist work has suggested that the horror film may present an interesting, and perhaps instructive, case of oscillation between masochistic and sadistic poles. This more recent argument, advanced by Carol J. Clover, has suggested that pleasure, for a masculine-identified viewer, oscillates between identifying with the initial passive powerlessness of the abject and terrorized girl-victim of horror and her later, active empowerment (Clover, 1987).

This argument holds that when the girl-victim of a film like *Halloween* finally grabs the phallic knife, or ax, or chain saw to turn the tables on the monster-killer, that viewer identification shifts from an "abject terror gendered feminine" to an active power with bisexual components. A gender-confused monster is foiled, often symbolically castrated by an "androgynous" "final girl" (Clover, 1987, 206–209). In slasher films, identification with victimization is a roller-coaster ride of sadomasochistic thrills.

We could thus initially schematize the perverse pleasures of these genres in the following way: pornography's appeal to its presumed male viewers would be characterized as sadistic, horror films' appeal to the emerging sexual identities of its (frequently adolescent) spectators would be sadomasochistic, and women's films appeal to presumed female viewers would be masochistic.

The masochistic component of viewing pleasure for women has been the most problematic term of perversion for feminist critics. It is interesting, for example, that most of our important studies of masochism – whether by Deleuze (1971), Silverman (1980; 1988), or Studlar (1985) – have all focused on the exoticism of masculine masochism rather than the familiarity of female masochism. Masochistic pleasure for women has paradoxically seemed either too normal – too much normal yet intolerable condition of women – or too perverse to be taken seriously as pleasure.

There is thus a real need to be clearer than we have been about what is in masochism for women – how power and pleasure operate in fantasies of domination which appeal to women. There is an equal need to be clearer than we have about what is in sadism for men. Here the initial opposition between these two most gendered genres – women's weepies and male heterosexual pornography – needs to be complicated. I have argued elsewhere, for example, that pornography has too simplistically been allied with a purely sadistic fantasy structure. Indeed, those troubling films and videos which deploy instruments of torture on the bodies of women have been allied so completely with masculine viewing pleasures that we have not paid enough attention to their appeal to women except to condemn such appeal as false consciousness (Williams, 1989, 184–228).

One important complication of the initial schema I have outlined would thus be to take a lesson from Clover's more bisexual model of viewer identification in horror film and stress the sadomasochistic component of each of these body genres through their various appropriations of melodramatic fantasies that are, in fact, basic to each. All of these genres could, for example, be said to offer highly melodramatic enactments of sexually charged, if not sexually explicit, relations. The subgenre of sadomasochistic pornography, with its suspension of pleasure over the course of prolonged sessions of dramatic suffering, offers a particularly intense, almost parodic, enactment of the classic melodramatic scenario of the passive and innocent female victim suffering at the hands of a leering villain. We can also see in horror films of tortured women a similar melodramatization of the innocent victim. An important difference, of course, lies in the component of the victim's overt sexual pleasure in the scenario of domination.

But even in the most extreme displays of feminine masochistic suffering, there is always a component of either power or pleasure for the woman victim. In slasher horror films we have seen how identification seems to oscillate between powerlessness and power. In sadomasochistic pornography and in melodramatic woman's weepies, feminine subject positions appear to be constructed which achieve a modicum of power and pleasure within the given limits of patriarchal constraints on women. It is worth noting as well that *non*-sadomasochistic pornography has historically been one of the few types of popular film that has not punished women for actively pursuing their sexual pleasure.

In the subgenre of sadomasochistic pornography, however, the female maso-chist in the scenario must be devious in her pursuit of pleasure. She plays the part of passive sufferer in order to obtain pleasure. Under a patriarchal double standard that has rigorously separated the sexually passive "good" girl from the sexually active "bad" girl, masochistic role-playing offers a way out of this dicho-tomy by combining the good girl with the bad: the passive "good girl" can prove to her witnesses (the super-ego who is her torturer) that she does will the pleasure that she receives. Yet the sexually active "bad" girl enjoys this pleasure and has knowingly arranged to endure the pain that earns it. The cultural law which decides that some girls are good and others are bad is not defeated but within its terms pleasure has been negotiated and "paid for" with a pain that conditions it. The "bad" girl is punished, but in return she receives pleasure.[4]

In contrast, the sadomasochistic teen horror films kill off the sexually active "bad" girls, allowing only the non-sexual "good" girls to survive. But these good girls become, as if in compensation, remarkably active, to the point of appro-priating phallic power to themselves. It is as if this phallic power is granted so long as it is rigorously separated from phallic or any other sort of pleasure. For these pleasures spell sure death in this genre.

In the melodramatic woman's film we might think to encounter a purer form of masochism on the part of female viewers. Yet even here the female viewer dose not seem to be invited to identify wholly with the sacrificing good woman, but rather with a variety of different subject positions, including those which empathically look on at her own suffering. While I would not argue that there is a very strong sadistic component to these films, I do argue that there is a strong mixture of passivity and activity, and a bisexual oscillation between the poles of each, in even this genre.

For example, the woman viewer of a maternal melodrama such as *Terms of Endearment* or *Steel Magnolias* does not simply identify with the suffering and dying heroines of each. She may equally identify with the powerful matriarchs, the surviving mothers who preside over the deaths of their daughters, experiencing the exhilaration and triumph of survival. The point is simply that identification is neither fixed nor entirely passive.

While there are certainly masculine and feminine, active and passive, poles to the left and right of the chart on which we might position these three genres (see table), the subject positions that appear to be constructed by each of the genres are not as gender-linked and as gender-fixed as has often been supposed. This is especially true today as hard-core pornography is gaining appeal with women viewers. Perhaps the most recent proof in this genre of the breakdown of rigid dichotomies of masculine and feminine, active and passive is the creation of an alternative, oscillating category of address to viewers. Although heterosexual hard core once addressed itself exclusively to heterosexual men, it has now begun to address itself to heterosexual couples and women as well; and in addition to homosexual hard core, which has addressed itself to gay and (to a lesser extent) lesbian viewers, there is now a new category of video called bisexual. In these videos men do it with women, women do it with women, men do it with men and then all do it with one another, in the process breaking down a fundamental taboo against male-to-male sex.[5]

A related interpenetration of once more separate categories of masculine and feminine is what has come to be known in some quarters as the "male weepie." These are mainstream melodramas engaged in the activation of the previously repressed emotions of men and in breaking the taboos against male-to-male hugs and embraces. The father-son embrace that concludes *Ordinary People* (1980) is exemplary. More recently, paternal weepies have begun to compete with the maternal – as in the conventional *Dad* (1989) or the less conventional, wild paternal displays of *Twin Peaks*.

The point is certainly not to admire the "sexual freedom" of this new fluidity and oscillation – the new femininity of men who hug and the new masculinity of women who leer – as if it represented any ultimate defeat of phallic power. Rather, the more useful lesson might be to see what this new fluidity and oscillation permits in the construction of feminine viewing pleasures once thought not to exist at all. (It is instructive, for example, that in the new bisexual pornography women characters are shown verbally articulating their visual pleasure as they watch men perform sex with men.)

An Anatomy of Film Bodies

Genre:	Pornography	Horror	Melodrama
Bodily excess	sex	violence	emotion
Ecstasy: shown by	ecstatic sex orgasm ejaculation	ecstatic violence shudder blood	ecstatic woe sob tears
Presumed audience:	men (active)	adolescent boys (active/passive)	girls, women (passive)
Perversion:	sadism	sadomasochism	masochism
Originary fantasy:	seduction	castration	origin
Temporality of fantasy:	on time!	too early!	too late!
Genre cycles: "classic"	stag films (20s–40s) *The Casting Couch*	"classic" horror: *Dracula* *Frankenstein* *Dr Jekyll/Mr Hyde* *King Kong*	"classic" women's films: maternal melodrama: *Stella Dallas* *Mildred Pierce* romance: *Back Street* *Letter from an Unknown Woman*
contemporary	feature-length hard core porn: *Deep Throat*, etc. *The Punishment of Anne* Femme Productions Bi-sexual Tri-sexual	post-*Psycho*: *Texas Chainsaw Massacre* *Halloween* *Dressed to Kill* *Videodrome*	male and female "weepies" *Steel Magnolias* *Stella* *Dad*

The deployment of sex, violence, and emotion would thus seem to have very precise functions in these body genres. Like all popular genres, they address persistent problems in our culture, in our sexualities, in our very identities. The deployment of sex, violence, and emotion is thus in no way gratuitous and in no way strictly limited to each of these genres; it is instead a cultural form of problem solving. As I have argued in *Hard Core*, pornographic films now tend to present sex as a problem, to which the performance of more, different or better sex is posed as the solution (Williams, 1989). In horror a violence related to sexual difference is the problem, more violence related to sexual difference is also, the solution. In women's films the pathos of loss is the problem, repetitions and variations of this loss are the generic solution.

Structures of Fantasy

All of these problems are linked to gender identity and might be usefully explored as genres of gender fantasy. It is appropriate to ask, then, not only about the structures of perversion, but also about the structures of fantasy in each of these genres. In doing so, we need to be clear about the nature of fantasy itself. For fantasies are not, as is sometimes thought, wish-fulfilling linear narratives of mastery and control leading to closure and the attainment of desire. They are marked, rather, by the prolongation of desire, and by the lack of fixed position with respect to the objects and events fantasized.

In their classic essay "Fantasy and the Origins of Sexuality," Jean Laplanche and J. B. Pontalis (1968) argue that fantasy is not so much a narrative that enacts the quest for an object of desire as it is a setting for desire, a place where conscious and unconscious, self and other, part and whole meet. Fantasy is the place where "desubjectified" subjectivities oscillate between self and other occupying no fixed place in the scenario (16).

In the three body genres discussed here, this fantasy component has probably been better understood in horror film, a genre often understood as belonging the "fantastic." However, it has been less well understood in pornography and women's film melodrama. Because these genres display fewer fantastic special effects and because they rely on certain conventions of realism – the activation of social problems in melodrama, the representation of real sexual acts in pornography – they seem less obviously fantastic. Yet the usual criticisms that these forms are improbable, that they lack psychological complexity and narrative closure, and that they are repetitious, become moot as evaluation if such features are intrinsic to their engagement with fantasy.

There is a link, in other words, between the appeal of these forms and their ability to address, if never *really* to "solve," basic problems related to sexual identity. Here, I would like to forge a connection between Laplanche and Pontalis's structural understanding of fantasies as myths of origins which try to cover the discrepancy between two moments in time and the distinctive temporal structure of these particular genres. Laplanche and Pontalis argue that fantasies which are myths of origins address the insoluble problem of the discrepancy between an irrecoverable original experience presumed to have actually taken place – as in the case, for example, of the historical primal scene – and the uncertainty of its hallucinatory revival. The discrepancy exists, in other words, between the actual existence of the lost object and the sign which evokes both this existence and its absence.

Laplanche and Pontalis maintain that the most basic fantasies are located at the juncture of an irrecoverable real event that took place somewhere in the past and a totally imaginary event that never took place. The "event" whose temporal and spatial existence can never be fixed is thus ultimately, according to Laplanche and Pontalis, that of "the origin of the subject" – an origin which psychoanalysts tell us cannot be separated from the discovery of sexual difference (11).

It is this contradictory temporal structure of being situated somewhere between "too early" and the "too late" of the knowledge of difference that generates desire that is most characteristic of fantasy. Freud introduced the concept of "original fantasy" to explain the mythic function of fantasies which seem to offer repetitions of and "solutions" to major enigmas confronting the child (Freud, 1915). These enigmas are located in three areas: the enigma of the origin of sexual desire, an enigma that is "solved," so to speak, by the fantasy of seduction; the enigma of sexual difference, "solved" by the fantasy of castration; and finally the enigma of the origin of self, "solved" by the fantasy of family romance or return to origins (Laplanche and Pontalis, 1968, 11).

Each of the three body genres I have been describing could be seen to correspond in important ways to one of these original fantasies: pornography, for example, is the genre that has seemed to endlessly repeat the fantasies of primal seduction, of meeting the other, seducing or being seduced by the other in an ideal "pornotopia" where, as Steven Marcus has noted, it is always bedtime (Marcus, 1964, 269). Horror is the genre that seems to endlessly repeat the trauma of castration as if to "explain," by repetitious mastery, the originary problem of sexual difference. And melodramatic weepie is the genre that seems to endlessly repeat our melancholic sense of the loss of origins – impossibly hoping to return to an earlier state which is perhaps most fundamentally represented by the body of the mother.

Of course each of these genres has a history and does not simply "endlessly repeat." The fantasies activated by these genres are repetitious, but not fixed and eternal. If traced back to origins each could probably be shown to have emerged with the formation of the bourgeois subject and the intensifying importance to this subject of specified sexualities. But the importance of repetition in each genre should not blind us to the very different temporal structure of repetition in each fantasy. It could be, in fact, that these different temporal structures constitute the different utopian component of problem-solving in each form. Thus the typical (non-sadomasochistic) pornographic fantasies of seduction operate to "solve" the problem of the origin of desire. Attempting to answer the insoluble question of whether desire is imposed from without through the seduction of the parent or whether it originates within the self, pornography answers this question by typically positing a fantasy of desire coming from within the subject *and* from without. Non-sadomasochistic pornography attempts to posit the utopian fantasy of perfect temporal coincidence: a subject and object (or seducer and seduced) who meet one another "on time!" and "now!" in shared moments of mutual pleasure that it is the special challenge of the genre to portray.

In contrast to pornography, the fantasy of recent teen horror corresponds to a temporal structure which raises the anxiety of not being ready, the problem, in effect, of "too early!" Some of the most violent and terrifying moments of the horror film genre occur in moments when the female victim meets the psycho-killer-monster unexpectedly, before she is ready. The female victims who are not ready for the attack die. This surprise encounter, too early, often takes place at a moment of sexual anticipation when the female victim thinks she is about to meet her boyfriend or lover. The monster's violent attack on the female victims vividly enacts a symbolic castration which often functions as a kind of punishment for an ill-timed exhibition of sexual desire. These victims are taken by surprise in the violent attacks which are then deeply felt by spectators (especially the adolescent male spectators drawn to the slasher subgenre) as linked to the knowledge of sexual difference. Again the key to the fantasy is timing – the way the knowledge of sexual difference too suddenly overtakes both characters and viewers, offering a knowledge for which we are never prepared.

Finally, in contrast to pornography's meeting "on time!" and horror's unexpected meeting "too early!," we can identify melodrama's pathos of the "too late!" In these fantasies the quest to return to and discover the origin of the self is manifest in the form of the child's fantasy of possessing ideal parents in the Freudian family romance, in the parental fantasy of possessing the child in maternal or paternal melodrama, and even in the lovers' fantasy of possessing one another in romantic weepies. In these fantasies the quest for connection is always tinged with the melancholy of loss. Origins are already lost, the encounters always take place too late, on death beds or over coffins. (Neale, 1986.)

Italian critic Franco Moretti has argued, for example, that literature that makes us cry operates via a special manipulation of temporality: what triggers our crying is not just the sadness or suffering of the character in the story but a very precise moment when characters in the story catch up with and realize what the audience already knows. We cry, Moretti argues, not just because the characters do, but at the precise moment when desire is finally recognized as futile. The release of tension produces tears – which become a kind of homage to a happiness that is kissed goodbye. Pathos is thus a surrender to reality but it is a surrender that pays homage to the ideal that tried to wage war on it (Moretti, 1983, 179). Moretti thus stresses a subversive, utopian component in what has often been considered a form of passive powerlessness. The fantasy of the meeting with the other that is always too late can thus be seen as based upon the utopian desire that it not be too late to remerge with the other who was once part of the self.

Obviously there is a great deal of work to be done to understand the form and function of these three body genres in relation to one another and in relation to the fundamental appeal as "original fantasies." Obviously also the most difficult work of understanding this relation between gender, genre, fantasy, and structures perversion will come in the attempt to relate original fantasies to historical context and specific generic history. However, there is one thing that already seems clear: these "gross" body genres which may seem so violent and inimical to women cannot be dismissed as evidence of a monolithic and unchanging misogyny, as either pure sadism for male viewers or masochism for females. Their very existence and popularity hinges upon rapid changes taking place in relations between the "sexes" and by rapidly changing notions of gender – of what it means to be a man or a woman. To dismiss them as bad excess whether of explicit sex, violence, or emotion, or as bad perversions, whether of masochism or sadism, is not to address their function as cultural problem-solving. Genres thrive, after all, on the persistence of the problems they address; but genres thrive also in their ability to recast the nature of these problems.

Finally, as I hope this most recent example of the melodrama of tears suggests, we may be wrong in our assumption that the bodies of spectators simply reproduce the sensations exhibited by bodies on the screen. Even those masochistic pleasures associated with the powerlessness of the "too late!" are not absolutely abject. Even tear jerkers do not operate to force a simple mimicry of the sensation exhibited on the screen. Powerful as the sensations of the jerk might be, we may only be beginning to understand how they are deployed in generic and gendered cultural forms.

Notes

I owe thanks to Rhona Berenstein, Leo Braudy, Ernest Callenbach, Paul Fitzgerald, Jane Gaines, Mandy Harris, Brian Henderson, Marsha Kinder, Eric Rentschler, and Pauline Yu for generous advice on drafts of this essay.

1 For an excellent summary of many of the issues involved with both film melodrama and the "women's film," see Christine Gledhill's introduction to the anthology *Home Is Where the Heart Is: Studies in Melodrama and the Woman's Film* (Gledhill, 1987). For a more general inquiry into the theatrical origins of melodrama, see Peter Brooks's (1976) *The Melodramatic Imagination.* And for an extended theoretical inquiry and analysis of a body of melodramatic women's films, see Mary Ann Doane (1987), *The Desire to Desire.*
2 Carol J. Clover (1987) discusses the meanings of this famous quote in her essay, "Her Body/Himself: Gender in the Slasher Film."
3 Dollimore (1990, 13). Dollimore's project, along with Teresa de Lauretis's more detailed examination of the term perversion in Freudian psychoanalysis (in progress) will be central to any more detailed attempts to understand the perverse pleasures of these gross body genres.
4 I discuss these issues at length in a chapter on sadomasochistic pornography in my book *Hard Core* (1989).
5 Titles of these relatively new (post 1986) hard-core videos include: *Bisexual Fantasies; Bi-Mistake; Karen's Bi-Line; Bi-Dacious; Bi-Night; Bi and Beyond; The Ultimate Fantasy; Bi and Beyond II; Bi and Beyond III: Hermaphrodites.*

Works Cited

Altman, Rick. 1989. "Dickens, Griffith, and Film Theory Today." *South Atlantic Quarterly* 88: 321–359.

Bordwell, David, Janet Staiger and Kristin Thompson. 1985. *The Classical Hollywood Cinema: Film Style and Mode of Production to 1960.* New York: Columbia University Press.

Brooks, Peter. 1976. *The Melodramatic Imagination*. New Haven, CT: Yale University Press.

Clover, Carol J. 1987. "Her Body, Himself: Gender in the Slasher Film." *Representations* 20 (Fall): 187–228.

Deleuze, Gilles. 1971. *Masochism: An Interpretation of Coldness and Cruelty*. Translated by Jean McNeil. New York: Braziller.

Doane, Mary Ann. 1987. *The Desire to Desire: The Woman's Film of the 1940s*. Bloomington: Indiana University Press.

Doane, Mary Ann, Patricia Mellencamp, and Linda Williams, eds. 1983. *Re-vision: Essays in Feminist Film Criticism*. American Film Institute Monograph Series, vol. 3. Frederick, MD: University Publications of America.

Dollimore, Jonathan. 1990. "The Cultural Politics of Perversion: Augustine, Shakespeare, Freud, Foucault." *Genders* 8.

Douglas, Ann. 1980. "Soft-Porn Culture." *The New Republic*, 30 August 1980.

Dworkin, Andrea. 1979. *Pornography: Men Possessing Women*. New York: Perigee Books.

Foucault, Michel. 1978. *The History of Sexuality* Vol. 1: *An Introduction*. Translated by Robert Hurley. New York: Pantheon Books.

Freud, Sigmund. 1915. "Instincts and their Vicissitudes." Vol. 14 of the *Standard Edition of The Complete Psychological Works of Sigmund Freud*. London: Hogarth. 14.

Gledhill, Christine. 1987. *Home Is Where the Heart Is: Studies in Melodrama and the Woman's Film*. London: British Film Institute.

Laplanche, Jean, J. B. Pontalis. 1968. "Fantasy and the Origins of Sexuality." *The International Journal of Psycho-Analysis*. 49: 1–18.

MacKinnon. 1987. *Feminism Unmodified: Discourses on Life and Law*. Cambridge, MA: Harvard University Press.

Marcus, Steven, 1964. *The Other Victorians: A Study of Sexuality and Pornography in Mid-Nineteenth Century England*. New York: New American Library.

Morgan, Robin. 1980. "Theory and Practice: Pornography and Rape." In *Take Back the Night: Women on Pornography*, edited by Laura Lederer. New York: Morrow.

Moretti, Franco. 1983. "Kindergarten." In *Signs Taken for Wonders*. London: Verso.

Mulvey, Laura. 1975. "Visual Pleasure and Narrative Cinema." *Screen* 16, no. 3: 6–18.

Neale, Steve. 1986. "Melodrama and Tears." *Screen* 27 (Nov.–Dec.): 6–22.

Silverman, Kaja. 1980. "Masochism and Subjectivity." *Framework* 12: 2–9.

——. 1988. "Masochism and Male Subjectivity." *Camera Obscura* 17: 31–66.

Studlar, Gaylyn. 1985. *In the Realm of Pleasure: Von Sternberg, Dietrich and the Masochistic Aesthetic*. Urbana: University of Illinois Press.

Twitchell, James. 1985. *Dreadful Pleasures: An Anatomy of Modern Horror*. New York: Oxford.

Williams, Linda. 1983. "When the Woman Looks." In *Re-Vision: Essays in Feminist Film Criticism*. See Doane (1983).

——. 1989. *Hard Core: Power, Pleasure and the "Frenzy of the Visible."* Berkeley: University of California Press.

3

The Body and Spain: Pedro Almodóvar's *All About My Mother*

Ernesto R. Acevedo-Muñoz

The critical and commercial success of *All About My Mother* (1999) in American theaters and at the Hollywood Oscars in 2000 has helped renew the critical interest in the films of Spanish director Pedro Almodóvar in this country. The director's gen(d)re-bending style has defined the identity of Spanish cinema since his debut film *Pepi, Lucy, Bom and Other Girls on the Heap* (1980) and especially outside of Spain after the international success of *Women on the Verge of a Nervous Breakdown* (1987) (Smith, 101–102). As Marvin D'Lugo asserts "Almodóvar's cinema represents . . . an unequivocal stylistic rupture with nearly every Spanish filmic tradition that precedes it" (48). Almodóvar's films are irreverent, self-reflexive, excessive explorations of identity, sexuality, repression and desire, sprinkled with rich generic allusions (melodrama, screwball comedy, thriller) and assorted media intersections (television commercials, billboard advertisements, popular songs, kitsch art). The melange of genre conventions (which peaked in the comedy/melodrama-musical/thriller *High Heels*, 1991) and the pastiche quality of Almodóvar's mise-en-scène helps to define the director's sense of narrative structure and visual style. Almodóvar's films from *Labyrinth of Passion* (1982) to *Kika* (1993) and *Live Flesh* (1997) seem to be stories in search of a format, always about to spin out of control but finally held together by their own unstable generic and formal rules. The search itself for a satisfactory formal identity and the films' dependency on intertextuality, camp appropriations of "Spanishness," and generic instability are among their defining characteristics.

Ernesto R. Acevedo-Muñoz, "The Body and Spain: Pedro Almodóvar's *All About My Mother*," pp. 25–38 from *Quarterly Review of Film and Video* 21:1 (2004) (Philadelphia and London: Taylor & Francis and Routledge). © 2004. Reprinted by permission of Taylor & Francis Group, LLC, http://www.taylorandfrancis.com

By shaping his films as ingenious celebrations of formal, generic, and sexual identity crises, Almodóvar addresses and explores Spain in the cultural and national transition period following the end of General Francisco Franco's regime (1936–1975). In his book *Un caníbal en Madrid: la sensibilidad camp y el reciclaje de la historia en el cine de Pedro Almodóvar* (1999) Alejandro Yarza argues that Almodóvar's films re-appropriate and recycle the cultural markers of Spain perpetuated (and perpetrated) by fascist iconography under Franco's rule. In his films of the 1980s (*Pepi, Lucy, Bom, Labyrinth of Passion, Dark Habits* [1983], *Matador* [1986]) Almodóvar revised and reinvented the Francoist images of a nation of toreadors, flamenco dancers, and Catholicism revealing and deconstructing its ideological function of cultural homogenization. Films like *Tie Me Up! Tie Me Down!* (1989) and *What Have I Done to Deserve This?* (1984) present the theme of rebellion against paternal figures and patriarchal order, violating the image of the overwhelming, powerful, all-knowing and yet benevolent Father figure for decades celebrated in Spanish cinema. Pedro Almodóvar's films challenge that representation by introducing "unorthodox," dysfunctional family units where fathers are absent, as in *The Law of Desire* (1986) and *High Heels*, or useless, as in *What Have I Done to Deserve This?* and *Kika*.

These films propose new, alternative familial and social models that seem appropriate to the heterogeneous, changing, "transitional" Spain of the 1980s (Yarza, 117–122). As Marsha Kinder argues, Almodóvar makes traditionally marginal characters and plot situations central (drugs, transvestites, terrorists), unmasking the manufactured centralized national identity seen in Francoist cinema while proposing a revision of Spain's cultural identity in the recent past (429–432). Almodóvar's films of the transition served an arguably therapeutic function at home, while revealing the new body of Spain to international audiences, since they dominated Spanish film exports abroad from 1982 to 1989 (Kinder, 433). In his films of this "transition" period, writes Yarza, Almodóvar "presents . . . signs of cultural anxiety derived from the national identity crisis resulting from Spain's process of integration into Europe" (174, my translation). In other words, Almodóvar and other artists of the period were concerned with how to rescue those cultural signs from their association with the nation's identity under the regime. After four decades of a dominant trend in national cinema focused on articulating a false sense of identity based on invented or abducted symbols of the national (for example, la españolada), Almodóvar's films reclaim those symbols and emphasize them as a masquerade that at once hides and defines the national. Marvin D'Lugo has argued that in Almodóvar's films of the 1980s the city of Madrid itself symbolizes the space of tolerance and "openness" of the transitional post-Francoist Spain. Almodóvar's visual and narrative fabrication of the city (its people, landmarks, movement, neighborhoods, attitudes) serves not only to "construct a new past" but also to revise the meaning of social and political institutions ("the family, the Church, the police") of the Franco regime (D'Lugo, 50).

There are recurring themes in Almodóvar's films through which the question of "cultural anxiety" arises. Among them are the stories of transvestites and transsexual characters seen in many of his films (Yarza, 89–91, Smith, 85–88). In *Labyrinth of Passion, Matador* (1986), *The Law of Desire* (1986), *Tie Me Up!, Tie Me Down!, High Heels*, and *Kika* central and marginal characters show "trans-itional," transvestite, transsexual and even "cyborg" characteristics (for example "Andrea Caracortada," played by Victoria Abril in *Kika*) which emphasize the human body as one of the locales of negotiation, tension, and trauma, suggesting the body itself as a sign of the social contradictions of a country involved in a process of profound cultural transition. There is a correlation between the generic excesses and the challenging of conventional sexual and physical roles played by transvestites and transsexuals in Almodóvar's films. Alejandro Yarza states that "the transvestite is the indicator of a crisis of the conventional sexual and cinematic taxonomic systems," a "monster" that, along with Almodóvar's generic cross-references, exemplifies the nation's "cultural anxiety" (90, my translation).

In his more mature, recent films, *The Flower of My Secret* (1996), *Live Flesh* (1997) and *All About My Mother*, Almodóvar's exploration of family and the national has been yet again revised into an equation where women and men constantly rearrange gender and/or familial roles, identity, and sexuality. Yet, in these three films there is some settling of the generic schizophrenia of earlier films into more definably melodramatic formats, a tendency partly visible already in *High Heels*. Generic "definition" has come with a volatile gender un-definition of key characters whose transitional identities are paradoxically symbolic of their stability and not of crisis. A character like the transgender "Agrado" in *All About My Mother*, played by Antonia San Juan, would probably be seen as "monstrous" and symbolic of traumatic identity crises in earlier Almodóvar films like *The Law of Desire*. But in *All About My Mother*, Agrado is clearly defined as a rational, "authentic" character who gradually gets rid of the traumas of her past. Thus arguably, Agrado's negotiation of the identity crisis hitherto represented by the transgender or transvestite characters is symbolically neutralized in *All About My Mother*.

In *All About My Mother* the role of transgender and transitory bodies of fathers, mothers, and children becomes a sign of Almodóvar's effort to resolve some issues of national identity seen in his previous films. My analysis of the story, some stylistic motifs, the use of theatrical spaces and performance, and of the extended body/nation metaphor in *All About My Mother* suggests a move toward an understanding of identity as something ambiguous (sexually, culturally) and problematic, yet ultimately functional. Furthermore, I argue that the film's narrative arch, the choices of locations and mobility, and the revised Oedipal trajectory (here a paternal search that leads to stability) propose a resolution to many of the nation's issues seen in Almodóvar's and other Spanish films of the previous two decades.

The main protagonist in *All About My Mother*, played by Argentine actress Cecilia Roth (*Pepi, Luci, Bom, Labyrinth of Passion*), is significantly a nurse in charge of transplant coordination in a Madrid hospital. From the opening-credit sequence the film concentrates on human bodies and their condition, starting with close-ups of a serum bag, a heart monitor and other life-support machines. We are thus introduced to Manuela, as she witnesses a patient's death and quickly goes to her office to arrange for a transplant of the man's heart, liver, etc. These early shots emphasize the sequence of events from death to the arrangement of organ donation without much emotional involvement: for Manuela at this point this is strictly a professional task. This is further emphasized by Manuela's agreement to take her son Esteban to the hospital the next day to watch her conducting a training seminar for hospital employees about how to deliver the news of death and ask for organ donations from the relatives of clinically dead patients. The scene is staged as seen in 1996 in Almodóvar's *The Flower of My Secret*. Manuela playacts the part of the relative, speaking with the physicians about the organ donation. Esteban observes Manuela from a television monitor in the next room. She pretends ignorance about the donation request, but ultimately understands the need for the transplant for someone's survival, even if it is not of her fictitious loved one. Meanwhile, Esteban, an aspiring author, writes in a notebook where he has begun to record "all about [his] mother," inspired by the title of the film *All About Eve* (Joseph L. Mankiewicz, 1950) which he had seen with Manuela the previous night.

The "staging" of Esteban's seemingly capricious desire to see his mother "perform" suggests two relevant things for understanding the film's position about the body and mise-en-scène. First, it underscores performance, as Manuela fakes her emotional reaction to the news of death and to the request for organ donation. It also brings up the question of mediation and mise-en-scène. The film resolves many of its conflicts and crises on or around the stage, either in theater dressing rooms, or in the presence of theatrical and cinematic intertexts, most prominently Tennessee Williams' *A Streetcar Named Desire* (1947) and Mankiewicz's *All About Eve*. Manuela's first performance in the film (with her son Esteban as audience) also foretells a type of corporeal intertextuality: the human body itself becomes a site for exchanges and rearrangements in the process of being reconstituted.

Nevertheless, Manuela's journey of reconstruction begins when she has to face reality and not theatricality. Esteban is killed by a car after attending a performance of *A Streetcar Named Desire* with her, and the story then returns to the hospital setting seen earlier. This time around, however, Manuela hears the request for her son's organs in reality, and without the mediation of acting and television. The scene appears for the third time in an Almodóvar film. Yet, unlike its implied performative and theatrical quality in *The Flower of My Secret* (where the character was also named Manuela) and the beginning of *All About My Mother*, the reality of Manuela's heartbreak here produces a believably moving melodramatic moment. In part, by removing the often present (and usually comic) media intersections seen in his films (television commercials, news broadcasts, magazine clippings, etc.) Almodóvar suggests an immediate and unmediated access to the character's feelings in *All About My Mother*. Sitting down in medium close-up with a friend (in contrast to the extreme close-up of her face seen before on the TV screen and reminiscent of television soap-opera mise-en-scène), Manuela screams and cries even before hearing the final news. In the previous version she had waited for the scene to run its course and had reacted as scripted. But here her unmediated reaction delivers a moment of authenticity, suggesting the frivolity of mediating elements. The sequence cuts to a shot of the hospital form where Manuela signs, donating her son's heart. We learn from their identical last names (Manuela and Esteban Colemán Echevarría) that he is unrecognized by his father. Here the identical names become a restatement of Almodóvar's previous references to absent (or useless) fatherly figures as seen in *Labyrinth of Passion*, *The Law of Desire* (1986), *High Heels, Matador* and *What Have I Done to Deserve This?* Instead of a rejection of "the name of the father" as in earlier films, Manuela and Esteban's trajectory in this film point towards reconciliation with the father, something hitherto unseen in Almodóvar's films since the satirical incestuous relationship ironically explored in *Labyrinth of Passion*.

Before tracing the paternal bloodline however, the story follows Esteban's heart in a montage sequence that goes from the ICU to the operating room in Madrid; from the donor's record (focusing on the word "heart") to the recipient getting ready to leave for his transplant; from the airport to the operating table itself. The sequence ends with the recipient leaving the provincial hospital in La Coruña, breathing new life as his relatives celebrate his eighteen-year-old heart. In an unusual change for Almodóvar, the "heart" of the story along with the heart of Esteban move away from Madrid, the city so prominently and symbolically featured in all his films. The move is especially significant because it underlines an uncharacteristic displacement of the action, here dramatically and violently taken away from the central plains of Madrid. Manuela first goes to the Galician city of La Coruña, on the northwestern coast of the country, only to briefly see the man who now bears her son's heart. She then goes to Barcelona on the northeastern coast, determined to find her former husband, honoring Esteban's request minutes before dying to be told "all about [his] father." Manuela is prevented by Esteban's sudden death from fulfilling his desire, expressed on his journal, of completing the "missing" part from his life, from knowing and perhaps reconciling with his father.

The significance of Manuela's travels cannot be underestimated. Galicia, where Esteban's heart goes, is a largely agricultural region, known to have been historically somewhat isolated from the "rest" of Spain by mountains and Celt heritage, with less Moorish influence than much of the rest of the country. In contrast, Barcelona has been considered, until recently, Spain's most modern, culturally dynamic and politically progressive city, with a past of anti-Francoist efforts during the Civil War of 1936–1939. By placing Esteban Jr's heart in La Coruña and Esteban Sr in Barcelona, Almodóvar not only displaces Madrid (considered "the center of the universe" in *Labyrinth of Passion*) as a synecdoche of all things Spanish, but also acknowledges a sense of inclusion of "other things Spanish" by reconciling this bi-coastal dyad. Galicia and Cataluña are steps in Manuela's process of healing in her search for and effort to "reorganize" the body of Spain.

The juxtaposition of these three locales in *All About My Mother* signals the harmonization of previously dislocated and seemingly ill-fitting parts of a single body. The film stresses this concept even further with the character of Agrado. She adds a fourth dramatically diverse Spanish region to the equation (actress Antonia San Juan is from La Palma, Canary Islands), and also a body literally composed of disparate parts, as we will see shortly. Finally Manuela's relocation to Barcelona in search of the father by train stresses the power of connections instead of separation; the railroad lines suggesting the interconnected veins inside a body going from "heart" to "brain" to every organ and member. Furthermore, Almodóvar subverts classic train imagery seen in films from John Ford (*The Iron Horse*, 1924) and Buster Keaton (*The General*, 1926) to Alfred Hitchcock (*North By Northwest*, 1959) and Luis Buñuel (*That Obscure Object of Desire*, 1977). While still emphasizing bodily metaphors, Almodóvar denies the customary phallic symbolism associated with this mode of transport in films, and directly opposes the "monstrous" characterization of the approaching train seen in Victor Erice's 1973 film *The Spirit of the Beehive* (Kinder, 130). In *All About My Mother*, the train is seen horizontally bisecting the screen rather than in the aggressive, slightly diagonal, "erect" fashion of other films. Before the anticipated arrival in Barcelona the camera is presumably placed in front of the train as it rides inside a tunnel. The camera tracks through the darkness of the tunnel, revealing the light of the exit slowly stretching ahead as we approach it. The shot is suggestive of the birth canal seen from the inside, and not of the customary action of penetration witnessed from outside and suggestive of the primal scene celebrated in films like Buñuel's *That Obscure Object of Desire* and Hitchcock's *North by Northwest* (L. Williams, 190–191; Brill, 20–21). Thus, instead of the classically traumatic vision of penetration much exploited in Freudian analysis and criticism, in *All About My Mother* the search for the father is anticipated by an allusion to maternity and birth. The unsuspecting father waits at the other end of this birth canal.

The introduction of Barcelona in the film, as we exit the "birth canal," comes in an aerial establishing shot of the city (incongruous in light of Manuela's arrival by train) in the early evening, cinema's magical hour. The city emerges from behind the hills looking at once welcoming and harmless. The most prominent city landmark that we are shown as Manuela rides around in a taxi is significantly the city's best known: the towers and façade of the Temple of the Sacred Family (Temple Expiatori de la Sagrada Familia). Manuela looks out the window of the back seat of her taxi; as the car briefly comes to a stop we see the temple's façade in a slow tracking shot. The reverse shot shows the temple's façade reflected on the car window through which we see Manuela. As she rolls down the window, her face replaces the image of the building. One of the most celebrated creations of Catalan architect Antonio Gaudí, (1852–1926), the Sacred Family is an important choice for Almodóvar in this film. Its title as a temple of "expiation" suggests the action of reconciliation (as the Catholic sacrament of "penance" has been known after the Vatican II council of the 1960s). Moreover, according to the Christian doctrine, Jesus offered his own body as sacrifice for humankind's sins. Meanwhile, the allusion to the sacred family of Joseph, Mary, and Jesus underscores Manuela's search for Esteban Sr as a similar act of reconcilement for her fragmented family. Gaudí's modernist creations, this temple itself, and other city landmarks like the Casa Vicens and the Parc and Palau Güell also metaphorically emphasize the topic of reconciliation. In Gaudí's dramatic combinations dissimilar shapes, spaces, and mismatching materials are often labored into harmony in an effort to give the buildings a natural, organic feeling. The sequence of Manuela's arrival in Barcelona, from "birth" to "sacred family" to reconciliation, arguably announces the narrative's direction toward a more harmonious, unaffected view of the family and the nation.

Manuela's transgender friend, Agrado, first appears immediately following the Sacred Family stop, which happens to be on the way to Barcelona's prostitute market, "el campo." The scene is reminiscent of the opening of Almodóvar's *Labyrinth of Passion*, in which the main characters, Sexi (also Cecilia Roth) and Riza (Imanol Arias) roam Madrid's largest flea market, "el Rastro" in search of men. The memorable sequence is composed of shots of Sexi's and Riza's faces in close-up, their gazes inconspicuously directed towards men's crotches and behinds. In *All About My Mother*, Manuela is driven around in a carrousel of johns window-shopping, while prostitutes and transvestites (everyone's "real" gender and identity kept a mystery) aggressively offer themselves, emphasizing their surgically altered bodies. Manuela's search for Esteban Sr (or "Lola" as he is henceforth known in the film), among the half-naked, counterfeit bodies, and not among the johns, suggests that the father is one of these "transitional" characters. Manuela does not locate Esteban's father, but finds instead her old friend Agrado, a transgender prostitute herself. Agrado's speech pattern and accent clearly place her origin in the Canary Islands. Manuela saves Agrado from a violent john who's attacking her, her face first shown badly bruised and bloody.

From this chance encounter on, Agrado's body, also surgically altered as she gleefully celebrates later on in the film, becomes the locus of reconstruction and restoration, of the search for stability. Their first sequence together reintroduces the theme of healing when they go to an all-night pharmacy (where Agrado in a marked accent greets the attendant in Catalan) to purchase "gauze, rubbing alcohol, iodine, suturing tape," and then go to Agrado's apartment where Manuela cures her friend's wounds. In this scene, Agrado sits in a chair while Manuela stands in front of her and applies the medications. While Manuela works on Agrado's bruised face, her friend finally offers some leads as to the whereabouts of Lola/Esteban. It emerges that some months ago, Agrado had picked up Lola whom she found in terrible shape due to a drug overdose. Agrado relates to Manuela her last meeting with the elusive "father," Lola: "one morning after returning from 'el campo,' she had robbed my house: watches, jewelry, '70s magazines where I draw inspiration, three hundred thousand pesetas." The symbolic action of healing is here associated with the pillages of "the father." Furthermore, Agrado's reference to the 1970s "for inspiration" (also suggested by her apartment's vivid decor, wallpaper, lamps, and furniture) emphasizes the camp value and re-appropriation of recent Spanish history so important for filmmakers since the cultural transition (as discussed by D'Lugo, Smith, Yarza, Kinder, etc.). With dialogue and mise-en-scène, Almodóvar revisits the theme of the absent and harmful father figure, temporally displaced back to the last decade of Franco's regime, and in doing so resumes the task of restoring the nation's body. The body has been initially fragmented and traumatized with Esteban Jr's death, and later put in motion with his organ donations and the geographical displacements of Manuela (from Madrid, to La Coruña, to Barcelona). The addition of Agrado reinforces these themes. She adds yet a fourth region of Spain to the equation (the Canary Islands), this one further distanced by not "belonging" to the peninsula. The choice may also suggest inclusion of Spain's transnational and diasporic elements, since the Islands are not only among the few remaining national territories outside of Europe, but were also a common stopping place for Spanish ships during the conquest and settling of its American colonies. Agrado thus suggests a more inclusive picture of the "body of Spain." Furthermore, Agrado's discourse about her body may also be representative of the process of reconciliation and of the settling of identity issues, since other critics have argued that transvestism and transsexuality have been seen as a sign of the nation's "anxiety" in Almodóvar's films (Yarza, 90; Smith, 87–88).

The problems of identity presented in *All About My Mother*, are not suggestive of actual "settled" identity but of the understanding and coming to terms with one's own "authenticity" even if that which is authentic is paradoxically marked by reinvention. As Agrado remarks in response to Manuela's compliments of her knock-off Chanel suit, "the only things I have that are real is my feelings, and the liters of silicone." When Manuela and Agrado decide to find legitimate work, they go to Sister Rosa, a beautiful young Catholic novice (Penélope Cruz, cast effectively against type) who works as a counselor in a support center for drug addicts, prostitutes and other "marginal" characters. As always, Agrado speaks her mind, this time about the competition in "el campo." She points out the differences between whores (women), "drags" (men in women's garb) and herself, a "pre-op" transgender. Tellingly, Agrado's problem with the "drags" is not cross-dressing, but the deceptive nature of their identity. She calls them "mamarrachas," (grotesque, ridiculous): "the drags" she says, "have mistaken transvestism with the circus; no, not the circus, but with mime . . . I can't stand them. . . ." The transvestite character in Almodóvar's films, as suggested earlier, has often been seen as "monstrous," as indicative of the traumatic identity of both the characters and the film's own generic definition (Yarza, 90). But as Agrado's sentence suggests the transvestite's problem lies not in the violation of classic systems of gender identification, but in that it is based in deception. By contrast, Agrado offers her transsexual character as "authentic" because her "feelings" are real, disparaging the "transvestite" action of deception. Different than the transsexual character of Tina (Carmen Maura) in *The Law of Desire*, who Paul Julian Smith declares is nostalgic "for a singular and unfissured identity" (87) Agrado does not show signs of insecurity, does not hold onto her previous sexuality as a part of her current self. She is firmly certain of her authenticity. In *The Law of Desire* Tina serves as an agent of "the acknowledgement of history as a communal project" (Smith, 88), mediating her brother Pablo's process of coming to terms with his own self and personal history after an amnesiac episode. For Pablo and Tina, this involves a final, definitive rupture with the memory of their abusive, incestuous father (Kinder, 247). In *All About My Mother*, by contrast, Agrado helps in the process of restoring relationships with the father since she is a connecting figure in Manuela's effort to find Lola and reconcile him/her with their son Esteban.

The process of paternal reconciliation in *All About My Mother* is seen through Sister Rosa's family (or families). We learn that Rosa's relationship with her immediate family is not very cordial. Rosa visits her mother with Manuela, and the brief scene is reminiscent of the treatment of family scenarios in earlier Almodóvar's films, such as *Matador*. Rosa's mother (referred to as Doña Rosa and played by Rosa María Sardá) is a cold woman, estranged from her daughter by the latter's choice of profession, and by Rosa's desire to leave for a mission to El Salvador. Rosa's mother calls the daughter's desire to leave "parricide" suggesting that the pain of separation will cause her father harm. She begs for Rosa to return home to help take care of her father, whose memory is impaired by senility or some unnamed mental disease. Doña Rosa's concerns however, are not only with the daughter's estrangement, but with the threat of being exposed as a fraud. In another inquiry into the question of identity and authenticity, it turns out that Doña Rosa is an art forger, specializing in falsifying paintings by Chagal. The choice characterizes Doña Rosa as someone who customarily passes something false for authentic, but who must herself be anonymous, undetected. The question of troubled identity is then here projected onto otherwise traditionally "adjusted" characters, the senile father, and the deceptive mother. Sister Rosa's estrangement from her parents stems from both disease and deception, and from the mother's own identity crisis as an art forger.

In this case, the father (Fernando Fernán Gómez) does not recognize his daughter and forfeits paternal responsibilities. Yet, he is at once harmless in his oblivion (in sharp contrast with fathers, present or not, in *What Have I Done to Deserve This?* and *The Law of Desire*), and immune from any feeling of pain or loss provoked by the daughter's absence. His abandonment is involuntary, unlike aforementioned paternal figures in Almodóvar's films. This familial division is governed not by the trauma of previous relations, but by more natural causes. Rosa loves her father, as we quickly learn, but is incapable of relating with him. But while Rosa is unable to reconnect with her father and unwilling to negotiate with her estranged mother, she does not want the same thing to happen to her unborn child.

Impregnated by Lola/Esteban during one of his drug crises, Rosa has been having problems with her pregnancy. Instead of going to her mother, she seeks Manuela's protection. Coincidentally, Rosa's plea to Manuela and her revelation that her child belongs to the same "lost father" as Esteban Jr coincides with the move to Barcelona of Huma Rojo's production of *A Streetcar Named Desire*.

This is the same production Manuela and her son saw the night he died. The narrative here seems to reconnect with itself. It suggests the inevitability of the confrontation (or reconciliation) with the elusive father, Lola, since Manuela left Madrid in search for him after Esteban's death. Structurally and thematically it stresses the circularity of the narrative, a common trait of melodrama. Manuela soon revisits the performance, finding in the familiar play some solace for the seat now empty beside her. Symbolically, it suggests the understanding of the theatrical space as authentic since Manuela seems to genuinely relive the pain of her son's death as she watches the play again. As with other suffering female characters like Tina and Becky in Almodóvar's *The Law of Desire* and *High Heels* respectively, Manuela seems ready to confront her pain and her loss by an evolution into the theatrical space and performance. But unlike the characters in previous films, Manuela is still removed from the stage, a member of the audience, vicariously living her pain through Williams' fictional characters.

It is off the stage, however, where the real drama takes place. After the performance, Manuela sneaks backstage to look for Huma, who is linked to her son's death. The scene takes place in the star's dressing room, recalling the earlier citation from Joseph L. Mankiewicz's *All About Eve*. In an interview with Annette Insdorf that accompanies the film's DVD release, Almodóvar himself states that the dressing room is where "reality occurs" in this film (as in Mankiewicz's), as opposed to the theater stage itself. Huma and Manuela become friends, as Huma repeats a famous line from Williams' play "Whoever you are – I have always depended on the kindness of strangers." The dialogue, mise-en-scène and intertextuality in this scene are significant as the setting for a revelation (Manuela learns that Nina, Huma's co-star and lover is a drug addict and needs help). The dialogue from *A Streetcar Named Desire*, the dressing room set alluding to *All About Eve*, posters of classic films with Elizabeth Taylor and other divas on the walls, photographs of Bette Davis, and Huma herself dressed-up and made-up in various roles, all point toward theatricality, performance, and intertextuality. Nonetheless, the moment is one of disclosure, of confession. What is suggested here, as in the scene where Manuela learns of Esteban's death, is that the theatrical/media intersections in this film do not really "mediate," because as Agrado would put it, "the feelings are real." There is no real separation between Huma (which coincidentally is not her real name) and her theatrical personas. The same actress, Marisa Paredes, who plays a singer and actress in Almodóvar's *High Heels*, confesses in that film that the only thing she really knows how to do "is perform." It is in her different roles, in her poses and performances that Huma is "real." Meanwhile, when not performing Huma is arguably still a masquerade; her false name, her orange-red dyed hair, excessive make-up and plagiarized lines of dialogue announcing an identity crisis. The use of theatrical situations as the locus of "authentic" disclosures in *All About My Mother* is reminiscent of Gilles Deleuze's discussion in *Cinema 2: The Time Image* of the theatrical space in films. For Deleuze, film characters in the theater, especially when not performing (rehearsing, for example), touch upon a deeper state of authenticity. In certain para-theatrical situations, writes Deleuze, "the characters spring to life again . . . and discover pure attitudes as independent of the theatrical role as they are of a real action, although echoing both of them" (194). In All *About My Mother*, there is a similar use of the theater and "para-theatrical" or theater-related spaces (such as Huma's dressing room) that leads to moments of revelation and unmasking of true feelings.

The confusion of theater with the authentic is also brought up in Manuela's substitution of Nina in the role of Stella (whom Manuela had played in her youth) in the Sunday matinee of *A Streetcar Named Desire*. Prepared for the part, because she "can lie very well," Manuela's Eve Harrington-style substitution of Nina (who is home, sick) proves a grand success on stage. We see the end of scene eight, in which Stanley Kowalski gives Blanche a bus ticket home and asks her to leave the house. In the middle of the ensuing argument over her sister, the pregnant Stella goes into labor. In Tennessee Williams' description of the scene, Stanley rants about their "happiness" before Blanche's arrival, while "Stella makes a slight movement. Her look goes suddenly inward, as if some interior voice had called her name" (112). Manuela is on stage in the role of Stella, and yet, seems not to be acting but reconnecting with the "interior voice" of her shattered maternity. She is indeed having a "real" moment, reliving the pain of Esteban's death, forever linked to the play, to performance, and to Huma. Manuela, although on the stage, is not a professional actress, and is expressing her real feelings. She grants the performance a transcendence that removes it from the inherent artificiality of the theater and from the burden of performance itself, of being an actor, a professional phony. The setting is artificial, the "feelings are real," and the moment is melodramatic twice over, both in Williams' text and in Almodóvar's appropriation of it.

Later confronted by Nina and accused of being "Eve Harrington," Manuela confesses to Huma and Nina her link to *A Streetcar Named Desire*. Of course, as Almodóvar has already established, the "real," confessional moment occurs again in Huma's dressing room. It is in this scene, as the two actresses listen to the "real" woman's story, that Almodóvar seems to be suggesting a settling of intertextuality and generic crisis. On one hand, *Streetcar* has marked Manuela's life, as she tells Huma and Nina. On the other hand, Esteban Jr's narrative of Manuela (the notebook entitled "All about my mother") underscores the reference to Mankiewicz, itself a text about theatricality and usurped identities. One fictional text (*Streetcar*), and one confessional or "testimonial" (Esteban's notebook), unleash and determine the structure and narrative of *All About My Mother*. Almodóvar seems to be attempting to settle these contrasting modes of "theatrical" fiction and testimonial narrative into something undivided, with less of the generic schizophrenia of earlier films like *Labyrinth of Passion, Women on the Verge, High Heels* and even *Live Flesh*. Thus, the theater question also addresses the issue of generic or formal identity, always present in Almodóvar's films. In his interview with Annette Insdorf, Almodóvar calls this new generic identity "screwball melodrama," combining the battle-of-the-sexes based comic tradition of Katharine Hepburn/Spencer Tracy, and the melodrama of longing, motherhood, hysteria, and inner suffering of classical Hollywood (Almodóvar 2000). Appropriately, the "screwball" part serves only as the adjective that describes the noun proper which is melodrama. The film stresses themes like Oedipal trajectory, sacrifice, motherhood, circular narrative and inner emotions, subjects generally treated in classic film melodrama (Hayward, 206–207).

In spite of the strong component of comedy, mainly present in Agrado's childlike, unbridled honesty, the melodramatic elements that converge either on the stage, in the dressing room, or around Manuela's life, are decisive for the generic settlement of the film. For example, it turns out that Sister Rosa, the pregnant nun, has contracted AIDS from the elusive Lola who is sick due to his history of intravenous drug use. Paradoxically, the celebrated body of actress Penélope Cruz is reclaimed by Almodóvar in this film and disrobed of its scopophilic and erotic function as seen in films like Bigas Luna's *Jamón, jamón* (1992). In that film, Cruz plays an "ideal" woman, everyone's object of desire, her sexuality and desirability exploited for the male characters' and our own voyeuristic pleasure. In *All About My Mother*, Almodóvar relieves Cruz of that duty by casting her against type and putting her to play a pregnant nun with AIDS. In classic melodramatic fashion, the woman's physical illness steps in to represent redemption, punishment, or healing as seen in films like *Letter from an Unknown Woman* (Max Ophüls, 1948) and *Camille* (George Cukor, 1936). In this case, as Rosa lies pregnant and seriously ill in Manuela's apartment, her estranged mother pays a visit, at Manuela's summons, and the mother and daughter reconcile. Manuela's apartment is itself a celebration of disparate themes; the decor and mise-en-scène are cluttered with geometric patterns, right angles and straight lines happily coexisting with circular forms, curved lines, oval shapes, contrasting colored wall paper, and vases and furniture placed around the rooms. Almodóvar is no novice to the use of symptomatic mise-en-scène, and here with the help of designer Antxón Gómez, the setting emphasizes the action of reconciliation between the two characters. Even in the privacy of the bedroom where they speak, the two Rosas are surrounded by disparate designs, framed in asymmetrical composition; even their blonde/brunette hair colors are a mismatch. And yet, this is the closest they ever come in the film to a reconciliation, admitting their faults, effectively reaching an understanding and mending their relationship.

It may never be all that happy, since Rosa will eventually die in keeping with classic melodramatic conventions, but the gesture of reconciliation with the mother announces the final reconciliation with the "father," a far more problematic figure in Spanish cinema after Franco. The scene is reminiscent of the ending of Almodóvar's *High Heels*, when the dying mother, Becky (Marisa Paredes), and her estranged daughter, Rebecca (Victoria Abril), also make peace. In that film however, the two Rebeccas reconcile over the corpses of several real and metaphoric father figures, since Rebecca has murdered both her stepfather and her husband, who was also Becky's lover. In search of her mother's love, Rebecca kills two father figures that have been sexually involved with her mother. In Almodóvar's films "family" usually means "mothers," and as it happens in *High*

Heels fathers often disrupt narrative coherence and family structures. As Marsha Kinder argues in her discussion of *High Heels* "mother love lies at the heart of all melodrama. . . . Therefore, the rebellious patricidal impulse must be redirected back toward the father, who remains merely a pawn or minor obstacle in the women's game" (Kinder, 253). The two Rosas' restatement of the two Rebeccas' meeting invites a revision of the earlier film's negotiation of the conflict with the father. In *All About My Mother*, Sister Rosa's (and Manuela's) desire is to reconcile with the father and to introduce their sons to him in spite of his previously destructive absence (from Esteban Jr's life) and presence (in Rosa's child's life). There is no "rebellious patricidal impulse" in *All About My Mother*, but a convincing effort to repair that troubled relationship of the past in favor of some redemption, of some rebuilding, of some reconstitution of the body of the nation through the reparation of the family.

It is quite significant, therefore, that Almodóvar juxtaposes Rosa's melodramatic bedridden reconciliation with her mother with the comic relief of Agrado's theatrical performance, once again suggesting a correlation between theatricality and the reality of feelings. At the end of the women's meeting, Manuela tells the story of her dead son to Doña Rosa. She exits the apartment leaving Manuela crying by the door and the scene cuts to the parallel space of the theater, to a tracking shot along the theater curtain. On the soundtrack we hear Agrado's footsteps announcing her arrival on stage. The shot ends with a close up of Agrado in profile as she steps out from the curtain. The choice is doubly significant; Almodóvar characterizes the close-up as "an image whose narrative content is highly complex and specific . . . an X-ray of the character [that] precludes all duplicity" (Almodóvar 1996, 34). While the close-up is customarily used to gain access to a character's subtleties and "real" value, the close-up in profile further emphasizes knowledge of his/her personality. As William Rothman states, the profile shot "announces that we have arrived at the limit of our access to the camera's subject" (33). Agrado's arrival on stage is thus a moment of revelation and unambiguous disclosure as for the character's meaning and arguably, a formal suggestion of "knowledge" in film language. Equally suggestive is Agrado's position on stage, in front of the closed curtain, removing herself from the performance space proper and facing the audience directly, which Deleuze argues is a "purer and more independent" state of authenticity (194). Agrado excuses Nina and Huma, who due to health reasons (they beat each other up in a fight), are unable to perform. Meanwhile the camera tracks through the center aisle of the theater toward her, her public visible in both sides of the symmetrical composition. As the camera approaches her, Agrado announces that the performance is suspended. Paradoxically, she offers in substitution "to tell the story of my life." The mise-en-scène emphasizes the contradiction, negating the theatricality of the performance space and offering "reality" instead. Under the spotlight, but removed from the stage, the "performer" offers authenticity while the curtain remains shut. Significantly, Agrado's life story," as she tells it, is one of assumed names, transformations, and alterations of the real body. In her own words:

They call me Agrado, because all my life I have only wanted to make life agreeable for others. Besides been agreeable, I am very authentic. Look at this body: all custom made. Eyes, 80 thousand (pesetas); nose two hundred . . . ; tits, two, *because I am no monster*, seventy each. Silicone: lips, forehead, cheekbones, hips, ass. . . . Laser hair removal (because women, like men, evolved from the monkeys) 60 thousand per session, depending on how hairy you are, because if you are "folkloric," you'll need more.

Agrado's speech is occasionally juxtaposed with the audience's enthusiastic reaction shots and crowned at the end with a satisfied round of applause. The public celebrates, laughs, and is mesmerized with Agrado's confession, which ultimately does not reveal anything about the "story of [her] life." "As I was saying," she concludes, "It costs a lot to be authentic, Lady, and for these things one shouldn't be stingy, because one is more authentic, the more you resemble that which you have dreamed of yourself." After the speech, the camera shows a close-up of Agrado visibly moved by the public's acceptance, by its celebration of her authenticity, even though not one of the performance's promises have been fulfilled. She is not "a monster," like similar characters in Almodóvar's films, she is whole and legitimate. Her performance offers no actors, no play, no (theatrical) mise-en-scène; what the public gets is a recognition of an identity based on the instability of transition, of acceptance, of authenticity centered on reinvention, on "what you have dreamed of yourself." The sequence ends with a long shot of the theater audience happily applauding, satisfied with the performance as it is.

In contrast to other theatrical scenes in Almodóvar's films, Agrado's performance, perhaps because it isn't, denotes neither crisis nor the making of counterfeit identities. The performance scene of Cocteau's *La Voix humane* and Jacques Brel's song "Ne me quitte pas" in *The Law of Desire*, in contrast is symbolic of the loss of the characters parents. Tina misses her abusive, incestuous father, and the girl, Ada, her ward has been abandoned by her mother. In *Women on the Verge of a Nervous Breakdown*, Pepa (Carmen Amura) collapses while in the recording studio dubbing Spanish dialogue for Joan Crawford in Nicholas Ray's *Johnny Guitar* (1953). The dialogue itself is a reflection of Pepa's doomed relationship and her fainting is symptomatic of her desperation at being abandoned by her lover while pregnant. And in *High Heels*, the young Rebecca breaks down and is arrested for confessing to her husband's murder on television, while her mother later collapses on stage singing Agustín Lara's song "Think of Me" to her daughter. Similar examples of moments of "crisis" (physical, emotional) and deceit while performing occur in *Tie Me Up! Tie Me Down!*, *What Have I Done . . . ?*, and twice more in *High Heels*. However, in *All About My Mother*, the theatrical space is re-appropriated by Manuela and Agrado as the locus of "authenticity" and relief, and not of performance or the "hysterical" symptoms of crisis. Agrado, removed from the purely theatrical space, effectively replaces the dysfunctional Kowalski-DuBois family of Williams' fiction, in favor of the symbolic "story of [her] life."

The conclusion of *All About My Mother* suggests Almodóvar's evolution into a stage in which history is no longer deconstructed to neutralize trauma and rebellion, but in which a concerted effort at reconciliation with Spain's past is dramatized. The third act begins with Rosa's apparent reconciliation with her father while en route to the hospital to give birth to Lola's son, Esteban III. Rosa requests the taxi driver stop at the Plaza de Medinaceli, where she encounters her oblivious father. Although he does not recognize her, she tenderly exclaims "adiós Papá" acknowledging the possibility that this is their last meeting. Rosa's father is a man with no historic memory, as mentioned above, a fact that perhaps allows for the reconciliation to occur since the trauma of recent history does not interfere with the process. Their history is not revisionist but forgotten, ignored, maybe overcome. After reconciling with her father, Rosa dies giving birth to Esteban III. She has fallen to the HIV acquired from her sexual affair with Lola. At Rosa's funeral, the elusive Lola finally appears, dressed in drag, "a monster," "an epidemic" as Manuela and Agrado refer to him. At the funeral, Lola learns of his first-born's death, the reason for Manuela's move to Barcelona. But in spite of her initial reaction, Manuela allows Lola to make peace with his two sons. They meet at a café off the Plaza de Medinaceli, where Rosa had symbolically made peace with her own father. Holding Esteban III in his arms, Lola, with his enormous breasts and his made-up face apologizes to the child for leaving him "such a bad inheritance." But Manuela informs him that the baby is not sick and has no reason to develop the disease. Manuela then shows Lola their son's photograph and the notebook where he had begun to write "All about my mother." The upper half of the composition is filled with the young Esteban's eyes framed within the frame looking directly into the camera, which takes Lola's point of view. The extreme close-up is another moment of recognition and revelation, Esteban II at once acknowledging, confronting, and symbolically reconciling with his father in spite of the latter's "monstrosity," absence, and sexual identity crisis. Lola reads Esteban's journal in which the young man (born around 1982, in the cultural transitional phase) states his desire to meet his father "no matter who he is, nor how he is, or how he behaved" and to find and complete the "missing half" of his life. It is ultimately Esteban's manuscript that resolves the paternal crisis, bringing the Oedipal trajectory to a closure, emphasizing his desire for reconciliation, his longing to know "all about his father," as he had once requested from Manuela. After reading aloud from the notebook, Lola metaphorically reconciles the two generations, suggesting the settlement of the paternal crisis often symbolic in Spanish cinema of the national trauma (Kinder, 197–198; Yarza, 111–113; Smith, 33–34). The conclusion is also circular, since the film begins with Esteban's interest in knowing "all about his mother," but ends in an encounter with the father. For Esteban II, what is important is reconciliation, to know and perhaps understand "all about his father." In *What Have I Done to Deserve This?*, *Matador* and *The Law of Desire* not only are fathers absent, abusive, or engaged in incestuous relationships with their children, but as seen in Almodóvar's symptomatic use of mise-en-scène and the appropriation of symbols of Spain's recent past (bullfighting culture, Catholicism, the Opus Dei), they are also symbolic of the nation's trauma under Franco. The "rebellious patricidal impulse" of Almodóvar's past is here clearly subverted in favor of reconciliation.

In the epilogue of *All About My Mother*, Manuela retraces the steps of her initial journey once again, having fled to Madrid with the baby, now returning to Barcelona. The image of the train returns, the same shot as in the beginning repeated from the inside of the tunnel. The second time around the shot suggests a rebirth, a new beginning. This circular closure repeats the motif of rebirth seen in *Live Flesh*. At the end of that film the protagonist, while en route to the hospital with his girlfriend in labor, observes the streets full of people out celebrating on a Christmas night. He warmly tells his unborn child to be patient and have no fears because, unlike 26 years ago when he was born, "luckily, in Spain it's been a long time since we've been afraid." José del Pino has argued that in *Kika, The Flower of My Secret* and *Tie Me Up! Tie Me Down!* Almodóvar attempts a similar effort to heal some previously troubling signs of identity by helping the transitory present reconnect with the past through the protagonists' visits to the country towns of their ancestors (del Pino, 168–169). The same is arguably true of *All About My Mother*, when the third Esteban retraces with his surrogate mother the trip back to his "fatherland."

In her internal monologue at the end of *All About My Mother*, Manuela's explains that Esteban III is cured, his body having "neutralized the (HIV) virus in record time." Lola, Rosa, and Esteban II are all dead, but their respective offspring and sibling is a medical wonder. In spite of his troubled conception and "bad inheritance," he is a symbol of the dramatic restoration and reconstruction that the extended bodily metaphor of the film suggests. Like Agrado's body, which is "authentic" and real because it is what she desires, what she has "dreamed of herself," Almodóvar offers a conclusion in *All About My Mother* that stabilizes the crises treated in his previous films. The film ultimately suggests the characters "transitional" or "artful" stages as their defining identities. In the very last scene, Huma leaves Manuela, Agrado, and Esteban II's photograph in the dressing room to go on stage, but what we see, reminiscent of Agrado's speech, is the closed theater curtain. Thus, both the melodramatic climax (Lola's reconciliation with his sons), and the epilogue (the cured baby and Huma's negated performance), offer symbolic "conclusions" to the generic, paternal, and identity crises that Almodóvar has explored in his films since 1980.

In the last twenty years, Spain has steadily moved toward more conservative politics, higher tolerance of its regional differences and cultural identities, an effective democratic political structure, and an important place in the economic community of the European Union. Equally, Almodóvar's revisionist historical approach has changed from an attempt to reinvent the past to the acceptance of the present, as the end of *Live Flesh* already establishes. As the director himself prophesized in 1994, "when one makes a film, writes a book or paints a picture, one can correct reality, improve on it" (Almodóvar 1996, 136). In *All About My*

Mother Almodóvar's twenty-year search for an understanding of the nation's identity crisis settles into the suggestion of ambiguity as Spain's strongest sign of current stability. Through the juxtaposed motifs of the body and the nation, Almodóvar suggests several conclusions that unequivocally point to a happy ending.

In *All About My Mother*, there is a reconstruction of the national geographical space, which begins with Manuela's journey from Madrid (the city synecdoche of the national reconstruction effort), to Barcelona, the liberal gateway to Europe. But the urban allegory is here extended to include also the province (Galicia), the overseas territories that Agrado contributes (the Canary Islands), and even the inclusive transnational dimension of the "new" Spain, seen in the two exiled characters, Lola and Manuela. The film draws a line of inclusion throughout the national territory. Moreover, Almodóvar emphasizes the reconstitution of the body in an allegory of settled identities, not only with Esteban III's miraculous cure from HIV (through his parents' symbolic sacrifice), but also with Agrado's recognition and celebration of her surgically altered self as a testimony of "authenticity." Finally, the theme of reconstruction and restoration is accentuated with the previously rejected option of reconciliation with the father. The film certainly celebrates motherly bonds between the assorted characters (Manuela and the two Estebans, Rosa, her mother and Manuela, Huma, Manuela and Agrado). But the strengthening of motherly relations is a step on the way to mending the much more problematic relations between children and their fathers (as we see with Rosa and her father, Lola and his sons, and even Manuela's visit to the Sacred Family temple while searching for Lola). In earlier films, Almodóvar stresses the contrasts and divisions between village and city, Spain and Europe, parents and children, men, women, and transgender. In this more mature film, however, traumatic identity, performance, geographic displacement, disease, and death serve as the vehicles through which the characters (and the nation by extension) find love, stability, identity, health, and finally, redemption. At once a synopsis and a reevaluation of his past career, in *All About My Mother* Almodóvar is reaching that point where art imitates, corrects and, indeed, improves on reality.

Works Cited

Almodóvar, Pedro. *Almodóvar on Almodóvar*, Frédéric Strauss, ed., Yves Baignères, translator, London: Faber and Faber, 1996.
——. Interview with Annette Insdorf, January 10, 2000, Columbia TriStar DVD, 2000.
Brill, Lesley. *The Hitchcock Romance*. Princeton: Princeton UP, 1988.
Deleuze, Gilles. *Cinema 2: The Time Image*. Minneapolis, MN: U of Minnesota P, 1991.
Del Pino, José M. "La tradición permanente: apuntes sobre casticismo y europeísmo en los fines de siglo," *Nuevas perspectivas sobre el '98*. John P. Gabrielle, ed., Madrid: Iberoamericana, 1999: 161–170.
D'Lugo, Marvin. "Almodóvar's City of Desire," *Quarterly Review of Film and Video* 13.4 (1991): 47–65.

Hayward, Susan. *Key Concepts in Cinema Studies.* London: Routledge, 1996.

Kinder, Marsha. *Blood Cinema: The Reconstruction of National Identity in Spain.* Berkeley: U of California P, 1993.

Rothman, William. *Hitchcock: The Murderous Gaze.* Cambridge: Harvard UP, 1982.

Smith, Paul, J. *Desire Unlimited: The Cinema of Pedro Almodóvar.* London: Verso, 1999.

Williams, Linda. *Figures of Desire: A Theory and Analysis of Surrealist Film.* Berkeley: U of California P, 1992.

Williams, Tennessee. *A Streetcar Named Desire.* 1947. New York: Signet, 1972.

Yarza, Alejandro. *Un caníbal en Madrid: la sensibilidad camp y el reciclaje de la historia en el cine de Pedro Almodóvar.* Madrid: Ediciones Libertarias, 1999.

4

Enjoy Your Fight! – *Fight Club* as a Symptom of the Network Society

Bülent Diken and Carsten Bagge Laustsen

> *How is it that all the examples of lines of flight . . . turn out so badly?*
> *(Deleuze and Parnet 1987: 140)*

Fight Club,[1] David Fincher's recent film, poses significant questions about "microfascism": the heterogeneous, subterranean "other" of political theory that, in spite of public denial, persists in the network society as sexism, racism, hooliganism, fundamentalism and other "passionate attachments".

Fight Club's protagonist, Jack (Edward Norton), is mobile: he has a career, travels in the space of flows, and fully but reflexively participates in consumerism. He is constantly on the move, yet his attitude toward his environment is *blasé*. As a spectator of his own life, he paradoxically lives in inertia in the midst of a mobile network society. Jack also suffers from insomnia, a typical pathology of the hyper-mobile network society. But, finding his pain negligible, his doctor does not want to give him sleeping pills: "You want to see pain? Swing by Meyer High on a Tuesday night and see the guys with testicular cancer." Jack does as the doctor says. Trying several therapy groups as a "tourist", he shares others' pain, which works as catharsis. He then starts to visit different self-help groups every day. In one of the groups he meets Marla (Helena Bonham Carter), the *femme fatale* who is to change his life. The real change, however, follows when the protagonist meets his *doppelgänger*, Tyler Durden (Brad Pitt), the embodiment of a colourful and dynamic contrast to Jack himself, his messianic alter-ego. One day Tyler asks

Bülent Diken and Carsten Bagge Laustsen, "Enjoy Your Fight! – 'Fight Club' as a Symptom of the Network Society," pp. 349–67 from *Cultural Values* 6:4 (2002) (London: Taylor & Francis and Routledge). © 2002 by Cultural Values. Reprinted by permission of Taylor & Francis.

Jack to hit him as hard as possible. Jack hits him and Tyler returns the favour. After repetitive fights, fighting becomes an addiction. They are exhilarated by violence and through fighting they discover the corporeality of their existence.

The most powerful twist in the film is when it becomes obvious that Jack is in fact schizophrenic, that Tyler is a product of his fantasy. Tyler thus materializes Jack's unconscious wishes. Together, Jack/Tyler creates a Fight Club: a secret, fraternity-like, rhizomatic group, open to males only. It functions as a line of flight from the stratified society. Through perversion and transgression, Fight Club aims at a critique of capitalism. Yet, in spite of a deterritorializing start, Fight Club ends up transforming into a fascist organization with a new name: Project Mayhem. Violence is now turned outwards, which culminates in a plan for "organized" terror to undermine the foundations of the consumerist society. Thus, Fight Club oscillates between liberation and servitude, between escape from society and micro-fascism. Indeed, it is as if in Fight Club everything subversive turns out to be repressive: Fight Club is a comedy of subversion. The emerging question is whether and in what ways the *critique* of capitalism, based on the idea of subversion (e.g. through nomadism) still can hold in network society. What if micro-fascism itself constitutes a subversive line of flight, a question which preoccupied Bataille and Deleuze? What happens to the idea/project of subversion when power goes nomadic in the network society? And what if the idea of subversion is accommodated by the "new spirit of capitalism" that thrives well in aesthetic forms of justification based on inspiration and creativity (Boltanski and Chiapello 1999)? Is it still possible and feasible to say "More perversion!" (Deleuze and Guattari 1983: 321), when perversion has already become a big business? *Fight Club* stages such global questions.

Capital and Its Subterranean Other

"The first rule of Fight Club is: you do not speak about Fight Club. The second rule of Fight Club is: you-do-not-speak-about-Fight-Club!" Yet, of course, prohibition is an invitation to transgress the rule: go and tell about Fight Club, but treat this knowledge as a dirty secret that unites "us", the community of sworn brothers! Fight Club knows well that it cannot exist without secrecy, that, if transgression becomes all too obvious, its attraction would disappear: there is no social order without an obscene supplement, and no social bond without a dark, invisible downside. The heterogeneous supplement does not negate a given order but, rather, as Fight Club demonstrates, serves as its positive condition of possibility.

Does not the downside of the social bond today often materialize itself in "explosive communities" (Bauman 2000: 193), in arenas for acting out perverted scenarios, finding its form and expression in sexism, racism, ethnic passions and so on? Such forms of sociality are based on acting out certain fantasy scenarios, which are definitely not only a subtext to their public roles. In the context of *Fight Club*, no Jack without a Tyler Durden! The normalized and law-abiding subject is haunted by a spectral double, by a subject that materializes the will to transgress the law in perverse enjoyment. Thus Tyler, Jack's ghostly double, says to him: "You were looking for a way to change your life. You could not do it on your own . . . I look like you want to look. I fuck like you want to fuck. I'm smart and capable, and most importantly, I'm free in all the ways you're not."

If the subject, as Freud claims, internalizes social norms through a superego, one should add that this superego itself is split in two distinct but interrelated figures of the law, between the two figures of the father. First, the father of the law, of the symbolic order, castrating the subject through the law and language, and second, the obscene father commanding no less than transgression and enjoyment. Whereas the first authority simply prohibits, "Don't!" the latter says: "You may!" (Žižek 2000: 132). Because the transgressor needs a law to transgress, and because the law is not destroyed but rather confirmed though the act of transgression, any attempt at balancing these two functions is doomed to be fragile. And an important tendency of the contemporary society, be it the "network society" (Castells 1996) of deterritorialized flows or the detraditionalized, reflexive "risk society" (Beck 1993), is the disturbance of this fragile balance. We are witnessing the demise of symbolic efficiency, or, the fall of the father (Žižek 1999: 322–34). Socially produced risks are unpredictable, and since there is no master in charge, which can reduce complexity, social spheres are "increasingly 'colonized' by reflexivity" (Žižek 1999: 336). Things are to be decided upon without a symbolic authority, without somebody who "really knows" (the big Other) and can bear the burden of choosing. Foucault's disciplinary society was about reproduction of power through "strategies without subject". Today we are confronted with the exact opposite situation, subjects caught in the consequences of their actions without a master that regulates their interactions (Žižek 1999: 340).

The de-traditionalized, increasingly reflexive individuals no longer have ready-made symbolic authorities, and they complain, as does Tyler in the Fight Club, "we are a generation of men raised by women". He never "knew his father" (Palahniuk 1997: 49). In the social space within which Fight Club emerges there is no father, only a ruse of signs, an experience of a smooth space without symbolic hierarchies – a place no longer determined by the law and tradition or by the solidity of a habitus. What follows is the burden of reflexivity as one has to choose one's place in the social, because identity is no longer a matter of occupying an already given subject position. Hence one desperately searches for a true identity, tries to find an objective correlate to being. "I loved my life. I loved my condo. I loved every stick of furniture. That was my whole life. Everything – the lamps, the chairs, the rugs – were me. The dishes were me. The plants were me. The television was me."

This "friction-free", smooth space is of course the space of contemporary capitalism, of flows. What is often overlooked is that in this social space fantasies are violated, not because they are forbidden but because they are not. Today fantasies are subsumed under capital, and a market for the extreme and the perverted is growing. In our post-Oedipal era, the paradigmatic mode of subjectivity is the "polymorphously perverse" subject that follows the command to enjoy; no longer the Oedipal subject integrated into the symbolic order through castration (Žižek 1999: 248). If, in the reflexive society, the symbolic father of the uncompromising "No!" is in retreat, the void is filled with either ersatz authorities (e.g. ethical committees) or authorities that make transgression or perversion of the Law a rule in the service of enjoyment. Thus, the standard situation of the disciplinary subject is reversed: "we no longer have the public Order of hierarchy, repression and severe regulation, subverted by the secret acts of liberating transgression . . . on the contrary, we have public social relations among free and equal individuals, where the 'passionate attachment' to some extreme form of strictly regulated domination and submission becomes the secret transgressive source of libidinal satisfaction, the obscene supplement to the public sphere of freedom and equality" (Žižek 1999: 345). The problem of authority today is not that of the symbolic authority that forbids enjoyment but that of the superego, of the obscene authority that enjoins one to enjoy. This is a scenario in which transgression does not result in freedom but in new, and even more rigid, authority structures.

The distinction between societies of discipline and societies of control, in which power goes nomadic, is illuminating here. Deleuze claims that capitalism is no longer characterized by panoptic, place-bounded discipline forcing people to overtake given subject positions, but by a permanent movement, in which the subject is always in a state of becoming. "Control", he says, "is short-term and rapidly shifting, but at the same time continuous and unbounded whereas discipline was long-term, infinite and discontinuous" (Deleuze 1995: 181). If the geography of discipline worked in terms of fixed points or positions, control operates in terms of mobility, speed, flexibility, anonymity and contingent identities, in terms of "the whatever" (Hardt 1998: 32). The symptom of control society is the collapse of the institutional walls: not that discipline ends with the deterritorialization of institutions. Rather, discipline, now freer than ever from territorial constraints, has become more immanent to the social field (Hardt and Negri 2000). In control society subjectivity is "produced simultaneously by numerous institutions in different combinations and doses"; hence social space tends to lose its delimitation: a person "is factory worker outside the factory, student outside the school, inmate outside prison, insane outside the asylum – all at the same time. It belongs to no identity and all of them – outside the institutions but even more intensely ruled by their disciplinary logics" (Hardt and Negri 2000: 331–2). This unfinished, constantly mutating status of everything does not bring with it freedom, but control, which corresponds to the immanent, axiomatic logic of capital.

Capitalism no longer functions according to the discourse of the master (Žižek 1999: 373). Control is not given by castration, that is, by a restriction of the subject's ability to move and to act, by a limitation in being. It pertains to flows; the universe of capitalism is immanent, infinite, without an end. As *Fight Club* says, living in it is like living in "The IBM Stellar Sphere, The Philip Morris Galaxy, Planet Starbucks". The source of anxiety in this open, smooth space is not lack of being; rather, too much pseudo-freedom, e.g. freedom to consume. "[T]he anxiety generated by the risk society is that of a superego: what character-izes the superego is precisely the absence of a 'proper measure' – one obeys its commands not enough/or too much; whatever one does, the result is wrong and one is guilty. The problem with the superego is that it can never be translated into a positive rule to be followed (Žižek 1999: 394). Thus, permitted enjoyment – You may! – turns into the prescriptive enjoyment – You must! (Žižek 2000: 133). In other words, the demise of the symbolic authority in no way implies the demise of authority as such, and herein lies the paradox of the theory of reflexivity, its blindness to the (re)emerging nonsymbolic forms of authority. This is the paradox of postmodern individuality: the injunction to be oneself, to realize one's creative potential, results in the exact opposite, that is, the feeling of the inauthenticity of all acts. No act, no commodity is really *it*. My "inner being" is not expressed *that* way, either (ibid. 22–3). Extreme individuality reverts to its opposite, causing the subject's experience to be uncertain and faceless, changing from mask to mask, trying to fill the void behind the mask by shifting between idiosyncratic hobbies (Žižek 1999: 373).

Undoing the Social Bond

Enter Jack's life in a rigidly segmented modern society. He is a white, male, middle-class member of generation X, "a slave to the IKEA nesting instinct". His cry is loud and clear: "My life just seemed too complete . . . Deliver me from Swedish furniture. Deliver me from clever art . . . May I never be content. May I never be complete. May I never be perfect. Deliver me" (Palahniuk 1997: 46, 52).

Enter Deleuze and Guattari: "We are segmented from all around and in every direction . . . Dwelling, getting around, working, playing: life is spatially and so-cially segmented" (Deleuze and Guattari 1987: 209). The "social" is segmented in two ways simultaneously: one molar/rigid, the other molecular/supple. *Masses* or *flows*, with their molecular segmentarity (based on mutations, deterritorialization, connections, and accelerations) are different from *classes* or *solids*, with their rigid segmentarity (binary organization, resonance, overcoding). Rhizomatic flow versus rigid structure, lines versus points/positions, micropolitics versus macro-politics: a qualitative distinction, not between "society" (macro) and the individual or mass phenomena (micro), but between the molar and the molecular segments, both traversing the "social" and the "individual" at the same time. The two dif-ferent segmentarities "are inseparable, they overlap, they are entangled . . . Every society, and every individual, are thus plied by both segmentarities simultaneously

. . . every politics is simultaneously a *macropolitics* and *micropolitics*" (Deleuze and Guattari 1987: 213). There is always something that flows, that escapes from social segmentation. Every creative potential, and every profound movement in society, originates from "escape", not from antagonisms or contradictions between rigid segments (Deleuze and Guattari 1987: 220). "What matters is to break through the wall" (Deleuze and Guattari 1987: 277).

Fight Club is constructed along a line of flight in the Deleuzian sense. Its lines of flight are attempts to escape segmentarity, be it molar or molecular, to disorganize the social bond. It is "only after you lose everything . . . that you're free to do anything . . . We have to break everything to make something better out of ourselves" (Palahniuk 1997: 70, 52). Fight Club seeks to attain a "Body without Organs", the zero-degree of symbolic difference, an undifferentiated body with no face, no privileged zones and forms: "a chaos so perfect, so pure, so complete that in it all differences, all articulations are effaced. Pure chaos, the undifferentiated reality" (Callinicos 1982: 95). Complete destratification. With Bataille, its principle is "expenditure", with Deleuze and Guattari "antiproduction", a universal tendency coexisting with exchange and production. Fight Club wants to "go back to zero". "The answer is not improvement but destruction, including self-destruction" (Palahniuk 1997: 49).

In his *Programme* from 1936 and his analysis of fascism, Bataille concludes that there is much the Left can learn from the organizational forms of fascism (Bataille 1997a, 1997b; Sørensen 2001). "Assume the function of destruction and decomposition . . . Take part in the destruction of the existing world . . . Fight for the decomposition . . . of all communities . . ." (Bataille 1997a: 121). Fight Club, too, seeks "a prematurely induced dark age . . . The complete and right-away destruction of civilization." (Palahniuk 1997: 125). Bataille had argued that it is necessary to affirm the "value of violence" and "to take upon oneself perversion and crime" (1997a: 121); and Fight Club, again, violently lifts the curse: "Yes, you're going to have to kill someone . . . No excuses and no lies . . . You are the same decaying organic matter as everyone else" (Palahniuk 1997: 125, 134). Fight Club wants the whole world to "hit the bottom" (Palahniuk 1997: 123). Echoing the French philosophy, especially the Situationist manifesto, it especially attacks the society of spectacle. "Fight club isn't about words . . . Fight club is not football on television. You aren't watching a bunch of men you don't know halfway around the world beating on each other live by satellite with a two-minute delay" (Palahniuk 1997: 50, 51). Fight Club is about street fights, urban anarchism, and strategies of subversion.

"Realize . . . the irony of the animal world", continues Bataille's *Programme* (1997a: 121). In his imagination, Jack walks up the entrance of a cave and out comes a penguin. "Slide", it says, smiling. "Without any effort, we slid through tunnels and galleries" (Palahniuk 1997: 20). It is no coincidence that the social space, in which Jack/penguin "slides", is a smooth social space. Losing the social bond is freedom, and in this sense Fight Club is a Deleuzian "war machine", a free assemblage oriented along a line of flight out of the repressive social machinery. It is that which cannot be contained in the striated, rigidly segmented social space; it consists of flows (speed), operates in a smooth space, and unties the social bond (codes) in multiplicity (mass-phenomena). In this respect "war", or "fight", is the surest mechanism against social organization: "just as Hobbes saw clearly that *the State was against war, so war is against the State*, and makes it impossible" (Deleuze and Guattari 1987: 357). It is crucial in this context that Deleuze and Guattari recognize a war machine as an assemblage that has as its object not war – war is only "the supplement" of the war machine – but the constitution of a creative line of flight, a smooth space. War is simply "a social state that wards off the State" (1987: 417). In this sense, violence is Fight Club's supplement, not necessarily its object; Fight Club is above all a social state that wards off "society". Fight Club proliferates in – or even better, constructs – a nomadic social space without zones, centres, segments: a flattened space, in which one can "slide" through connections: "and" . . . "and" . . . "and". Lines rather than points; connection rather than conjugation. Fight Club does not have a fixed spatiality, a permanent address; it grows like a rhizome, through discontinuous jumps. And temporally, it "exists only in the hours between when fight club starts and when fight club ends" (Palahniuk 1997: 48).

Fight Club is a film about mobility and mobilization. However, it depicts mobility as a paradoxical topic. "You wake up at Air Harbor International . . . You wake up at O'Hare. You wake up at LaGuardia. You wake up at Logan . . . you wake up and have to ask where you are . . . You wake up, and you're nowhere" (25, 33). Jack's extreme geographical mobility leads to "inertia" *à la* Virilio's theory (2000). Yet *Fight Club*'s nomadism is not (only) geographical mobility. It is, rather, a nomadism in the Deleuzian sense, which is related to *deviation*, however slowly, from fixation and linear movement (Deleuze and Guattari 1987: 371). It is by staying nonsocialized, by deviation, and not necessarily by physical movement, that the nomad creates his own space. That is, *Fight Club*'s nomadism is also spiritual: "Keep moving, never stop moving, motionless voyage, desubjectification" (Deleuze and Guattari 1987: 159). A sort of metaphysical mobility, a schizophrenic connectionism, in search of new possibilities that are to (be)come. "Let the chips fall where they may," says *Fight Club*.

As a whole, the film *Fight Club* constantly makes use of a schizo-logic. For instance, the motif of "decomposition" throughout the movie is a double reference to the poststructuralist French philosophy and to postapocalyptic primitivism *à la The Planet of the Apes* and *Twelve Monkeys*. The film is both a commercial blockbuster and a critique of consumer society. It demonstrates both modernist techniques (e.g. flashbacks-in-flashbacks, Brechtian epic cuts in which the narrator directly addresses the audience by breaking dramatic illusions, and so on) and pop-art. It is simultaneously loaded with motifs of the Christ (e.g. fights take place in parking lots and basements as the early Christian meetings in caves) and Nietzschean motifs of the anti-Christ. It refers both to the Frankfurt style pessimism/elitism (may I never be content, deliver me from . . .) and mass movement (fascism), and so on. *Fight Club* is both violence and comedy, both popular culture and avant garde art, both philosophy and pop-philosophy at the same time, in the same schizophrenic package. As a commentator put it, "For all its revolutionary, fuck-it-up fervor *Fight Club*'s dirty little secret is it's one of the best comedies of the decade. Forget the blood, the explosions, the Nietzschean verbal jousting, the weird gender mutation . . . this is some funny, subversive stuff" (Savlov 2000).

Microfascism

Lines of flight, emphasize Deleuze and Guattari, are neither good nor bad in themselves; they are open-ended processes. There is not a dichotomy between schizophrenia and paranoia, between the rhizome and the tree, between the strata and lines of flight. And then it is not enough to be against the strata, to oppose the strata (organization) and the lines of flight (becoming body without organs) to one another. Lines of flight have their own dangers, which are interesting in relation to *Fight Club*.

The first danger is that a line of flight can become restratified: in the fear of complete destratification, rigid segmentation and segregation may seem attractive. Whenever a line of flight is stopped by an organization, institution, interpretation, a black hole, etc., a "reterritorialization" takes place. In spite of the fact that *Fight Club* makes a mockery of an "illusion of safety" in the beginning, its line of flight is followed by reterritorialization. It evolves into a *project*, Project Mayhem. Becoming a "bureaucracy of anarchy" (Palahniuk 1997: 119), Project Mayhem is the point at which Fight Club reterritorializes as "the paranoid position of the mass subject, with all the identifications of the individual with the group, the group with the leader, and the leader with the group" (Deleuze and Guattari 1987: 34). In comparison with Fight Club, Project Mayhem is centralized around Jack/Tyler who gives the multiplicity of lines of escape a resonance. Methods change too: "We have to show these men and women freedom by enslaving them, and show them courage by frightening them" (ibid. 149). The new rules are: "You don't ask questions"; "You have to trust Tyler", and so on (ibid. 125). Fight Club was a gang, Project Mayhem is more like an army. Fight Club produces a microcosm of the affections of the rigid: it deterritorializes, massifies, but only in order to stop deterritorialization, to invent new territorializations.

The second danger of the line of flight, which is less obvious but more interesting, is "clarity". Clarity arises when one attains a perception of the molecular texture of the "social", when the holes in it are revealed. What used to be compact and whole seems now to be leaking, a texture that enables dedifferentiations, overlappings, migrations, hybridizations. Clarity emerges with the transformation of Fight Club into Project Mayhem. "Everything is nothing, and it's cool to be enlightened" (Palahniuk 1997: 64). Clarity is also the reason why Fight Club fascinates its members. In this sense, Fight Club does not only reproduce the dangers of the rigid in a miniature scale; it is *micro*-fascism. "Instead of the great paranoid fear, we are trapped in a thousand little monomanias, self-evident truths, and clarities that gush from every black hole and no longer form a system, but are only rumble and buzz, blinding lights giving any and everybody the mission of self-appointed judge, dispenser of the justice, policeman, neighbourhood SS man" (Deleuze and Guattari 1987: 228).

Interestingly, whereas the movie clearly makes a self-reflexive mockery of Project Mayhem in the context of the first danger (macro-fascism), the aspects of Fight Club that do not resonate in Project Mayhem (that is, its micro-fascist aspects) escape its ironic perspective. It seems as if the movie assumes that power pre-dominantly pertains to molar lines. But lines of flight are not exempted from power relations, and there is a micro-fascism in Fight Club that cannot be con-fined to Project Mayhem. It is in this context remarkable that Fight Club oper-ates as a deterritorialized line of flight, as a war machine that is violently opposed to the state; its members are not merely the Oedipalized paranoiacs of the cap-italist state order. Its micro-fascism can be understood best as a transgressive delirium. "What makes fascism dangerous is its molecular or micropolitical power, for it is a mass movement", a proliferation of molecular interactions, "skipping from point to point, *before* beginning to resonate together in the National Socialist State" (Deleuze and Guattari 1987: 214–15). If Project Mayhem is the ridiculous Nazi-type organization with unreflexive skinheads who just repeat Tyler's orders, Fight Club is the molecular face of fascism.

The third danger: a line of flight can lose its creative potentials and become a line of death. This is precisely what happens in Fight Club: "the line of flight crossing the wall, getting out of the black holes, but instead of connecting with other lines and each time augmenting its valence, *turning to destruction, abolition pure and simple, the passion for abolition*" (Deleuze and Guattari 1987: 229). In fact, fascism is the result of an intense line of flight that becomes a line of death, wanting self-destruction and "death through the death of others" (Deleuze and Guattari 1987: 230). A line of flight that desires its own repression. The point at which escape becomes a line of death is the point at which war (destruction) becomes the main object of the war machine rather than its supplement. Fight Club, transforming into Project Mayhem, becomes an instrument of pure destruction and violence, of complete destratification, a war machine that has war as its object. In other words, the regression to the undifferentiated or complete disorganization is as dangerous as transcendence and organization. Tyler, the alluring and charismatic, the free-wheeling pervert of Fight Club, is as dangerous as society. If there are two dangers, the strata and complete destratification, suicide, Fight Club fights only the first. Therefore a relevant question, never asked by micro-fascists, is whether it is not "necessary to retain a minimum of strata, a minimum of forms and functions, a minimal subject from which to extract materials, affects, and assemblages?" (Deleuze and Guattari 1987: 270). The test of desire is not denouncing false desires but distinguishing between that which pertains to the strata, complete destratification, and that which pertains to line of flight, a test, which Fight Club does not pass (Deleuze and Guattari 1987: 165). Let's qualify this point by investigating the way the logic of the cut works in the film.

The Cut

In insomnia Jack feels nothing real. Everything seems distant and far away. Everything is like "a copy of a copy of a copy". Merely following a career and striving for unnecessary commodities are felt as a sign of lack of "real" experience. Much action takes place, but never a genuine act. Life passes by. "We're virgins. Neither one of us has ever been hit." Fight Club is not merely about physical pain; physical pain is sublated into affirmative joy. Through physical pain a sublime body arises: a living body. Fighting is a way to be hit by life. "You weren't alive anywhere like you were alive at Fight Club."

Our central concern in this context is the way Fight Club's depiction of the lack of real life experience juxtaposes the body and words. "Fight club isn't about words." Fighting is not communication; it is not, for instance, a way of saying "I hate you, I want to destroy you." In fact, the members of Fight Club are solipsists: they only feel the pain in their own bodies. Tyler is, one is tempted to say, wrong, when he stresses that after a few nights in Fight Club men are hardened like wood. The aim is not to become immune towards pain but to live through it. Being hit and feeling pain is a way to re-conquer life. The practice of Fight Club invokes a life with scars. "I don't want to die without any scars", Jack says.

Why the body and why scars? The body is that which is not just a "copy of a copy of a copy". And it is *my* body. However, one should also stress capitalism as a background for such practices. If capitalism is given by the logic of accumulation, the production of still more goods, the reaction must necessarily take the form of a useless expenditure: potlatch, destruction, or senseless pain. "Self-improvement is masturbation. Self-destruction is the answer", in Fight Club's terminology. The answer to a one-eyed universe driven by a utilitarian logic is destruction. Furthermore, the scar on the body is lasting. It cannot be changed like clothes or like postmodern life-forms can. If the experience has disappeared, bodily harm offers an experience of life (and death). Through fighting, fighters feel the finality of life, and life itself.

The relationship between the body, pain and existence is, however, more complicated. We witness in Fight Club a gradual process of sublation of pain. First, when Jack visits different self-help groups, pain is experienced through sharing others' pain, at a safe distance so to speak. Then it is recognized that the other's pain basically mirrors one's own, that one does not need the other and his pain at all. Later in the film, pain is sublated into terror when it is recognized that the solipsism of pain has the capitalist system as its frame. To cure one's pain one needs to demolish the system that creates it, which is the purpose of Project Mayhem. Yet, when the direction of violence changes from inwards to outwards, it becomes a hard task to distinguish between fascism and benevolent terror. Both are carried out for the sake of a greater cause. The difference is the subject serving as the agent of violence. Does the subject heroically accept its role as a vanishing mediator? Does the revolutionary act transform the subject? Or, does it lay the ground for a regime of terror sustained by an unchanged subject?

The crucial shift between the four forms of violence identified so far is the one from inward pain to outward terror. It is a change from subject to cause. Or better, it is a question whether the reality of pain is inscribed in the imaginary or the symbolic order. In the first, pain seeks to "harden" a *subject*; in the latter, it has as its goal to install new community. To clarify this difference, let's investigate the different rites of initiation described in the film. What is the difference between the scars obtained through fighting in Fight Club, and the scars burned on the right hand of the space monkeys? What is the logic of the cut? The first cut has, as mentioned before, the wish to escape from the imaginary simulacra dominating our society (Salecl 1998: 159–60). Mutilation of the body is a way of creating the body as a work of art. Piercing and tattooing are other similar techniques for the same purpose. What is crucial to remember is that it is a cut on *my* body, a way through which *I* feel my existence. The cut does not mark an inclusion in a society, but rather a movement away from it, it is narcissistic, signalling that I can do whatever I want to my body. My body is my possession.

In this sense, *Fight Club* remains within the confines of what it criticizes. It criticizes capitalism for reducing everything to imaginary simulacra, but paradoxically it is entrapped within the imaginary register itself. Tyler is a soap expert. The best soap is made from human fat because the balance of salt is just right, he claims. Jack and Tyler steal fat from a liposuction clinic with the sign *Body Sculpting Clinic* on the front. The inter-textual references are here dense. Producing soap from human fat is of course a reference to a Nazi practice; as Tyler puts it, "I make and sell soap – a yardstick for civilization." At the same time, as a critique of capitalism, fat refers to greed, to useless consumption. "We were selling rich women their own fat." The irony is that the fat is stolen from a body *sculpting* clinic. But isn't Fight Club also about a sculpting of the body, creating oneself as a work of art? Does self-creation not in this case mirror what it attempts to criticize? The postmodern cut is different from the traditional one:

> the traditional cut ran in the direction *from the Real to the Symbolic*, while the postmodern cut runs in the opposite direction, *from the symbolic to the Real*. The aim of the traditional cut was to inscribe the symbolic form on the raw flesh, to "gentrify" raw flesh, to mark its inclusion into the big Other, its subjection to it; the aim of postmodern sado-maso practices of bodily mutilation is, rather, the opposite one – to guarantee, to give access to the "pain of existence", the minimum of the bodily Real in the universe of symbolic simulacra. In other words, the function of today's 'postmodern' cut in the body is to serve not as the mark of symbolic castration but,

rather, as its exact opposite: to designate the body's resistance against submission to the socio-symbolic Law. (Žižek 1999: 372)

Another way to approach the problem of the postmodern cut is to focus on the notion of masochism. Obviously, the practice of Fight Club is masochistic. As Salecl reminds us, the masochist is the executioner of his own law. However, this law is not that of the symbolic but that of the imaginary. A masochist is the one who longs for the cut of castration. He wishes to feel the pressure of the law, and hence accepts to install it himself. Since for the masochist castration is not completed – that is, the symbolic is not fully operative – in his rituals of torture the masochist stages castration, trying to operationalize the law. But he finds "enjoyment in the punishment imposed by the law that he himself establishes. Since he lacks the symbolic prohibition, the masochist becomes his own executioner" (Salecl 1998: 156). It is important to note that the fundamental fantasy of masochism is one of identity, of *existens* (Žižek 1999: 281). It is a version of Descartes' doxa for tough men: *I hurt, therefore I am.* Indeed, one of the major sequences of the film is the scene that reveals that Jack is in fact fighting himself (that Tyler is his own creation).

The scars obtained in Fight Club are, however, not the only example of the cut in the film. One day, producing soap at home, Tyler kisses Jack's hand and puts some lye on it. Lye and water make a chemical reaction whereupon the substance rises up to 200 degrees. Such a burn is of course a source of terrible pain and it does leave a scar. Yet, we do not see any trace of pleasure in Jack's face during this act, neither is this related to masochism or sadism. It is a cut of another kind. Later in the film, in Project Mayhem we find out that all members have a burn like Jack's on their right hands. This wound, remembered by any and every member, marks the membership of a community. It signals that one has passed through an initiation ritual. The passage regarding the question of whether the real of the cut is inscribed in the imaginary or in the symbolic reflects a change in the structure of Fight Club too: from being a rhizomatic structure it is now transformed into a stratified, segmented structure.

Regarding the cut, Elias' description of the practice of duelling resembles Fight Club. In *Germans*, Elias (1997) argues that duels were constitutive of the German upper class. Of course one was born into this social strata, yet membership still had to be confirmed, which took place through duelling, with a visible cut on the flesh as a mark of membership. Upper-class men would never fight lower classes. Importantly, the duel had to be kept secret; what mattered to show was the scar itself, a proof of the willingness to risk death. Fighting was forbidden and hence sublimated as a transgression of a rule, as is the case with Fight Club. The crucial difference between the duel and fighting in Fight Club, however, is that in the duel the scar marked a membership of a social strata, whereas Fight Club is more a *mass* phenomenon until it is transformed into Project Mayhem. In this respect, Fight Club is the undifferentiated mass resembling Canetti's "crowd" (1996), while Project Mayhem is internally stratified in line with Freud's "mass" (1976).

In Freud's theory, the mass is organized like a family: it has a father, a leader or a master, and the members' being is constituted through identification with this father. Such an internal differentiation also emerges within Fight Club when its rules shift from commanding secrecy to obedience, when Jack/Tyler, as a Fascist leader, becomes an object of desire and of identification.

Fight Club as Critique

Chuck Palahniuk is celebrated as an "anti-institutional writer" (see Spear 2001: 37). At first sight *Fight Club* does not really fit into the universe of Hollywood. Indeed, publishers initially refused the first version of the book, claiming it to be too dark, too offensive and too risky. Yet, as a response, Palahniuk only took its violence to the extreme rather than toning it down: "I made it even darker and riskier and more offensive, all the things they didn't want . . . And it turns out, boom – they loved it" (quoted in Tomlinson 1999). Why? Why does "more" excess sell beter? Is the aesthetic critique of capitalism, which *Fight Club* enjoins, really "anti-institutional", or subversive, in today's world? It is the poststructuralist French philosophers who most visibly opposed capitalism and power with an aesthetic critique: inspiration, perversion and transgression versus the power of inertia, paranoia and the law. Nomadism versus sedentariness; situationism versus the society of spectacle. Yet, what *Fight Club* ironically highlights once more is that lines of flight emanating from critique are open-ended and that they can be accommodated by a power which itself goes nomadic today.

In the contemporary network society real geography is to a large extent cancelled by the deterritorialized logic of flows (Virilio 2000: 8; Castells 1996). Power works according to the principle of mobility: the fast eat the slow (see Bauman 2000: 188). Ours is a "nomad capitalism" (Williams 1989: 124); it justifies itself and advertises its products also with reference to the aesthetic regime of inspiration: "Be Inspired", as Siemens says. Meanwhile, capitalists them-selves boast in new ways – "I am such a nomad, I am such a tramp" (A. Roddick, the owner of Body Shop, quoted in Kaplan 1995: 54) – and a new capitalist discourse based on metaphors of mobility is emerging in business organizations, promoting the notion of a "constant adaptive movement" and flexible organiza-tional forms that can "go with the flow" (Thrift 1997: 38–9). In a nutshell, today "we are witnessing the revenge of nomadism over the principle of ter-ritoriality and settlement" (Bauman 2000: 13) We are today "condemned to nomadism, at the very moment that we think we can make displacement the most effective means of subversion" (Lotringer and Virilio 1997: 74). And it is increasingly becoming visible that the "new spirit of capitalism" is based on a compromise between hitherto separated regimes of justification and critique, between the aesthetic regime of inspiration, of industry, and of the market (see Boltanski and Chiapello 1999).

Aesthetic creativity, which is related to the idea of transgressing oneself, industrialist productivity, and the market's grandeur, willingness to take risks, are no longer exclusive worlds. Boltanski and Chiapello call this new compromise "project regime", a new regime of justification and critique adjusted to network mobility whose grandeur is connectionism, always being on the move towards a new project, new ideas, living a life of simultaneous and successive projects. In this connectionist, reticular world, in which a pre-established habitus is not desirable, one "should be physically and intellectually mobile" and be able to respond to the call of "a moving world": the "grand person is mobile. Nothing must disturb his displacements" (Boltanski and Chiapello 1999: 168, 183, quoted in Albertsen and Diken 2001: 19–20).

The development of the contemporary society confirms that critique is not a peripheral activity; rather, it contributes to capitalist innovations that assimilate critique, which is constantly confronted with the danger of becoming dysfunctional. Capitalism had received mainly two forms of critique until the 1970s: the social critique from the Marxist camp (exploitation) and the aesthetic critique from the new French philosophy (nomadism). Since the 1970s capitalism has found new forms of legitimation in the artist critique, which resulted in a "transfer of competencies from leftist radicalism toward management" (Boltanski and Chiapello; quoted in Guilhot 2000: 360). Consequently, the aesthetic critique has dissolved into a post-Fordist normative regime of justification, the notion of creativity is re-coded in terms of flexibility, and difference is commercialized. This is perhaps nowhere more visible than in the production process of the movie *Fight Club* itself as an aesthetic commodity: "David [Fincher] said to me, 'You know, Chuck, we're not just selling the movie *Fight Club*. We're selling the idea of fight clubs'" (Palahniuk, quoted in Sult 1999).

Thus *Fight Club* is hardly an "anti-institutional" response to contemporary capitalism, just as creativity, perversion or transgression are not necessarily emancipatory today. Power has already evacuated the bastion *Fight Club* is attacking and it can effortlessly support *Fight Club*'s assault on sedentariness. Palahniuk says:

> We really have no freedom about creating our identities, because we are trained to want what we want. What is it going to take to *break out* and establish some modicum of *freedom*, despite all the cultural training that's been our entire existence? It's about doing the things that are completely *forbidden*, that we are trained not to want to do. (quoted in Jenkins 1999)

What Palahniuk enjoys the luxury of overseeing here is precisely that such strategies are emancipatory only insofar as power poses hierarchy exclusively through essentialism and stable binary divisions. But many of the concepts romanticized by Palahniuk's *Fight Club* find a correspondence in the network capitalism and its aesthetic Mecca, Hollywood, today.

As Deleuze and Guattari repeatedly emphasized, smooth space and nomadism do not have an irresistible revolutionary calling but change meaning drastically depending on the context (see 1987: 387). Neither mobility nor immobility are liberatory in themselves. Subversion or liberation can only be related to taking control of the production of mobility and statis (Hardt and Negri 2000: 156). In this respect, *Fight Club*'s aesthetic critique sounds, if not cynical, naive. Asked by CNN if he is amused by the irony that Hollywood decided to make a violent movie about anti-consumerism by spending millions of dollars, Palahniuk answers that "it seems like the ultimate absurd joke. In a way it's funnier than the movie itself" (CNN 1999). Yes indeed; but as we tried to show, there are reasons why it is so.

Palahniuk himself emphasizes *Fight Club*'s social critique. "The system is more frightened of our anti-consumerist message than they are of our violence. The violence is just an excuse to trash us" (Palahniuk in CNN interview, 1999). Right. *Fight Club* overtly takes issue with strategies of social critique too and launches an articulated critique of the contemporary society. While Marx is disregarded by much mainstream academia, his philosophy seems to reappear as a Hollywood brand. Indeed, although *Fight Club* has been called "nihilism for dummies" by some reviewers, it is perhaps more adequate to label it "Marxism for dummies". Let's begin with the most basic form of social critique: the critique of commodity fetishism, of sublimation of objects that are treated as objects of desire and not as use-value. A commodity is simultaneously determined according to its use-value, its exchange-value, and its fetish- or sign-value (that is, according to its status as an object of desire), and *Fight Club* articulates its anti-consumerist critique as a critique of exchange and fetish value with reference to use value. "Generations have been working in jobs they hate, just so they can buy what they don't really need." The value of what one really needs, use-value, is considered to be exterior to the consumer society. Following this, *Fight Club*'s critique takes two moves: first, it experiments with (aesthetic) sublimation of violence as an alternative to commodity fetishism, and second, it calls for a (social) potlach that aims at the destruction of the exchange system, as an escape from the lure of the commodity form. What both have in common is of course a search for an outside, for what is exterior to capitalism.

Regarding the first, *Fight Club* perfectly illustrates that what is threatened in contemporary society in which the aesthetic critique is increasingly accommodated by capital is sublimation itself. Not only because it is difficult to create sublime objects, but in an even more radical sense. In the contemporary society:

> the very fundamental matrix of sublimation, that of the central Void, the empty ("sacred") place of the Thing exempted from the circuit of everyday economy, which is then filled in by a positive object that is thereby "elevated to the dignity of the Thing" (Lacan's definition of sublimation), seems to be increasingly under threat; what is threatened is the very gap between the empty Place and the (positive) element filling it in. (Žižek 2000: 26)

In the face of this threat, the strategy which *Fight Club* adopts is that of sustaining the void – "so it is as if, paradoxically, the only way to sustain the (Sacred)

Place is to fill it up with trash, with an excremental abject" (Žižek 2000). Thus the "abjective" quality of violence, "the last real form of honesty" (Palahniuk, quoted in Sult 1999). Seen in this way, *Fight Club* is trying to save the logic of sublimation. The problem is that the collapse of the sublimated element, violence, into the Void – that is, the destruction of the gap between the element and the void – brings with it a psychotic collapse of the symbolic order. When the Thing, or the Real, becomes directly present, the symbolic order (the impersonal set of rules that coordinate social existence) is destroyed, the reason why the intervention of the Real is a source of anxiety. Without sublimation, that is, *objet petit a* as a stand-in for the Real, the symbolic order is not possible; but if the gap is not sustained, "the social" disintegrates: welcome to the Real, post-Oedipal sociality of the "men raised by women". Thus, although Palahniuk sees *Fight Club* as a "convenient, short-term psychosis" in a "consensual controlled situation" (quoted in Tomlinson 1999), the traumatic impact of violence in *Fight Club* is so strong that it cannot be located within the horizon sustained by the void of the Real. In *Fight Club* the Real is no longer absent, or present as a void, as the background of events, but is directly present (see Žižek 2000: 39).

The second strategy *Fight Club* adopts is, desperately searching for a nonconsumerist domain *outside* capitalist exchange, heading toward a total anti-production, a potlatch. The destruction of Jack's perfectly appointed condo, his moving into Tyler's dilapidated mansion on the edge of a toxic-waste dump, terrorizing the food industry, blowing up the financial buildings to sabotage the credit-card society, and so on. The ultimate aim of all this is the destruction of capitalism. Capitalism survives by sublimating commodities, transforming them into objects of desire, and *Fight Club* is obsessed by the desire to escape from the lure of the commodity form. Yet, is this desire for ant-production not the other side of the very capitalist fantasy? The reverse case of commodity fetishism is waste: the object devoid of its fetish-value; totally decommodified and desublimated object, which is indeed, according to Jacques-Alain Miller, the main production of contemporary capitalism. What makes *Fight Club* postmodern is precisely the realization that all consumption artefacts will become obsolete before being used and end as waste, transforming the earth into a gigantic waste land, which is a permanent feature of the capitalist drive (see Žižek 2000: 40–1).

Waste is a sign of the growing significance of desublimation in contemporary capitalism. Herein lies also *Fight Club*'s mistake: the idea that use-value could be sustained without surplus-value production, that objects of desire would remain without their fetish value, that is, *objet petit a* (see Žižek 2000: 19, 21). *Fight Club*'s anti-consumerism is in this sense capitalism's inherent fantasy, concealing the fact that capitalism without surplus-value production (and without surplus-enjoyment based on sublimation) is impossible. When the object is delivered from the sublime *objet petit a*, it becomes waste. Waste produced by *Fight Club* itself is thus the melancholy of capitalism insofar as melancholy defines the subject's relation to objects that are deprived of their aura.

Therefore *Fight Club*'s "sacrifice" is not subversive but supportive of capitalist desire. The paradox of *Fight Club* is that it makes an excess of sacrifice. It invests sacrifice itself with desire. "And it is only *this* desire, the very anti-desire, that is desire *par excellence*" (Žižek 2001: 41). *Fight Club*'s secret is then the culmination of the fetish character of the commodity. "The opaque character of the object *a* in the imaginary fantasy determines it in its most pronounced forms as the pole of perverse desire" (Lacan, quoted in Žižek 2001: 42). If avoidance of excess itself generates an excess, "surplus enjoyment", what Lacan calls the "temptation of sacrifice", is to ascertain that there is some symbolic authority, some Other, even if it does not grant what I want (see Žižek 2001: 64–5). Enter Fight Club: "getting God's attention for being bad was better than getting no attention at all . . . God's hate is better than His indifference" (Palahniuk 1997: 141). Again, *Fight Club*'s social critique is trapped in the framework of the symbolic order.

Does the domain outside exchange, which *Fight Club* seeks to find, really exist in the network society? No. "There is no more outside" (Hardt and Negri 2000: 187). With the "real subsumption" of society under capital, "capital has become a world. Use value and all the other references to values and processes of valorization that were conceived to be outside the capitalist mode of production have progressively vanished" (386). The dialectic between "society" and "nature", the "modern" and the "primitive", the "mind" and the "drives", the "public" and the "private" has come to an end. What we have in the contemporary society is "a non-place of politics", a spectacle, a virtual place, which is at once diffuse and unified (Hardt and Negri 2000: 188–9). The smooth space, which is created by Fight Club, is in a sense also the space of the network society and its powers to be. Perhaps there is no topological contradiction between the *ou-topia* of the network society and the *utopia* of Fight Club. In this sense, Fight Club is the truth, or the symptom, of the reticular world.

But Fight Club is in many respects typical of contemporary social movements. The masses in the contemporary society are driven by a desire for mobility: desertion, exodus and nomadism. Whereas resistance took the form of sabotage (direct/dialectical opposition) in the disciplinary era, in the contemporary era of control, resistance takes the form of desertion (flight, battles through subtraction, defection). Indeed, the mobility of the multitude, the migration of the masses is the new "spectre" that haunts today's reticular world (Hardt and Negri 2000: 213). The new terrain of political struggle is mobility (214). Yet, as is the case with Fight Club, contemporary political struggles proliferate in an age of communication but they are "incommunicable". But what they tend to lose regarding extension, duration and communicability, they gain regarding intensity. "They are forced to leap vertically and touch immediately on the global level" (Hardt and Negri 2000: 54–5). Insofar as capital extends its networks, singular points of revolt tend to become more powerful: "Empire presents a superficial world, the virtual center of which can be accessed immediately from any point across the surface"; in the depthless, spectacle-ized society every point is potentially a center (58). Which means that, for immanent struggles *au milieu*, the desire to be against, or disobedience to authorities, is no longer an obvious notion. Palahniuk argues that "Tyler plays the devil's advocate against society . . . Tyler's motivation is perhaps to be against something, anything" (in CNN 1999). Yet, being against is not enough; as is the case with Fight Club, the problem of the network society is, rather, "how to determine the enemy against which to rebel" (Hardt and Negri 2000: 211).

Act?

How is an ethical and political act possible when there is no outside? It is relevant in this context, that the narrator of *Fight Club*, Jack/Tyler, speaks from an impossible position, namely the position of the dead. Speaking from this phantasmatic outside, he places himself outside the symbolic order. In this sense, *Fight Club* exempts itself from the concrete historical context and from an actual involvement with politics. Rather than a political act, Fight Club thus seems to be a trancelike subjective experience, a kind of pseudo-Bakhtinian carnivalesque activity in which the rhythm of everyday life is only temporarily suspended. "You know the rage is coming out some way. And if this stuff can be sort of vented in a consensual controlled situation like a fight club, I just see that as an improvement" (Palahniuk, quoted in Tomlinson 1999). *This* transgressive character accounts for the "surplus-enjoyment" Fight Club gets from excess. However, as we already pointed out, in Jack/Tyler's suicide, there is an act in the proper sense of the word. The *act* differs from *action* in that it radically transforms the agent, that is why suicide the act *par excellence*. In the act,

> the subject is annihilated and subsequently reborn (or not), i.e., the act involves a kind of temporary eclipse, *aphanisis*, of the subject. Which is why every act worthy of this name is "mad" in the sense of radical *unaccountability*: by means of it, I put at stake everything, including myself, my symbolic identity; the act is therefore always a "crime," a "trangression," namely of the limit of the symbolic community to which I belong. (Žižek 1992: 44)

Regarding Jack's suicide (and thus attempt at killing Tyler) it is important to delimit two kinds of sacrifice/suicide. The first aims at securing a position within the symbolic order. The second, and the more radical one, aims at the denial of this very place within the symbolic. The radical act sacrifices the sacrifice itself, condemning the actor, excluding him or her from the symbolic order. Killing himself, and thus Tyler, who is posed throughout the film as an object of desire and of identification, Jack sacrifices the social bond (Fight Club), assuming the limit-position of the impossible zero-level of symbolization. As such he is, while still alive, regarding the symbolic order already dead and excluded.

The Lacanian concept of drive is crucial in this context. Drive enables desire to break out from the framework of fantasy, which freezes the metonym of desire in fixed coordinates. It is a line of flight that escapes from a given economy of desire. In a sense, the death drive is really about life. "Dying people are so alive", as Jack says. Yet, the death drive is also about death: it "kills" the old subject in order to give birth to a new one. The death drive is the force enabling the subject to redefine itself, and it is in this sense that "destruction makes way for the character to evolve into a better, stronger person, not so hampered by their past" (Palahniuk, quoted in PageOne 1999: 3). Here is, again, the difference between *action* (orientated toward and conditioned by the symbolic space) and an *act* (that destroys the symbolic space and the fantasy that sustains it). In other words, the final scene of *Fight Club* is not about desire or enjoyment, but about drive. Trying to commit suicide, Jack goes through fantasy. As a tragic hero he uncouples himself from the symbolic through a process of subjective destitution.

Yet, an act is not beyond the "reality principle"; rather it is an envelovement with changing the very coordinates of the "reality principle", of social reality; it is not "beyond the Good", it redefines what is defined as "Good" (Žižek 2001: 167). In this context, one could say that Fight Club is radically critical of the dominant economy of desire, but it does not attempt a re-definition of a new, another economy: at redefinition of the value of values as well as a destruction of them. A new economy is necessary, for there is no escape from the symbolic order: there is no outside, only lines of flight, a moment of death, sacrifice, and revolution that can subvert the old economy and install a new one. Without this insight it is impossible to distinguish act and terror, flight and micro-fascism, experience of immanence and Fight Club.

> for Lacan, a true act does not only retroactively change the rules of the symbolic space; it also disturbs the underlying fantasy – and here, concerning *this* crucial dimension, Fascism emphatically does *not* pass the criterion of act. Fascist "Revolution" is, on the contrary, the paradigmatic case of a pseudo-Event, of a spectacular turmoil destined to conceal the fact that, on the most fundamental level (that of the relations of production), *nothing really changes* . . . far from disturbing/"traversing" the fantasy that underlies and sustains the capitalist social edifice, Fascist ideological revolution merely brings to the light the phantasmic inherent transgression of the "normal" bourgeois ideological situation (the set of implicit racist, sexist, etc., "prejudices" that effectively determine the activity of individuals in it, although they are not publicly recognized). (Žižek 1999: 200)

There is much action but not much act in *Fight Club*. It is in this respect thought-provoking that, when asked about "consumerism is bad . . . but what is good?", Palahniuk can only reply with irony: "Haha. I want to sidestep that one! Seriously, buy my book . . . or better yet . . . just send me gobs of money. Please don't make me wrestle that intellectual greased pig any more" (Palahniuk, in CNN 1999). The problem with *Fight Club* is that it falls into the trap of presenting its problematic, violence, from a cynical distance. *Fight Club* is of course extremely reflexive and ironic. It can even be said that it is an irony on Fascism. Thus of course it should not be taken literally. Further, does not Fight Club even deny its own existence?

> Then a magazine editor, another magazine editor, calls me, angry and ranting because he wants to send a writer to the underground fight club in his area. "It's cool, man," he says from New York. "You can tell me where. We won't screw it up." I tell him there's no such place. There's no secret society of clubs where guys bash each other and gripe about their empty lives, their hollow careers, their absent fathers. Fight clubs are make-believe. You can't go there. I made them up. (Palahniuk 1999)

It is perhaps the case that "today's neo-Fascism is more and more 'postmodern', civilized, playful, involving ironic self-distance . . . *yet no less Fascist for all that*" (Žižek 1997: 64).

Note

1   The film is based on a novel by Chuck Palahniuk with the same title. Obviously, the screenwriter Jim Uhls adapted the book with considerable fidelity. In this article the quotations from the book refer to Palahniuk (1997), while the quotations from the film appear in the text without a specific reference. Thanks to Civan Gürel for useful comments.

References

Albertsen, N. and Diken, B. (2001) "Mobility, Justification, and the City", *Nordic Journal of Architectural Research*, 14(1), 13–24.

Bataille, G. (1997a) "Programme (Relative to Acéphale)" in F. Botting and S. Wilson (eds), *The Bataille Reader*, London: Blackwell, 121–2.

Bataille, G. (1997b) "The Psychological Structure of Fascism" in F. Botting and S. Wilson (eds), *The Bataille Reader*, London: Blackwell, 122–46.

Bauman, Z. (2000) *Liquid Modernity*, London: Polity.

Beck, U. (1993) *Risk Society*, London: Sage.

Bogard, W. (1998) "Sense and Segmentarity: Some Markers of a Deleuzian-Guattarian Sociology", *Sociological Theory*, 16(1), 52–74.

Boltanski, L. and Chiapello, È. (1999) *Le Nouvel Esprit du Capitalisme*, Paris: Callimard.

Callinicos, A. (1982) *Is There a Future for Marxism?*, London: The Macmillan Press.

Canetti, E. (1996) *Masse og Magt*, Copenhagen: Raevens Sorte Bibliotek.

Castells, M. (1996) *The Information Age. Volume I: The Rise of Network Society*, Oxford: Blackwell.

ChildCare Action Project, Christian Analysis of American Culture (2000) "Entertainment Media Analysis Report. Fight Club", http://www.capalert.com/capreports/fightclub.htm

CNN (1999) CNN Chat Transcript "*Fight Club* Author Chuck Palahniuk", http://www.joblo.com/fightclubchat.htm

Conrads, U. (1986) *Programs and Manifestoes on 20th Century Architecture*, Cambridge: The MIT Press.

Deleuze, G. (1995) *Negotiations*, New York: Columbia University Press.

Deleuze, G. and Guattari, F. (1983) *Anti-Oedipus. Capitalism and Schizophrenia I*, Minneapolis and London: University of Minnesota Press.

Deleuze, G. and Guattari, F. (1987) *A Thousand Plateaus. Capitalism and Schizophrenia II*, Minneapolis and London: University of Minnesota Press.

Deleuze, G. and Parnet, C. (1987) *Dialogues*, New York: Columbia University Press.

Elias, N. (1997) *Germans, The Power Struggles and the Development of Habitus in the Nineteenth and Twentieth Centuries*, London: Polity Press.

Fincher, D. (1999) *Fight Club*, Twentieth Century-Fox.

Freud, S. (1976) "Massepsykologi og jeg-analyse", *Metapsykologi II*, København: Hans Reitzel, 77–152.

Guilhot, N. (2000) "Review of Luc Boltanski & Eve Chiapello's *Le Nouvel Esprit du Capitalisme*", *European Journal of Social Theory*, 3(3), 355–64.

Hardt, M. (1998) "The Withering Civil Society" in E. Kaufman and K. J. Heller (eds), *Deleuze and Guattari. New Mappings in Politics, Philosophy, and Culture*.

Hardt, M. and Negri, A. (2000) *Empire*, London: Cambridge.

Jenkins, E. (1999) "Extreme Sport. An Interview With Thrill-Seeking Novelist Chuck Palahniuk", http://www.villagevoice.com/issues/9941/jenkins.php

Kaplan, C. (1995) "'A World Without Boundaries'. The Body Shop's Trans/National Geographics", *Social Text*, 12(2), 45–66.

Lotringer, S. and Virilio, P. (1997) *Pure War*, Semiotex(e), New York: Columbia University Press.

OnAir (2001) "Inside Fight Club", interview with Chuck Palahniuk, http://204.202.137.113/onair/DailyNews/chat-palahniuk991116.html

PageOne (1999) The Official PageOne Literary Newsletter Website, http://www.pageonelit.com/interviews/chuckP.html

Palahniuk, C. (1997) *Fight Club*, London: Vintage.

Palahniuk, C. (1999) LA Times Memoir: "I Made Most of It Up, Honest", http://www.chuckpalahniuk.net/essays/latimes.htm

Salecl, R. (1998) *(Per)versions of Love and Hate*, London: Verso.

Savlov, M. (2000) "Fight Club", a review of *Fight Club*, http://www.auschron.com/film/pages/movies/9207.html

Sørensen, A. (2001) "At tage laere af Fascismen: Mellem Modstand og Analyse" in M. S. Jacobsen, M. Carleheden and S. Kristiansen (eds), *Tradition og Fornyelse – en Problem-orienteret Teorihistorie for Sociologien*, Aalborg: Aalborg Universitetsforlag, 241–60.

Spear, R. (2001) "Chuck Palahniuk: Ben Aslinda Tatil Kitabi Yazmak Istiyordum", *Varlik*, 69(1127), 36–9.

Sult, E. (1999) "To Get Famous, Punch Somebody. Fight Club Rains Down on Chuck Palahniuk", http://192.245.12.37/1999–10–21.bookguide5.html

Thrift, N. (1997) "The Rise of Soft Capitalism", *Cultural Values* 1(1), 29–57.

Tomlinson, S. (1999) "Is It Fistfighting, or Just Multi-Tasking?", http://www.salon.com/ent/movies/int/1999/10/13/palahniuk/index.html

Virilio, P. (2000) *The Information Bomb*, London: Verso.

Williams, R. (1989) *Resources of Hope*, London: Verso.

Žižek, S. (1992) *Enjoy Your Symptom! Jacques Lacan in Hollywwod and Out.* London: Routledge.

Žižek, S. (1997) *The Plague of Fantasies*, London: Verso.

Žižek, S. (1999) *The Ticklish Subject*, London: Verso.

Žižek, S. (2000) *The Fragile Absolute*, London: Verso.

Žižek, S. (2001) *Did Somebody Say Totalitarianism?*, London: Verso.

5

Film and Changing Technologies

Laura Kipnis

The problem in writing this chapter is that by the time you read it, everything will have changed radically, once again. Electronic and digital technologies are having seismic, unsettling effects on the film industry, and film production practices are being transformed and retransformed on practically a monthly basis. Computers are increasingly affecting every stage of production. Traditional filmic processes are disappearing, replaced by new forms of digital image manipulation. Everyone connected with film is waging a valiant struggle to keep up with rapidly changing technologies, trying to make sense of the present, while simultaneously hazarding calculated guesses about the future. Professional organs like *American Cinematographer*, which always viewed encroaching electronic technologies (such as video) with barely contained suspicion, are now suffused with free-floating anxiety, their articles permeated with loss and pathos about film's potentially diminished stature in the digital age. One can hardly help but notice the emotional and at times overwrought language brought to bear on the topic within the world of film production.

The anxiety is not confined to the industry either. At a film studies conference in Chicago in 1996, academic panellists fretted about 'the death of the camera', and 'the end of film'. Academics involved in teaching new technologies routinely speculate about the 'end of narrative', given the various forms of non-linear temporality and interactivity that new digital technologies have made possible. And how is our curriculum supposed to reflect the end of narrative, when we can't even figure out what production technologies to invest in, given that every

Laura Kipnis, "Film and Changing Technologies," pp. 211–20 from John Hill and Pamela Church Gibson (eds), *World Cinema: Critical Approaches* (Oxford: Oxford University Press, 2000). © 2000 John Hill and Pamela Church Gibson. Reprinted by permission of Oxford University Press.

time you look up, another one is being phased out? And these changes aren't entirely welcome ones. To the great detriment of independent filmmakers, Super-8 film is now virtually extinct (although still making special guest appearances in features like Oliver Stone's *Natural Born Killers* (1994) to signal 'experimentation'), killed off quickly by the introduction of affordable and easy-to-use VHS camcorders *circa* 1985. (On the subject of technological change and uncertainty, let's not even get into the panoply of video formats that have come and gone over the last two decades, and how many carcasses of dead or dying production technologies litter our equipment rooms.)

Even the future of 16mm seems precarious, with support services – labs, sound services, projector-manufacturing – rapidly crumbling. Once Betacam camcorders hit the scene in 1982, news-gathering changed immediately to video, as did industrial and corporate film, as well as much documentary production aimed for broadcast. Eastman Kodak, the world's largest film manufacturer, has been struggling schizophrenically to keep up with these technological changes, shifting corporate strategies virtually from week to week – first moving into videotape, then shoring up film production and fighting to ensure that film would remain the favoured origination medium in image-based mass entertainment, now jumping feet first into digital imaging. Kodak has laid off at least 17,000 employees in the United States and over 30,000 workers abroad since the mid-1980s, in corporate belt-tightening occasioned by a series of bad forecasts about new technologies and heavy world-wide losses. Kodak's Rochester workforce has been downsized – to use the current euphemism – by 40 per cent in the same period. Rochester, NY, had long been something of a company town treated by Kodak like a favourite nephew; more recently the company has vastly retreated from this century-long civic commitment. These changes in technology don't affect filmmakers alone or happen in a social vacuum: they have had sweeping repercussions everywhere, from international markets to local issues like health care for Kodak's retirees – even down to the specifics of the number of hospital charity beds available for the poor in Rochester.

In short, the language of crisis, loss, and uncertainty is endemic to anything connected to film these days. It may be that these are the linguistics of any period of rapid technological transformation, and that at the birth of radio, or of film itself, or the introduction of film sound, or the invention of television and early computers, similar anxieties reigned. Or it may be that digital technology will transform all things, including film, beyond recognition and that what we are hearing now are merely small rumblings compared to the thunder of stampeding elephants coming over the horizon.

At the same time as technological changes in film-related industries are having sweeping material effects in terms of jobs and markets, transformations in image-making procedures brought about by digital technologies are spawning complex theoretical questions about the ontological status of the filmic image itself. Can a photograph be considered *evidence* of anything in the digital age, and if not, what does this mean – aesthetically, socially, or juridically? It has now become routine, via the magic of digital manipulation, to see long-dead cult actors like Humphrey Bogart or Jimmy Cagney 'interacting' with live actors in commercials; or to witness 'character replacement' – for *In the Line of Fire* (1993), footage of George and Barbara Bush disembarking from Air Force One was digitally scanned, and actors playing the First Couple were composited into the image. The truth-status of any given image is anyone's guess. Or if there is no 'original' but only endless perfect digital clones, does this have implications for how value and meaning are assigned or experienced? How photographic technologies work and how they make images available to audiences – questions of reception – open onto an array of impossibly large questions about referentiality and indexicality, onto questions about mimesis and realism. Issues of photographic reproducton, as Walter Benjamin has so famously pointed out, are inseparable from even larger issues of modernity, capital, and their respective ideologies. And *will* the new modes of interactivity make linear narrative obsolete? This is certainly a question with ramifications far beyond film studies, as narrative seems to be one of those basic categories of human conceptualization.

Or, taking the long view, are interactivity, non-linearity, and the 'digital revolution' a bit over-hyped, and are we falling into a romantic and narrow technological determinism if we envision that new technologies alone will alter something so indelible as narrative, or vastly change something so much a facet of contemporary culture as film? And is all of this really so new? After all, the mute button on your television remote control is an interactive technology. Non-linear narrative has been a staple of modernist experimentation for most of this century (or since the invention of the unconscious, if you consider dreams a media form). And are computer-generated images so completely different from the use of models, mattes, optical effects, rear projection, and a host of other ways of inventing and manipulating images that have long been staples of cinematic technology? In other words, did the photographic or filmic image ever have any particular rela-tion to truth or evidence to begin with? And does it really matter whether those dinosaurs are miniatures or computer-generated, optically printed or shot against blue screen or digitally composited? *Should* the mode of production of the image change the kinds of theoretical question we ask about it? So, for example, if a filmic image no longer originates in a 'pro-filmic event', but is generated by a computer, does that necessitate revisions in theories about realism and reception? If a character in a film isn't portrayed by an actor acting, but is the result of manipulating scanned images of numerous faces or bodies, for instance, do new theories about identification need to be devised?

But as technological changes are provoking or reprovoking such epistemo-logical uncertainties, let us remember that these revolutionary new technologies are *social* technologies, meaning that their revolutionary potential is limited to the uses that surrounding social institutions and economic forces allow to be made of them. The captains of industry have a lot invested, in all senses of the word, in hooking us on ideologies of continual technological obsolescence and change: if, as in one proposed scenario for the future, movie theatres stop projecting film and convert to screening high-definition television (HDTV) signals beamed in by satellite, some lucky captain of industry and his stockholders stand to make a megafortune on the deal. Or, will HDTV – the latest much-hyped thing – eventually go the way of 3-D film, into the trash-heap of technological also-rans with all those cute little cardboard 3-D glasses? And do consumers really *care* about television images with better resolution, or do they care to the tune of the several thousand dollars they'll have to spend to convert to the new system, *if* it ever gets off the ground, which still seems doubtful? Do you? It is estimated that consumers will be forced to spend $75 billion to upgrade old television sets once the conversion to HDTV is complete.

But before you whip out your credit card, keep in mind that much of the fascination with newness and innovation, our beliefs in progress and the necessity of change, have ideological implications and serve specific interests, namely those of capitalism's ongoing necessity for new markets and fresh innovations to keep itself viable. And despite the hype about interactivity and revolution, the centres of cultural influence and power are not likely to change one bit, and neither is the direction of the flow of cultural products, or the move towards global domination of cultural markets by big capital. Rather, digital reproduction will most likely simply aid the penetration of new markets by multinational media conglomerates, creating new delivery systems for not-very-new and hardly-very-different images and information.

So if film studies has been somewhat slow to come to terms with a changing apparatus, or to theorize the shifts in film language and grammar that technological change seems to have so rapidly brought about, the reasons are understandable. As I have tried to indicate, these are impossibly large questions, and unfortunately this article too cannot even begin to attempt to answer them: predicting the future, or revamping film theory, or performing large-scale social analysis, or even offering detailed comparative historical casestudies in previous technological changes are all beyond my scope. Instead, let us call this chapter both a case-study in technological innovation (and particularly in the anxiety of technological innova-tion), *and* an experiment in how to write about technological innovation from within the midst of the maelstrom, where things are both nebulous and hopping about drastically from one moment to the next, like Silicon Valley techno-nerds on No-Doz and caffeine highballs.

Film and Video

But another reason for the hesitation around technological change is that film studies is, to a large extent, premised on an understanding of film as a discrete technology. The same understanding permeates the industry's discourse about itself. I would like to suggest that, historically, film has constructed an identity for itself that was maintained by erecting a somewhat fictive separation between itself and neighbouring electronic technologies, and that changes in technology are making this separation increasingly problematic.

One of the ways that film studies has been able to achieve credibility as an academic discipline in the humanities is precisely to distinguish itself from television, to claim (and produce) a more elevated and more high-minded status for itself, that is to distinguish film as art – or 'Film Art' (the title of a well-known introductory film textbook) – from the noisy lower orders of video and television. Perhaps this imperative even factors into which film theories achieve success as paradigms for the field, and which fade away: the emphasis on film as
• a discrete technology and on cinematic specificity seems to be maintained within the dominant traditions of contemporary film theory, such as apparatus theory (Rosen 1986).

What will be the fate of dominant film studies paradigms in the face of technological shifts that attenuate the distinctions between the film and electronic technologies? It now makes less sense than ever to speak of 'film' as though it were a discrete technology. But, in fact, if you examine the recent history of film technology, it appears that, despite the conventional academic separation of film and television studies, in *practice* film and video have been quite interdependent and increasingly proximate for at least the last twenty years, that is, ever since the introduction of the Rank-Cintel Flying Spot Scanner in 1972. What the Rank-Cintel did was obviate the difference in frame rates between film (24 frames per second) and video (30 frames per second) in film-to-video transfers. You don't really care how – the important point is that this opened the possibility of reinventing the entire method of film post-production and distribution in North America, because now origination medium wouldn't necessarily determine the finishing medium. In other words, something could be shot on film, and edited and finished on videotape, and released on either film *or* video.

The advent of digital non-linear editing (the Avid is the best-known example) has pretty much finished off film editing: even films that are theatrically released on film are almost universally edited electronically (either on tape, or on a non-linear system) before being reconformed on film. And of course film-to-video transfers opened up the possibility of the home rental market, which has had a major transforming effect on all aspects of film financing, production, and viewership, not to mention transforming film studies and education, given the new access and availability of film. The unfortunate casualty has been the 16mm film print business, pretty much dead and buried.

Other major intersections of the two technologies are video assist on film cameras, in which a video tap on the film camera allows the image (or a black-and-white version of it) to be viewed on a television monitor on the film set, instead of waiting for the film to be processed, printed, and returned from the lab the next day. This, as you can imagine, has had a decisive effect on the directorial process, and on film sets. Francis Ford Coppola now directs from an electronically rigged trailer off the set, where he can view the unfolding scene on television monitors, rather than, as was once the practice, from on the set, and in proximity to the actors.

The ever-greater commingling of film and video seems to provoke a certain state of alarm, and indeed acrimony, on the part of the film profession, or so you would infer from the language used to describe the experience. 'Video technology is encroaching on traditional film production techniques from several directions . . . advances in video assist and addressing the dreams – and nightmares – of many directors of photography' (Brandt 1991: 93). Or 'A lot of film shooters and editors come to video with a queasy feeling, a sense that they're about to surrender control of their work.' Film folk get the 'flutters' when they approach video, according to this author, who begs his reader not to conclude that he has been seduced by the 'mindless and endless proliferation of video technology' (Roland 1992: 53–4). So while there is no argument that computer-based random access editing – which is to video editing what word-processing is to typing on a typewriter – is incredibly convenient *and* allows editors increased flexibility and creativity, it is still an experience fraught with risk. According to *American Cinematographer*, 'It's only natural for an experienced professional to feel some trepidation towards new technology, especially in a historically hands-on task like film editing. One [film] editor who recently tried our system for the first time was very, very nervous,' recalls the vice-president of a company manufacturing digital editing systems; 'He actually got a piece of film and attached it to his desk, so he'd still be able to touch film' (Pizzelo 1994: 22). Or, 'Rostock, like most film editors, initially resisted the idea of editing film on tape . . . She still has fond memories of film cutting, however. "There's this whole cosmic thing about wanting to touch the film, which I still miss, and you can't mark tape with a grease pencil"' (Comer 1992: 26–7). Anecdotes of this sort are quite typical of the curiously *emotional* tone of much of the writing about new technologies from within the film profession – as is the somewhat talismanic and weirdly occult status accorded to film in these accounts. And I can personally testify that one quite often *does* hear filmmakers, when discussing the inferiority of video editing to film editing, invoking this loss of 'touching film' as if editing film were a conduit to something deeply personal, even religious, to which punching buttons on a video edit controller can't compete. (For those unfamiliar with the video-editing process, touching tape is *verboten* and you don't physically splice the tape; rather, an electromagnetic signal is transferred from one piece of tape to another, or, in the case of digital editing, onto computer hard drives before being laid off to tape.)

The film-to-tape transfer – also known as the telecine process – and the site of greatest full-body contact between film and electronic technology, becomes, perhaps predictably, a scene of particular fretting and distinction-making. One reason, of course, is that film and video still do have different aspect ratios, one of the problems HDTV is meant to solve. Film has a wider frame than video, and when transferred to video, only the centre of the film frame makes it to your living-room. To compensate, especially on the widest-screen film formats, video engineers often add camera movements the director never intended (this is known as 'pan and scan'), by panning to the edges of the film frame itself during the transfer process, thus enabling viewers at least to see any crucial action instead of lopping it off. This is a less than happy solution, but so is 'letter-boxing', in which widescreen films are shown full width, but squeezed down to microscopic size, with bands of black at the top and bottom of the video frame. Most directors, knowing their films are eventually destined for television, simply do not employ the edges of the frame for significant story information, in a routine compliance of aesthetics with commerce – another defeat of film's breadth by video's narrow frame.

It is these resonances and connotations that need to be pointed out, rather than focusing on the obvious material differences between film and video. The more interesting question is one of assigned differences: how does value come to be attached to what are mere distinctions, and how has film's discourse about itself relied on hierarchizing such distinctions into relations of value and merit? Like the penchant for touching film, when you start looking closely at these things, they can start to seem rather odd.

In reading over the last ten years of *American Cinematographer* on the subject of film's relation to electronic technologies, one can't help but notice that the vocabulary brought to bear on the subject – which often relies on metaphors involving the lack of a 'shared language' and corresponding concerns about 'relationships', 'communication problems', and 'incompatibility' – seems oddly reminiscent of the vocabularies associated with other hotbed issues involving cultural confrontations with 'others' like race or immigration, in which language differences also become a way of articulating boundary anxieties. And language issues are also typically a mechanism through which the 'other' is imbricated into a structure in which dissimilarity is redefined as inferiority, and in which cultural differences are rearticulated as hierarchized oppositions. So the fact that, from within film discourse, video didn't speak the right language is significant in its fall from value. It is not simply a *different* technology, it is figured as a social inferior. My point here is not that the film–video opposition has crashing social significance on the order of race or immigration issues, or that we should bring humanistic empathy to bear on video's plight, but that discourses about social technologies can be seen to follow certain conventions of the social and linguistic contexts they inhabit. And I am suggesting that these discursive conventions *have* had significance in both the film profession and film studies, and that current shifts in technologies – in which video and electronic technologies are permeating film far more than ever before (and perhaps eventually displacing it) – are making this more apparent.

Typically, an article in the March 1993 *American Cinematographer* on 'Telecine: The Tools and how to Use Them' (Harrell 1993) focused less on material differences like the 'pan and scan' problem than on the cultural differences – the shared-language problem. Film people just don't know how to talk to telecine operators. The kind of 'close relationship' that exists between a film's director of photography and the film's colourist, that is, between two film professionals from the same world 'is very much a personal relationship'. But, conversely, 'telecine color correction and movie color timing are two different worlds'. The shared 'terminology that has been honed and developed for nearly a hundred years [in film] hasn't yet been fully developed'. And, in that what makes film an *art* is the photographic intent of the film, or what director of photography Conrad Hall calls 'the artistic use of color, grain, sharpness, darkness and motion', the fear is that, left to the mercy of the telecine colourist, this art will be lost. So, 'It is up to the telecine operator to make film *art* work for video *technology*' (my emphasis).

So the language difficulties become a way of erecting an art–technology opposition, and that opposition is one of the most frequent ways that film figures its distinction from, and hierarchizes its relation to, video. I think this is worth a closer look. The typical form this distinction takes is that film is human, sensuous, and creative, while video is dominated by machines, engineers, and technocrats. (Thus the control panels of the telecine colourist are described in the *American Cinematographer* article as looking like 'the cockpit of a 747'.)

To those outside the field, film's aversion to video, or its relegation of video to the sphere of technology, might be seen as merely an instance of what Freud referred to as the narcissism of small differences. Many people can't even tell the difference between something shot on film and something shot on video, particularly on broadcast television, which reduces the appearance of the difference anyway, by squashing the number of lines of resolution (a measurement of the quality of picture information) down to television's bandwidth. (If you are one of those who can't tell them apart, think about news, soap operas, live sports: that's video. Hour-long dramas, movies of the week: that's film. See the difference?) The difference between the look of the two is diminishing with the advent of digital video cameras, which feature controls that allow you to shape the look of the picture to make it resemble film, adding grain, flicker, and diffusion.

But video does look different from film. It is not only its lower resolution: video can't reproduce the same contrast ratio from lights to darks, meaning that it has less range, and gives less detail at either end of the light–dark spectrum. A consequence is that there are certain technical rules about how light your video whites can be and how dark your video blacks can be, and how vast a difference between the two there can be, particularly in broadcast situations. So video is routinely bad-mouthed in film discourses for allowing less latitude to the cinematographer, and thus less creative freedom, and less 'art'. And the fact that television engineers do get the final say about what may or may not be broadcast leads to no end of carping by cinematographers that video is a medium overruled by control-room engineers and soulless technocrats, not artists, because if your blacks are below 7.5 and your whites above 100 on a horrible contraption called a waveform monitor, you may have won an Oscar for cinematography, but your masterpiece won't go on the air.

So when filmmakers approach video, it has usually been with great trepidation about losing their souls in a devil's pact with technology. The arm's-length distancing is evident in the jacket copy from a widely used 1985 (that is, pre-digital) American Society of Cinematographers handbook whose project was exactly to forge some heretofore unknown *rapprochement* between film and video via what would have previously been thought an oxymoronic title: *Electronic Cinematography: Achieving Photographic Control over the Video Image*. The jacket reassures the nervous cinematographer:

> Here's a book that *uniquely* demystifies video and reveals its creative potential. The authors, who have worked in both film and video, approach electronic cinematography from the point of view of the *cinematographer*, rather than that of the engineer . . . If you are interested in combining the refinements of motion picture film techniques and aesthetics with the technology of video, you will find a wealth of applications . . .

The book requires 'no previous electronics experience', the reader is assured. Once again, film is the realm of aesthetics, video is technology.

But let's get real. Shooting film can *hardly* be considered less technocratic than shooting video, and is actually far *more* technically difficult, requiring precise measurement of light, detailed knowledge of arcane things like sensitometry, and a somewhat overstructured relation to numbers: between film stocks (7287, 5298), film speeds (250, 500 . . .), frame rates, f-stops, lenses, filters, the Kelvin scale (a measurement of colour temperature), footcandles (a measurement of light intensity), and wattage (the power drawn by lights). These hardly seem less 'technological' or more sensuously personal than anything you would encounter on a video shoot.

Perhaps the art–technology distinction starts to seem a little more iffy. Now a hard-core film buff will probably intervene at this point to insist that we talk about the quality of the image, and the 'artfulness' possible with film that simply can't be achieved with video. And video often does look different from film, but that is also largely the result of the uses to which it is put. Video does do a technically less precise job of directly reproducing reality with the same degree of detail and verisimilitude, even though it tends to have a 'harder edge' and a more 'real' look. But this look of 'realness' is, to a great degree, a product of video's historic association with electronic news-gathering, or ENG: it is a convention, not an essence. When videographers want to make video look more like film, they will actually try to fuzz that hard edge somehow: by using diffusion or filtration. Film may tend to look more beautiful, but this is also, to a great degree, a matter of conventions: it is generally lit differently (low-key or arty, as opposed to high-key and functional), and for different purposes.

But the issue is the way in which material distinctions and differences between film and video become expressed as relations of value, and the issue of value is never far away from any discussion of film–video distinctions. One reason may be that, as one filmmaker philosopher put it, 'In shooting on film you're shooting on precious metal, that is, silver. With video technologies, you're shooting on silicon, which is essentially dirt.' It may not be exactly the silver–dirt distinction that lends film its aura of preciousness, but the fact that this makes film costs subject to fluctuations in the silver market. Film *does* cost more to shoot and process. Consequently, video is often shot in situations where money needs to be saved, for example lower-status genres like sitcoms or soap operas, or to advertise lower-status consumer commodities like used cars or down-market furniture, or in live (and thus usually more passing and disposable) programming like news or sports. So it may be that video has come to be associated with cheapness, with the momentary, the real, the quotidian. So it starts to *look* cheap, while film, by contrast, comes away with higher-class status. It starts to look richer, and this, I'd suggest, is a *sub rosa* aspect of the romance about film. And, of course, you only see video on television, for free, in your home, whereas the optimal film-viewing experience is after you have travelled somewhere and paid for your seat. So, in short, the film–video distinction has come to have certain class connotations that are piled on top of the other oppositions already in play: art–technology, silver–dirt, higher genres–lower genres, and cinema–television (even though 75 to 85 per cent of what is broadcast on prime time US television is shot on film).

Film, Video, and Digital Culture

This brings us back to the present, and to the vast changes sweeping the world of production. How exactly do they affect and trouble the status of film? Well, a new generation of digital video cameras has recently been introduced by Sony that is said to rival 35mm film in terms of image quality. New advances in digital cinematography software allow camerapersons to simulate different film stocks on video, by selectively adding graininess or other film characteristics, to boost particular highlights, alter colours, change the overall tonal scale or contrast ratio – all previously activities proprietary to the 'art' of cinematography. The first all-digital live-action filmless movie was shown at last year's Sundance Film Festival, about which *American Cinematographer* wrote, 'The Berlin Wall between film and video may or may not be tumbling down. But if the recent all-digital production of *Mail Bonding* is any indication, there may be some serious cracks in the separation between these two media' (Kaufman 1995: 50). It is interesting to note, though, that three years earlier the magazine's editor had announced breathlessly, 'Cinematography now stands at the crossroads of film, video and computer technologies' (Heuring 1992: 25). The film world still seems unsure, regarding electronic technology, whether the Cold War rages still or *détente* has been achieved: should we pull up the drawbridge or welcome the invaders with cake and punch? Even though video technology has been in bed with film for at least twenty years, the profession, with a certain symptomatic disavowal ('yes I know, but . . .'), seems to keep greeting it anew.

Anxiety and disavowal are typical responses to unwelcome change, but what might also make film particularly prone to a current sense of instability is that, as

I have suggested, it had never completely habituated itself to the presence of electronic technologies to begin with, and the technological changes currently under way seriously muck up the distinctions that have traditionally structured film's own discourse about itself. If digital technologies will allow video to rival 35mm film in terms of image quality, positioning electronic technologies to share in 'film art', perhaps it starts to become more apparent that the deeply held conviction that film is art, not technology, is something of a smokescreen for another material issue: that film is, of course, really, a vast business. It is economics, not art, that drives the development of these new technologies and their applications, just as it is economics that has driven the film industry from its inception. It seems fairly clear that one way film has played out its art–commerce ambivalence is by assigning all forms of such crudeness to the realm of video, while clinging to the notion of itself as somehow purer, an 'art form'. Even film academics, who might seem less likely to buy into the art thing in any wholesale way, can regularly be heard disparaging and distancing themselves from television studies. The Society for Cinema Studies, the leading film studies professional organization, has only recently contemplated changing its name to allow some allusion to television.

It may be that film *is* on its last legs. Speculation is currently running high that economic forces will inevitably lead to electronic distribution of theatrical features, and to the demise of projected film. That is because it is ultimately cheaper to distribute electronic images and sound via satellite, fibre optics lines, or another carrier than it is to mass-produce film prints and physically deliver them to theatres. And instant home distribution of first releases by satellite (with pay-per-view by credit card) is even more financially advantageous because producers could recoup on their investments almost immediately. If 60 per cent of revenues are now generated by video distribution a year after a theatrical release, financiers are carrying those debts until the features hit the home viewer. Why wait so long? The most dire scenario for film is that there won't be sufficient economic incentive for film manufacturers to compete, and that there will even ultimately be a transition away from film as an origination medium, as digital cameras achieve greater and greater sophistication.

Whether or not this is the future is anyone's guess. As I said, a general sense of impending loss permeates much of these discussions. What seems to provoke ambivalence about so much of this technological change is the sense that something 'human' is being lost, or shunted aside. There is a definite loss of older crafts and craft knowledge: film editing is virtually dead, as are special effects crafts like mould-making, casting, modelling, drawing, not to mention optical compositing and effects. Matte painting is on its way out, replaced by computer workstations. One response has been a defiant quasi-Luddite return to older technologies: Tim Burton's *The Nightmare before Christmas* (1993) had a cast entirely composed of puppets, bringing stop-motion photography back from the edge of extinction because many older technologies like stop-motion, according to Ray Harryhousen – one of the big names in traditional special effects – lend a certain strangeness to fantasy films which is lost if you make a film too realistic: 'You lose that dream quality.' Other special effects old-timers compare the cleanliness of computer workstations to 'accounting procedures' (Magrid 1994: 26–8). Perhaps there *is* the loss of something ineffably human in these new technologies. The two big hits of summer 1996, *Independence Day* (which had the largest opening grosses of any film in history) and *Twister*, are both noted for replacing 'star power' with massive computer-generated special effects. New computer software, such as the infamous 'morphing' technique of *Terminator 2* (1991), become the star of the big new blockbusters, which now tend increasingly to be written around new special effects rather than special effects being used organically to help tell a compelling story.

There has also been much post-*Jurassic Park* (1993) speculation that computer technologies will ultimately replace actors, sets, and locations with digital simulacra; that 'If an actor's too fat to do movie number four, his head can be grafted onto somebody else's body or recreated digitally'. Whether or not this is the wave of the future, *Jurassic Park* did, in fact, feature a computer-generated actor portraying a human: for the final seconds of the shot in which the T-rex devours the attorney Gennaro head first, a computer re-creation of the actor was used (Magrid 1994: 30). Certainly cutting costs by eliminating actors is always an incentive. In *Forrest Gump* (1994) an anti-war protest scene involved a crowd of 200,000; all but 1,000 of them were digital replicants. Spiralling mega-salaries are the largest factor in out-of-control film costs, and film executives are starting to notice that big stars don't necessarily generate big profits.

Forrest Gump was, of course, the breakthrough movie that digitally put words in former presidents' mouths by 'repixillating' their lips, leading to much commentary and concern about the propagandistic or manipulative potential made available by digital technologies, in which every pixel in a frame can be endlessly manipulated and transformed. Says special effects artist Ken Ralston, '*Forrest Gump's* shots of Hanks interacting with historical figures definitely pushes the outer edges of effects work, dabbling with what were supposed to be photographic documentations of history. When seeing is no longer believing, the concept of photography as proof of anything seems on the verge of extinction. Here's the technology to do really dangerous work.'

Political and cultural theorists have been writing about the loss of a sense of history for some time now. So does a society get the technology it deserves, or technologies that make its own dominant ideologies more visible, more livable? As *American Cinematographer* wrote with some excitement regarding the then revolutionary morphing techniques in *Terminator 2* (you can now buy a similar programme for your home computer for under $100), 'The big news was that the audience accepted an incredible illusion as reality, and they loved it.' Well, it hardly seems like news, following on the heels of Reagan–Thatcherism, that audiences will accept incredible illusions as reality, or that the relationship between technologies and social ideologies has a certain quality of identity.

The task is then, as usual, for independent image-makers to work to utilize these new technologies to create images and contents that *aren't* simply business as usual. Technology needs to be demystified, as do silly manufactured oppositions between this or that technology on the basis of false notions of 'value'. Instead, technology can be utilized to contest the forces of social amnesia, rather than reproducing the industry's incessant bottom-line drive towards newer, bigger, shinier tech. What does it matter if independents produce more 'artistic' but equally tunnel-visioned technological reveries, that is, succumb to experimentation as an end in itself? Too many young film- and videomakers have got caught up in mastering each successive new technology, each new computer-imaging program, and end up producing pretty, technically competent wallpaper. Many of the most talented students seem to be producing the most vapid work, spending endless hours manipulating pixels into submission without stepping back to wonder what for.

Instead, now that it's possible to alter landscapes digitally, perhaps we can think about using these 'revolutionary' technologies as tools to alter social landscapes in more permanent and even more unsettling ways, rather than being seduced into quiescence by the lure of the new.

Bibliography

Benjamin, Walter (1936/1969) 'The Work of Art in the Age of Mechanical Reproduction', trans. Harry Zohn in *Illuminations* (New York: Schocken Books).

Bordwell, David, and Kristin Thompson (1990) *Film Art: An Introduction* (New York: McGraw-Hill).

Brandt, James B. (1991) 'Video Assist: Past, Present and Future', *American Cinematographer*, 72/6 (June), 93–8.

Comer, Brooke (1992) 'Incident at Oglala: Advancing the Art of Editing', *American Cinematographer*, 73/4 (Apr.), 26–32.

Film Art: An Introduction (1990) (New York: McGraw-Hill).

Harrell, Alfred D. (1993) 'Telecine: The Tools and how to Use Them', *American Cinematographer*, 74/3: 61–6.

Hayward, Philip, and Tana Wollen (eds.) (1993) *Future Visions: New Technologies of the Screen* (London: British Film Institute).

Heuring, David (1992) 'When "Post" Becomes the Main Event', *American Cinematographer*, 73/9 (Sept.), 22–3.

Kaufman, Debra (1995) 'Mail Bonding: Foray into Digital Filmmaking', *American Cinematographer*, 76/4 (Apr.) 50–4.

Lister, Martin (ed.) (1995) *The Photographic Image in Digital Culture* (London: Routledge).

Magrid, Ron (1994) 'Exploring the Future of Special Effects', *American Cinematographer*, 75/2 (Feb.), 52–6.

Millennium Film Journal (1995) Special Issue: *Interactivities*, 28 (Spring).

Petro, Patrice (ed.) (1995) *Fugitive Images: From Photography to Video* (Bloomington: Indiana University Press).

Pizzelo, Chris (1994) 'Forecasting the Digital Future', *American Cinematographer*, 73/9 (Mar.), 25–30.

Roland, Fritz (1992) 'Making Peace with Technology', *American Cinematographer*, 73/9 (Sept.), 53–7.

Rosen, Phillip (ed.) (1986) *Narrative, Apparatus, Ideology* (New York: Columbia University Press).

Williams, Raymond (1975) *Television: Technology and Cultural Form* (New York: Schocken Books).

6

Postmodern Cinema and Hollywood Culture in an Age of Corporate Colonization

Carl Boggs and Tom Pollard

The art and business of filmmaking, along with the experience of film viewing, have become integral to the discourses of modernity and postmodernity which have shaped virtually every realm of social life in North America over the past few decades. Thanks in part to significant new advances in technology (videotapes, cable TV, the Internet) as well as the immense global power of US corporate capital, American cinema has reached broader audiences, both in the US and around the world, than probably any other cultural medium; it has become more dynamic, aesthetically integrated, and multifaceted than forms such as music, architecture, painting, literature, and television. One of the defining characteristics of the film enterprise today is its capacity to assimilate these other forms into its increasingly wide scope of aspirations, technical powers, and aesthetic sensibilities. As a vital element of media culture, film has done much to transform – for better or worse – the general public sphere, constituting in the process what Norman Denzin calls a 'new visual legacy'[1] and what George Ritzer refers to as a 'new cathedral of consciousness'.[2] Viewed in historical terms, cinema occupies a space where the global forces of corporate domination, consumerism, technology, and popular culture merge into a hegemonically powerful *ensemble*.

Both within and outside the film legacy, what can be defined as the postmodern shift represents – in its vast complexity and diffuseness – a fundamental trend in American society, first taking hold in the 1970s as a deep response to ongoing structural changes: the post-Fordist economy, globalization, the informational revolution, heightened patterns of consumption, increasing social atomization. This shift was readily visible in the spheres of art and architecture, academia, mass media, popular culture, even politics.[3] Perhaps nowhere was it more detectable than in the world of cinema that, in its elaborate celebration of images, glamour, and spectacles, arguably contained strong elements of the postmodern ethos from its very inception at the turn of the century. The well-chronicled history of Hollywood moviemaking has been one long testimony to the immense power of visual images to evoke popular emotional responses, indeed to reflect and influence processes of social change, within a seemingly endless parade of texts, discourses, narratives, social themes, and technical innovations.

This article explores the unique role of film in shaping contemporary history, politics, and culture within an unfolding melange of forces that not only helps mold but also *reflects* dominant themes of popular consciousness, stretching from the 1970s to the start of the new millennium. Viewed thus, cinema inevitably enters into the main ideological discourses of the period, even if those discourses are not always overt statements by producers, directors, writers, and other creative figures involved in filmmaking. As Zavarzedeh correctly insists, cinema always tends to revolve around 'sites of ideological investment'[4] insofar as it represents particular images of the social life-world: class and material relations; gender, romance, and sexuality; race and ethnicity; the power of national ideals; a vision of hero-protagonists; the place of violence in society; and so forth. It upholds a sense of the past, present, and future – directly, indirectly, or just metaphorically. What seems rather noteworthy about the postmodern shift, however, is that longstanding ideological boundaries and conflicts have become increasingly blurred or refracted, a motif that underlies much of our argument.

The social context of postmodern cinema is a highly-rationalized yet extremely turbulent world dominated by multinational corporations with enough reach in power and wealth to control the bulk of the world's resources, labor markets, flow of capital, and the long-term fate of the planetary environment. These same corporations exercise colonizing power over mass media and popular culture of vast proportions, especially in the most industrialized nations. The capacity of huge business empires, banking systems, and governments to manage economic, political, and cultural life coincides, ironically, with a civic life that is anything but stable and orderly. Indeed institutionalization at the commanding heights coexists with a growing *disorder*, even chaos, within civil society increasingly rife with anarchic planlessness, social dislocation, class polarization, poverty, violence, and ecological crisis. As global capitalist patterns of production and consumption responsible for this Hobbesian morass veer toward ever more predatory and destructive outcomes, mechanisms that could block or reverse such trends are nowhere to be found. In the absence of even minimal international Keynesian methods, the huge multinationals move to further globalize, downsize, techno-logically restructure, and merge while continuously sharpening their exploitative capabilities. In this milieu, intensifying social and 'natural' contradictions give rise to a popular mood of anxiety, fear, pessimism, and cynicism about a future that seems increasingly filled with images of doom and apocalypse. Born out of this historical crisis and shaped by the contours of corporate colonization, postmodern cinema both mirrors and helps reproduce the mood of the time, lending it an aesthetics aptly described by Mike Davis as the 'glamour of decay'.[5]

The Crisis of Modernity

The gradual appearance of postmodernism in cultural, intellectual, and political life – and specifically within Hollywood cinema – is probably best understood as part of an intensifying crisis of modernity linked to the gradual eclipse of Enlightenment rationality. For at least two centuries modernity has been forged through a coherent set of beliefs and norms shaped by the industrial revolution and tied to notions of progress through sustained scientific, technological, and economic development – ideals that reached their pinnacle at the time of the English, French, and American revolutions, including above all individual freedom and rights, popular governance, a rational–legal administrative order separated from the *ancien regime* and its hegemony located in the aristocracy, Church, and state bureaucracy. Modernity was always an optimistic, forward-looking, rationalizing ethos, part of the 'great transformation' that supplanted the traditional order with the rapid spread of market relations to every corner of society. By mid-20th century this modernizing impulse, no longer strictly tied to the liberal-capitalist order, followed the route not only of commodity production but also of bureaucratic and technological expansion, whether under the aegis of US corporate capitalism, European social democracy, fascism, or Soviet-style communism. The 19th-century ideologies of liberalism, nationalism, and Marxist socialism, whatever their differences, converged within a matrix of assumptions regarding a more or less linear, progressive view of history grounded in sustained industrial and technological development, the domination of nature, and optimistic expectations about the future. Where Enlightenment ideals gained a powerful stronghold, as in the US, modernization would shape and reshape the entire social terrain along lines anticipated by such diverse thinkers as Marx, Comte, J. S. Mill, Durkheim, Veblen, and Weber. It would be a universe in which the main protagonists stood for a clear set of rational beliefs and agendas linked to continuous material growth and national regeneration.

Within this historical labyrinth, cultural modernism meant a break with time-honored pre-industrial traditions combined with a furtive move toward (still limited) mass constituencies that would, fitfully and unevenly, attach themselves to the rationalizing and commodifying impulses of urban, industrial society. Whether in photography, art, architecture, literature, or music, cultural modernism became deeply inscribed in forms of (generally elite or avant-garde) artistic creativity if not yet of popular consciousness. In the world of cinema, which achieved a mass audience no earlier than the period of the First World War, modernism took hold not only in the US (with the innovations of D. W. Griffith) but in Europe (with the breakthroughs of directors like Eisenstein, Pudovkin, Murnau, and Renoir), being loosely allied with an ethic of social realism involving efforts by filmmakers to capture vital elements of social reality on screen. Such realism was depicted, for example, in the epic struggles of the Russian Revolution, classic depictions of poverty, exploitation, and upheaval within capitalist society, scenes from the American Civil War and later wars, and the various corruptions of ruling elites. Over time, both modernism and realism followed the path of photographic representation, visible in a plethora of documentaries, quasi-documentaries, docudramas, historical dramas, and other forays into *cinéma vérité*.

While Hollywood modernist fare such as Westerns, combat movies, detective thrillers, historical dramas, and certain sci-fi adventures often entered into the business of mythmaking, in the end, films of this sort usually incorporated a mixture of visual images, literary narratives, and social 'facts' or 'experiences', presumably dug out of the actual everyday world, enabling the viewer to identify (often subliminally) with protagonists and ideals that were encoded within definite ideological messages. (Historically, of course, we know that the bulk of Hollywood cinema gave expression to mainly status-quo ideals and messages.) The power of film to evoke deep, emotional popular responses by means of deft screenwriting, directing, cinematography, special effects, and acting performance was always one of its most seductive qualities. The modernizing ethic spawned by Enlightenment rationality and 20th-century industrialism intersected with a cinematic modernism that remained firmly hegemonic in the film industry through at least the 1960s. Cinematic modernism drew not only from the seminal influences of Griffith, Chaplin, Eisenstein, Pudovkin, and then later such widely divergent filmmakers as Ford, Capra, Huston, Visconti, DeSica, and (in a very mixed sense) Welles. This ethic set out to depict historic struggles between good and evil in a world where (typically male) protagonists stood for coherent values and where redemption (both individual and collective) always seemed possible. It was a world inhabited by characters whose representations of modernity were linked to their sense of historical mission – a mission perhaps most graphically visible in the classic Western and combat genres popular from the 1930s to the 1960s. Within modernism, the hero (however flawed or tragic) was invested with the capacity to decisively influence or transform society, or at least stand tall against enormous odds, exemplified by Frank Capra's *Mr Smith Goes to Washington* (1939), John Ford's *Stagecoach* (1939) and *Grapes of Wrath* (1940), and Fred Zinnemann's *High Noon* (1952).

One way to approach the crisis of modernity within advanced industrial society is to reflect upon the deterioration of ideological discourses associated with historically modernizing forces such as the nation-state, urban industrialism, bureaucracy, and material growth: above all liberalism, nationalism, socialism, communism. In one way or another these ideologies celebrate the historic impetus toward economic, technological, and bureaucratic rationalization which, since the 1960s, has generated a series of localized counter-responses visible in the new left and counterculture of the 1960s, the new social movements (notably feminism and ecology), identity politics, various modes of populism, and finally postmodernism itself. These counter-responses were made possible by deep fissures, contradictions, and conflicts arising out of modernity: class divisions and social dislocations, the unprecedented turbulence of urban life, bureaucratic domination, the global ecological crisis. Established ideological discourses, going back to the early phases of capitalist development, upheld an optimistic, transformative view of history inspired by visionary ideals and protagonists, while the backlash against modernity moved through a less certain, more ambiguous, increasingly dystopic understanding of historical process; the supposedly positive consequences of modernity were thrown into question.[6] Such sentiments came to permeate much of political and intellectual life in the US, and ultimately its cultural life as well.

While there is little evidence to suggest that the 'age of ideology' is totally exhausted, as writers like Fukuyama and Schwartzmantel argue,[7] it seems reasonable to conclude that particular ideologies connected with modernity have been on a downward spiral for many decades. What seems equally obvious is that cultural and aesthetic impulses connected in some way to modernity are likewise in profound crisis – a major reason postmodern cinema has taken off in so many directions through the 1980s and 1990s. While modernism as such has scarcely disappeared, many influential filmmakers of this period (Coppola, Scorsese, Altman, Allen, Stone, Lee, Tarantino, and Waters to name the most prominent) have been drawn to postmodernism in one form or another – a move that seems to correspond to the transformed historical situation.

Here postmodern film builds upon a revulsion within and outside mainstream studio production against tightly-structured, formulaic, commercialized methods historically linked to the studio system, although the issue of working independently of corporate production, marketing, and distribution has never been resolved or even confronted. The breakdown of unbridled studio control by the 1960s ushered in a new era of filmmaking that opened up creative space for writers, directors, cinematographers, actors, and editors, even as corporate power was being reconsolidated. Given the deep changes at work in American society, it now became possible for innovative, experimental movie production to develop alongside the quest (often successful, as it turned out) for new mass audiences. These audiences were generally more receptive to creative, path-breaking, even offbeat cinematic methods and themes of the sort earlier pioneered by independent filmmakers like John Cassavetes; indeed the dividing line between 'mainstream' and 'independent' productions often became blurred, as was visible in the work of experimental directors able to maintain a creative presence (and perhaps celebrity status) within a film industry that had come under critical assault. The postmodern shift tore down, gradually and inexorably, some well-established boundaries – not only between 'low' and 'high' culture (a questionable division from the outset), but also between realism and formalism, between conservative and progressive, between and among the many conventional genres (drama, comedy, thriller, gangster, etc.).

If postmodern cinema became subversive of many longstanding Hollywood codes, methods, and rituals, its distinctly *social* or political meaning was typically more ambiguous: in certain ways it cuts across familiar bipolar divisions of left vs. right, liberal vs. conservative, oppositional vs. conformist, innovative vs. traditional, one reason postmodern auteurs have been so difficult to classify along conventional ideological or political lines. What can be said, however, is that the same trends underlying post-Fordist transformations (technological restructuring, increased differentiation of the workforce, civic privatization, consumerism, urban dislocation, etc.) are simultaneously behind the postmodern shift in cinema. In the midst of a universe of uncertainty, dispersion, and ambiguity scores of films have appeared, including some of the best, that call into question established traditions associated with corporate, family, religious, and patriotic values (even if there is scant evidence of any politically transformative impulses in the vast majority of these films). However, to the degree this postmodern shift can be understood as part of a deepening aesthetic revolt – much like cubism or German Expressionism in painting or *cinema verite* in film – its cultural *and* political consequences could in time be rather explosive. We know that its artistic and intellectual precursors go back many decades, encompassing the influences of German Expressionism, Dada, surrealism, existentialism, the seminal work of Welles and Hitchcock, film noir, and the neo-noir revival that began in the 1970s.

Today it is the larger historical context that endows postmodern cinema with such an abundance of cultural exuberance and creativity. As Jameson observes, there is unquestionably a powerful linkage between globalization of the capitalist economy (a process greatly intensified since the 1970s) and growing concentration of corporate power within the film industry, a linkage that recasts virtually every cinematic development in the US. Viewed thus, postmodern cinema can be situated within a framework of corporate mergers, restructuring, and product diversification as tendencies forcing adoption of novel production and marketing strategies that demand technological innovation, thematic difference, and cultural diversity within an increasingly competitive international market.[8] Whereas postmodernism suggests a condition and outlook attuned to indeterminate change and turbulence, it further signifies a creative *response* to the essentially coherent, rationalized workings of a developed corporate order. Modernism typically assumed progress or what is systemically rational, but postmodernism fixated instead upon what is localized, micro, and diffuse. If modernism embraced the positive, visionary, transformative side of Enlightenment ideology, postmodernism follows the path of its crisis and dissolution.

The breakdown of cultural modernism and the emergence of postmodern film coincides with the appearance of a full-blown cinematic age where the restless search for new epistemological and aesthetic paradigms – a search often veering toward chaos and even apocalypse – has infused the spirit of Hollywood. This quest makes abundantly good sense in a crisis-ridden world of urban chaos, civic violence, hyper-real media culture, ecological crisis, and a progressively disordered international politics. Here the conditions of postmodernity involve nothing less than development (or refinement) of new ways of seeing the world, a new cinematic 'voyeurism' (to use Denzin's reference, in *The Cinematic Society*, chs 2 and 3) appropriate to the society of the spectacle.

Film and the Postmodern Ethos

The limited but nonetheless ongoing postmodern assault on Enlightenment values has called into question the familiar inclination to locate simple moral or epistemological truths that might be distilled from historical experience. In the US of the late 1960s and early 1970s a powerful national mood of angst and insecurity took hold, reflecting all the ambiguity, fear, turbulence, and pessimism of a noir world shaped by the specter of the cold-war balance of nuclear terror, political assassinations, post-Vietnam syndrome, and the continuous deterioration of urban life.[9] Such images, of course, seemed appropriate to the highly-modernized yet socially fragile world of late capitalism – except that, for reasons suggested above, they resonate more fully with the specific conditions of contemporary American society: post-Fordism, informational revolution, economic globalization, ecological and urban crisis, the collapse of universal ideologies. In this milieu, postmodernism has evolved into much less a unified theory or belief system than an amorphous congeries of attitudes, feelings, and reactions – often surrounded by philosophical assumptions – that resist any facile theoretical or political conceptualization. In any event, it would exert a profound influence on intellectual, cultural, and political life in the US, and this would be felt nowhere more than in the film scene.[10] And if postmodernism appears to lack the coherence and specificity of earlier traditions, it is nonetheless possible to identify within it a number of broad themes and trends that allow for the kinds of generalizations we employ here.

Postmodern cinema moves along diverse planes and assumes many disparate expressions in a setting where the film-going public may remain scarcely aware of the kind of cinematic distinctions employed here. We identify five general trends within cinematic postmodernism, as follows:

1   The blockbuster-spectacle (the *Star Wars* episodes, *Batman*, *Jurassic Park*, *Titanic*, etc.), which has introduced the most hyper-real, super-commodified of media productions extending far beyond the movie experience itself;
2   The theme of existential morass earlier present in some film noir and neo-noir classics (*Out of the Past*, *Touch of Evil*, *Taxi Driver*, *Chinatown*) and more recently given fuller expression in the films of Woody Allen;
3   Emphasis on a distinctive American experience of historical quagmire, accompanied by a vanishing of the classic hero-protagonist, perhaps best developed in the dystopic films of Oliver Stone (*Born on the Fourth of July*, *The Doors*, *El Salvador*, *Talkradio*, and especially *JFK*);

4 What might be called a cinema of mayhem involving a turn toward motifs of Hobbesian civic turbulence visible in directors like Scorsese (*Mean Streets, Taxi Driver, Casino*), Brian DePalma (*Dressed to Kill*), and more recently Quentin Tarantino (*Reservoir Dogs, Pulp Fiction*);

5 Embellishment of 'ludic' or playful cinema where little seems to be valued or sacred, where established norms and codes are subject to irreverent mockery, as in the work of John Waters (*Hairspray, Cry Baby, Serial Mom, Pecker*).

While these motifs cover a vast cultural terrain, some narrative structures and social themes do in fact recur throughout – a turn toward nostalgia and romantic pastiche, death of the conventional hero, a disintegrating urban scene, images of tormented human relationships, dystopic (pessimistic, fearful, mordant) visions of the future. True to the postmodern ethos, it would be hard to arrive at *political* generalizations that would cut across the divergent motifs; coherence of this sort is entirely lacking.

We can say that recent technical and aesthetic innovations in cinema have given rise to a body of work that is uniquely experimental, irreverent, eclectic, even subversive in its cultural sensibilities. Postmodern film builds upon the loose associational principles taken from Griffith and Soviet directors of the early period, using the montage approach to assemble a barrage of shots, images, and scenes that are meant to convey a jumble of social reality that is not always readily discernible, as in Tarantino's *Pulp Fiction* or Stone's *JFK*. As postmodern montage conveys dynamic, sometimes amorphous patterns of social and psychological experience, filmmaking inevitably places greater emphasis on the art of cinematography (whether or not digitally aided) and of course editing. Space and time – the whole field of objects depicted in cinema – wind up increasingly mediated and refracted, far beyond what the classic auteurs might have anticipated. While such innovations are not always associated with postmodern culture, they have in a variety of guises come to dominate the filmmaking landscape of the past two or three decades.

Within this epic (if gradual) transformation the classic modalities of 'real' and 'unreal' have lost much of their distinctive character as the old schemes and methods enter into crisis and then begin to vanish – witness, for example, the downward trajectory of *cinéma vérité* that was always one of the cornerstones of modernism. Largely within but also outside the mainstream film industry, postmodernism has created new space for creativity and self-reflection, difference and pluralism, critique of and resistance to hierarchy, though largely within the parameters of a corporate studio system that is now increasingly globalized. Here the glamorized role of the auteur, still quite visible and powerful within the spreading postmodern haze, furnishes new creative leverage for filmmaking even as it works assiduously under the watchful eye of huge business interests. The reality is that many auteurs today have become recognized as public intellectuals in a fashion more or less unknown during the studio era, reflected in the careers (uneven and often conflicted) of such directors as Coppola, Scorsese, Altman,

Lee, Allen, Stone, Sayles, and Tarantino. Yet if the new generation of auteurs is free to direct films that make profound aesthetic and social statements, its supposed autonomy is still limited, falling well short of the cinematic architectonics celebrated by classic auteur theory. Whereas postmodern sensibilities permit wider zones of creativity and difference, they join a cultural process that is nowadays inevitably collaborative, as reflected in the enormous power wielded by producers, actors, writers, cinematographers, and editors owing in part to rebirth of the star system, in part to the growing importance of sophisticated techniques.[11]

This blurring of directorial functions, along with eroding distinctions between the real and the illusory, between mainstream and alternative, between the historical and the present, is magnified by further postmodern murkiness in the area of narratives, plot structures, editing techniques, and the general power of cinematic images. The pervasive sense of ambiguity surrounding postmodern culture enters into most contemporary filmmaking, regardless of style or 'genre'. This helps explain why, at a time of expanding corporate power within the culture industry as a whole, there is an abundance of films made in opposition to long-revered Hollywood formulas and codes, often motivated by a deep critical spirit. American films of the 1980s and 1990s more often than not express a jaundiced view of many hallowed institutions, as conservatives never tire of repeating: the family, big business, law enforcement, the military, religion.[12] Even relatively mainstream films may relate a disenchantment with US military adventures abroad, corruption in city hall, the bankruptcy of electoral politics, the vicious predatory culture of Wall Street, or corporate destruction of the environment – witness Stone's *Wall Street, Born on the Fourth of July* and *JFK*, *Silkwood* (Mike Nichols), *The Milagro Beanfield War* (Robert Redford), *Bob Roberts* (Tim Robbins), *Wag the Dog* (Barry Levinson), and *Erin Brockovich* (Steve Soderbergh).

Yet only rarely do such films, shaped by culturally radical sensibilities as they might be, embrace any distinctly *political* conclusions or alternatives; like so much of American society itself, they remain depoliticized to the extent their artistic insurgency is hardly ever translated into a *political* radicalism. Insofar as postmodern styles of cinematic representation can be viewed as part of a strongly pessimistic turn in social and political life, they offer no exit from deepening contradictions of late capitalism where the prevailing mood is one of fear, anxiety, and hopelessness. No doubt the ethos itself disparages such an attempt, lest it be assimilated into a universal (therefore potentially transformative) discourse. As individual alienation from the structures and ideologies of modernity intensifies, it reinforces powerful trends toward privatized lifestyles involving a retreat from explicitly social and political forms of engagement; civic culture disintegrates.[13] It would be rather surprising if this mood did not infect postmodern cinema, in even its most 'radical' expressions – for example, in such films as *Bob Roberts, Dave, Wag the Dog, Primary Colors,* and *Bulworth.* The overwhelmingly cynical, often detached and socially opaque nature of even the best contemporary American filmmaking should hardly be astonishing given the politically amorphous nature of most postmodern art, from the work of Andy Warhol to punk rock, the music of Philip

Glass, the architecture of Robert Venturi, and the literature of William Burroughs. Much the same could be said of the European intellectual founders of post-modernism (notably Michel Foucault, Jacques Derrida, and Jean Baudrillard) who, though at one point clearly theorists of the left, wound up embracing themes and concepts calling into question the very *possibility* of radical politics.[14] Earlier cinema that appears to have coincided with the postmodern turn – including above all the work of Fellini, Godard, and Fassbinder – fits the same pattern.

The advent of postmodern cinema has so transformed ways of making, seeing, and interpreting film that old conceptual distinctions (auteur theory, realism vs. formalism, genre theory, semiotics) have become rather archaic. Take 'auteur theory', which first gained currency in Europe during the 1950s: what does our understanding of director as single galvanizing force in filmmaking mean today when media culture and communications is shaped by far-reaching expert collaboration, diversification, and the ubiquitous power of the commodity? In the postmodern era actors, for example, seem to have achieved nearly unlimited power to influence script and performance. At the same time, cinematographers, sound technicians, and especially film editors can exercise a decisive influence on the final cut of a movie, while producers and directors – now more than ever working in a globalized and highly-competitive market – are forced to combine their efforts out of fear their project will atrophy. Further, it is evident that film-going audiences have become more interested in images and spectacles than in any particular creative dynamics brought to the screen by even the most celebrated directors. Despite their status, few directors today possess the auteurial nobility of all-powerful figures like Chaplin, Ford, Hitchcock, Welles, Hawks, and Wilder, all of whom managed their film sets with near-dictatorial powers. Neither the authority nor the style of even the most distinctly auteur-like contemporary directors (Coppola, Allen, Stone, Lee, Altman, Scorsese) can be said to reach such powerful dimensions, since neither the culture nor the technology will permit it. While directors who might be broadly defined as postmodern can still aspire to the status of recognized and well-paid filmmakers, perhaps even as distinguished 'public intellectuals' in the fashion of Welles and Hitchcock, their autonomy is compromised at different stages of their work. From this standpoint 'auteur theory' inevitably loses its capacity to provide any special insights into the dynamics of contemporary filmmaking.

The introduction of digital technology must be addressed here insofar as it threatens to alter many of the basic formulas and methods that enter into creative filmmaking by transforming the way in which images are established and conveyed. 'Reality' becomes easily malleable where digitalization is employed. Many observers predict it will soon be possible to replace actors as well as crucial parts of the set design with computer-created images that cannot be distinguished from the real thing. If true, there will be nothing to prevent future films from being 'shot' exclusively through computers, enabling filmmakers to get rid of movie sets, studio lighting, and expensive actors. Such 'virtual films' could be released over the Internet as well as other non-theater venues, an outcome that would result in chaos for the Hollywood movie industry. Among other things, digital imaging separates film from photography and allows filmmakers to contrive alternative realities at will, rendering the older definitions of cinematic 'reality' obsolete.

The postmodern assault on long-established traditions, discourses, and techniques calls forth a full-scale reconsideration of modernist theories and concepts – in film as in the rest of social and cultural life. Defenders of the modernist faith, whether in politics or aesthetics, are forced to occupy a narrower terrain as the transformative optimism rooted in Enlightenment rationality gives way to deepening conflicts, fissures, and challenges that will not soon disappear. The age of postmodern cinema, though hardly monolithic in its own right, is above all a period marked by unprecedented historical novelty shaped by vast economic, technological, and international changes. To fully grasp this phenomenon we will need more than an analysis of 'texts', 'codes', and 'signs' viewed apart from the flow of historical conditions and events. Compounding all of this is the fact that postmodernism, in theory or in film, does not constitute a unified philosophical or theoretical alternative to modernism since, among other things, its own tenets serve to undermine such coherence: local knowledge, a decentered universe of meaning, a multi-perspective outlook, opposition to master discourses, and so forth.

Modernism in the sphere of art both reflected and transcended the structures and ideologies of modernity linked to industrialism, technology, and bureaucratic organization – structures and ideologies theoretically elaborated by the great social and political theorists of the Enlightenment. Cultural modernism simultaneously embraced and questioned the power of the commodity, a conflicted dualism that further extends to its stance toward technology. Viewed accordingly, modernity enters into daily life through the products and artifacts of consumer society, the system of mass production, a large mainstream audience, and dynamic forms of technological reproduction – all elements of what would strongly impact media culture. Yet these very rationalizing trends have developed to the point of near-implosion, generating *counter*-trends favoring discourses of fragmentation, localism, and diversity. For those on the extreme fringes of postmodernism, the new conditions have given rise to a paradigm of historical novelty and difference requiring new categories of analysis along lines initially suggested by Debord, McLuhan, Baudrillard, Foucault, and (more recently) Jameson. Insofar as such historical novelty embellishes genuine cultural change, there can be no turning back to the simpler discourses of modernism that, in film, recalls the Hollywood studio system and the work of classic auteurs like Ford, Hawks, Capra, and Kazan.[15]

Mass Audience and Media Culture

In historical terms, the full expansion of media culture in the US has its origins in the post-Second World War era, when rapid technological change generated sophisticated communications systems that would impact all spheres of artistic life. Although the culture industry was critically interrogated as early as the 1930s by such Frankfurt School theorists as Benjamin, Horkheimer, and Adorno,[16] what might be described as a more full-blown media empire did not appear until the maturation of television, when 'cultural' products began to colonize everyday life. Since the 1950s American society has been literally overwhelmed by a multitude of technological novelties: big-screen TV, cable and satellite TV, video recorders, multimedia consumer products of every sort, and more recently the Internet with its endless assortment of on-line entertainment forms. Within this huge panoply of consumer items and outlets film culture too has evolved and matured – always within the parameters of media culture – thus enhancing both the quality of its product and the scope of its audience. Media culture has evolved into a commodified system of production and distribution, in which everything is done for profit by giant corporations seeking mass audiences, and expanded market shares. It is a culture defined by the steady flow of images, sounds, and spectacles, that bombard relatively passive consumers with great regularity, in the process shaping identities, loyalties, and leisurely preferences to a degree scarcely imagined in human history. Owners and managers of media conglomerates like Disney, Time-Warner, Sony, and Viacom, geared toward reaching large audiences in a highly-competitive market, remain fearful of offending any significant constituencies or interests. The predictable result is formulaic, conformist fare that is either ideologically sanitized or winds up avoiding social or political issues altogether. Still, this is only part of the story. As Ritzer argues, the spread of media culture – of mass consumption in general – functions to 're-enchant', to make more humanly livable, a social existence that has become otherwise cold, rationalized, and bureaucratic. Re-enchantment enables the system to open itself up to novelty, leisure, entertainment, experimentation, and new forms of eroticism at precisely the moment when commodity production (and to a lesser extent governmental regulation) intensifies its hold over an increasingly passive and cynical citizenry.[17] With this the capitalist market opens itself up to powerful new influences and pressures. As Kellner points out:

> . . . precisely the need to sell their artifacts means that the products of the culture industries must resonate to social experience, must attract large audiences, and must thus offer attractive products which may shock, break with conventions, contain social critique, or articulate current ideas that may be the product of progressive social movements.[18]

This duality lies at the very heart of postmodern cinema.

It is precisely this duality which helps explain why, at a time of intensified corporate colonization of social and cultural life, the film industry has been able to nourish emergent (often postmodern) trends that resist and sometimes transcend the old traditions and codes, indicating that in crucial respects media culture must be understood as contested terrain. Some of the biggest risk-taking producers, directors, writers, cinematographers, even editors and actors have often felt free to push their own agendas – agendas often conflicting with bottom-line priorities of the mega-corporations. For this reason it is no longer surprising to see films with unconventional or radical sensibilities produced and/or distributed within the Hollywood studio structure: *Malcolm X, The Player, JFK, Bulworth, Norma Rae, The Milagro Beanfield War, The Insider,* and *Erin Brockovich* to name only a few. In the face of unprecedented corporate media power, postmodern cinema breaks with simple formulas and is ambivalent toward the notion of film as commodity. The new trends, however, fall short of any real assault on corporate domination or market-defined imperatives, an impossibility within existing arrangements in any case. The point here is that increasingly diversified audiences, along with plural artistic impulses, manage to coexist with corporate hegemony just as with book and music production. What the postmodern shift reveals is that film production is shaped more by a diffuse consumerism than by a tightly-administered managerial structure, a development that clashes with the standard audience-manipulation/propaganda model of the culture industry.

Media culture embraces constituent elements of the liberal-capitalist order: hierarchy mixed with unbridled individualism, commodification mixed with diversity, an urban industrialism fused with social atomization and psychological alienation. The multiple expressions of decay, violence, and chaos endemic to Hobbesian civic disorder are reflected in every form of media – TV, music, graphic arts, theatre, videos, computer games, and perhaps most of all film. While modernity remains shrouded in longstanding myths of individual heroism, great technological feats, and national redemption, cultural modernism has yielded to a postmodern ethos that appears to question everything before it, often fueled by the darkest currents of anti-Enlightenment ideology. In cases where a critique of the status quo is given dramatic representation, it is frequently merged with depictions of rampant egoism, pessimism, or nihilism that, while energized by dystopic feelings, makes sense within a society so immersed in rapidly-moving visual images. Trapped in the social immediacy of the present, images attached to the spectacle tend to obliterate a collective sense of past and future. Media culture thrives on fabricated images and sounds largely detached from *historical* context and meaning, obliterating any understanding of deeper social patterns that unfold over time. Whether the cinematic moment is *Star Wars* or *The Truman Show* or *Titanic* or *Eyes Wide Shut*, all attention is fixed upon the momentary, fleeting, and spectacular even where social content is obviously incorporated into the whole. Personalities, melodrama, surface images, outlandish scenes, and of course technical special effects take precedence over historical narrative regardless of ideological definition or cinematic style. Here the much-ballyhooed informational revolution is short-circuited by superficial representations (and distortions) intrinsic to the media culture we have, although exceptions can readily be found both within and outside the discourse of postmodern cinema.

Film enters into and reproduces media culture as a dramatic, visual, and technological medium nowadays given to a marked *rapidity* of shot sequences, image manipulation, and innovative montage constructions that play on the viewer's sensory impulses. In part this dynamic is built into the logic of cinema itself, clearly visible in the earliest Hollywood classics, but has achieved its fullest expression only with the maturation of postmodern cinema. Each tendency within postmodern filmmaking we have identified – blockbuster spectacle, existential morass, historical impasse, Hobbesian chaos, ludic playfulness – is energized by the disparate elements of media culture. Yet media culture dictates a certain objectification process that reinforces the passivity of film audiences: aesthetic experience is shaped by and for the commodity, attuned to the passive consumer, thus devaluing audience engagement or interaction. Viewed from this angle, media culture and postmodern cinema can be seen as simultaneous manifestations of a deteriorating public sphere in which genuine popular engagement (democratic participation in its myriad forms) is more subverted than bolstered. The progressive side of economic and technological change is undermined by a darker, more cynical side that (implicitly at least) rejects the very possibility of fulfilling any historical mission grounded in universal values and goals.

At this juncture Baudrillard has theorized that dramatic historical moments are usually transformed into hyper-real spectacles by the mass media and culture industry, which instinctively blurs the distinctions between fact and fiction, reality and perception, subject and object to a point where all conceptual boundaries seem to have disappeared. Influenced by Debord's *Society of the Spectacle*, Baudrillard's work has come to approximate what we now understand as 'postmodern', in both politics and culture.[19] Although one-dimensional in his monolithic view of media culture, Baudrillard provides insights into the evolution of contemporary American cinema not to mention the broader contours of the culture industry. Events like the Persian Gulf War, the O. J. Simpson trials, the Unabomber saga, the White House sex scandal, and the 1999 NATO bombing of Yugoslavia have taken on such hyper-real status that they are perhaps best grasped as media 'events'. What may be less obvious, however, is the growing intrusion of the hyper-real into filmmaking and film viewing, a phenomenon reflective of the general postmodern shift. Many critically-acclaimed films since the 1970s have confronted, in quite different ways, the meaning of spectacle – or at least all-consuming images – in what can only be described as the postmodern setting: *Being There, The Player, Network, Zelig, Bob Roberts, The Truman Show*, and *Wag the Dog*, to name the most obvious. Less transparent expressions of the hyper-real can be found in films such as *Taxi Driver, Chinatown, Apocalypse Now, Stardust Memories*, and *Bulworth*.

The hyper-real aspect of postmodern cinema becomes all the more intelligible in the context of the industry's perpetual drive for larger and, in many cases, more specialized or culturally diverse audiences. This suggests that filmmakers and viewers are bound together within the labyrinthine maze of media culture, tied to the logic of the postmodern shift. Of course the interests, attitudes, and preferences of producers and audiences alike have changed sharply with altered historical circumstances; one need only compare the decades of the 1930s, 1970s, and 1990s, both stylistically and thematically, to visualize this profound cultural transformation. We know that film viewing has become increasingly vital to the larger process of socialization, mirroring the power of a media culture that competes with (and sometimes dwarfs) other arenas of socialization: family, peer groups, educational context, work, government, and the legal system. Beginning with early childhood, people assimilate images of patriotic loyalty, heroism, violence, sexuality, individual styles, and mundane everyday language from the world of cinema – blurred, ambiguous, or conflicted as such images might be. A central feature of postmodern cinema, of course, is that film images have often become murky and disjointed given that styles, themes, and social roles are now devoid of the coherence they once possessed in modernist genres like the Western, gangster, and combat movies.

If media culture reproduces and extends the hyper-real, individual personalities are bound to establish a special attachment to big-screen images, suggesting that such images have a distinct socializing power that has yet to be fully understood. Baudrillard's famous conception of the hyper-real suggests a media-saturated world in which images become spectacles and spectacles (much like the cathedrals of consumption) become so much larger-than-life that they begin to overwhelm and redefine 'reality' itself, as with Disneyland and Las Vegas. Perhaps nothing fits the hyper-real better than Hollywood blockbusters like *Star Wars, Jurassic Park, Batman*, and *Titanic*. Here it might be useful to introduce Jacques Lacan's well-known 'mirror stage' of early development whereby children learn to differentiate personalities by viewing the self as if in the reflection of a mirror, where in effect the self contemplates the 'self'. Lacan's interest was mainly in early childhood socialization, but the reflection metaphor can be applied to later developmental stages, above all where the molding of consciousness occurs largely *outside* the family and kinship realms. From this standpoint media culture can be understood as furnishing a kind of mirror of the self, serving as an assemblage of 'mirrors' where audiences can reflect back on their supposedly 'real' selves and experiences in the midst of vicariously identifying with any number of fictional or imagined 'selves'. The result is a series of far-reaching psychological transformations and upheavals that in part can be traced back to the influences of postmodern cinema, as conventional formulas, narratives, schemes, and 'role models' give way to a more diffuse, fragmented, and confusing parade of images. If such 'action heroes' as Arnold Schwartzenegger, Chuck Norris, and Sylvester Stallone represent the contemporary incarnation of John Wayne and Errol Flynn (in classic Western and combat roles), the postmodern emphasis on the dispersed, atomized self with its confusion of social roles is readily visible in such films as *Trading Places, Thelma and Louise, Tootsie, Zelig, The Joy Luck Club, The Truman Show*, and *American Beauty*. (We might note here that Billy Wilder's 1960 classic *Some Like it Hot* has been referred to as the first postmodern film.)

Consumerism, Media, and the Spectacle

The past few decades have witnessed dramatic growth in what Ritzer calls the 'new means of consumption' – mass consumerism, advertising, credit purchasing, and leisure pursuits – mostly defined through and shaped by the culture industry.[20] The expanded 'cathedrals of consumption' refers to shopping malls, Disneyland-style theme parks, casinos, cruise ships, special tourist attractions including glitzy museums, and massive entertainment meccas like Las Vegas, Atlantic City, and Disneyworld.

As we have seen, Ritzer argues that these modes of hyper-consumption, available to broadening sectors of the population, function to soften the harsh and alienating features of advanced capitalist production and work, 're-enchanting' an economic system that people otherwise experience as oppressive. Post-Fordist capitalism becomes more attractive to those who can consume, who have the means to enter the hallowed cathedrals of consumption. What needs to be incorporated into Ritzer's analysis is the role of media culture that fosters convergence of commodity and the spectacle. Consumerism and the hyper-real reinforce each other in a world of simulations and visual images transmitted via TV, music, the Internet, and above all the movies. Postmodern cinema has a dynamic relationship with the new modes of consumption, serving to re-enchant a public longing for identity, purpose, and engagement – a process, however, that turns out to be mostly illusory.

This re-enchantment of capitalism is made possible by a powerful shift in the system linking economics and culture, production and everyday life, material relations and the hyper-real that is increasingly framed by and within the media and culture industry. Ronald Inglehart defines this shift as one favoring 'postmaterialist' concerns of lifestyle, leisure, entertainment, and so forth – that is, favoring 'quality-of-life' over material priorities connected to work, public services, and survival.[21] While distinctly 'modern' features of growth, productivity, efficiency, and technological innovation live on, they are complemented – in some cases superseded – by 'postmodern' emphasis on diversity, creativity, and autonomy, which Inglehart sees as the logical outgrowth of mature industrialism. 'Postmodern' values of this sort have been given shape by different expressions of 1960s radicalism, the counterculture, and later new social movements (especially feminism and ecology), and were crucial to the New Hollywood ferment of the 1970s.[22]

Media culture rides the crest of these epochal transformations within capitalist industrialism and American society in general. In such an explosive milieu the spectacle, as Debord was the first to thoroughly explore, lies at the focal point of social and institutional changes, giving expression to hegemonic forms of cultural life.[23] The spectacle converges with postmodern cinema to the degree it celebrates what is visual, ephemeral, and illusory, what is reproduced at the level of surface appearances, through 'its very monopolization of the realm of appearances'.[24] What makes the spectacle so overpowering for Debord is its organic linkage to mass consumption: 'The spectacle corresponds to the historical moment at which the commodity completes its colonization of social life'.[25] Thus, while media culture seems to reflect a universe of integration, it is grounded in an economic system that fosters dislocation and alienation as it colonizes social life through the all-powerful commodity. Thus: 'The spectacle's function in society is the concrete manifestation of isolation'.[26] This gives rise to erasure of the dividing line between self and society, between self and the spectacle in a world where the separation between true and false, real and unreal, fact and fiction, seem to be effectively obliterated.[27]

In the footsteps of Debord, Baudrillard observes that it is the spheres of media and mass consumption where individuals seek out some form of identity and social involvement, hoping to 'participate' in what has become a completely reconstituted public realm. While this occurs, however, the relentless proliferation of signs and symbols characteristic of postmodern culture works to dissolve the core of social meaning, blurring distinctions between media-driven images and real-life experiences. Here the great expansion of media culture and consumerism endemic to modernization turns back on itself, imploding as it engulfs new arenas of social life. This epochal marriage of technology, media, and commodity amounts to the ultimate triumph of form over content, style over substance, going well beyond what Marshall McLuhan had anticipated with his groundbreaking media theorizing of the 1950s. If Debord and Baudrillard exaggerate this phenomenon, the attention they devote to the historic merger of media culture and commodity furnishes the kind of conceptual insights we need to understand more fully the origins and consequences of postmodern cinema at the turn of the century. Our eyes focused on the dynamics of a simulated environment, we can begin to grasp the deep, destabilizing, often threatening forces operating within the popular culture. Viewed within this context, we can see that the vaunted informational revolution proceeds on two levels, de-differentiating or dissolving old boundaries while also colonizing society as a whole.

It is here that Ritzer's preoccupation with new cathedrals of consumption makes sense, for the postmodernity of simulations, images, and commodities counters the rationalizing thrust of modernity outlined by epic theorists like Marx and Weber, especially in the realm of popular culture. We know that the entire industrial, managerial, and political structure is governed by strong rationalizing impulses that show no signs of diminishing. In crucial ways the spectacle and the commodity give rise to their own contradictions: their illusory yet re-enchanting features can easily soften the impact of alienation and powerlessness, often taking people into a world that is quite magical, mysterious, dreamy, fantastic – the very stuff of Las Vegas, Disneyworld, the Super Bowl, and *Star Wars* blockbusters. Among other things, this shift blurs familiar modernist' distinctions between the actual and the illusory. In Ritzer's words:

> If in the modern world everything seems pretty clear-cut, on the cusp of the
> postmodern world many things seem quite hazy. This is especially true in the realm

of consumption. . . . Virtually every means of consumption in a simulated setting, or has simulated elements, or simulated people, or simulated products. Even those things that still seem real have an increasing number of unreal elements. As a result, it is no longer so clear what is real and what is unreal.[28]

As the convergence of media spectacle and corporate power reshapes popular culture, it simultaneously atomizes social life and undermines the public sphere; it is thoroughly depoliticizing, subverting citizenship at every level. At the same time, even if it turns out to be little more than commercialized entertainment, the postmodern shift does allow for limited autonomy where aesthetic creativity, diversity even cultural opposition can find space. While the corporate media and popular culture reinforce dominant institutions, ideologies, and practices, the total-manipulation model is much too overdrawn. Neither completely one-dimensional nor monolithic, the cultural sphere (no matter how commodified) represents a contested terrain where corporate agendas and simulated messages can be questioned, diverted, distorted, and overturned. Perhaps more than any other discourse, postmodern cinema constitutes precisely such a contested terrain. If the separation between the real and illusory, fact and fiction is being dissolved through the workings of media culture, then attempts to identify concrete expressions of 'truth' or 'knowledge' in the complex and shifting visual field become all the more elusive. Here postmodern cinema evolves as part of what is best described as an epistemological movement in which, fueled by merger of the spectacle and commodity, it seems that little 'reality' can exist independent of discourses and symbols constituted within and through media culture.[29] With the visual element so integral to postmodernism, cinema reproduces itself in such a way as to embellish the world of the 'voyeur', a development fueled by the general mood of anxiety, impotence, and passivity that popular culture helps sustain. A cinematic realism dependent upon the capacity of filmmakers to depict and unravel 'essential structures of meaning' is undermined by the advent of new technologies which help to sustain an opaque, simulated environment where (in Denzin's words):

> . . . the everyday is now defined by the cinematic. The two can no longer be separated. A single epistemological regime governs both fields. The hegemony of the camera's eye, with its fine-grained realism, elevates to new heights the visual gaze and the narrative text that contains and explains what is seen. Cinema not only created the spectator in its own eye; it created what the eye of the spectator would see. It then subjected that eye and its vision to the unrelenting criteria of realism and the realistic image of reality given in the camera's eye.[30]

Here again 'knowing' is fully equated with a perception, always arbitrary – of visual representations within media culture.

The collapse of any systematic distinction between simulated images and the realities of everyday life gives rise to forms of social interaction and civic participation which themselves are refracted and illusory. What media culture does provide, of course, is a definite *sense* of being part of something larger: social identities and consumer preferences are channeled through larger-than-life images and spectacles endemic to the simulated environment. Much the same holds for our understanding of work, family, sexuality, politics, violence, even foreign or military policy. Sense of purpose and meaning for most people, feeling insignificant in a society colonized by corporate and market priorities, is readily obtained through a variety of fantasies and romanticized images of the sort purveyed by media culture. For better or worse, individuals may carve out 'selves' defined by representations of media personae – the rich and famous, superstar athletes, rock personalities, TV sit-com celebrities, and, of course, film stars who may ultimately come to dwarf their cinematic vehicles (*Star Wars, Batman, Titanic, Jurassic Park, Saturday Night Fever*, etc.)

These developments are magnified at precisely the moment when old Hollywood institutional restraints and codes have been breaking down, opening the gates of independence and creativity to a new wave of film producers, directors, writers, and actors who defined the 'New Hollywood' sensibility and built the artistic and intellectual foundations of postmodern cinema. Even while ensconced in a hyper-real setting, an emergent cultural elite was able to generate tremendous power and status through its mobilization of compelling narratives, images, and themes associated with an extensive body of original and experimental cinema, much of it shaped by rebellious, anti-status quo ideas and values. At a time when the power of cinema to impact popular consciousness had grown beyond anything previously imagined, where everyday life is saturated with media culture, filmmakers in the postmodern idiom often hold views that are harshly critical of both the Hollywood establishment and the larger power structure (or culture). The familiar notion that Hollywood was always a bastion of deeply-conservative ideology cannot be sustained in the face of much evidence to the contrary, especially today.[31] Film audiences, meanwhile, have become younger, more affluent, better educated, more cinematically sophisticated, more attuned to new ideas, techniques, and motifs, and more accustomed to a generation of actors famous for their nonconformist or 'outlaw' roles (including Brando, Pacino, DeNiro, Beatty, Dunaway, Penn, Nicholson, Hoffman, Jane and Peter Fonda). Viewers have been weaned on films dwelling upon corruption, family breakdown, tormented sexuality, violence, and above all social chaos, themes inspired by an outlook hostile to most institutions of the status quo. Yet such ideological hostility could go only so far: innovation, change, and diversity inevitably wound up confined to the (always-shifting) parameters of media culture and the commodity.

Historical Mise-en-Scène

In *Ecology of Fear*, Mike Davis writes of a 'Blade Runner' society where ecological catastrophes, mounting social crises, and the plain misery of everyday urban life

will converge to produce an impending nightmarish future for sprawling, fragmented cities like Los Angeles. Reflecting upon historical conditions we have come
to associate with a post-Fordist, globalized capitalist system, Davis pointedly
asks: 'Is there any need to explain *why* fear eats at the soul of Los Angeles?'[32]
Los Angeles, of course, is the city of Raymond Chandler, James L. Cain, the rich
Hollywood noir tradition – not to mention the upheavals surrounding the bombing of the *Los Angeles Times* building prior to the First World War, the Black
Dahlia murder, two major riots (in 1965 and 1992), the Rodney King episode,
the Charles Manson killings, the O. J. Simpson spectacle, and the more recent
LAPD scandal as well as periodic earthquakes, fires, and floods. The unsettling
scenario painted by Davis far transcends anything imagined by the great architects
of noir or standard dystopic postmodernism, but it does suggest a milieu (within
and far outside of Los Angeles) in which contemporary film directors like Tarantino,
the Coen Brothers, John Badham, Bryan Singer, Mike Figgis, and the Oliver
Stone of *Natural Born Killers* and *JFK* will routinely discover abundant non-
fictional material. Today, Los Angeles is the main locus of a renewed noir tradition based in the work of African-American writers like Walter Mosley and Gary
Phillips. Although a vital task of film directors is to give a semblance of order and
meaning to artistic projects, the logic of both Hobbesian society and postmodern
culture works directly in opposition to this: disorder and chaos define much of
the social and political landscape, occupying and helping determine the very
center of the filmmaking enterprise we refer to as postmodern – always remem-
bering that the enterprise is not especially conscious or planned by the creative
agents involved. At a time of intensified economic globalization and expanding
media culture, the merging of historical trends and creative forces within cinema
mirrors yet another phenomenon – namely, the profound and astonishingly rapid
disintegration of American politics.

We thus arrive at one of the crucial dimensions of postmodern cinema, at least
in the US – its abiding hostility to the world of political thought and action. We
know that postmodernism as a general trend is antagonistic toward the idea of
fixed discourses, identities, and meanings, and is even more fiercely hostile to the
Enlightenment faith in modernity and its basically optimistic vision of the future
that extends across the ideological spectrum. Here it is possible to see in the crisis
of modernity a parallel crisis of the public sphere, with postmodernism taking on
something of the character of the 'post-political'.[33] In the realm of cinema the
future is given to contemporary audiences as murky, frightening, hard to decipher, much like those dystopic scenarios in *Blade Runner, Brazil, Pulp Fiction,
Natural Born Killers*, and *The End of Violence*. As we have seen, the postmodern
era is one where social life appears increasingly destabilized, purposeless, dominated by images of chaos, quite at odds with the requirements of coherent
ideological discourse and political action. This helps to explain why the work of
most postmodern filmmakers turns out to be so politically elusive, so difficult to
locate along the ideological spectrum; it can be simultaneously 'conservative' and
'radical' or 'liberal', critical of the status quo (and the film industry), yet impotent

to embrace anything resembling collective action or social change, to identify alternatives to the present corruptions and nightmares. In their anti-political ethos, postmodern film narratives and styles tend to be broken, discontinuous, and pastiche-like, perhaps aesthetically compelling, but rarely consonant with anything but the most ludic or surreal discourses. Nietzsche's famous 19th-century 'death of God' pronouncement turns into a more contemporary statement about the 'death of the hero' and finally the 'death of politics' as we begin the 21st century.

The historical trend toward depoliticization finds its expression in contemporary Hollywood filmmaking just as in other areas of social and cultural life. Postmodern cinema inherits and builds upon a long tradition of American hostility to politics, upon such trends as noir and neo-noir where suspicion, fear, and paranoia rule, where political ideals and good works are scoffed at, where the public sphere is riddled with corruption, greed, distrust, cynicism, and violence. A good many films in the pre-New Hollywood era echoed this motif, including *Dr. Strangelove*, *The Manchurian Candidate*, *Seven Days in May*, and *Easy Rider*. Later, films like Brian DePalma's *Blow Out* (1981) and Alan Pakula's *All the President's Men* (1976) embellished themes of political skullduggery, conspiracy, and cover-ups that, in the Vietnam and post-Vietnam periods, became staples of American politics. DePalma's work, including also *Obsession* (1976) and his more recent *Snake Eyes* (1998), dwelled especially upon themes of paranoia, surveillance, and voyeurism made commonplace by the advent of new technology. Today, even films that engage politics in some fashion – *Bob Roberts*, *Wag the Dog*, *Enemy of the State*, *Primary Colors*, *Bulworth* – present distinctly alienated, jaundiced views of government, politics, and politicians. Other pictures with clearly progressive agendas – *A Civil Action*, *The Insider*, *Erin Brockovich*, *Ghosts of Mississippi* – offer images of collective action that fall considerably short of *political* engagement; they uphold the idea of citizen initiatives only within a localized, delimited sphere.

With the postmodern turn we encounter a more heightened spirit of anti-politics, one immersed in a Hobbesian state of nature where chaos, violence, and dystopic images of the future seem increasingly *de rigeur*. Here Oliver Stone's masterpiece, *JFK*, offers a quintessential example of a motion picture that sets out to explore the deep quagmire of recent US history and politics. Stone of course indicts a broad network of groups in the murder of President Kennedy, including the Mafia, CIA, anti-Castro Cubans, even sectors of the power structure itself, along with others involved in the cover-up (the Warren Commission, politicians, journalists, *et al.*). The brilliant cinematography employed by Stone and Bill Richardson reinforces a mood of fear, paranoia, turbulence, and dystopia that characterizes not only the momentary events but also much of contemporary US history. Stone makes the case here, as he has in films like *Salvador*, *Born on the Fourth of July*, and *Talk Radio*, that politics amounts to nothing more than a cesspool of immorality, corruption, and futility, with seemingly no exit out of the morass. Other postmodern-style films of the 1990s featured and indeed celebrated this ethos of anti-politics, reflective of pervasive trends in American society: loss of civic idealism, eroding public trust in government and politicians, privatization of social life, trivialization of political debates, ideological convergence of the two major parties, the corrosive influence of corporations and money in politics. Where modernist cinema generally celebrated the liberal-capitalist tradition, postmodernism embraces a far more jaundiced view of the public sphere. Tim Robbins' savagely satirical treatment of American electoral politics, *Bob Roberts* (1992) furnishes a case in point. With Citizen Kane-type hubris, Roberts (played by Tim Robbins) is a right-wing folk singer running against liberal Brickley Paiste (Gore Vidal) for US senate, using his celebrity status to blast liberals and their big-spending social programs as the source of all problems. The 'campaign' unfolds in surreal fashion, with contrived debates, phony scandals, candidate pratfalls, silly everyday crises, a desperate attempt to murder Roberts, and of course plenty of music. In the end, the media spectacle outdoes itself but nothing of political substance is ever discussed; American politics is revealed as a farcical interlude in people's daily lives. In a similar vein, *Wag the Dog* (Barry Levinson, 1997) satirizes both government and mass media, showing how a President who needs to worm his way out of a sex scandal employs a team of advisors and media consultants to manufacture a foreign 'crisis'. A fierce patriotic campaign is orchestrated against a demonic enemy (tiny Albania) with hopes of distracting popular attention away from the scandal and thus ensuring the President's reelection two weeks hence. The shrewd figure behind all this is Hollywood producer Hanley Motss (Dustin Hoffman), whose manipulative skills are so powerful he is able to dupe an entire nation.

The outright contempt for American politics evoked in these films turns out to be very close to the way ordinary people experience government, politicians, and their phony 'debates' and controversies. Mike Nichols' *Primary Colors* (1998) and Warren Beatty's *Bulworth* (1998) continue this tradition, as do such documentaries as *American Dream, A Perfect Candidate*, and *The Big One*. Beatty's approach to American politics is essentially a surreal assault on everything that corrodes the body politic, all squarely within the spirit of postmodern cinema: empty promises, boring speeches, phony personalities, corporate deceit, media manipulation, and racism. The 'post-political' aspect of postmodern filmmaking goes beyond direct encounters with politics as such, extending above all into the arena of media culture where the vast power of images and spectacles contributes so much to the depoliticization of American society. Interesting enough, those films mentioned above all dwell upon the famous marriage of politics and media, which by the 1990s had become more intimate and hegemonic than earlier media theorists like McLuhan, Debord, and Baudrillard might have imagined.

Postmodern cinema constitutes a (partial and uneven) revolutionary break with Hollywood tradition rooted in modernist values and the studio system. The fact that its break has been partial and uneven is unavoidable given its place, however ambivalent, within the globalized corporate system. A more thorough cultural, not to mention political, departure would require a fundamental move away from corporate-industrial structures and priorities that continue to shape the bulk of mainstream and 'indie' filmmaking – a move that hardly seems imminent. Even the most creative, experimental, indeed progressive filmmaking will for the most part give expression, therefore, to that very Hobbesian state of nature which corporate colonization so systematically fosters.

At its deepest level, postmodern cinema, in particular, and postmodern culture, in general, so devalues universal discourses – and with it coherent social and political narratives – that the dynamics of public life are quickly diminished if not forgotten. Depoliticization is built into the very logic of such 'post-political' motifs, in film as elsewhere. In the highly splintered, discontinuous postmodern milieu, social bonds and feelings of community are profoundly weakened as the vital linkage between everyday personal life and the public sphere is increasingly severed; politics becomes the object of suspicion, distrust, fear, and hostility. In part the legacy of a liberal-capitalist ethos that seems so firmly entrenched in American history, this narrowing of politics coincides with a precipitous loss of public and moral vision, and with the absence of countervailing mechanisms strong enough to reverse the corporate colonization of the world. We are left with those images furnished by motion pictures, mainly accurate, of a society in which the corporate pursuit of material self-interest, wealth, and power reproduces institutional domination at the same time that it generates a culture immersed in chaos, violence, decay, and dystopia.

Notes

1 Norman Denzin, *The Cinematic Society* (London: Sage, 1995), p. 13.

2 George Ritzer, *Enchanting a Disenchanted World* (Thousand Oaks, CA: Pine Forge, 1999), p. xi.

3 Steven Best and Douglas Kellner, *The Postmodern Turn* (New York: Guilford, 1997), introduction.

4 Mas'ud Zavarzadeh, *Seeing Films Politically* (Albany, NY: SUNY Press, 1991), p. 1.

5 Mike Davis, *Ecology of Fear* (New York: Henry Holt, 1998), p. 278.

6 See William Ophuls, *Requiem for Modern Politics* (Boulder, CO: Westview Press, 1997), chapter 1.

7 See Francis Fukuyama, *The End of History and the Last Man* (New York: The Free Press, 1992), chapter 1, and John Schwartzmantel, *The Age of Ideology* (New York: NYU Press, 1998), p. 9.

8 Fredric Jameson, *Postmodernism, or the Cultural Logic of Late Capitalism* (Durham: Duke University Press, 1995).

9 Nicholas Christopher, *Somewhere in the Night* (New York: Henry Holt, 1997), chapter 2.

10 See especially Timothy Corrigan, 'Auteurs and the New Hollywood', in Jon Lewis (ed.), *The New American Cinema* (Durham, NC: Duke University Press, 1998), pp. 38–63.

11 Walter Murch, *In the Blink of an Eye* (Los Angeles: Silman-James Press, 1995), passim.

12 This point is made emphatically, and for the most part persuasively, by Michael Medved in his *Hollywood vs. America* (New York: HarperCollins, 1992).

13 On the theme of civic disengagement in American politics, see Carl Boggs, *The End of Politics* (New York: Guilford, 2000), chapter 1.

14 Best and Kellner, *The Postmodern Turn*, pp. 4–6.

15 On this point see Sam Girgus' excellent account in *Hollywood Renaissance* (New York: Cambridge University Press, 1998), chapter 1.

16 See, for example, Max Horkheimer's analysis in 'Art and Mass Culture', in *Critical Theory* (New York: Seabury, 1972), pp. 273–90.

17 See Ritzer, *Enchanting*, chapter 5.

18 Douglas Kellner, *Media Culture* (New York: Routledge, 1995), p. 16.

19 Among other sources, see Jean Baudrillard, *The Consumer Society* (London: Sage, 1998 [1970]).

20 Ritzer, *Enchanting*, pp. 172–86.

21 Ronald Inglehart, *Modernization and Postmodernization* (Princeton, NJ: Princeton University Press, 1997), p. 22.

22 Peter Biskind, *Easy Riders, Raging Bulls* (New York: McGraw-Hill, 1998).

23 Guy Debord, *Society of the Spectacle* (New York: Zone Press, 1995), p. 13.

24 Debord, *Society of the Spectacle*, p. 15.

25 Debord, *Society of the Spectacle*, p. 29.

26 Debord, *Society of the Spectacle*, p. 23.

27 Debord, *Society of the Spectacle*, p. 153.

28 Ritzer, *Enchanting*.

29 Denzin, *The Cinematic Society*, p. 201.

30 Denzin, *The Cinematic Society*, p. 36.

31 Stephen Powers, David J. Rothman and Stanley Rothman, *Hollywood's America* (Boulder, CO: Westview Press, 1996).

32 Davis, *Ecology of Fear*, p. 363.

33 Boggs, *The End of Politics*, chapter 7.

Part II
Genders: More than Two

Introduction

Gender issues in culture and in film began to surface as a visible and discursive topic in the political activism of the 1960s in the United States and Europe. In academia women's studies programs appeared in this and subsequent decades, and some programs later changed their designation to gender studies as a result of the growing attention to new studies in masculinity in many fields in the humanities and social sciences since the 1980s.

Feminists have argued that gender is socially constructed and defined, and is not biologically determined. Feminist studies of culture largely focused on content – images of women, social limitations, sexual identities (e.g. "good" and "bad" girls/women), and the lives of actresses on and off screen. Laura Mulvey's groundbreaking essay "Visual Pleasure and Narrative Cinema" (in Mulvey, 1989, pp. 14–29) offered an analysis of the female spectator's identification with filmic characters' roles and identities on screen. Mulvey opened up a focus for film studies on film's psychoanalytic processes, a field also innovatively explored in conjunction with gender issues by Kaja Silverman. Some feminists drew upon Jacques Lacan's psychoanalytic theories in which the film creates a "gaze" that, bearing the social order and conventions, subjugates the viewer who is induced to desire what is on the screen. These theories stress the viewer's desire for a wholeness of self, like the idealistic self we see in the mirror (Lacan's theory of the infant's mirror stage). We viewers project this desire onto the screen, but it is always illusionary. Mulvey assumed that film (and mass culture in general) forms spectators into subjects that fit conventional social categories of gender. Mulvey concluded that men and women are differentially positioned by cinema: men as subjects identifying with agents who drive film narrative; women as objects for masculine desire and fetishistic gazing.

Employing Lacanian psychoanalysis to account for gendered subjectivity, desire, and visual pleasure, Mulvey did not acknowledge spectatorship as a possible site of resistance or of critical viewing. She later reconsidered her theories and acknowledged spectators' differences from each other and from fixed film identities, recognizing spectators as active participants who respond in many ways, including resistance and revision, to gendered identities and expectations projected by film genres. In her second essay, "Afterthoughts on 'Visual Pleasure and Narrative Cinema,'" Mulvey refines some of her ideas, focusing on the film *Duel in the Sun* (1946). Recent feminist theorists continue to explore diverse accounts of spectators' self, agency, identity, and viewing circumstances both as individuals (psychoanalysis) and as social/socialized beings. These nuanced theories try to account for viewers' unpredictable reception and interpretations of films outside of the intended meanings in films' conventional representations.

Gender, a social formation distinct from one's biological sex, offers a variety of viewing situations for all spectators. Studies of masculinity have revised gender studies, most notably by denying a standard masculine position or gaze, and by recognizing the instability and fragility of masculine identities, shaped and reshaped by mass culture. Masculinity studies also reinvested the notion of genre, as in analyses of male "weepies," or melodramas, usually considered a "female" genre, or of the dominance of women in recent action films (e.g. *Lara Croft: Tomb Raider*, 2001, or *Alien*, 1979), a genre usually filled with men only. In addition, scholars have demonstrated that war films, usually assumed to be heavily invested in conventional masculine ideals, are more complex, offering multiple gender identities and modes of masculinity. To complicate matters, the physical ideals for men and for women change, too, from the slender male ideals of the 1940s to the muscle-bound fighters played by Arnold Schwarzenegger or Sylvester Stallone, or in the many variations on ideal female bodies, personalities, and faces in films.

What are "gender" films? There is hardly an obvious category of gender films; gender arises as an issue in almost all films. There are films full of male characters (e.g. war films) in which women are absent or serve as imaginary evidence (photos of sweethearts, for example) of male heterosexuality. These and "cop" films play with masculine ideals as buddies in these films often go through a variety of emotions, usually resolved in a macho conclusion. Men may have a variety of responses to masculine situations of war and be measured on a scale of masculinity (e.g. *The Deer Hunter*, 1978, in which the gentle soldier (John Savage) and the sensualist (Christopher Walken) are seen as unmanly and "punished" by death or crippling/castration by the film's end). Other films on Vietnam presented war and masculinity as complex, resistant to machismo, and varied (*Coming Home*, 1978; *Platoon*, 1986; *Full Metal Jacket*, 1987; *Born on the Fourth of July*, 1989). In science fiction the conventional male hero of many 1950s sci-fi films was replaced by a female hero, as in *Alien*. In Westerns, men may withdraw from the demands of machismo (*The Man Who Shot Liberty Valance*, 1962; *The Shootist*, 1976) and women often take submissive domestic roles, but these can be overturned (Joan Crawford and Mercedes McCambridge as the dueling pair in *Johnny Guitar*, 1954) or challenged (*Duel in the Sun*, 1946, with its dueling pair of Jennifer Jones and Gregory Peck). An assertive, spunky actress like Jean Arthur can make female roles strong, as a wife with unconsummated extramarital desires in the Western *Shane* (1953) or as a equal to the male lead who is often more naive than she is (*Mr Smith Goes to Washington*, 1939; *Mr Deeds Goes to Town*, 1936). In "screwball comedies" of the 1940s, for example, women often were assertive and matched their male cohorts in wit and energy (e.g. Rosalind Russell in *His Girl Friday*, 1940). Many movies can assert female agency in professions (Geneviève Bujold as a doctor in *Coma*, 1978, or the women in *Nine to Five*, 1980), as well as use class to divide women (Sigourney Weaver versus Melanie Griffith in *Working Girl*, 1988, in which power is restored to the male character Harrison Ford). Melodramatic "weepies," presumed to appeal only to women, can represent strong women with agency and undomesticated sexual desires (such as the classics *Now, Voyager*, 1942, and *Brief Encounter*, 1945). Films that focus on domestic life or all-women casts may endorse traditional gender roles (*Terms of Endearment*, 1983, with its maudlin, operatic death of the female) but can also endorse multiple gender roles (*Steel Magnolias*, 1989) and explore, like male war films, a range of options for women. The power of stardom, too, can affect gender identities on the screen, as in the strong roles of Katherine Hepburn, Bette Davis, and Susan Sarandon in many of their movies or in the cases of Meryl Streep and Glenn Close, who refuse to do nude scenes, which almost always mean female nudity and rarely male nudity, a clear indication of the asymmetry in bodily exposure that reflects appeals to male viewers and the submission of female actors to audience voyeurism. Remakes are often interesting for measuring changes in attitudes toward gender, as in *The Stepford Wives* (1975 and 2004). Finally, films have recently pursued the exploration of homosexuality, transsexuality, and gender bending in films, some of them with major stars: *The Killing of Sister George* (1968, (Susannah York), *The Bitter Tears of Petra Von Kant* (1972), *La Cage aux Folles* (1978), *The Crying Game* (1992), *Philadelphia* (1993, Tom Hanks), *Ed Wood* (1994, Johnny

Depp), films by John Waters, *The Incredibly True Adventure of Two Girls in Love* (1995), *Bastard out of Carolina* (1996, Jennifer Jason Leigh), *Gods and Monsters* (1998, Ian McKellen), *Boys Don't Cry* (1999, Hilary Swank), *Best in Show* (2000), *Before Night Falls* (2000, Javier Bardem), *Mulholland Drive* (2001, Naomi Watts), *Monster* (2003, Charlize Theron), and *Brokeback Mountain* (2005).

Perhaps the most important consequence of the new gender studies and the recent focus on masculinity is the realization that genders include a range of identities beyond conventional heterosexual masculine (weak/strong dichotomy) and feminine (mother/prostitute dichotomy) identities. Genders also embrace "unconventional" heterosexual, bisexual, and homosexual identities as subjects of films and of spectators' experiences on and off screen. Further complicating these categories are sexual identities mixed with race (e.g. Black masculinity or Black femininity), which are more than the sum of their parts, gendering in other cultures and ethnicities now represented in films, and gender representations by diverse groups currently making films. Inspiring this opening up of notions of gender is the realization that in addition to being socially constructed, as feminist scholars have explained, genders are relational, meaning that they are unstable and shifting according to changing social, historical, and technological circumstances, e.g. changed status for women or homosexuals, the critical mass of diasporic communities in which genders are differently defined, and even new medical options like transsexual surgeries. Masculinity and femininity have social and symbolic meanings in relationship to each other and each is a conglomerate of multiple gender identities (each may include heterosexual, homosexual, transsexual, racial, historical, gendered identities).

Masculinity studies employ Freudian and Lacanian psychoanalytic theories of gendered identities earlier deployed in feminist film criticism a generation ago. These theories emphasize how important fantasies and desire are in spectators' receptions of film and in the very experience of watching film. Films can function like cultural mirrors: their large scale and iconic close-up of faces can feed our desires and fantasies of sexual fulfillment and sexual identities. The dark theatre can turn the public space into a private intimacy between individual spectator and screen image, thus linking film viewing with our visual fantasies, dreams, and voyeurism.

The focus in feminist studies has moved from an emphasis on images of women in film through psychoanalytic theory to the study of women filmmakers' diverse images of women, women in films from around the world, the fluidity of female images on the screen and in the audience, and rhetorical and cognitive approaches that draw on theories of the learned nature of emotional behavior so readily touched by films. Just as gender permeates genre issues (e.g. melodrama), it also is embedded in a host of issues in world cinema in which gender issues vary widely. The representation of gender is now identified with an array of aesthetic and alternative modes of production that emphasize the interrelatedness of race, gender, and class, further complicating notions of any one of these. What unites many of these films, as Robin and Jaffe (1999, p. 2) note, is the "privileging of difference," a new aesthetic that rejects hierarchies of identity for an open field in which pluralism is explored, celebrated, and represented. Interestingly, world cinema produced films made by women generations before such production in the USA or Europe (e.g. Mexican women's filmmaking beginning in the 1920s), further unseating Western European and North American concepts of their own "progress" and "equality" for women. Robin and Jaffe identify several new issues in feminist and women's films: new positions and power for women in various roles in filmmaking, representations of women's subjectivities and histories, women's communal identities and roles, women's collective film production companies, and women's assertive opposition to domination and colonial circumstances (Robin and Jaffe, 1999, p. 13).

Some theorists argue that the spectator is dissolved into the film's system of identification, which partly explains the power of film and the omnipresence of Hollywood films. But this supposes the passivity of the audience. What gender studies reveals is that spectators are active and have multiple gender positions to inhabit in film viewing – spectators can identify with characters unlike themselves or with several identities simultaneously in a single film. Spectators do not exclusively inhabit any single mode of seeing, as the seers or the seen, or any predetermined identification. Films offer imaginary and imagined identities, after all, and the pleasure of watching films is the fluidity of the identities we can try on as we view films. Likewise, the pain of viewing is the other side of seeing a mode of our identity treated in sexist or racist ways on film, as identities can be unavoidable in cases of extreme prejudice on film. Audiences tend to bring their historical circumstances, current problems, and social conditions to bear on the films they watch, as well as projecting their own fantasies and imaginary identities. Susan Torrey Barber (1993) examines films by Stephen Frears made in England during the 1980s regime of the Conservative Prime Minister Margaret Thatcher to emphasize the historical conditions in which gender identities are defined and redefined as they cross with racial and ethnic identities during a time of political conservatism.

To talk about gender (or race or national identity) is to talk about reception, how spectators make decisions about the identities in films and their own identifications with filmic identities. What spectators bring and know contributes not only to the context of a film as we usually presume, but also to the content of the film, as it is the lens through which spectators "read" and interpret films. This content is made up of spectators' interpretive strategies drawn from their experiences, fantasies, choices, and expectations. These varied and often indeterminate strategies are what Janet Staiger (2000, p. 32) calls "perversities" of spectators – spectators finding their own meanings and pleasures in film, unpredictable and without norms.

Developments from feminist to gender studies and the attention to masculinity and homosexuality have emphasized the physical body as a site for meanings that are often complex and contradictory. The body is located in a complex pattern of multiple identities – historical, gendered, racial, ethnic, and national – all at the same time. The body is a powerful social and historical site, not just a biological entity, so it becomes perhaps the most powerful image for spectator identification, a mirroring of spectators' real and imaginary identities and the identities they can inhabit unconsciously. Essays in this part raise a range of gender issues, including new ones, as suggested by Williams's "body genre" idea in part I and Sharma's study of how the body in films may suggest new gendered and generic possibilities, focusing on Mira Nair's films, which introduce and overlap with issues of race and world cinema in parts III and IV. Two essays on *The Crying Game* serve to offer multiple views of this film, in which gender is portrayed as complex and disruptive. Flanagan, Pidduck, and Tasker examine gender bending in literary (from Virginia Woolf's *Orlando*) or action films with women protagonists, and Flanagan includes a consideration of technological changes on the gendering of images and characters in film.

Further Reading

Barber, Susan Torry (1993) "Insurmountable difficulties and moments of ecstasy: crossing class, ethnic, and sexual barriers in the films of Stephen Frears." In Lester Friedman (ed.), *Fires Were Started: British Cinema and Thatcherism*. Minneapolis: University of Minnesota Press, pp. 221–36.

Carson, D., Dittmar, L. and Welsch, J. R. (eds) (1994) *Multiple Voices in Feminist Film Criticism*. Minneapolis: University of Minnesota Press.

Cohan, Steven and Hark, Ina Rae (1993) *Screening the Male: Exploring Masculinities in Hollywood Cinema*. New York: Routledge.

Denzin, Norman K. (1995) *The Cinematic Society: The Voyeur's Gaze*. London: Sage.

Erens, Patricia (ed.) (1991) *Issues in Feminist Film Criticism*. Bloomington: Indiana University Press.

Grant, Barry Keith (ed.) (1996) *The Dread of Difference: Gender and the Horror Film*. Austin: University of Texas Press.

Haas, L., Bell, Elizabeth and Sells, Laura (eds) (1995) *From Mouse to Mermaid: The Politics of Film, Gender, and Culture*. Bloomington: Indiana University Press.

Kaplan, E. Ann (2000) *Feminism and Film*. Oxford: Oxford University Press.

Kirkam, Pat and Thumin, Janet (eds) (1995) *Me Jane: Masculinity, Movies, and Women*. London: Lawrence and Wishart.

Lehman, Peter (ed.) (2001) *Masculinity: Bodies, Movies, Culture*. New York and London: Routledge.

Mulvey, Laura (1989) *Visual and Other Pleasures*. Bloomington: Indiana University Press.

Pomerance, Murray (ed.) (2001) *Ladies and Gentlemen, Boys and Girls: Gender in Film at the End of the Twentieth Century*. Albany: State University of New York Press.

Robin, Diana and Jaffe, Ira (eds) (1999) *Redirecting the Gaze: Gender, Theory, and Cinema in the Third World*. Albany: State University of New York Press.

Staiger, Janet (2000) *Perverse Spectators: The Practices of Film Reception*. New York: New York University Press.

7

Mobile Identities, Digital Stars, and Post Cinematic Selves

Mary Flanagan

Molly Haskell noted that "The closer women come to claiming their rights and achieving independence in real life, the more loudly and stridently films tell us it's a man's world."[1] Women's relationship to technology is perhaps the most threatening relationship the West has known. Unlike issues of property ownership, the right to vote, wage discrepancies, and other calculable inequities, the use of technology by women is dangerous because it not only allows for immediate access to information but because it is also immeasurable. What an ironic image, then, to have the emerging personalities of the new millennium – female digital stars – created by the technology that "real" women are denied.

Lara Croft, the 3-D star of the action game series *Tomb Raider*, has become the most popular computer game character ever. Created by Core Design in England, Lara's game series *Tomb Raider* (I, II, III, IV: The Last Revalation, and soon to be released *Tomb Raider Chronicles*), distributed by Eidos Interactive, has helped create a new star system in the arena of electronic gaming. Since premiering in 1996, her games have sold over six million copies – some of the best-selling video game titles in history. In the game, players control Lara Croft, a female Indiana Jones-style swashbuckling archaeologist on a global quest to whisk away artifacts from "exotic" locales in epic, colonialist CD ROM adventures. She is the best-known computer generated character in the world and her creation has brought into existence a virtual star system. As the millennial icon, she has been featured on the cover of over eighty magazines with characters such as Bill Gates and America Online CEO Steve Case, and touted as one of the fifty "cyber elite."

Mary Flanagan, "Mobile Identities, Digital Stars, and Post Cinematic Selves," pp. 77–93 from *Wide Angle* 21:1 (1999) (Baltimore: The Johns Hopkins University Press). © 1999 by Wide Angle. Reprinted by permission of The Ohio University School of Film.

Lara is more than a character; she is a celebrity. "She's developed a persona," says Keith Boesky of game publisher Eidos Interactive. "She's the first digital character that's really treated like a person."[2] Lara Croft might be compared to a person, but she is much more onscreen. Lara wields amazing physical prowess and multiple firearms. She is capable of any physical activity demanded by the game's incredible situations: back-flipping out of buildings, swimming underwater, punching tigers, round-housing monks, and even biting foes (blood/gore included) – while barely clad in scanty, skin-tight "explorer" clothing. In addition to her superhuman traits, Lara is precise, rides in great vehicles, and, unless there is user error, never needs a second take.

Inevitably, the comparison has to be made between this new star system and film history's account of stars and star discourse. A review of this material will help us understand how and why the cinematic star as a culturally produced body has evolved into a digital star system in which signifiers, identities, and bodies themselves are called into question. More than the indulgence of looking in at these stars within filmic worlds, we now embrace the very real pleasure of controlling these desired bodies: Lara is at the apex of a system in which looking manifests into doing, into action. The digital star is the location on which fantasies of desire and control are projected; they embody the fears, desires, and excess of our culture in the form of obnoxiously sexualized female stars. The subject, object, audience, director, viewer, participant, creator, and user tangle and double over; these roles blur into a new phenomenon that refuses to take on a shape.

Lara is clearly our first digital star,[3] and the role of information and technology in the construction of the digital star cannot be ignored. Rob Milthorp has pointed out that the lure of the video game fantasy is "that of a vicarious escapist experience that also responds to men's technological passion."[4] Beyond the attraction of technology, however, this essay suggests that it is through the excess of information and sexuality, the absence of the "authentic," and the development of an intricate subject/object relationship that these fantasies have organized into a truly new form of star system "personified" through Lara Croft. Using Lara Croft and other digitally-rendered female images – Kyoko Date, Kiss Dolls, and Ultravixen – as examples, this essay seeks to expose and complicate new manifestations of the coded subject/object positions examined by feminist scholars of popular media for the last twenty years. I will show that "cults of personality" could only develop from the electronic entertainment industry when virtual personalities embodied a marketable, consumable, idealized, and entirely "man-made" female form. It is through the recognition, representation, and redefinition of this body and the understanding of the shaping of the subject within the digital star system that our position as users and our technologically produced, multiple subjectivities can be understood.

Seeing Stars

In his essay "The Emergence of the Star System in America," Richard deCordova distinguishes phases in the development of the classical Hollywood star system. His concepts are useful when comparing the "cults of personality" that developed almost a century before the digital star system. Starting with discourse on legitimate stage acting and comparing it with "performing" (as opposed to acting) for the camera, he describes the differences between a "picture personality" and the "star." There was a marked difference between personalities and stars in the way they related to discourse and products. Popular film magazines included quizzes about the players' names and listed their filmographies; however, actor-centered dialogue was always second to the discourse on the films themselves. DeCordova notes, "The picture personality was to be the principal site of product individuation"[5] and by 1907, the star system had evolved, making the name of the star more important than the films in which they starred. Thus, a decade into the twentieth century, pressure increased for extra-filmic information beyond that of the professional existence of the performer – interest grew about his or her private lives. The interest in the private lives of screen performers – and the excess of biographical information sold about a performer's personal life – created the star system, and with it a commodification of an actor's biographical data. This focus on an individual actor's life and family may have helped to legitimize the cinema and its practices – as deCordova notes, "The private lives of the stars emerged as a new site of knowledge and truth"[6] and, of course, commodity.

The star system evolved as an important component in the development of the information age by blurring distinctions between the personal and the private. Technology-bound, technologically determined, both digital stars and cinema stars were birthed in an environment of spectacle. If we think about technology not as a purely mechanical tool but as a systematic apparatus of production which includes extra-media dialogues (such as fan discourse, advertising, company/studio press releases, and other cultural phenomena) we see a certain kind of technological determinism both media share. The star system produced the personality as commodity to be consumed by audiences – a product to be desired, and ultimately, acquired.

Like the arcades of electronic gaming, early cinema was exhibited in predominantly male spaces, but exhibition practices are not the only shared elements between the star systems. The first stars in both films and computer games are females: the marketable names of Florence Lawrence (the first popular screen player at Biograph Studios) and Lara Croft have drawn large audiences. But from the picture personality "Biograph Girl" (Lawrence) to the star "IMP Girl" (Lawrence's name at her next studio) to the "Bit Girl"[7] the representation of biographical excess and overt sexuality changed dramatically. While the "innocent" early film stars gradually evolved into more sexual and objectified stars, Lara Croft and clone characters are immediately coded as sexual objects upon arrival.

Star Sex

Scott Bukatman points out that contemporary culture "eroticizes the techno-logical";[8] and thus in addition to her appearance, Lara Croft is by virtue of her existence bound to erotic codes and interpretation through the means of her production. A look at the first cinematic sex symbol, Theda Bara, gives historical insight into the design of the sex object screen star. Fox Studios director Frank Powell cast her as a vampire in the film version of *A Fool There Was* (1915). She became Fox's biggest star, appearing in as many as ten feature films per year.[9] Theda Bara's success as a sex symbol stems from her construction as a persona without a fixed personal history. A key factor in her design as a sex symbol was the mystification of her true, "authentic" identity. Though she was almost thirty and obviously had a personal history of her own, Fox Studios created a fictional personal history for her with each film role she played. At hundreds of press conferences, Theda Bara acted out these roles, dressing in veils, furs and silks, petting snakes or eating exotic fruits. The media played along with the spectacle and printed as fact obviously jumbled biographies. According to one report, Theda Bara was born under Egypt's pyramids, the daughter of a French actress and an Italian artist.[10] Similarly, Lara Croft's past is also recreated, multiplied, and retold. Her lack of a true history is masked by the excess of life stories created by multiple agencies – Eidos' marketing department, gaming magazines, and count-less fan fiction sites. Like Theda Bara, Lara's excessive biographies are filled with impossible fictions.[11] Yet while Theda's histories were concocted to create a media stir for the studio, Lara's past continues to be filled in by fans across the world. Internet sites such as *Lara's Scrapbook* and *Lara's Oasis* fill in details continually. This act of viewer/user/participant generation of these histories is significant as they multiply Lara's "reality" into many fictions which represent multiple realities. While each fan community may have its own version of her story, no one story is considered more or less true than any other. This works in part because of the immensity of the interested group: six or seven million fans can create "regional" narratives of the hero in what ends up being localized oral, written, and pictorial histories – legends.

Lara and Theda are alike in that they both embody excess and spectacle and exist in a duality between the text (the films, games) and in sub-texts and extra-texts. Their personal histories are coded as "exotic," vague, and undecipherable. Their bodies with their assorted histories are fractured into multiple fictions to act as shells for a viewer's desire. In his study of male fantasy and the image of woman, Klaus Theweleit writes:

> The fictive body of woman has become an imaginary arena for the fantasies of deter-ritorializations, while actual male–female relationships have continued to serve . . . as focal points for the implementation of massive reterritorializations. Exotic women, and women of the ruling class, have provided the raw material for those fictions.[12]

Stars of the cinema share qualities with computer-generated stars; not static or fixed in time and space, they inhabit screen worlds. A star system draws upon the separation between the image and the body, the public and private, the historical, biographical persona and the location of many fictional biographies, between the scripted and the "real," to create a culture of consumption around the "persona." The representation of Lara Croft's body is essential to understand the issues of (dis)embodiment of computer personalities and the particular place of gender in these embodiment relationships. Lara's body is an interesting culmination of numerous western ideals. Box art, press releases, and fans describe her as "icy" and "sexy." She shoots, climbs, and runs with mechanical precision; controlling her body is like driving a fine machine. In addition, Lara Croft has an over-idealized female physique. She is a self-less body created from 540 polygons.[13] With beyond-Barbie statistics (pushing Lara as a pin-up icon, Eidos has claimed her measurements are 88–24–84),[14] Lara is an over-idealized construction of EuroAmerican standards of beauty.[15] Modeled with brown hair and eyes and a deep skin tone, Lara could be one of the few non-white characters within Euro-American-dominated games. However, Lara is perceived most often by her fans as Caucasian.[16] Creator company Eidos provides only a rough sketch of Lara's life, and as a result there should be few elements which remain stable about her biography. But even within the reinterpretations of Lara's history, she is consistently read by fans to come from a position of economic privilege: well-bred, educated, and feminine even as she guns down attackers. She is the idealized privileged white female image of Theweleit's writing.

Lara is young and beautiful – and she will always be. Lara will not know physical age. She will, however, be subject to the outdating of her technology. Any digital star's repertoire will consist of a set of obsolete file formats on aged media storage devices. As the body coordinates and texture maps are refined through the years – remapped, refracted, holographed into the technology of the time – her previous incarnations will grow more and more obsolete.

However, she will stay eternally young; reborn, more perfect than before, with each technological advance. The experience of a digital star, then, is one of continued present. The technology of the present is the only way to maintain the star. Lara represents the circumstance described by Gilles Deleuze as the process of "becoming." She exists not as an identity but as a site of becoming – winning or losing the game, adventuring, controlling, pleasuring, moving, fighting. In his essay "What is Becoming?" Deleuze describes a state of event-centered being that is a useful way to examine interactive experiences.[17] The characters, landscape, and entire world of Tomb *Raider* are a continuous, data-driven event. The artificial is always a copy of a copy,"[18] data looping and changing in a viral manner. Lara, as a pure data loop, makes discourse about the concept of the authentic, the "instance," impossible. Thus, the absence of a physical body means the absence of history, the lack of a "real" biography; the data is the entirety of the star. Her female identity further complicates this intersection. Judith Butler argues that the very position of "woman" is a construction within this constant flux as well: "Woman itself is a term in process, a becoming, a constructing that cannot rightfully be said to originate or end."[19]

Set Prototypes

What we see on the screen of a digital star – the body, the gender, the matrix of social and cultural ties – is as much as we get. Or is it? Postmodernism brought us the disintegration of the subject, the fragmented receptor constantly in flux. The boundaries between humans and machines are becoming irretrievably blurred. So too have the boundaries between the subject and object, the voyeur and the object of the gaze, the user/participant and the avatar representation of that user in a virtual world. The blurring of boundaries that has come to fruition in Lara Croft can be traced through three important evolutionary stages.

Kyoko Date

To begin looking at existing examples of prototypical digital stars and under-standing the apparatus, the technological means that have pre-shaped us as sub-jects, we can examine one of the first internationally known virtual beings, the Japanese character Kyoko Date. Of all prototypical digital personas, Kyoko may be the best known. Called the "Daughter of technology" by some fans,[20] Kyoko Date or "DK-96" (DK for "Digital Kids") was the first virtual idol. Created by the Japanese entertainment company Hori Productions, Inc., Date is a 3-D model consisting of over 40,000 polygons; it is easy to mistake printouts of Date for photographs of human subjects. The production of Date was enormous: ten designers at HoriPro alone worked on her facial features.[21] Kyoko is physically attractive; but she is not solely touted for her sex appeal. According to CNN/fn's news reporter John Lewis, Kyoko "has just that desired mix of purity and lost innocence, she has the cute pout down pat, and she's fashionably slender in all the right places."[22] Kyoko Date was not based on an existing media personality, nor was she created in order to further the media career of a human star. And while Kyoko Date did not erupt from a computer game, toy, television program, or movie, she quickly became an influential media figure through commercials, music videos, and pop songs. HoriPro chose to make its star as "real" as possible using an abundance of "normal" human references. Kyoko Date "grew up" in the suburbs; the "girl-next-door" image behind the media blitz was constructed to make her as human as possible. She is represented as a typical sixteen-year-old entertainer and lives with her parents just outside of Tokyo. Kyoko is said to have one sister, a year younger than herself, and works at her parents' family-run restaurant in Tokyo.

130

It is important to note that the fame of Kyoko Date was not perennial. Kyoko was the prototype for the digital star system, but her meticulously detailed personalized history created more of a "self" than a digital personality can have. Fans have dropped some of her websites and others are no longer maintained. She was too well-defined to sustain interest.

Kiss dolls

A big hit in Japan since the early 1990s and a swelling American phenomenon, Kiss games are electronic drag-and-drop paper doll computer games that one plays on the computer. Kiss dolls are an interactive strip show with the goal of exposing and eroticizing images of anime characters and barely pubescent girls. Available in the underground software scene,[23] the creation, production, and distribution of KISS are performed by fanatics, technicians and programmers – not corporate pornographic agencies. Newer KISS dolls, dubbed "FKISS," can incorporate limited animation and sound; this movement most often manifests as blinking eyes, animated clothing, giggling sounds, or animated sex toys. The interaction – the user has power over the doll and is able to click and drag items off or onto the body of the doll – compels the user to play. The significance of the animated paper dolls lies in the type of control offered to users and the animations embedded in the files. The user not only controls the female image and visual identity through clothing and hair, but the user can actually act upon this body – shave it, make it wet, and ultimately rape it with objects found in the scene. One animated doll, Sailor Mars, features a young anime-style female figure, about nine years old, wearing a Japanese school uniform: white top and a grey skirt. When the player clicks on the doll's skirt, the skirt bunches up to expose the girl's underwear, as though the hand of an adult has reached under the skirt to expose her. Similarly, when the player clicks on the girl's shirt, the shirt pops open but stays on the body. Clicking on the underwear results in the underwear bunching down to expose the giri's genitalia. Meanwhile, the drawing stays expressionless, the cartoon child returning the gaze of the player, her eyes, wide and shiny, blinking passively. Through clicking repeatedly on the figure, a player can gain access to the body through this scrunching and unbuttoning. The choice to leave the clothes astrew on the body, skirt hiked up instead of neatly removed, is a design choice to grant users the opportunity to molest the young female image. Thus while Kiss dolls offer virtual, "manipulate-able" striptease shows for the users, this particular doll confronts, albeit passively, the manipulation of the female image directly.

It is critical that many authors of the animated dolls choose to focus their animation on the blinking eyes in contrast to animating more sexually coded areas of the body. The doll eyes that look out directly at the user and blink as though alive and aware result in the digital character's passive recognition of her victimization. These digital paper dolls, who consciously watch while they are manipulated for the user's pleasure, reflect our possession and control over the female image. Unlike other kinds of pornography, the dolls arrive to the user as innocents and it is through interactivity that they are inscribed as erotic. As Zimmerman and Gorfinkel point out, they constitute "a curious double sexuality; at once garishly innocent adolescents and hyper-sexualized porn objects, a complicity of awkward pubescence and demure seduction."[24] Kiss dolls seem to arrive to us as innocents but leave as sexualized objects of desire produced by the actions of the user. Kiss dolls, as anonymous shells upon which users can play out a fantasy of control and desire, are "safe" precisely because of their lack of authenticity. Users do not, however, manipulate the girls' bodies (except for the few dolls accompanied by sex toys); rather, users can decide the level of exposure (indecent or otherwise). Kiss dolls incorporate a level of control that is defined by exposure of the body rather than the direct manipulation of it. As anonymous electronic strip shows, they exist in between worlds and experiences as "trading cards of desire." Their lack of history, their spoiled innocence that is completely at the service of the user for the pleasure of the user alone, and their capacity to fulfill the fantasy of the visible by maneuvering the image within interactive technology leads to the fulfillment of user desire.

Ultravixen

Ariel, aka Ultravixen, is the "hypersexy superheroine of the 21st century" in the "world's first Internet Anime Sex Game."[25] Created by Pixis Interactive, purple-haired hero Ariel is billed as the "super-hot sci-fi sex star." The story on the Pixis website begins with her torture and rape at the hands of a professor. Her powers emerge as the result of the rape. Ariel becomes the Ultravixen, the bearer of the "super climax": an orgasm capable of warping time and space. Her sexual "weapon" is the means of defeating an evil Overlord from the future, who uses a time travel network to acquire girls and enslave them in his maniacal sex machines. The role of the user is to play her "lover" and serve as the operator of these sexual torture devices. Players manipulate the "sex machines" to arouse Ultravixen to the point of orgasm so that she may in turn destroy the machine, and with it, the Overlord.

While the narrative makes the Overlord into a diabolical character because of his rape of women and dominance over the girls using sex machines, the game is designed so that players must duplicate his actions to save the world. The interaction in Ultravixen is a complex set of objectifications: the user controls elements in the game (implements of torture) which in turn gives the user power over the sex object, Ariel. Yet as players we are absolved of any moral guilt as the narrative clearly tells us that Ariel wants to be tortured. She appears in a machine, and the user is told that Ariel desires "pleasure." Ultravixen represents the point at which the gaze is given the power of manipulation, a place where the gaze MUST manifest into sexual control and abuse in order to play and finish the game. Consequently, torture is legitimized and sanctioned by positing the relationship between user, machine, and victim as a consensual act. This "rape and rescue" fantasy is used to justify the subjugation of the disenfranchised female body. In one level of the game, Ariel travels to Nazi Germany and is subjected to torture and mutilation resembling the "experimentation" upon Jewish women while imprisoned in Death Camps. She is even crucified to a swastika. This analogy is more than disturbing. Though the portrayal in Ultravixen is abusive and negative, the user does not directly control Ariel – control is mediated through the sex machine. In comparison, even though Lara Croft exists in a game which does not submit her to torture, she is submissive to the direct control of the user.[26]

These three examples show varying degrees of the creation of the digitally-rendered female image's overt sexuality. Each one bears marks of the evolution towards the digital star system. On the surface, Kyoko Date seems to be a digital star: she is a three dimensional artificial character created to sell media work While her name differentiates and sells products, she is created with a grounded, stable history – not created from excess but rather from "satisfactory" spheres of knowledge. She becomes too "realistic" and historically situated to be the site at which we play out fantasies. Kiss Dolls are crude examples of the enactment of anonymous control fantasies. An individual doll's identity is not as important as the power to manipulate the doll, and thus product differentiation relies more on the features of a particular doll set versus the character depicted therein. Ultravixen has little identity and exists for the player's pleasure alone; the only way we relate to her is through manipulation somewhat removed from the game world. These digital prototypes help form the conditions necessary for a star system to develop but are not digital stars unto themselves. The economic, racial, and gender hierarchies embedded in these electronic games "allegorize" the social relationships in our time much like cinema,[27] creating a-historical digital female imagery for the fulfillment of fantasy. Each of these examples offers us a few of the elements which contributed to the construction of the digital star system, yet they do not each bear enough elements to fully launch it.

Objects/Subjects

The games above feature prototypical digital stars. A central reason that they could not offer true stardom to their characters is that they did not offer complex subject positioning for players. The ability to feel as though one is shifting viewpoints while manipulating a character one identifies with in a variety of ways offers tremendous possibilities for theories about subject/object relationships. The space between experiencing first hand (inside) a virtual character, to controlling the avatar as a separate object is like Deleuze's phantasm: the movement by which the ego opens itself up to surfaces and "liberates" the halted differences contained (such as point of view);[28] "the phantasm covers the distance between psychic systems with ease, going from consciousness to the unconscious and vice versa – from the inner to the outer and conversely."[29]

More than an inner and outer dichotomy, we can identify five points of action/identification/subject positioning within a three-dimensional gaming environment like *Tomb Raider*. First, through the keyboard, players make Lara act. Second, she acts – sometimes on her own accord, through pre-scripted animation, and sometimes as an extension to our influence. Third, as players we act with her or next to her as a friend or companion. Fourth, we act through her/within her in the first person. In other words, we become Lara. Finally, we react to her. For example, players respond to her positions in the game, whether in fear or with mirth. Never before has there been a figure in any media that has become such a unique axis of complex identification with the audience. We move from the first person position – sitting in front of the monitor using the keyboard – to the third person simultaneity of being inside the game worlds with our characters. We are again in first person controlling the gaming experience through the characters – we can actually become them and see the world through their eyes; then with a keystroke, we can move to the third person omniscient perspective in order to control the character like a puppet. Through this network of positions, the boundaries between subject and object, the delineation between various points of view, and the notion of self and other are inextricably intertwined.

Though players physically interact in *Tomb Raider* through keyboard keys, Lara is the means by which the user is extended into the virtual environment. Users have control over her body, true; but users identify with her body in a variety of ways, Of Lara Croft, Herz notes, "In *Tomb Raider*, Lara Croft is the protagonist, the hero. When a boy plays the game, Lara is not the object, as she would have been in older games: she is the game. The boy who plays the game plays it as a woman."[30] Herz, while showing the potential of the technology to experience truly "virtual realities," exposes the cultural confusion about subjectivity in electronic games. Herz's words confuse the manipulation of a female object with becoming the very object manipulated. But the situation is even more complex, because there are women and girls who do enjoy playing the game. Interviewing a young woman "newbie," Mark Snider includes "At first I was teasing (my dad) about playing *Tomb Raider* because there was a half-naked woman in it," but when she began to play the game, she became a fan. "You don't just feel like you're playing the game, you're going adventuring with Lara Croft."[31] So while Lara is an object to manipulate, she is also a friend or partner. Different players relate to this simultaneity in different ways. The subject/object relationships exemplified by the interactive Lara Croft experience do represent a new model for discovering female or alternative subjectivity, but this model has not been used with feminist content. Through the player/character relationship exemplified by *Tomb Raider*, we may someday be able to have multiple experiences of reality and identify sites at which we can adequately be addressed as subjects. The development of the sheer numbers of points of view may create an alternate subject position that could address the largely excluded female audience. These alternate spaces, exemplified within the postmodern subject position offered in *Tomb Raider*, expose fissures in which alternate subject positions, or new combinations of subjective positions, will gain footing and representation. Thus (perhaps even *more so* for female players), the multiplication of the subject position offers an opportunity at which new ways of gaming (and more) could develop. True digital stars, that is, stars without need of their own physical body, did not exist until our culture was ready to rethink the body in the context of technology, and until the technology could present this body in a pleasing, "hyperreal" aesthetic. It also took a female digital character in a female body to spark these conventions. These female bodies are not bound by physical, biological traits of race and gender, but rather are bodies which are entirely technologically and culturally determined.[32] The digital star system arose, like cinema's star system, through the development of an intricate subject/object, through an excess of information and sexuality, and alongside the absence of the "authentic," but it is an evolving and changing phenomenon. The current narratives offered on the gaming market, however, work against these possibilities by offering hyper-sexual or victim characters. Even though they suggest that multiple points of view can be destabilizing, right now they remake stereotypical female sex objects. This is popular media's chance for opposition or total dissolution of conventional ideas of the self through the destabilization of the subject, to create selves in the relationship between the user and the narrative through gameplay and interactivity design in electronic media. The incorporation of movement, agency, and multiplicity within virtual worlds has tremendous possibilities for repositioning the subject and opening up narratives to non-stereotyped female roles and helping users find their favorite spot among a spectrum of viewpoints and subject positions.

Notes

1   Quoted in C. Brunson, *Films for Women* (London: BFI, 1986), p. 131.
2   Mark Snider, "Tomb Raider Blasts into Virtual Stardom," *USA Today*, 17 December 1997, 1D.
3   "Girl Trouble," *Next Generation*, 4.37, January 1998, 98–102.
4   Rob Milthorp, "Fascination, Masculinity, and Cyberspace," in Mary Anne Moser and Douglas MacLeon (eds), *Immersed in Technology* (Cambridge, MA, and London: MIT Press, 1996), p. 143.
5   Richard DeCordova, "Emergence of the Star System," in Christine Gledhill (ed.), *Stardom: Industry of Desire* (London and New York: Routledge, 1991), p. 24.
6   Ibid., p. 26.
7   N'Gail Croal and Janes Hughes, "Lara Croft, the Bit Girl: How a Game Star Became a 90s Icon," *Newsweek*, 10 November 1997, 82.
8   Scott Bukatman, *Terminal Identity* (Durham, NC: Duke University Press, 1993), p. 328.
9   Glen Pringle, *Theda Bara: Silent Star of May 1996*. www.cs.monash.edu.au/~pringle/silent/ssotm/May96/ (accessed 1 July 1998).

10 Ibid.

11 Bowen H. Greenwood, *Lara Croft's Tales of Beauty and Power*. http://network.ctimes.net/tales (accessed 20 July 1999).

12 Klaus Theweleit, *Male Fantasies, Volume 1: Women, Floods, Bodies, History*, trans. Stephen Conway (Minneapolis: University of Minnesota Press, 1987), pp. 298–9.

13 Croal and Hughes, 82.

14 Croal and Hughes, 82.

15 Snider, 1D.

16 Robert Wheeler, *The Tomb Raider Archive*. http://trarchive.ctimes.net/index.html (accessed 31 July 1999).

17 Gilles Deleuze, *The Deleuze Reader*, trans. Constantine V. Boundas (New York: Columbia University Press, 1993), pp. 39–41.

18 Gilles Deleuze, *The Logic of Sense*, trans. Constantine V. Boundas (New York: Columbia University Press, 1990), p. 265.

19 Judith Butler, *Gender Trouble: Feminism and the Subversion of Identity* (New York and London: Routledge, 1990), p. 38.

20 *Kyoto Date Website*. http://111.etud.insa-tlse.fr/~mdumas/kyoko.html

21 HoriPro, Inc., "Notes on the Development of Virtual Idol DK-96," www.dhw.co.jp/horipro/talent/DK96/dev-e.html (accessed 31 July 1999).

22 John Lewis, "Virtual Reality Entertainment in Japan," CNNf/n News in Play: Video Transcript, Cable News Network, Inc., 5 February 1997.

23 Kiss Dolls are a huge net phenomenon and can be found at sites such as http://otakuworld.com and *The Blue Page H'n'H Times Supplement* issues 5–11, ed. Dominatrix, www.terra.es/personal/domina/hnhtimes.htm (accessed June 1999).

24 E. Zimmerman and E. Gorfinkel, "KISS and Tell," *21C Magazine* January 1997, 74.

25 Pixis Interactive, "Ultravixen Website," www2.ultravixen.com/choose.html (accessed August 1999).

26 Moira Muldoon, "Growing up in Gameland," *Salon* www1.salonmagazine.com/21st/feature/1998/06/02featureb.html (accessed July 1998).

27 Ella Shohat, "Gender and Culture of Empire: Towards a Feminist Ethnography of the Cinema," *Quarterly Review of Film and Video* 13:1–3 (May–October 1991), 45.

28 Deleuze, *The Logic of Sense*, p. 213.

29 Deleuze, *The Logic of Sense*, p. 217.

30 Quoted in Gregory Kallenberg, "J. C. Herz: What's in a Game," *Austin-American Statesman*, www.austin360.com/tech/browser/071097.htm (accessed 10 July 1997).

31 Snider, 1D

32 Anne Balsamo, *Technologies of the Gendered Body* (Durham, NC, and London: Duke University Press, 1996), p. 5.

8

"Nothing Is as It Seems": Re-viewing *The Crying Game*

Lola Young

> *How has sexuality come to be considered the privileged place where our deepest 'truth' is read and expressed?*[1]

This essay is focused on three areas of interest suggested by Neil Jordan's fantasy, *The Crying Game* (UK, 1992): firstly, the relationship between the representation of racial difference and sexuality; secondly, the possible meanings of the text's use of cross-dressing and thirdly, the ways in which the press reviews of the film, treated these themes. One reason for concentrating on these areas is to consider the question of how a generally conservative and anti-intellectual British press responded to a film which ostensibly posits a radical sexual politics and attempts to address questions of national, racial and political identity and commitment.

The notion that it was the sexual conundrum at the centre of *The Crying Game* which held the key to the film's meaning was fundamental to most discussions of it. Perverse sexuality – epitomised by homosexuality and transvestism – figured through an interracial relationship involving two men would not appear, on the face of it, to be obvious material for mainstream cinema, yet *The Crying Game* was a critical and – after a slow start – box-office success. Through the use of a narrative device which was not only clever in terms of its dramatic execution but also in terms of the allusion to, and concealment of, that plot development in the reviews, the film generated much speculation about the sexual secret at its core.

Lola Young, "'Nothing Is as It Seems': Re-viewing *The Crying Game*," pp. 273–85 from Pat Kirkham and Janet Thumin (eds), *Me Jane: Masculinity, Movies and Women* (London: Lawrence and Wishart, 1995). © 1995 by Lola Young. Reprinted by permission of Lawrence and Wishart.

Even before filming on *The Crying Game* began, controversy about the casting was reported. It was claimed by the film's producers that Forest Whitaker would attract the necessary North American finance because he was a star of international repute. Members of the actors' union, Equity, argued that a black British actor should be given this rare opportunity to take a major role in a British film but the financial argument won, and the African-American was cast as a black soldier from north London. Apparently, a deal was struck between Equity and the film-makers that if Whitaker was accepted by the union, a role of similar status would go to a black British actor. The *Daily Telegraph* reported that, on hearing that 'the role eventually offered was that of a transvestite, Equity reversed its position.'[2] It would appear that a feminised man did not count as sufficient recompense.

The Crying Game begins as a story about the kidnapping of Jody/Forest Whitaker, a black soldier in the British army serving in Northern Ireland. Enticed by a politically motivated young white woman, Jude/Miranda Richardson, Jody is taken hostage by Irish political activitists. Jude has no sympathy for Jody and treats him brutally, but it is Fergus/Stephen Rea who has the main responsibility for guarding Jody. They strike up a relationship as a result of which Fergus promises to visit Jody's partner who lives in London. The photograph which Jody shows to Fergus is, apparently, of an attractive young black woman. Whilst trying to escape, Jody is killed, not by his captors but, significantly, by the British troops who are searching for him. Fergus manages to escape the raid, eventually crossing over to England. Once in London, he searches for and finds Dil/Jaye Davidson, Jody's lover. Dil and Fergus come to depend on each other and embark on a sexual relationship. Before long it is revealed that, anatomically, Dil is a young man, and the relationship temporarily breaks down. Jude turns up in London and makes it clear that in order to compensate for his previous lack of political commitment, Fergus has to participate in what is effectively a suicide mission: he must shoot a judge. In order to protect Dil whom Jude threatens, Fergus agrees but is prevented from carrying out the deed by Dil. The assassination goes ahead anyway and Jude seeks revenge for yet another betrayal on Fergus' part. Jude is shot by Dil and Fergus takes responsibility for the crime. In prison, Fergus is faithfully visited by Dil.

Transsexual/Transvestite . . . Transgressive?

One of the principal constituents of the film as far as most reviewers were concerned was the promise of a shocking revelation: that this shock turned out to be both sexualised and racialised made it all the more intriguing. Interestingly, though, reference to the racialisation of sexual transgression was rarely explicit in the critiques. In fact, both within the film and the reviews, 'race' is the great unspoken, the repressed discourse which returns, represented by two black male sexual transgressors.

Bisexuals, homosexuals and transvestites have to be read as transgressive forms of sexual expression because, despite attempts to discuss and understand the complexities and inconsistencies of sexual identity, society remains conservative in regard to the roles and behaviour considered appropriate for women and men. The boundaries of such behaviour – whether in the social or the sexual realm – are still rigorously monitored and policed.

Attitudes to sexual norms are anchored by the external evidence of gender offered by clothing, hairstyle, physical bearing and so on. Wearing clothes considered as inappropriate to one's sex is often read as a disruption of sexual boundaries, a rebellion against the constricting conformity of societal norms. Interestingly, both within and outside of cinematic representation, it is male to female transvestism to which most frequent reference is made. Cross-dressed men signify a defiance of sexual norms and assume an emblematic status that cross-dressed women do not enjoy.

In a sense, both transvestites and transsexuals contest the fixity of sex ascription, albeit in different terms. Whereas it is acknowledged that many male transvestites are heterosexual or bisexual, and that they often spend time – because of both societal pressures, and personal choice – dressed in men's clothing, male transsexuals express the necessity to be regarded as female. Transsexualism is used to refer to those who feel that the way in which they experience their gender is at variance with their biological/anatomical sex: those who attempt to 'pass' as members of the opposite sex.[3] Whether the character of Dil is transvestite or transsexual is not really elaborated in the text but in the context of a discussion of the metaphorical status of gender cross-identification, it may be important, since transsexualism indicates the absence of choice in the matter of gender identification and the impossibility of a return to biologically defined sexual origins. Transsexualism speaks of necessity rather than choice. However, the very lack of clarity regarding Dil's sexual trajectory adds another layer of ambiguity to the film and the sense that it is an understanding of his/her sexuality and others' attitudes towards it that will facilitate our understanding of the text.

The trope of 'passing', which informs an interesting essay by Judith Shapiro on transsexualism, is most often associated with racial passing which refers to a 'light-skinned' black person who can 'pass' as white. Such ambiguous racial positioning may serve to re-confirm the legitimacy of racial categorisations whilst simultaneously problematising it. With regard to 'race' the act of passing, whilst potentially undermining absolutist notions of racial categorisation, is ultimately necessary because of these fixed, prescriptive racial taxonomies.

Passing – whether racial or sexual – has radical potential in terms of its unsettling of defining norms framed by social, scientific, and legal discourses, and in terms of undermining the privileging of visual proof and knowledge. What you see may not actually be what you get, something made clear on a number of occasions during *The Crying Game*. However, not every act of passing may realise that radical potential since there are frequently deeply conservative elements involved. For women with black ancestry who claim whiteness – and most fictional accounts of 'passing' do refer to women – denial of the past and fear of the future characterise their experience. In regard to cross-dressing, it is often the case that representations of men passing as women assume the most conspicuously 'feminine' accoutrements – false eyelashes, heavy amounts of coloured eyeshadow, over-elaborate coiffures and so on: these excessively 'feminine' external signifiers take on a performative, parodic role which does not necessarily suggest convention-breaking notions of womanhood.

The notion that it is somehow necessarily politically progressive to adopt the external appearance of the Other is problematic. However, Shapiro posits that:

> . . . we might see male to female transsexualism in Euro-American society as reflecting the fact that those who intentionally move down in the system are more threatening to its values than those seeking to move up. The latter may constitute a threat to the group concerned with maintaining its privileges, but the former constitute a threat to the principles on which the hierarchy itself is based.[4]

This analysis oversimplifies what is at stake, especially when racial difference is implicated in the sex/gender matrix, since ideologies of racial and cultural inferiority and superiority inform social and gender hierarchies. Further, it may also be the case that 'moving up' is profoundly disruptive because it undermines the essentialist claims of the exclusivity of the dominant, privileged group: the privilege based on the external signs of 'race' or sex is demonstrated as being something which is appropriated rather than a natural and inevitable situation. 'Moving down' is not inherently more radical or subversive, as it may be read as a surrendering of power in order to abdicate responsibility. In addition, with regard to the transsexual, there is also the point that beyond the anatomical external characteristics of gender, it is implied that there are distinctive female and male essences which struggle to emerge from within the confines of the inappropriately genitalised body.

In her critical account of the stage play *M Butterfly* – a narrative concerned with the fallibility of visible 'proof' of gender identity, and racial fantasies/ cultural stereotypes regarding sexuality – Marjorie Garber notes

> . . . the fact of transvestism as both a personal and a political as well as an aesthetic and theatrical, mode of self-construction. Once again, as so often, the transvestite is looked through or away from, appropriated to tell another kind of story, a story less disturbing and dangerous, because less problematic and undecidable.[5]

Garber points to a 'category crisis' (i.e. a failure of definitional distinction) once a borderline which has been assumed impervious but that becomes permeable, permits crossings from one (apparently distinct) category to another. Once again, the trope of 'passing' is invoked to indicate the fluidity of sexual positions which defy reductionist ascriptions of masculinity or femininity. The presence of the undefinable sexual subject – the transvestite – in a text, in a culture, Garber claims, may signal a crisis of definition elsewhere.[6] The 'crisis' suggested but not elaborated in *The Crying Game* is linked to 'race' but not explicated in racial terms.

With regard to cinematic play with transvestism, many of the roles which call upon men to play women have not done so in a manner which explicitly calls into question their heterosexual, masculine integrity. When Tony Curtis dresses as a woman in *Some Like It Hot* (Billy Wilder, US, 1959) it is clear that his pursuit of Marilyn Monroe is not sisterly. The situation with Jack Lemmon's cross-dressing in the same film, is rather more complicated, since we are left to ponder what will become of his relationship with an elderly rich, male suitor. Even in this instance though, Lemmon's performance is conducted with a good deal of knowingness about his deception which is, after all, economically expedient: the joke is on the old man, who in the quest for the perfect female partner, falls for a man in drag.

Other often cited examples of male cross-dressing in mainstream popular cinema where the male concerned makes clear his heterosexuality are Cary Grant in *I Was a Male War Bride* (Howard Hawks, US, 1949) and Dustin Hoffman in *Tootsie* (Sidney Pollack, US, 1982). More recently, in *Mrs Doubtfire* (Chris Columbus, US, 1993), despite proving that he is better at mothering than his wife, Robin Williams, in the central role, retains his heterosexual masculinity throughout.

According to Chris Straayer, in these instances '[A]t the level of performance, feminine garb ironically both accentuates the male's secondary sex characteristic, thus signalling his "nature", and keeps his biological genital out of view.'[7] In the case of Dil however, this does not hold true. In this instance, it is his femininity which is consistently emphasised, suggesting that 'he' is really 'she'. Furthermore, Dil's male genitals are fully exposed and the sexual incongruity foregrounded. Straayer argues that the absence of the penis invisibilises male sexuality, whereas women's sexuality is inscribed on the female body through constant exposure of the secondary sexual characteristics such as breasts:

> the historic absence from view of the penis in cinema has allowed the male body an independence from sexual anatomical verification. It is his charging about that has identified a male film character as male, yet it is his penis that has invested him with the cultural right to charge about – the signifier *in absentia*.[8]

Straayer contends that the male cross-dresser has 'the *potential* for an intense double signification of sexuality, containing both macho male sexuality via the unseen penis, and female sexuality displaced onto visible display via masquerade.'[9] The masquerade which is evidenced in *The Crying Game*, is of a different order: here the intensity of the signification of sexuality is achieved through the penis being stripped of its macho resonance as a consequence of its appropriation by the (constructed) femininity of Dil.[10]

Dil's physical image as both feminine and phallic helps to negate the disturbing notion of sexual difference and castration anxiety. It is significant that the big secret that reviewers were asked to withhold from the public was the sighting of a *black* man's penis. One of the few close-up images of a penis outside of porno-graphic films just happens to be that of a homo/transsexual black man masquerad-ing as a woman: three kinds of Otherness captured in one. The anxious desire to look at the dimensions of the black male's penis is satisfied by its disclosure, and, as the black penis belongs to an ersatz woman, it is rendered harmless by its feminisation.

Critical Interventions

> To understand the real social/sexual meanings of drag . . . I would argue that you must look not so much at the *men* who dress as women, or the *women* who dress as men, but at the 'feminine' or 'masculine' characteristics they adopt, and the values placed on these, no matter who 'wears' them.[11]

It is necessary to look at the men involved, however, when considering how racial identity is implicated in the cross-dressing in *The Crying Game*. In both *M Butterfly* and *The Crying Game*, the cross-dressing men are doubly Other because they are Chinese and black respectively. At work here are not only gender stereotypes but racial ones too. In order to develop this point further, it is instructive to examine how Dil/Davidson is discussed in the reviews.

Jaye Davidson's film acting debut caused a stir, eliciting much praise: 'stunning' was a well-used term but quite what Davidson contributed apart from sexual enigma is hard to elicit from the citations. *Gay Times'* commented that 'the film really belongs to newcomer Jaye Davidson as Dil; the impact of this, her debut film appearance, will be at least equal to that made by Cathy Tyson in *Mona Lisa* (Neil Jordan, GB, 1986).'[12] The comparison is appropriate since Jaye Davidson is dressed and made up to be similar in appearance to Cathy Tyson's performance as Simone, and the shoot-out towards the end of *The Crying Game* bears similarities to that of *Mona Lisa*. *Gay Times'* positive review was somewhat reticent about the sexual games played in the film, refusing to mention the 'secret'. Such a strategy may be read as being consistent with the film's rejection of sexual essen-tialism, although it could be argued that such a ploy is undermined by referring unproblematically to Dil/Davidson as 'she'. By not engaging with the question of gender and sexual identity, and making only one reference to racial identity, however, this account of the film serves to highlight the fact that, without the racialised sexual shock, the text has little allure.

Fascination with Dil/Davidson is demonstrated in *Forum Art* where Hilton Als writes, 'One image that is in between: Jaye Davidson. Between colored and not colored, male and not female, kindness and not kindness.'[13] Designated by

Als as racially liminal, Dil/Davidson becomes a literalisation of the phallic mother as Als asks 'Would I eventually ask Jaye Davidson the baby question I ask of everyone: Are you my mother?'[14] It is Dil/Davidson's perceived 'in betweenness' that allows him to become a screen onto which these fantasies of maternal and sexual desire may be projected.

In the same magazine, Molly Nesbitt in a discussion of both Sally Potter's film *Orlando* (GB, 1993) and *The Crying Game*, states that 'The Body without Organs is a beyond. A friendly, forthcoming beyond that can help explain how an Irish man who loves women can continue to love a man who appears with a woman's surface.'[15] Fergus is seemingly attracted by Dil's intriguing manner and the 'surface' of her/his body as well as being motivated by the guilt he feels at having been involved in Jody's death. Notably, however, this character elaboration is only accorded to Fergus by Nesbitt: apparently no explanation is required of Jody's motivation, even though the narrative demonstrates that he too 'loves women'. In any case, according to normative perceptions rather than being a body 'without organs' Dil has an excess of sexual organs.

The actor who played the transvestite Chinese spy in *M Butterfly* was billed in such a way that his gender could not be identified. Similarly, the sexual ambiguity of the name 'Jaye' Davidson served to obscure gender signs. It was reported that the film – the original working title of which was *The Soldier's Wife* – was made on a closed set and that no-one was allowed to divulge the 'secret' of Davidson's anatomical sex. This play on gender/sexual ambiguity was further emphasised in reviews of the film, where apparently critics were requested not to divulge Dil/Davidson's sex. To further confound the speculation, it was suggested that Davidson should be nominated for an Oscar under the 'best supporting actress' category. Undoubtedly these strategies ensured a good deal of publicity for, and curiosity about, the film.

In Jonathan Romney's *Sight and Sound* review – which begins by mistakenly attributing both the accounts of an allegory about a scorpion to Fergus rather than acknowledging that the first telling is by Jody during his captivity – Jody's remark to Fergus about his posting in the British army is quoted: 'I get sent to the one place where they call you a nigger to your face' which constitutes a rare explicit reference to black/white antagonisms in the text.[16] Leaving aside the question of the lack of correspondence of this remark to black people's actual experiences, the fact that this comment is singled out as being a summary of 'the film's theme of perceived identities and their naming' is of interest since it does not appear to me to be given a great deal of significance in the course the narrative.[17] Rather it seems more like a necessary but reluctant acknowledgement of the contradictory position of black soldiers in the British armed forces, fighting for a country which often rejects them and renders their presence problematic. However, locating the racial politics both of the film and its critics is not easy since racial themes are so under-elaborated that they constitute a structuring absence.[18]

The film's publicity clearly emphasises its potentially controversial themes but, despite this, it was not generally perceived in the press as politically controversial.

This is quite an achievement for a film which features Irish Republicanism. In fact, I suspect that the absence in the text of a distinctly articulated political position contributed to the film's appreciative reception by most reviewers. There is certainly evidence of this in Sheridan Morley's review when he claims that the film is 'about personal politics, about states of mind rather than states on a map.' And again, as he states, 'This is not a film about the IRA or Northern Ireland except in its early sequences: rather it is a film about what we mean when we take on people and assignments'.[19] The political is adeptly reconstituted as the non-threatening, personal, in contrast to the listings guide, *What's On*, which somehow manages to claim that the film 'deals with politics and race and sexual obsession . . .'.[20] By keeping interracial sexual relationships, homosexuality, transvestism and the moral corruption of the judiciary to the realm of the private, individual act and choice, *The Crying Game* is on much safer ground.

This desire for a 'safe' text is not confined to the British press: in the New York publication *Village Voice*, Georgia Brown claims that *The Crying Game* 'handles the matter of race in a refreshingly natural way. Jody is black and so is Dil. But only in the opening scene, when drunken Jody drapes himself around the blond Jude (at a carnival in Northern Ireland where everyone else is white) was I conscious of him as a black man.'[21] Brown's sigh of relief is almost audible here, relief that she was not forced to think of Jody's predicament as a lone black man in a hostile environment. The insinuation here is that treating 'race' in a 'natural' way means not drawing attention to structures of dominance and subordination, or to individual and communal acts of racism. Dil *is* in an interracial sexual relationship with Jody's former captor Fergus, but the focal point for the audience's view of the relationship is not that of racial difference but that of transgressive sexuality. Significantly, for Brown, Jody's blackness is troublesome and obtrusive when he engages in a heterosexual act with a 'blond' white woman. When his head is obscured by a sack or when he is implicated in a sexual relationship with a black male transvestite, he is not so dangerous.

Brown positions Fergus as 'the product of a racist culture' and also quotes Jody's line about being called a 'nigger' to his face. She continues 'yet he's [Fergus] a gentleman to the core and doesn't seem to make distinctions according to race' – all of which serves to allay Brown's racial anxieties. It is a tribute to Jordan's script and direction and to Stephen Rea's acting that several critics point to Fergus' humanity and *kindliness*, overlooking his participation in terrorist activities and the fact that he was instrumental in Jody's death.

Despite citing a lack of pretension in the treatment of racial difference here, Brown manages to reconstruct *Crying Game* as a 'racial allegory', explaining that 'Jody and Dil are twins, extensions of each other, magical and real.' There is a brief moment when Brown questions whether the two black characters are merely marginal, not autonomous subjects but mysterious objects constructed for the white male gaze. Fergus is redeemed by his behaviour towards Jody and Dil: the process of his humanisation is demonstrated by his benevolence to black people who are indeed otherwise marginal. The black man's role – in the character of Dil and Jody – is to draw out Fergus' sexual and political ambivalences. In this sense Dil represents an intensification of the common function assigned to black women, black men, and white women: that of a backdrop for white male experiences.

It was refreshing to read Cynthia Heimel's statement: 'I personally think that the appearance of a bigger-than-life penis right in our faces is what got everyone excited'. She links this fascination with the phallic to women's lack of substantial roles in the cinema in general.[22] Philip French describes Miranda Richardson's characterisation of Jude as 'sexuality transformed into lethal politics' implying that for her, political commitment is a sublimation of sexual energy which accounts for her intense fanaticism. Jude's shrill characterisation as the ideologically dogmatic political gangster's moll, wielding a retributive gun stands in stark contrast to Dil, the soft voiced transvestite version of femininity.

One of the few female reviewers of *The Crying Game* in the British press. Anne Billson, also comments on the representation of women in the film. Referring to the men's relationships, she argues 'it's no wonder they go in for this male bonding, when the token women on display are such dubious specimens.'[23] The 'best woman' turns out to be Dil: after all, Dil is faithful to Fergus to the end, and after, whilst Jude uses her sexuality to deceive Jody and abandons Fergus when he fails to demonstrate his political commitment.

The awe and fascination engendered by the film is hyperbolically exemplified by Terrence Rafferty's review in the *New Yorker*.[24] The critical appreciation is titled 'Knight in Armor' which gives an indication of the mythical status that Rafferty confers on the film. *The Crying Game* is compared to various literary categories – myths, legends, short stories, fables and fairy tales – and to dramas. The film's alleged universal appeal is further emphasised by Rafferty's emphatic use of the all-encompassing 'we' which is deployed to conceal his imperial 'I'/ eye. The sense of Rafferty's imperial I/eye meshing with that of Jordan's is suggested in the following: 'Jordan keeps trying to see to the bottom of things, to plunge into the mysteries of his own nature, and in recent films his vision has seemed to cut through the murk and shadows of modern life like a searchlight beam.'[25] Rafferty's task as a critic is analgous to that of Jordan since Rafferty guides 'us' through the 'dark interior', consisting of black, homosexual and female sexualities. Perhaps Rafferty's presumptuous use of 'we' indicates an over-identification with what he describes as Jordan's task – to assist 'us' in 'our' understanding of the mysterious processes of sexual identification and identity. As is so often the case, these 'explanations' are necessary in order to explore the central enigma of white, male sexuality. It is that theme which is constantly and obsessively explored in texts, and although *The Crying Game* attempts to shift the parameters of this discussion, it still foregrounds white male experience at the expense of others.

The significance of the sexual revelation is rarely in doubt, although some reviewers attempted to underplay it. Although he fixes on the sexual shock, a 'huge, jaw-dropping surprise – a revelation that changes utterly our understanding of everything that has gone before', Rafferty claims that the revelation is not merely a narrative device. Similarly, Sheridan Morley's critique for the *Sunday Express* is full of praise for Jordan's drama but the giveaway is the italicised, indented paragraph which states:

> *The plot turns on two shocks of stunning impact, neither of which it would be fair to reveal, and either of which I defy you to forecast.*[26]

He observes later, in similar style:

> *Nothing is now what it may have seemed at the outset.*

The Crying Game self-consciously presents us with a disruption of sexual binarism whilst evading and failing to address racial binarisms. It may be the case that the attempt to problematise sexual categories is intended to make audiences question national and racial dichotomies, but it is on the visual, sexual spectacle of the male cross-dresser that the film is fixated. Jody's brief, physical relationship with Jude is both a diversionary tactic to lead us to an assumption of his hetero-sexuality, and a reiteration of assumptions about that black male sexuality which is apparently unable to resist the temptations that white women offer. Black women are apparently so troublesome that they have to be written out completely, replaced by a black man 'passing' as a woman.

The narrative is centrally concerned with a white male identity, that of a man whose political affiliations have afforded him companionship and a heterosexual relationship but little by way of coherent political philosophy or emotional com-mitment. Black men here are serviceable Others, created in order to form a setting against which Fergus may explore his personal and political dilemmas. Jordan compulsively re-explores some of the same ground tentatively covered in *Mona Lisa* regarding black sexuality, a point emphasised by the similarity of the look of Cathy Tyson and Jaye Davidson. Unfortunately, *The Crying Game* is too preoccupied with its own fantasies to be able to effectively comment on, and engage with that fascination and its provenance.

Given the current state of the press, I suppose it is not surprising that none of film critics writing on *The Crying Game* that I read, appear to have developed a perspective on 'race', gender and sexuality as both discrete and intersecting areas of discussion in contemporary cinema: serious, perceptive, and accessible film criticism is currently very scarce indeed.

Notes

1   Lawrence D Kritzman (ed), *Michel Foucault: Politics, Philosophy, Culture: Interviews and Other Writings, 1977–1984*, Routledge, London, 1988, p110.
2   The *Daily Telegraph*, 21 October 1991, p3.

3   For an extended discussion of the significance of transsexualism, see Judith Shapiro 'Transsexualism: Reflections on the Persistence of Gender and the Mutability of Sex'; Julia Epstein and Kristina Straub (eds), *Body Guards: The Cultural Politics of Gender Ambiguity*, Routledge, London, 1991, p248.

4   *Ibid.*, p270.

5   Marjorie Garber, 'The Occidental Tourist: *M Butterfly* and the Scandal of Transvestism' in Andrew Parker et al. (eds), *Nationalisms and Sexualities*, Routledge, 1991, p123.

6   *Ibid.*, p125.

7   Chris Straayer, 'The She-man: Postmodern Bi-sexed Performance in Film and Video', *Screen*, Volume 31, Number 3, Autumn 1990, p262.

8   *Ibid.*, p262.

9   *Ibid.*, p263.

10 The notion of 'feminine masquerade' is a concept developed by Joan Riviere in her often cited essay, 'Womanliness as Masquerade' published by Hendrik M Ruitenbeek (ed), *Psychoanalysis and Female Subjectivity*, College and University Press, New Haven, 1966.

11 Judith Williamson, *Consuming Passions: The Dynamics of Popular Culture*, Marion Boyars, London, 1987, p47.

12 *Gay Times*, October 1992, pp78–79.

13 Hilton Als, 'A Fan's Notes', *ArtForum*, Summer 1993, p95. This is not a review of the film but a rather self-indulgent eulogy centred on Dil/Davidson.

14 *Ibid.*, p95.

15 Molly Nesbitt, 'Apart Without a Face: *Orlando* and the *Crying Game*', *ArtForum*, Summer 1993, p95.

16 *Sight and Sound*, November 1992, p40.

17 *Ibid.*

18 This term is useful in considering how some issues and representations are both present and absent. For an explanation of the term, see Richard Dyer's '*Victim*: Hegemonic Project' in *The Matter of Images: Essays on Representation*, Routledge, London, 1993, p105.

19 Sheridan Morley, *Sunday Express*, 1 November 1992, p45.

20 *What's On*, 28 October 1992, p8.

21 *Village Voice*, 1 December 1992, p24.

22 See *The Independent on Sunday*, 28 March 1993, p43.

23 See *The Sunday Telegraph*, 1 November 1992, p41.

24 *The New Yorker*, 16 November 1992, pp127–130.

25 Terrence Rafferty. *Ibid.*, p130.

26 Morley, *op.cit.*

9

Crying over the Melodramatic Penis: Melodrama and Male Nudity in Films of the 90s

Peter Lehman

Over the opening credit sequence of Neil Jordan's *The Crying Game* (1992), we hear Percy Sledge singing "When a Man Loves a Woman." The song we later learn is used ironically since the film deals centrally with Fergus, a man who discovers that Dil, the woman he loves, is really a man. The song points to how carefully Jordan uses music in the film. Over the film's closing credit sequence, for example, he returns to ironic use of music with Lyle Lovett's cover version of the Tammy Wynette classic, "Stand by Your Man." Clever as this selection of songs is, however, it is the title song, "The Crying Game," that points to a significant central feature of the film: melodrama and the male body.

Traditionally, melodrama has been associated with women and the female spectator. There are, however, interesting traditions of male melodrama and one of them is a somewhat minor and overlooked pop/rock music tradition, songs which frequently have the word "crying" in their titles. Johnnie Ray's "Cry" (1952) probably marks the beginning of that tradition, and many of Roy Orbison's songs, including his classic hit "Crying" (1962), are the most artistically significant recordings within that tradition. Perhaps not coincidentally, Orbison himself recorded a cover version of "Cry."[1] Jordan's choice of Dave Berry's "The Crying Game" (1964) as the title song of his film invokes this male melodramatic rock tradition, and it does so in a manner which relates to the film's shocking and now famous revelation scene.

In *Running Scared: Masculinity and the Representation of the Male Body*, I argued that images of men and the male body are caught within a polarity not

Peter Lehman, "Crying over the Melodramatic Penis: Melodrama and Male Nudity in Films of the 90s," pp. 25–41 from Peter Lehman (ed.), *Masculinity: Bodies, Movies, Culture* (London: Routledge, 2001). © 2001 by Routledge. Reprinted by permission of Routledge/ Taylor & Francis Group, LLC.

unlike the mother/whore dichotomy which structures so many representations of women. At one pole, we have the powerful, awesome spectacle of phallic masculinity, and at the other its vulnerable, pitiable, and frequently comic collapse. The stars of male action films (e.g., John Wayne, Clint Eastwood, Arnold Schwarzenegger, Sylvester Stallone) and hard-core porn (John Holmes and Jamie Gillis), for example, typify the former. Short actors with rounded bodies (e.g., Edward G. Robinson, Peter Lorre), certain comic actors (e.g., Dudley Moore and Woody Allen) as well as the countless characters who are the butt of penis-size jokes typify the latter. This polarity not surprisingly also structures much of the representation of the penis in those rare instances when it is represented. The oft-noted requirement that porn stars be well endowed stems from the manner in which hard-core porn attempts to represent the male as an awesome, phallic spectacle. With the exception of such stars as John Holmes who are unusually large even when flaccid, hard-core porn generally minimizes or even totally elides flaccid penises, favoring an emphasis on large erections. The opposite side of the coin is the epidemic of penis-size jokes in US films of the '80s and '90s (e.g., "Pee Wee" in *Porky's*, 1981, and the Pierce Brosnan character in *Mrs Doubtfire*, 1993) in which characters with small penises, never seen, become the butts of such jokes. Implicitly, the message is that if the penis is going to be shown it had better be an impressive spectacle or, if it fails to live up to that standard, it had better be the unrepresented object of scornful humor.

While I still believe that such a polarity functions centrally within current Western representations of the penis, the extreme critical praise and box-office success surrounding David Henry Hwang's play *M Butterfly* and Neil Jordan's film *The Crying Game* suggest the emergence of a third category which I call the melodramatic penis. These representations of the penis, which are neither the phallic spectacle nor its pitiable and/or comic collapse, on the one hand challenge conventional representations, and on the other hand constitute a troubled site of representation that contains disturbing contradictions. The much-publicized Bobbitt case that centered on a severed and reattached penis is part of this melodramatic penis discourse. Penises, it seems, must elicit an extremely strong response from us, and if awe and laughter do not define the full range of such responses, melodrama is standing by.

Why is the sight of the penis such a problem, and what significance does the mini-epidemic of melodramatic penises that I will analyze below have? There are three major reasons for the difficulty of representing the penis in our culture. First, because of the gap between the penis and the phallus, the latter threatens to underwhelm the former. In Richard Dyer's memorable words, "the penis isn't a patch on the phallus" (274). The privileged signifier of the phallus most easily retains its awe and mystique when the penis is hidden. The sight of the actual organ threatens to deflate and make ludicrous the symbolic phallus. Second, since so many areas of representation in our culture, including mainstream cinema, are male dominated, two other problems arise, one linked to heterosexuality and one to homosexuality. Men may fear that the representation of the penis gives women a basis for comparison and judgment and, although men have long engaged in such behavior toward women, the thought of the tables being turned on them is close to unbearable. Finally, the representation of the penis creates a great deal of anxiety for homophobic men who may become intensely disturbed at finding themselves fascinated by it or deriving pleasure from looking at it.

Within this triple layer of fearfulness, the easiest thing to do is not represent the penis but, if the penis must be shown or even spoken about, its representation must be carefully regulated. Various discourses have sprung up to fulfill precisely that function; they include a medical discourse, an artistic discourse, a porno-graphic discourse, and even a comic discourse. In a desperate attempt to collapse the distinction between the penis and the phallus, pornography limits the re-presentation of the penis to the large, ever-present, long-lasting erection. This, pornography asserts, is what women want and need. Twentieth-century medical discourse, on the other hand, virtually fetishizes the normal, average penis, which it defines statistically as the 4-inch flaccid penis and the 6-inch erection, with a normal range of 5 to 7 inches. Such discourse assures nearly everyone that their penis is normal and limits its photographs, diagrams, drawings, and so on, to penises within this normal range. Penis-size jokes, on the other hand, seem to acknowledge that not all penises are in fact so much the same and that some look noticeably smaller than others. In most of that humor, however, the small penis is the butt of the joke. In a sense, penis-size jokes are the other side of the pornography coin: if the latter affirms the penis as the glorious phallus, the former ridicules those penises that, though invisible in representation, fall short of maintaining the sight of the penis as a dramatic spectacle. Small, retracted, shriveled penises are pathetic objects of ridicule, unworthy of being worshiped on the pornographic throne of the phallic penis or even the medical throne of the normal penis.

How does the melodramatic penis fit into these discourses and why has it made its appearance at this moment? Precisely because the penis has remained hidden for so long, in some ways it has become the last great taboo in our culture. The media typically maintain a tense contradictory relationship with such taboos: on the one hand, there are cultural imperatives for respecting the taboo and, on the other hand, there are the journalistic and artistic motives for breaking the taboos by creating new images which bring attention to themselves, sometimes in a shocking manner. Indeed, John Wayne Bobbitt's penis may well be the ultimate melodramatic penis: first it is severed, then it is lost, then it is found, then it is miraculously reattached, then it becomes a star in porn films, and then it is enlarged! While I am hard put to imagine what other melodramatic events can befall that penis, it is important to note the obsessive media coverage of this story. In 1993, for the first time, the word *penis* became common in much journalistic discourse, including prime-time, network newscasts (Grindstaff and McGaughey). In one sense, the Bobbitt case gave the media the opportunity they needed to assault the last taboo and utter the word *penis*. We are currently undergoing a media feeding frenzy about penises. No sooner had the Bobbitt case died down than the media began detailed coverage of new techniques in penis-enlargement surgery. Indeed, the *Wall Street Journal* gave front page coverage to the penis-enlargement business in 1996! I have been interviewed and quoted countless times about the representation of the penis by the media since publishing *Running Scared*.

This flurry of media attention to the penis clearly relates to the representation of the penis in films of the '90s. There is currently a widespread assault on this taboo and, of course, work like my own within academia is part of that context: scholars, artists, and journalists alike contribute to the total picture. It is worth noting that the films I will analyze here are extremely diverse: *Cobb* (1994) and *Boogie Nights* (1997) are mainstream Hollywood productions; *Angels and Insects* (1995) and *The Crying Game* (1992) have strong affinities with the European art cinema; *Carried Away* (1996) is an American independent, low-budget feature directed by Bruno Barretta, a Brazilian filmmaker; and *The Governess* (1999) is a British costume drama written and directed by a woman, Sandra Goldbacher.

I begin my analysis with *The Crying Game* since that film inaugurated this cycle. The opening scene of the film contains a conventional reference to penises when Jody urinates at a fair. He stands in such a manner that the view of his body is blocked by a tent, though he remarks that he has never urinated while holding a woman's hand. A similar scene occurs when he is held captive and has to urinate. The camera is positioned in such a manner that his genitals are offscreen at the bottom of the frame. Yet the unusual circumstances of the scene bring extraordinary attention to his penis. Since he is handcuffed, he asks Fergus, his guard, to unzip his pants, take out his penis, and hold it while he urinates. Fergus eventually does so, but only with great reluctance and discomfort. These scenes lull the audience into a false sense of conventional expectations – no matter how much talk of and attention to the penis, the film positions its spectators to expect that the organ will not be shown. No experience in the film, in other words, has shattered the expectation that the conventions will be followed. This even further heightens what would under any circumstances be the shockingly unexpected representation of the penis in the revelation scene. In a film where we are positioned to expect to not see the penis even when we hear about it, we are hardly prepared to see it in a scene where we do not even know it is present. Not surprisingly, that scene is one of intense melodrama.

After going to Dil's apartment, Fergus lies back on the bed as Dil goes into the bathroom preparatory to lovemaking. Dil reemerges, comes over to the bed, and Fergus rises, kisses her, and begins to take her robe off. As he slides it down he sits on the edge of the bed. With the camera placed behind him we see both him looking and the sight of male genitals simultaneously; his stunned reaction coincides with ours. This camera positioning doubly heightens what is already a highly dramatic moment. Jordan could, of course, easily have shot the scene in a conventional manner where the spectator would have learned that Dil is a man without seeing his genitals or, in a less conventional scenario, at least have learned that information before seeing the genitals. Jordan's strategy maximizes the shock value of the moment by making it a perceptual experience for the spectator. This is further heightened by keeping Fergus in the frame, since the spectator's shock is intensified through character identification with the heterosexual man who finds himself in this distressful situation.

At this point, the more conventional moments of melodrama begin. Fergus becomes violently ill. As he jumps up from the bed to rush to the bathroom, he pushes Dil over, and we see Dil fall to the bed. We hear the sounds of off-screen vomiting and then cut to a graphic medium shot of Fergus vomiting into the bathroom sink. Cut to a long shot with the bathroom at the far left rear of the frame. Dil sits on a sofa in the foreground, blood trickling from his nose. As Dil speaks we continue to see Fergus vomiting through the open bathroom door. He then slams it shut. When he emerges, apologizes, and prepares to leave, he walks past Dil, who grabs his pants and is pulled to the floor, begging, "Don't go, say something." Fergus does not respond and Dil falls from supporting his upper body with his hands on the floor to lying completely prostrate with his head on the floor. As he falls to this position, non-diegetic music reappears to heighten the moment. He says, "Jesus," as Fergus leaves, and the shot holds for a moment after the door in the rear of the frame has closed, and we are left with the sight of Dil lying distraught in the left foreground of the frame.

Several elements in this scene are reminiscent of classic melodrama, the most obvious being illness and images of bodies being knocked down and lying prostrate (e.g., *Way Down East*, 1920). The violence with which Fergus knocks Dil down the first time and bloodies his nose, the manner in which Dil gets pulled to the floor and remains partially propped up before fully collapsing, and the explicit imagery of Fergus vomiting combine to create a melodramatic spectacle. Camera positioning and the use of the soundtrack further mark the scene's melodrama stylistically. The sounds of Fergus's retching are a constant reminder of how violently sick he becomes, and the last shot of the scene, as he exits, is extremely unbalanced in a manner characteristic of classical melodrama. Thomas Elsaesser has shown how the tensions in Hollywood melodrama are frequently reflected in compositions that give extreme emphasis to foregrounded objects. In Jordan's variation, rather than an object such as a liquor bottle, Dil's body looms in the left foreground. Had Jordan placed the camera further back or, in a more likely variation, changed the angle and the distance so that, for example, Dil lies in the center of the frame as Fergus walks off to the right, the melodramatic effect would have been lessened. All stylistic decisions in the revelation scene, however, convert the drama inherent in the moment to melodrama, which appears to be the only mode appropriate to the unexpected sight of the penis.

David Henry Hwang's play *M Butterfly* supplies a similar moment in a seemingly opposite context since there the sight of the penis, far from being a surprise, is expected by both the character in the play and the audience. The revelation that Song, one of the play's central characters, is a man rather than a woman comes near the end of the play. When the play opened it was, however, widely known that it dramatized an internationally publicized case that led to the arrests of a French diplomat and a Chinese opera singer on espionage charges. Being unaware of Chinese opera performance traditions, the male diplomat mistakenly believed that the singer with whom he fell in love was a woman. Whereas the advertising campaign for *The Crying Game* was built around the secret which it urged all who had seen the film to keep to themselves, *M Butterfly* opened in 1988 amid publicity which referred to the then well-known story. Rather than being caught unaware, theater-goers were positioned to wonder how such a thing could happen.

The scene itself is further structured as a kind of dramatized striptease. Song appears before Gallimard, the diplomat, after the latter has learned of his true identity. Referring to Gallimard's request years earlier that Butterfly (as he calls her) strip for him, Song promises to do it now. Although Gallimard begs him not to do it, Song strips. The stage directions are simple: "Song drops his briefs. He is naked" (Hwang, 88). There are no prior stage directions indicating how Song has come to be in his briefs. He has previously been described as wearing a "well-cut suit" (80). As the scene is commonly staged, however, the play comes to a virtual halt as Song announces, "Monsieur Gallimard – the wait is over" (88) and slowly and deliberately takes off his tie, shirt, and suit before dropping his underpants. Both Gallimard and the audience watch in mounting suspense for what they know is coming. Song is positioned frontally for both Gallimard and the audience and the scene is fully lit. Song remains naked for the remainder of the scene until the stage directions indicate, "He puts on his briefs and slacks" (90) before Gallimard removes him from the stage.

Patterns of showing and/or talking about the penis in general within the theater are, not surprisingly, linked closely to that of movies. *The Shock of Recognition* by Robert Anderson, a brief one-act play written in 1966 and produced in New York in 1967 as part of the play *You Know I Can't Hear You when the Water Is Running*, almost ludicrously summarizes the "problem" presented by showing the penis in the theater at that time. Indeed, the play is about nothing else! It concerns a playwright who has the shocking idea of showing a naked man on stage. Much of the play is taken up with discussion by the playwright, the producer and others about how unacceptable this is, with particular emphasis given to the issue of showing the penis. What actor could possibly agree to do it? What do women think of penises? What do men think of penises? Although no penis is shown in this play, the play is about virtually nothing else but the seemingly revolutionary idea of doing so.

The Shock of Recognition, so titled because the playwright wanted the nude actor to be an Everyman rather than a masculine ideal, is dated in the worst and most extreme sense of the term. What is of interest today about the play is that it was written and staged in 1966 and 1967 – the last possible moment in US history when such a play could be written. Soon the Broadway production of *Hair* would conclude with the entire cast of men and women coming out on stage completely nude and lined up facing the audience. Other plays such as *Tom*

Paine and *Oh! Calcutta* would quickly follow. The whole notion of making such a big deal out of frontal male nudity was suddenly ancient history, part of another era. This coincided with a larger cultural climate of late '60s and '70s casual male nudity that had faded by the '90s. The melodramatic revelation of the penis is the polar opposite of casual (Lehman and Hunt).

Heather MacDonald's *Dream of a Common Language* (1993), for example, also stages male nudity in a highly melodramatic way. In the play, set in 1874, Clovis, the wife of a well-known artist and herself a former artist, asks Marc, a male friend, to pose nude for her. Even though he is an artist himself, he doesn't understand at first why a woman would want a completely nude model, and he only begins to fully disrobe after Clovis holds a gun on him. According to the stage directions, "Clovis points the gun at each garment indicating which he should remove next" (88). He stops with his underwear still on and she fires a shot to get him to continue. The other major characters, all of whom are offstage, hear the shots and rush onstage. When he understands the gravity of the situation, Victor, her husband, starts to disrobe while Marc remarks, "You want to point guns at men, make us take off our clothes" (90). The stage directions then read, "Victor has removed all his clothing and stands naked, wide open to Clovis" (90). She then poses and paints the nude man.

This melodramatic scene of a seemingly crazed woman artist waving a gun at a man to get him to strip for her is the climax of the play, which ends shortly afterward. In this play, the appearance of the penis is motivated by the historical setting, a time during which it was unacceptable for female artists to paint male nudes. That is, it appears that all the gun waving, drum-beating melodrama surrounding the penis belongs to the late nineteenth century, but it speaks loudly and clearly to the '90s. Indeed, the parallels with *M Butterfly* are most interesting: the latter motivates its male nudity with reference to actual recent events and leads up to it with a striptease; the former motivates its male nudity with general reference to an earlier era and leads up to it with an enforced version of a striptease. In both cases, the audience *of* the plays watches in rapt attention along with the characters *in* the plays as the slow removal of clothing leading up to the revelation of the penis takes place.

It is difficult to imagine scenes being structured in a manner that would bring more attention to a penis than these. Indeed, much of *M Butterfly* leads up to this moment of revelation where Gallimard is faced with the indisputable evidence that both he and the audience find so incredible. As in *The Crying Game*, the revelation also produces a strong response from the heterosexual male character in the scene. According to the stage directions, after Song is naked, "Sound cue out. Slowly we and Song come to realize that what we had thought to be Gallimard's sobbing is actually laughter" (88). Once again, the scene could easily have been staged in a much more conventional manner. Song could, for example, stand with his back to the audience so that only Gallimard sees his genitals. As with *The Crying Game*, the audience who has been watching this "woman" throughout the play is now forced to acknowledge that physiologically "she" is a he. Song's penis is not the butt of Gallimard's laughter as in a penis-size joke; the laughter, rather, is directed at the situation in which he finds himself.

Clearly, neither Jordan nor Hwang position the spectator to view the penis as an awesome spectacle of phallic power nor as its pitiable or comic collapse. Nor do they fall into the equally conventional and limiting position of not showing the spectator the penis that is the center of such dramatic attention within their narratives (as in, for example, *The Full Monty*, 1997, which, as many critics pointed out, does not deliver the full monty to the spectators of the film). Something of the limitation of this latter position ironically emerges in David Cronenberg's film of *M Butterfly* (1993) which was written and produced by Hwang. Since unlike the play, the film adopts a linear narrative which fits the classical Hollywood style, perhaps it comes as no surprise that the revelation scene is shot in such a manner that Song is seen nude only from behind or from the waist up. This conventional approach simply contributes to the awe and mystique of the penis by keeping it hidden.

When the penis is represented or shown or even referred to it is nearly always part of a discourse which attempts to carefully regulate that representation or reference: hard-core porn represents large, mostly erect penises; sexology represents statistically average, "normal" penises; penis-size jokes usually refer to small inadequate penises. What is lost amid all this careful regulation is the variety of actual penises that are not asked to bear the burden of representing anything other than what they are – penises, in other words, which are neither more nor less than penises. While the recent emergence of what I have called the melodramatic penis at least challenges norms of representation, it perpetuates the cultural assumption that the sight of the penis has to be provoked by an extraordinary event that guarantees the sight will have a major impact. These are still penises that are not just penises.[2]

When *The Crying Game* appeared in 1992, its representation of the penis was, to say the least, unique in the history of mainstream feature filmmaking; no other films had similarly shown the "shocking" revelation of a penis where the spectator didn't expect one. As I have indicated, at that time, the larger cultural significance of the representation of the penis in that film seemed to relate to a Broadway play and a news story, not other films. Things, however, have changed drastically in the last seven years. After *The Crying Game*, at least five other films with related melodramatic representations of the penis had appeared by 1999. Two of them, *Cobb* (1994) and *Angels and Insects* (1995), are closely related in that the scenes in question are not only shocking surprises but excessively melodramatic. The others, *Carried Away* (1996), *Boogie Nights* (1997), and *The Governess* (1998), are more closely related to the theatrical version of *M Butterfly*.

Cobb is an unusual sports biopic about the famous baseball player Ty Cobb. What makes the film unusual is its dark representation of one of the greatest heroes of America's national pastime. Cobb is portrayed as an unappealing, out-of-control, mentally disturbed, racist, anti-Semitic, misogynistic egomaniac – hardly the stuff of conventional hero worship. As he recounts his life's story to a reporter, he talks about how wonderful his father was and reveals that he was murdered. We then see a brief image of a man falling. Later, Cobb returns to the subject and we see a full flashback of his father's murder, including the brief snippet we had earlier seen. Now he narrates that his father, suspecting his mother of having an affair, tells his wife that he is going out of town on a business trip. He sneaks back to the house at night and approaches the bedroom window through which we see a naked woman. Upon discovering the intruder, the woman grabs a rifle and shoots him. When we return to the frame story, the reporter blurts out with astonishment, "Your mother killed your father!" From the flashback we surmise this has been an accident since she is startled by the intruder and acts in what appears to be self-defense.

Within Hollywood convention, we always accept flashbacks as revealing the truth, something that, as Kristin Thompson has argued, makes Alfred Hitchcock's *Stage Fright* (1950) transgressive. Similarly, near the end of *Cobb*, when we finally learn the truth about Cobb's father's death, an already classically melodramatic scene is made more shockingly so by the simultaneous revelation that we, the spectators of the film, have been tricked by the earlier lying flashback and are only now learning the truth. The situation is pure classic melodrama: once again, we are told that Cobb's father suspects his wife of infidelity, announces a business trip and, on a stormy night, sneaks home to spy on her activities. This time, however, when he watches through the bedroom window, he catches his wife in the act of adultery – the melodramatic moment *par excellence*. Precisely at this moment we get the shocking view not only of what is going on inside the room but simultaneously we see the lover in frontal nudity as he picks up a rifle and shoots Cobb's father. The melodramatic moment par excellence, a spouse catching a partner in the act of adultery, is displaced by the only thing that could top it: someone being murdered on the spot.

The unexpected sight of the penis here clearly contributes to and is embedded within an intensely melodramatic moment. The audience is already in something of a state of shock from the double whammy of the lying flashback and the revelation of the adulterous act when it is treated in quick succession to the surprising spectacle of frontal male nudity followed quickly by murder.[3] The film does offer a motive for the lying flashback: Cobb, a psychological wreck of a man, cannot easily admit to the true nature of his mother's adultery and his father's death. In an attempt to preserve his own legend, he tries to conceal the truth. The lying flashback, however, creates yet another parallel with *The Crying Game*. I mentioned above that in the latter film, the audience is lulled into conventional expectations by two earlier urination scenes that no penis will be shown. The lying flashback similarly lulls the audience since it leads us to believe that Cobb's mother is alone in her bedroom. She is the only person we have seen in the previous flashback. The last thing we expect to see the next time we revisit the scene is a man, let alone a penis. In one sense, then, we are just as surprised to see a man in the scene in *Cobb* as we are in *The Crying Game*. The added shock of surprise intensifies the melodramatic effect in both films.

Between the revelation that a woman is a man in *The Crying Game* and the revelation that a man we thought was shot without malice was in fact killed by his wife's lover after catching them together, it would seem we have pretty well reached the peaks of melodramatic possibilities for the surprise appearance of the penis: what, after all, can equal transvestism and adultery/murder for supplying such juicy melodramatic contexts? Incest can. *Angels and Insects*, set during the Victorian era, involves a young man who is a long-term visitor in a family that includes a brother and sister. He falls in love with the young woman, and they are married. Suddenly, however, she withdraws her sexual favors from her husband and even sleeps in another room. One day the husband leaves the house but returns home unexpectedly. He frantically searches through the house, looking for his wife. When he enters a bedroom, he interrupts her in the midst of intercourse with her brother. The brother turns around and frontally faces the camera, his genitals fully exposed.

The scene has a quite literal parallel with the nude scene in *Cobb* since it is structured around a husband returning home unexpectedly and discovering his wife in the act of adultery. Once again, it is not just the central character who is shocked in this film but also the spectators. Indeed, once again we have been lulled into complacency since everything we have seen about this family fits an image of propriety and extreme sexual repression. We are once again doubly shocked: no sooner do we realize that the wife is having sex with her brother than we are presented with the spectacle of his penis, this time erect. Much like we were shocked to discover the presence of the male lover in the bedroom during the last flashback in *Cobb*, here we are shocked to discover the presence of the brother. It is precisely these contexts of a similar series of shocks in which we see the penis that make these moments so similar in all three films. On the surface, the penis itself never appears to be the cause of the shocks but, rather, accompanies the revelation of something shocking: transvestism, adultery, and incest.

Carried Away tells the story of a relationship between two middle-aged schoolteachers. The man lives with his aging mother, and the woman lives alone. The man has a torrid affair with one of his high school students which leads him to question the nature of his relationship with the schoolteacher. In one scene, he goes over to her house and confronts her about his dissatisfactions: they have a boring, predictable love life, and since they make love in the dark they have never even seen each other's nude bodies. Working himself into a virtual hysteria about this state of affairs, he begins to dramatically turn on all the lights in the room and to disrobe in front of her until he stands naked. He repeatedly tells her to look at him and then commands her to undress, which she does. Throughout the scene there are several well-lit, frontal and sideview long shots of the man's body as he stands waiting for her to look at him and then undress and join him. The scene ends as they embrace and fall to the floor to make love.

In some ways, this scene appears to be nearly the opposite of the scenes in *The Crying Game*, *Cobb*, and *Angels and Insects*, rather than the sudden unexpected appearance of the penis surprising us, its appearance is announced with great flourish. Indeed, *Carried Away* beats drums and literally shines spotlights on the penis. Furthermore, unlike the scenes in those other films, this scene lacks excessive melodrama. Nothing more dramatic happens than the lovers taking off their clothes, embracing, and falling to the floor – no one intrudes with a gun, for example.

Within the context of *Carried Away*, however, the nude scene is in fact fairly melodramatic; it, like the scene in *Cobb*, even takes place during a thunderstorm, a fairly classic element of melodrama. Furthermore, throughout much of the film, the Dennis Hopper character is quite staid; he thus appears quite agitated, indeed nearly hysterical, during this scene. One of the very points of *Carried Away* is that, contrary to genre conventions, affairs and sexual transgressions do not have to end in melodramatic excess. This is seen in several ways. The climax of the film occurs after everyone has learned of the affair between the man and the teenage girl. In the expectation that the girl's father will attempt to kill him, the man takes a rifle and prepares himself for the inevitable, violent confrontation. Yet, when the father, accompanied by the mother, arrive, all they want to do is talk. They do not threaten physical violence or legal action. Indeed the film ends with no severe consequences for any of the three lovers; the girl returns to her family, and the teachers are reunited as a couple. There is not even any suggestion that the underage girl has been traumatized by her sexual experiences with the much older man. The closest thing to conventional melodrama occurs when the girl sets fire to a horse barn.

Within the context of this film, then, the love scene between the teachers is in fact marked as somewhat excessive. More important, however, the strategy of virtually announcing the penis will be revealed before actually showing it has a curiously similar effect to its surprise appearance: it imbues the sight of the penis with a sense of great significance. Far from being casual, this is a nearly overwhelming moment.

The notorious "dick" shot in *Boogie Nights* (1997) can also best be understood within this '90s discourse of the melodramatic penis (Lehman, 1998). The need to talk about and show the penis is everywhere, including an entire episode of *Ally McBeal* during the 1997–98 season and *Chicago Hope* during the 1998–99 season. In this regard, Paul Thomas Anderson's dwelling on it throughout the film and showing it in the last shot can best be understood as part of the time in which his film was made, rather than the time period it represents. In 1975 or even 1985 it is highly unlikely that a Hollywood film that spoke of its central character's penis would end with a graphic shot of it.

On the surface, it might seem that the final shot of *Boogie Nights* falls not into the melodramatic category but, rather, that of the awesome spectacle of phallic power. But within the context of a Hollywood film, the shot is also quite melodramatic – a sort of hybrid of the two categories. After soliloquizing in front of a mirror while waiting to shoot a porn scene, Dirk Diggler (Mark Wahlberg) unzips his pants and pulls out his penis, which we see as a frontal, close shot in the mirror. And what a penis it is – there is no question that part of the shot's effect derives from this "impressive" spectacle. I have argued elsewhere that this kind of emphasis on the large flaccid penis results from a slippage of the erect penis onto the flaccid penis (Lehman, 1993). If we are going to show the flaccid penis, in other words, it had better look as much like the supposed awesome spectacle of an erection as possible. And, indeed, the flaccid penis in *Boogie Nights* seems virtually indistinguishable from the 13-inch erection we have been hearing about. The brutally frontal, nearly confrontational manner in which the penis is directly revealed for the camera relates the shot to the excesses of melodrama I have described in the other films. Like the scenes in *Carried Away* and the theatrical version of *M Butterfly*, this scene is structured in such a manner that the revelation of the penis is much heralded.

In a newspaper article devoted entirely to discussing the penis shot in *Boogie Nights*, journalist Barry Koltnow discusses moments in the history of film that have "shocked" audiences sexually: Clark Gable removing his shirt in *It Happened One Night* and Sharon Stone crossing her legs in *Basic Instinct*. "This time the shocking moment will come in the last few frames," Koltnow notes. It is precisely this element of shock that aligns the last shot of *Boogie Nights* with the melodramatic shocks of transvestism, adultery, murder, and incest in the films described above.

The Governess, written and directed by Sandra Goldbacher, supplies yet another variation on the above pattern. In this film, Minnie Driver plays a young Jewish woman who hides her true identity and takes a job as a governess in the home of a wealthy family. The husband, a scientist and inventor, is working on the discovery of the photographic process. The governess ingratiates herself with her employer, and they work together and have an affair. On one occasion, he passes out after too much drink, and she takes nude pictures of him. She leaves them for him in the spirit of a lover's gift. Later, however, we see him examining the pictures with a magnifying glass. He seems focused on the image of his penis, and a deeply disturbed expression appears on his face.

The penis is shown both in the photo-session scene and later in the photograph as the man studies his image. Neither is a particularly melodramatic moment. Indeed, during the session, the woman enjoys herself and suffers no response at all from the sleeping man. And although the man is troubled as he looks at the picture, nothing further happens at that moment. The pause, however, is brief. The appearance of the penis precipitates the most intense melodrama for the remainder of the film.[4] First, the employer immediately banishes the governess from his laboratory and breaks off his entire relationship with her, both as a coworker and a lover. In further retribution, he denies her contribution to their joint research and takes full credit himself within scientific circles for work they shared. In revenge for these actions, the governess melodramatically disrupts a family dinner by marching in with a print of the nude photograph and giving it to the wife.

The Governess departs slightly from the pattern in the above films in two ways. First, the penis is neither a big shock nor is it a highly heralded event. Second, when it appears it seems anything but melodramatic – there is a brief pause before the melodrama erupts. Like *Dream of a Common Language*, *The Governess* thematizes the melodramatic penis within an historical context – all the turmoil surrounding it appears attributable to the nineteenth century. And even though the film supplies a profound investigation into historical issues of gender and representation (it is a highly accomplished, important film), it also nevertheless speaks to the contemporary context I have been describing.[5]

All of these films and plays featuring melodramatic penises certainly suggest that the taboo against showing the penis is crumbling. Yet, this is not a simple occasion for joy. The melodramatic penis may in part be a reaction to the women's movement. At a time when women have made major inroads upon areas of male privilege such as the workplace, politics, and the military, asserting the importance of the penis seems to affirm the significance of the one thing women can't have (Lehman and Hunt).

The current moment involves tension between conflicting ideologies in a manner that recalls the nineteenth century and the invention of photography and then cinema. Stephen Heath has noted that, prior to the invention of photography, the problem of anxiety produced by representing the female genitals was avoided in art by painting and sculpting the female body as complete without any sign of the genitals, not even the suggestion of a slit or opening in the body. The main drive behind the invention of photography, however, was to reveal everything, including what the naked eye could not see. Suddenly, photography demanded that female genitals be open, exposed to view and ceaselessly explored. Linda Williams has shown how early hard-core film pornography was similarly driven by a need to show everything. Thus, the camera's ideology of showing everything conflicted with the cultural tradition of representing the female body as complete without being fully sexed. From such a perspective, acknowledging the female genitals gave rise to castration anxieties and the resultant representations had to develop strategies to contain those anxieties – various forms of fetishism, for example, and scenarios of narrative reassurance.

Something similar is happening in the late twentieth century, but now it is the penis and not the vagina that is the site of the anxiety producing conflict. The dominant ideological drive to retain the awe and mystique surrounding the penis is crumbling before the journalistic and artistic drive to break down the final taboo. The melodramatic penis is the result. The melodrama surrounding the representation of the penis paradoxically cries out to reaffirm the spectacular importance of the penis even as the very assault on the taboo seeks to dislodge that importance. The melodramatic penis can, on the one hand, be read in a positive manner as avoiding such simple structuring dichotomies as the large, awesome phallic spectacle versus its pathetic, comic collapse. In that sense, the melodramatic penis is far removed from either the pornographic phallic penis or the small penis that is the butt of jokes. On the other hand, the melodramatic penis continues to insist that the very act of representing the penis is somehow monumental. The penis may no longer be called upon to look impressive or sound pathetic but in a different manner it is still marked as being of extraordinary significance. The discourse of the melodramatic penis still seeks to block a penis from merely being a penis. In this regard the seemingly opposite strategies of surprise in *The Crying Game, Cobb*, and *Angels and Insects* and prior expectation in *M Butterfly, Carried Away, Boogie Nights*, and *The Governess* are really the same: whether by shocking us or preparing us, all these works insist that showing the penis is of excessive dramatic importance. That is something to cry about.

Notes

1   Jordan titled his film *In Dreams* (1999), after a Roy Orbison song, which he used over the closing credits.

2   Signifificantly, *The Crying Came, M Butterfly* and the Bobbitt case all involve racial and crosscultural elements. From the perspective of issues of the male body to which I have limited my remarks here, I think that all of these examples would remain fundamentally unchanged if all the characters were white. Narratives and images of racial and cultural difference that center strongly on the penis, however, suggest that racial and sexual difference frequently become intertwined, as with Robert Mapplethorpe's photographs and the media coverage of the controversy surrounding them.

   Since writing this essay, Richard Lucht has brought to my attention the 1983 teen slasher film *Sleepaway Camp*. It ends in a graphically shocking scene with full frontal nudity revealing that the central female character is a teenage boy, not a girl. Given the often radical vitality of the "disreputable" slasher genre, it is not surprising to find a film in it prefigure the melodramatic penis nearly a decade before an "art" film such as *The Crying Game*.

3   Although my main interest in this scene at the moment relates to the connection between the surprising revelation of the penis and melodramatic excess within the narrative, the scene includes another peculiar element in relationship to the representation of the male genitals. If the sight of the male genitals is rare enough in any context within the Hollywood cinema, the sight of a naked man holding a rifle may be unique. The reason this image is particularly bizarre is due to a certain redundancy within Hollywood logic whereby a rifle is commonly viewed as a phallic symbol. The usual rules of representation governing masculinity and the male body preclude simultaneously revealing both the literal organ, the penis, and its symbolic dimension, the phallus, in this case represented by the rifle. As we shall see, this risks opening a ludicrous space between the penis and the phallus, a space which patriarchy desperately tries to deny. Indeed, the scene in *Cobb* minimizes the penis/phallus contrast by showing both only briefly as the lover receives the rifle from the woman and moves toward her; the very phallic shots of him pointing the shotgun at and shooting Cobb's father are mid-shots.

4   *American History X* (1998) also fits this pattern. During what appears to be a peaceful shower scene in a prison, we see several apparently casual shots of the penises of showering inmates, including that of the main character. Moments later, however, he is the victim of a shocking and graphic rape.

5   *The Governess* also includes another scene of male nudity. The son in the family is a young man who falls in love with the governess and is rejected by her. Near the end of

the film, after she leaves the family, we see the distraught young man emerging naked from a swim in the ocean. The glimpse of his penis in this shot is tied to the emotional anguish highly visible on his face. His nakedness, a sign of excessive vulnerability, along with his behavior and intense emotional distress are signs of melodramatic illness.

Works Cited

Anderson, Robert. 1967. *You Know I Can't Hear You when the Water's Running*. New York: Dramatists Play Service Inc.

Dyer, Richard. [1982] 1992. "Don't Look Now." In *The Sexual Subject: A Screen Reader in Sexuality*, 265–76. London: Routledge.

Elsaesser, Thomas. [1972] 1985. "Tales of Sound and Fury: Observations on the Family Melodrama." In *Movies and Methods, Vol. 2*, ed. Bill Nichols, 166–89. Berkeley: University of California Press.

Grindstaff, Maura, and Martha McGaughey. 1998. "Feminism, Psychoanalysis, and (Male) Hysteria over John Bobbitt's Missing Manhood." *Men and Masculinities* 1, 2 (October): 173–92.

Heath, Stephen. [1978] 1992. "Difference." In *The Sexual Subject: A Screen Reader in Sexuality*, 47–106. London: Routledge.

Hwang, David Henry. 1994. *M. Butterfly*. New York: Penguin.

Koltnow, Barry. 1997. "BOOGIE NIGHTS Leaves a Big Question" *Orange County Register*, Oct. 20, Knight-Ridder/Tribune Information Services.

Lehman, Peter. 1993. *Running Scared: Masculinity and the Representation of the Male Body*. Philadelphia: Temple University Press.

——. 1998. "Will the Real Dirk Diggler Please Stand Up?" *Jump Cut* 42: 32–38.

Lehman, Peter, and Susan Hunt. 1999. "From Casual to Melodramatic: Changing Representations of the Penis in Films of the 70s and 90s." *Framework* 40 (April): 69–84.

MacDonald, Heather. 1993. *Dream of a Common Language*. New York: Samuel French.

Thompson, Kristin. 1988. *Breaking the Glass Armor: NeoFormalist Film Analysis*. Princeton, NJ: Princeton University Press.

Williams, Linda. 1989. *Hardcore: Power, Pleasure, and the "Frenzy of the Visible."* Berkeley: University of California Press.

10

Travels with Sally Potter's *Orlando*: Gender, Narrative, Movement

Julianne Pidduck

In her essay 'Desire in narrative', Teresa de Lauretis[1] identifies an overarching structural narrative economy of gendered stasis and movement. This formula scripts the male subject as dynamic hero who moves through narrative time and space: meanwhile, back in the kitchen, the female term typically represents stasis, home and hearth. The female character, then, is figured as social and imaginative constraint – a threshold or destination for the male protagonist's inner and outer journeys of self-realization and social transformation. Mary Ann Doane[2] extends such a gendered economy to spatiotemporal patterns of genre. She suggests that the more dynamic narratives and open landscapes signifying freedom of movement and possibility correspond to male address, while cluttered interiors and narrative constraint correspond to female address. The notion of female narrative constraint is manifested textually and historically in gendered codes of corporeal and geographical mobility – a skewed actual and imagined access to social space and agency.

Doane cites the Western as the 'masculine' genre *par excellence*, while the costume drama, with its precise attention to costume and set design, and a meandering, detail-rich, languorous quality of event may be seen according to this schema as a quintessentially 'female' genre. Observing the costume drama's obsession with the alternatively luscious and claustrophobic subtleties of decorum and visual style, it could be argued this genre intimately explores a particular historical quality of white, bourgeois, social constraint – an experience rendered explicitly around gender relations and femininity. However, Sally Potter's *Orlando*

Julianne Pidduck, "Travels with Sally Potter's Orlando: Gender, Narrative, Movement," pp. 172–89 from *Screen* 38:2 (Summer 1997) (Oxford: Oxford University Press). © 1997 by The John Logie Baird Centre. Reprinted by permission of the author and Oxford University Press.

(1992) does not fit neatly as a 'typical' costume drama. Perhaps the general descriptive terms of movement and constraint are qualified, fleshed out, problematized when applied to a particular text. What has come to fascinate me in this film is the attenuated dynamism of character movement traced out by a protagonist who changes, at least on the surface, from male to female. Even as she/he undertakes an audacious journey through four hundred years of English bourgeois and imperial history, Orlando proves for the most part a rather inept protagonist.

The slowness and uncertainty of Orlando's progress coincides with what I believe to be an explicit play (in both Virginia Woolf's source novel and Potter's film adaptation) upon gendered conventions of narrative movement. According to de Lauretis, part of the project of feminist film criticism and filmmaking has been the production of new forms of discourse, new forms of narrative which can 'construct the terms of reference of another measure of desire'. Potter's *Orlando*, like her earlier projects *Thriller* (1979) and *The Gold Diggers* (1984), playfully takes up this challenge. The following detailed account of the film's precise – and in some ways idiosyncratic – treatment of gendered space, time and movement raises interesting questions about these emergent feminist desires. Further, as an exception can illuminate the rule, this filmmaker's deliberate tinkering with general patterns of narrative and film form as well as with the particular conventions of costume drama, foregrounds cinematic norms of gendered movement and constraint.

In this essay, I will elucidate several different qualities of gendered movement in *Orlando*. Through the term 'movement' I address, variably, the spatiotemporal issues of costume, decor and narrative tempo and the psychological dimension of character development, as well as narrative and imaginative historical and geographical voyages. Working from literary accounts of the pull of narrative through time and space, I first develop a detailed description of these layers of movement and stillness. Then, using Mikhail Bakhtin's notion of chronotope as a bridge, I work outwards from textual issues of narrative movement towards a 'preferred' audience for this text: a dispersed feminist audience. Drawing from the notion of the journey as a structuring logic of narrative, I would even go so far as to say that *Orlando* develops a utopian feminist voyage of 'becoming' which can delicately 'move', inspire or amuse this audience. In a sense, Potter updates and screens Woolf's iconic feminist text through Tilda Swinton's feminist heroine who strides, at times with difficulty, through four centuries of English bourgeois and colonial history. In the process the dry theoretical problem of gendered narrative movement becomes an explicitly collective project of social critique – and above all, an exploration of a feminist utopian journey.

However, to extend the theoretical questions raised by de Lauretis and Doane, I follow Orlando's awkward bumbling through historical social and aesthetic vignettes into the imaginative imperialist encounter with the Khan of Khiva. In the final section of the essay, then, I look at Orlando's sojourn in colonial space as an instance which calls into question the binary logic of a gendered narrative/social allocation of movement and constraint. In the process, I begin to explore the implications of a seemingly self-evident feminist aspiration for access to the (white masculine) dream of unhindered mobility.

In 'Forms of time and chronotope in the novel', Mikhail Bakhtin describes the different articulations of time and space within historical literary genres as 'chronotopes':

> In the literary artistic chronotope, spatial and temporal indicators are fused into one carefully thought-out, concrete whole. Time, as it were, thickens, takes on flesh, becomes artistically visible; likewise, space becomes charged and responsive to the movements of time, plot and history. This intersection of axes and fusion of indicators characterizes the artistic chronotope.[3]

Bakhtin describes a classical Greek form, the 'adventure novel of everyday life', which evokes the inner machinations of plot-time/space in *Orlando*. This form twins a biographical narrative of human identity, crisis and metamorphosis with an adventure structure chronicling a protagonist's 'actual course of travel' or journey. For Bakhtin, this chronotope combines the epic adventure time of the Greek romance with the everyday time of human biography: 'The factor of the journey itself, the *itinerary*, is an actual one: it imparts to the temporal sequence of the novel a real and essential organizing center. In such novels, finally, biography is the crucial organizing principle for time.'[4] The adventure time (space) through which the literary and cinematic protagonist Orlando gambols wide-eyed follows a highly selective and ironic account of four hundred years of English aristocratic gender and social relations. The subtitle of Woolf's novel, 'a biography', indicates that *Orlando* was written as a *roman à clef* shadowing the life of Woolf's friend and lover Vita Sackville-West.[5] To complicate further the structuring frame of biography, Woolf's (and Potter's) character Orlando may be read as a stand-in for, or a witness to, the historical experience of bourgeois English women. I will return below to this point.

Following the framework of the adventure novel of everyday life, Potter's adaptation of Woolf combines the characteristic forms of segmentation and passage. Intertitled signposts mark off a sequence of seven semi-autonomous episodes: '1600 DEATH'; '1610 LOVE'; '1650 POETRY'; '1700 POLITICS'; '1750 SOCIETY'; '1800 SEX'; and 'BIRTH' (not dated, but presumably Potter's present day, even as Woolf's novel ended in her time, 1928). Bold white capitals on a black screen, these intertitles effectively frame, foreground and methodically *interrupt* the film's narrative flow. The two elements (dates and events) within the titles signal the doubled spatial–temporal articulation of the adventure novel of everyday life. Crass episodal tags from death to (re)birth frame formative moments in Orlando's life according to traditional biographical developmental stages. Orlando's 'biographical' journey involves her/his passage through the clearly delineated historical episodes referenced by the dates. The protagonist, then, literally 'moves' through clearly differentiated tableaux, from the dotage of Elizabeth I

(1600) to an ambassadorial appointment in the Orient (1700) and into the mid twentieth century. Orlando's passage through these stylized historical chrono-topes links the film's narrative movement with an allegorical 'history' of British (bourgeois, white) womanhood.

I shall call these segments 'tableaux' or, better, 'movements': in reference to the composition of musical texts, each 'movement' carries its own colorations and mood. These movements offer a clue to the bare bones of *Orlando*'s narrative structure. Each episode encapsulates a particular aesthetic/historical space–time. Each movement presents a stylistically and narratively semi-autonomous segment. Visually, these tableaux are set apart by a distinct array of period costumes and decor which evoke and exaggerate the 'feel' of an era. Working with a particular room in the Great House, the Duchess's drawing room, or the stylized exteriors of the ice court, fragments of space metonymically reproduce a certain aesthetic/historical moment. In keeping with a theme of property-holding, Orlando's travels continually return to the family seat, the Great House itself. While the bold black and white flagstones of the Great Hall, the manor's exterior architecture, and the great oak tree in the field which bookends the film ('enduring old England') remain constant, particular rooms are redecorated (like Orlando/Tilda Swinton's changing garb) to signal historical shifts.

These historical moments are not produced, though, through the conventions of realism (even as applied within more traditional costume drama), but rather through the metonymic excess of elaborate set design and splendid overblown costume. The staged fantastical setting of each movement calls attention to the film's irreality. For example, the encounter with the Muscovites occurs not within a castle, but in the magical space of the ice court; Orlando's ambassadorial mission to Central Asia occurs within a grove of pillars, or out in the windblown desert. The excess of the costumes and ridiculousness of the infinite ritual and pomp offer a kind of ongoing visual satire of the historical conventions of bourgeois English manners, gender comportment and, less rigorously, empire. For example, consider the British ambassadorial contingent in Khiva at the onset of the battle, parading around in enormous hats with obscene plumage, skinny stockinged legs and coyly, hugely buckled shoes. The pomposity of these wigs and costumes and the self-important mannerisms which accompany them offer a running visual commentary on the project of empire. The impracticality of the clothes, the attitudes and the disingenuous policies brought along in the huge spatial movement of colonialism highlight the polite ridiculousness (if not the tragedy) of the colonial venture. I will return to this point at greater length below.

In parallel (and perhaps more eloquently), the sheer crippling unmanageability of Orlando's bourgeois female attire speaks volumes to the 'structure of feeling' of upper-class British womanhood – the limits on physical and social mobility. The newly-corseted Orlando in her voluminous stiff white gown minces with difficulty around the dust-draped furniture in what had been her own parlour. the whiteness and volume of her skirt resemble the abandoned furniture which has been draped awaiting the return of the Lord of the Manor. Similarly, in the

'Society' parlour scene, Orlando is immobilized like one elaborate, frosted blue cake on a love seat. Complete with an unlikely sculpted headdress, she becomes a porcelain figurine, hampered equally by costume and convention from moving or responding to the routine snubs of the male 'wits'. The awkwardness of these overblown costumes is reinforced through a consistent use of perfectly orchestrated balanced visual compositions and long static shots which create a luscious stage on which to observe the actors going through their painstakingly choreographed, if meaningless, paces.

This self-conscious artifice of set and costume emphasizes a divergence from the conventions of realist period film – and a refusal of its implicit claim to represent a historically 'authentic' narrative space. On this subject, Sally Potter remarks: 'I always said to the design teams: this is not a costume drama, this is not a historical film, it's a film about now that happens to move through these periods. Research and find out all the things we can and then throw them away. We're going to stylize, we're going to leave out, exclude certain colours or textures or shapes. The usual approach to costume drama is in the genre of realism. . . . But the premise of *Orlando* is that all history is imagined history and leaves out all the most important bits anyway.'[6]

Such an approach relates to ironic reworkings of the genre in contemporary British cinema: *The Draughtsman's Contract* (Peter Greenaway, 1982) or *The Madness of King George* (Nicholas Hytner, 1994). British queer rewritings of history and costume drama (Derek Jarman's *Caravaggio* (1986) and *Edward II* (1991)[7] or Isaac Julien's *Looking for Langston* (1989)) offer a further aesthetic and political context for *Orlando*. Finally, Potter's project coincides interestingly with emergent feminist interest in costume drama, including Ulrike Ottinger's extravagant *oeuvre* (notably *Johanna d'Arc of Mongolia* (1989)), Jane Campion's *The Piano* (1993), and Julie Dash's *Daughters of the Dust* (1991).

In relation to my central preoccupation with gender and movement, the latter feminist films offer the most intriguing point of contact with *Orlando*. To a considerable degree, as my analysis points out, the ironic costume, gesture and character movement employed by Potter here highlight issues of gendered physical and social mobility and constraint. As Stella Bruzzi argues, *The Piano* presents another feminist treatment of costume which emphasizes historical, social and sexual constraint through clothing.[8] By situating *Orlando* beside these other feminist costume dramas, an interesting range of cinematic expressions of femininity, movement, constraint – and indeed race and class – emerge. While such an analysis lies outside the scope of this essay, the above reading of costume and set in *Orlando* offers a point of departure from which to consider these questions in other feminist costume dramas.

Moving from this discussion of the screen spaces of segmentation, I would like now to delve into the more temporal problem of movement and passage. Roland Barthes's essay on the 'Structural analysis of narratives' offers precise terms for describing the movement, interruption, ellipsis, and expansion of narrative. For

Barthes, the 'functional units' of narrative describe the actions and events which advance the plotline. He divides these units into the primary 'cardinal functions' and 'catalysers'. Cardinal functions correspond to the key plot points within narrative, while catalysers describe the secondary events which fill the space between the moments of risk or plot development. In Barthes's terms, 'cardinal functions are the risky moments of a narrative. Between these points of altern-ative, these "dispatchers", the catalysers, lay out areas of safety, rests, luxuries.'[9]

While this schema seems to lend itself most immediately to conventional narratives such as the Bond detective novels analysed by Barthes, it applies also to a more leisurely, digressing structure such as that of *Orlando*. The cardinal functions – the critical episodes of risk, of ordeal traversed by the protagonist – correspond neatly to the intertitled episodes. The titles are shorthand for the significant action of each movement, from the death of Queen Elizabeth to Orlando's love for Sasha. In a sense, very little 'happens' in this film, as its events can be condensed into the string of intertitles. Within the genre of costume drama, the cardinal functions appear secondary to the real 'meat' of the story – the subtleties of gesture, a sidelong glance, the flick of a fan. As in costume drama generally, a great deal of the meaningfulness, the richness, of *Orlando* is conveyed through a micro-economy of polite silences, gestures and looks. Within this genre, these secondary actions do far more than 'embellish' the narrative events. As Barthes so perceptively points out, these catalysers are intrinsic to the 'economy of the message'. The 'dilatory sign', this 'apparently merely expletive notation always has a discursive function: it accelerates, delays, gives fresh impetus to the discourse, it summarizes, anticipates and sometimes even leads astray'.[10]

The triumph of the dilatory sign in *Orlando* indicates a key quality of the text's narrative movement, its tempo. Potter creates a languorous, digressing and stately progression of perfectly choreographed tableaux: the splash of a red and gold tunic in a golden field as the long-legged Orlando sprawls under a tree. Here, the category of secondary plot points spills over into Barthes's second category of units, known as 'indices'. Indices relate to another descriptive level of narrative, having to do with character or setting. Cardinal functions form the narrative framework, which functions according to the logic of plot or story, while catalysers and indices serve as narrative *distortion* and *expansion*. The centrality afforded details of costume, setting and atmosphere in *Orlando*, as in other costume dramas, helps explain the pleasures of this slow-moving genre. A consistent use of long takes and meaningful stillnesses allow the leisure to enjoy the film's ample textures and colours, while the precise 'punch' of the film speaks through the pointed, sharp dialogue, and through Orlando's addresses and looks to the camera. For example, seemingly little 'happens' in the late twentieth-century sequence in which Orlando takes her manuscript to the publisher, who says to her:

> This is really very good. Written from the heart. I think it will sell. Provided you rewrite a little. You know, develop the love interest and give it a happy ending.
> By the way, how long did this draft take you . . . ?

In response, Orlando merely looks quizzically into the camera. The pith of the moment, the richness of its irony speaks eloquently through Orlando's mute look. Perhaps the most singular stylistic device in the film, these carefully orchestrated looks and addresses to the camera reach outside of the diegetic action to create a moment of complicity with the audience. In a sense, the absurd constraints on bourgeois femininity so precisely recreated in the film's visual language prompt a leap to a different level of discourse for commentary. Swinton's quick looks and witty rejoinders brilliantly rupture the potential claustrophobia and preciousness resulting from a deliberately slow pacing.

Barthes points out that cardinal functions correspond to 'metonymic relata', while indices refer to 'metaphoric relata; the former correspond to a functionality of doing, the latter to a functionality of being'.[11] Clearly, this polarity of being and doing signals the question of the gendering of narrative and genre. While detective, Western or action genres (traditionally coded as 'masculine') privilege the metonymic plane of physical and spectacular *doing*, of action and decision, the more 'feminine' melodrama or costume drama genres lean more heavily towards the metaphorical level of *being* – a micro-economy of gesture, and a rich audiovisual array of colour, harmony, pattern, texture, rhythm and melody. In 'Entertainment and Utopia', Richard Dyer calls these elements 'non-representational signs' which may be treated as a mere function of narrative, but which operate at a level of 'feeling' or 'sensibility', rather than of linear plot progression.[12] And even though these non-representational signs may call attention to themselves within female-coded genres (Dyer focuses on the musical), they certainly form an integral part of the semiotic system of all genres.

Of course, as Dyer reminds us, generic conventions and the 'structure of feeling' they evoke correspond to very real systems of marketing and social relations. Mary Ann Doane points out that the gendering of genre articulates the former category of traditionally 'male' genres precisely with the level of action, of doing – a linear and energetic narrative 'drive' traversing topographies of open space, possibility, agency, movement.[13] 'Female' genres such as the melodrama, on the other hand, tend to function at a more subtle, immobile level, incorporating (for Doane) claustrophobic, cluttered internal spaces, and a corresponding stifling, hysterically immobilized temporality.

On one level, then, *Orlando*'s chosen genre of the costume drama, with its attention to setting, costume and subtle conventions of look and gesture, draws heavily on such 'female'-coded generic conventions rather than on the muscular striding of a protagonist through space and time, as suggested by the quintessential male genres. Even so, the audacity of Orlando's journey through four hundred years of British history links the adventure to motion, transformation, change on the heroic scale of *Gulliver's Travels*, or *Around the World in Eighty Days*. If this generic tension between the gendered economies of being and doing holds, how then can we describe the attenuated narrative movement of *Orlando*?

Thus far I have described a plot structure which follows a dilatory, languorous pattern of sequential segments of (in)action. Each segment sketches out a perfectly orchestrated, self-contained little world of set, costume and micronarrative. These 'movements' are strung together by the physical presence, if not the forceful subjectivity, of Orlando in her/his passage *through*, destination unknown.

For Bakhtin, the 'journey' provides a stock narrative code which corresponds to the movement of the character through time and space. The metaphor of narrative as journey is an old one: but more than a mere artistic trope, the journey has been described as the structuring code of narrative. Teresa de Lauretis follows from Greimas to suggest that 'the semantic structure of all narrative is the movement of an actant-subject toward an actant-object.'[14] De Lauretis writes that the movement of narrative 'seems to be that of a passage, a transformation predicated on the figure of a hero, a mythical subject.'[15] Yet as she points out, this journey, the seeming substance of all manner of narrative from folkloric tales to Sophocles's (and Freud's) tale of Oedipus, does not spring spontaneously, ahistorically and neutrally from Zeus's brow, but carries traces of the places and times through which it travels. In short, the narrative journey is historical, culturally specific, and, perhaps most importantly, gendered. De Lauretis contends, then, that 'the work of narrative . . . is a mapping of differences, and specifically, first and foremost, of sexual difference into each text; and hence, by a sort of accumulation, into the universe of meaning fiction and history represented by the literary-artistic tradition and all the texts of culture'.[16]

For de Lauretis this structuralist binary coding of differences functions according to a gendered economy of stasis and movement. Here she cites Lotman who describes two fundamental character types: 'those who are mobile, who enjoy freedom with regard to plot-space, who can change their place in the structure of the artistic world and cross the frontier, the basic topological feature of this space, and those who are immobile, who represent, in fact, a function of this space'.[17] Following this binary division of narrative freedoms, it becomes immediately evident who must be the adventuring protagonist – and who stays home to mend socks. For de Lauretis, this binarism of mobile/immobile positions within narrative describes perhaps

> the fundamental opposition between boundary and passage; and if passage may be in either direction, from inside to outside or vice versa, from life to death or vice versa, nonetheless all these terms are predicated on the *single* figure of the hero who crosses the boundary and penetrates the other space. In so doing the hero, the mythical subject, is constructed as human being and as male; he is creator of differences. Female is what is not susceptible to transformation, to life or death; she (it) is an element of plot-space, a topos, a resistance, matrix and matter.[18]

'Immobile' (female) characters are seen to exist solely as functions of male becoming, providing landmarks and diversions in the all-important, hopelessly self-involved journey of Our Hero. Yet when we look at *Orlando*, the binary gendering of movement and agency within the narrative becomes problematic. Orlando becomes, almost in spite of her/himself, *mobile*, as she/he moves through different historical circumstances. But hers/his is a fickle quality of agency, reliant on the whims of chance.

The film's narrative eschews the conventional motors of character motivation, or a subtly orchestrated sequence of conflicts (dilemma, action, reaction), in favour of a progress according to what Bakhtin calls 'the logic of chance': 'This logic is one of *random contingency*, which is to say chance *simultaneity* [meetings] and *chance rupture* [nonmeetings], that is, a logic of random *disjunctions* in time as well.'[19] *Orlando*'s plot moves do not work through the psychological, progressive logic of character development, but rather, sail on the fickle winds of circumstance. Orlando's acquisition of immortality, for example, springs from his chance meeting with Queen Elizabeth who upon her deathbed simply wills away the ruins of time. In the film's second movement, Our Hero chances to meet Sasha, daughter of the Muscovite ambassador, amidst the pomp of the magical ice-court, and courts her only for the time granted by the insubstantial ice the revellers skim over so beautifully. Waiting under the bridge for Sasha to steal away with him forever, Orlando is once again subject to chance as the rain breaks up the ice, allowing the Muscovite ship to set sail. Similarly, after Orlando's encounter with Shelmerdine, her lover's departure is signalled by a change in the wind.

Intriguingly, Orlando's biographical journey does not entirely correspond to the 'adventure novel of everyday life' in which the hero must weather crisis and emerge transformed, a better (or worse) version of himself. Rather, Orlando proves a uniquely melancholic and lethargic hero who, within each plot movement and within the film as a whole, fails most of the trials of manliness (or womanliness). In this way, the closure of conventional narrative convention is constantly denied: Orlando does not get his girl; he proves a self-indulgent and mediocre 'dabbling' poet; faced with the enemies at the gate of Khiva, Orlando fails the test of manly valour and flees the site of battle; when she meets Shelmerdine, Orlando lets him go again and forgoes marriage (and the possibility of keeping her land); when she gives birth, she bears not a son, who would allow her to keep her beloved property, but a daughter.

This constant frustration within the micronarrative of each movement forms a recursive structure which defies conventional narrative closure – both the classic heterosexual closure of marriage, and the capitalist drive towards regaining what was owned and lost, Orlando's property. Orlando's biographical journey transpires very slowly, as she/he lingers in lengthy melancholic adolescence for some 350 years before becoming a young woman. Digressing from the centrality of metamorphosis in Bakhtin's biographical passage, the drama and significance of this transformation is played down.

According to Rachel Blau DuPlessis's analysis of Woolf's *Orlando*, 'Orlando's perpetual youth – at any rate, her astonishingly slow rate of growth – seems to challenge Freud's idea of the progress of the psyche from bisexual dramas to heterosexual object choice.'[20] In the novel, the affirmation of androgyny and homosexual desire undercuts the Freudian development model of female sexuality current in the 1920s. The newly-female Orlando finds in Shelmerdine a mate who is very womanly, played by a sensual and 'feminine' Billy Zane resplendent with long flowing locks and sensuous lips. Through moments like this, and especially through Swinton's self-conscious performance of Orlando's man-becoming-woman, Potter's film toys incessantly with the arbitrariness of gender.

The uncertain status of gender in *Orlando* is echoed in a hesitancy at the level of action. As Orlando never entirely rids herself/himself of gender ambiguity, she/he never achieves full status as a mobile adventurer. As a woman, she experiences at a stroke the constraints levied against bourgeois females through law, apparel and social codes of conduct. For example, in the 'Society' movement, when ambassador Orlando awakes to find himself a her, she is unceremoniously bundled off home on the back of a camel, only to discover upon arrival that she must now marry or lose her property. As many gendered conventions of narrative closure (romance, heroism, property) fall by the wayside, the outcome becomes indeterminate. The hero as androgyne is no longer guaranteed to get 'his' girl; while the girl might unexpectedly sprout a penis and set out on an adventure of 'her' own.

Such a reading of gendered movement in *Orlando* must be informed by the understanding that Woolf and Potter are on some level explicitly out to usurp such conventions. Even as critics commonly identify *Orlando* as a 'crossdressing' film (in reference to the concurrent sensation *The Crying Game* [Neil Jordan, 1993]), Potter explicitly underplays the significance of gender. Upon realizing her change of sex, Orlando comments drily to the camera: 'Same person. No difference at all. Just a different sex.' In this vein, Orlando moves through the film virtually unchanged. What transformation occurs does not change the 'essence' of Orlando/Tilda Swinton, but registers at the level of costume and hairstyle, or, in the case of the sex change, is etched on the body surface. On some level, Potter's Orlando speaks always through Tilda Swinton's singular *female* performance. Woolf and Potter remind us that gender is superficial and matters not a whit. At the same time, however, the film's irony arises from its constant demonstration that gender is made to matter very, very much through absurd social convention. In this vein it is absolutely pivotal that Orlando is played by a woman, not a man. Orlando's enigmatic address to the camera must be absolutely female, and feminist.

Through a bravura performance, and through her addresses and looks to the camera, Orlando/Swinton periodically punctures the film's diegetic action. In the process, she achieves a certain immunity to the perils of either position as she/he journeys more as witness than active participant. Through her looks and addresses to the camera, Swinton's Orlando usurps and comments upon the constraints of narrative and social codes. Much of the pleasure of *Orlando* for a feminist audience arises from these juxtapositions of narrative situation and commentary and from the simultaneous dramatization and unbinding of gendered constraints of bourgeois history. In the next section, I will return to Bakhtin's chronotope to link *Orlando*'s textual world to the social space of international feminist audiences which forms one context in which the film circulates.

Tracing the transposition of Woolf's *Orlando* into another medium and another historical era, the chronotopic model insists on the specificity of each textual and social time–space, and on the dynamic relation between the living, breathing text and 'the completely real-life time–space where the work resonates'.[21] Bakhtin's dialogism sketches a porous membrane between text and specific historical–social formations. Orlando's 'look', then, provides the chronotopic doorway, if you like, between the textual chronotope (the intricacies of plot structure, character and 'narrative movement' through textual space–time as described in the first half of the present essay) and the meaning-making process undertaken by situated historical subjects. Swinton's looks and addresses construct a bridge, a link of sensibility, offering a humorous phatic contact which continually invites the spectator back into Orlando's journey.[22] Thus beckoning, the in-joke speaks with a particular inflection through the codes of a particular feminist tradition. By evoking Woolf's iconic feminist text and authorial voice, *Orlando* speaks to and from the dispersed and varied contexts of (western, English-speaking) feminism. (Of course, this is not the only audience for the film, but I am reading the film here in terms of a privileged and pointed address to a 'model reader'.) Woolf and Potter respectively harness the collective, utopic and transformative power of narrative movement, specifically the trope of an allegorical biographical journey. Hardly disturbing the times through which she travels, Orlando bears witness to the absurdity of these quasihistorical tableaux, pausing periodically to 'report back' to the 1990s audience. Swinton's Orlando becomes a time-travelling feminist observer – and ultimately a protagonist journeying towards herself, towards artistic creation.

Throughout her adventures, the cinematic Orlando retains a certain blank quality, the hard smooth surface of impressionable youth, where her full subjectivity as protagonist should be recorded. Further, she remains to some audiences Tilda (a British avant-garde theatre and film persona), while her witty asides carry an implicit homage to Woolf. The address and the adventure straddle the 'once upon a time' inflection of fabled mythical subject and a more complex collective project of feminist movement, where Orlando offers a quizzical screen onto which the audience can project a utopic feminist fable of becoming. For Duplessis,

> [Woolf's] *Orlando* is at least a parodic biography, a female history of Britain, a feminist apologue – an insouciant break with conventional norms surrounding gender, sexual identity, and narrative. In this work, the Ages of England have become the Ages of Woman, scrutinized with two questions in mind: whether the protagonist can undertake work and whether she can enjoy love. Until the present, these satisfactions are divided, and love is separated from quest.[23]

Potter's changes to key aspects of Woolf's plotline (especially its resolutions) offer clues to the 1990s feminist exigencies which inform her adaptation. Woolf's novel, a wish-fulfilling spoof biography of Vita Sackville-West, ends with green lights on all counts: in love, in the work of writing, and in the restoration of the lost property to its rightful owner. Transposed into the terms of contemporary feminism, Potter's film also ends on a hopeful note, but dispenses with the romantic closure of married life with Shelmerdine, gives up the bourgeois privilege of property, and trades a daughter for the son. The symbolic achievement of artistic self-expression, the birthright of a new generation of daughters, becomes the key focus of resolution and utopic future vision. The film closes in the field under the oak tree where it began with the unbearded youth trying to write poetry. Only now, in the present, Orlando stares coolly into the camera in a final lingering closeup, as her daughter plays with a camcorder (a none-too-subtle symbol of feminist self-representation). A cherubic Jimmy Somerville floats somewhere above. The field, the oak tree and Somerville's otherworldly angel falsetto bookend the film, enclosing it in the pleasing wrapper of 'once upon a time' and 'happily ever after'.

Looping back to the earlier discussion of narrative movement, then, through the looks to the camera the audience shares the pithy pauses, the ridiculous uncertainties, of Orlando's progress through the ages. After all of Orlando's masculine bumbling lassitude, it is only in the present day, as a woman in the late twentieth century, that she finds artistic (and presumably in the process, social) recognition. In keeping with the film's curious tempo of attenuated dynamism, *Orlando* ends where it began. After all of her wardrobe changes Orlando remains essentially the same, only as the final voice-over attests: 'she is no longer trapped by destiny'. Ultimately, Potter stakes the allegorical project of feminist becoming almost entirely on the feminist tradition of critical high art, a bourgeois tradition exemplified by Woolf and continued in Potter and Swinton. Orlando's 'arrival' is a return to the English oak tree, an evocation of interconnected generations of feminist artistic creators. A field of their own, perhaps?

Now, in this quest for the 'movement' within *Orlando*'s narrative structure, we hit a snag. What I have described so far indicates stasis or, at best, pleasurable (spatiotemporal) lingering, or temporal digression at the core of the film's structure. Transposing Orlando's journey onto this structure, I had hoped to arrive at a semblance of dynamism which seems necessary to a feminist journey of becoming. But if I were to report this dynamism, with Orlando/Swinton/Woolf/Potter voyaging purposefully through the centuries setting things right, I would be manipulating the text to my own ends.

Rather, we find ourselves at a kind of rest station, stuck in what Margaret Morse describes as a 'paradoxical feeling of stasis and motion'.[24] What I am constantly craving, what was so splendid and rare about, say, *Thelma and Louise* (Ridley Scott, 1991), or even *The River Wild* (Curtis Hanson, 1994), was the female embodiment-in-journey: the subversive act of what Kirsten Marthe Lenz calls 'changing the script' – hijacking that muscular male drive, and somehow making it our own, a female journey of metamorphosis, and, ultimately, we hope, arrival somewhere *better*,[25] where we find ourselves miraculously 'transformed' (Bakhtin's term) into something less damaged, more dynamic. But this is not the flavour of pleasure offered by *Orlando*. Potter and Woolf present a more subtle project of critique – a kind of attenuated 'doing' or extended, aesthetically vibrant, 'being'.

In the above detailed analysis of gendered movement, Orlando's curious lassitude seems to spring from her/his indeterminate gender. But after all that, I am left wondering about the completeness of this binary argument about gendered stasis and motion. Reconsidering the film, widening my perspective, I think I have missed something. As is so often the case, where de Lauretis's argument illuminates some patterns in narrative, it obscures others. In brief, as *Orlando* speaks so eloquently to a particular English bourgeois experience of gender, I have overlooked other dynamics of stasis and movement operative within the text. In fact, in one interview,[26] in the midst of a long and detailed discussion of feminism, Sally Potter cites colonialism as the subtext of *Orlando*. But how does the profound historical and geographical movement of imperialism complicate the genesis and impetus of Orlando's utopian feminist journey?

In *Culture and Imperialism*, Edward W. Said writes of the imperialist ethos, 'a structure of attitude and reference' which strongly informs the spatial imaginary of the English novel. Not concerned only with works set explicitly in the colonies, Said describes the constitutive outside provided by empire even in novels set in England. 'As a reference, as a point of definition, as an easily assumed place of travel, wealth, and service, the empire functions for much of the European nineteenth century as a codified, if only marginally visible, presence in fiction.[27] In this literature, young English men are commonly sent off to sow their wild oats in the constantly available, lucrative and exotic playground of 'the colonies'. Along these lines, Woolf's Orlando voyages to Turkey to escape a persistent suitor, and the author wryly describes: 'He did what any other young man would have done in his place, and asked King Charles to send him as Ambassador Extraordinary to Constantinople'.[28] *Orlando* the novel adds a layer of satirical commentary to the trope of colonial adventure, an engagement taken up by Potter in the cinematic language of 1990s arthouse cinema.

The gentle irony of Orlando's self-indulgent sojourn in Khiva (shot in Khiva, Uzbekistan) emerges perhaps most directly in the stock trope of the adventure novel, the 'encounter' with the Other. In Potter's *Orlando* the initial encounter with the Khan of Khiva cuts directly to the quick of the matter:

KHAN: Why are you here?
ORLANDO: I am here as a representative of His Majesty's government. . . .
KHAN: Yes. It has been said to me that the English make a habit of collecting
             . . . countries.

This scene, as well as the following one where the Khan exchanges toasts with Orlando under the blistering sun, offer a brilliant sendup of the ceremonious imperial encounter. Surely the casting of Québécois actor Lothaire Bluteau as 'Khan' of a generic Orientalist kingdom can be no coincidence here. Potter slyly brings the breadth and arbitrariness of British imperialism into relief here, as one colonial subject is made, tongue in cheek, to stand in for another.

Visually, these encounters are composed of perfectly symmetrical balanced shots which play up the formality of imperial exchange against the exaggerated quality of the costumes and the explicit irony of the dialogue. The Khan, for example, is resplendent in a blue 'eastern' outfit, flanked by his twin turbanned lieutenants and columns aligned perfectly behind. This shot corresponds to an equally formal Orlando with his enormous (hot) white flowing wig, backed up by his effeminate soldiers. The absolute theatricality of these matched shots, the stasis of both camera (long still shots) and actors (constant formal choreographing of purposefully pointless marching) concisely satirises the imperial encounter with strategies similar to those Potter employs elsewhere to address gender. Yet there is an uncomfortable edge to this ironic take on colonialism.

I would suggest that part of the narrative uncertainty of *Orlando* (particularly in the 'Politics' movement) springs not only from indeterminate gender but also from a certain 'stuckness' which extends beyond feminism into bourgeois imperialist history proper: How now are westerners to represent critically the project of empire? What exactly are/were Orlando (and through him our collective historical imaginations) doing in Khiva? According to Woolf, 'We can only testify that Orlando was kept busy, what with his wax and seals, his various coloured ribbons which had to be diversely attached, his engrossing of titles and making of flourishes round capital letters, till luncheon came – a splendid meal of perhaps thirty courses'.[29] In cinematic language, Potter also focuses on empty ceremonious detail and luxury. She visualizes the lassitude and general uselessness of what Woolf calls Orlando's 'career' in the constant parading of the Ambassador and his henchmen through the dusty streets of the walled city. Then, after a time in his new post, Ambassador Orlando is pictured posed in rapturous meditation beside a 'Turkish' bath wrapped in a middle-eastern shift, his hair up in a towel. Apparently our Orlando has 'gone native'. In his polite, well-meaning way, Orlando fulfils all the cliches of westerners who 'discover' themselves in the Orient.

In imperialist literature, the encounter often facilitates some deeper knowledge of self. The Other, like the female term in de Lauretis's equation, marks a threshold for the protagonist's passage. Even as we find Orlando in Khiva ultimately, narcissistically, alone (suggesting that a rendezvous with self seems the logical fruition of the colonial encounter), such a critique can only be about Englishness. (The delightful scene with the Muscovites offers another superb vignette on English attitudes to 'foreigners'.) As in E. M. Forster's soulsearching tales of colonial relations, the window into another world ultimately only brings Orlando back to her 'true' (female) self.

Personal and political crisis strikes for Orlando only when the Khan's enemies are at the city gates, and the English guests are called upon to prove their mettle. Significantly, the incomprehensible battle raging between heathen forces offers the backdrop and the catalyst to Orlando's gender transformation. At this key juncture in the film, the site of narrative critique shifts from the awkwardness of the colonial encounter back to issues of gender, and Orlando is abruptly transported back to 'Society'. Crisis of empire becomes crisis in masculinity, a timely disengagement from distasteful matters of statesmanship and empire. Woolf's point, of course, is that British women have historically been excluded from 'the public life of Orlando's country'. In Potter's contemporary adaptation, the contested quality of imperial space presents a limit, a vanishing point for a critical feminist costume drama. Perhaps feminist costume drama can most powerfully and precisely address a particular white, bourgeois experience of English femininity. More generally, perhaps the polite, understated mannered form of this genre, conceived in European bourgeois social experience, does not translate well to address the savagery of bloody colonial conflict?

Finally, I sense an aesthetic limit to the critical possibilities of a certain quality of European art cinema, particularly (though not exclusively) in relation to colonialism. While *Orlando* springs from and continually returns to the preoccupations of English history and landscape, in the 'Love' and 'Politics' movements Potter digresses into the 'foreign' landscapes of St Petersburg and Uzbekhistan respectively. To a certain degree, like other European arthouse coproductions, *Orlando* relies for its appeal on an absolutely lush quality of set and costume – and on the spectacle of historically or culturally 'other' landscapes, costumes, peoples and customs. Potter draws from this contemporary cultural repertoire of international image–space, even as she inserts moments of incisive self-critique of English xenophobia. For both book and film, the conceptual sweep of a bumbling feminist journey through vast tracts of space and time provides part of the delight, the *élan*, the sense of movement and possibility of the project. These exotic backdrops may provide one element of de Lauretis's 'plot-space, a topos, a resistance, matrix and matter' to mark the passage of the feminist adventurer. And while Potter is cognizant of many of the contradictions of this backdrop, I find that other feminist projects such as *The Piano* and *Johanna d'Arc of Mongolia*[30] share in a generalizable neocolonial tendency of other arthouse (not to mention Hollywood) films, from *City of Joy* (Roland Joffe, 1992) to *Indochine* (Regis Wargnier, 1993). These films, whatever their political inflections (which of course require careful attention in and of themselves), continue to perpetuate and refurbish cinematically Said's 'structure of [imperialist] attitude and reference'.

Placed alongside the broader cultural plundering of neocolonial space, the voyages taken by feminist costume drama in search of self and narrative agency may be considered in a new light. Ultimately I am not interested in assigning blame here, but rather in interrogating and extending feminist work around movement and constraint in narrative. I believe that the question of colonial movement, as well as other key issues around race and class mobility and constraint, must inform a feminist reading of these issues. Further, as Richard Dyer's work on the racial inflections of cinematic space suggests, these meditations on the social renderings of cultural/textual space and time can provide a productive perspective on a range of overlapping accounts of identity and representation.[31]

Through a close reading of Sally Potter's film, *Orlando*, this essay has explored an intuitive link between narrative and imaginative movement, and the sociohistorical feminist desires for agency and transformation (specifically the utopian drive of feminist journeying as expressed in cultural texts). By juxtaposing a consideration of how colonialism facilitates and undercuts these feminist aspirations to geographical and imaginative mobility, I come to reconsider the implications of a certain quality of desired 'feminist movement'. In detailing the precise qualities of narrative and imaginative movement in *Orlando*, I have suggested productive avenues of inquiry which may be extended to other costume dramas. More generally, I have sketched out a rich area of inquiry which speaks to, but is no means limited to, feminist costume drama or arthouse cinema – an area of inquiry which addresses the particular gendered qualities of movement in cinematic texts.

Notes

1   Teresa de Lauretis, 'Desire in narrative', in *Alice Doesn't: Feminism, Semiotics, Cinema* (Bloomington: Indiana University Press, 1984), pp. 103–57.

2   Mary Ann Doane, 'The moving image: pathos and the maternal', in *The Desire to Desire: The Woman's Film of the 1940s* (Bloomington: Indiana University Press, 1984), pp. 70–95.

3   Mikhail Bakhtin, 'Forms of time and chronotope in the novel', in M. Holquist (ed.), *The Dialogic Imagination: Four Essays*, trans. C. Emerson and M. Holquist (Austin: University of Texas Press, 1981), p. 84.

4   Ibid., p. 104.

5   See Sandra M. Gilbert, 'Introduction', in Virginia Woolf, *Orlando: a Biography* (London: Penguin, 1993), pp. xi–xl.

6   Penny Florence, 'A conversation with Sally Potter', *Screen*, vol. 34, no. 3 (1993), pp. 276–7.

7   *Orlando* borrows some of its lush layering of colour and texture and its theatrical, episodic structure from recent British avant-garde cinema. In fact, the film's production designers Ben Van Os and Jan Roelfs have worked extensively with Peter Greenaway; and Sandy Powell, veteran of Derek Jarman's *Caravaggio*, provides a superlative array of costumes. Also, actress Tilda Swinton is featured prominently in Derek Jarman's films.

8   Stella Bruzzi, 'Tempestuous petticoats: costume and desire in *The Piano*', *Screen*, vol. 36, no. 3 (1995), pp. 257–66.

9   Roland Barthes, 'The structural analysis of narratives', in S. Heath (ed.), *Image – Music – Text*, trans. S. Heath (New York: The Noonday Press, 1977), pp. 17–34.

10 Ibid., p. 95.

11 Ibid., p. 93.

12 See Richard Dyer, 'Entertainment and Utopia', in *Only Entertainment* (London: Routledge, 1992), pp. 271–83.

13 Doane, 'The moving image: pathos and the maternal'.

14 de Lauretis, 'Desire in narrative', p. 112.

15 Ibid., p. 113.

16 Ibid., p. 121.

17 Ibid., p. 118.

18 Ibid., p. 119.

19 Bakhtin, 'Forms of time and chronotope in the novel', p. 92.

20 Rachel Blau DuPlessis, *Writing beyond the Ending: Narrative Strategies of Twentieth-Century Women Writers* (Bloomington: Indiana University Press, 1985), p. 64.

21 Bakhtin, 'Forms of time and chronotope in the novel', p. 252.

22 In the introduction to the published script of *Orlando*, Sally Potter notes how she and Swinton settled on the device of these looks and addresses to the camera 'to convert Virginia Woolf's literary wit into a cinematic humour . . . I hoped that this direct address would create a golden thread that would connect the [1990s] audience . . . with Orlando.' See Sally Potter, 'Introduction', in *Orlando* (London: Faber and Faber, 1994), p. xiii.

23 DuPlessis, *Writing beyond the Ending*, p. 61.

24 See Margaret Morse, 'An ontology of everyday distraction: the freeway, the mall, and television,' in Patricia Mellenkamp (ed.), *The Logics of Television: Essays in Cultural Criticism* (London: British Film Institute, 1990), pp. 193–221.

25 See Kirsten Marthe Lenz, 'The popular pleasures of female revenge (or rage bursting in a blaze of gunfire)', *Cultural Studies*, vol. 7, no. 3 (1993), pp. 371–405.

26 Florence, 'A conversation with Sally Potter', p. 284.

27 Edward W. Said, *Culture and Imperialism* (London: Chatto and Windus, 1993), p. 63.

28 Woolf, *Orlando: a Biography*, p. 82.

29 Ibid., p. 85.

30 See Linda Dyson, 'The return of the repressed? Whiteness, femininity and colonialism in *The Piano*', *Screen*, vol. 36, no. 3 (1995), pp. 267–76. For an insightful discussion of the complex relations of East and West in *Joan of Arc of Mongolia*, see Julia Knight, 'Observing rituals: Ulrika Ottinger's *Johanna d'Arc of Mongolia*' (paper presented at the *Screen* conference, June 1996).

31 See Richard Dyer, *Whiteness* (London: Routledge, 1997).

11

Body Matters: The Politics of Provocation in Mira Nair's Films

Alpana Sharma

Since she began making films in 1979, Mira Nair has flaunted her ability to provoke viewers, western and non-western, into various stances of angry criticism or frank admiration or even both. Her entire filmography to date, while certainly not produced expressly with the intent to shock, characterizes Nair as a non-traditional filmmaker unafraid of controversy. Her short black-and-white film, *Jama Masjid Street Journal* (1979), documented Muslim men and women's reactions to her alien presence as a filmmaker in their traditional Indian community; *So Far from India* (1983) delineated a young man's painful acculturation process as a working-class Indian immigrant in New York with a pregnant wife back home; *Children of a Desired Sex* (1985) examined the use of ultrasound for the purpose of sex determination and female foeticide in India; *India Cabaret* (1986) sought to give voice to cabaret dancers or strippers in Bombay in a documentary fashion; *Salaam Bombay!* (1988), a cinema-verite style film employing actual street children, depicted the urban devastation wrought by poverty and prostitution; *Mississippi Masala* (1991) trod upon interracial ground, depicting the scandalous romance between an Indian woman and an African American man in the American South; *The Perez Family* (1995) followed Cuban refugees fleeing to Miami in search of a better life; *Kama Sutra* (1997) transformed India's ancient love manual into a theatrical tale about friendship, passion, and revenge. Her most recent film, *My Own Country* (1998; based on a book by medical doctor and author Abraham Verghese), is no less venturesome in treading new ground:

Alpana Sharma, "Body Matters: The Politics of Provocation in Mira Nair's Films," pp. 91–103 from *Quarterly Review of Film and Video* 18:1 (Philadelphia and London: Taylor & Francis and Routledge, 2001). © 2001. Reprinted by permission of Taylor & Francis Group, LLC, http://www.taylorandfrancis.com

here, the camera's subject is an India-born specialist in infectious diseases in the American deep and rural South who finds himself educating the underground gay community about HIV and AIDS whilst undergoing psychic transformation himself. Summing up her risk-ridden approach to film in a 1993 interview, Nair has stated her case rather directly; when asked whether filmmaking is a political tool for her, she replied:

> My job is to provoke you into something, into re-examining something, or looking at something differently. I may provoke you into being shocked or being moved in some other way. Generally speaking, I don't get drawn to pieces of fluff. But film is not like an agenda or instrument. I think that approach is generally reductive. I think the most exciting so-called political tools are those that catch up to you, that steal up from behind and make you think about something in an oblique way, rather than being direct. (Nair 1993: 151)

A similar valuing of subtlety and obliqueness over heavy-handed politics is reflected in Nair's response to some critics' view that the men frequenting cabarets in her documentary film, India Cabaret, escape censure by her:

> It was unsettling to some that there were no out-and-out villains in the film. Granted the men were "exposed" in their hypocrisies and double standards and the women were shown as ostracized by a morally corrupt society, but no character in the film is portrayed as totally Good or totally Bad. Life is like that! A subtle approach is seen as almost morally wrong. I can understand the reasons why people would be more comfortable with simple dichotomies, because we live in a situation which is black and white in many ways: class differences are huge, exploitative hierarchies rampant, discrepancies enormous. So I can see why someone would choose to show a situation without any grey areas. I respect such work but am personally more interested in revealing the world in all its complexity, irony, and contradictions. If one can reflect ambiguity effectively, questions are evoked in viewers' minds, and perhaps the film will live inside them a little longer. Someone has said, the essence of tyranny is the absence of complexity. (Nair 1986–7: 66)

By her own admission, then, Nair approaches filmmaking with a high level of tolerance for complexity, irony, contradiction, and ambiguity, qualities, in short, which demand a subtle, sideways approach. Of course, as we may well imagine, it is precisely the admixture of a certain spontaneity and subtlety, the valuing of a kind of improvisational creativity over a priori political agendas, that has led to some controversy over Nair's films. Criticisms of her have generally targeted her orientation towards the West, maintaining that her films are made with an eye to western consumption; she has been accused of a class-based replication of racist colonial gestures; her increasing use of Hollywood-style budgets and formulas of glamour and romance has also come under attack, as has her presumed arrogance in assuming she can speak for those who cannot speak for themselves (the disenfranchised subaltern classes of strippers, prostitutes, drug dealers, pimps, etc., who are so often at the center of her films; see Dayal 1992; Arora 1994; Ballal 1998).

Without dismissing these criticisms out of hand, this essay argues differently. Nair's filmmaking is more careful and canny than critics have allowed. Her camera opens out both ways: it asks us to look at its subject just as frankly as we look at ourselves looking, in the process breaking down the dialectic of inside and outside, subject and object, viewer and viewee. Specifically, I would argue that Nair's politics of provocation are wedded to a belief in the agency of the body as this body materializes itself in a set of regulatory practices that at once define the body and set the body free. In her films, it is the literal fact of the body's taking up and occupying space – one might say, materiality at ground zero – that simply cannot be thought away. Indeed, the body's entire giving itself over to the work of pain and pleasure constitutes a key motif in Nair's work. The unashamed, frank bodies of the cabaret dancers in *India Cabaret* as they undulate and strip onstage, as they sit on the laps of their clients afterwards, as they clothe, feed, and recuper- ate in their homes afterwards; the small, emaciated torso of Krishna/Chaipau in *Salaam Bombay!* supported by the pair of skinny legs with which he scurries about performing the menial chores of his daily life on the streets of Bombay; his playmate, in a fit of childish jealousy, hiding while she rapidly and surreptitiously devours the gift of biscuits he asked her to deliver to his sweetheart "Sweet Sixteen"; the drug pusher-addict Chillum out of whose wasted, very eloquent body surprisingly emanate the lyrics, "pistol-packing mama, lay your pistol down"; in *Mississippi Masala*, the luscious naked bodies of Meena (Sarita Choudhury) and Demetrius (Denzel Washington) as they bring each other to filmic sexual climax; again, this time in *Kama Sutra*, sultry naked people pleasuring one another in a way that renders sexual climax irrelevant; against the backdrop of their eroticized bodies, in stark and poignant contrast, the twisted and misshapen body of rival lover Vikram Singh, in search of a union never to be: in all of these examples, what we see is an insistent spatial presencing of the human body engaged in the daily bodily rituals that simultaneously sustain and constrain it, a way of the body's mattering that is only reinforced by the powerful exteriority of the medium of film, film's ability to show plainly on the surface what lies just below the skin.

I use the word "mattering," mindful, of course, of Butler's profound medita- tion in *Bodies that Matter*. In it, Butler explores the following sorts of questions: how and why do bodies matter? Mattering here turns on two meanings: how and why do bodies "mean" what they mean as well as how and why do they "mater- ialize"? And further, what is the gendered genealogy of their mattering (32)? As part of this meditation, Butler takes on the whole concept of the body's presumed irreducibility. Traditional thinking would posit the body as irreducible, as preceding signification, but, on another register of thought, even this positing or signifying as prior participates in the very production of the body that is being signified as prior. The body is, then, an effect of signification, in which case, argues Butler, the mimetic or representational status of language, which claims that signs follow bodies as their necessary mirrors, is not mimetic at all. On the contrary, it is productive, constitutive, one might even argue performative, inasmuch as this signifying act delimits and contours the body that it then claims to find prior to any and all signification. (30)

Butler is interested in rewriting the body's imagined pre-discursive condition (its occurring before language, its irreducibility) as itself a function of a kind of discursive practice that fixes the body along a gendered matrix and then covers over this gendered materiality in the name of irreducibility. In the process of such a reconfiguring, language comes to be seen as what it already was: constitutive and performative rather than simply imitative ("mimetic") and causal; as it names, it brings into being that which it names. Butler is quick to clarify that the body understood in this way is not a mere linguistic device reduced only to language. For language itself is driven by its lacunae; because it is never fully present to itself, it is impelled by that which it cannot fully name, signified severed from signifier in a way that would render any desire to fully signify fundamentally nostalgic and absurd. Rather, Butler draws attention to the double bind accompanying signification: we speak in language about something, setting into motion a "that which" which is motivated by a "that without which" (67). And, in a sense, there is an irretrievable materiality of the sign that prevents us from positing a pure materiality from without: "It is not that one cannot get outside of language to grasp materiality in and of itself; rather, every effort to refer to materiality takes place through a signifying process which, in its phenomenality, is always already material" (68). Hence, language and materiality are not opposed to one another, but by that very token they are not identical to one another either; language both is and refers to the material, and the material always, in part, emerges from the signifying process (68).

The political consequences of thinking through the body's mattering in this different way are many. For example, if a habitual way of thinking about something is seriously challenged, particularly when its customariness helps produce established and institutional pieties (Foucault's "regimes of truth"), it can no longer constitute the ground for discourse in quite the same authoritative way again, and an entire critical reorientation becomes not only possible but also necessary. As Butler puts it: "To call a presupposition into question is not the same as doing away with it; rather, it is to free it from its metaphysical lodgings in order to understand what political interests were secured in and by that metaphysical placing, and thereby to permit the term to occupy and to serve very different political aims" (30). Hence, for instance, putting into crisis Lacan's symbolization of the penis as phallus (by carefully noting that a symbol is a symbol precisely because it is ontologically removed from that which it symbolizes), Butler not only uncovers the (arbitrary) privileging of male body parts in Lacan's masculinist lexicon but also then posits the notion of a "lesbian phallus"; the phallus, after all, is not an originary term of privilege but part of an endless chain of signification and resignification, allowing also a crucial resignification of the body, indeed, sexual difference itself, in a feminist vein (89).

I am not interested in mapping a neat applicability of Butler's theories of the body's mattering to Nair's own body of work and the bodies this work proffers. Not only would this prove a tedious exercise for writer, reader, and viewer, but it would also do disservice to both Butler and Nair, who, it must be said, work in different mediums and critical vocabularies. But there is something compelling about the idea that both philosopher and filmmaker seem agreed that the materiality of the body cannot be thought away; according to both, the gendered body is formed along the axis of a multitude of competing drives and power relations; and, for both, the overriding possibility of the body's mattering is one that coalesces performativity and political critique. A scene from *Salaam Bombay!* comes to mind: Krishna/Chaipau has been beaten down repeatedly by the dark forces in his life – his tea-shop boss, the pimp, the death of his best friend Chillum, the loss of innocence of his sweetheart Sweet Sixteen as she is sucked into a life of prostitution – until, in a terribly bold gesture of bodily excess, he stabs the pimp from behind and runs away, leaving him for dead. The final sequence of the film shows him running through street crowds, then stopping, sitting, spinning a top, and finally simply staring, his tiny chest heaving with the strain of both physical stress and impending tears. The stabbing of the pimp – extreme yet, in a way, absolutely mandatory – of course necessitates a return of the social order whose very logic the act of murder put into question: can punishment be far behind? Yet it is the moment of stabbing, of suddenly and improperly penetrating someone's body with a foreign object so as to take charge and arrest that body's motility, that stays in the mind, its liberatory power recalling another powerful text, Egyptian novelist Nawal El Saadawi's *Woman at Point Zero*. It is a true account of Egypt's most (in)famous prostitute, Firdaus, who went on trial for murdering her pimp; her refusal of a presidential pardon that would revert her death sentence turned her into a cause célèbre in Egypt. Firdaus's life, as narrated by her to the author, consists of the most unimaginable physical and psychological duress: abandoned by her parents as a child, raped by her uncle, married off to an older abusive man, shackled and turned into a sex slave by the man whom she thought had rescued her from her husband, prostituted, betrayed, repeatedly insulted, but still alive and fighting at the point when a pimp takes over her life and life earnings. Firdaus reacts to the pimp's invasion of her desperately guarded privacy and autonomy with cold anger – as he reaches for his knife, she grabs it from him and proceeds to stab him repeatedly:

> I raised the knife and buried it deep in his neck, pulled it out of his neck and then thrust it deep into his chest, pulled it out of his chest and plunged it deep into his belly. I stuck the knife into almost every part of his body. I was astonished to find how easily my hand moved as I thrust the knife into his flesh, and pulled it out almost without effort. My surprise was all the greater since I had never done what I was doing before. A question flashed through my mind. Why was it that I had

never stabbed a man before? I realized that I had been afraid, and that the fear had been within me all the time, until the fleeting moment when I read fear in his eyes. (Saadawi, 96)

Of particular interest in this passage is the obsessively descriptive, even performative, aspect to the killing act, Firdaus's hand penetrating, phallus-like, the pimp's body easily and smoothly, moving from neck to chest to belly to everywhere else in a spontaneous yet systematic way, even implying a particular pleasure in this act of killing. The scene is repeated on page 102 with the same obsessive features: "The movement of my hand upwards and then downwards destroyed my fear. . . . [It] had become very easy, and everything in my hand could be moved with a natural ease, even if it were a sharp knife which I thrust into a chest and then withdrew. It would penetrate in and come out with the natural ease of air entering the lungs and then flowing out. I am speaking the truth now without difficulty." Both Krishna/Chaipau and Firdaus react to the operations of power headquartered in the pimp's body by reaching for a weapon and using it. Surely the spontaneity of the act of killing should not disguise the political critique being offered here, albeit indirectly and obliquely: in the exchange system of prostitution, which relies on the full use of the prostitute's body by the body of her client, the one extraneous body that circulates – extraneous because it does not enter the sexual exchange between bodies except by way of parasitical reliance upon this exchange for non-sexual value – is that of the pimp. In this sense, then, one might say that the pimp's body is dispensable.

Having posited the body as a site for insinuating a dialogue between Nair and Butler, I would also like to point out that Nair's politics of provocation are grounded in a diasporic space that brings with it certain privileges of impiety and non-conformity: hers is a reinvented, playful discourse that plays fast and loose with the rules. An exemplary diasporic, Nair was born in Bhubaneshwar, Orissa, educated at Harvard, and is now settled in Uganda while working on films in Africa, India, and the United States. By reinvention, I do not invoke a kind of remaking for its own sake. Such diasporic writers as Bharati Mukherjee, for instance, make a living for themselves by celebrating the United States' potential for soliciting a free-form reinvention of the immigrant self: as the old, worn-out adage goes, in "America," you are free to be anyone you choose to be, etc. But not for Nair a formless reinvention of the self that would elide the self's painful yet necessary construction in the social order. Rather, I would say that when she plays fast and loose with the rules, the rules themselves paradoxically usurp the scene of representation. Bodily pleasures are indulged, not wholly but guardedly, with an eye to their transgressive powers and the constant need to leash in these powers at the very moment during which their release is imminent. Why else is Nair so preoccupied with the punitive aspects which invariably accompany the body's giving itself over to complete abandon? Why is there always such a high price to be paid for the sexual pleasures of the body (male guilt and denial over frequenting strip joints in *India Cabaret*; the cabaret dancers' own sense of shame and exile from their traditional communities; social ostracism in *Mississippi Masala*; ostracism and death in *Kama Sutra*)? It would appear, then, that a diasporic location, while it organizes the playful and experimental ground upon which Nair crafts her films, also brings with it a certain kind of rigor or price that is best symptomatized by the ritualized punishment of the body as this body is caught in the act of obeying its own laws of desire. This is what I would term Nair's politics of provocation: it is in the performance of the transgressive act – not before or after it – that the political critique is embedded as a kind of surprise that may be missed altogether, or worse, misperceived as Nair's catering to mere shock value. This performance takes as its site the spectacle of the body as its excesses of pleasure and pain call attention to the social codes of normativity at the same time as these codes are transgressed.

What is produced out of this double movement is a new (human) subject that, even as it may obey the summons of ideology, is no longer in the proper place to be adequately interpellated by ideology; it finds itself elsewhere. Just such a new subject is in the process of emerging at the end of *Kama Sutra*. Through all the vicissitudes in Maya's life – the highest of highs, the lowest of lows – her character is not merely destroyed but remade. The regulatory functions of pain and pleasure have been breached by an unruly desire, leaving a emptied subjectivity which still affirms at the point of negation: "Knowing love, I will allow all things to come and go, to be as supple as the wind, and take everything that comes with great courage. As Rasa would say, life is right in any case. My heart is as open as the sky."

It must by now be clear that I wish to recuperate Nair's work in a different arena, away from the "typical" scolding that has set the tone of much of the critical reception of her work, most noticeably by viewers from the subcontinent. This is not to say that critical reception does not matter. Filmmakers are public artists, and critical reception – even at its most hostile and negative – is an indispensable gauge for measuring not only the quality of their work but, equally importantly, how, in Nair's case especially, her films constitute a flashpoint for a postcolonial global culture addressing the difficult issues of our current moment: the imbrications – both minute (within the human subject, insofar as this subject can be delineated) and broad (within the massive historical formations of which the human subject is but a symptom) – of race, gender, sexuality, nationalism, transnationalism, migration, class, tradition, and modernity, to name just a few discursive sites of current cultural interrogation and transformation. A politically engaged diasporic artist coming of age at the end of the twentieth century cannot avoid addressing these issues; but by the same token, she is also not simply a mouthpiece for her time and generation, reduced and answerable only to the exigencies of her historical moment. This point seems relevant in the context of rising Hindu fundamentalism in India, where the realm of art has been especially singled out for attack and censorship. For instance, Deepa Mehta did not make *Fire* as a "lesbian film" yet this was the only label it retained when it played to great public protest and demonstrations in Bombay and Delhi, some of these extremely violent and destructive. (In February of 2000, the shooting of Mehta's *Water* came under similar Hindutva attack for its supposedly negative portrayal of widows in the holy city of Benaras.) In the face of reductive readings, I would insist on the particularity of Nair's craft, suggesting that there are aspects irreducible to only political readings; for instance, the many pressing reasons why the camera pauses, pans, cuts away, or zooms in when it does, have their own merit. Agreed that these reasons too bear historical meaning and ideological force. But that the craft of Nair's work is meaningful only to the extent that it serves some monolithic political purpose is an unfortunate reflection of the heavy burden that, for a variety of complicated reasons, postcolonial criticism has now come to bear. Many of its practitioners seem bent on joining a thought police that marches through time, texts, and images with the sole intent of tracking down the Enemy. I am mindful here of Anne McClintock's comment that, after all, "post-colonialism" may well be just another p-c word (McClintock, 299). Who can deny the logic of postcolonial critics' demand for adequate attention paid to the historical structure of oppression unleashed upon the world by modern forms of Euro-American imperialism and neoimperialism? But when their demand takes on the shape of an ideological sledgehammer that blunts or flattens the subtleties, nuances, and surprises of Nair's work, I would want to look elsewhere for strategies of recuperation.

An example of such unfortunate criticism comes from Poonam Arora's "The Production of Third World Subjects for First World Consumption: *Salaam Bombay!* and *Parama*." Arora's scholarship on postcolonial film is groundbreaking, but her critique of Nair ignores Nair's politics of provocation. In her essay, Arora argues that *Salaam Bombay!* conforms to the "representational codes" (294) of the West by insufficiently historicizing its subject(s): the characters themselves, the "social ills" of child labor, the drug trade, prostitution, and so on. Nair's film is contrasted negatively to Aparna Sen's *Parama*, which properly specifies its subject: how the concept of the "Indian housewife" is produced for Western consumption by a *Life* magazine photographer-ethnographer operating under the delusionary quest for authenticity and indigenity. The former film's failure is charted along the following course: first, the locale of Bombay and the character of Krishna/Chaipau are treated by Nair as interchangeable, generic types of third world oppression; Arora's second bone of contention is that the viewer targeted is from the first world – s/he is "unimplicated" (295) in the events of the film and all that is asked of her/him is sympathy. On the first count – lack of specificity, or interchangeability of places and identities – it would appear that this is part of the point Nair is making. The genericness of names – Chaipau for teaboy (Krishna), Chillum for marijuana pipe (the drug addict-pusher), Sweet Sixteen for pretty young girl (the abducted prostitute), etc. – serves to accentuate the fact that while people may outlive their use value, value as such remains and will always find another use to attach itself to. The metonymic interchangeability of identities in the chain of signification and resignification released under the sign of power means that power is not only produced but also, more importantly, reproduced. The body as a site for power relations – Foucault's thesis in *Discipline and Punish* – means that it is not so much a question of who has or doesn't have power (i.e., who is and is not named) as it is an issue about bodies systematically providing the ground which power traverses. Further, as Foucault has argued in *Discipline and Punish* and volume one of *The History of Sexuality* – convincingly, according to this reader – power is not something someone owns or possesses; it is everywhere produced and reproduced in its exercise, and it is maintained even by those who do not have it. Located within its operations, we do not have a vantage point from which to contest it unilaterally for there is no position outside it; rather, resistance ought to be produced from within power's own operations. On the second count, by assuming that the sole viewership of the film is Western-based, is Arora not granting more power and ubiquity to the West than, strategically, it should be accorded? What about the force of her own critique, coming as it does from the position of a US-based Indian academic not quite circumscribed by the unthinking, merely sympathetic response she attributes to Western viewers? Why assume merely sympathy is required of these viewers? Why not a sense of their complicity in the power structures outlined by the film, why not a measure of discomfort?

A scene Arora refers to only briefly is worth elaborating here. Krishna/Chaipau and Chillum peddle dope to a naive American tourist who is conned into paying them a high price. The sudden windfall is cause for celebration, and Krishna/Chaipau not only gets high for the first time but also seals his friendship with Chillum. The two stumble along unsteadily in the dark, arm in arm, singing ("pistol-packing mama, lay your pistol down") and recalling, in a fit of irreverent merriment, the foolishness of the American tourist. Arora considers this sequence a regrettably "brief irruption into the text of the dynamism of a more contemporary economic reality" (296), neglecting to mention that it is the extra money Chillum made from this encounter with the American tourist that proves his undoing and, ultimately, his death. Baba, the drug dealer and pimp, learns of the incident, is convinced that Chillum is withholding the profits from his drug deals, and hence summarily fires him. Without the wherewithal to restart his already fading life, in the chills and shakes of an agonizing withdrawal from drugs, Chillum descends rapidly into hell, almost touchingly eager to hasten the inevitable process of decay and disintegration and so erase from view the specter of his wasted body and naked, searching eyes. In the exchange between first and third worlds epitomized by Chillum's encounter with the American tourist, then, celebration degenerates into death, grief, and mourning. If the brutal logic of the first world prevails – it is the American tourist who has the last word, after all – at least Nair has set into motion an interrogation of the very "international geopolitics" and "dynamism of a more contemporary reality" (296) that Arora finds missing in the film.

Critics have also been drawn to another aspect of Nair's films: their willingness – for better or worse – to represent those without privilege and voice. These marginalized characters, whether real or fictive, have come, for some viewers, to mean specifically gendered subalterns, the very figures whose absence caused Gayatri Spivak to chastize the Subaltern Studies group for their radical yet blinkered historiographic project to rewrite Indian history from the perspective of the (male) subaltern. Sweet Sixteen, the older prostitute Rekha, and Rekha's daughter Manju in *Salaam Bombay!*; the cabaret dancers in *India Cabaret*: all accede to varying levels of representation and agency, from virtual silence to covert resistance to exuberant assertion of selfhood. Many of these characters make the journey from the margins of society to the center of Nair's films in a way that strikes some as insufficiently problematized and unself-reflexive. Samir Dayal puts it this way: "[*Salaam Bombay!*] seems to present itself as a forum where the subaltern could speak, but wherever it might succeed in its aim it reverts instead to the elite, and sentimental, figurations of the subaltern. There is no sense in Nair's film . . . that the prostitute wields a certain power over the client as well as some measure of control over her own destiny" (28). Dayal resists Nair's pessimistic commentary on the crippling and permanently debilitating circumstances of the prostitutes' lives, searching (I think rightly) for interventionist concepts such as agency and empowerment. Yet a film like *India Cabaret* shows very well how vocal the dancers themselves are, how boldly they handle their bodies, indeed, how their own tenacious and tough understanding of their subject position is often at odds with the entire sentimental discourse of submission and victimhood informing other parts of the film. In keeping with the spirit of the film, Gwendolyn Foster's astute reading of Nair's "speaking subalterns" in *India Cabaret* simply refuses to participate in the silencing of subaltern voices:

> Nair brings forth the active subjectivities of women as speaking subalterns . . . by foregrounding identity in first-person address, in the "naming" of her subjects . . . and the manner in which she avoids the disembodied knowledge of the standard documentary voice-over. In *India Cabaret*, the dancers speak directly to the audience; telling their own stories, witnessing failures and joys and their very corporeality. In one of the opening shots, Lovina flirts with the gaze of the camera as she applies her makeup. Rekha tells us of her dancing ability in a distinctly bragging tone, then explains the double standard toward strippers, "Everybody goes to cabarets but won't admit it." (Foster, 113)

Rekha's retelling of a folktale in which the god of death, Yamaraj, asks three women about their life on earth suggests something of her wit and vivacity. The first woman confesses to leaving one man for another, pledging total fidelity to the second man, and gets the silver gates from Yamaraj; the second attests to fidelity to only one man throughout her marriage and receives the golden gates. The third woman, a cabaret dancer, tells him: "'Sir, down there I made no man unhappy. I gave pleasure to every man, to every man I brought ecstasy. To all the men in the world I brought happiness.' 'Give her the keys to my room!' the Lord said. 'Down there you made so many men happy, now up here you can make me happy too.' What did the virtuous virgins get? One got a lousy silver door. The other got a lousy golden door. Only Rekha got the keys to the Lord himself!"

(Nair 1986–87: 58). By inserting herself into the fable as this third woman, this cabaret dancer, Rekha claims a pride that can only amount to "a certain power over the client as well as some measure of control over her own destiny" (Dayal, 28). Again, Rekha, this time on the concept of shame:

REKHA: Shame? Why shame? You should leave shame behind when you enter this profession.

VASANTI: When I go out at night, sometimes a customer sees me and says, "Look, there goes that naked dancing girl, that whore!" I say, motherfucker, you enjoyed me on stage and now you say this! That's when I feel shame.

REKHA: If somebody said that to me, I'd say, here's my address, come see me tonight! (Nair 1986–87: 62–63)

Hence, Foster's accurate assessment, as she picks up on Nair's characteristic motif of the body: "Rekha refuses to be invisible, refuses to be objectified by an ethnographic gaze. Her knowledge is distinctly bodied and underscored by the presence of her body language. She tells us the fable as she glares at us, smoking, laughing, gesturing, refusing the mantle of the polluted subaltern" (114).

Arguably the most notorious of her films, *Kama Sutra* bears all the character-istic trademarks of a Nair film: a bold valuing of understatement and subtlety; a blatant disregard for the naysayers; and, above all, an extended visualization of the body in all its extremes of pain, pleasure, and punishment. The film's premise is impudent: Nair wanted to portray "love and sexuality before it was messed up with shame and 'honor'" (interview; Patel, 79); in a feminist spirit, she also wanted to rewrite the ancient love manual along the lines of women's sexual desire, "not the male-oriented pleasure stuff" (Patel, 79). Interestingly, the film is set in the sixteenth century: an obvious attempt to predate British colonialism, which ushered in the era of sexual taboos. Yet *Kama Sutra* is a palimpsest incorporating many other literary and historical influences, at least two of which come from Wajida Tabassum's "Utran" ("Hand Me Downs"; 1975) and Salman Rushdie's "The Perforated Sheet," from his novel *Midnight's Children* (1980), respectively. Tabassum's ingeniously conceived short story details the humiliating fate of a servant girl, the young Chamki, who is forced throughout her life to wear the used clothes of the rich and pampered Shehzadi Pasha and to suffer all the debilitating effects of a neglected childhood. As she was Pasha's wet nurse, even the mother's milk was handed down to Chamki secondhand. Aware of the many uses of a young body – a body which Shehzadi Pasha's used clothing served only to conceal – Chamki gets back at Pasha (or, as the text puts it, she "plunders" all three of them [Tabassum, 41]) by seducing her future husband the night before their wedding: "'Pasha, all my life I have lived with your used things, but now you, too . . .' She laughed like one possessed '. . . all your life something that I have used is for you . . .' Her manic laughter wouldn't stop. Everyone thought the sorrow of parting from her childhood playmate had temporarily unhinged Chamki" (Tabassum, 42). The concept of the used husband constitutes, of course, the premise of Kama Sutra, while Rushdie's chapter, "The Perforated Sheet," in which the young doctor Aadam Aziz gets to know his future wife, her imaginary ailments, and body parts through the holes of a sheet, is repeated in the film when Tara's sexuality, shrouded under a bedsheet, comes alive before the groping hands of a physician.

Given these postcolonial overtones, it would appear impossible for Nair to achieve a truly pre-colonial text, one untainted by Victorian prudery's imposition of "shame and 'honor'" upon the history of Indian eroticism. That this imposition occurred with far-reaching results is undeniable. A compelling example, in the form of eighteenth-century Telugu court poet Muddupalani, is detailed by editors Susie Tharu and K. Lalita in their Introduction to the 2-volume anthology, *Women Writing in India* (1–12). In the aesthetic mode dictated by Indian classical thought, Muddupalani's poetry attempted an evocation of the nine *rasas* ("essences" of human emotions, including erotic pleasure). Here was a female poet who, in sexually frank poems such as *Radhika Santwanam* (*Appeasing Radhika*), placed female eros, even a young girl's first experience of sex, at the center of her work. While in her own time her poetry seemed well received, in 1910, when accomplished artist and courtesan Bangalore Nagaratnamma proceeded to publish Muddupalani's poetry, she encountered a wall of controversy so thick that eventually the book was banned (the ban was only lifted in 1947). As Tharu and Lalita point out, it was the economic, political, and ideological changes wrought by British imperialism that were responsible for this marked shift in critical reception. Commercial monopoly, a new bourgeois standard dictating female sexual propriety, an Orientalist rewriting of the Indian canon, all shaped how women wrote and how their writing was received through the nineteenth century (7–11).

In such a loaded historical context, one may well ask: how, feasibly, in 1997, can a filmmaker appropriate the subject of Vatsayana's *Kama Sutra* without in any way indexing the colonial history by which erotic expressions of Indian sexuality were censored, rerouted, domesticated, or otherwise exoticized? Nair's response is characteristically bold: given that the history of the exotic itself has come to inform what we know about India's erotic past, the exotic must be taken seriously in order, finally, to be dispensed with as an inadequate means of representation. This is why its status in Nair's oeuvre, most especially and problematically in *Kama Sutra* – all those sultry silk-clad, jewel-encased bodies some viewers likened to an endless fashion parade in an upscale emporium! – is of a different order than the exotic as a mere fetishistic colonial construction of fixity. Again bearing Butler in mind, we may understand Nair's species of exoticization as part of the materializing process by which bodies come to matter. As a specific way of the body's mattering/materializing, Nair's exotic is on display not as an occasion for mindless consumption of bodies but as an invitation to re-examine the obvious, or, as she puts it, the "banal."

Responding to the controversy unleashed by the film in India (the Central Board Of Film Certification refused to clear it, and when Nair sought the Board's

Tribunal intervention to get the film cleared with a minimum of cuts, it was still rejected, then banned, and then the ban was repealed), Nair insists that the film is about "sexual politics, not sexual positions. It's as far from pornography as you can get, but it's about women who are not afraid to express themselves sexually" (Braun interview). The interview unfolds the complicated point that what was so risky about the project is also what makes it so radical. Nair wanted, she says, to see "the eros in the banal . . . [to integrate] the mundane things with the actual love, [treating both] equally." As she puts it, "The sensuality in this film is within the mundane, the everyday, the banal. . . . For the film to work as a Kama Sutric situation, it is about the art of living, not just the act of sex." In other words, if in Vatsayana's time the erotic was treated as part of the everyday, the mundane, the banal, then Nair's political point is to represent this very banality such that our relationship to the immediate present – not only to the past – undergoes a productive reassessment: as we are estranged from the erotic past of Vatsayana's *Kama Sutra* (as if we could any longer imagine sex as an everyday art!) we also look anew at our present moment in which the erotic has grown exotic and Other, taboo, secret, furtive, private. The erotic is accessed via the exotic; there is no way to look at the past except through the lens of the present. The film is not, then, an attempt to recreate the past as such; it is "an ancient/modern film, a look at the past in a contemporary way" (Braun interview).

But where the film reaches its own limit is when it appears to impose a heterosexual compulsory upon the sexual relationships that constitute its subject. Three scenes allude to a lesbian unconscious which is foreclosed by the film's dominant logic of heterosexuality. There is the under-water opening sequence in which the two girls Tara and Maya are not yet sexually individuated as rivals but are linked amniotically in a kind of feminine continuum. The second scene invokes the first; in this one, the grown and unhappily married Tara is found by Maya in a pool of her own blood, and as Maya holds her the film cuts to an early under-water shot of the two girls, the point being to show a certain contrast now that the two women negotiate their sexuality via men, who are increasingly the adjudicators in relations between women. Finally, there is the scene in which both women look in a mirror as Maya teaches Tara how best to seduce her husband. Maya to Tara: "I will show you how to . . . mark him. But first I will mark you. He'll know a woman made these marks and it will excite him." Hence, female desire appears secondary and sexuality itself normalized as heterosexual. Over and against such normalizations masquerading as "natural," Butler would posit gender as a kind of imitation lacking an original. In one way of thinking about it, homosexuality does not derive from heterosexuality as its imperfect copy; rather, heterosexuality itself needs homosexuality in the way that origins need secondary consequences to establish themselves as origins. Further, repetitions of heterosexuality that only produce heterosexuality as an effect are normalizing performances premised on the possibility of their own failure: what if they should fail to repeat?

. . . if repetition is the way in which power works to construct the illusion of a seamless heterosexual identity, if heterosexuality is compelled to repeat itself in order to establish the illusion of its own uniformity and identity, then this is an identity permanently at risk, for what if it fails to repeat, or if the very exercise of repetition is redeployed for a very different performative purpose? If there is . . . always a compulsion to repeat, repetition never fully accomplishes identity. That there is a need for a repetition at all is a sign that identity is not self-identical. (Butler 1991: 24)

Kama Sutra does not fully avail itself of slippages in gender construction/repetition but instead repeats performances that may well end up reinforcing and not radically questioning normative heterosexuality. This is not to fault Nair for not having read Butler. The issues are larger, extending beyond sexual orientation as such to the ways in which identities, gendered or sexual, in so far as they are compelled to repeat their perceived truths, are fundamentally unstable, and, given this, how they may repeat differently. Why is it necessary to divert female relationships onto phallocentric tracks? There is a more unruly and radical subtext that is unexplored – woman's desire for woman – in which men's bodies are treated secondarily or, at best, as conduits for conveying this desire between women. This is not simply to invert the binary man/woman, as this would only reinscribe power relations; this is perhaps to clear the way for a new and as yet relatively unexplored space in mainstream postcolonial film (if we can yet imagine such a genre, going by the uneven successes of Hanif Kureishi, Shekhar Kapur, and the like): one that critiques the very ideological structures it is itself heavily invested in.

Works Cited

Arora, Poonam (1994) "The Production of Third World Subjects for First World Consumption," in Carson, Dittmar and Welsch (eds), *Multiple Voices in Feminist Film Criticism.* Minneapolis: University of Minnesota Press, pp. 293–304.

Ballal, Pratiti Punja (1998) "Illiberal Masala: The Diasporic Distortions of Mira Nair and Dinesh D'Souza," *Weber Studies* 15:1 (Winter), 95–104.

Butler, Judith (1991) "Imitation and Gender Subordination," in Diana Fuss (ed.), *Inside/Out: Lesbian Theories, Gay Theories.* New York: Routledge, pp. 13–31.

Butler, Judith (1993) *Bodies that Matter: On the Discursive Limits of "Sex."* New York and London: Routledge.

Dayal, Samir (1992) "The Subaltern Does not Speak: Mira Nair's *Salaam Bombay!* as a Postcolonial Text," *Genders* 14 (Fall), 16–32.

Foster, Gwendolyn Audrey (1997) *Women Filmmakers of the African and Asian Diaspora: Decolonizing the Gaze, Locating Subjectivity.* Carbondale and Edwardsville: Southern Illinois University Press.

McClintock, Anne (1994) "The Angel of Progress: Pitfalls of the Term 'Post-Colonialism,'" in Patrick Williams and Laura Chrisman (eds), *Colonial Discourse and Post-Colonial Theory: A Reader.* New York: Columbia University Press, pp. 291–304.

Nair, Mira (1986–7) "*India Cabaret*: Reflections and Reactions," *Discourse* 8 (Fall/Winter), 58–71.

Nair, Mira (1993) "Interview," in Janis Cole and Holly Dale (eds), *Calling the Shots: Profiles of Women Filmmakers*. Kingston, Ontario: Quarry Press, pp. 143–54.

Nair, Mira (1997) "For Filmmaker Nair, Eros Is Human," interview with Liz Braun, *Toronto Sun* 15 May (www.clive.canoe.ca/JamMoviesArtistsNair%5fmira.html).

Patel Vibhuti (1997) "Making a Woman's Kama Sutra," *Ms.* May/June, 79.

Saadawi, Nawal El (1983) *Woman at Point Zero*. London: Zed Books.

Shah, Amit (1987) "A Dweller in Two Lands: Mira Nair, Filmmaker," *Cineaste* 15:3, 22–3.

Tabassum, Wajida (1994) "Hand-Me-Downs," trans. Manisha Chaudbry, in Chandra Talpade Mohanty and Satya Mohanty (eds), *The Slate of Life: More Contemporary Stories by Women Writers of India*. New York: Feminist Press, pp. 37–42.

Tharu, Susie and Lalita, K. (1990, 1993) *Women Writing in India: 600 bc to the Present*, 2 volumes. New York: Feminist Press.

12

Cowgirl Tales

Yvonne Tasker

The idea of a 'female Western' may be both as useful, and as risible, as that of 'male melodrama', both formulations being predicated on a supposed exclusivity of terms which are actually closely entwined. Gendered identities, the meaning, experience and parameters of masculinities and femininities, are at issue in both the Western and the melodrama, regardless of whether the fiction revolves around men or women. The perception that genres might in some senses be gendered has nonetheless persisted with narratives of crime, science-fiction, adventure and the Western acquiring and retaining a reputation as male spaces. Yet, as Pam Cook points out, women have had a long and a significant role in the genre. Writing in 1988, she indicated that women's historical role in the west, at least as far as the Western was concerned, had forgone the 'dubious luxury of a liberal reassessment', adding that it is:

> tempting to put this down, as many critics have, to the male Oedipal bias of the Western, a narrative based on a masculine quest for sexual and national identity which marginalizes women. Fruitful though this approach may be, it has not really come to terms with the dual, contradictory role of women. On the one hand she is peripheral. . . . On the other hand she is central (Buscombe 1988: 241).

The significance of women in the 'traditional' Western, with its insistent inscription of sexual difference in the context of homosocial bonds between men, lies, as Cook suggests, in this peculiar position of marginal centrality. Discourses of masculinity in the Western are defined in relation to female figures such as the showgirl, and a structuring opposition between wives and whores, just as much as on the national, racial and ethnic hierarchies (implicit or explicit) within which white men and women of the Western both battle and depend on native, Black, Chinese, Mexican, Irish, Scandinavian (and other) Americans.

It may come as no surprise that the saloon-owning, business-savvy Vienna in *Johnny Guitar* (1954) is styled as a self-made woman whose status, it is implied, has been achieved through sexual performance. Her success in business marks her as 'working girl' in both sexual and economic senses. Like Joan Crawford's star image, Vienna's costumes and costume changes (first butch, then femme, then butch again) suggest her mobility in terms of gendered signifiers.[1] The stylised geography of the saloon (Vienna's itself) both offers up and questions the division between gendered spaces of business, sexual performance and sex as business. In the Western, women 'upstairs' in a saloon are typically prostitutes, a convention reiterated in such recent movies as *Bad Girls*. Yet Crawford's Vienna insists 'down there I sell whiskey and cards: all you can buy up these stairs is a bullet in the head'. If the representation of white womanhood in the Western is structured in terms of an opposition between wives and whores, it is not the case that individual female characters or protagonists are simply fixed in one position. Just as critics need to acknowledge the significance of women's role in the genre, Cook insists, any 'demand for more realistic images of women' should also take account of:

> the fact that what lingers in the memory, refusing to be dismissed, is a series of extraordinary heroines, from Mae West's Klondike Annie and Doris Day's Calamity Jane, to Joan Crawford's Vienna and Barbara Stanwyck's Jessica Drummond. The search for realism is perhaps self-defeating in a genre which is more concerned with myth than historical accuracy. It might be more illuminating to shuffle the deck (bearing in mind that female card-sharps in the Western are few and far between) and see what permutations emerge. (Buscombe 1988: 241)

Ten years on, these comments have a resonance for an examination of the latest batch of revisionist Westerns to revisit the myths of the open range. We might note that the only female card-sharp to appear in recent Westerns is the decidedly femme Annabelle Branford in Richard Donner's *Maverick* (1994), a film that produces the unexpected spectacle of Jodie Foster, known from her days as a child actor for her tomboy roles, as a fraudulent Southern belle romancing Maverick Junior (Mel Gibson) and Senior (James Garner).

Cook's litany of strong women (stars and roles), whether 'masculinised', aggressively sexual or some composite of the two, provides a frame through which to consider those recent Westerns with female protagonists including *The Ballad of Little Jo, Bad Girls, The Quick and the Dead* (1995) and *Buffalo Girls*. The combination of sexuality and bravado in movies of both past (*Johnny Guitar*) and present (Sharon Stone in *The Quick and the Dead*) can also be understood in terms of the extent to which the Western has been a prime genre for the eroticised display of masculinities as spectacle, a spectacle typically enacted over the male body.[2] The genre's long history includes dandified singing cowboys who rub shoulders with glamorous stars such as Marlene Dietrich, Marilyn Monroe and Angie Dickinson. The Wild West show, paperback fictions, comics and songs all contributed to the production of the 'cowboy' as a spectacle of masculinity even in the nineteenth century within which many of the films are set. Indeed the production of the west as spectacle, and the relation of this production to truth and history has been a regular concern of the cinematic Western itself.[3] The Western as a cinematic genre has been understood as a set of fictions articulating discourses of American history. Yet it is also rather camp and is centrally concerned with the activities (however earnest) of dressing up and putting on a show. The androgynous eroticism of such images as Doris Day in/as *Calamity Jane* (1953) or Crawford in *Johnny Guitar* (in her battle with Mercedes McCambridge) also provides a context within which to consider the lesbian connotations of the cowgirl/female gunslinger.[4]

If the Western is noteworthy for its foregrounding of masculinity as a form of performance which, at least potentially, links the showgirl and the cowboy, it is also and pre-eminently a genre in which freedom is the central term. The Western is a genre in which white men and women achieve a freedom in class terms that is simply unimaginable in other genres. Though some Westerns have worked to open up the role of African-Americans, this has tended to focus on men. *Posse* (1993), for example, features Pam Grier, an action star of the 1970s. Yet she does little more than fire off a few rounds, relegated to cutaway shots.[5] The Western then, offers a (limited) textual space for tomboys/cowgirls to flourish, producing the set of archetypal roles that Cook refers to. Within the rhetoric and imagery of freedom, which is in turn bound up with colonial expansion, vagrancy has a romance attached to it (the open range). The vagrant/wandering Western hero(ine) signifies the freedom that stems from colonial expansion whilst not necessarily being an explicit part of it (as a property owner for example). The romanticism of the vagrant/wanderer provides a framework within which the double meaning of the word 'tramp' is also quite suggestive. Or rather the term means something distinct when applied to women, with tramp taking on sexual connotations (ironic then that Vienna's trouble stems from her desire to settle down). A strong element of the loss involved in the framing 'present-day' sequences of Ford's *The Man Who Shot Liberty Valence* (1962) is the contrast between a slow, restrained, repressed Hallie (Vera Miles) and her younger self which has been lost with the development of the west. This loss is not only to do with the passage of time (as ageing) but a loss of mobility, energy and agency. As Hallie has become literate she has lost her voice. The white woman in the Western has, at least some of the time, a strength and an independence to match the struggles that she faces.

Outlaws and Gunslingers

Styled by B. Ruby Rich as 'the closest thing to a female Western so far', Ridley Scott's *Thelma and Louise* (1991) successfully deployed the iconography of the Western within a narrative that explored the genre's themes of self-reliance and self-discovery (1993: 20). The film's reworking of the road movie format around two women (Susan Sarandon and Geena Davis), which provoked substantial critical and popular debate, called up the history and imagery of the Western (through costume, gunplay and the desert) whilst also touching on a series of other generic reference points. *Thelma and Louise* mobilises a powerful imagery involving the movement of its 'outlaw' protagonists into an 'empty' landscape that operates as an environment for self-discovery, with the women heading towards a mythicised Mexico that they never ultimately reach. The scene in which their car drives through the night, illuminated from within, recalls the campfires of the stylised movie Western landscape (sharing a sense of human isolation within nature). The climax set in Monument Valley is also rich in Western connotations. At a thematic level, the representation of Thelma and Louise as outlaws by default, their actions the result of circumstances as much as intent, makes sense not only within feminist discourses about sexual violence but in terms of the conventions of the Western. Scott's film both capitalises on and contributes to an iconography of independence associated with signifiers such as guns, country and western music and denim, signifiers which also define the figure of the cowgirl. Just so, films and television movies of the 1990s, including *Bad Girls*, *Buffalo Girls*, *The Ballad of Little Jo* and *The Quick and the Dead*, have in quite different ways situated women as protagonists within the Western. Moreover, again as with *Thelma and Louise*, they have intersected with a broader reappropriation and redefinition of the cowgirl style by lesbian audiences and within music (new country) and advertising.

Just as *Thelma and Louise* was greeted with some ambivalence on its release, of the movies cited in this chapter, only *The Ballad of Little Jo*, with its distinctly arthouse touches, has received much favourable response (or indeed any response at all) from feminist critics. Leslie Felperin's *Sight and Sound* review asserts that: '*Bad Girls* is about as politically correct as a L'Oréal hair mousse commercial, which it resembles far more than *The Searchers* or *Johnny Guitar*.' Of course she is right, since the feminist discourses on which the movie draws are those also deployed in advertising: that is, your right to choose the way you want to be.[6] Critics such as Hilary Radner have commented, in this context, on consumer culture's particular articulation of feminism as identity politics, consumption as self-production (Collins *et al.* 1993). If *Bad Girls* was not the type of Western which feminist critics might have looked for neither was it, according to Felperin, the movie that was initially envisaged, having been conceived originally as a more experimental affair directed by Tamra Davis.[7] The film's exploitation of sexual violence, toying with glossy magazine versions of both femme lesbianism and feminist posturing, for example, were almost guaranteed to produce the kind of uneasy response which greeted it. Whilst *Bad Girls* betrays self-consciousness about its project, most evident in its references to *Johnny Guitar* (the bank robbery, for instance), the fact that women are central to the Western landscape is not played for comedy. They are not, that is, *out of place. Bad Girls* has its precedents and reference points not only in a sexy cowgirl chic or the stylised figures of strong women found in Westerns of the 1950s and in country music, but in the comic book characters of the 1940s and 1950s such as those discussed by Jack Shadoian (1979), including Buffalo Belle and Rhoda Trail. From this basis, the film introduces the stereotype of the independent woman, more often located in an urban environment, and the themes associated with her into the Western setting: the struggle to be financially independent from men, a feminist-inspired critique of violence and of women as property.

This juxtaposition of the 'independent woman' and the Western setting is also prefigured in an earlier, slow-paced film, Alan Pakula's *Comes a Horseman* (1978). Set during the end of the Second World War, the film stars Jane Fonda as Ella, a tough woman who is struggling to keep her ranch going through another season. She is helped by an old man, Dodger (Richard Farnsworth) and, later, by Frank (James Caan), an outsider recovering from a gunshot wound. The movie re-hearses a melodramatic terrain in which Ella is pitted against Ewing (Jason Robards) who wants her land at the same time, it is revealed, that he is in danger of losing his own. The familiar opposition of farmer versus cattle is supplanted by cattle versus oil as the ranchers attempt to hold out against the drilling of their land. At the same time, the film addresses the implications of its female protagonist (very much a 'novelty') through its use of both Fonda's star image and the iconography of the Western. Citing diverse examples, including *The Doll's House, Nine to Five* and *Coming Home*, Tessa Perkins characterises Fonda's films of the 1970s as scenarios in which her character, through the course of the film, 'changes and moves closer to the Jane Fonda star-image of an enlightened, independent, radical woman' (Gledhill 1990: 247). Here, though, from the outset she is defined as tough, independent, but also isolated. The film charts Ella's struggle with Ewing alongside her movement from a silent, gruff figure to a warmer persona through her developing relationship with Frank. The portrayal of the work of the ranch is central to the film providing, with the expanse of the landscape, a key element of its spectacle. Yet Ella is also frequently positioned in the house, her face looking out (in close-up) from behind net curtains. It is not until Frank has begun to work with her that we see Ella on horseback, linked firmly with the iconography of the Western. The sequence in which they agree to work together has Ella in her car (noisy, awkward in the landscape) driving alongside Frank on his horse. Both are small figures within the landscape. Their first kiss follows their efforts to contain a stampede, an image that both sublim-ates their energy into their work and provides a counterpoint to the low-key scenes of the couple which follow. Pakula's film is not only concerned to situate its female protagonist within the Western, but to bring out contemporary aspects of the genre: the returning soldiers of the war refer back in terms of the genre to the Civil War and, in contemporary terms to Vietnam. Ella's precarious but iconic position, her enmity with Ewing and his destruction of her house (the movie ends with her and Frank building a new place) locate the film's themes, through gendered and generic discourses, in terms of an opposition between inside and out, past and present, tradition and modernity.

The opening shot of *Bad Girls* echoes the contradictory positioning of Ella/Fonda both within the landscape and within the house, seen through net curtains. The camera is positioned outside a saloon window, revealing both Anita (Mary Stuart Masterson) inside with a client (whose death will trigger the women's flight) and, superimposed, the Western landscape reflected in the glass. The movie begins in Echo City with the four women working as prostitutes. Eileen (Andie McDowell taunts the Christian marchers gathered on the street below. If, within the classic Western, the woman poses a problem for the hero, here the narrative 'problem' is posed (fairly loosely) in terms of sexual violence and exploitation. Kaplan's movie followed the success of Clint Eastwood's *Unforgiven* (1992), an exercise in demystification the narrative of which is triggered by a knife attack on a prostitute, Delilah. When Gene Hackman's 'Little Bill', Sheriff of Big Whiskey, demands that the cowboys responsible should bring the brothel-owner horses in exchange for damaging his property, the women team together to pay for a gunfighter to avenge them. Here then the motivating factor is the women's refusal to agree with the definition of themselves as property. Similarly, when a customer hits Anita in the opening sequence of *Bad Girls*, Cody shoots him, an action which leads (almost instantaneously) to the mobilisation of a Christian-led lynch mob, her rescue by the other three women, and their subsequent efforts to escape pursuers including Pinkerton detectives and Kid Jarrett. Thus the four women's stylised struggle for independence begins in a brothel. Here, as in *Klute*, prostitution simultaneously stands in for some notion of sexual 'liberation' and exploitation. The opposition between 'bad girls' and citizens of the town works in terms of a contrast between moral freedom and restriction expressed as absolutes. The association between the lynch mob and the Christians (dressed in funereal black) confirms their delight in death over life. The film thus foregrounds and pursues themes of status, property and justice in order to establish the inevitability (and the legitimacy) of their outlaw status. (Anita's deed to 'her' land is worthless without her husband: prostitution and marriage are both envisaged as forms of exchange). The move from barely sanctioned role of 'bad girl' (prostitute) to outlaw evolves through the women's reliance on each other and themselves, rather than either of the 'communities' associated with men encountered in the film (Jarret's outlaw gang, Tucker's ranch). The individual stories that gradually emerge relate to familiar narratives in which women take on 'male' responsibilities following the loss or failure of a significant man. Cody Zamora's (Madeleine Stowe) past was with a gang of outlaws who picked her up as a teenager. Anita had travelled west with her husband to stake a claim. His death leaves her without legal claim to their land. Eileen left her father's small Texas farm when it was taken by the bank. Lilly (Drew Barrymore) was left with the debts of her father's Wild West show in which he had been a famous trick rider. In providing motivation for their outlaw status, the film combines the women's anger at the (sexual) violence to which they are subject with long-standing Western themes of the individual pitted against the institutions and finance and government: banks, the law and small-town morality.

The climax of *Bad Girls* features the four protagonists in a *Wild Bunch*-style gunfight in which Cody wishes to exchange a captive for her lover, Josh (a 'pretty boy' who helps her elude capture and later takes care of her). The gang kill him anyway and, after a long fight, Cody challenges chief villain, Kid Jarrett, to a gunfight that is simultaneously parodic and conducted in earnest (throwing him a bullet she drawls, 'pick it up, put it in; die like a man'). If *Bad Girls* seems at times parodic, it nonetheless draws upon and rearticulates the iconography, themes and narrative concerns of the Western. Its distinctiveness stems from the other sources on which it draws: the iconography of country and western, advertising images, soft pornography and fantasy comics. At the same time, however, its use of a group of women as central characters involves renegotiating the terms of the genre at some level. *Bad Girls* was marketed as a (sexy) post-feminist Western, employing a language of liberation and independence, of women's right to control their own bodies in an uneasy combination with cleavage shots and the fetishistic use of whips and weaponry. It is in this context we can understand the film's rather exploitative aspects – the sexualised display of the female leads in their various prostitute costumes, the hint of an undeveloped lesbian relationship between Lilly and Eileen, the images of sexual violence. Though the film's 'novelty value' was undoubtedly central to its marketing, *Bad Girls* also depends to an extent on a generic basis for its intelligibility. However, its exuberant production of a girl-gang Western results in an avoidance of the complexities of the iconography that it invokes, sidestepping any interrogation of the Western itself.

Sam Raimi's *The Quick and the Dead* stars Sharon Stone as Ellen, an 'enigmatic stranger', referred to through most of the film as 'The Lady', a designation which suggests a femininity quite at odds with her gunslinging image (leather pants, cheroots and even shades in one scene). From the opening scene in the desert through her arrival in and triumphant departure from the small town of Redemption, the film operates a sustained pastiche of the spaghetti Western which casts Stone, strong and silent, as a figure beset by doubt and the desire for revenge. *The Quick and the Dead* capitalises on the iconic status Stone, who also co-produced, has accrued as signifier of a strong, independent and dangerous sexuality through her early role in *Total Recall* and, most notoriously, in *Basic Instinct*. Like the prostitutes-turned-outlaws of *Bad Girls*, Ellen as The Lady offers a sexualised version of female strength defined in relation to the positions of 'Lady' and whore. On arrival she rides into Redemption, walks into a bar and asks for a room. Still an unknown quantity, she is met with the response 'whores next door' from a barman who doesn't even turn round to look at her. Ellen's response is to kick his chair out from under him, catching a bottle of beer with bravado. Here, as in the scene in which she reveals her shooting skills (rescuing outlaw-turned-preacher, Cort), the film reprises a familiar scenario in which the hero's powers and abilities are at first kept hidden. While the unknown male is designated weak (subject to laughter), the unknown female is designated a prostitute, as just another working girl. The comic exchange in which Ellen replies to the invitation 'I need a woman' with the put down 'You need a bath' further situates her in relation to the terse one-liners associated with cinematic tough-guys. This in contrast to the spectacular Ace (Lance Henrikson) whose bravado and dandy costume is revealed to be an imposture.

If the movie refutes a wife/whore opposition, Ellen's 'masculine' status does not render her asexual (something that Stone's image might not allow). The night before the final contest, Ellen storms into the brothel where Cort (Russell Crowe) is being held and takes him for herself since they may both be dead the next day. As in *Bad Girls*, it is suggested that her character can use her sexuality. 'You Can't Resist Her', the posters proclaimed, conflating her sexual attraction with her capacity for violence. The motivation for Ellen's actions is uncertain at the film's outset. She seems distant from the other gunfighters who are in town for an annual competition organised by its boss, Herod (Gene Hackman). This is in part because of her sex (and, of course, she is the only female gunfighter in the film: construed as exceptional). Apparently repelled by violence, she leaves town after the first round, turning her back on plans for vengeance. Her fury at the sexual exploitation of the bar-owner's daughter (she 'wriggled like a fish' gloats her attacker) leads her to kill him, effectively going through to the next round of the contest. Clearly there is some affection or empathy between Ellen and the young girl, expressed in a series of looks. Yet when she seeks to idolise Ellen ('I think you're great'), she is dismissed and is told to 'grow up'. Just as *Bad Girls* picks up and runs with the commodified images of female rebellion familiar from advertising, magazines and music video, *The Quick and the Dead* looks to other popular cultural reference points: the black humour of director Sam Raimi exercised in the horror classic *The Evil Dead*. Here the Western combined with more than a little of the conventions of the horror/slasher film enables Stone to function as a kind of composite of the Eastwood/Bronson gunslinger and the 'final girl' identified by Carol Clover (1992) in the slasher movie. For once, the woman with a past is not seeking to avenge her own sexual violation, though the theme is nonetheless invoked in the figure of the young girl Ellen avenges. Instead she is her father's daughter, acting in his stead. Towards the end of the film, however, it is revealed that as a young child Ellen inadvertently shot her father when offered a chance to save him by shooting through the rope by which he was to hang. The revelation produces an ironic comment on the masculine woman's supposed identification with the father. There is also a generic reference here in the allusion to Bronson's 'harmonica man' in *Once Upon a Time in the West* (1968).

Cross-dressers and Tomboys in the Western

The Western has long been a privileged site for gendered cross-dressing. Whether or not she seeks to pass as a man, the 'masculine' Western heroine, as tomboy, gunslinger or cowgirl, is a recurrent figure in the genre, past and present, with Calamity Jane perhaps the best-known example. 'Male' attire serves to further underline her strength and independence, drawing on the physical freedom which working clothes suggest in advertising images, a freedom constructed in relation to 'feminine' costumes of restraint. Ella's costume of cowboy hat, jeans and plaid shirt in *Comes a Horseman*, Vienna's more stylised 'gunfighter' look in *Johnny Guitar*, Ellen's Eastwood-style garb in *The Quick and the Dead*, all function as appropriations of cowboy clothes that signify the uncertain status of the heroine. Transgressive in her refusal of her place, the tomboy is typically explained and contained in terms of her relationship to her father. Her 'masculine' qualities stem from a distorted upbringing in which she has had to rely on herself, whether this is expressed in terms of the loss of the mother or an identification with the father deemed excessive for a woman. The four 'bad girls' all tell different stories which define them, as we've seen, in relation to failed or absent men. Frank tells Ella in *Comes a Horseman*: 'Lady, you got balls the size of grapefruit.' Later, in a cowboy bar, old-hand Dodger explains how Ella's father had raised her: 'tried to make her a son that he needed but he never did have – she was weaned on war; she never knew nothing else'. Ellen in *The Quick and the Dead* produces herself as gunfighter to avenge her father. Neither does she have any ambitions to embody the law, tossing her father's Sheriff badge to Cort before riding out of town.

Though tomboy types are often 'explained' in terms of their relationship to men/fathers, they are also iconographically lesbian figures. In this way Barbara Creed terms *Calamity Jane* (1953) a 'lesbian Western', commenting on the Oedipal narrative of transformation in which Doris Day 'relinquishes her men's clothing, foul language, guns and horse for a dress, feminine demeanour, sweet talk and a man'. This movement also involves giving up Alice, the woman 'with whom she has set up house and whom she clearly loves' (1995: 95). Pam Cook also identifies a 'characteristic trajectory of the Western heroine from tomboy to wife' (Buscombe 1988: 243). The distinctiveness of at least some recent Western narratives involving female protagonists lies in their refusal of that Oedipal trajectory. Or, more precisely, a refusal of its implications: such as the renunciation of activity for passivity, masculinity for femininity, female friends for a man. Like Crawford's Vienna, both Ellen and the 'bad girls' of Kaplan's film shift between butch and femme guises. The construction of Ellen, for example, involves no contradiction between her 'masculinity' and her active sexuality. Fonda's Ella may wear a frock to dance with Frank, in a scene that emphasises their happiness as a couple, but his first gift to her is a set of chaps. If these protagonists are tomboys or cross-dressers, they are not, it seems, necessarily destined to give up pleasure for marriage.

In the CBS mini-series *Buffalo Girls* Anjelica Huston stars as the cross-dressed heroine Calamity Jane, from whose point of view the sprawling narrative of the 'Old Wild West' is told. She is one of a range of stock characters (including Wild Bill Hickock, Buffalo Bill Cody, General Custer, Annie Oakley, Sitting Bull and so on) in a production which seems at times to be a Wild West show itself. Calamity's voice-over addresses this history to her daughter Jane who, during the course of the film, she gives up to a wealthy English couple travelling in the west. At the very beginning of the narrative she speaks of her adoption of male clothing thus:

> In them days, Jane, there was only two ways for a woman to survive out west; 'wife-ing' and whoring. As I wasn't cut out for either one, I had to find my own way of surviving. So I lived like a man and sometimes even passed myself off as one. Got a little sticky at times but give me a kind of freedom that few women ever knew.

Later, Jane 'tells' her daughter that 'I never really thought of myself as a woman'. Her cross-dressing is, once more, explicitly to do with status and work. The opening sequence has Calamity/Huston passing as male to get work in Custer's army. Shuffling her feet, she is a tall, gawky figure who looks at the ground. But when challenged, Calamity wields a whip to flick the cap off the recruiting officer and thus demonstrates her prowess. On discovery (her breasts give her away whilst washing in the river), Calamity is set to 'humiliating women's work' washing clothes. If there seems to be something of necessity in Calamity's cross-dressing, this is no rites of passage tale in which she will ultimately adopt female clothes and institutionalised heterosexuality. Indeed in the final sequence, left caring for the baby of her buddy Dora (Melanie Griffith), Calamity is still in her male garb, in mythic tones telling of how she needs to just take off sometimes and ride in the hills. Even Ellen Barkin's lovesick Calamity in Walter Hill's *Wild Bill* is at a distance from the roles of wife or whore (though she spends the film mooning over Bill Hickock).[8]

In Maggie Greenwald's *The Ballad of Little Jo*, Josephine Monaghan (Suzy Amis) finds a space out west as a small man ('little' Jo). She has been expelled from a position of femininity, designated 'society girl', which is clearly marked within the film as a class position through the expression of her sexuality (she has given birth to an illegitimate child). Having lost her class position she goes west, engages in the colonial adventure and becomes a man, owner of land and a 'husband' of sorts. Living in a hidden relationship with Tinman Wong (David Chung), who s/he has saved from the townsmen, Jo takes on the role of patriarch. Jo's choice, like that of Calamity Jane is mapped in relation to the two options of marriage and prostitution. Thus the promotion for Greenwald's film ran: 'In the Old Wild West, a woman had only two choices. She could be a wife or she could be a whore. Josephine Monaghan chose to be a man'. But of course the line means a 'poor white woman'. Rather than live as a working-class woman (as classless) s/he scars herself and sets out on a life as a small man, needing patronage but independent after a fashion. Jo's decision is not really constructed within the film as a matter of choice. The opening sequence shows her in woman's clothes, walking down a busy road, haughty but encumbered by her luggage and her parasol. 'I'm not a vagrant' she declares, but does not know where she is going. She is given a ride by a salesman, Mr Hollander, who betrays her, selling her to some soldiers from whom she escapes, her clothes torn. Mr Hollander seems to offer one possible career. She sells a chair on his behalf and is delighted when he pays her: 'the first money I've ever earned' she tells him. The scene underlines the dangers of remaining Josephine, though the woman who runs the store where she buys men's clothes (there are no dresses to be had) tells her 'it's against the law to dress improper to your sex'. Jo's transformation, in which she undresses, cuts her hair and scars her face, is intercut with flashbacks that tell her story. The sequence is eroticised, the first shots framed as if through a window, spying on her. The intercutting suggests a relationship of cause and effect between past and present, the conception of an illegitimate child, her father's condemnation of her as a 'whore': all of which produce her decision to become male. Later in the film the undertaker's undressing of her dead body is intercut with Jo's friends reminiscing in the saloon bar, a reminiscence disrupted by the news that 'Little Jo' was a woman.

As do other cross-dressing narratives, *The Ballad of Little Jo* takes pleasure in mapping Jo's successful disguise, while at the same time is haunted by the threat of discovery. This threat leads to isolation, for example with Jo taking the job of shepherding, the loneliness of which would drive other men crazy. Revelation does indeed bring danger, as Percy Corcoran's (Ian McKellen) angry attack demonstrates. Corcoran's earlier attack on Elvira, a deaf-mute prostitute who is led into the town on horseback, indicates the precarious position of women among this community of men. The final revelation of Jo as Josephine, in death, brings humiliation as his erstwhile friends marvel at the female corpse, dressing it up and setting it on a horse to be photographed. Jo's cross-dressing generates a cinematic commentary on masculinity and on the Western, with the restrictions within which other female characters operate framed through her perspective. We watch her/him learning how to eat like a man, acquiring shooting skills to protect the sheep s/he is guarding. Her gun also protects her from Percy and from the incursion of the land-hungry cattle company. Though a 'little' man, Jo gains respect within Ruby City by situating himself outside of it: 'You are a free white man now', Tinman tells Jo. She has saved his life of course, though Frank spares him on the condition she hires him to cook and clean. Jo thus gains, and at least initially exercises, power over Tinman, shutting him out in the rain to protect her own identity, to hide her secret.

If Greenwald's film thus involves the movement towards heterosexuality characteristic of the 'tomboy' scenario, this movement is problematically located in terms of the hierarchical relationship between Jo and Tinman, relations of master/servant (the parts they play when Frank visits) which also intersect with discourses of gender and with the portrayal of their inter-racial romance in a genre that is, as Pam Cook notes, 'haunted by the fear of miscegenation'

(Buscombe 1988: 242). Their romance does not involve Jo returning to the role of woman. As they lie in bed together, she shows him a small, framed photograph of herself as 'society girl', formal and posed. Tinman prefers her as she is, saying 'this white girl would never do this with me'. Later, Jo angrily demands he leave the house, dressing herself as a woman and trying to make a pie: 'What man would want you?' he asks. Frank's perception of Tinman as a housekeeper disguises his role as Jo's lover, just as he cannot see Jo for what s/he is (though he repeatedly terms him 'peculiar', 'unfriendly'). The film draws on, and to some extent cuts across the Hollywood cinema's recurrent inscription of Chinese men in terms of 'femininity'.[9] Jo's 'male' guise, her short hair, is set against Tinman's long hair; her scarred face against his body, scarred from assaults and from years of work on the railroad. Their developing relationship is constituted and functions in terms of their shared exclusion from the society of white men: both face the threat of violence and fear the town. Of the three occasions on which her secret is discovered, the moment when Tinman recognises Jo as a woman ('You are not Mr Jo') is defined not by violence but mutual interest, one in which they both ask each other for their 'real' names (his mispronounced, hers shortened).

The classic Western rarely portrays women together. The fact that *Buffalo Girls* is a television production, albeit a big budget, all-star movie, allows the narrative to focus more directly on its female protagonists than is usual in the Western.[10] Indeed, the friendship between Calamity (Anjelica Huston) and Dora (Melanie Griffith) structures the film. Dora is an ultra-femme madam, to whose (whore)house/saloon Jane continually returns and who has known her, we are told, for twenty years. Unlike the cinema's many male-bonding movies, the sexual implications of this butch/femme friendship are not disavowed through comedy. Arriving at Dora's place in Deadwood for the first time in the movie, Jane enters her bedroom where she is asleep with romantic interest Gabriel Byrne, and leaps on the bed, embracing them both, at which point Byrne's character retreats to another room. While Dora immediately uncovers the secret of Jane's love for Hickock (whilst cleaning her up with a bath), it is their relationship that is constant. When Jane wants to seduce Wild Bill Hickock, Dora lends her woman's clothes. This is one of only two occasions when she will be dressed as a woman – contemplating herself in the mirror she expresses her wonder: 'I don't look anything like myself'. She must learn to walk like a woman (just as Jo in *The Ballad of Little Jo* must learn to act like a man), but her greatest humiliation also comes in these clothes as Hickock announces her identity to the bar and she becomes an object of ridicule.

If the first time Jane self-consciously dresses in female clothing is as a prospective lover, the second is in her role as mother, during an ill-fated trip to London to reclaim her daughter. She is quite out of place in the context of the 'old world', a lack of place played for comedy when she shoots up a pub. The contrast is further underlined as she looks on (unacknowledged) at her daughter riding a pony in the park, sat 'gracefully' and quite different to her mother. And in their final meeting Jane gives her daughter a horse, so much associated with the Western, which they ride together. Yet the film does not suggest that somehow Calamity's masculine dress and behaviour is an impediment to motherhood. When Dora dies in childbirth (the seemingly inevitable corollary to female friendship) Jane takes on the job of raising her baby. If the two women operate as a kind of butch/femme couple, it's also worth noting that Dora too keeps moving from town to town, as restless in her own way as Calamity. She consistently refuses marriage to the man she loves, a refusal that Calamity explains to him/us as a fear of being trapped on a ranch, of being away from the town. Yet Dora's independence and her friendship with Jane also suggest another story, one which reinvents the familiar Western relationship of cowboy and townswoman in terms of an eroticised female friendship. The image of the cowgirl, tomboy cross-dresser that she is, evokes the figure of the lesbian. Perhaps wary of these connotations, Hollywood movies have frequently cast her either as an isolated figure or set within an Oedipal narrative that ultimately produces her as a wife. Sharon Stone's Ellen is a solitary, revenge-driven figure in *The Quick and the Dead*, while Ellen Barkin's lovesick Calamity Jane in Walter Hill's *Wild Bill* exists only in relation to Hickock: dashing upstairs in the saloon to fetch him her guns, she hands over her power to him. As a movie about a group of four women, *Bad Girls* can, it seems, spare one of them for domesticity/heterosexuality whilst retaining the image of the remaining three women riding off into the sunset together to the sounds of an upbeat soundtrack. Eileen's decision to stay on the ranch with William Tucker at the end of *Bad Girls*, though it is also a rejection of tomboy Lilly (with whom she shares kisses), stems from a 'femme' persona that is constructed as extreme, artificial and out of place. Her allusions to her status as 'a fine Southern lady' are undercut by Lilly, for example, repeatedly emphasising the artificiality of her performance.

The appropriation of 'masculine' clothing that defines the cowgirl produces her as a transgressive figure who is frequently androgynous, sometimes decidedly butch. *Even Cowgirls Get the Blues* (1994), Gus Van Sant's adaptation of Tom Robbins' book, offers a loving rendition of the lesbian/cowgirl scenario on the Rubber Rose Ranch complete with a k.d. lang soundtrack including such songs as 'Cowgirl Pride'. The Western/road movie provides a generic setting for a parodic tale of transformation, politics and lesbian love in which Sissy Hankshaw (Uma Thurman), a hitch-hiking misfit falls for cowgirl Bonanza Jellybean (Rain Phoenix). B Ruby Rich links the film's uneven critical reception to divisions of 'gender and generation', with straight male critics left cold by the humour and the film's lesbian/cowgirl articulation of the road movie/Western, reading the film as dated rather than as a commentary on 1970s-style collectivism (1993: 21). Van Sant's explicit appropriation of Western iconography and the figure of the cowgirl for a lesbian love story picks up on the genre's (increasingly) evident homoeroticism. *Johnny Guitar* constructs and exploits what Victor Perkins (1996) terms the 'eroticism of hatred' between Vienna and Emma, a move that, in Paula Graham's words, both underlines and draws on 'the lesbian-erotic implications of the "cat-fight", which in turn draws on homoerotic subtextual elements in Westerns' (Wilton 1995: 175).

In turn country music, whence cowgirl chic was long banished, both operates and undercuts extremes of (white) gendered identities, partly through its array of strong (often tragic) womanhood.[11] Louise Allen notes that k.d. lang's 'fame as a country singer has helped to popularize a country and western style lesbian style', whilst cowboy/girl iconography also features 'specifically within gay and lesbian cultural production' including *Desert Hearts* and Van Sant's earlier *My Own Private Idaho* (1991) (Wilton 1995: 81). Elsewhere Rosa Ainley and Sarah Cooper show how New Country has attracted a lesbian audience by keeping the elements of country and western that hold a 'camp' appeal (its ' "spunky" women per-formers, and great clothes', for example) whilst offering an updated 'cowgirl brand of feminism that was first seen in numbers like Dolly Parton's "Dumb Blonde?" ' (Budge and Hamer 1994: 47). The comic fantasy sequence in which Dolly Parton's character in *Nine to Five* pursues, lassoes and ropes her sexist boss (Dabney Coleman) comes to mind. Parton's elaborate performance of femininity (she has observed more than once that 'if I hadn't been a woman, I would have been a drag queen') has its counterpoint in k.d. lang's androgynous, latterly out-lesbian persona (her latest release is titled 'Drag').[12] Madonna famously referred to k.d. lang's androgyny as 'Elvis is alive and is she ever beautiful', a phrase that signals both her gender ambiguity and the strong element of performance in her image.[13] Performance in the sense that, as Marjorie Garber notes, '[i]t is almost as if tile word "impersonator", in contemporary popular culture, can be modified *either* by "female" *or* by "Elvis" ' (1992: 372). Of course Elvis was an ambivalent figure who articulated a peculiar feminised, objectifying version of white working-class masculinity as aggressive sexual display. Presley's image was built on a sexual and racial ambiguity that produced him as both feminised and macho, appropriat-ing black American music for the white mainstream. One of his two Westerns, *Flaming Star* (Don Siegel, 1960), picked up on the sense of racial ambiguity associated with the Elvis persona, casting him as a son of white/Native-American ancestry who is torn between two identities.[14]

If the cowgirl is already a type of cross-dresser, the Western is a genre in which an elaborate, ritualistic performance of masculinity and activities of dressing up are central. In this context it may be no surprise that Jackie Stacey terms *Desert Hearts* a 'fantasy of transformative and successful lesbian romance' (Wilton 1995: 94). She suggests that the cumulative effect of the Western setting, and the juxtaposition of the country soundtrack with this narrative of lesbian romance is ironic, drawing attention to the conventions of Hollywood romance. Already stylised when played by a man, women's enactment of the cowboy/girl image only heightens the element of self-conscious performance, of a dressing up often associated with childhood. The framing of the romantic couple, Cay and Vivian, serves to contradict 'the meaning of the "Wild West" as the place where anything goes', reminding the viewer 'that, for lesbians, romance always take place within the "frame" of heterosexual culture' (ibid.: 109). It is surely significant that *Desert Hearts, Even Cowgirls Get the Blues* and *Thelma and Louise* (three movies that draw on the lesbian connotations of the cowgirl, country music and the Western) involve journeys, using the metaphor of travel as escape from social convention (transformation) set alongside the development of a strong central relationship between two women. In a quite different way to the sort of revisionist Western typified most recently by *Unforgiven*, the evocation of the cowgirl here works to question assumptions made in the Western about violence or about gender. *The Ballad of Little Jo* adopts both strategies, framing its gritty (revisionist) portrayal of the west through the eyes of a woman from the east who is living as a western man. Whether stylised, comic, musical or revisionist the Western still has stories to tell.

Notes

1   Victor Perkins (1996) discusses the film in terms of Crawford's career.

2   See Neale (Cohan and Hark 1993) for a discussion of masculinity in the Western.

3   Ford's *The Man Who Shot Liberty Valence* (1962), Lang's *The Return of Frank James* (1940) or Peckinpah's *Guns in the Afternoon/Ride the High Country* (1962) are obvious examples. Eastwood's *Unforgiven* (1992) features a writer who learns that death in the west lacks the nobility he seeks to attribute to it.

4   Andy Warhol's *Lonesome Cowboys* (1968) has fun with the homoeroticism of the Western. Jackie Stacey (1994) discusses Doris Day in *Calamity Jane*, while Paula Graham writes of the complex lesbian appeal of *Johnny Guitar* (Wilton 1995).

5   Though questions of ethnicity, gender and sexuality are central to the Western, the female gunslingers in recent Westerns are exclusively white. Native-American women are caught up in overdetermined structures of passivity, whilst the clichés of an overdetermining sexuality frame Mexican women in the genre (the stereotypes that frame *Duel in the Sun* (1946), for example). The decision not to subtitle the Chinese woman healer in *Bad Girls* seems all too typical. The contemporary Western, revisionist or otherwise, is not by definition a white woman's game, however. The genre has the potential at least to tell a wider range of stories.

6   Advertising culture is quite evidently a source for independent woman imagery in *Bad Girls* – the kind associated in Britain with the Peugeot car 'Thelma and Louise' spoofs and tampon commercials which feature bright (usually white) young women being athletic.

7   Leslie Felperin, *Sight and Sound*, July 1994: 38. As both Felperin and B Ruby Rich recount, the project lost director Davis (whose cult hit *Guncrazy* (1992) had featured Drew Barrymore) and performer Cynda Williams to become a more mainstream (and all-white) affair. Lizzie Francke cites the movie as an example of the restrictions produced by studio interference (1994: 141).

8   Sexual encounters are often constructed in terms of vulnerability, leaving a hero weak or, in the horror film, couples subject to violence. *Wild Bill* has Bill Hickock caught by Jack McCall as he and Calamity Jane (half-dressed) are having sex on a saloon table.

9   See King-Kok Cheung on Chinese-American masculinities in Hirsch and Keller (1990). I also discuss this in Stecopoulous and Mebel (1997).

10 Schulze's arguments about the television movie (Balio 1990) are discussed in my introduction.

11 In turn these life stories are recycled in such movies as *The Coal Miner's Daughter* (1980) with Sissy Spacek as Loretta Lynn or *Sweet Dreams* (1985) with Jessica Lange as Patsy Cline. Speculation about the loves and lives of country and western performers runs rife: by the time k. d. lang came out as a lesbian performer, she had already been framed in terms of transgression of country codes of dress and performance. Dolly Parton is regularly quizzed about her sexuality (Parton reproduces this as one of the most asked questions at the end of her autobiography), perhaps suggesting the peculiar effect of the 'femininity' she enacts.

12 See Dolly Parton (1994: 309). k. d. lang's *Drag* puns on drag as impersonation and drag as smoking, with a collection of tunes all related to cigarettes in some way. The cover image has lang in drag, hand poised but no cigarette.

13 Victoria Starr, *k. d. lang* (1993: 138).

14 Elvis' other Western was *Love Me Tender* (1956), his feature film debut.

Works Cited

Balio, Tino (ed.) (1990) *Hollywood in the Age of Television*. London: Unwin Hyman.

Budge, Belinda and Hamer, Diane (eds) (1994) *The Good and the Gorgeous: Popular Culture's Romance with Lesbianism*. London: Pandora Press.

Buscombe, Ed (ed.) (1988) *The BFI Companion to the Western*. London: BFI.

Clover, Carol (1992) *Men, Women and Chainsaws: Gender in the Modern Horror Film*. London: BFI.

Cohan, Steve and Hark, Ina Rae (1993) *Screening the Male: Exploring Masculinities in Hollywood Cinema*. London: Routledge.

Collins, Jim, Radner, Hilary and Preacher Collins, Ava (eds) (1993) *Film Theory Goes to the Movies*. London: Routledge.

Creed, Barbara (1995) Lesbian bodies: tribades, tomboys and tarts. In E. Grosz and E. Probyn (eds), *Sexy Bodies: The Strange Carnalities of Feminism*. London: Routledge.

Francke, Lizzie (1994) *Script Girls: Women Screenwriting in Hollywood*. London: Routledge.

Garber, Marjorie (1992) *Vested Interests: Cross-dressing and Cultural Anxiety*. London: Routledge.

Gledhill, Christine (ed.) (1990) *Stardom: Industry of Desire*. London: Routledge.

Hirsch, M. and Keller, E. F. (1990) *Conflicts in Feminism*. London: Routledge.

Parton, Dolly (1994) *Dolly: My Life and Other Unfinished Business*. New York: HarperCollins.

Perkins, Victor (1996) Johnny Guitar. In I. Cameron and D. Pye (eds), *The Movie Book of the Western*. London: Studio Vista.

Rich, B Ruby (1993) At home on the range. *Sight and Sound*, October, 19–22.

Shadoian, Jack (1979) Yuh got pecos! Doggone Belle, yuh're as good as two men! *Journal of Popular Culture*, 12(4), 721–36.

Stacey, Jackie (1994) *Star Gazing: Hollywood Cinema and Female Spectatorship*. London: Routledge.

Starr, Victoria (1994) *k. d. lang.* New York: St Martin's Press.

Stecopoulous, Harry and Uebel, Michael (eds) (1997) *Race and the Subject of Masculinities.* Durham, NC: Duke University Press.

Wilton, Tamsin (ed.) (1995) *Immortal, Invisible: Lesbians and the Moving Image.* London: Routledge.

Part III
Race: Stereotypes and Multiple Realisms

Introduction

It may appear obvious what race is, but in fact race is a complex term, defined not by biology as much as by politics, history, fear, and social hierarchies. Often these forces are disguised as science, in order to assert their authority as "objective." The "objectivity" assumed to reside in photographic media, including film, makes it apparent why filmic images of race have such power and authority. As Lola Young (1996, p. 3) notes, "cinema is complicit in the structuring and naturalizing of power relations between Black and white people." In the past, color or race applied to any kind of "otherness," and even Jews, Irish, and Italians (in the USA), groups defined as ethnic (tribal or national cultural identities), were considered another "race," even "Black." Race is an ideological term bearing imagined stereotyped social and behavioral qualities, or, as Mark Reid (2005, p. 1) notes, race is "an ever-changing sociocultural construction." Race is applied to many groups – Africans, African Americans, Native Americans, Asian Americans, Hispanics, and Blacks and Asians living in Europe – and blurs with cultural uses of "white" and "black" as metaphors of good and bad, respectively. Racial stereotypes have consequences for notions of "normal" gender identities, too, as race, gender, and sexuality are intimately intertwined. "Deviant" sexuality (lust, impotence) is often projected onto racial "others."

Race is rarely applied to "whites," who are presumed the "norm" against which differences are measured, just as gender has been presumed to be a "woman's" issue. While gender is now examined in studies of masculinity, homosexuality, and femininity, there are now emerging corresponding applications of race to whites. Film scholar Richard Dyer in 1988 was among the first to treat whiteness as a racial category, followed by other scholarly studies (see bibliography). Today "race" is still usually limited to people of color, without corresponding complementary and dialogic application to "whites." Such dialogic complementarity can be readily examined in the film studies classroom.

Stereotypes become "normal" or "naturalized," i.e. so often repeated that we don't think critically about their accuracy, authenticity, or causes. Stereotypes are so interwoven within cultural assumptions that we assume unquestioningly that they are "true." One source of their naturalization is that until the past few decades white actors played Blacks ("Blackface"), Indians, and Asians ("yellowface"). White performers often exaggerated stereotypes to essentialize racial types, like the sly Asian, the submissive Black, or the lusty Latin, demonstrating how representation and power work together to institutionalize racial prejudices.

Black stereotypes have a long history in American entertainment back to nineteenth-century minstrel shows. D. W. Griffith's 1912 *The Birth of a Nation* was emphatically racist and pro-Ku Klux Klan as it purported to be historical and heroic. Even Griffith felt the need to repudiate this interpretation through his film *Intolerance*, critical of European civilization. *The Birth of a Nation* provoked a Black film industry that paralleled mainstream films and sometimes influenced all-Black casts in Hollywood films (e.g. *Hallelujah*, 1929; *Cabin in the Sky*, 1943). Films in the 1960s sometimes openly addressed racism (*Raisin in the Sun*, 1961; *Guess Who's Coming to Dinner*, 1967; *To Sir with Love*, 1967) and in the 1970s appealed to Black audiences directly (*Cotton Comes to Harlem*, 1970; *Shaft*, 1971; *Sounder*, 1972; *Superfly*, 1972; *Pressure*, 1975, by Horace Ové and the first Black film made in Britain). From the 1980s on, Black actors rose in the star system, even appearing in films not about race.

Films protesting racial inequalities may replicate gender inequalities, limiting and stereotyping women characters (mammies, femme fatales) by creating a male coming of age narrative to define racial behaviors and identities solely through male characters. Films which foreground race *and* gender often focus on female bonding (*Passion Fish*, 1992; *Waiting to Exhale*, 1995; *Eve's Bayou*, 1997). Spike Lee's films offer multiple commentaries on US race relations, sometimes at the expense of women who, lacking agency, are subdued in his films by rape (*She's Gotta Have It*, 1986; *School Daze*, 1988), and of other racial and ethnic groups (Jews, Koreans). Lee's films deploy a Hollywood style and scale to represent heterogeneity in Black communities, including class and color differences. Lee interrogates conventional notions of protagonists, heroes, villains, and genres, while unhinging notions of racial "progress" (resurrected Blackface in *Bamboozled*, 2000). His sophisticated camera, editing, and lighting techniques combined with Black imagery, music (rap and jazz), historical allusions, and iconic figures (Martin Luther King, Malcolm X) have opened up a space for the discourse of race in mainstream films and for the employment and participation of Black actors, cinematographers, musicians, and other filmmaking professionals. Carl Franklin's 1995 *Devil in a Blue Dress* focuses on the Black community seen from within, as does *Compensation* (1995) by Zeinabu Irene Davis, a silent film about two deaf mutes. African American films in the 1990s sophisticatedly combined themes, styles, and techniques from both popular and independent films, focusing on a range of topics including the inner city, Black youth, middle-class Black life, family struggles in divided communities, and playful rap films, addressing a mixed audience of whites and Blacks and crossing generations (see Reid, 2000, pp. 22–6).

"Hispanic" or "Latino/a" embraces many national identities throughout Central and Latin America. Mexicans became stereotyped in Westerns as lawless, greedy, lusty, and murderous revolutionaries. Protests against these types began in 1913, after a spate of racist films. Cuban and Brazilian characters tended to appear more benign (e.g. Desi Arnaz or Carmen Miranda, respectively), connected to lively music and dance. Political changes, like Franklin Roosevelt's Good Neighbor Policy, mitigated Hispanic stereotypes only slightly. Challenges to stereotypes and fears of miscegenation appeared in *El Norte* (1983) and *The Ballad of Gregorio Cortez* (1984), followed by 1980s Hispanic "hood" movies and films that criticized US intervention in Latin American politics. The "new" Hispanic Hollywood's films focused on internal communities (*Mambo Kings*, 1992; *Mi Vida Loca*, 1994; *Mi Familia*, 1995), and more recently on "border cinema" about Indian/Spanish mestizo communities, leaving Anglo culture out of the narrative.

Native Americans/Indians began appearing in silent films made by William "Buffalo Bill" Cody, whose "Wild West Show" traveled throughout the USA and Europe "performing" a narrative of US history. His film company began making films in 1914. In 1912 Griffith made *A Pueblo Legend*, invoking the noble savage stereotype, and in 1913 his *The Battle at Elderbrush Gulch* evoked the brutal savage stereotype. The novelist Zane Grey made films sympathetic to Indians exploited by whites, but his views were thwarted by Paramount Pictures' revisions, in which Indians lose the Darwinian struggle for survival (*The Vanishing American*, 1926). Telling American history of the West usually meant demeaning Indians to make heroes and martyrs of Custer, the cavalry, and the pioneers. The myth of Indians as savages (paralleling the "untamed" wilderness) supported the myth of white Americans' righteous "destined" domination. Such "histories" were compulsively repeated, making the Western the most popular genre by far, seen by most Americans from childhood and also seen around the world, making these films especially pernicious. Films often put tribes together in places where they never lived, and Indians from one tribe play Indians from another in generic "Indian" dress.

Before the 1980s some sympathetic films appeared (*Fort Apache*, 1948; *Broken Arrow*, 1950; *Tell Them Willie Boy Is Here*, 1969), while some that claimed accuracy indulged in racism (*A Man Called Horse*, 1970). Films were inflected by the American Indian Movement protest at Wounded Knee, 1973, and subsequent Indian reactions to attempts to erode their autonomy and cut reservation funds (*Incident at Oglala*, 1992). Films still indulge in the plot of the white man who becomes a better Indian than the Indians (*The Emerald Forest*, 1985; *The Last of the Mohicans*, 1993). One such film, *Dances with Wolves* (1990), presented Lakotas sympathetically and speaking their own languages, but made Pawnees the "bloodthirsty savage" stereotype. In these films, "natives" need whites to protect them from evildoers, what Jacquelyn Kilpatrick (1999, p. 129) calls the theme of "Great White Hunter in League with the Natural Ecologies." Historical revisionism, including eroticization of Indian women, appears most appallingly in the Disney Studio's *Pocahontas* (1995), in which the pre-pubescent girl, as Pocahontas actually was, becomes a buxom woman with a desire for white men.

Native Americans began making their own films, including short historical features by directors Victor Masayesva Jr in the 1980s and George Burdeau in the 1990s. Recently *War Party* (1988), *Powwow Highway* (1989), *The Sunchaser* (1996), *War Code: Navajo Code Talkers* (1996), *Smoke Signals* (1998), and *The Fast Runner* (2002) use largely or exclusively Native actors sometimes speaking Native languages, often set in the twentieth century. Some movies draw on literature by Native authors such as Sherman Alexie (*Smoke Signals*) and M. Scott Momaday (*House of Dawn*, 1972). Robert Redford's Sundance Institute helped to make several of these films.

Stereotypes of Asians ("the yellow peril," "inscrutable") pre-date films, going back to early European contacts with Asians. "Asian" embraces many national identities, including Chinese, Japanese, Filipino, Korean, Vietnamese, Cambodian, Indian, and Pakistani, among others. The Japanese were targets of Second World War films, even after the war was over, and the Chinese, targets of Cold War films. Stereotypes like the emasculated Japanese houseboy or the geisha were common in the 1950s and 1960s. During and after the Vietnam War, the Vietnamese became the bad guys (e.g. *The Deer Hunter*, 1978). Other typical anxieties associated with Asians were danger (film noir, *Chinatown*, 1974), the Orient as a site of decadent opium smoking (*McCabe and Mrs Miller*, 1971), the presumed erotic (the rape theme in

Griffith's *Broken Blossoms*, 1919; suicidal Butterfly or exotic Suzie Wong), deception and trickery (e.g. "evil" Fu Manchu played by Boris Karloff!). Asian characters appeared in Westerns (Chinese running restaurants or laundries), crime, war, spy, and mystery films ("inscrutable" Charlie Chan played by Swedish actor Warner Oland). The martial arts fighter for justice in popular Bruce Lee films of the 1970s was revived in the 1990s in comedic Jackie Chan films. The first Asian film made in Britain appeared in 1975 (*A Private Enterprise*).

The 1980s and 1990s were rich and diverse in Asian representations. The 1980s was a decade that included war films (*The Year of Living Dangerously*, 1982; *The Killing Fields*, 1984) and epics (*Heat and Dust*, 1982; *Gandhi*, 1982; *A Passage to India*, 1984; *Ping Pong*, 1986; *The Last Emperor*, 1987). In the 1990s more nuanced films appeared, many by Asian directors (*Bhaji on the Beach*, 1993; *Farewell My Concubine*, 1993; *Chungking Express*, 1994; *Eat Drink Man Woman*, 1994; *Peggy Su!*, 1998; *East Is East*, 1999). More recently such films as *Bend It Like Beckham* (2002) and *The Warrior* (2002) have been commercial successes. The "white savior" plot, however, persists as recently as *The Last Samurai* (2003), in which Tom Cruise becomes a better (and the only surviving) Samurai than all the Japanese who trained him!

Some Asian filmmakers have put a pan-Asian identity above particular Asian identities to gain political clout and acknowledge changing Asian identities through new emigration and large diasporic communities established in the USA and Europe for decades or even centuries. Asian, Asian American, and Asian European directors do not always focus on Asian subjects (Ang Lee's *Sense and Sensibility*, 1995, and Mira Nair's *Vanity Fair*, 2004).

A central issue of racial identity politics is how to counter stereotypes. Through stereotyping, individual characters often bear the role of representatives of an entire race, something never expected of "white" characters. So-called "good" images are often flat, reductive, and idealized, still dominated by stereotypes they try to correct or replace. Often "good" means helping whites: "good" Indians help white soldiers or settlers defeat "bad" Indians who resist white domination and colonization, and "good" Blacks submit to white domination or identify with their white compatriots or masters (e.g. *Gone with the Wind*, 1939).

One way around the political content of race is to make race identities and relationships (friendships, marriage, etc.) appear matters of individual choice, not institutional imposition. Ideologies based on personal choice often represent "good" Blacks as trying to improve themselves, helped by "good" white race "missionaries," while "bad" Blacks pursue "'hood" activities, and "bad" whites express racism. These plots present white society as open to anyone willing to work hard and live within the law, failing to note the nuances of choices made by ghetto/barrio residents and the real obstacles to making such "free" choices. In such films racism is mediated away as a non-problem or blamed on "bad" people, hoping to lead spectators to presume mistakenly that racism has been overcome.

Narrative conventions and frameworks place stereotypes in larger cultural narratives and current history, in which individuals may be members of overlapping groups, not all of which cohere monolithically in beliefs and experiences. Representations do not represent anything fixed, nor does the receiver necessarily have to "read" the image in the same way as the sender intended. Think, for example, of Black spectators viewing *Gone with the Wind* – they would, and do, have a very different view of the characters and film than do white spectators. Spectators' interpretations are constituted by the images themselves, the current historical circumstances and events in the lives of spectators, and the spectators' individual conditions of race, gender, region, etc. Images not only reflect experience, but also shape and *create* experiences by adding new contexts and reiterations to our experiences through filmic representations. Racial political positions include integration, pluralism, assimilation, and separatism, suggested by filmmakers from a range of racial and political identities.

One foremost issue is who has the authority to represent a particular racial group. Filmmakers of color insert historical characters and events previously ignored in historical accounts (*Zoot Suit*, 1981; *Glory*, 1989; *Amistad*, 1997), promote ethnic success stories (*La Bamba*, 1987; *Selena*, 1997), or "reveal" the hitherto invisible life in racial communities (*Do the Right Thing*, 1989). Does being "inside" that community privilege a director, screenwriter or actor, or can anyone represent any racial content or communities? Some films appeal to both minorities and whites, including cop buddy films (*Lethal Weapon*, 1987; *Pulp Fiction*, 1994; *The Shawshank Redemption*, 1994; *Men in Black*, 1997), female friends movies (*Bhaji on the Beach*, 1993; *The Joy Luck Club*, 1993; *Mi Vida Loca*, 1994; *How Stella Got Her Groove Back*, 1998; *Bend It Like Beckham*, 2002), films of interracial romance (*Jungle Fever*, 1991; *Mississippi Masala*, 1992; *Monster's Ball*, 2001), or films of familial-like ties (*Driving Miss Daisy*, 1989; *Passion Fish*, 1992; *White Men Can't Jump*, 1992; *Secrets and Lies*, 1996). Some focus on single communities (*Dim Sum*, 1985; *School Daze*, 1988; *Tap*, 1989; *The Five Heartbeats*, 1991; *The Wedding Banquet*, 1993; *My Son the Fanatic*, 1997). In the 1990s, as racial minorities began making and producing films, narratives increasingly embraced multiple identities in communities (*Stand and Deliver*, 1988; *Boyz N the Hood*, 1991; *Barbershop*, 2002). Related to this is the ghettoizing notion that a director or actor of color must only make films about people of color, which is not required of them, of course. Mark Reid (2005, p. 1) uses the term "Black-oriented film" to describe films with a focus on Black issues and characters, but not made by black directors or screenwriters.

Filmic associations of ethnicity with violence (starting in the 1970s with blaxploitation films of gangs and Black mafia) have persisted (*Zoot Suit*, 1981; *The Color Purple*, 1985; *Colors*, 1988; *American Me*, 1992), reinforcing fears about ethnic groups and reviving nineteenth-century notions of people of color as "savage." The aesthetic of cinematic violence may also work against moral messages (*New Jack City*, 1991). But these films can also offer explanations of how violence is constructed out of political, social, and economic inequities, themselves violent institutional forces. Unlike blaxploitation films of the 1970s, with their relatively static characters, Black films of the 1990s offer complex character development, often through rites of passage that integrate ghetto survivors into society. These films are dystopian *and* utopian in exploring violence as a social problem constructed by the state. As S. Craig Watkins (1998, pp. 196–218) notes, representations of post-industrial ghetto life in music and film (e.g. *Menace II Society*, 1993) can present counter-discourses that cannot be spoken in other films. Debates continue about whether these films highlight ghetto nihilism or critique the larger society.

Directors of color must still work within systems of visual and cinematic conventions, ideologies, and expectations, even to find different voices, activist aesthetics, and new representations. Hollywood movies' changing structural and institutional factors affect representations of race, as they do of gender. Genre, in turn, is engaged in racial representations (e.g. Native Americans and Mexicans in Westerns). Racial films test, intervene, parody, modify, or create new genres. In the film *El Mariachi* (1993) the ethnicity of the protagonists affects the "warrior adventure" film genre, indicating not only genres' categorical fluidity, but also how changes in protagonists' race and ethnicity (and gender) affect generic structures and spectators' expectations. Structure and content inflect each other and viewers' expectations, beliefs, and prejudices. Many films simultaneously parody, invert, and resist stereotypes and genres (*Hollywood Shuffle*, 1987; film noir in *Chan Is Missing*, 1982; musicals in *Malcolm X*, 1992) to introduce resistant images of racially identified characters, sites (ghetto or barrio), and stories (rags-to-riches, morality versus materialism, assimilation versus racial community identity).

Race films have a special relationship to "realism," perhaps parallel to the relationship of gender representation to sexual fantasies. Realism, as some scholars have pointed out, is often tied to the depiction of a gritty world.

But realism, the representation of what is presumed to be "real," is a construct that reflects political structures and domination, not some objective "truth." What is considered realism often imposes closure on issues that in our experience remain unstable, unresolved, and unexamined. Realism assumes a passive audience that does not question the hierarchy, "truths," and beliefs privileged in the cultural work as "true" or "real."

Audience interpretations are inflected by their own historical experiences: race issues in the USA (where slavery defined racial histories and relations) are different from representations in the UK (where colonialism, including the slave trade, defined racial histories and relations). Audiences' interpretations depend on their individual experiences and their group identities, which are plural, overlapping, or even contradictory (e.g. a white female may have power as white but be subordinate as female and experience and identify with both culturally represented identities). Films construct spectators as national, gendered, racialized, generational beings and do so differently from film to film, or differently within a single film. Many studies find profound differences among responses by white, Black, Latino, and Asian audiences to the same films, news clips, TV shows. Spectators have their own "raced ways of seeing," to use Darnell Hunt's phrase (Hunt, 1996, p. 144).

Reception plays an important role in the content of films with racial content and in the films' perceived ironies, parodies, and politics. Race in films is always in dialogue with current political and social policies, such as US anti-Asian immigration policies in 1882 against the Chinese and in 1908 against the Japanese and Koreans, the civil rights movement from the late 1950s through the 1970s, UCLA's 1968 Ethno-Communications program and its offshoot the Asian American Visual Communications group, the American Indian Movement in the 1980s, various film collectives in the UK, and conservative politics of the 1980s in the USA and the UK. Social changes may revert to prejudicial attitudes, even after years of "progress," as happened in the USA and Europe in the 1980s.

Readings in this part touch on multiple racial issues and groups, as well as on the intersection of race with genre (Dan Florry on film noir and Nicola Evans on the interracial family genre) and with gender (Gina Marchetti's essay examines homosexuality in the Chinese American community). Strong's essay addresses animated films for children in which stereotypes are especially insidious and their messages subliminal in perpetuating racism. Most of these essays question sharp divisions of race and the hyphenated nature of racial and national identities (African American, Asian American, Asian British). Gilroy explores how an oral tradition in some Native American cultures can be incorporated into film, an issue that also anticipates topics of world cinema in part IV.

Further Reading

Benshoff, Harry and Griffin, Sean (eds) (2004) *America on Film: Representing Race, Class, Gender and Sexuality at the Movies.* Oxford: Blackwell.

Berg, Charles Ramirez (1996) "Ethnic Ingenuity and Mainstream Cinema: Robert Rodríguez's *Bedhead* (1990) and *El Mariachi* (1993)." In Chon A. Noriega and Ana M. López (eds), *The Ethnic Eye: Latino Media Arts.* Minneapolis: University of Minnesota Press, pp. 107–28.

Bernardi, Daniel (ed.) (1996) *The Birth of Whiteness: Race and the Emergence of US Cinema.* New Brunswick, NJ: Rutgers University Press.

Bernardi, Daniel (ed.) (2001) *Classic Hollywood, Classic Whiteness.* Minneapolis: University of Minnesota Press.

Bird, S. Elizabeth (ed.) (1996) *Dressing in Feathers: The Construction of the Indian in American Popular Culture.* Boulder, CO: Westview Press.

Churchill, Ward (1988) *Fantasies of the Master Race: Literature, Cinema and the Colonization of American Indians.* San Francisco: City Lights.

Denzin, Norman K. (2002) *Reading Race: Hollywood and the Cinema of Racial Violence.* London: Sage.

Diawara, Mantia (ed.) (1993) *Black American Cinema.* New York: Routledge.

Dyer, Richard (1998) "White." *Screen*, 29(4), 44–65; also chapter 13 in Dyer (2002) *The Matter of Images: Essays on Representations*, 2nd edn. London: Routledge, pp. 126–48.

Feng, Peter (2002) *Identities in Motion: Asian American Film and Video.* Durham, NC, and London: Duke University Press.

Fine, Michelle et al. (eds) (2004) *Off White: Readings on Power, Privilege, and Resistance*, 2nd edn. London: Routledge.

Fregoso, Rosa Linda (1993) *The Bronze Screen: Chicana and Chicano Film Culture.* Minneapolis: University of Minnesota Press.

Friedman, Lester (ed.) (1991) *Unspeakable Images: Ethnicity and the American Cinema.* Urbana: University of Illinois Press.

Guerrero, Ed (1993) *Framing Blackness: The African American Image in Film.* Philadelphia: Temple University Press.

Hall, Stuart (1998) "What Is This 'Black' in Black Popular Culture?" In Valerie Smith (ed.), *Representing Blackness: Issues in Film and Video.* London: Routledge, pp. 123–33.

Hamilton, Marsha J. and Block, Eleanor S. (2003) *Projecting Ethnicity and Race: An Annotated Bibliography of Studies on Imagery in American Film.* Westport, CT, and London: Praeger.

Hunt, Darnell (1996) *Screening the Los Angeles "Riots."* New York: Cambridge University Press.

Kilpatrick, Jacquelyn (1999) *Celluloid Indians: Native Americans and Film.* Lincoln: University of Nebraska Press.

McKelly, James (1998) "Raising Cain in a Down Eden: *Menace II Society* and the Death of Signifyin(g)." *Screen*, 39(1), 36–52.

Marchetti, Gina (1993) *Romance and the "Yellow Peril."* Berkeley: University of California Press.

Massood, Paula J. (2003) *Black City: African American Urban Experiences in Film*. Philadelphia: Temple University Press.

Noriega, Chon A. (1992) *Chicanos and Film: Essays on Chicano Representation and Resistance*. New York and London: Garland.

Noriega, Chon A. (2000) *Shot in America: Television, the State, and the Rise of Chicano Cinema*. Minneapolis: University of Minnesota Press.

Noriega, Chon A. and López, Ana M. (eds) (1996) *The Ethnic Eye: Latino Media Arts*. Minneapolis: University of Minnesota Press.

Reid, Mark A. (1993) *Redefining Black Film*. Berkeley: University of California Press.

Reid, Mark A. (ed.) (1997) *Spike Lee's Do the Right Thing*. Cambridge: Cambridge Film Handbooks.

Reid, Mark A. (2000) "New Wave Black Cinema in the 1990s." In Wheeler Winston Dixon (ed.), *Film/Genre 2000*. Albany: State University of New York Press, pp. 13–28.

Reid, Mark A. (2005) *Black Lenses, Black Voices: African American Film Now*. Lanham, MD: Rowman and Littlefield.

Slethuag, Gordon E. (2003) "Hurricanes and Fires: Chaotics in Sherman Alexie's 'Smoke Signals' and 'The Lone Ranger and Tonto Fistfight in Heaven'." *Literature Film Quarterly*, 31, 130–40.

Tsung-Yi Huang (2001) "*Chungking Express*: Walking with a Map of Desire in the Mirage of the Global City." *Quarterly Review of Film and Video*, 18, 129–42.

Voss, Karen (1998) "Replacing LA: *Mi Familia, Devil in a Blue Dress*, and Screening the Other Los Angeles." *Wide Angle*, 20(3), 157–81.

Watkins, S. Craig (1998) *Representing: Hip Hop Culture and the Production of Black Cinema*. Chicago: University of Chicago Press.

Willis, Sharon (1997) *High Contrast: Race and Gender in Contemporary Hollywood Film*. Durham, NC, and London: Duke University Press.

Wong, Eugene (1979) *On Visual Media Racism: Asians in the American Motion Pictures*. Manchester, NH: Ayer Company Publishers.

Xing, Jun (1998) "Cinematic Asian Representation." In Jun Xing (ed.), *Asian America through the Lens: History, Representations, and Identity*. London: Altamira/Sage, pp. 53–86.

Xing, Jun and Hirabayashi, Lane Ryo (eds) (2003) *Reversing the Lens: Ethnicity, Race, Gender and Sexuality through Film*. Boulder: University of Colorado Press.

Young, Lola (1996) *Fear of the Dark: "Race," Gender and Sexuality in the Cinema*. London: Routledge.

13

The Family Changes Colour: Interracial Families in Contemporary Hollywood Cinema

Nicola Evans

How profound the hatred, how deep the bigotry . . . that wakens in this image of black life blooming within white. . . . It is an image that squeezes racism out from the pores of people who deny they are racist.

Patricia Williams[1]

In December 1998, DNA tests identified Thomas Jefferson as the father of at least one child with his black slave woman Sally Hemings. The discovery spawned numerous commentaries in the media on the significance of this finding and many large claims were made. Superficially what was at stake was the right of Hemings's descendants to claim Jefferson as an ancestor and to be buried in the Monticello family plot, a right long contested by some of Jefferson's white descendants who control the foundation and the graveyard. But there were many who saw the decision as symbolic not just of a past that the USA had erased, but a future towards which it might tend. For Lucian Truscott IV, a white Jeffersonian descendant who supports the Hemings's claim, the finding affirmed that this country 'is a family not only in democratic theory, but in blood'.[2] Allusions to the national family were quickly buttressed by parallels drawn between Jefferson and William Jefferson Clinton, another president accused of extramarital liaisons, whose 1992 campaign was attended by rumours that he had fathered a black child.[3] Lisa Jones, writing in the *Village Voice*, summed up the tenor of many commentaries by declaring 'I can't think of a more potent metaphor of American race relations at the millennium than the battle over graveyard space at Monticello'.[4]

Nicola Evans, "The Family Changes Colour: Interracial Families in Contemporary Hollywood Cinema," pp. 271–92 from *Screen* 43:3 (Oxford: Oxford University Press, Autumn 2002). © 2002 by The John Logie Baird Centre. Reprinted by permission of the author and Oxford University Press.

The findings of the Monticello committee capped a decade in which a surprising number of films, both mainstream and art-house, began to explore familial ties that cross the colour line. Some of these films, such as *Made in America* (Richard Benjamin, 1993), *Secrets and Lies* (Mike Leigh, 1996) and *A Family Thing* (Richard Pearce, 1996), have plots reminiscent of abolitionist literature, in which the discovery of an interracial relationship in the past throws the family into melodramatic disarray. Other films, including *Six Degrees of Separation* (Fred Schepisi, 1993), *Smoke* (Wayne Wang, 1995), *Losing Isaiah* (Stephen Gyllenhaal, 1995) and *Finding Forrester* (Gus van Sant, 2000), feature whites who become symbolic parents to black children, often with the suggestion that these metaphorical ties are more rewarding than the relationships the parents have with their own white children. The question this paper considers is whether the growing screen presence of the interracial family is a step forward in the task of imagining more democratic race relations. If our concept of the family changed colour – from white to something more multicoloured – would this strengthen and improve interracial bonds as many activists through history have insisted, or is the fight for inclusion in the family plot indeed a fight for graveyard space?

For mainstream films to be considering interracial relations at all is a departure. When it comes to race Hollywood has toed the colour line, producing either all-black films, or white-cast films with token representation of African-Americans. The rare instances in which interracial relations occur are designed to be temporary, or to end tragically.[5] Even the black and white buddy movie, the most popular format for including interraciality, typically suppresses or evades racial issues through rousing paeans to the race-transcendent bonds of masculinity.[6] For mainstream films to be exploring interracial families is startling. Both on screen and off, the taboo against race-mixing within the family has seemed particularly strong. In the quotation that heads this paper, Patricia Williams suggests that the image of a mother suckling a child of another race is an idea that sticks in the gullet of even those who are most liberal on race issues. Benetton, a company famous for its taboo-breaking advertisements, appeared to agree when in 1989 they cancelled a campaign that proposed to feature a poster of a black mother breast-feeding a white child.[7] What is special about the family that makes the imagination balk at the prospect of race-mixing here, even when cautiously permissive of interracial friendships outside the family?

Until recently, the censorship of interraciality on screen was matched by a paucity of interracial studies in scholarship. Gregory Stephens notes the tendency among scholars to pathologize interraciality, viewing every relationship that crosses racial lines as inevitably exploitative or oppressive. As Stephens points out, such an assumption enforces the colour line by making 'any interracial relations beyond rape or genocide unimaginable'.[8] Citing Frederick Douglass's definition of racism as 'diseased imagination', Stephens calls us to begin the task of creating more affirmative scripts for interraciality. It is in the spirit of this work that I examine the representation of interracial families on film. While aiming to stay alert to ways such representations may recycle racist scenarios, my goal is to see whether there is material here with which to envision more equitable relations between blacks and whites across the unnatural chasm of the racial divide.

Although this essay will focus on film, I begin with the Monticello affair because it suggests why the family is such an explosive site for the exploration of race issues. Specifically the Monticello case points to three aspects of the family as an ideological entity: the family as a primary measure of social well-being, the interdependency of family and narrative, and the historical opposition between family values and race values.

The Family Trope

The reverberations of the Jefferson–Hemings story, especially the inclination to read this family affair as a comment on the state of democracy, points to the family's privileged status as the yardstick by which the quality of other social institutions is assessed. Jacques Donzolet refers to what has become 'an essential ritual of our societies to scrutinize the countenance of the family at regular intervals in order to decipher our destiny, glimpsing in the death of the family an impending return to barbarism, the letting go of our reasons for living'.[9] In Roddey Reid's analysis of public discourse on the family, an even stronger claim is made. The family, he suggests, is regarded as the principal institution for 'keeping human beings human'.[10] That is, our value as human beings is determined principally by our performance as family members. Reid traces this idea to the end of the eighteenth century, when people began to be judged less by their social rank and more by their fulfillment of familial responsibilities: 'The question was less "What is your station?" . . . but rather "What kind of father or mother are you?" '[11]

The easy way in which family becomes a surrogate for 'humanity' is suggested by the predominance of family metaphors in new social movements. For the various men's movements of the 1990s, for example, creating a more acceptable form of masculinity meant inventing a more acceptable form of fatherhood. In the cinema, the quest for a gentler, kinder version of manhood produced numerous films in which action heroes learn the importance of paternal values.[12] In everyday situations, too, we use familial language to encourage people to behave more humanely – for example, a woman objecting to a sexual slur may ask the offender whether he would like to see his mother or sister treated that way.[13] Conversely, not having a family – or having the wrong kind – becomes a vehicle of dehumanization. As Kay Weston notes, the equation 'straight is to gay as family is to non-family' has long served as a means by which gays and lesbians are rendered less than human.[14] Small wonder then that the stakes surrounding the family are extremely high when membership in the normative family qualifies you as a human being. Does this make a case for regarding the introduction of interracial families to the screen as an intrinsically progressive move for race

225

relations? If the question 'would you want your daughter to marry one' has been a sticking point for racists, should recognition of interracial families be seen as a powerful countermove, the first step towards bringing down barriers in other areas of social life?

One problem with this idea is that as an ideological unit, the family is repeatedly imagined as divorced from social life, an oasis of intimacy in an unfriendly world. In a brilliant *exposé* of familial ideology, Michele Barrett and Mary McIntosh explain how characterizing the family as the exclusive source of genuine emotion and caring, nurturing relationships works to 'suck the juice out of other institutions'.[15] Making the nuclear family the primary model for human relationships succeeds not just in denigrating other kinds of family arrangements, but also in undermining other forms of sociality. The community, for example, becomes at best a weak imitation of the true and lasting bonds we are supposed to share with family members. In a similar vein, Paul Gilroy points to the problems associated with the popularity of the kinship trope in African-American political discourse.[16] Conceiving of the black community as a family of 'brothers' and 'sisters' works to delegitimize other forms of political agency and association (strengthening the black public sphere, forging transnational solidarities, and so on), and too often supports claims that ending structural discrimination is a matter of reviving the black family.

The family acquires ideological force insofar as it seems to turn its back on other social institutions and can be clearly differentiated from them, retaining its status as a 'natural' and therefore privileged association predicated on the involuntary ties of blood. Yet to a significant degree, the family idealized by the discourse of family values is a narrative entity, constructed in opposition to the ties of blood. This becomes evident in considering what counts as a family.

The Family Circle

The idea that Jefferson had fathered Hemings's children had been a matter of family lore among Hemings's black descendants, preserved through oral narratives, necessarily, because slaves were forbidden to write. Confirmation of a DNA linkage provided support for the oral storyline, against the rival narrative of Jefferson's white descendants who had been able to draw on written documentation to back their version of the family tree. The Monticello affair reveals to what degree families are structures that are kept alive and maintained through stories rather than through blood ties. The shape of this particular family, how far it extended and whom it counted as members, depended very literally on whose story was heard and on which story received social support.

In some well-known lines written for the preface to *Roderick Hudson*, Henry James observes 'Really, universally, relations stop nowhere, and the exquisite problem of the artist is eternally but to draw, by a geometry of his own, the circle within which they shall happily appear to do so'.[17] James is here talking about the problems of narrative, of how in this, his first novel, he experienced the tussle between holding fast to his subject and 'the ache of fear, that was to become so familiar, of being unduly tempted and led on by "developments"'. James attempts to resolve this problem by centring his novel in the consciousness of Rowland Mallett, so that 'this whole was to be the sum of what "happened" to him'.[18]

The strategy adopted by James to resolve the problem of narrative control is similar to the strategy used to solve the problem of kinship relations that really stop nowhere. Anglo-American culture draws the line tightly around a core nuclear unit centred on the father, cutting off more distant kin and designating this small configuration above all others as necessary to individual and social health. Not only is the nuclear family an arbitrary selection from a larger web of blood connections, it is also a unit frequently constructed in opposition to blood relations. Adoption agencies for example, often prefer to place a child with an unrelated set of parents rather than allowing the child to live with members of the extended family, revealing a preference for something that looks like a nuclear family over actual blood ties.[19] As is well documented, families that do not look nuclear – families headed by a single woman, for example – are considered dangerous and disorderly places to raise children, despite the presence of a blood tie. The foundations of the nuclear family are forged out of stories and images, not blood. In her discussion of photography, Susan Sontag observes that parents who do not take pictures of their children are likely to be perceived as inadequate, even unloving parents.[20] Similarly, the breaking of a family tie may be signalled by the name that is never mentioned at dinner, the torn wedding photo, the picture excised from the family album. More than other institutions, the family relies heavily upon its self-representations to stay alive. But the most dramatic example of how little blood matters to the construction of families is the historic opposition between family and race. The line that encircles the nuclear unit, separating off extended relations and dividing family from nonfamily, is also, crucially, a colour line.

Race versus the Family

In a study of interracial literature, Werner Sollors traces the opposition between race and the family to the racial technology developed to support slavery.[21] The prescription of slave status for anyone with a black ancestor, irrespective of the presence of white relatives, allowed racial ancestry to overrule kinship, bringing these two institutions into conflict. The enforcement of a colour line between free whites and subhuman blacks was a line that would cut through the ties of family in the event of interracial unions. White slave owners who fathered children with black women created 'shadow families' of mulatto relatives who could not be acknowledged as kin. If race could erase portions of the family tree, causing close kin to disappear from view because they were the wrong colour, it could also reveal familial relations where none were presumed to exist. A popular theme of interracial literature involved the birth of a black child to white parents. Like a flame that passes over the page to reveal lines of invisible writing, the birth of a black child subverts the official family narrative, pointing to the presence of unknown black grandfathers, or giving rise to the suspicion of extramarital affairs.

The themes that Sollors isolates in abolitionist literature clarify how much the opposition to slavery was rooted in the perception of the way that slavery endangered the family. A favourite storyline in abolitionist literature featured the villainous white patriarch who bred and sold mulatto children for profit, violating the sacred bonds between parents and children. The discovery of unwitting incest, another favoured plot device, served as a warning to supporters of slavery that the colour line was a threat to the sexual sanctity of the family, increasing the risk that whites would commit incest with the half-white brothers, sisters and daughters they did not know they possessed.

Ironically, as Sollors points out, the colour line also threatened patriarchy. Because slave status depended on maternal descent, white men could not pass on their name or inheritance to their mulatto sons, hence interfering in the normal transmission of property that the institution of marriage and family was designed to accomplish. In another way, too, race acted to disrupt the hierarchies of power that governed the nuclear family. The birth of a dusky child to white parents was an immediate source of information on the separate contributions of father and mother to a child. Racial complexion thus challenged the subordination of female identity to patriarchy by providing visible testimony of the importance of both parents to the production of offspring.[22]

In history and in fiction, the exclusion of racial difference from the family narrative makes race into the family's worst enemy, undermining patriarchal control, subverting the orderly distribution of power within the family, registering the presence of forces and relations both outside and inside the family that distract from the orderly succession of father to son. The opposition of race and family continues to mark contemporary debates on racial issues, although now the pressure to deny family members out of loyalty to one's racial community is as likely to come from blacks as from whites. When, for example, the National Association for the Advancement of Colored People called upon biracial individuals in the USA to identify themselves as African-American on the 2000 Census, they were requiring that race should trump family; that what was owed to white family members should be suppressed in favour of allegiance to the black community. Conversely, when advocates of transracial adoption recommend that black children should be placed with white families when no black family is available, they presume that family trumps race – that the value of living in a family outweighs the value of contacts with one's racial heritage.[23]

The tension between race and family is a pervasive presence in the films discussed here. In the first two films, a white man comes into contact with his 'shadow family' and undergoes a personal transformation as a result. Although these two films ostensibly celebrate an antiracist perspective, the perception of the family as the private property of a white patriarch turns the interracial family into a device for rejuvenating white male authority at the expense of black men. Family functions in these films as the outer boundary of racial progress, drawing a line between what can be accomplished in personal relationships and the supposedly irresolvable racial tensions of the public sphere. In the second two films, race interferes more productively with our notions of what constitutes a family, inviting reflection on what families are for, why they are dangerous, and how the tension between race and family loyalties might be renegotiated.

White Fathers, Black Donors

The plot of *Made in America* turns on the discovery by Zorah, a black high school student, that her mother gave birth to her through a sperm donor. A visit to the sperm bank produces the information that Zorah's biological father is a white car salesman called Hal (Ted Danson). The news horrifies Zorah and her mother Sarah (Whoopi Goldberg), both highly educated, professional women. Zorah, a gifted science student, has by the close of the film won a scholarship to MIT, Sarah runs a store in Berkeley specializing in African books and artefacts. Following the discovery, both Zorah and her mother make several inexplicable visits to Hal's truck emporium, inexplicable because Hal would seem a poor object for their enthusiasm. As a salesman of all-American trucks, Hal looks like a Marlboro man gone to seed. His job consists of dressing up in gaudy cowboy gear to participate in television commercials featuring circus animals. Zorah is nonetheless keen to claim him. The pull of biological ties is, we are led to believe, sufficient to override racial and class differences.

Hal offers us an image of a white male icon depleted and reduced by the marketplace into a commercial joke. We first encounter Hal lying in bed exhausted after a vigorous bout of lovemaking with his girlfriend, a fanatic aerobics instructor. Commercially Hal is not doing well either. His girlfriend suggests that he start another enterprise, marketing classical violin music with a rap beat, because rap, unlike the white-identified classical music, is big business. The title of the film, *Made in America*, continues the theme of commerce by alluding to a product, and the product most obviously declining in value is Hal, whose name has become part of a cheesy slogan to sell his All-American trucks ('Hal's your pal!'). The thrust of the film is to give Hal back his name, by elevating him to the more respectable position of fatherhood. As Hal's interest in his biological daughter grows, and as he forms a relationship with Sarah, he cleans up his act, throwing out the junk food, pouring away the whisky and giving up cigarettes. In the final scene of the film, when Zorah accepts her scholarship at a graduation ceremony, Hal receives public affirmation of his role as father by Zorah in front of a jubilant crowd.

However, the title of the film also refers to Zorah's conception. She was not born but *made* in a test tube with sperm bought from a *bank*. The narrative of the film works to rewrite her origins and to remove the taint of the marketplace from the family by restoring to Zorah a father who falls conveniently in love with her mother. It is no coincidence that each time Zorah and Sarah visit Hal's truck emporium they interrupt a financial transaction. On her first trip, Zorah causes havoc in the commercial that Hal is shooting with a bear. After Zorah's visit, Sarah arrives to disrupt a commercial that Hal is shooting with an elephant. The entrance of kin is in this way staged to interfere with profit, underlining the sacred, noncommercial status of family relations.

Whereas Hal is rejuvenated by finding his lost family, the effects on the black women are damaging. The rehabilitation of Hal requires that he be given back not only his name but also his patriarchal authority. And this means curtailing, symbolically, the freedom of the black woman whose choice of a sperm bank threatens to sideline the contributions of men to procreation. Sarah begins the film as an independent, politically aware black woman, riding her bicycle through the lively multicultural streets of Berkeley to her store, The African Queen. By the end of the film she is on crutches. As Hal cleans up his act we watch Sarah get drunk, crash her bicycle and eventually end up in hospital, affording Hal the opportunity to step into the role of provider. The restoration of the family diminishes the woman – after Sarah becomes involved with Marlboro Man Hal she is increasingly featured in the home, engaged in domestic tasks such as sewing.

Meanwhile Hal's paternal responsibilities towards his putative daughter appear to consist largely in protecting her sexuality. Zorah's sexual vulnerability is accordingly overemphasized to spell out the need for a paternal protector. She has a date with a Latino man that ends in an attempted seduction, but because the Latino is Hal's employee we are assured that she can be protected from him. Even in hospital a black doctor gratuitously remarks that Zorah is 'hot', giving Hal the opportunity to assert himself as her father and silence the doctor.

The unpleasant spectacle of a white man assuming paternal rights at the expense of nonwhite men cast as sexual predators is foreshadowed early on in the film during the visit to the sperm bank. While Zorah attempts to gain access to the computer records, we glimpse a heavy-set muscular black man leaving down the corridor after having made an apparently successful donation of sperm. Immediately following this scene we are introduced to Hal as a middle-aged man exhausted from the physical effort of satisfying his young girlfriend. The pairing of these scenes institutes a hierarchy between black men who furnish the biological materials for family and white men who, not able to compete sexually, are nonetheless presented as the best candidates for fatherhood. To ensure that this contest is no contest, the only black men featured in *Made in America* are either gay (Sarah's assistant at the store), feminized (Zorah's would-be boyfriend, the hapless T-cake) or dead (Sarah's first husband). In a plot twist at the end of the film we discover that the computer records were faulty and that Zorah's father is in fact black. But he remains anonymous, like the donor we glimpse at the sperm bank. The discovery does not prompt Zorah to initiate a new search. Instead, the film would have us believe that Hal has so successfully embodied paternity that the actual black father is unnecessary. The fiction of natural blood ties sufficient to override racial difference is exposed as a preference for something that looks like a family, a unit headed by a white man.

At a pivotal moment in the film, Hal is shown watching *The Little Princess* on television, the sentimental children's story in which Shirley Temple loses her father and finds a new one. As Hal watches the scene, he looks at a photo of Zorah. The substitution of a white daughter for a black one is revealing. Although *Made in America* would have us believe that family transcends racial difference, the care taken by the film to avoid interracial sex suggests that race matters enormously. There are three moments in the film when the possibility of interracial sex is explicitly disavowed. The first is the mistake made by the sperm bank in using a white donor for a black woman's conception, a mistake that turns out not to have been made. The second occurs during Hal's first encounter with Zorah and before he knows that she may be his daughter. Hal has trouble with the zipper in his pants and Zorah kneels down to help him. The frightened face of the secretary who catches them in this position gives the audience the chance to confuse shock at the sight of fellatio with shock at the sight of a mixed race couple. Furthermore, since the audience believes that Zorah is Hal's daughter, the spectre of incest offers another reason to justify discomfort with this scene and motivates the desire to see Hal publicly acknowledged as Zorah's father. The third way in which this film denies the interraciality that it ostensibly embraces is through the casting of Whoopi Goldberg. As Tania Modleski has observed, the career of this actress on screen is marked by a certain gender ambiguity, reinforced by the number of films in which she is literally or metaphorically substituting for a man (for example, *Jumpin' Jack Flash* [Penny Marshall, 1986], *Ghost* [Jerry Zucker, 1990] and *The Associate* [Donald Petrie, 1996]).[24] In other films, Goldberg plays the nanny whose task is to nurse the white boy (*Clara's Heart* [Robert Mulligan, 1988]) or the white man (*Corrinna, Corrinna* [Jessie Nelson, 1994]) through trauma. The choice of Whoopi Goldberg as the romantic partner for Ted Danson, best known as the infantile Sam from the television comedy *Cheers* (Paramount, tx 1982–93), may suggest the degree to which her desexualized persona and her reputation as a comic provides a safety net for the audience, insulating them from having to accept that anything sexual will ever take place.[25]

The construction of the interracial family as a defence against racial difference and as a refuge for white men is particularly evident in *A Family Thing*. Earl (Robert Duvall) runs a hardware store in Arkansas. Following the death of his mother he discovers that his real mother was a black maid coerced into sex by his father. The discovery effectively deprives Earl of his rights to white masculinity and it will be the task of the film to restore him to his former status. When Earl journeys to Chicago to meet his black half-brother Ray (James Earl Jones), he suffers a series of humiliations that emphasize his fall from grace. He is beaten up by a group of young black men, stripped of his wallet (and identity), thrown out of a bar when seen to be bothering a black family, and ultimately spends a night sleeping with the homeless under a bridge. Earl's vulnerability in the city streets is repeatedly contrasted with the superior urban know-how of Ray, a policeman working in downtown Chicago. Once again the interracial family offers the white man a means of rehabilitation and a way to prevail in these racial rivalries. As Earl takes refuge from the dangerous streets by staying with Ray and his family, he gradually replaces his black brother as the head of the household by taking over paternal responsibilities for Ray's troubled son Virgil. The transfer of fathers is captured in a scene in which Earl dispenses paternal advice to Virgil on how to put his life back together (advice given, significantly, in the form of a story about a man who adopted a son). Once more a family thing becomes a male thing – Earl's trip to Chicago to see Ray begins with the death of his white mother, and ends at the grave of his black biological mother, the two men bonding as they gaze at her tombstone. And by emphasizing the family as a haven from the racial tensions of the public sphere, the film makes the interracial family anti-social, as the exceptional and only place where racial tensions can be resolved (in favour of white men), not the first step towards remaking race relations in society.

Made in America and *A Family Thing* are classical Hollywood narratives. The problem of a racial transgression that upsets race and gender hierarchies prompts a quest for order that is successfully completed by the restoration of the family unit. The two films considered in the next section turn this equation on its head, making family the problem, not the solution to questions of race. More formally complex, both *Six Degrees of Separation* and *Smoke* disturb temporal continuities to challenge the orderly succession of generations that is part of the official understanding of how families are meant to work. Both films take the act of narration as their subject. The characters of these films borrow, steal and trade stories in order to secure a place in a variety of relational configurations, making explicit the connection between making families and telling stories and questioning the inevitability of the nuclear master plot. In *Six Degrees* and *Smoke*, relations really stop nowhere, an idea that invites us to consider the dangers of making families such exclusive enclosures and to ask whether crossing the colour line might entail breaching the family circle.

White Parents, Black Sons

Six Degrees of Separation relates the story of a young black man, Paul (Will Smith), who inveigles his way into the homes of rich white families by pretending to be the son of Sydney Poitier. The first home we see him entering belongs to an art dealer and his wife, Flan and Ouisa Kittredge (Donald Sutherland and Stockard Channing), who narrate the story piece by piece to various sets of people in their elite social circle. The story, as they tell it, begins one evening in their New York apartment. The Kittredges are playing host to a rich white South African, Jeffrey, hoping that he will lend them two million dollars for a deal that Flan is brokering to buy a Cezanne. When the talk turns to the prospect of a visit to South Africa, the Kittredges trade quips about the racial privileges they enjoy – the problems of talking about oppressed blacks from a comfortable penthouse on the East Side. Already in these remarks there is a hint of the liberal guilt that this film will exploit. If they went to South Africa, Ouisa remarks, they would see only what they expected to see – the poor suffering blacks, a tourist's view of apartheid. The desire for 'real' difference appears to be answered when a young black man bursts in, claiming to be a friend of their children, the son of Sydney Poitier, and the victim of a street mugging which has caused him to seek the help of the Kittredge couple. Just how much 'difference' the Kittredges are capable of tolerating is a question raised by the film's careful choreography of this arrival. Flan and his financier are admiring a print of the Cezanne painting. We see a closeup of the painting as Flan rhapsodizes on Cezanne's artistry in making a burst of colour 'carry the weight of the whole picture'. Gradually the painting goes out of focus, and as it is lowered, the camera refocuses on Paul standing behind it, framed in the doorway supported by the doorman and Ouisa. The timing of Paul's entrance to coincide with Flan's discussion of colour instructs us in the superficiality of Flan's understanding of racial difference and in the aesthetic appreciation that will dominate his responses to Paul. As the explanations begin, the camera cuts to a long shot in which the two groups, Flan and the financier at one end, his wife with Paul and the doorman at the other, appear to be standing at a great distance from one another. The separation of the wealthy white men from those who too often depend on them is a subtle reminder of the true chasm that such superficial good intentions will never cross.

Throughout the evening, 'Paul Poitier' charms his hosts. Dressed in preppy clothes, he cooks them an exquisite dinner, alludes to a childhood in Switzerland, offers them parts in his father's new movie of *Cats*, and concludes with a rendition of his thesis on the subject of J. D. Salinger's book *Catcher in the Rye*, discoursing so eloquently on the debasement of the imagination in modern literature that he moves Flan to tears. Next morning, Ouisa discovers Paul in bed with a white male hustler and in panic and anger the Kittredges eject him from the apartment. As the plot unfolds, the Kittredges discover they are the not the only ones to have been romanced by Paul: another white couple has played host to the son of Poitier, and subsequently they meet a third victim, a white Jewish doctor who also invited Paul home believing that he was a friend of his son.

Paul enters the lives of these white families as the perfect son, everything that their own children are not. When the Kittredges team up with Paul's other victims to solve the mystery of Paul's visits, we are treated to multiple scenes of vituperative family quarrels. Each of the couples we meet is locked into a bitter battle with their children. The Kittredge children rage and snarl at their parents. The doctor's son taunts his father for his stupidity, his lack of virility and his divorce. 'Your father was right, you are a fool!' screams the waitress at her boyfriend, the last couple that Paul visits and charms. Paul with his deference, his polished manners, his intelligence and his eagerness to learn about art is very obviously the son that Flan does not have – that no-one has. Significantly, after his visit to the Kittredge couple Paul changes his act and begins to pass himself off as Flan Kittredge's illegitimate black son. The film offers us other signs of Paul's symbolic filial status. In a dream that Ouisa narrates, she sees Paul outside her bedroom window, inflicting a wound on his side that echoes the figure of Jesus, the ultimate ideal son. Finally, as the unexpected guest at the Kittredge dinner party, Paul mimics the most famous role of the man he claims as father, the role of talented son-in-law to white parents played by Sydney Poitier in *Guess Who's Coming To Dinner* (Stanley Kramer, 1967).

The battle for power between parents and children finds an analogy in the unravelling of narrative authority. The Kittredges are the chief narrators of these events, but they are not in control of the story they tell, any more than they can control their children. The first discovery that the Kittredges make is that their encounter is part of a larger plot that started earlier; they are merely second-to-last in the sequence of Paul's impersonations. And what they discover about the origins of this masquerade presents a further challenge to both familial and narrative hierarchy. Enlisting the help of their children, the Kittredges track down a white gay man, Trent Conway, who was a friend of their children at boarding school. It was Trent who picked Paul up in the street and, in an attack of Pygmalion fever, made him over, teaching him how to talk, how to act among the rich and sharing with him information about his friends and their families in return for sexual favours. In a sense the story that the Kittredges tell of meeting the son of Sydney Poitier was authored by their children, who passed it on to their friend, Trent, who created the Paul Poitier who arrived to rock the house that Flan built. 'You have no secrets', Paul tells Ouisa on the phone – her children have told them all.

The degree to which the Kittredges are part of a larger plot that exceeds their narrative grasp is foregrounded in the flashbacks that are woven into their story. For example, their account of the evening of Paul's visit is interspersed with scenes of Paul rehearsing his performance to the gay man who picked him up, emphasizing that the stories Paul tells them are the product of stories he was told, just as his eloquent discourse on Salinger turns out to be borrowed from a commencement address at Groton. However, if the story that the Kittredges tell is part of a larger network of narratives, crossing class and age lines, this larger narrative stops abruptly at the racial borders. What nobody in the film can discover is Paul's real name and background. Paul enters the film as a white fiction, the product of the white gay man who worked the makeover. His own background and origins remain hidden.[26] What the Kittredges see in Paul is an image that was tailored to their specifications, calculated to appeal to them on the basis of what Trent knew from their own children. The film thus draws the family circle tight again, so that the black man becomes a white invention, a story authored by the Kittredge children and handed on through various mediators. When the Kittredges think they are reaching out to help a young black man, they are merely responding to a reflection that they themselves produce. The proliferating narrators and expanding stories remain locked within a racially homogenous family circle. It is this claustrophobic reduction of families that the film works to uncover and oppose.

Paul's exclusion from the family narrative is dramatized by his ending. Like his origins, the story of what happens to Paul in the end eludes the film's narration. Having promised to help him and to treat him as her son, Ouisa agrees to accompany Paul to the police. But she arrives too late and Paul disappears into the criminal justice system. As Ouisa trudges from precinct to precinct, she is told she cannot track Paul because she does not know his name and 'he is not family'. Paul's story remains in darkness, outside the incestuous inbreeding of stories in *Six Degrees*. Family becomes emblematic of the chasm existing between white and black worlds, a mechanism for keeping racial difference out. By the end of the film Ouisa is voicing her dissatisfaction with both her stories and her family.

Throughout *Six Degrees* our attention is drawn to the disjuncture between the act of narration and the events that are to be narrated. The film shifts between two and sometimes three time-zones, using flashbacks to shuttle us back and forth between the events that happened to the Kittredges, their account of these events to various acquaintances, and Paul's rehearsals with Trent. The foregrounding of the act of narration accomplishes two things. First, it emphasizes that Paul is a fictional creation of white people meant to serve their own interests. The tale of Paul Poitier is a story on which the Kittredges dine out and which increases their value at the social functions integral to Flan's business as an art dealer. This is one of the accusations that Ouisa hurls at Flan in the film's denouement. Having been invited to once more sing for their supper, Ouisa reproaches herself and Flan for the way they have packaged and sold Paul as a story: 'And we turned him into an anecdote to dine out on . . . have we become these human jukeboxes spilling out these anecdotes?' The Kittredges are not the only culprits in this regard. In the flashbacks to Paul's rehearsals he stares directly into the camera while he practises his story and begins to take off his clothing. Trent remains out of frame, his presence in that room not revealed until much later. Paul's seductive routine is thus aimed at the offscreen audience as well as the wealthy couples he targets, a move that may encourage some viewers of this film to reflect on their own complicity in accepting racial difference when it comes in forms that are palatable to whites.[27]

The second thing accomplished by the separation of tale from teller is to highlight the discrepancy between where the Kittredges begin their story and where the film chooses to begin. The Kittredge story follows the order of their discoveries, starting with their evening playing host to Jeffrey and their gradual discovery of the larger story of which they are a part. The film, conversely, opens on a scene of panic. The Kittredges are rushing around their apartment, crying out that they could have been killed, frantically checking to see whether any of their most valuable art possessions have been stolen. Only later do we learn that these moments of chaos are the result of discovering Paul in bed with a white hustler. The opening of the film thus grants an originary force to the revelation that Paul is gay. Moreover, the scene in which Ouisa goes to wake Paul, hears the sounds of lovemaking as she approaches the bedroom door, and shrieks at the sight of Paul in the arms of a white man – this scene plays very much like a primal scene. However, not only is the order of the primal scene inverted – it is a parent who happens on the lovemaking of a man in her son's bedroom – but the substitution of homosexual for heterosexual copulation rattles the entire structure of the nuclear family. The film invokes homosexual couplings twice more. The last couple that Paul visits, a pair of young would-be actors, is an affair that ends tragically when Paul seduces the young man who later commits suicide. During the final dinner party, Ouisa again evokes a homoerotic dimension, accusing her husband Flan of being attracted to Paul. Although her words are ambiguous, Flan's immediate and abrupt denial ('Oh please, cut me out of that pathology right now') successfully allows the homosexual dimension to emerge as a latent possibility.

What Paul brings to the Kittredge couple is the potential for relations outside the airless box of the family structure. 'There was colour in my life', Ouisa mourns at the end, and her words recall the careful rhyming of Paul's arrival in the Kittredge home with the discussion of colour in the Cezanne painting. As 'coloured man' and as gay man, Paul occupies an extrafamilial position. The image of a black and a white man embracing powerfully summons up that alternative American love story described by Leslie Fiedler, in which the American hero departs family and civilization to find redemption in the arms of a black man.[28] The relegation of black and white unions to the wilderness reflects an inability to imagine anything beyond the family. This inability is represented in the Kittredge's prize possession: a double-sided Kandinsky, one side showing geometric precision, the other, abstract chaos. There are apparently only two options, either the excruciating claustrophobia of the ordered white family, or the chaos imagined to occur when race and sexual difference are allowed in, nothing in between.

In *Six Degrees*, the entrance of a black man into the closely-knit world of upper-class whites acts like a stone flung into a pond. Although the ripples spread and widen to encompass more and more people, the pattern they create monotonously repeats itself, demonstrating the difficulties of breaking out of the family circle. The eager adoption of Paul by this succession of white couples points to a yearning for an alternative to the nuclear family. But while *Six Degrees* lays bare the dysfunction of these families and the tight and ultimately degenerate insularity of the world they produce, it can only gesture towards what might lie beyond.

Reinventing the Family: *Smoke*

A white man meanders along a sidewalk in New York. Colours are drab, washed-out and the air is dense with the haze of a hot summer in the city. As the man steps off the pavement a black hand reaches into the frame like the hand of fate and pulls him out of the path of an approaching truck. The camera pauses for the barest instant on the two men, one black, one white, lying on the ground and then cuts quickly to the aftermath, as the white man earnestly asks if he can buy his rescuer a cup of coffee to 'balance the scales'. This scene from early in the film *Smoke* suggests the similarities between *Smoke* and *Six Degrees* as well as some of the more crucial differences. Both films have plots centred on fortuitous connections forged between strangers as the result of an encounter with a young black man. The white man in the scene described above is a middle-aged writer called Paul Benjamin (William Hurt). Like Paul Poitier in *Six Degrees*, the arrival of a young black man, Rashid Cole (Harold Perrineau), injects 'colour' and 'vitality' into the lives of the white characters. Once Rashid moves into Benjamin's apartment, the seedy browns and off-whites that have dominated the colour scheme until now are replaced with dark, rich reds, greens, and the dazzling light of early morning sunshine coming through the apartment bay window. However, there the resemblances end, for there is a significant tonal difference in the way that *Smoke* handles quite similar material. Whereas *Six Degrees* inhabits a hyperemotional terrain, punctuating the action with heated outbursts and intense confrontations, the interactions in *Smoke* are more muted. Confrontations are rare, and when a moment of drama occurs, as in the narrowly avoided accident described above, it is over almost before it begins, quietly allowed to fizzle out or dwindle into a cup of coffee in a cafe. This shift in tone is indicative of where the film locates itself – somewhere in-between the overwrought, pressured intimacies of the nuclear family and the lighter, more casual emotions we reserve for strangers on the street. The temporal structure of the film helps to locate it in everyday life. Although *Smoke* follows a roughly linear chronology, the division of the film into five sections, each named after one of the five major characters, pulls against the forward movement of the narrative. Furthermore, the absence of clear demarcations in time, the blending of days and weeks, and the looping of certain incidents that recur in the characters' lives effectively capture the mix of routine and invention that characterizes the rhythms of the everyday. The sense we have throughout *Smoke* of associations formed by chance, relationships subject to the vagaries of time, place and good fortune, is strengthened by the camera movements. Using mostly long takes, the camera approaches its characters from lovely oblique angles. Frequently the characters are positioned at an angle to one another, just slightly off the axis of action, creating the sense of connections that are tenuous and contingent and that could easily have been missed. By such means *Smoke* permits more complex and open-ended versions of family to emerge.

The world to which *Smoke* introduces us initially is cluttered with the debris of family disasters. Each of the five main characters whose stories are interwoven bears wounds from disintegrating families. Benjamin is a writer who has had trouble completing a novel since the death of his pregnant wife in a street shoot-out. Rashid's mother is dead and his father, Cirus, abandoned him at the age of eight. When Rashid locates Cirus at a run-down garage outside the city, he finds a man who has a hook for a left arm as a reminder of the car crash that killed his wife. Perhaps the happiest character is Augie, owner of the small corner store in New York which acts as the hub of the wheel around which these characters revolve. But Augie, too, will come face to face with family wreckage when he receives a visit from Ruby, an old girlfriend who informs Augie that he may be the father of a drug addict who has just had an abortion.

Each of the characters in *Smoke* is immobilized by their family troubles. Benjamin has writer's block, Augie's hobby is taking pictures of the street corner outside his store, every day at the same time, a powerful suggestion of creativity trapped and penned by routine. Ruby and Cirus carry permanent marks of former failures in the exaggerated disfigurements of their body – a black patch for an eye, a hook for an arm. Of all these characters, only Rashid seems in motion, his restless state marked by the three name changes he undergoes through the film. At their first meeting, the young black man introduces himself to Benjamin as Rashid Cole. His aunt reintroduces him as 'Thomas Jefferson Cole' who has run away from home after hearing that his father has been spotted. And when Rashid finds his father he shifts again, introducing himself this time as 'Paul Benjamin'. The three names with their overdetermined intimations of fatherhood – black fathers, white fathers, founding fathers – seem to suspend Rashid between black worlds and white worlds like a floating signifier in search of an anchor.

Rashid's role in this film carries the sense of liminality that Bill Nichols associates with the portrayal of sons in the cinema.[29] In search of an image of acceptable, non-patriarchal masculinity, Nichols finds potential in the young son who hovers on the point of maturity. He is, in Nichols's view, one of film's more empathetic visions of masculinity, because he is so often shown as poised between the genders, uncertain whether to accept the Law of the Father or to retain his allegiance to the more feminine attributes of relationship and nurturing. It would be tempting to see Rashid as similarly confronting a choice not between genders, but between races, between his black father Cirus and Benjamin, the white man who becomes his substitute father. It is Benjamin who takes Rashid in after their chance encounter in the street, giving him a place to stay, and it is Benjamin's name that Rashid takes when confronting his biological father. After Rashid sees no room for himself in Cirus's new family, he returns to his writer friend, bringing with him a television so that Benjamin and Rashid can sit together watching baseball and smoking cigars, a paradigmatic scene of father–son bonding. And when the gang members who are chasing Rashid visit Benjamin's apartment and beat him up, the writer emerges with his left arm in a sling in a muted echo of the wound that Rashid's black father incurred, as though to signal Benjamin's acceptance of symbolic fatherhood to Rashid. Does *Smoke* then return us to that racist familial narrative in which white men teach the rules of patriarchy to black men, graciously allow them into the family in the subordinate position of admiring sons?

There are in fact several interesting inversions in *Smoke* that militate against such a reading. Is Rashid Benjamin's symbolic son, or is he Benjamin's symbolic father? At one point Benjamin tells Rashid a story that shakes our certainty about the placement of these characters in the family hierarchy. The story concerns a man who goes skiing and is caught by an avalanche, suffocating under the snow. Years later the man's son comes across the body of his father perfectly preserved under the ice, so perfectly that the son is now older than his father. In the following scene Rashid playfully takes up this story when he introduces himself to a woman in the bookstore as Benjamin's father. The story of the man preserved in the ice under snow may refer us to Benjamin's life. He is also iced-in, unable to move forward with his writing or away from the death of his wife, a state from which the encounter with Rashid rescues him. The story is told in the manner of a father passing on what he knows to his son, but the story itself also suggests the viewpoint of a son, imaging the subtle shifts in power that occur in families as children come to feel older than their parents and the gifts of nurture, advice and material support begin to flow in the opposite direction. In this moment, *Smoke* invites us to see family as a dynamic structure in which power is flexible and the order of membership shifts as the family unit ages.

The inversion of hierarchical relationships across racial lines is built into the narrative structure of *Smoke*, which, like *Six Degrees*, spins a web of accidental connections to link its main characters. Consider the trail of money that brings the protagonists of *Smoke* together. Rashid is on the run; he witnessed a robbery and picked up the money dropped by one of the thieves, a member of a black gang which is now pursuing him. Through Benjamin, Rashid finds a job in Augie's cigar store where he accidentally destroys a case of cigars that Augie had illegally imported from Cuba. Rashid gives Augie the money to pay for the cigars and Augie gives the money to his old girlfriend Ruby, a gift that helps to offset the tensions and injuries of their past relationship. Money that began as stolen goods is gradually laundered through these exchanges until it becomes a gift signalling affection. Even when Benjamin has his arm broken by the gang chasing Rashid, he jokes that he will use this incident in a story, making the medical expenses tax-deductible and bringing the chain of gifts full circle.

This complicated pattern of exchanges, debts, thefts and gifts is repeated at the end of the film. Benjamin has been commissioned by the *New York Times* to write a Christmas story and Augie tells him a story that begins very much like Rashid's. This time it is Augie, running after a young black boy who stole from his store, who picks up something the thief dropped, which turns out to be his wallet. Augie's anger is softened by the family photos he finds in die wallet and he decides to return it to an address in the projects on Christmas Day. There he meets Ethel, the boy's black grandmother, who appears to mistake Augie for her grandson because she is blind. Augie falls in with the deception. 'It was as if', he says, 'we both decided to play this game, without having to discuss the rules. I mean, she knew wasn't her grandson . . . but it made her happy to pretend.' He purchases some food and they have Christmas dinner together. In the old woman's bathroom Augie finds a stack of new cameras, probably stolen, one of which he steals. His theft will then become the story that he gives to Benjamin to write for the *New York Times*. The parallels with Rashid's story cannot be missed.

If Rashid's encounter with thieves led him to Benjamin, whose son he pretended to be, Augie's encounter with a thief leads him to Ethel, whose grandson he pretends to be. Both stories involve numerous economic and affective transactions across the colour line, but so deliberately confusing are the transactions that it becomes difficult to sort out who is the creditor and who the debtor, who stole and who gave, since everyone steals and gives, incurring debts that cannot be calculated. Rashid is father and son to the white author Benjamin, he takes from him and also gives back, as Augie is grandson to a black woman Ethel and takes and gives back to her.

This is an apt account of both familial and narrative relations. Acts of 'relating', as Hillis Miller points out, whether through words or through relationships, 'incur an infinite debt which like that in all intimate, human relationships, can never be paid off'.[30] Throughout *Smoke* we find characters attempting to measure the value of things conventionally thought of as priceless. From Benjamin's initial story about attempts to measure the weight of smoke, through his attempts to 'balance the scales' and thank Rashid for saving his life, through the bargains that Rashid strikes with his biological father over the price of a drawing, and his no less complex gift of a television to Benjamin, the network of familial relationships is mixed up with the economy of value in a way that prevents us from consigning the family to some mythic realm separate from commerce.

At the conceptual core of this film are the photographs that Augie takes each morning at eight o'clock of the corner in front of his store. The photographs are in black and white and they include any people who happen to be passing by at that particular time. They are of course photographs that – we learn by the end of the film – were taken with the camera that Augie stole from the black woman Ethel. The importance of these photographs is signalled by a temporary interruption of the narrative during the scene in which Augie shows his photographs to Benjamin. We are first shown these photographs from Benjamin's point of view, in medium-shot, and as inert pictures pasted onto a page they look as uninteresting as he declares them to be. The camera then cuts to a closeup, allowing the contents of the photograph to fill the screen, and a series of beautiful dissolves moves us from one photograph to the next, endowing the still photo with movement and depth and taking us momentarily out of the diegesis. This movement out of the film is reinforced by the only other occasion in which the director uses black and white, namely the reenactment of Augie's story about how he obtained the camera, shown at the end of the film to accompany the credits. In guiding us out of the diegesis, the photos comment self-reflexively on the operation of the film as a whole. Like the people who appear in Augie's photographs by chance as they pass by a street corner at a particular hour of the day, the people who make up the interracial family of *Smoke* are linked by chance encounters in a particular location. Augie's photographs, transformed into a living procession of people by the director's dissolves, reanimate the 'dead time' of everyday routines and furnish a model for the different kind of family that *Smoke* constructs. The number of people who pass by his store is not finite, no line can be drawn to fix this family in the frozen postures of a single portrait. Unlike the family album which turns its gaze inward, towards domestic interiors, Augie's album is filled with photos that look outward into public space, turning the family inside out to face the street. Indeed the possibility of distinguishing between public and private space is called into question when Augie shows his photographs to Benjamin. At first Benjamin is mystified, 'They're all the same', he says, until Augie tells him to look more closely. The camera zooms in for a closeup of a woman carrying an umbrella and this time Benjamin does see something: a picture of his deceased wife on her way to work, which causes him to break down in tears.[31] The discovery of a personal connection among the anonymous strangers on the street is precisely the kind of connection that Augie's store facilitates. The store is located at the intersection between public and private, its boundaries metaphorically enlarged by Augie's photos of 'his' street corner. The store is a place of trade, but also the common ground where people come to find and remake their families.

Whereas in *Made in America* and *A Family Thing* race is used to pull the drawbridge up on the family in order to resuscitate white paternity, *Smoke* uses race to contest and undermine the frozen hierarchies of the nuclear family, loosening the stranglehold of the family circle. In this film we glimpse an idea of family where hierarchies are flexible and changing, where the lines between public and private responsibility are blurred, and where the complex intertwining of debts, thefts and gifts that takes place in the family becomes a way to imagine relations between whites and blacks beyond the punitive, zero-sum games of racial competition. *Smoke* offers us a vision of a thoroughly social family, one that might help to expand our imagination of what is possible in relationships that cross the colour line.

Notes

1   Patricia Williams, *The Alchemy of Race and Rights* (Cambridge, MA: Harvard University Press, 1991), p. 189.
2   Cited in Lisa Jones, 'Grave matters at Monticello', *Village Voice*, 5 January 1999.
3   *New York Times*, 13 February 2000; *New Statesman*, 6 November 1998.
4   Jones, 'Grave matters at Monticello'.
5   Ed Guerrero, 'Spike Lee and the fever in the racial jungle', in Jim Collins, Hilary Radner and Ava Preacher Collins (eds), *Film Theory Goes to the Movies* (New York: Routledge, 1993).
6   Robyn Wiegman, 'Black bodies/American commodities', in Lester D. Friedman (ed.), *Unspeakable Images: Ethnicity and the American Cinema* (Urbana and Chicago: University of Illinois Press, 1991).
7   *Mother Jones*, January 1990.
8   Gregory Stephens, *On Racial Frontiers: the New Culture of Frederick Douglass, Ralph Ellison, and Bob Marley* (Cambridge: Cambridge University Press, 1999), p. 6.
9   Jacques Donzolet, *The Policing of Families* (New York: Pantheon Books, 1979), p. 4.

10 Roddey Reid, 'Death of the family, or, keeping human beings human', in Judith Halbarstam and Ira Livingston (eds), *Posthuman Bodies* (Bloomington: Indiana University Press, 1995).

11 Ibid., p. 187.

12 Susan Jeffords, 'Can masculinity be terminated?', in Steve Cohan and Ira Rae Hark (eds), *Screening the Male: Exploring Masculinities in Hollywood Cinema* (New York: Routledge, 1993).

13 Of course the ironic assumption that mothers and sisters are treated better is symptomatic of how familial ideology functions to mask the violence within families.

14 Kay Weston, *Families We Choose: Lesbians, Gays, Kinship* (New York: Columbia University Press, 1991).

15 Michelle Barrett and Mary McIntosh, *The Anti-Social Family* (New York: Verso, 1982).

16 Paul Gilroy, 'It's a family affair', in *Small Acts: Thoughts on the Politics of Black Culture* (New York: Serpent's Tail, 1995).

17 Henry James, *Roderick Hudson* (1909) (New York: Harper, 1960), p. xli.

18 Ibid., p. li.

19 Barrett and McIntosh, *The Anti-Social Family*.

20 Susan Sontag, *On Photography* (New York: Farrar, Strauss and Giroux, 1977).

21 Werner Sollors, *Neither Black nor White yet Both: Thematic Explorations of Interracial Literature* (Cambridge, MA: Harvard University Press, 1997).

22 Ibid., p. 41.

23 Janet Farrell Smith, 'Analyzing ethical conflict in the transracial adoption debate: three conflicts involving community', *Hypatia*, vol. 11, no. 2 (1996), pp. 1–33.

24 Tania Modleski, *Feminism without Women* (New York: Routledge, 1991).

25 The only romantic encounter between Sarah and Hal is played for laughs and conveniently interrupted by the return of her daughter.

26 Compare *Secrets and Lies*, in which the discovery of a black daughter similarly exposes the wounds festering in a white working-class family resulting in a triumphant celebration of communication within the family. However, although many secrets are revealed, the black woman's origins remain a mystery – her mother refuses to tell her about her father, hinting at horrors that permit the reemergence of the stereotype of the black rapist, and the nuclear family doors swing shut once again.

27 The casting of Will Smith cannily exploits extracinematic material here. At the time, Smith was defending himself from accusations of being too white, based on his transition from urban rapper to the star of the hit television sitcom *Fresh Prince of Bel-Air* (where he plays a black man who goes to live with his wealthy relatives). These are accusations that Sydney Poitier before him had also fielded. David Ritz, 'Will power', *Essence*, February 1993.

28 Leslie Fielder, *Love and Death in the American Novel* (New York: Dell, 1969).

29 Bill Nichols, 'Sons at the brink of manhood: utopian moments in male subjectivity', *East-West Film Journal*, vol. 4, no. 1 (1989), pp. 27–43.

30 J. Hillis Miller, 'The two relativisms: point of view and indeterminacy in the novel *Absalom, Absalom!*', in B. J. Craige (ed.), *Relativism in the Arts* (Athens: University of Georgia Press, 1983), pp. 163–4.

31 Although the family conceived in *Smoke* is constructed along more generous lines than the white nuclear circle, it is still an account of male bonds cemented across the bodies of absent women.

14

Black on White: *Film Noir* and the Epistemology of Race in Recent African American Cinema

Dan Flory

Noir's most recent renaissance has produced some remarkable pieces of work, both cinematically and critically. From *After Dark, My Sweet* to *LA Confidential*,[1] and from J. P. Telotte's *Voices in the Dark* to James Naremore's *More Than Night*,[2] striking filmic as well as critical examples have proliferated. However, one strand of production that has lacked extensive critical scrutiny is African American filmmakers' use of *film noir* techniques and themes. These filmmakers have found *noir* conventions crucial for the portrayal and interrogation of struggles African Americans face daily in their efforts to confront the white supremacism deeply rooted in American society. In this fashion *film noir* has allowed into the Hollywood mainstream depictions of the power structures or "micro-physics" of racism's dominant form.[3] Such presentations of black experience's typical features permit viewers access to perspectives and knowledge that are sorely needed if the subtleties of white privilege are to be properly understood and overcome, for these films make explicit the extraordinary injustices that often constitute everyday African American existence. Through constructing narratives by means of typical *film noir* conventions, black filmmakers have offered audiences ways of knowing about American society that are highly critical of it, yet that also promise to make insights into the dissolution of its unconscious white supremacism easier to formulate.

Moreover, these films reveal in stark detail features of African American life that are virtually unknown to most philosophers and in so doing articulate distinctively critical perspectives on standardly accepted moral presuppositions. That is,

Dan Flory, "Black on White: *Film Noir* and the Epistemology of Race in Recent African American Cinema," pp. 82–90; 96–108 plus 110–14, 15–16 (notes) from *Journal of Social Philosophy* 31:1. © 2000 by Blackwell Publishing Ltd.

because these films acutely address what Charles W. Mills has called an "epistemology of ignorance" by telling "white people things they do not know and do not want to know,"[4] the cinematic works to be described here demand philosophical attention as well. Their narrative details contain crucial insights the incorporation of which would require substantially augmented systems of moral knowledge capable of reflecting many hitherto unaccounted for shades and nuances. These films introduce viewers to many specific aspects of an alternative system of knowing the structures of (white) power through dramatizing perceptions, moral actions, and values that stand in direct opposition to those of white privilege. Through their narrative details, these recent examples of African American cinema offer philosophers sustained access to what Mills and others have described as an overlapping yet distinct parallel universe of experience, where racist oppression is imposed on everyday black life through its perceived normalcy from the perspective of white privilege.[5] As Mills argues, the content of such experience's criticisms of the white status quo demands a reconceptualization and redirection of one's moral vision, because typical features of African American experience have had little or no part in the abstract representations of European or European American philosophers.[6] By depicting features of racist oppression from the underside in such specificity, these films represent elements that are fundamental to the development of more comprehensive moral epistemologies as well as enhanced senses of social justice, for African American filmmakers' "internalist critique of the dominant culture" and that culture's underlying epistemology undercut those systems of knowledge presently supporting most philosophical thinking on such matters.[7]

To make these films' philosophical importance clearer, I will first outline some commonly used narrative themes and techniques in *film noir* that have not only sustained critical and viewer interest, but that African American filmmakers have found it profitable to employ in their efforts to lay bare the foundations of racist forms of thinking and acting. Then, I will focus on how *noir* conventions arise in particular films by Bill Duke, Carl Franklin, Charles Burnett, and Spike Lee. These filmmakers' works explore issues of race and African American experience in ways seldom done in earlier *films noirs* – or for that matter, American film in general. One could cite isolated cases such as Joseph Mankiewicz's *No Way Out* (Twentieth Century Fox, 1950) or Robert Wise's *Odds against Tomorrow* (United Artists, 1959), in which themes of race and prejudice figure significantly in the narrative, but in more recent films by African Americans, characters confront the confines and exclusions imposed on them by white supremacism in still more explicit and explicitly *film noir*–derived ways. Narrative conventions deployed in these films often tacitly recall tropes found in such classic *noir* texts as *Double Indemnity*, *Phantom Lady*, *Detour*, *The Killers*, *Out of the Past*, *The Big Clock*, and *The Asphalt Jungle*,[8] all works in which typical *noir* features such as unknown or inadequately understood forces far more powerful than the protagonists either marginalize them or box them into fates from which there seems no escape. These cinematic tropes of power, confinement, determinism, and marginalization reappear in many African American filmmakers' efforts of the 1990s. Yet their efforts deploy these filmic conventions in ways new to American cinema, for *film noir* tropes become transformed through the category of race, and this transformation reveals their usefulness as analytic tools in efforts to disclose the inadequacies of typical philosophical conceptions of justice and morality, a point I hope to make clear in my discussions of the films and in a final section assessing their implications.

The Epistemology of *Film Noir*

First, however, I will outline the general understanding of *film noir* to be used in this article. Like many critics, I believe that *film noir* is best understood not as a genre, mood, movement, or visual style, but rather as discourse.[9] "Genre," for example, is a term borrowed from literary studies and focuses on classifying things ontologically; that is, categorizing them by means of the formal properties they allegedly possess, always the bane of *noir* studies because it has never been agreed precisely what properties make a film *noir*. Moreover, generic classifications elide such matters as the fact that until very recently *films noirs* were categorized and promoted as "women's films," "problem-pictures," "gangster films," "crime films," "thrillers," and in other ways. The French term has largely operated as a retrospective classification imposed in hindsight.[10] Efforts to characterize *film noir* as a visual style, mood, or movement might be seen as attempts to respond to the unsatisfactory nature of genre classification, but all fall victim to similar difficulties. Exemplary cases such as *Laura*, *The Big Sleep*, *The Postman Always Rings Twice*, and *Key Largo* are too brightly lit and too conventionally shot to be categorized along with, say, *T-Men* or *Touch of Evil* as *films noirs* by means of visual style; nor do all of these films seem to be in the same "mood" or part of the same movement.[11] Such characterizations fail to capture satisfactorily the many facets of *film noir*.[12]

Treating *film noir* discursively, however, promises to escape these problems by shifting the grounds of discussion from ontology to discourse itself, which opens up possibilities for examining dispersions of the term *film noir* as well as its history.[13] For example, if we look at *film noir*'s genealogy, we can see that post–World War II French critics developed it a as portmanteau term in order to describe primarily the forties' cycle of American crime genre and gangster films.[14] Since its invention, however, the expression has disseminated and become a valuable term of art for filmmakers, critics, and viewers in discussing many different sorts of motion pictures.[15] Thus, in contrast to Joan Copjec's view, it seems that the "positivist fiction"[16] involved in describing the discursive field for *film noir* may be constructively employed when one understands its dispersed and protean character. Instead of idealistically seeking the necessary and/or sufficient conditions for *film noir* so that we might establish its categorical bounds once and for all, we would much more usefully direct our energies, as critics like Naremore and Telotte have, toward determining its deployment in the discursive practices and actions of its users and utilizing those determinations in our subsequent examination of possible further instances.[17]

Naremore in particular notes that "*film noir* belongs to the history of ideas as much as to the history of cinema" and that it "is both an important cinematic legacy and an idea we have projected onto the past."[18] Thus our sense of *noir* should include an understanding of it as a discourse involving aesthetic ideologies, theoretical movements, ways of reading, and historical moods as well as one involving films. Naremore provides a much-needed discursive background for the term's French cultural roots and concludes that "the discourse of *noir* was initiated by two generations of Parisian intellectuals."[19] The term's origins are usually located in Nino Frank and other French critics' use of it to signify what they saw as "a series of narrative, stylistic and thematic departures from the Hollywood cinema of the prewar years,"[20] yet the term also figured into the "*serie noir*" of American thrillers and "hard-boiled" crime fiction that at that time had been recently translated into French and published under the direction of Marcel Duchamel,[21] as well as echoing still earlier uses of "*roman noir*" to describe British Gothic novels of a century before.[22] Some French critics also related these American films to prewar French productions that had already been termed *films noirs*.[23] Naremore traces French discussions of *noir* such as these still further to their backgrounds in surrealism, existentialism, and critical reactions to developments in American literature and film (revealing, among other things, a long-obscured racial element that the films to be discussed here might be seen as transformatively reinstating).[24] The real value of Naremore's work is in locating critical examination of *film noir* in the context of cultural and discursive history, not merely Hollywood history, for his analysis reveals a dispersal of the term *noir* and its related discourse at a level other critics have merely acknowledged, but seldom explored.[25] Much remains to be done, but in order to achieve any sort of reasonable grasp of *film noir* we will need fuller recognition such as his work initiates of those discourses that continue to give depth and resonance to critical discussions of American film from the 1940s onward.

Following Naremore's lead, one item we should further explore is something that Frank and other early French critics failed to adequately notice and that has dogged discussion of American *film noir* since its initiation in 1946. Specifically, these early critics overlooked how strongly, in spite of their claims to the contrary, the films they originally designated as *noir* (*The Maltese Falcon, Murder, My Sweet, Double Indemnity, Laura*, and *The Woman in the Window*)[26] and those that followed constituted a continuation of traditional prewar Hollywood cinema. Rather than departing radically from it, *film noir* used techniques and explored themes that had long been part of Hollywood narrative, in some cases from D. W. Griffith's days at Biograph. Marc Vernet, among others, catalogs many such techniques, and Jonathan Munby argues convincingly that *film noir* directly continued the exploration of themes probed earlier in such gangster films as *Little*

Caesar, Public Enemy, and *Scarface*.[27] As Munby points out, in some cases the trade magazines of the era virtually identified these 1940s crime pictures as what he calls "*ersatz* gangster films."[28]

Many critics have played lip service to this link,[29] but the thematic continuity between these works of the 1940s and their 1930s ancestors constitutes an absolutely critical trait to recognize in order to properly understand *film noir* in the overall context of Hollywood cinema. In the early thirties gangster films were huge commercial successes,[30] taking in impressive grosses and engendering innumerable imitation contests of such stars as James Cagney and Edward G. Robinson.[31] Yet these films also constituted a threat to the established order through their typically sympathetic and seductive presentation of illegal activities, their sensitive and nuanced portrayals of urban immigrant life, and their implicit criticisms of existing law and uptight WASP sensibilities.[32] Their use of urban immigrant argot, for example, helped to legitimate this way of speaking for audiences otherwise pressured to conform to accepted WASP forms of speech.[33] Gangster films' casual acceptance of alcohol consumption, on the other hand, implicitly endorsed a form of lower-class behavior that WASPs had just worked mightily to illegalize.[34] Moreover, because these subversive tendencies were at that time so much a part of the genre, gangster films (along with Mae West) principally engendered in 1933 the creation of the Motion Picture Production Code Administration (PCA),[35] and in 1935 the PCA declared a moratorium on making gangster films because they constituted such a threat to the sensibilities of those in power.[36] In the cases of *Public Enemy* and *Little Caesar,* for example, these films went unscreened for eighteen years because they were denied approval by the PCA office, and even in 1953 their re-release was restricted to domestic markets.[37]

Yet in spite of the ban, because gangster films were such attractive moneymakers film studios continued to seek ways to make them in alternative forms, casting them as nostalgia (e.g., *Roaring Twenties*), incorporating them into social problem films (e.g., *Dead End*), merging them with comedies (e.g., *A Slight Case of Murder*), and other ways.[38] In addition, the personas of stars such as Cagney, Bogart, and Robinson often helped associate films in which they acted with the gangster genre. In Cagney and Robinson's case, it was often by merely switching sides from being gangsters to G-men.[39] In other instances these stars helped to incorporate gangster themes into *film noir* itself. Bogart's past history of playing thugs, crooked bosses, and criminals gave many *films noirs* in which he acted continuity with gangster pictures.[40] Similarly, Cagney and Robinson's bodies of work helped to associate *noirs* such as *White Heat* and *Key Largo* with themes that gangster pictures had explored in the thirties.[41] *Film noir* greatly augmented Hollywood's efforts to get around its own in-house censors at the PCA office to the established moneymaking (and at times subversive) genre of gangster films through being such an effective and consistent strategy around self-imposed censorship rules, particularly from the mid-1940s and into the 1950s.[42]

Beyond features of continuity with gangster films, however, one could further argue that *film noir*'s novel convergence of different techniques and themes not only constituted an especially interesting and successful cluster of means around the PCA office, but also became an entrenched way of manipulating themes of criminality and lawbreaking that otherwise might have offended too many audience members to be profitable. Beginning in the 1940s, American crime and gangster films entered a cycle in which significant audiences paid to see,[43] among other things, shady wisecracking detectives function as substitute gangsters and deal with criminals or visit gangland hangouts to obtain information. Protagonists often crossed lines of bourgeois acceptability and transgressed established laws or their underlying moral codes. Characters were also portrayed as excluded or confined to outlaw groups by the genteel society who mostly watched these films. Moreover, the unfairly doomed fates of many characters frequently reflected an implicit dissatisfaction felt against oppressive established orders. These films typically used psychological doubling, voice-over, and flashbacks to tell their stories, had convoluted plots, and often caused audiences to sympathize with transgressions both moral and legal as well as underworld economies. Many of the works in which these narrative and technical features arose later came to be known as *film noir*, movies like *A Double Life, The Dark Mirror, Hollow Triumph, Out of the Past, Murder, My Sweet, The Reckless Moment, Phantom Lady, Possessed, The Lady from Shanghai*, and many others.[44]

In addition to its links with gangster pictures, a further element of *film noir* we should note is its typical connection to epistemology. Acquiring, having, or withholding knowledge characteristically drives *noir* narratives. From Sam Spade and Kaspar Gutman playing cat and mouse over who knew where and what the black bird was to Jake Gittes trying to figure out whether Evelyn and Katherine Mulray were sisters or mother and daughter, *noir* has regularly exploited epistemological themes in order to keep audiences interested and following its narratives. Partly because *noir* protagonists have often been seekers of knowledge such as detectives, individuals ignorant of their circumstances, or people trying desperately to make sense of their lives, partly because efforts to create an understanding of events in film automatically produces narrative tension and drive, knowledge construction has typically played a fundamental role in creating the *noir* sensibility. In *Out of the Past* Jeff Bailey/Markham seeks to understand how Whit Sterling has framed him and what information Kathie Moffatt has provided so that Jeff will be made powerless to do anything about it. In *Murder, My Sweet* Phillip Marlowe seeks through his voice-over to make narrative sense of the events that took place in the case of his efforts to find Moose Malloy's girlfriend, Velma Valento. In *Dead Reckoning* Rip Murdock confesses to the ex-paratrooper Father Logan ("the jumping padre, always the first one out of the plane") his efforts to put together the pieces of the puzzle surrounding Johnny Drake's death and Coral Chandler's role in it. In *Double Indemnity* Walter Neff works to coherently tell his story of obsessive entanglement with Phyllis Dietrichson and their killing of her husband to his friend Barton Keyes' Dictaphone. In *Phantom Lady* Carol "Kansas" Richman tracks every lead she can find in an effort to clear her former boss of a murder she is convinced he did not commit. In *Undercurrent*

Ann Hamilton (played by Katharine Hepburn, of all people) works to discover the truth behind the Garroway brothers and the source of her husband Alan's psychological instability. In *Sudden Fear* Myra Hudson slowly realizes that her new spouse has married her for money and greedily plans to kill her for it. In *The Killers* insurance investigator James Reardon seeks to reassemble the Swede's life and understand why he would lose the desire to live and passively allow two thugs to kill him.[45] The search for and construction of knowledge in a *noir* world thus regularly constitute one of its most distinctive features. *Noir* protagonists typically work to understand situations in which they or other characters find themselves. This work thrusts unto them epistemological tasks: they must seek to acquire knowledge they do not have, put it together with other items they uncover, and often try to devise ways to use it so that circumstances may be changed or appropriate actions taken.

Noir epistemological work also typically involves coming to know things that others would prefer left unknown. The kind of information sought by *noir* characters might reveal the swinish cruelty of everyday life or evil lurking inside the family (e.g., *Shadow of a Doubt, Uncle Harry, Mildred Pierce, Secret Beyond the Door, Caught, Chinatown*); it might reveal activities that must be kept from the law's knowledge (e.g., *Detour, Scandal Sheet, Where the Sidewalk Ends, Criss Cross, The Reckless Moment, Love Crimes, The Last Seduction, Bound*); or it might uncover knowledge that endangers those who possess it (e.g., *Sorry, Wrong Number, Phantom Lady, Somewhere in the Night, The Big Heat, Kiss Me Deadly, Black Angel, Lost Highway*).[46] Through its capacity to foreground that which many would prefer left unknown, *noir* (like its early thirties ancestor, pre-PCA gangster films) possesses a potential for subversive criticism, especially when directed toward oppressive, dominant social structures. The knowledge uncovered can thus throw into question what was previously known, disrupt once secure points of view, and force characters to do things or face circumstances in opposition to the status quo. At times the knowledge revealed may shatter the foundations of knowledge itself and force characters to see the world in wholly new ways and act accordingly. Thus in *Force of Evil* this propensity fuels an implicit critique of capitalism that eventually causes the main character to act against those principles by which he has previously lived his life; in *Crossfire* it criticizes what was at that time commonplace anti-Semitism; in *Chinatown* it reveals a pervasive corruption constituent of the ordinary way many municipalities are run; *In A Lonely Place* uncovers the latent violence of a not atypical masculinity that destroys the love two people have for one another; and *The Stranger* illustrates how fascism may lurk beneath the surface of small-town (and boarding school) day-to-day life.[47] As narrative elements these bits of subversive knowledge challenge viewers to examine and reconstitute their own epistemologies, to change fundamentally their standard ways of knowing the world and how they live in it.

In spite of this subversive critical capacity, however, Mike Davis and others have argued correctly that overall forties' *film noir* was "an ideologically ambiguous aesthetic" (*City of Quartz*, 41) that was just as frequently employed in the service of reactionary politics, as may be seen in pitifully transparent Howard Hughes productions like *I Married A Communist for the FBI*, as well as squadrons of authority-loving police procedurals such as *Between Midnight and Dawn*.[48] Moreover, the denatured form of many recent *films noirs* (e.g., *Final Analysis, Dead Again*),[49] which offer little criticism of our increasingly mean-spirited version of the American Dream during the last two decades, further confirm this general ambiguity in the *noir* aesthetic. In such recent deployments, as Davis points out, *noir* functions as little more than "ambiance shorn of its 1940s radical affinities" (21). In addition, many novels that became part of Duchamel's *serie noir* were "produced by writers under contract to the studio system" of Hollywood (37), never quite the hotbed of radical insurgency that J. Parnell Thomas, Estes Kefauver, or Joe McCarthy thought it was. Although these novels frequently criticized the status quo, they did not typically offer utopic communistic visions of how human beings might live together; if anything, they usually depicted the opposite. Yet despite such narrative ambiguity, Davis admiringly describes both many literary and cinematic versions of what we in retrospect call *noir* as "a fantastic convergence of American tough guy realism, Weimar expressionism, and existentialized Marxism" (18), a mix that often constituted "one of the most acute critiques of the culture of late capitalism" and exposed "how the [American] dream had become nightmare" (20). At its best, "*noir* was like a transformational grammar turning each charming ingredient of the [American] arcadia into a sinister equivalent" (38).[50]

Noir, then, can cut both ways, although I would want to argue that it is noticeably duller as anticommunist or right-wing critique. Moreover, like Davis and many others I find its radical affinities more attractive.[51] These affinities are also the ones African American filmmakers have sought to recuperate in their work. In one of the few in-depth articles written thus far describing this appropriation,[52] Manthia Diawara notes that over forty years ago the French film critics Raymonde Borde and Etienne Chaumeton described *film noir*'s use of black and darkness tropes as metaphors for (white) characters' moral transgressions and falls from grace in the eyes of acceptable, middle-class society.[53] Many recent films by African Americans, on the other hand, redeploy these same tropes to highlight social injustice against African Americans and the need for its rectification (263). Rather than merely highlighting transgression, black and darkness tropes foreground the oppression forced on African Americans from above by white society and its supporting institutional structures. Using Chester Himes's novel *A Rage in Harlem* as a paradigmatic model through which to understand new urban black films, Diawara seeks to illustrate how African American directors have reconfigured *film noir* (272). Arguing for a content-based form of *film noir* criticism as opposed to the more formalist accounts offered by Marxist or feminist perspectives (262–3), Diawara explains that such narrative themes of darkness and shadow no longer signify mere moral transgression or alienation from mainstream society, but now constitute a method through which African American life and culture may be made visible (263). Through thus depicting black life, these films deconstruct white racism and its many intricacies by exposing the ways in which forces of privilege fracture and distort African American existence (263), thereby making possible improved reflections for audience members regarding the immorality of these institutions and their implicit social injustice.

In his analysis Diawara focuses particularly on roles that black rage, freedom, and criminality may play in narratives portraying African Americans. For example, as Himes's *A Rage in Harlem* makes clear, blacks often "are choked by powerlessness, economic deprivation, and captivity" (266). In narrative contexts rage thus becomes "an expressive act against incarceration" by oppressive social structures (269). Diawara explains that black characters' violence may be understood as communicative acts deployed in frustration and "aimed at people who are perceived as obstacles to freedom or economic empowerment" (268). Trains, on the other hand, Diawara argues, are "associated with escape and freedom for black people" (269). The symbol of the train "is so powerful because of its mobility; nothing hinders its traversing of Harlem and thus its movement into the white world that connotes power, economic prosperity, and freedom" (268). Moreover, the hidden economy of crime offers African American characters a sphere in which to realize visions of themselves free from the oppression of white society: it manifests "an opportunity to beat the system that is inhospitable to them" (272). Often confined to meager and misery-ridden spaces by the institutions servicing white America, black lawbreakers may thus be seen as heroes "in the black community where the black life world is colonized by the police and other institutions. To break the law is to fight one's captivity, and to claim the right to invent oneself. Lawbreakers are usually the first to challenge the status quo and to generate new ways of being that later become styles for the community [or] symbols of freedom" (271–2). Diawara identifies these symbolic possibilities as reasons why black filmmakers have turned "to the structure of *film noir* where lawbreakers are not simply bad guys, and identification with them is possible." *Film noir* themes and techniques may serve as channels for "black rage against the colonization of the black life world in the 1980s and 1990s" and as ways to show how institutions of white authority often impose criminality and lawbreaking on African Americans that they then seek to appropriate as their own (272).

[. . .]

Devil in a Blue Dress

Rather than portraying contemporary events and the current established order in Los Angeles, Carl Franklin's 1995 *Devil in a Blue Dress* (Tristar) explicitly recreates a 1940s-era detective story, complete with voice-over, convoluted plot, and passages into a criminal underworld where the main character, Easy Rawlins, must obtain information essential to his case. Set primarily in Los Angeles's black community, the film aims to depict the everyday oppression and harm done to African Americans trying to live unexceptional lives in the years after World War II. In this manner the film embroiders elements in Lewis Gordon's Fanonian description of racist oppression: "the imposition of extraordinary conditions of the ordinary upon individuals in the course of their effort to live 'ordinary' lives."[54] Having followed Horace Greeley's advice and gone West to evade the poverty and crime-ridden life of Houston's Fifth Ward, Easy finds to his dismay that California as well promises such miseries for African Americans. At first escape to an ordinary life must have seemed possible: Easy had secured a job at one of Los Angeles's many aircraft plants, bought a house, and began settling into the working-class neighborhood of Watts. But as the film opens Easy's voice-over tells us, "It was summer 1948 and I needed money." As last hired, first fired, he has just been laid off and has no idea how he will pay his mortgage, already two months overdue. To make his payments, he takes a detecting job that in typical *noir* fashion he doesn't want from a sleazy white "businessman" named Albright, who does "favors for friends."

In contrast to many white *noir* heroes, Easy makes every effort to escape lawbreaking and live a respectable, morally principled life. As his friend Joppy says, "Easy's always trying to do better" and overcome his rough background. But Easy finds that the color of his skin forces him into crime's hidden economy. His fate is to be sucked into a life he does not want to live, that he has explicitly rejected, because he is confined to such spaces and denied access to others, such as that of unremarkably working at a factory and puttering with the fruit trees around his house. At first desperate for money to pay his mortgage and later a suspect in two murders, he has no choice but to help Albright find Daphne Monet, even though Easy senses his employer is a gangster and would himself prefer to see Daphne go her own way. Eventually, in angry response to being pushed around by the cops, Albright, and various others, he calls for help on his old friend Mouse, a trigger-happy murderer who is one of many things Easy had hoped to escape by moving from Houston to Los Angeles. Together they find Daphne and resolve Easy's dilemma with Albright and the police, although Easy must restrain Mouse every step of the way from acting out Easy's rage and shooting anyone who even slightly crosses either one of them. This *noir* doubling, as Ed Guerrero has pointed out, works "Easy and Mouse in psychological counterpoint,"[55] but instead of serving to indicate Easy's darker side it points to his humanity, restraint, and desire to escape the rage lurking in his heart. In this way, *Devil* contrasts with many other *films noirs*, illustrating Easy's efforts to "do better" rather than succumbing to a fatalistic determinism that maintains human beings will inevitably do worse, if only given the chance (such as in, say, Fritz Lang's *Scarlet Street, The Woman in the Window, Clash by Night,* or *Beyond a Reasonable Doubt*).[56]

Devil in a Blue Dress means to present its viewers with the general validity of the idea that, even when African Americans try to escape the criminalistic *noir* world, it often exerts its power to pull them back into its influence, as it does on

Easy. Yet its power, as the film takes pains to point out, is not due to the inherent evil of human beings, but to a thoroughly corrupt and corrupting racial order imposed on African Americans by white power and privilege. The fate of Daphne Monet, the femme fatale, reinforces this point. Literally the *Devil in a Blue Dress*, she is so not because she is bad or evil, but because she is Creole and has "passed" for white. Initially engaged to Todd Carter, a rich and powerful white man, she finds herself being blackmailed by a politician opposing Carter in the mayoral race. In order to thwart this blackmail and keep her secret hidden, she purchases photographs showing her fiancé's political rival to be a pederast who molests young boys. It is this political rival who has actually hired Albright to find Daphne, obtain the photos, and probably kill her. In the end, Daphne must tell Carter of efforts to hide her racial transgression in order to explain why the events in the film have happened, and even though Carter loves her, he is unwilling to cross the color line and marry her once he finds out she is not white. She, too, remains confined to the spaces reserved for people of color in 1948. She has motivated all the film's killing and criminality not from inherent evil, but through her efforts to cross an unjust social barrier and escape the confinements imposed on her by race.

The film's setting also provides critical background information for many more recent events (such as various riots in Los Angeles) by underscoring the historical depth of ongoing problems, including the imposition of extraordinary conditions like criminality on the African American community and African Americans' confinement to misery-ridden spaces on urban maps. In this way *Devil in a Blue Dress* seeks to reveal the hidden history of white supremacism's seamy underside and challenge viewers to rethink their place in its moral institutions as well as their view of its commonly accepted presumptions, history, and consequences. Once again, in presenting these matters the film's narrative parallels claims advanced by Mills and Goldberg that ideas of race fundamentally affect typical thinking about morality as well as space. As Mills writes, "part of the purpose of the color bar/the color line/apartheid/jim crow is to maintain [racialized] spaces . . . to have the checkerboard of virtue and vice, light and dark space, *ours* and *theirs*, clearly demarcated."[57] Similarly, Goldberg argues that "racisms become institutionally normalized in and through spatial configuration . . . being conceived and defined in racial terms." Moreover, "the concept of race has served, and silently continues to serve, as a boundary constraint upon the applicability of moral principle."[58] Through its vivid portrayal of spatial and moral demarcations by means of imposed ideas about race, *Devil in a Blue Dress* serves to illustrate and enliven the same territory of white supremacy's unfairness and injustice as that indicated by these thinkers. Easy's character, for example, works to obscure the moral boundary set out for him by race, to show its artificiality, by contrasting his principled and restrained responses with those of Mouse. Thus, whereas Mouse embraces imposed criminality and lawbreaking with comically maniacal relish, Easy resists these pressures and responds with horror to Mouse's many evil deeds, such as his killing of Joppy for a serious but understandable indiscretion. Moreover, as viewers become identified with Easy through the narrative, they come to see more clearly white supremacy's moral bankruptcy, its unfair imposition on African Americans and the places where they live, its fundamental immorality, its continued and long-standing injustices. Such an implicitly corrupt and corrupting social order, the film implies, requires immediate moral dedication to its improvement, to the eradication of its damaging privilege and power, so that something better may actually be possible for those whose lives it affects, just as Mills, Goldberg, and other philosophical theorists of race urge on the basis of similar observations.

Clockers

Returning again to a contemporary setting, in Spike Lee's film *Clockers* (Universal/ Forty Acres and A Mule, 1995) *noir* conventions serve to reveal the way in which drug culture may appear to offer alluring ways out of seemingly hopeless traps of poverty and unemployment for desperate young African Americans, in much the same way 1930s gangster films such as *Public Enemy* and *Little Caesar* depicted the ways in which other oppressed minorities of a past era – Italians and the Irish – sought to use the drug culture of alcohol to create ways out of similar traps of misery and joblessness. From its opening scene in the flagpole court, *Clockers* characterizes this alternative's allure as "the most glamorous and remunerative life option for black adolescents"[59] that is within their severely circumscribed experience. It does this through the way in which it focuses on intimately detailing the drug trade, its allure, and the culture of desperation surrounding these adolescents' lives, as well as the distorted ways in which knowledge and teaching permeate much teenage African American experience.

After a montage under the credits of reproduced crime scene photographs depicting half-grown teenagers dead from gunshot wounds intercut with murals dedicated to fallen children and spectators peering curiously over crime scene tape, the film opens in the courtyard of a Brooklyn project with a group of young teenagers arguing about Chuck D., Tupac Shakur, and the issue of whether or not being a hard-core rapper requires committing actual violence. But Strike, the main character, rudely breaks up this argument among his crew and orders them to get to work, pointing out they have to get about their business and make some money, which is their main purpose for being out there. A customer soon appears interested in buying some product. One of Strike's crew gets off the benches and inquires what he would like to purchase. Like any cost-conscious shopper, the customer asks what the specials are for today ("red caps") and decides to buy two of them. The whole crew looks around carefully and after an elaborate exchange of signals to indicate that no one is watching, another crew member fetches the product from a safe apartment and deposits it in a trash can for the customer to pick up. Everything is done so that these activities will attract as little attention as possible, so that the actual events taking place will escape detection by those who do not have the special knowledge to spot it. As Leonard Quart observes, this detailed depiction of drug-dealing dynamics clearly shows "how much intelligence is wasted in the elaborate and furtive process of making a sale,"[60] while also implicitly showing how much potential exists in these kids for far more constructive activities.

Of course, the hidden knowledge required by these illegal activities is two-sided: it must be both unknown and known, for otherwise such commerce is not possible. The price Strike and these other round-the-clock drug-dealers must pay for staying in business is constant surveillance and harassment by the police. Arriving immediately on the heels of this opening scene but too late to stop any actual sales, the cops instead humiliate these young adolescents. Strike, for example, must submit to a public body cavity search while his mother watches from her apartment window. When the cops come up empty-handed, they turn to insulting and roughing him up. While such harassment typically produces no arrests, the stress of them gives Strike ulcer attacks that he tries vainly to calm with milky soft drinks.

Nor is this the only kind of surveillance to which these young entrepreneurs must submit: Strike's boss Rodney Little cruises the projects like an overseer to make sure that his crews are not goofing off, that they are always working hard to make him money. And if the police are one kind of oppressive presence, that of Rodney is quite another. Thinking of himself as the divinely inspired general of his juvenile drug dealer army, Rodney represents the paternal taken to insane extremes. By turns kind and violent, Rodney both sweet-talks and badgers Strike and the other clockers, showing a father's concern at one moment and a pimp's heartlessness the next. He tells Strike that he regards his clockers as his children and Strike in particular as the son who will be his sword and his staff. Later he buys Strike Mylanta to soothe his raging ulcer and advises him to see a doctor about it, sermonizing, "You got to take care of yourself." Yet Rodney also keeps Strike on the benches supervising fourteen-year-olds selling crack vials to desperate addicts while others work the easy jobs of selling cocaine to suburbanites from the order windows of fast-food restaurants. Rodney further admits to bloodying Strike on Daryl Adams's murder, so that he will have "something personal" on Strike, so that his knowledge of Strike's involvement will act as insurance that Strike will never turn Rodney in – and will always keep Strike working for him. Ever manipulative, Rodney uses knowledge deftly as a weapon. More than once he tells Strike, "Don't you know I know everything?" thereby seeking to characterize his knowledge of Strike as an additional tool of confinement. Moreover, as one of the few available male role models around the projects, he knows Strike looks up to him, so he uses it against Strike, subverting the younger man's admiration for his own personal gain. He knows, for example, that Strike and the others desperately seek a way out of the projects, so he modulates his pitch for the drug trade in those terms by means of a speech so familiar to Strike he can mouth it from memory whenever he hears Rodney launch into it. The older man lectures the many children who hang out in his candy store that they can buy houses for their mothers and acquire the wealth and status they crave through clocking.

African American confinement is shown in a different way through Strike's older brother Victor. As Strike's *noir* double,[61] Victor has chosen the "legitimate" route to try escaping the ghetto. Instead of dealing drugs, he works two jobs, saves all the money he can, and is "never late" to work in order to find a way out for his family. As he tells the cops, "I'm really trying to move us out of the projects . . . I'm working, I'm saving . . . [trying to] provide those ends." Yet Victor, too, is not undamaged by the pressures and confinements that impinge on project inhabitants. He becomes ill when a clocker several years his junior offers him a month's wages every week just so drugs may be sold on the premises of the fast-food restaurant that Victor manages, yet hates. In his second job as a security guard, Victor must enforce many of the stereotypes he hopes to escape: as some-one who can "speak their language," he is paid to find peaceful ways to turn away black teens who his employer thinks might rob her store. Yet the overwhelming pressures of these constricting roles and the easy money from the drug trade belittle Victor's tremendous efforts to get his family out of the projects legitim-ately, driving him to drown his sorrows with Scotch at the local bar. As Quart notes, this inner-city world is one "where violence and desperation are the norm . . . living in the projects is like being under constant siege, and escaping it demands an enormous act of will."[62] For Victor, "the very construction of employment, health care, safe housing, raising children, and a great number of the mundane features of 'reasonable' day-to-day living demands extraordinary choices and efforts to be lived mundanely," as Gordon writes in *Fanon and the Crisis of European Man* (42). Victor shows the strains of these extraordinary acts of will that he must perform every day by seeking solace in a bottle. He, too, is filled with rage and frustration that he feels compelled to dampen with his drug of choice, an alternative the ineffectiveness of which is reflected by Victor's involvement in Daryl Adams's murder.

In still another case of *noir* doubling, this time of Rodney, Errol Barnes, formerly a drug addict and stone killer, now in the final stages of AIDS, functions like some demented Elijah who uses his threatening reputation to buttonhole children into listening to his prophecies involving the evils of drugs and the crushing inevitability of the streets. Once Rodney's teacher in the hows and whys of street killings, he has turned his final mental energies to warning kids like Strike or the youngster Tyrone about the fatal inescapability of street life. "You'll end up like me – or worse," he predicts to Strike. To Tyrone he lectures, "Where you momma at? . . . She know you out here? . . . When you elders talkin' to you, boy, you listen." Errol is clearly in the later stages of AIDS dementia, but through his insanity some truth escapes. When Strike confesses his ignorance about Victor's involvement in the Daryl Adams case, Errol reminds him, "He yo' brother. You s'posed to know." Of having AIDS he tells Strike, "You can't cheat this shit." Finally, after telling Strike about the prophecy his father made to him about taking drugs ("'You gonna pay fo' that'"), Errol notes, "He was right." Errol's narrative function in these contexts is to sum up what he has come to know at the end of his drug-wasted life: that it was not worth it, and that other paths he could have taken, such as being an accountant (something he had studied at one time), would have been a better choice. But just as he is a bad role model for these children who instinctively avoid him and feel more attracted to Rodney, as a teacher Errol is not taken seriously. His lessons fall on deaf ears.

In concert with its utilization of other typical *noir* features, then, *Clockers* is also an epistemological film, one in which imparting or acquiring knowledge and contemplating change in one's fundamental system of belief and actions are major components of its characters' lives. What characters know and do not know, for example, continually arises as objects of desire or investigation. Police detective Rocco Klein, as he is reflected in a shot of Victor Dunham's eye, demands, "I want to see what you see," to which Victor at last wearily closes his eye as if to say, "You can't." Later Rocco tells Strike, "I want to know what you know," but this time Strike explodes in anger, "You don't know a motherfuckin' thing about me . . . you don't know how it is for brothers out here . . . and you . . . definitely don't know nothing about what's going on out here [in the streets]!" After twenty years as an urban detective Rocco thinks he is capable of knowing and seeing the world through African American experience, but one primary thrust of the film is to show that he does not, that his consciousness of African American existence is severely truncated. His experience of looking at dead African American children has not broadened his knowledge, but hardened it so that all he can see and think are what his calcified stereotypical prejudices allow. He is blind to the many truths before him. For instance, his implicit assumption (and by implication much of the audience's) is that Victor could not have shot Daryl Adams as he had confessed. In Rocco's view "something's not right," so he refuses to shut the case on the Daryl Adams murder and continues to investigate, against the advice of his partner Mazilli. Rather than Victor, he believes that Strike, the "bad" brother, was the murderer. After pressuring Strike through much of the film and at the end of his rope in his effort to incriminate the drug-dealing brother, Rocco yells at him, "You're a lowdown, cold-blooded, evil junkyard nigger like I've never seen in my life . . . I read you like a Marvel fucking Spiderman comic book . . . I been inside your ball-pea brain since you were born! Twenty fucking years!" Of Victor, on the other hand, Rocco thinks "he's one of the decent ones," one of the few "Yos" or "Nubians" who seeks to get out of the projects legitimately and make a better life for himself and his family.

Yet Rocco's cognitive blindness, which leads him to the Manichean conclusion just noted, also causes him to miss crucial features of the case, such as Strike's fundamental inability to commit murder or the pressures affecting all who live in the projects, even the "decent ones," not just those who sell drugs. He fails to see, for example, that these pressures could help to explain how the truth is already before him, that Victor was "just sick and tired," simply could not take the pressure anymore, and had to make somebody "pay" for the misery he felt. Victor's anger got the better of him one night he felt particularly bad and he lashed out at the nearest object he could focus his frustrations on: his "competition" at Ahab's restaurant and a drug dealer to boot, Daryl Adams. As Mazilli coldly explains it, the murder was "like the capper on a bad day" for Victor. But in Rocco's search for a more "reasonable answer," he is blind to the fact that, as Victor exclaims in frustration during his interrogation, "The truth is looking at you, man!" Victor really did shoot Daryl Adams and has confessed to it, yet Rocco fails to recognize this until the senior Mrs Dunham carefully explains to the detective what happened to her son that night and commands Rocco (and implicitly the audience), "Believe him!"

Rocco's cognitive blindness here also points to an epistemological double bind often imposed on African Americans. On the one hand, he does not recognize the truth of Victor's statements; on the other, he does not believe Strike, either. As Strike puts it, "Black man say he didn't do something, you don't believe him. Black man say he did do something, you still don't believe him." Rocco cannot believe the truth of what African Americans tell him because their statements do not fit into his limited schema of what the truth should be. As a case-hardened police detective, Rocco thinks that he knows what is going on in the projects and that his task consists of coercing the appropriately incriminating statements out of black people to show it. Thus he pressures Strike throughout the narrative in order to force his version of the truth out of the young drug dealer. But the truth is far more complicated than Rocco's simple schema for it may comprehend. The truth is that even "one of the decent ones" like Victor can be capable of killing someone, so great are the pressures and confinements exerted on people in the projects. The truth is that even drug dealers are capable of sympathetic fellow-feeling and concern for others, as Strike shows through such actions as his inability to kill Daryl (during interrogation by Rocco, Strike confesses he "didn't have the heart for it") and by trying to help bail Victor out of jail (an explicit change from the novel). Rocco mouths the usual platitudes about how he understands the difficulties facing young African Americans through the history of slavery, racism, no jobs, and so forth, but these admissions serve no function in his truncated consciousness of African American experience. Instead, a simplistic, Manichean distinction between good and bad brothers, combined with a sclerotic view of people of color, frames and directs his search for truth. He is accurate to believe that "something's not right," but the fault lies with his own uncomprehending and foreshortened view of his fellow human beings, not with the truth-telling capacities of African Americans.

Like most urban-area cops, Rocco probably lives in the suburbs or somewhere equally separated from life in the projects, going there to do a policing job among people with whom he has no association except as victims, suspects, or criminals.[63] His view of them, then, is accordingly limited. Thus he falls easily into thinking about them as "Yos" and "Nubians" who rarely tell him anything truthful or intelligent unless he is able to force them into doing it. As he taunts a bystander named Chucky (played by Spike Lee himself, making a Hitchcock-like appearance) who tells Rocco that because he did not witness the murder just committed he cannot speak intelligently about it, "I wouldn't want you to not speak *intelligently*," Rocco seems to believe that sentences uttered by African Americans are all but incapable of achieving that level of mental competence. At one point he tells Strike that he even has trouble telling black people apart in the daytime, let alone at night; and one reason he begins to suspect Strike in the first place is that he mistakes his picture for Victor's at the local bar while checking up on Victor's confession.

Moreover, when a uniform cop complains at the scene of another murder that "they should blow these projects to Timbuktu," Rocco's partner Mazilli replies, "Why bother? They kill themselves anyway. Like one of those self-cleaning ovens . . . That's how the Nubians do it, man . . . cycle of shit." Rocco's views are nothing out of the ordinary for the people who must police the projects, who consider a child's murder just "another stain on the sidewalk" and taunt their onlooking friends with comments like, "Nothing you ain't seen before, huh fellas?" and "Could be you next." It is true that urban police have enormously difficult jobs and are asked by society to contain problems of profound complexity, but rigid and bigoted cynicism such as this, while on the one hand perhaps a protective mask that helps them to deal with the unimaginable brutality they see every day, also constitutes an epistemology of racist belief that far too often prevents them from seeing the truth before their eyes. This is precisely Rocco's problem. He sees "Justice in Black and White" as the headline for *The Final Call* announces to him at the end of the film; as he looks at it he subtly nods in agreement. For Rocco justice is simple. As he mumbles to a bystander (Spike Lee again) while trudging off to begin investigating still another murder, "What's so scientific [about it]?" Yet to be "scientific" – to seek knowledge that could potentially change one's system of belief and to have the capacity to then alter one's perceptions and actions in light of the knowledge one finds – constitutes a major feature of the film, as Rocco's negative example shows. His truncated view of African American life, shared by many audience members, illustrates a typical system of belief from the perspective of white privilege. It is, as Mills describes it, an epistemology of ignorance, a way of knowing that structurally excludes perception of African Americans as full-fledged human beings.[64] One thing *Clockers* hopes to make clear, however, is that such epistemological perspectives are morally bankrupt and inherently unjust and would require fundamental reconstitution before they could be made fair.

Passing knowledge on through teaching constitutes another major theme in the film. For example, like his own substitute father Rodney, Strike, too, hopes to be a teacher and role model to those younger than him. That is why he takes Tyrone under his wing: he wants the opportunity to pass on what he knows to someone. Thus he begins tutoring Tyrone in the ways of drug dealing. "Profit's all in the cut – don't *never* forget that," he commands his new charge. He also lectures him on the etiquette of proper dealing (i.e., don't ever use the drugs you sell) and the cold hard economic facts of life: "Any flyshit you want in this world, it costs money – and this is how you get it: hustling. And don't never forget that shit, neither." He quizzes Tyrone on the mathematics of drug sales, asking him how much profit will be made on the current deal by way of arguing that Tyrone should stay in school (bizarrely, in order to be a better drug dealer) and gives him a street name ("Shorty") as well as gifts to curry his favor and show the economic power of hustling. All this is strangely mixed with more innocent instruction, such as Strike's lecture about the history of Lionel trains and when to say "thank you" for gifts, as well as a dead serious lecture about guns, street violence, and Errol Barnes. Strike intones, "if [Errol] ever try to creep up on me, I'm mo' gat his ass, and you best be ready to do the same shit, too," thereby planting in Tyrone instructions that he will so tragically follow later in the film. Finally, however, due to pressures from Tyrone's mother and Andre, a local cop who lives in the projects and tries to help kids find alternatives to the streets, Strike rejects Tyrone from his crew.[65] For this Tyrone reproaches him, "You shouldn't have taught me," which reminds the audience of the misguided way of looking at the world he has already learned from Strike and that he will put to use in the film's final act.

However, Spike Lee is in no way interested in glamorizing the knowledge Strike and others like him possess in the film. Strike's shortcomings as a teacher and a role model are explicitly pointed out. As Andre tells him angrily when he discovers Strike's tutelage of Tyrone's downfall, "You motherfucker, you don't know nothing about nothing. 'It's not my fault!' Well, I'm not hearing that bullshit no more. It's motherfuckers like you who mugged Rosa Parks." As if to prove his point, Strike responds, "Who the fuck is Rosa Parks?" Neither is Lee interested in portraying Strike as any sort of role model. Rather, through depicting Rodney and Strike's horrifying efforts to pass on what they know Lee means to show that in the absence of other accessible teachers, project kids turn to available sources like dealers for knowledge because they are the ones achieving the greatest obvious success out on the streets and who in young adolescents' eyes seem logical sources to which to turn as examples to emulate in their efforts to gain the wealth and power needed to escape the torment of living in the projects. Strike and Rodney's severely limited views of human alternatives are shown with all their flaws and inhumanity in order to illustrate the perverse effects that an epistemology of ignorance may have on African Americans themselves.[66] Yet Lee also portrays this ignorance in ways that imply it could be eliminated through proper teaching and education, which is presumably why Lee places such fundamental stress on these matters in the narrative.

Moreover, because *Clockers* is such a despairing and unrelenting film, Lee felt the need to offer audience members some hope at its conclusion.[67] He does this partly through the symbolism of trains, which as Diawara has pointed out represent freedom for African Americans stuck in the urban misery of New York ghettoes. In a breathtaking finale Strike escapes the pressures around him by taking the Santa Fe Limited to an uncertain but clearly brighter future than he would have had in New York. Trading his Lionel trains and the "toy freedom" of drug dealing for the genuine article, we see him in the last scene riding a real train for the first time in his life and looking out at the Southwestern landscape of possibility, a place where whites for the last century have found redemption and renewal through the iconography of Westerns – so why not blacks too?[68] Victor as well is miraculously freed from jail and rejoins his family in a scene that offers hope that he, like his brother, may also find a way out of his difficulties.

However, there is a deeper purpose to this final admission of hope than to simply make people feel good, for Lee's use of *noir* determinism is also thereby transposed. Life in the projects may produce the kind of hopelessness that leads to drug abuse or trafficking, but Lee wishes to stress that it is not inescapable. Strike's flight to New Mexico, Victor's release from jail, even Tyrone's adoption of Strike's model train set in the film's final moments all represent the inspiration that could potentially take people out of the projects and on to better things. The bleak determinism of inner-city life is one imposed on African Americans by white society and enforced by institutional forces such as the police. It includes features like Rocco's cognitive incomprehension of the events and people there as well as presumptions of criminality for its inhabitants on the part of various institutions supporting white power. Yet escaping it, Lee hopes to make clear, must come from within by one's recognizing these institutions for what they are and consciously changing one's life in light of that knowledge.

In a turn toward asserting the need for personal responsibility and autonomy, Lee's film implies that the task of getting out from under these racially imposed circumstances lies within the capacity of African Americans to generate and implement for themselves. For example, in *Clockers* Lee clearly holds Strike responsible for Tyrone's shooting of Errol Barnes, respects Victor's choice to legitimately work his way out of the projects, and finds honorable Andre's attempts to keep children off the streets. This sense of responsibility for one's own actions as well as one's community are also why the at times intrusive shots of billboards commanding "No More Packing" repeatedly flash by: Lee seeks to impress on those living in the projects that they simply can not passively wait for white America to make the sort of changes that will improve ghetto circumstances and free its inhabitants of the misery in their lives. Rather, they must take responsibility for themselves by consciously recognizing the forces shaping their existence and making choices to alter them. Cries of racism go only so far, as Lee has sometimes noted;[69] after that people trapped in the projects must work to understand and counteract their problems themselves because white society as a whole is unlikely to change drastically in the near future and give up its power merely for the sake of fairness. Such a change has to be motivated by and come from within spaces such as the black community, as did civil rights; and it will come, according to the logic of the film, only when those in the projects – in particular, young teenagers – begin to understand and take responsibility for their own lives through making difficult choices such as walking away from challenges to their manhood and eschewing violence rather than responding to it or seeking it out. The intercuts of "No More Packing," then, signify the first step to be taken in order to eliminate those problems and allow teenagers to take control of their lives. Clearly, this is an arduous path to set before them, but it is the only immediately viable one according to the film that may be adopted in such desperate straits. Young African Americans, it is implied, must invent their own ways out from under white supremacism, in much the same way that in the past they have used lawbreaking and criminality as means to escape the pressures of white power, to find an independent sphere in which to create new ways of being and identities for themselves.

Through a transformative use of *noir* conventions, then, Spike Lee has sought to turn *film noir* on its head in order to show a way out of criminality and lawbreaking rather than merely a way in. By recognizing the imposed nature of project circumstances, inhabitants can come to see the possibility of creating their own lives independently of that which white power has so often imposed on them – namely, criminality and lawbreaking – and devise new forms of African American existence apart from such determinants. Liberation, to use Lewis Gordon's explanation of Fanon's view, depends on people's grasping the extraordinary circumstances that have been imposed on them and seeking ways to transform perceptions of those circumstances into their appropriate form. The "ordinary" conditions of African American existence must therefore be given their proper characterizations as forms of injustice, pathology, abnormality, and misanthropy, and this transformation has to occur from the bottom up if it is to be successful. Only through the work of those experiencing the oppression themselves to alter views of these "everyday" conditions from being seen as ordinary to their proper perception as extraordinary injustices may such conditions be successfully and permanently changed, for without such whole-scale transformations rooted in the very conditions to be altered, the changes will not stick.[70] Through grasping this aspect of the film's narrative one may see how the racially transformed conventions of *film noir* that Lee deploys are meant to point the way to freedom and liberation, not merely confinement, marginalization, and the sort of fatalism that results in drug addiction or trafficking.

Noir implications for moral epistemology

As Diawara notes, other motion pictures might also be cited as examples of reconfigured *noirs* by *noirs*: *New Jack City, A Rage in Harlem, Juice, Chameleon Street*, and others (see Copjec (ed.), 273–277).[71] Moreover, to this list could be added works such as the Hughes brothers' *noir*ish *Menace II Society* and *Dead Presidents*, as well as films more explicitly in the gangster genre like *Set It Off* and *Hoodlum*, or even HBO releases like *Always Outnumbered, Always Outgunned*.[72] These films use techniques such as voice-over, flashbacks, heavily determinist narratives, multiple naming, sympathy for criminality, and a consciousness of the deeply oppressive forces in American society in order to depict African American experience as ruptured and distorted by white power. These forces inhibit most hopes and expectations to live anything resembling a decent moral life that African Americans might otherwise long to achieve. Yet like many white filmmakers in the years following the Depression and World War II, in the last decade African American filmmakers have found the narrative conventions that ultimately came to be characterized as *film noir* useful in conveying this oppression to mainstream audiences and calling for changes in viewers' ways of seeing the world in light of the knowledge presented.

African American directors' uses of these *film noir* conventions have thus transposed, revived, and reinvigorated the radical critical possibilities latent in *noir* conventions described by such critics as Mike Davis in *City of Quartz* and, for that matter, noted in 1950 by C. L. R. James of gangster films, particularly those of the early 1930s.[73] Of course, as Davis notes, the use of *noir* conventions, at least in literary contexts, is nothing new for African Americans: he points out that Chester Himes employed them in his Los Angeles novels *If He Hollers Let Him Go* (1945) and *Lonely Crusade* (1947); Diawara builds his interpretation of recent appropriations of *noir* filmic conventions on *A Rage in Harlem*; Jonathan Munby notes their later deployment in "black experience" novels written by Donald Goines and Robert Beck; and Walter Mosley utilizes *noir* themes and conventions in his Easy Rawlins mysteries.[74] Moreover, Naremore's reference to the French fascination with racial otherness earlier in the century and its relation to *film noir*'s discourse constitutes an additional contributing factor here that deserves further investigation and elaboration, as do Eric Lott's analysis of racial and ethnic prejudice in many American *film noir* classics, E. Ann Kaplan's explorations of *film noir*'s racial metaphors, and others.[75] Through building on the aforementioned literary antecedents and borrowing from standard Hollywood cinema, the redeployment of *film noir* conventions by African American filmmakers has made them effective tools in portraying the consequences of a supremacist system of knowing and acting in which many whites hardly realize they participate. These deployments of *noir* conventions in films by and about African Americans thus serve to give audiences – in particular, white audiences, if they are willing to be receptive – startling insights into the depth of white privilege's immorality and the degree to which it is embedded in everyday thought and action, while also offering surprising examples of how classic *film noir* conventions may be transformed and used as precision investigative tools to teach us new lessons about "invisible" facts and culturally embedded beliefs. As in many *films noirs* of the 1940s and 1950s, the search for and construction of knowledge in these later films lead to the discovery of factors that not only challenge hitherto secure perspectives of morality and social justice, but demand wholescale changes if such knowledge is to be properly accommodated. One's moral epistemology becomes not merely disrupted or called into question, but requires the sort of fundamental reconstitution that Charles Mills notes is necessary, if one is to adequately reconcile the sorts of knowledge, perspectives, and experiences presented by means of these film narratives with typical conceptions of morality and justice that have for so long been a part of the dominant culture in the United States, as well as that culture's foundations.[76]

Through articulating in such depth a distinctly critical African American moral vision that depicts perceptions, values, and social experiences in direct opposition to those of white privilege, then, these films offer criticisms that bear directly on philosophy's own efforts to develop more comprehensive and inclusive moral systems of belief. These films' presentations of the overlapping yet distinct parallel universe of lived African American experience regarding such things as power, criminality, determinism, and confinement vividly show that, in Lewis Gordon's words, "there is the mundane for the white and the mundane for the black."[77] The films can thus be characterized as depicting moral and social features of human existence that, once recognized, cannot but require reconsideration and consequent alteration of the fundamental systems of knowing that underlie many traditional moral concepts and values. Such alteration is required, according to Charles Mills, because the structuring logic of the racial contract is largely unaccounted for in typical philosophical conceptions of justice and morality;[78] and that different structuring logic is explicitly foregrounded by these *films noirs* by *noirs.* The depth and resonance given in these works to the complexity of both white American and African American life as well as their constituent possibilities illuminate aspects of human moral life that philosophers may ignore only at the risk of furthering those beliefs, values, and actions that have enabled white privilege for so long, and that philosophers must confront, as Mills points out, if they are to fairly and properly reconceptualize moral epistemologies that accurately reflect as many shadings and dimensions of human experience as possible, and that may then generate actions that accommodate to the greatest extent the scope and magnitude of human moral existence.[79]

[. . .]

Notes

1   *After Dark, My Sweet* (Avenue Pictures, James Foley, 1990); and *LA Confidential* (Regency/Warner Brothers, Curtis Hanson, 1997). (In this article I will cite the production company, director, and year in which a film was made with the first mention of its title.) See also the filmography for "*neo-noir*" in *Film Noir: An Encyclopedic Reference to the American Style* (Woodstock, N.Y.: Overlook Press, 1992), 3rd ed., Alain Silver and Elizabeth Ward (eds.), Carl Macek, Robert Porfirio, and James Ursini (coeditors), 423–440.

2   J. P. Telotte, *Voices in the Dark: The Narrative Patterns of Film Noir* (Urbana: University of Illinois Press, 1989); and James Naremore, *More Than Night: Film Noir in Its Contexts* (Berkeley and Los Angeles: University of California Press, 1998). See also (among others) Mike Davis, "Sunshine or *Noir?*" in *City of Quartz* [1990] (New York: Vintage, 1992), 17–97; Frank Krutnik, *In a Lonely Street* (London: Routledge, 1991); Colin McArthur, *The Big Heat* (London: BFI Publishing, 1992); Slavoj Žižek, *Enjoy Your Symptom! Jacques Lacan in Hollywood and Out* (New York: Routledge, 1992), 149–165; Brian Neve, *Film and Politics in America: A Social Tradition*

(London: Routledge, 1992), 145–170; *The Book of Film Noir* [1992] (New York: Continuum, 1993), Ian Cameron (ed.); *Shades of Noir* (London: Verso, 1993), Joan Copjec (ed.); Slavoj Zizek, *Tarrying with the Negative: Kant, Hegel, and the Critique of Ideology* (Durham: Duke University Press, 1993), 9ff.; Dana Polan, *In a Lonely Place* (London: BFI Publishing, 1993); Robin Buss, *French Film Noir* (London: Marion Boyars, 1994); R. Barton Palmer, *Hollywood's Dark Cinema: The American Film Noir* (New York: Twayne Publishers, 1994); and *Women in Film Noir* (London: BFI Publishing, 1998), new ed., E. Ann Kaplan (ed.).

3   Regarding the "micro-physics" of power, see Michel Foucault, *Discipline and Punish* (New York: Vintage, 1979), trans. Alan Sheridan, 26ff.

4   Charles W. Mills, *The Racial Contract* (Ithaca: Cornell University Press, 1997), 18, and "Non-Cartesian *Sums*: Philosophy and the African-American Experience," *Teaching Philosophy* 17 (1994), 227.

5   See, e.g., Mills, *The Racial Contract*, 131–132, "Non-Cartesian *Sums*," 225; and Henry Louis Gates, Jr., *The Signifying Monkey: A Theory of African-American Literary Criticism* (New York: Oxford University Press, 1988), 49.

6   See Mills, *The Racial Contract*, esp. 2–7, 109–133, and "Non-Cartesian *Sums*," 225.

7   See Mills, *The Racial Contract*, esp. 62–133. (Phrase quoted from Mills's "Non-Cartesian *Sums*," 225.)

8   *Double Indemnity* (Paramount, Billy Wilder, 1944); *Phantom Lady* (Universal, Robert Siodmak, 1944); *Detour* (PRC, Edgar Ulmer, 1945); *The Killers* (Mark Hellinger Productions, Robert Siodmak, 1946); *The Dark Corner* (Twentieth Century Fox, Henry Hathaway, 1946); *The Big Clock* (Paramount, John Farrow, 1947); *Out of the Past* (RKO, Jacques Tourneur, 1947); and *The Asphalt Jungle* (MGM, John Huston, 1950).

9   Works debating the status of *film noir* are legion. Two classic texts are Paul Schrader, "Notes on *Film Noir*," *Film Comment* 8:1 (1972), 8–13, and J. A. Place and L. S. Peterson, "Some Visual Motifs of *Film Noir*," *Film Comment* 10:1 (1974), 30–35. These and other classical discussions have now been collected in the *Film Noir Reader* (New York: Limelight Editions, 1996), Alain Silver and James Ursini (eds.). For recent critical over-views of the debate, see Naremore, *More Than Night*, 9–39; Davis, *City of Quartz*, 17–54; Krutnik, *In a Lonely Street*, 16–17; E. Ann Kaplan, "Introduction to New Edition" in *Women in Film Noir*, Kaplan (ed.), 4–14; Telotte, *Voices in the Dark*, 9–36; Marc Vernet, "*Film Noir* on the Edge of Doom," in *Shades of Noir*, Copjec (ed.), 1–31; Palmer, *Hollywood's Dark Cinema*, 7–31; and David Bordwell, "The Case of *Film Noir*," in Bordwell, Janet Staiger, and Kristin Thompson, *The Classical Hollywood Cinema: Film Style and Mode of Production* (New York: Columbia University Press, 1985), 74–77.

10   See, for example, Krutnik, *In a Lonely Street*, 17; and Jonathan Munby, *Public Enemies, Public Heroes: Screening the Gangster from "Little Caesar" to "Touch of Evil"* (Chicago: University of Chicago Press, 1999), esp. 142–143. Todd Erickson's "Kill Me Again: Movement Becomes Genre" (in *Film Noir Reader*, Silver and Ursini (eds.), 307–329) notes that director Dennis Hopper's *The Hot Spot* (Orion, 1990) was the first theatrical release to actually be promoted as a *film noir* (307, 326).

11   *Laura* (Twentieth Century Fox, Otto Preminger, 1944); *The Big Sleep* (Warner Brothers, Howard Hawks, 1946); *The Postman Always Rings Twice* (MGM, Tay Garrnett, 1946); *Key Largo* (Warner Brothers, John Huston, 1948); *T-Men*

(Eagle-Lion, Anthony Mann, 1948); and *Touch of Evil* (Albert Zugsmith/Universal International, Orson Welles, 1958).

12 The details regarding why *film noir* is not a genre, mood, movement, or visual style have been frequently rehearsed and need not delay us here. For more on this matter see the critical overviews mentioned in note 9.

13 For more on the possibilities of examining dispersions and discursive histories of terms, see Michel Foucault, *The Archeology of Knowledge* (New York: Pantheon Books, 1982), trans. A. M. Sheridan Smith, esp. 31–39.

14 See, for example, Krutnik, *In a Lonely Street*, 15–29; Vernet, "*Film Noir* on the Edge of Doom"; and Jonathan Munby, *Public Enemies, Public Heroes*, 115–220.

15 See Naremore, *More Than Night*, esp. 10–11, 34–39.

16 See Copjec (ed.), "Introduction," *Shades of Noir*, xi.

17 See Telotte, *Voices in the Dark*, esp. 1–40; and Naremore, *More Than Night*, 9–39.

18 Naremore, *More Than Night*, 11.

19 Naremore, *More Than Night*, 27.

20 Krutnik, *In a Lonely Street*, 15. (See also Bordwell, "The Case of *Film Noir*," 75; and Palmer, *Hollywood's Dark Cinema*, 7–20.)

21 Krutnik, *In a Lonely Street*, 15; Palmer, *Hollywood's Dark Cinema*, 7–8; and Etienne Borgers, "Serie Noir," in *The Big Book of Noir* (New York: Carroll and Graf Publishers, 1998), Lee Server, Ed Gorman, and Martin H. Greenberg (eds.), 237–244.

22 See *The Film Encyclopedia* (New York: Harper Collins, 1994), 2nd ed., Ephraim Katz (ed.), 452.

23 See Bordwell, "The Case of *Film Noir*," 75; and Palmer, *Hollywood's Dark Cinema*, 9–10. This French connection has been explored in still greater detail by Charles O'Brien, "*Film Noir* in France: Before the Liberation," *Iris* 21 (1996), 7–20; Janice Morgan, "Scarlet Streets: *Noir* Realism from Berlin to Paris to Hollywood," *Iris* 21 (1996), 31–53; Ginette Vincendeau, "*Noir* is Also a French Word: The French Antecedents of *Film Noir*," in *The Book of Film Noir*, Cameron (ed.), 49–58; and Buss, *French Film Noir*, 7ff.

24 Naremore, *More Than Night*, 11–13, 233–253.

25 See Naremore, *More Than Night*, esp. 36–39, 220–277.

26 *The Maltese Falcon* (Warner Brothers, John Huston, 1941); *Murder, My Sweet* (RKO, Edward Dmytryk, 1944); and *The Woman in the Window* (RKO/International, Fritz Lang, 1945). (See, for example, Krutnik, *In a Lonely Street*, 15; and Palmer, *Hollywood's Dark Cinema*, 8.)

27 *Little Caesar* (Warner Brothers, Mervyn LeRoy, 1930); *Public Enemy* (Warner Brothers, William Wellman, 1931); and *Scarface* (Howard Hughes Productions, Howard Hawks, 1932). See Vernet, "*Film Noir* on the Edge of Doom"; and Munby, *Public Enemies, Public Heroes*, 115–220, and "The 'Un-American' Film Art: Robert Siodmak and the Political Significance of *Film Noir*'s German Connection," *Iris* 21 (1996), 76. (See also Bordwell, "The Case of *Film Noir*," 74–77.)

28 Munby, *Public Enemies, Public Heroes*, 156–166.

29 E.g., Krutnik, *In a Lonely Street*, 197–202; and "Appendix A1," in *Film Noir: An Encyclopedic Reference*, Silver and Ward (eds.), 323–325.

30 See Garth Jowett, "Beer, Bullets, and the Hays Office: *Public Enemy* (1931)," in *American History, American Film: Interpreting the Hollywood Image* (New York: Ungar, 1980), John E. O'Connor and Martin A. Jackson (eds.), 60; Robert Sklar,

City Boys (Princeton: Princeton University Press, 1992), 7–9; John Izod, *Hollywood and the Box Office* (New York: Columbia University Press, 1988), 86; and Munby, "The 'Un-American' Film Art," 76–77.

31 See, for example, Munby, *Public Enemies, Public Heroes*, 55; Sklar, *City Boys*, 11–17; and Izod, *Hollywood and the Box Office*, 105.

32 See Munby, "*Manhattan Melodrama*'s 'Art of the Weak': Telling History from the Other Side in the 1930s Talking Gangster Film," *Journal of American Studies* 30 (1996), 101–118, and *Public Enemies, Public Heroes*, 19–82; and Izod, *Hollywood and the Box Office*, 105.

33 Munby, *Public Enemies, Public Heroes*, esp. 41–51, 61–73, and "*Manhattan Melodrama*'s 'Art of the Weak,'" 101–108.

34 Munby, *Public Enemies, Public Heroes*, 27–38, and "*Manhattan Melodrama*'s 'Art of the Weak,'" 104, 114–115.

35 See Munby, *Public Enemies, Public Heroes*, esp. 110–125, "*Manhattan Melodrama*'s 'Art of the Weak,'" 115–118, and "The 'Un-American' Film Art," 76; and Izod, *Hollywood and the Box Office*, 105–108.

36 In particular, it should be noted that President Franklin D. Roosevelt himself asked that production of gangster films cease. See Munby, "*Manhattan Melodrama*'s 'Art of the Weak,'" 103, "The 'Un-American' Film Art," 76, and *Public Enemies, Public Heroes*, esp. 83–114; and Izod, *Hollywood and the Box Office*, 105–108.

37 Munby, *Public Enemies, Public Heroes*, esp. 107–108, and "The 'Un-American' Film Art," 76. In the case of *Scarface* re-release took even longer. It was shown to audiences after its original release only in 1979 [see Joseph McBride, *Hawks on Hawks* (Berkeley and Los Angeles: University of California Press, 1982), 44]. This was partly due to the tangled finances of producer Howard Hughes's estate, but the PCA's restrictions contributed significantly as well.

38 *Roaring Twenties* (Warner Brothers, Raoul Walsh, 1939), *Dead End* (MGM, William Wyler, 1937), *A Slight Case of Murder* (Warner Brothers, Lloyd Bacon, 1938). See Munby, *Public Enemies, Public Heroes*, esp. 110–114, 134–143, and "The 'Un-American' Film Art," 76–78.

39 See Munby, *Public Enemies, Public Heroes*, 66n2, and "*Manhattan Melodrama*'s 'Art of the Weak,'" 110n9; and Izod, *Hollywood and the Box Office*, 107. (The most salient examples are Warner Brothers' *G-Men* (1935) and *Bullets or Ballots* (1936), both directed by William Keighley and starring Cagney and Robinson, respectively.)

40 See, for example, Sklar, *City Boys*, 117; and Munby, *Public Enemies, Public Heroes*, 75n9.

41 *White Heat* (Warner Brothers, Raoul Walsh, 1949). (See, e.g., Munby, *Public Enemies, Public Heroes*, 115–121, 156–158, and "The 'Un-American' Film Art," 84–85.)

42 See Munby, *Public Enemies, Public Heroes*, 115–220, and "The 'Un-American' Film Art," esp. 84–85; and Neve, *Film and Politics in America*, 147–170.

43 See, for example, Izod, *Hollywood and the Box Office*, 121; Neve, *Film and Politics in America*, 145; and Munby, "The 'Un-American' Film Art," 76–78.

44 *A Double Life* (Kanin Productions, George Cukor, 1948), *The Dark Mirror* (Inter-John, Inc., Robert Siodmak, 1946), *Hollow Triumph* (Hollow Triumph, Inc., Steve Sekeley, 1948), *The Reckless Moment* (Wayne Wanger Productions, Max Ophuls, 1949); *Possessed* (Warner Brothers, Curtis Burnhardt, 1947); *The Lady from Shanghai* (Columbia, Orson Welles, 1948).

45 *Dead Reckoning* (Columbia, John Cromwell, 1947); *Undercurrent* (MGM, Vincente Minnelli, 1946); and *Sudden Fear* (Joseph Kaufmann Productions, David Miller, 1952).

46 *Shadow of a Doubt* (Universal, Alfred Hitchcock, 1944); *Uncle Harry* (Universal, Robert Siodmak, 1945); *Mildred Pierce* (Warner Brothers, Michael Curtiz, 1945); *Secret Beyond the Door* (Universal-Diana, Fritz Lang, 1948); *Caught* (Enterprise, Max Ophuls, 1949); *Chinatown* (Robert Evans, Roman Polanski, 1974); *Scandal Sheet* (Columbia, Phil Karlson, 1952); *Where the Sidewalk Ends* (Twentieth Century Fox, Otto Preminger, 1950); *Criss Cross* (Universal International, Robert Siodmak, 1949); *Love Crimes* (Millimeter/Sovereign, Lizzie Borden, 1992); *The Last Seduction* (ITC, John Dahl, 1994); *Bound* (Spelling Productions, Andy and Larry Wachowski, 1996); *Sorry, Wrong Number* (Paramount, Anatole Litvak, 1948); *Somewhere in the Night* (Twentieth Century Fox, Joseph L. Mankewicz, 1946); *The Big Heat* (Columbia, Fritz Lang, 1953); *Kiss Me Deadly* (United Artists, Robert Aldrich, 1955); *Black Angel* (Universal, Roy Neill, 1946); and *Lost Highway* (Lost Highway/CiBy 2000/ Asymmetrical Production, David Lynch, 1996).

47 *Force of Evil* (Roberts Productions, Abraham Polonsky, 1948); *Crossfire* (RKO, Edward Dmytryk, 1947); *In a Lonely Place* (Santana Productions, Nicholas Ray, 1950); and *The Stranger* (Independent Releasing Corporation, Orson Welles, 1946).

48 In *I Married A Communist for the FBI* (aka *The Woman On Pier 13*) (RKO, Robert Stevenson, 1949), Robert Ryan plays a former unionist longshoreman who must betray every leftist he knows in order to clear himself of his "troubled" past. *Between Midnight and Dawn* (Columbia, Gordon Douglas, 1950) is a mundane *policier* in which "buddy" officers track a singularly evil crook who later kills one of them. Documentary-style procedurals of this era often glorified the police by endorsing their use of brutality and intrusive surveillance techniques. Many critics have seriously questioned their status as "authentic" *noir* [see, for example, Jon Tuska, *Dark Cinema: American Film Noir in Cultural Perspective* (Westport: Greenwood Press, 1984), 192], but these arguments regarding the *noir* authenticity of police procedurals miss the point of *noir's* fundamental ideological ambiguity. For broader discussion of such films, see Krutnik, *In a Lonely Street*, 202–208; and Telotte, *Voices in the Dark*, 134–178.

49 *Final Analysis* (Warner Brothers, Phil Joanou, 1992); and *Dead Again* (Paramount/ Mirage, Kenneth Branagh, 1991).

50 Davis describes here only the literary version of *noir*, but the point applies equally well to the more progressive forms of its filmic equivalents. For more on the political texture of *film noir* and its limits, see also Neve, *Film and Politics in America*, 145–170; Richard Maltby, "The Politics of the Maladjusted Text," in *The Book of Film Noir*, Cameron (ed.), 39–48; and Munby, *Public Enemies, Public Heroes*, 186–226, and "The 'Un-American' Film Art," 74–88.

51 See also, for example, Neve, *Film and Politics in America*, 145–170.

52 Significantly, African American appropriation of *film noir* has begun to receive further recognition. See, for example, B. Ruby Rich, "Dumb Lugs and Femmes Fatales," *Sight and Sound* 5:11 (November 1995), 6–10; Ed Guerrero, Review of *Devil in a Blue Dress*, *Cineaste* 22:1 (1996), 38, 40–41; Diawara's "*Noir* by *Noirs*: Towards a New Realism in Black Cinema," *African-American Review* 27 (1993), 525–537; Richard Martin, *Mean Streets and Raging Bulls: The Legacy of Film Noir in Contemporary American Cinema* (Lanham, MD: Scarecrow Press, 1999), 137–143; and Jans

B. Wager, *Dangerous Dames: Women and Representation in the Weimar Street Film and Film Noir* (Athens: Ohio University Press, 1999), 124–127.

53 Manthia Diawara, "*Noir* by *Noirs*: Toward a New Realism in Black Cinema," in *Shades of Noir*, Copjec (ed.), 262; further page citations will be in the text. See also Raymond Borde and Etienne Chaumeton, "Towards a Definition of *Film Noir*" (trans. Alain Silver), in *Film Noir Reader*, Silver and Ursini (eds.), esp. 19–25.

54 Lewis R. Gordon, *Fanon and the Crisis of European Man: An Essay on Philosophy and the Human Sciences* (New York: Routledge, 1995), 41.

55 Guerrero, Review of *Devil In A Blue Dress*, 40.

56 *Scarlet Street* (Diana/Universal, 1945), *Clash By Night* (RKO, 1952), and *Beyond a Reasonable Doubt* (RKO, 1956), all directed by Fritz Lang.

57 Mills, *The Racial Contract*, 48.

58 Goldberg, *Racist Culture*, 185, 28.

59 Leonard Quart, Review of *Clockers*, *Cineaste* 21:4 (1995), 64.

60 See Leonard Quart, "Spike Lee's *Clockers*: A Lament for the Urban Ghetto," *Cineaste* 22:1 (1996), 10.

61 See screenwriter Richard Price's comment on the good brother/bad brother structure of his story in "A Novelist and Screenwriter Eyeballs the Inner City: An Interview with Richard Price," by Leonard Quart and Albert Auster, *Cineaste* 22:1 (1996), 17.

62 "Quart, Spike Lee's *Clockers*: A Lament for the Urban Ghetto," 9.

63 See Price's comments on Jersey City cops like Rocco in "A Novelist and Screenwriter Eyeballs the Inner City: An Interview with Richard Price," by Quart and Auster, 14. [In Price's novel, Rocco lives in a posh Manhattan apartment; see *Clockers* (New York: Avon Books, 1993), 45.]

64 See Mills, *The Racial Contract*, 56–61, 91–109.

65 Evidence exists for Strike doing this for altruistic reasons as well. In their scenes together he seems to honestly like Tyrone: his most relaxed moments are spent with him and he appears to genuinely enjoy his time joking with and lecturing the younger boy. I am inclined to believe that late in the film Strike also has Tyrone's best interests in mind when he kicks him out of the crew, tells him to go home to his mother, and begins to call him "Ty" rather than by his street name, but admittedly the support for that belief is not conclusive.

66 See Mills, *The Racial Contract*, 87–89, for a description of how such an epistemology can affect those who live under its conditions.

67 See Richard Price's comments on the ending of *Clockers* in "A Novelist and Screenwriter Eyeballs the Inner City: An Interview with Richard Price," by Quart and Auster, 17.

68 To be fair, the place of blacks in the American West has been noted by many, even through film; see, e.g., *Harlem Rides the Range* (Hollywood Productions, Richard C. Kahn, 1939), the first of several Herbert Jefferies Westerns, and more recently *Posse* (Working Title Productions, Mario van Peebles, 1993). My point, however, is that except for Woody Strode and Sidney Poitier's occasional appearances, mainstream American cinema has constructed the Western almost exclusively as a space for white possibilities.

69 For example, Lee made such comments during a CNN interview in April 1996; in addition, Quart alludes to similar comments in "Spike Lee's *Clockers*: A Lament for the Urban Ghetto," 9–11.

70 Gordon, *Fanon and the Crisis of European Man*, 62–63.

71 *New Jack City* (Warner Brothers, Mario van Peebles, 1991); *A Rage in Harlem* (Miramax, Bill Duke, 1992); *Juice* (Paramount/Island, Ernest Dickerson, 1992); and *Chameleon Street* (Prismatic One, Wendell Harris, 1989).

72 *Menace II Society* (New Line, 1993), *Dead Presidents* (Underworld Entertainment, 1995), both directed by Albert and Allan Hughes; *Hoodlum* (United Artists, Bill Duke, 1997); and *Always Outnumbered, Always Outgunned* (Palomar Pictures, Michael Apted, 1998), which was executive produced by its writer, Walter Mosley, and star, Lawrence Fishburne.

73 See Davis, *City of Quartz*, 21ff.; and James, *American Civilization* (London: Blackwell, 1993), esp. 118–132. [James believed that the gangster in films constituted a "derisive symbol of the contrast between ideals and reality" (127) for most Americans.]

74 See Davis, *City of Quartz*, 43–44; and Munby, *Public Enemies, Public Heroes*, 225–226 (also in personal conversation). See also Chester Himes, *If He Hollers Let Him Go* [1945] (New York: Thunder's Mouth Press, 1990), *Lonely Crusade* [1947] (New York: Thunder's Mouth Press, 1986), and *A Rage in Harlem* [1965; aka *For Love of Imabelle*] (New York: Signet, 1974); Donald Goines, *Dopefiend* (Los Angeles: Holloway House, 1971), *Black Girl Lost* (Los Angeles: Holloway House, 1973), *Daddy Cool* (Los Angeles: Holloway House, 1974), *White Man's Justice, Black Man's Grief* (Los Angeles: Holloway House, 1973); Robert Beck, *Trick Baby* (Los Angeles: Holloway House, 1967); and Walter Mosley, *Devil in a Blue Dress* (New York: Pocket Books, 1991), and *A Little Yellow Dog* (New York: W. W. Norton, 1996). Also worth noting is Mark A. Reid's connection of similar themes to early African American gangster films: see his "The Black Gangster Film," *Journal of Social Philosophy* 24 (1993), 143–154, esp. 152.

75 See Naremore, *More Than Night*, 11–13; Eric Lott, "The Whiteness of *Film Noir*," *American Literary History* 9 (1997), 542–566; and E. Ann Kaplan, "'The Dark Continent of Film Noir': Race, Displacement and Metaphor in Tourneur's *Cat People* (1942) and Welles' *The Lady from Shanghai* (1948)," in *Women in Film Noir*, Kaplan (ed.), 183–201. Also worth noting are Wanda Coleman, "Guys, Dolls and Bit Players," in her *Native in a Strange Land: Trials and Tremors* (Santa Rosa, CA: Black Sparrow, 1996), 159–161; and Julian Murphet's "*Film Noir* and the Racial Unconscious," *Screen* 39 (1998), 22–35.

76 See Mills, *The Racial Contract*, esp. 62–133, and "Non-Cartesian *Sums*," 223–231.

77 Gordon, *Fanon and the Crisis of European Man*, 42.

78 Mills, *The Racial Contract*, esp. 9–19, 53–77, 91–107, 109–120, and "Non-Cartesian *Sums*," 225.

79 Mills, *The Racial Contract*, esp. 77–79, 107–109, 120–133, and "Non-Cartesian *Sums*," 231.

15

Becoming Asian American: Chan Is Missing

Peter X Feng

It was almost ten years ago. A small group of us perched on the rickety chairs at the old Collective for Living Cinema loft in Manhattan got a first glimpse at a low-budget, black-and-white feature by then experimental filmmaker, Wayne Wang. The appeal of Chan Is Missing *(1981) went beyond its social relevance or the familiarity of the characters and themes. There was something original about the film, and something very Asian American.*

Renee Tajima, "Moving the Image"

Where's our jazz? Where's our blues? Where's our ain't-taking-no-shit-from-nobody street-strutting language?

Wittman Ah Sing, in Maxine Hong Kingston, *Tripmaster Monkey*

Sometime in the early 1980s, sometime between the inauguration of Ronald Reagan and the murder of Vincent Chin, a new voice began to intrude on the cultural consciousness of the United States. That voice belonged, depending on who named it, to Wayne Wang, a Hong Kong–born Chinese American filmmaker; to Asian American filmmakers as a group; or to Asian Americans as a filmgoing community. The film *Chan Is Missing* (1981) announced that Asian Americans could be artists, could be commercial filmmakers, and could support Asian American filmmaking, as well as successfully market Asian American films to wider audiences.

Peter X Feng, "Being Chinese American, Becoming Asian American: Chan Is Missing," pp. 88–118 from *Cinema Journal* 35:4 (Austin: University of Texas Press, Summer 1996). © 1996 by the University of Texas Press, PO Box 7819, Austin, TX 78713-7819. This revised version was published as "Becoming Asian American" in *Identities in Motion: Asian American Film and Video* (Durham, NC: Duke University Press, 2002). Reprinted by permission of the author and University of Texas Press.

Part 1 of this book interrogated attempts to delimit Asian American history through a variety of cinematic modes: ethnography, romance narratives, and home movies. The contrasting formal approaches that characterize each of these modes determine the ways the Americanness of Asian Americans is evaluated. In Part 2, travelogue films provide the occasion for reassessment of Western discourses about Asia, exploring the impossibility of seeing Asia through a lens that can be separated from the Western cinematic apparatus. Can cinema express Asian American identities that escape containment by Western regimes of vision and discourses of citizenship? Part 3 of this book examines films that attempt to trace identities in motion, subjectivities in the process of redefining Asian Americanness and the Asian diaspora, films that attempt to convey the heterogeneity of Asian American experiences without delimiting them. Given this diversity of experience, how can there be a voice that is distinctively Asian American?

Chan Is Missing works to destabilize notions of Chinese American identity, even while the film is marketed as an Asian American text; ultimately, I argue, the destabilization of Chinese American identity not only allows for, but actually contributes to the construction of Asian American subjectivity. This can be accomplished only by focusing on process rather than end result, on the act of "becoming" rather than the state of "being," otherwise we risk arguing "merely" that *Chan Is Missing* elaborates the fragmentation of Chinese American identity without suggesting what it offers in its place.[1]

Chan Is Missing is a useful text for examining the contingency of identity, for the film lends itself to multiple reading formations, generic and otherwise. Surely the appeal of *Chan Is Missing* to those of us who teach film is due in no small part to the different cinematic traditions the film evokes. Its narrative structure allows us to discuss it as an arthouse film; the film plays with the conventions of detective fiction, and thus contributes to a discussion of investigative narrative structures and epistemology; its claustrophobic visual style, combined with grainy black-and-white cinematography, suggests film noir; the film's low-budget aesthetic intersects with an auteur-based approach (insofar as it can be compared with other first features like Spike Lee's *She's Gotta Have It* [1986]); scenes that draw on direct cinema conventions locate the film in a tradition of international "new wave" films (such as John Cassavetes's *Faces* [1968]); and so on. Just as the identities of its characters are destablized by the film, so the identity of *Chan Is Missing* is destablized by a multiplicity of interpretations drawing on different aspects of cinematic history. But how many subject positions can one film occupy?

The Interval: Being and Becoming

In the introduction to his study of literatures of subjective fragmentation and alienation, Phillip Brian Harper argues that postmodernism erases certain markers of difference (race, class, gender, and sometimes sexual orientation) in its effort to decenter white male subjectivity.[2] Critiquing Habermas, Lyotard, and Jameson, Harper notes that "however differently they might interpret the political meaning of subjective fragmentation . . . [these three] theorists conceive of that meaning in terms of macro-level social and economic structures, leaving aside considerations of more contingent political phenomena, in particular those having to do with the social identities of the various subjects who manifest fragmentation in the post-modern context" (1994, 9). In Harper's analysis, social identities are contingent political phenomena, which is to say that social identities function instrumentally and are therefore already fragmented insofar as they are not essential.

Chan Is Missing foregrounds the heterogeneity of Chinese American subject-ivities, thereby arguing for the fluidity of Chinese American identity. If the film did no more than that, it would simply exemplify postmodern fragmentation, and its discourse would be recuperable by postmodern discourses that efface markers of social marginality. But *Chan Is Missing* also suggests the *contingency* of Chin-ese American subjectivities, and in so doing paves the way for Asian American subjectivities that might learn from Chinese American heterogeneity. To describe subjectivity as contingent suggests that subjectivity is not a thing to be located, but a process from which the world is perceived. Instead of positing subjectivity as that which seeks closure, the contingent subjectivity foregrounds its own impermanence, its inadequacy as a coherent identity formation. In a different context, Trinh T. Minh-ha notes: "Meaning can neither be imposed nor denied. Although every film is in itself a form of ordering and closing, each closure can defy its own closure, opening onto other closures, thereby emphasizing the inter-val between apertures and creating a space in which meaning remains fascinated by what escapes and exceeds it" (1991, 49). Like the progressive documentary film practice that Trinh describes, contingent identities maintain an instrumental gap between subject and object, creating and maintaining the space where meaning is exceeded. That space is akin to the space between "Asian" and "American," a space I have refused to bridge with a hyphen.

The presence/absence of the hyphen underscores the need to stabilize moment-arily a position from which to speak, and to destabilize that position immedi-ately. Taking a text such as *Chan Is Missing* and discussing the ways it mobilizes notions of hyphenate identity is "[to venture] into that distance that has not been abolished but expanded to infinity by postmodern criticism: the gap between the politics of production, and of regimes of consumption" (Morris, 1988, 268). To seize on a text is yet another attempt to hold together and keep apart the terms on either side of a hyphen; that is the distance or gap to which Morris alludes. We who would discuss hyphenate identity seize on Wang's film to do so, but our interpretations of the text must not lock down the range of meanings found in the gap between text and reader, but take advantage of the gap between the production of the term and the uses to which we put it. The question then becomes how exactly to mobilize such a label.

In *Chan Is Missing*, many courses of action are identified as being Chinese and others as being American, but a Chinese American course of action is difficult to identify. The realm of Chinese American – the gap between production and consumption – cannot be named, because it is constantly being negotiated by the characters in the film. Being Chinese American is not a matter of resolving a duality, for proposing to draw from two cultures inevitably results in not belonging to either. George, director of the Newcomers' Language Center, points to an apple pie baked by the Sun Wah Kuu bakery as an example of Chinese American negotiation: "It is a definite American form, you know, pie, okay. And it looks just like any other apple pie, but it doesn't *taste* like any other apple pie, you eat it. And that's because many Chinese baking technique has gone into it, and when we deal with our everyday lives, that's what we have to do."[3] But ultimately, such a negotiation proves untenable because it does not create anything new; it merely borrows forms.[4] Jo rejects the apple pie analogy, referring to it as George's "spiel," in his quest for a notion of identity that does see the duality, but creates a space in the gap between the two terms. As Trinh notes in *When the Moon Waxes Red*, "There is indeed little hope of speaking this simultaneously outside-inside actuality into existence in simple, polarizing black-and-white terms. The challenge of the hyphenated reality lies in the hyphen itself: the *becoming* Asian-American" (1991, 157). The apple pie cannot be Asian American because it does not manifest the process of "becoming": it is an expression of the uneasy encounter of two cultures, not revealing the process of accommodation so much as revising Asian techniques to produce American goods. To be Chinese American is to be constantly in the process of becoming, to negotiate the relationship between cultures; to be a Chinese American artist (whether baker or filmmaker) one must do more than introduce Asian themes into American forms: the artist must reveal the process that produces new cultural expressions and thereby preserve a sense of contingency. When an artist asserts that there is one way successfully to balance Chinese and American influences, that artist implicitly asserts that Chinese Americans exist in a fixed space, fulfill a fixed role. Rote actions are successful only when events operate predictably, and with rote responses one will not discover anything new, will not evolve, will not accept the challenge of becoming Asian American.

How, then, is the challenge of becoming Asian American explored by a film that draws on film noir conventions? Is a detective film with Chinese American characters simply an apple pie made in a Chinese bakery? Don't genre films, with their predictable events, call for the very rote actions (on the part of characters, and indeed, on the part of filmmakers as well) that fix their characters in a state of being rather than a process of becoming? When Jo and Steve argue about their course of action, Steve asserts: "Hey, I understand the situation man. . . . Here's how I see it. If you're sick, you go see a doctor, right? If you're going nuts, you go see a shrink. If you need some money, man, you go to a bank or a loan company. You know, somebody rips off your money, if you don't have no friends who can take care of it, you go to the cops and let *them* take care of it" (Wang, 1984, 64). Steve thus advocates a rote response: if someone does this, then you do that. He is frustrated by the lack of results, and so advocates conventional methods of resolving his problem. Jo, on the other hand, does not believe that conventional methods will work; "It's none of their [the police's] damn business" (64), he says, for he knows that Chan's disappearance is not conventional and therefore the police (who are bound by rote responses) will not be successful. When Jo says, "I'm no Charlie Chan," he is also saying. This only appears to be a Charlie Chan case, a genre film; but we don't know what will happen next, we're just making this up as we go along. In other words, Jo is willing to wait and see what happens next, what kind of a film this is "becoming."

One way of reading *Chan Is Missing*'s critique refuses to fixate on the questions it poses about the nature of hyphenate identity, and instead emphasizes the process of becoming. The film affirms through its textuality the impossibility of being, the insistence on becoming – in its refusal of closure, and by questioning identity, appropriation, narrative, and temporality. (These terms overlap; for example, appropriation is narrativized, temporality is expressed narratively, identities are appropriated as means to narrative and other ends.) But although *Chan Is Missing* may critique fixed notions of identity, it must be emphasized that many of the discourses that surrounded the film, discourses that contextualized its position in the marketplace, located it in relation to putatively fixed identity constructions. These discourses of the popular media place Wayne Wang's films between the constructed poles of Asian American and mainstream American film markets.

Wayne Wang[5] was born in Hong Kong in 1949 ("Really I was born when Hong Kong was born" [Thomson, 1985, 24]); his father named him after John Wayne (Wang, 1984, 101–2). He came to the United States to attend college in the late 1960s, earning a bachelor's degree in painting at the California College of Arts and Crafts, where he also studied film history and production. Returning to Hong Kong in the early 1970s, Wang quickly found work as a director for a Hong Kong television comedy, but he was not satisfied working in the Hong Kong industry. He returned to the San Francisco Bay Area and became an administrator and English teacher for a Chinatown community organization (experiences he would draw on for *Chan Is Missing*); during this period he also learned "how to write grants and turn them in on time." Wang also developed a program for KRON-TV and occasionally worked on Loni Ding's *Bean Sprouts*, a series of half-hour programs for Chinese American children (Thomson, 1985).

Wang's first film after returning from Hong Kong was supposed to be a thirty-minute video documentary on cab drivers. After securing $10,000 from the American Film Institute, he decided to make a feature instead. He and his crew shot the film over ten successive weekends and then settled down for the arduous process of editing and postproduction, going steadily deeper into debt; during this period, Wang supported himself by writing bilingual science curricula for San Francisco State University (Chiu, 1982, 17). Eventually securing a grant from the NEA, Wang completed the film on a budget of $22,500. After good response at a few festivals (key among them the New Directors/New Films festival in New York), the movie was picked up by New Yorker Films (Patterson, 1983). The result was an extremely rough, immensely likable film that earned critical raves and more than recovered its investment.

According to Sterritt, "Though its initial audience has not been an ethnic one, Chinese viewers are being wooed through newspaper ads, and Wang would like to see a trial run in a Chinatown theater" (1982, 18). This statement, though anecdotal, indicates the underdevelopment (or outright absence) of venues for Asian American feature films in 1982. *Chan Is Missing* succeeded because it appealed to arthouse audiences and also brought Asian Americans into the theaters. In Asian American newspapers, articles about *Chan Is Missing* and its director often cited its mainstream success and quoted reviewers in mainstream publications (e.g., Lam, 1981), as if to announce to the Asian American audience that, first, the film is not an amateurish production, and second, this is the film that is teaching whites about Chinese Americans. Reviews in the Asian American press often simply advertise the screenings (Lam, 1981); but the lengthier reviews usually refer to how white reviewers see Chinese Americans and how Asian American texts are received by non-Asian audiences (Lau, 1982).[6] Wing Tek Lum points out that many texts produced by Asian Americans are not produced *for* Asian Americans: "*Chan Is Missing* . . . does not have the same tone of voice as some of the other artistic works which have come out of [the Chinese American] community – the grossest examples being the tour guides and cookbooks – where one again has the feeling that the readership which the author has chosen to write to is really the larger society, there being so much explaining, so many footnotes, sometimes so much apology for not being white" (1982, 9). Lum takes care to point out that the tourist mentality can be found in texts, not just in their reception; he thus positions *Chan Is Missing* as *from* and *for* the Chinese American community.

By contrast, the majority of mainstream reviewers take one of two critical approaches, and often include both approaches despite their seeming incompatibility. The first approach is to locate the film within a tradition of filmmaking represented by "canonical" US films and foreign films that had arthouse success in the United States: several reviewers compare the film to *Citizen Kane* (Ansen, 1982; Seitz, 1982) and mention *The Third Man* (Denby, 1982; Ebert, 1982); the *Variety* review cites *L'Avventura* ("Caught," 1982), and Hatch (1982) reviews *Bob le Flambeur* in the same column, emphasizing *Chan*'s appropriation of gangster iconography. The film is often positioned vis-à-vis arthouse cinema through references to its low budget, often favorably (Ansen; Denby; Ebert, 1982; Hatch; Kauffmann, 1982; Sterritt, 1982; *Variety*) but not necessarily so (O'Toole, 1982; Seitz), and/or through reference to the film's release strategy; one reviewer (Siskel, 1982) even alludes to the manner in which other reviewers have hyped the film's budget. The second approach is to describe the authenticity of Wang's film and praise it for presenting a "true portrait" of Chinatown (Ebert, Hatch, Siskel), often citing a specific stereotype that the film challenges; in other words, by addressing certain stereotypes head on, the film is perceived by mainstream reviewers as representing an authentic Chinese American perspective.[7] The first approach locates *Chan Is Missing* in a tradition of arthouse cinema; the second asserts the essential uniqueness of the film. Although seemingly contradictory, these two approaches are of course entirely compatible, and indeed correspond to complementary marketing strategies.

Charlie Chan Is Dead – Long Live Charlie Chan!

When *Chan Is Missing* begins, two San Francisco cab drivers, Jo and Steve, are searching for their friend, Chan Hung, who has apparently absconded with $4,000. When the film ends, the money has been recovered but Chan has not been found, and Jo no longer knows who Chan Hung is. Each clue they find only raises more questions – indeed, the clues aren't even real clues: they include a gun that may or may not have been fired, a newspaper with the important article torn out, a spot on the wall where a picture used to hang, a series of former addresses no longer occupied by Chan, and a Polaroid photo in which Chan's face is obscured by shadows. Given the inconclusiveness of these clues, Jo is forced to rely on the testimonies he gathers from various people who knew Chan, but the incompatibility of these stories evacuates them of any explanatory force.

Chan Is Missing can be interpreted as a revisionist Charlie Chan film; indeed, the marketing of the videocassette release of the film refers to Jo and Steve as "two 'subgumshoes'" who are "walking self-mockingly in the footsteps of Charlie Chan and his Number One Son." At one point, Steve introduces himself by pointing to Jo and saying, "That's Charlie Chan, and I'm his Number One Son – The Fly!" (Wang, 1984, 52). The videocassette's "self-mocking" label seems appropriate; the characters themselves seem aware that they are trapped in a pop culture stereotype – trapped, not in the sense that they have been placed there by the dominant, but in Linda Hutcheon's sense of a strange kind of critique, purveying and challenging their position. Later, while puttering around in his kitchen, Jo invokes Charlie Chan in voice-over: "I guess I'm no gourmet Chinese cook, and I'm no Charlie Chan either, although I did start watching some of his reruns for cheap laughs. Charlie says, 'When superior man have no clue, be patient. Maybe he become lucky!' The next night, I was cleaning out the cab Chan Hung was driving the day he disappeared. I found a letter in Chinese and a gun under the front seat" (57–58). In this scene, it is not only Jo who mocks his adopted role of Charlie Chan, but the narrative itself that is bound up in the complicitous critique. Jo asks for a clue, and he gets one; the film's soundtrack underscores this moment of deus ex machina by hammering out melodramatic music when the gun is discovered. The overdetermined emphasis on this narrative moment mocks the unfolding of the narrative, and thus mocks the generic expectations of a Charlie Chan film.[8]

In 1935's *Charlie Chan in Paris*, Charlie whimsically notes, "Perfect crime like perfect doughnut – always has hole!" Charlie's doughnut reference alludes to the inevitable slip that will allow the detectives to capture the criminal, but I prefer to think of the doughnut in another way: as a metaphor for a mystery with a missing center. Whereas the typical Classical Hollywood detective drama[9] is characterized by a relentless narrative acquisition of clues that eventually climaxes in the solution of the mystery, in *Chan Is Missing* each clue seems to take the narrative farther from a possible solution. Rather than closing down the narrative possibilities, each clue opens up the range of possible answers to the question Where is Chan Hung? Jenny, Chan's daughter, further deflates the narrative tension by returning the money to Jo and Steve, thereby removing the impetus to find Chan. If Jo's investigation continues, it is because the real problem posed by the narrative is not Where is Chan Hung? but Who is Chan Hung? As Jo states at the end of the film, "I've already given up on finding out what happened to Chan Hung, but what bothers me is that I no longer know who Chan Hung is" (Wang, 1984, 73–74). If no one knows who Chan Hung is, then who can know if he has been found?

> Mr Lee says Chan Hung and immigrants like him need to be taught everything as if they were children. Mr Fong thinks anyone who can invent a word processing system in Chinese must be a genius. Steve thinks that Chan Hung is slow-witted, but sly when it comes to money. Jenny thinks that her father is honest and trustworthy. Mrs Chan thinks her husband is a failure because he isn't rich. Amy thinks he's a hot-headed political activist. The old man thinks Chan Hung's just a paranoid person. Henry thinks Chan Hung is patriotic, and has gone back to the mainland to serve the people. Frankie thinks Chan Hung worries a lot about money and his inheritance. He thinks Chan Hung's back in Taiwan fighting with his brother over the partition of some property. George thinks Chan Hung's too Chinese, and unwilling to change. Presco thinks he's an eccentric who likes mariachi music. (74)

Jo's investigation, rather than closing in on Chan, serves only to widen the hole in the doughnut.

Chan Is Missing's lack of closure is a manifestation of the process of becoming which the narrative describes. Any definitive answer to the questions Who or where is Chan Hung? would serve to close off the process of becoming and solidify the film into a "became." That the narrative of the film is closely tied to the notion of hyphenate identity is underlined by the two questions which are actually the same question: Who is Chan? and Where is Chan? Textually, the tie between narrative and identity is manifested in the destabilization of the identities of the various characters who seek to hypostatize Chan. As the narrative "progresses," for example, Steve's identity begins to evaporate, as if the increasing indeterminacy of Chan's identity undermines everyone else's identity. The reasons for this are underlined in the suggestion Presco offers to Jo and Steve in their search for Chan: "Look in the puddle" (Wang, 1984, 34) – look to your reflection to answer your question.

Early in their investigation, Steve asks Jo if his feelings about Chan Hung are being influenced by his feelings for his ex-wife; both were FOB (fresh off the boat). By doing so, Steve reveals an assumption that all FOBs are alike, or more specifically, that Jo would react to all FOBs in the same way. Steve tells a story about Chan that reveals how the older man's inability to acculturate himself embarrasses the supposedly well-adapted Steve: after seeing Chan take off his jacket and give it to a friend who had admired it, Steve told Chan that he liked his pants – was he going to take them off, too? Jo tells us in voice-over, "Steve doesn't realize that the joke about the pants is really on him. Chan Hung told me he sometimes play up being an FOB just to make Steve mad" (Wang, 1984, 28).

The encounter between Steve and Chan is a drama that resonates throughout the Chinese American community and has been dramatized before in playwright David Henry Hwang's *FOB*. In the prologue to *FOB*, an assimilated Chinese American "lectures like a university professor" at a blackboard:

> F–O–B. Fresh Off the Boat. FOB. What words can you think of that characterize the FOB? Clumsy, ugly, greasy FOB. Loud, stupid, four-eyed FOB. Big feet. Horny. Like Lenny in *Of Mice and Men*. Very good. A literary reference. High-water pants. Floods, to be exact. Someone you wouldn't want your sister to marry. If you are a sister, someone you wouldn't want to marry. That assumes we're talking about boy FOBs, of course. But girl FOBs aren't really as . . . FOBish. Boy FOBs are the worst, the . . . pits. They are the sworn enemies of all ABC – oh, that's "American Born Chinese" – of all ABC girls. Before an ABC girl will be seen on Friday night with a boy FOB in Westwood, she would rather burn off her face.
>
> . . . How can you spot a FOB? Look out! If you can't answer that, you might be one. (1990, 6–7)

In the course of Hwang's play, the ABC is forced to revise his estimation of FOBs; meanwhile, the audience comes to understand that the image of the FOB is entirely a creation of the ABC, and a creation that the ABC depends on to stabilize his or her own sense of identity. Similarly, Steve's identity is threatened by the destabilization of Chan Hung: Chan's process of becoming forces Steve to confront the fact that his identity is not fixed, that he too is in the process of becoming rather than being. As the investigation continues, and Jo begins to speculate about Chan's identity crisis, Steve becomes more and more adamant: "That's a bunch of bullshit, man. That identity shit, man – that's old news, man, that happened ten years ago" (Wang, 1984, 62). Jo asserts that the identity crisis is never over (that hyphenate peoples like Steve as well as Chan are always becoming), to which Steve replies that everybody has a role in "the game." Steve tells a story about an old friend of his, and then invokes his experience in Vietnam, "getting shot at by my own peo – ; 'ey! The Chinese are all over this city. Why are you tripping so heavy on this one dude, man?" (63) Steve almost refers to the Vietnamese as his own people,[10] but he stops himself; is it because he realizes that he is Chinese, not Vietnamese? Or is it because Marc Hayashi, the actor who plays Steve, realizes that he is Japanese?[11]

The instability of Steve's identity – and that of the ABC in Hwang's play – is clearly tied to his insecure masculinity. Steve's references to combat in Vietnam, not to mention his repeated use of the interjection "man," hint at the threat to his masculine identity posed by Chan Hung. Chan's inability to assimilate threatens Steve's perception of himself as American and as a man. Similarly, the ABC in Hwang's play reveals his biases when he allows that "girl FOBs aren't really as . . . FOBish." Juxtaposed with his claim that "Boy FOBs . . . are the sworn enemies . . . of all ABC girls," the boy ABC reveals that he thinks it is okay for ABCs to date FOB girls, but that FOB boys should stay away from ABC girls. The FOB stereotype, as articulated by Hwang's character, is rooted in the exchange of women in a sexual economy: women assimilate more easily than men, because women are sexual possessions and can be more easily absorbed into US society.[12] *Chan Is Missing* reveals a similar logic; for example, Chan Hung's wife rejects her husband because he was unable to assimilate ("He doesn't even want to apply for American citizen. He's too Chinese" [Wang, 1984, 46]), and Chan's daughter Jenny mocks Steve when he uses American idioms awkwardly (see below). As is often the case, the more Steve's masculinity is threatened, the more recourse he has to masculine posturing, as evidenced by his assertion that he understands "the game" better than Jo or Chan.

Steve's metaphor of "the game" suggests that everyone's actions are prescribed by certain rules, that interpersonal dynamics are reducible to a repertoire of gambits. "The game" is Steve's description of his own reliance on situationally determined rote responses: "If you're sick, you go see a doctor." For Steve, succeeding in the game is a matter not of always reacting the same way, but of recognizing and adjusting to the situation at hand; indeed, whenever Steve encounters someone new, he immediately riffs off the situation. When Jo and Steve visit Chan's hotel room, they are given some information by one of Chan's neighbors, who calls out to them from behind a closed door. The unseen speaker queries, "You Chinese, Jo?" Steve turns the question around: "Are you Chinese?" Then the voice asks, "Hey Jo, you police?" When the voice refuses to answer their questions, Steve squats down, makes a gun with his hand, and says "Let's go in the other way – got your magnum?" (Wang, 1984, 41–43). Steve adopts the posture of a cop, assuming the identity that the voice suggested for him.

The fluidity with which Steve shifts should not he mistaken for the process of negotiation that I have described as the process of becoming; instead, Steve reserves the right to shift from one fixed subject position to another. The fixity of the subject positions that he serially inhabits is emphasized by their mediated quality: each subjectivity is made available to him from pop culture. When I say that Steve adopts the posture of a cop, the word "posture" should remind us that such role playing involves the performance of visible actions metonymically asso-ciated with the roles in question. What, then, does it mean to say that Steve is a self-mocking Charlie Chan?

To celebrate Steve as a deconstructed Charlie Chan is to privilege the notion of postmodern critique. Such a reading assumes that Steve's situationally driven role playing displays his virtuosity. But Steve does not maintain any of his roles long enough to explore its uniqueness; instead, he isolates each subjectivity from its unique sociocultural context, so that it is evacuated of any political force. Instead of restoring markers of difference and hence historical specificity to the center, he confirms the emptiness of the postmodern subjectivity: the hole in the doughnut. This is evident in the reactions he elicits. The key scene in which Steve identifies himself as Chan's "Number One Son – The Fly!" begins with his misidentifying himself: "I'm Steve Chan – Choy – Chan – Choy" (Wang, 1984, 52). Even the spectator who does not already know that *Chan Is Missing* evolved from an improvised script is likely to read this line as a "blooper," a moment of rupture. In the spirit of improvisation, the other actors modify the trajectory of the scene to account for the dialogue: the scene continues with Jenny's friend mocking, "This dude doesn't even know his name!" While shaking her hand, Steve adopts the posture of a streetwise ghetto kid, clasping her wrist and rapping, "What's happening!" He then goes on a riff about Mrs Chong's mahjong club, to which the girls reply, "Who do you think you are, anyway, you think you're Richard Pryor, something like that?" Steve reverts to his "normal" voice until they say goodbye, when he suddenly shifts into Chinese Uncle mode: "I got some spare change, go get yourself an ice cream cone, man." The offer is rejected: "Who do you think we are, kids?" (51–54). The girls refuse to play along with him, to accept the roles that he is suggesting for them, leaving him trying on various identities, hoping he will find one that works. Steve's self-conscious awareness of his position as a mock Charlie Chan does not occasion a critique of that role, but instead reveals that he accepts the terms that the text lays out for him. Steve is trapped in a generically defined role.

"I'm Steve Chan – Choy – Chan – Choy. . . ." Steve's Chinese American identity is not in a process of becoming (of evolving from position to position), but of shifting from subjectivity to subjectivity, just as he oscillates between Choy and Chan. His character emblematizes the process by which Chinese American identity is interrogated by the film. His various subject positions are deployed in response to interpellation ("Are you police?") and situation ("What's happening!" to begin a conversation; "Get yourself some ice cream" to end one) and, most important, in contradistinction to Chan Hung, Steve's FOB other. This last dynamic is reversed by Presco's suggestion to "Look in the puddle": he advises that Chan Hung is best found by examining oneself. And indeed, everyone who offers an opinion of Chan first looks in the puddle – defines his or her own identity – and then depicts Chan as he best complements that identity. Steve sees Chan as an FOB; Chan's wife sees him as an unsuccessful, unassimilated Taiwanese; Mr Lee sees him as a small child who needs to be led by the hand. Each person sees Chan as the thing that he or she is not, or does not want to be. As such, each person sees Chan as something to get beyond, or rather, as something to avoid. "To get beyond" suggests that subjectivities exist on a continuum of becoming, emphasizing process and movement. However, each of the characters in *Chan Is Missing*, with the possible exception of Jo, attempts to fix Chan's identity, and in so doing fixes his or her own identity. It is crucial that the differing opinions about Chan are all expressed in his absence: Chan becomes the "other" who can be made to stand in for all insecurities, and through him the Chinese Americans can momentarily become one with the dominant.

It is telling that the suggestion to "look in the puddle" does not come from within the Chinese American community, but from Presco, who runs the Manilatown Senior Center.[13] At the Center, where Chan Hung went to enjoy mariachi music, the Filipinos know Chan as "Hi Ho" for the crackers he carries in his pockets. Thus, it would be wrong to suggest that the Filipino American community is more aware of the processes of becoming, for they too have as-signed Chan a stable identity (as Hi Ho). By suggesting that Jo and Steve "look in the puddle," Presco does not abandon his own understanding of Chan, nor does he ask Jo and Steve to accept his own interpretation. However, by taking the advice from Manilatown to Chinatown, Jo is provided with an opportunity to seek Chan in the interval between Chan's Filipino and Chinese identities. And it is in this interval where Chan has been lost, and where Asian American subjectivity may be found.

Voicing the Interval

If the figure of Steve emblematizes the paradoxes that attend to the performance of multiple identities, Steve also emphasizes the link between identity and the acquisition of a voice.[14] Given the multiplicity of voices in the film, what is the distinctively Asian American voice that Renee Tajima heard when she first saw *Chan Is Missing* in 1981? If there is such a thing as an Asian American voice, what does it have to say?

The characters in *Chan Is Missing* repeat themselves over and over again; it seems that everybody whom Jo encounters has a favorite rap. George uses the anecdote of the apple pie and has a rehearsed spiel about Chinatown politics. Henry talks about solidarity with the people in China (except when cooking, when he sings "Fry me to the moon" over and over). Mr Lee gives advice over the phone on how to make business arrangements with Chinese people. Frankie says, "You don't know the Oriental people – when they say they haven't got it, they got something" (Wang, 1984, 31–32). The faceless voice of Chan's neighhor recycles clichés from television shows like *Dragnet* and *The Rockford Files*. Everyone who is asked to speak to the specificity of Chan Hung's position instead takes refuge in prefabricated speeches.

The need to find a voice is expressed in the tension between the two epigraphs that began this essay. Wittman Ah Sing, the protagonist of Maxine Hong King-ston's *Tripmaster Monkey*, refers to African American culture and bemoans the lack of similar hyphenate cultural expression for Chinese Americans. Wittman can conceive of an Asian American voice only in terms of already existing voices of subcultural expression, which would seem to ally him with Steve and his various appropriated identities. But both *Chan Is Missing* and *Tripmaster Monkey* demonstrate the ultimate untenability of appropriating voices; it is as if the characters seize on the first thing at hand in an effort to plug the doughnut hole, without really understanding what that doughnut is. By romanticizing African American cultural forms as resistant ("ain't-taking-no-shit-from-nobody street-strutting language"), Wittman and Steve fail to interrogate the extent to which American culture has absorbed African American cultural forms, as well as the specific processes of negotiation and contestation that produced African American culture(s).

The conflict between different modes of expression – between different voices – is described in *Chan Is Missing* by a lawyer (Judi Nihei) researching a paper on "the legal implications of cross-cultural misunderstandings" (Wang, 1984, 17). When a police officer asked Chan, "You didn't stop at the stop sign, did you?" Chan answered, "No." In Chinese grammar, the answer must agree with the logic of the question ("No, I did not *not stop*"), whereas most native speakers of American English understand answers to agree with the logic of the statement ("No, I *did not* stop"). The lawyer, interested in the misunderstandings that result from this encounter, explicates the cross-cultural confusion in an attempt (presumably) to foster cross-cultural understanding. On the one hand, her voice is put in service of the two voices that preceded hers; on the other, her voice intervenes in their conversation, taking advantage of the confusion occasioned by the meeting of two voices to convey her own message.[15]

Following from this example of the interaction of hierarchized voices, it is important to maintain a distinction between the voice of *Chan IS Missing* and the voices of its characters, for the one contains and mediates the others. This is the only way I can make sense of Tajima's claim that there is something very Asian American about *Chan Is Missing*. If we understand hyphenate identity in the terms Trinh T. Minh-ha proposes, as a process of becoming, there can be no hypostatized Asian American voice, just encounters between difficult-to-place voices that can be interpreted by third parties as Asian American. I can understand my own voice to be Asian American only by standing apart from it, for if I try to arrest the process of becoming that my voice is undergoing, I remove myself from the realm of hyphenate identity and assert that I have a position somewhere. Perhaps, then, the importance of *Chan Is Missing* for the Asian American community is that it forces Asian Americans to reevaluate our own positions vis-à-vis our own identities.

I have argued that Asian American subjectivity cannot be founded on any notion of stability; this is especially true given the diversity of Asian Americans, who represent a wide range of Asian ethnicities and cultures, different histories in the United States, and different generational removes from Asia. In this, I am echoing Lisa Lowe, who suggests that "it is possible to utilize specific signifiers of ethnic identity, such as Asian American, for the purpose of contesting and disrupting the discourses that exclude Asian Americans, while simultaneously revealing the internal contradictions and slippages of [the term] Asian American. . . . I am not suggesting that we can or should do away with the notion of Asian American identity . . . [but that we] explore the hybridities concealed beneath the desire of identity" (1991, 39).[16] Wayne Wang's films explore the contradictions of Chinese American identity, and in so doing propose a space for Asian American subjectivity. *Chan Is Missing* takes the interrogation of identity as its central project, presenting a variety of perspectives on Chan Hung from a variety of puddles. Detective films are frequently described as if they were jigsaw puzzles; I have proposed the metaphor of the doughnut. Each character in *Chan Is Missing* holds a doughnut that contains the possibilities for Chinese American identity in its center; each character glances in the puddle and takes one bite from the doughnut in an attempt to find his or her access to the center. The big doughnut made up of all the little doughnuts – a doughnut akin to the construction of Chinese American identity that the spectator viewing *Chan Is Missing* is left with – is almost meaningless, almost wholly "hole." Whereas each character fixes Chan in an attempt to fix his or her own identity, the spectator is not allowed to occupy any one of these fixed perspectives but instead must negotiate all of them. Thus, each character's bite out of the doughnut, each character's attempt to limit the range of identities for Chan Hung opens up the interval in the spectator's doughnut, widening the space for spectatorial subjectivity and, by extension, Asian American subjectivity. By showing us why it is impossible to know precisely who we are as Chinese Americans, *Chan Is Missing* shows us how we might discover how we can become Asian Americans.

But while *Chan Is Missing* may emphasize the process of becoming, setting identities in motion, evolving subjectivities encounter resistance from those who are invested in affirming the legitimacy and solidity of established identity formations. At the end of *From Hollywood to Hanoi*, when Tiana returns to the United States with a helmet that is meant to signal her ironic relationship to the line drawn between North and South Vietnam, her father refuses to adjust his own identity as a South Vietnamese government official in exile. *Chan Is Missing* may show us how Asian American cinematic identity can be spoken from the interval, from liminal space, but we must not forget that even liminality is faced with recuperation by identity formations that are founded on the myth of origins and essences.

In this chapter I have attempted a reading that continually opens up the figure of Chan Hung, but it is more often the case that movies are interpreted in the light of fixed categories of identity; after all, Steve does not welcome the destabilizing of his identity, for it threatens the stability of his worldview. . . .

Notes

1   In this chapter, my use of the concept of "becoming" is drawn primarily from Trinh Minh-ha's formulation. The concepts of being and becoming are famously explored by Stuart Hall in an essay that appeared in *Framework* in 1989 under the title "Cultural Identity and Cinematic Representation." It has been reprinted often under

the title "Cultural Identity and Diaspora" (1994). Hall argues that cinema does not merely record identities but constitutes them. *Chan Is Missing* both documents Asian American identity's process of becoming and embodies that process; further, to the extent that *Chan Is Missing* helped usher Asian American cinema into public consciousness, the film marks the becoming of Asian American cinema itself. Bakhtin also uses the word "becoming" to refer to an individual's process of coming to consciousness vis-à-vis ideological discourses (1981, 342).

2 Craig Owens notes, "Postmodernism is usually treated, by its protagonists and antagonists alike, as a crisis of cultural authority, specifically of the authority vested in Western culture and its institutions" (1992, 166).

3 W. Wang, 1984, 50. Page references for quotations from the film's dialogue refer to Wang's published continuity script; however, when the script as published conflicts with what I hear on the soundtrack of the video release, I have opted to notate what I hear. My notations differ primarily in the way I have punctuated: I have attempted to indicate the rhythms of speech rather than grammatical logic. Although the continuity script has been an invaluable reference, it is no more than that – as is the script of any highly improvised movie. The principle actors (Wood Moy and Marc Hayashi) as well as some of the supporting players (in particular, Peter Wang and Judi Nihei) deserve credit for "rewriting" the initial script written by Wayne Wang, Isaac Cronin, and Terrel Seltzer.

4 The apple pie example does not combine American form with Chinese content – that might arguably result in something Chinese American – but rather combines American form with Chinese technique. Technique is not content, but another manifestation of form. Trinh tells us, "To excel only in the mechanics of a language, be it verbal, visual, or musical is to excel only in imitation – the part that can be formulated, hence enclosed in formulas. Form as formulas can only express form; it cannot free itself from the form–content divide" (1991, 162). (Chinese content would perhaps be Chinese ingredients, but not baking techniques.)

5 Wang's name rhymes with "hang." Whereas some Chinese Americans with Wang's surname pronounce their name "wong," which is closer to the correct Cantonese pronunciation, other Chinese Americans accept the Americanized pronunciation; in this, Wang is not unlike the descendents of European immigrants who have Anglicized or shortened their surname.

6 Wang's published script for *Chan Is Missing* includes a detailed bibliography of reviews, of which I was able to track down only a small fraction, as Asian American newspapers have limited regional circulation. My thanks to the staff of Seattle's *International Examiner* for locating back issues for me, and to the University of Iowa's Interlibrary Loan staff.

7 In analyzing the mainstream appeal of Amy Tan's novels, Sau-ling Cynthia Wong argues that counter-Orientalist rhetoric (e.g., when characters directly refute stereotypes) exists alongside hints of Chinatown exoticism, and together the two discourses constitute a "complex, unstable interplay of possibilities [that] makes for a larger readership" (1995, 191). I would go further: the voicing of a counter-Orientalist position legitimates the novels' "authenticity" and reframes their own tendencies to exoticize Chinese culture. Such a rhetorical approach appeals strongly to progressive whites because it condemns overt racism while celebrating (unassimilable) ethnic difference.

8 It is ironic to cite the music as underlining and mocking a moment of intertextual reference in the film, for the score itself has been lifted from Michel Legrand's score

for *The Go-Between* (1971). The musical quotation would suggest that the film's narrative approach belongs more in the realm of pastiche than of parody, to use Fredric Jameson's terminology (The excerpt is not noted in the credits.)

9 I do not mean to imply that there is any such thing as a typical detective movie; rather, I have chosen this locution in the absence of satisfactory generic terminology. I am uncertain whether the detective film is best described as a genre, a mode, or a tendency, and the conflation of the terms film noir and hardboiled detective drama only adds to the confusion. Insofar as this chapter is concerned with destabilizing terminology and the process of becoming, it rejects the notion that a rigorous definition of the detective film would assist us. Thus, I have used the word typical to call attention to the fluidity of the detective film.

10 Another interpretation: when Steve says he was shot at by his own people, he is referring to US soldiers.

11 For more on cross-ethnic casting in Wayne Wang's films, refer to the discussion of *The Joy Luck Club* in Chapter 8.

12 The implication that women assimilate more easily than men is, of course, tied up with the US attitude that it is more acceptable for white males to associate with women of color than it is for white women to associate with men of color. For a discussion of how these attitudes play out in US films about romances between Asians and whites, see Gina Marchetti's *Romance and the "Yellow Peril"* (1994). Marchetti discusses the roots of this attitude in, for example, rape narratives and captivity stories, two genres that revolved around attitudes toward non-Asian people of color, and how those genres were inflected when Asians were inserted.

13 Presco is played by Bay Area writer Presco Tabios. For an audience familiar with Tabios's poetry, the figure of Presco marks a space where actor and character are not distinct and separable. More than in in-joke, the casting of Tabios as Presco underlines the self-reflexive advice that Presco dispenses.

14 Galperin refers to Steve as "the most attractive and accessible of the film's characters . . . [because] Steve attracts our fallen nature, makes us realize who we are and more important what we must resign to become like Jo or to imitate the still greater example of Chan Hung" (1987, 1167). I agree with Galperin that Steve's character exhibits the contradictions of hyphenate identity most visibly, but I resist the implication that Jo represents a more successful negotiation of Chinese and American cultures. To speak of how Steve has "fallen" and what Jo has "resigned" suggests not only a cultural hierarchy, but also that the process of becoming forecloses even a partial "return."

Norman Denzin, on the other hand, is interested less in the voice than the gaze. Denzin's reading focuses on Jo and pays Steve only lip-service, which is perhaps inevitable given Denzin's argument: he discusses *Chan Is Missing* as an interrogation of the Charlie Chan movies, in which he (reasonably) privileges Chan over his various sons. He argues that Charlie is "rational, virtuous, mature, normal" when contrasted with "irrational, depraved, childish, violent, immature Westerners" (1994, 67), and he further notes, "Of course in the Chan series Number One Son played the part of the immature, irrational, childish Asian; yet even this conduct was neutralized, by having Charlie act as the traditional-white-paternal father figure" (86 n. 17). I would take Denzin's argument one step further: not only is Charlie the "Asian male [who] knew who he was, knew his place in society" (74), but by disciplining his awkwardly acculturated sons he does not merely "act as" a white *patriarch* but serves to enforce white *patriarchy*. Unlike the Number One Son, however, Steve is not contained by Jo, as revealed by Jo's attempts to explain Steve to Steve ("Two-faced, schizophrenic Chinaman" [W. Wang, 1984, 48]). Just as we should resist the temptation to read Chan Hung as a symbol of the diversity of Asian America, so should we as critics avoid reducing Jo and/or Steve to points of identification for the audience. Furthermore, we should not assume that our critical activity positions us as representatives of a unitary audience (a move Galperin risks) nor as completely divorced from it (which Denzin risks when he argues that in *Chan Is Missing* "this self has become so thoroughly Westernized, no otherness is any longer possible" [1994, 79]).

15 Of course, the alternately bored, confused, and bemused expressions on Jo's and Steve's faces suggest that the graduate student is not communicating as effectively as she might hope, either.

16 In personal conversation, Lowe revealed her desire to rewrite her essay, which relies heavily on Chinese American and Japanese American texts to interrogate Asian American subjectivity, However, I have argued that the deconstruction of the cultural term Chinese American opens up the interval in which we might locate the political term Asian American. I therefore contend that neither Lowe's nor my project reduces Asian America to its Chinese American components, but rather attempts to destabilize Chinese American texts in favor of Asian American subjectivity. (By contrast, Denzin's analysis conflates Asian American and Chinese American terms, e.g., "the Asian-American must take a stand on the American experience that is either Pro-Taiwan and assimilationist, or anti-American and pro-People's Republic of China" [1994, 76]. The flip side is that Denzin conflates *Blowup*, *The Conversation*, *Sex, Lies, and Videotape*, and *JFK* as "Hollywood" films [83].)

Works Cited

Ansen, David (1982) "Chinese Puzzle." Review of *Chan Is Missing*. *Newsweek*, 21 June, 65–6.

Bakhtin, M. M. (1981) *The Dialogic Imagination*, ed. Michael Holquist, trans. Caryl Emerson and Michael Holquist. Austin, University of Texas Press.

"Caught at Filmex in LA." (1982) Review of *Chan Is Missing*. *Variety*, 31 March, 26.

Chiu, Tony (1982) "Wayne Wang: He Made the Year's Unlikeliest Hit." *New York Times*, 30 May, 17.

Denby, David (1982) Review of *Chan Is Missing*. *New York*, 7 June, 72.

Denzin, Norman K. (1994) "*Chan Is Missing*: The Asian Eye Examines Cultural Studies." *Symbolic Interaction*, 17, no. 1, 63–89.

Ebert, Roger (1982) "'Chan Is Missing' Journeys through Real Chinatown." *Chicago Sun-Times*, 10 September, 47.

Galperin, William (1987) "'Bad for the Glass': Representation and Filmic Deconstruction in *Chinatown* and *Chan Is Missing*." *MLN*, 102, no. 5, 1151–70.

Hall, Stuart (1994) "Cultural Identity and Diaspora," in Patrick Williams and Laura Chrisman (eds) *Colonial Discourse and Post-Colonial Theory*. New York: Columbia University Press, 392–403.

Harper, Phillip Brian (1994) *Framing the Margins: The Social Logic of Postmodern Culture.* New York: Oxford University Press.

Hatch, Robert (1982) "Films." Review of *Chan Is Missing. The Nation*, 3 July, 26–7.

Hwang, David Henry (1990) *FOB and Other Plays.* New York: Plume.

Kaufmann, Stanley (1982) "Mysteries, Comic and Otherwise." Review of *Chan Is Missing. The New Republic*, 16 June, 24–5.

Lam, Michael (1981) "Program Notes: *Chan Is Missing*: Hard-edged, Gutsy." *East/West*, 2 December, 11.

Lau, Alan Chong (1982) "State of the Art." Review of *Chan Is Missing. International Examiner*, 9, no. 14, 4.

Lowe, Lisa (1991) "heterogeneity, Hybridity, Multiplicity: Marking Asian American Differences." *Diaspora*, 1, no. 1, 24–44.

Morris, Meaghan (1988) *The Pirate's Fiancée: Feminism, Reading, Postmodernism.* London: Verso.

O'Toole, Lawrence (1982) "Chinese Translations." Review of *Chan Is Missing. MacLean's*, 95, no. 36, 54.

Owens, Craig (1992) *Beyond Recognition: Representation, Power, and Culture.* Berkeley: University of California Press.

Patterson, Richard (1983) "Chan Is Missing, or How to Make a Successful Feature for $22,315.92." *American Cinematographer*, February, 32–9.

Seitz, Michael H. (1982) "The Unhyped." Review of *Chan Is Missing. The Progressive*, July, 50–1.

Siskel, Gene (1982) "'Chan Reflects Life, not Stereotypes." *Chicago Tribune*, 10 September, sec. 3, 1.

Sterritt, David (1982) "Lively, Enchanting Tale of the Chinese-American Experience." Review of *Chan Is Missing. Christian Science Monitor*, 1 July, 18.

Thomson, David (1985) "Chinese Takeout: Wayne Wang Interviewed." *Film Comment*, 21, no. 5, 23–8.

Trinh T. Minh-ha (1991) *When the Moon Waxes Red: Representation, Gender, and Cultural Politics.* New York: Routledge.

Wang, Wayne (1984) *Chan Is Missing*, ed. Diane Mei Lin Mark. Honolulu: Bamboo Ridge Press.

Lum, Wing Tek (1982) "*Chan Is Missing* Marks New Age of Asian American Film." *East/West*, 28 July, 9–10.

Wong, Sau-Ling C. (1995) "Denationalization Reconsidered: Asian American Cultural Criticism at a Theoretical Crossroads." *Amerasia Journal*, 21, nos 1–2, 1–27.

16

The Wedding Banquet: Global Chinese Cinema and the Asian American Experience

Gina Marchetti

According to *Variety, The Wedding Banquet* (Lee 1993) was the most "commercially successful" film of 1993 (Klady 1994). Given its modest budget, recouping production costs did not prove difficult; therefore, a greater percentage of the film's gross could be counted as profit, thus outstripping *Jurassic Park* (Spielberg 1993), which was released the same year. However, *The Wedding Banquet* also proved itself a critical success, winning accolades from reviewers as well as the prestigious Golden Bear award at the Berlin Film Festival. A commercial success in Asia and an "art house" favorite in the United States, *The Wedding Banquet* found an enthusiastic audience around the globe.

The Wedding Banquet tells the tale of Gao Wai-tung (Winston Chao), a gay man living in New York City with his lover Simon (Mitchell Lichtenstein). Wai-tung's family presses him from abroad to settle down and get married. Spurred by his father's stroke, Wai-tung agrees on a "green card" marriage of convenience with one of his tenants, Wei-wei (May Chin), a starving artist from Shanghai. When Mr and Mrs Gao (Sihung Lung and Ah-Leh Gua) arrive from Taiwan, they are appalled by the quickie, city-hall wedding between their son and Wei-wei. An old army acquaintance of Mr Gao's, who runs a restaurant in New York, insists on giving the couple a proper wedding banquet. Wai-tung and Wei-wei have intercourse on their wedding night, and Wei-wei becomes pregnant.

As Mr Gao stays on in New York to recover from a second stroke, all of the plot's complications surface and find resolution: Simon threatens to leave Wai-tung but finally stays. Wei-wei threatens to have an abortion but finally

Gina Marchetti, "*The Wedding Banquet*: Global Chinese Cinema and the Asian American Experience," pp. 275–97 from Darrell Y. Hamamoto and Sandra Liu (eds), *Countervisions: Asian American Film Criticism* (Philadelphia: Temple University Press, 2000). © 2000 by Temple University. Reprinted by permission of Temple University Press. All rights reserved.

decides to keep the baby and asks Simon to be the "co-father." Wai-tung comes out to his mother but agrees to keep his sexual orientation a secret from his father. Mr Gao "comes out" to Simon and tells him that he knows Simon is his son's lover and accepts it, but asks that Simon keep this knowledge from Wai-tung. *The Wedding Banquet*, then, ends "happily." Wei-wei gets a green card and a family. Wai-tung gets a "son" and keeps his lover. Mr and Mrs Gao see the continuation of their family line through the anticipated birth of a grandchild as they leave to return to Taiwan.

Although the basic narrative is straightforward, *The Wedding Banquet* proves difficult to classify. In fact, perhaps part of the reason for the success of *The Wedding Banquet* comes from a fundamental contradiction concerning its classification. On the one hand, it fits easily into several categories, and therefore can be marketed to a variety of audiences as an Asian film, a Chinese film, a Taiwanese film, an Asian American film,[1] a Chinese American film, a New York Chinatown film, a "green-card" story, a popular comedy, a melodrama, an "art" film, a gay film, an "ethnic" family film, or a "multi-cultural" feature designed to raise the consciousness of viewers. On the other hand, *The Wedding Banquet* may have been able to find an audience because it defies all of these classifications and the political configurations connected with many of them. In other words, just as the film appears to applaud the tenderness of a gay romance, the plot twists to uphold the values of the traditional, extended family. Just as the narrative seems to take a radical turn toward celebrating women's autonomy, very bourgeois notions of class and family culture intrude to shore up decaying values. While the film may hint that sexuality and sexual orientation are socially constructed fictions, those fictions determine the "happy ending" promised by the comedy.

Ang Lee (a.k.a. Lee Ang),[2] from Taiwan and educated in the cinema at New York University, has established himself internationally with films that feature family and romantic relationships. *Sense and Sensibility* (1995) and *The Ice Storm* (1997) have received wide acclaim. His earlier work includes *Pushing Hands* (1992), on Chinese immigrants in the United States, made before *The Wedding Banquet*, and *Eat Drink Man Woman* (1994), on contemporary life in Taiwan, made after *The Wedding Banquet*. With *The Wedding Banquet*, he proved himself adept at orchestrating the various threads of transnational production and distribution. *The Wedding Banquet*'s polyglot script ambitiously deals with the edges of the New York gay subculture, characters from the Republic of China (Taiwan) and the People's Republic of China, the solid middle class, and the margins of the illegal working classes. With this film, Lee demonstrates an ability to bring ethnic issues and issues of sexual orientation into the mainstream. One of the characters in the film remarks, "This is a cross-cultural event. Everything goes." It can be argued that the film works for its various audiences because of this overload of "difference" rather than in spite of it.

This analysis looks closely at *The Wedding Banquet* in the transnational context of its production and reception in order to elucidate the ways in which it straddles the borders that outline the various American and global Chinese communities it treats.[3] By looking at the film in the context of Asian American screen culture, this chapter explores the edges of that classification and the elusive nature of identity in an increasingly complex global culture industry.

China, Taiwan, and Chinatown

Ang Lee calls *The Wedding Banquet* a "comedy about identity" (Central Motion Pictures Corporation 1993). Indeed, the film does seem to have a certain relationship to the director's own sense of identity, particularly Lee's sense of himself as the child of those displaced by the outcome of the Chinese civil war in 1949. Lee characterizes himself as follows: "To me, I'm a mixture of many things and a confusion of many things. . . . I'm not a native Taiwanese, so we're alien in Taiwan today, with the native Taiwanese pushing for independence. But when we go back to China, we're Taiwanese. Then, I live in the States; I'm a sort of foreigner everywhere. It's hard to find a real identity" (quoted in Berry 1993, 54).

If the search for *The Wedding Banquet*'s identity begins at the very beginning of the film, the first credit listed for Central Motion Picture Corporation provides the initial entry into the movie's production history. As John Lent (1990, 68) points out: "Central Motion Picture Corporation is the largest producer of motion pictures in Taiwan. Owned by the government and controlled by the Cultural Department of the Kuomindang [KMT], CMPC's structure includes a board of chairmen with a general manager in charge. . . . CMPC now expects young directors intending to make a company-funded film to prove its marketability, including overseas."

While government funding from the Republic of China might conjure up martial-law policies precluding the treatment of homosexuality and serious intercourse between the mainland and ROC citizens, *The Wedding Banquet* stands as a successful document of a thaw. A homosexual and a mainlander (from the People's Republic of China) have intercourse (quite literally). The film is a meeting of strange bedfellows on all levels. Taiwan and the mainland meet; the PRC and the ROC agree to a symbolic marriage. However, that marriage is false, based on deceptions, a play to "pass" for straight and to get that ever-elusive green card and all it means as a ticket to the American Dream.

To begin with the often quoted observation by Fredric Jameson that all literature from the Third World (and Jameson does include Taiwan–China in that category) by necessity is "national allegory" (Jameson 1986), then *The Wedding Banquet*, extending the argument from literature to film, can be looked at as involving a national allegory. Given the financial involvement of the ROC government in this particular case, the investment of Lee in a narrative of China as a nation, from a particular Taiwanese perspective, may not be too far-fetched.

From this standpoint, details of the script stand out for those viewers invested in reading the film as a political allegory. Indeed, parts of the dialogue in Mandarin concerning relations between Taiwan and the mainland are not subtitled, so that the political allegory is highlighted for Mandarin-speaking viewers and considerably lessened for the English speakers.[4]

From the credit sequence, the voiceover of Mrs Gao reminding her son of his failure to get married and produce a son reveals other details. For example, she mentions Mr Gao's retirement from the army and the fact that he went to Taiwan with the KMT forces at the end of the civil war. Later, Mr Gao reminds his son that the entire family was wiped out during the war. (Although it could have been during the fighting with the Japanese, there is the implication that communist forces overran the family.)[5] Still later in the film, Mrs Gao mentions that she, too, went to Taiwan after 1949, so the entire family finds itself in that ambivalent category of exiles–conquerors–liberators with the KMT forces and their supporters.

Because of this, Wai-tung's decision to settle in America is over-determined ideologically. His settling in the United States takes him away from direct family pressure to lead a heterosexual lifestyle. However, his decision to settle abroad also takes him away from the uncertainties of Taiwan's status as a nation and the further uncertainties of his own position as the offspring of the 1949 "mainlanders." While the Hokkien-speaking majority of Han Chinese were also "mainlanders" at some point, centuries of living on the island, which has gone through a series of foreign conquests (most notably, its roughly fifty-year occupation by Japan), makes separatist sentiments run very strong. Only recently have these sentiments been allowed expression in Taiwan.[6]

While some feel that these second-generation KMT mainlanders have been assimilated into the mainstream of Taiwanese society, others note a difference and a certain tendency for many of these well-educated, well-to-do children of the KMT forces to settle abroad. In the 1940s, then, Mr Gao found himself in a situation similar to his own son's. As the script reveals, Mr Gao joined the KMT forces not simply out of political fervor to rid the country of the Japanese (and, implicitly, the communists), but also because he, too, was fleeing from an arranged marriage. Only years later did Mr Gao settle down to "do his duty" and produce an heir for the otherwise extinct Gao family. Like his father, Wai-tung has a political and a personal reason to leave China (mainland and Taiwan) behind.

Wai-tung, in his marriage of convenience, fulfills a political desire for national integrity. The marriage reunites Taiwan with the mainland, leaving the Hokkien majority (and the even more marginal, non-Han aborigines) completely out of the picture. A great deal of nostalgia and a certain amount of melancholy are associated with the KMT old guard. Even after retirement and a stroke, Mr Gao sticks to his old, military routine of brisk morning exercise. He, Mrs Gao, and Wai-tung speak fondly of an old army servant who is still attached to the family as cook and housekeeper. The appearance of Old Chen (Tien Pien) as a successful restaurateur in New York City, who still feels uncomfortable sitting in the presence of his former army commander, confirms that these old relationships continue. Actually, both Mr Gao and Old Chen's experiences with America have turned their initial relationship of superior to subordinate on its head. However, Old

Chen still bows to Commander Gao, and he only reluctantly shakes his hand (a gesture too intimate and familiar for their former relationship).

One of the most significant nails in the coffin of KMT authority came with the United States' recognition of the PRC as "China." While economic and other ties continued (including significant military connections), political legitimacy fell by the wayside. In this case, Old Chen has abandoned the "sinking ship" to make a successful go at life in New York. His bankrolling of the wedding banquet pays tribute to the industry of ROC citizens abroad. While treating the old political guard with respect, the film makes clear that this is the respect shown to an already dead regime. Old Chen's bow to Gao, and Gao's forcing Chen to shake his hand, concretizes the melancholic sentiment associated with their relationship. The future is away from the old politics, away from the old countries, away from the old guard, in an America dedicated to making money. As in Wai-tung's case, Old Chen's future and continued prosperity lie outside of both Chinas.

In a somewhat Confucian turn, the national–political and the familial–private get confused. Confucius took the patriarchal family and its hierarchy of members as a metaphor for the ideal state ruled by the emperor and kept intact by a series of duties and obligations between superior and subordinate. Similarly, *The Wedding Banquet* tries to keep intact a vision of the traditional, heterosexual family, even when it is revealed as an utter sham. Just as the KMT in Taipei tried to continue the impossible illusion that it would return to the mainland as the ruling party of a united China, all the principals of *The Wedding Banquet* do their best to put forward a face of the "traditional" heterosexual family.

To continue with the allegory a bit more, in any intercourse between the two Chinas (embodied by Wai-tung and Wei-wei), America (Simon) plays a critical role. America ambivalently brings the Chinas together (i.e., Simon suggests the marriage of convenience to Wai-tung as a way to solve both his and Wei-wei's problems) and pushes them apart (i.e., Simon threatens to leave Wai-tung when he learns that his lover has had sex with Wei-wei, which, in turn, pushes a lovelorn Wai-tung to distance himself from Wei-wei, the cause of the problem). As both Mr and Mrs Gao learn about Wai-tung's homosexual relationship with Simon, each comes to accept Simon in his or her own way. Mrs Gao, using Wei-wei as an interpreter, tries to make sense of Simon's complex family (since it is now intimately connected to her own).[7] Mr Gao more simply gives Simon a *hong bao*, a traditional red envelope filled with cash, to show that he is an accepted part of the Gao family. America may not be to everyone's liking, but allegorically it is accepted, in this case, as a bedfellow.

Wei-wei, as the final element of the allegory, embodies the PRC – or, rather, the ROC vision of the mainland. She is multiply marginalized and subordinated in the film – that is, as a woman, as an artist, as an illegal alien, as working class, as coming from economically underdeveloped and politically "backward" Communist China. To a wealthy and militarily and technologically advanced Taiwan, she plays the poor mainland relation. Throughout the film, a lot of the verbal play revolves around her national origin. Playing the peasant to Wai-tung's landlord, her first words to Wai-tung in the script are, "This floor has been liberated." She is called "*tong zhi*" (comrade) jokingly, and, as she straddles Wai-tung on their wedding night, she proclaims, "I'm liberating you." The nature of this "liberation" remains uncertain: is Taiwan, the wayward province, returned to the motherland, or is Taiwan, the bourgeois, decadent (homosexual) spawn of intercourse with America, returned to a "true," "Chinese" (heterosexual) path? Or is Wai-tung, ironically, really "liberating" Wei-wei from communism?

The allegorical dimension of *The Wedding Banquet* extends beyond the national, however, into the realm of ethnicity. The film's logo, for example, is an artificially created "triple happiness" character. The usual Chinese character for matrimonial bliss is a double "*xi*" (the character for "happiness"). In other words, this film presents a new version of the "double" happiness of marriage by adding a third element. The comic dimension of this nonsense character would not be lost on any literate Chinese viewer, and it serves as a reminder that this film has a transnational Chinese dimension. In other words, this national allegory is also an ethnic allegory, investigating the meaning of being "Chinese" beyond national affiliation.[8] Despite all the forces acting against a sense of Chinese tradition (embodied by the family over the nation), this allegory still manages to bring together a divided China by working with, rather than against, feminism, homosexuality, cultural imperialism, and the diaspora. However, this vision of a China elevated beyond the PRC and the ROC, reconciling communist and capitalist, fertile, and producing a new generation to erase historical differences, remains a comic vision, easily laughed at, ridiculed, and dismissed.

This allegorical reading of *The Wedding Banquet* tells only part of the story – that is, it favors a view of the KMT as a fading relic and the future of a united China on American terms. However, *The Wedding Banquet* offers other entry points into its interpretation. In fact, as the box office outside Taiwan demonstrates, many viewers of the film probably ignored elements of its national allegory for a reading that favors the perspective of a more globalized audience.[9]

To move from the modern national allegory to the postmodern fiction, the slippage between comedy and melodrama becomes telling in the film. The film's tone varies greatly. In one scene, Wai-tung finds Mr Gao slumped in a chair. An extreme close-up shows Wai-tung putting his finger under his father's mustached nose to check his breathing. A close-up of Mr Gao's still, vulnerable, aging face and another of Wai-tung's concerned expression follow. Then, Mr Gao suddenly awakes, and the mood lightens again. As this moment shows, *The Wedding Banquet* does not shy away from presenting darker emotions and possibilities that are associated with the melodrama rather than the comedy.

Even as these changes of tone mark shifts between genres, another question can be posed: slippage between what kind or kinds of comedy and what kind or kinds of melodrama? Is *The Wedding Banquet* a sex farce involving classic cases of mistaken identity and a few rounds of "musical beds"? Is it a gay comedy for straight audiences, like *La Cage aux Folles* (Molinaro 1978) and its American equivalents? Is the film a social satire on prevailing sexual mores? Is it a "romantic" melodrama, a family melodrama, or an "ethnic" family melodrama?[10] If, generally speaking, both the comedy and the melodrama work to keep heterosexuality and the patriarchy going, with a "successful" mating achieved after obstacles are overcome and progeny produced, then *The Wedding Banquet* need not be too firmly placed in one genre or the other. Its narrative resolution satisfies the aims of both. Rather, the question becomes whether anything exists in the film that exceeds the boundaries of allegory and genre.

On Photos, Phones, and Pictures of the Closet

Can *The Wedding Banquet* be looked at as camp? If so, is there a point of address in the film that can be said to target an "implied" gay viewer? Or does the film presuppose a straight audience by advancing a voyeuristic gaze onto an exotic, homosexual world for a "sympathetic," but decidedly "Other," spectator?

One Taiwanese commentator on the film laments the fact that no "gay mentality" exists in *The Wedding Banquet*, which the reviewer sees as a testing of traditional Chinese values in an alien environment rather than as a statement on gay life.[11] Indeed, the film's director, Ang Lee, married with children, does not identify himself as "gay."[12]

A few comments posted on the World Wide Web cover a range of perspectives by gay viewers. Gary Nygaard (1995) expresses the following view:

> I had heard good word-of-mouth about it, so eagerly I rented *The Wedding Banquet* within days of its appearance in video stores. But as I watched this film, which is billed as a gay comedy, I became uncomfortable and increasingly angry. . . . The lesson here, then, is that gay relationships must compromise themselves and bow to traditional, straight values and family structures. . . . Part of me can understand why this picture would catch on. The characters are generally likable – even the father, who I believe is the villain of the piece – and the film's tone is light with just enough emotional depth to engage. For a straight audience, the premise and the resolution are pretty non-threatening; and for a gay audience hungry to see gay and lesbian characters in the movies, this film does present "good-guy" gay men. But it makes me very sad that *The Wedding Banquet* has been so popular because, ultimately, I see it as a film that pretends to portray the lives of gays in a positive light, while really reinforcing old homophobic ideas and attitudes. Whether or not that was the filmmaker's intent, we don't need yet another movie which distorts us and demeans us.

Another review takes the opposite point of view:

> My favorite movie of all time has to be *The Wedding Banquet*!!! . . . An *absolute must* see for *any* in an Asian/Caucasian cross-cultural gay relationship, and a wonderfully entertaining comedy even if you're not :-). [DarkWhite n.d.]

Yet another gay viewer saw the film less as a campy comedy and more as a family melodrama:

> When I first saw the film, I was quite moved by it, especially the family relationships it portrays. I think that is something that is often ignored in straight perceptions of queers – family relationships actually do mean something to us. So I was very moved by mama's trying to understand what Wai-tung's life was, and father's quiet accepting of Simon's importance to his son. I think there is some universality there. [Anonymous 1997]

To begin again at the beginning with the opening credits for the producer and scriptwriter, Ted Hope and James Schamus have been involved with a number of projects involving gay issues, including *Poison* (1991) by Todd Haynes, as well as pieces on Roy Cohn, work by the lesbian filmmaker Jan Oxenburg, and more. Their production company, Good Machine, favors foreign art films and independent American gay–lesbian productions. *The Wedding Banquet* could fit into either camp. There seems to be enough in the text, too, to merit a careful consideration of an address to queer (particularly gay male) viewers.

One of the homoerotic visual themes begins in the opening scene. Wai-tung is introduced through a series of shots focusing first on close-ups of exercise-machine gears and pulleys and moving to shots of his body parts, with the emphasis on straining, sweat-drenched muscles. When looked at in the context of film history and its representation of the body as spectacle, these images tend to invite an erotic contemplation.[13] These shots can be taken as an invitation for a gay gaze at Wai-tung's semi-nude body. Other moments support this invitation to look pleasurably at men's bodies. In one scene after the wedding, for example, Wai-tung and Simon, thinking everyone else is out of the house, try to sneak in an afternoon sex romp. They kiss in the foyer and take off each other's clothes on the way upstairs. However, this brief respite from the closet ends abruptly when the two discover Mr Gao upstairs.

These moments of possible gay erotic contemplation find themselves undercut or countered in various ways throughout the film. For example, the opening scene also includes the plaintive voiceover cassette letter from Mrs Gao to her son, begging him to find a bride. Likewise, if there is an invitation to look at men as erotic spectacle, there is also a very open invitation to look at women in a similar way. Two bodies are "built up" in *The Wedding Banquet*: Wei-wei as the object of a presumably male heterosexual gaze and Wai-tung as the object of a presumably male homosexual gaze.

Wei-wei (played by a popular Taiwanese music personality who is unquestioningly taken as "attractive" by the public) enters the film with a series of shots that are strikingly similar to those that introduce Wai-tung. Living in an overheated loft, Wei-wei cools down with a sponge bath and a bottle of liquor. Like Wai-tung, she is introduced to the viewer through a series of moistly provocative, scantily clad body parts, and the mood is set with a blast of romantic Taiwanese pop music. Her disheveled appearance softens with the hazy, warm yellow-orange lighting used to convey a sense of "heat" in the flat. Throughout the remainder of the scene, she flirts with Wai-tung, trying to barter her painting, called *Heat*, for that month's rent.

In his business suit and tie, Wai-tung no longer holds center screen as an object of erotic contemplation. Wei-wei takes over that role, and Wai-tung, sweating and clearly uncomfortable in her presence, offers the possibility of straight identification for the viewer. In fact, it is this play with Wai-tung as a locus of identification for a heterosexual contemplation of Wei-wei that provides the specular working out of the plot's apparently irreconcilable incongruities.

Both scenes introducing Wai-tung and Wei-wei feature a split between the display of the male and female body, respectively, and a soundtrack with a less sexual and more sentimental bent. This split – between the carnal and the emotional, symbolized by the split between the body–spectacle and the voice–melodrama – continues throughout the film. Human relationships are organized around photographs (still images that construct and freeze a particular way of looking at things) and the telephone and tape recorder that connect disembodied voices (causing a split between the carnal and the sentimental). The drama revolves around the play between visual and aural (mis)communication.

The Wedding Banquet is a film about the "closet," defining the closet, constructing the closet, legitimizing the closet, coming out of the closet, staying in the closet, hiding behind the closet, and exposing the closet. As Jack Babuscio and others have pointed out,[14] camp humor revolves around issues associated with gay men's closeted lives, including a sense of irony, theatricality, and delight in surfaces. This aesthetic sensibility resonates with a life revolving around "false" appearances and a public "straight" persona needed to survive in the workplace, in the traditional family, and within a homophobic straight world. In *The Wedding Banquet*, both phones and photos serve to construct and deconstruct the closet.

For example, telephones in the film both illustrate gay intimacy and enable the closet to exist and adversely affect that intimacy. Wai-tung's love for Simon is introduced through a phone conversation. Their first screen kiss occurs after the two, sitting side by side, have a phone conversation to test the portable phone Simon has given Wai-tung as a gift. Also, Simon's decision to stay with Wai-tung is visualized through a shot of his tenderly replacing the receiver on the phone hook for an exhausted Wai-tung, who has fallen asleep in mid-conversation. However, the telephone also enables the closet to function. Mr and Mrs Gao's presence is felt in Wai-tung and Simon's relationship, long before the plane arrives from Taiwan, through long-distance late-night calls that interrupt the couple's sleep.[15]

The telephone, then, helps to create a gay relationship that can be disembodied and sentimentalized, but that can also, perhaps on a more positive note, be free of a perception of gay sexuality as "only sex" – that is, as unemotional, cold, and sterile. The telephone brings characters together and underscores their isolation and ignorance of each other's emotions. However, it is also important to note that the telephone enables the closet to function for Wai-tung. Disembodied communication allows for the distance necessary for the closet to keep going.

Scenes featuring still photographs punctuate the film and serve both to reaffirm Wai-tung's gay identity and to keep that identity in the closet. For example, when Wai-tung, Simon, and Wei-wei learn that the Gao parents will appear in New York for the wedding, they all do a lot of "house cleaning." Shown through a montage marked as conventionally comic by the use of up-beat, non-diegetic brass music played over the short takes, the construction of the closet is depicted primarily through the exchange of photographs. A photo of a nude Wai-tung is replaced with a photo of him in his Taiwan national service uniform.[16] Intimate photos of Simon and Wai-tung are replaced with photos of a distant-looking Wai-tung and Wei-wei. The scene comes to a climax with the unfolding of calligraphy scrolls in rapid succession. Gay New York has been replaced pictorially by ROC nationalism and Chinese tradition.

Later, in a striking shot, the camera takes the perspective of these scrolls (created by Mr Gao) as they are admired by Wei-wei and the rest of the family. Wei-wei has a long speech in which she details the merits of the scrolls, their relationship to various schools of Chinese calligraphy and their overall aesthetic significance. The film viewer looks at her looking at the camera (scrolls) and admires her admiring the viewer–camera–scrolls. She becomes the visual, aural, and dramatic cynosure of the closet as she wins over all commanded by her gaze – including the silent scrolls symbolizing Chinese order, tradition, a father's loving handiwork, and, implicitly, heterosexual patriarchy. Mr Gao comments that her expertise far exceeds Wai-tung's in this area, and he, as well as the scrolls–camera–viewer, is won over. Her voice and vision have legitimated the closet.

Wei-wei's association with the traditional connoisseur's eye finds its parallel in Simon's association with the eye of the modern photographer. During Wai-tung and Wei-wei's civil marriage ceremony at the court office, Simon takes on the role of photographer. He snaps pictures during the comic ceremony in which the nervous Wei-wei mangles the English wedding vows. Afterward, Simon rushes ahead of the rest of the family to take a group photograph. As the camera (the spectator's vision) shows Simon's view through the viewfinder, and the shot goes in and out of focus as Simon presumably fiddles with the lens, Mrs Gao melts into tears. Simon's photographic documentation of the wedding, to show the closet to US immigration and the Gaos' circle back in Taiwan, is disrupted.

Later, Simon's role as the gay eye on the marriage is usurped by a professional photographer. Indeed, Simon becomes blind to the transformation of the closet into a constructed and artificial, but surprisingly functional, heterosexuality. When Wai-tung, Simon (now in the role of "best man"), and the photographer approach the elaborately outfitted Wei-wei before the wedding banquet, a snap of the camera shutter underscores Wei-wei's desirability as the "beautiful" bride. A close shot of Wai-tung shows an interested look; Simon, in the background, remains oblivious. The presumed libidinous significance of Wai-tung's look finds further confirmation in a knowing glance and wink at Wai-tung from one of Wei-wei's bridesmaids. As Wei-wei has been built up to be a bride and her position has been captured and confirmed by the photographic eye, Wai-tung falls into line as the groom by taking on the specular position of the heterosexual viewer (a position underscored by the legitimizing presence of the fictitious still photographer). He looks, sees a conventionally constructed image of female desirability, and identifies with the straight way of seeing.

The construction of the heterosexual couple continues during a montage sequence that features the requisite studio shots of the bride, groom, and wedding party. The montage begins with the professional photographer orchestrating the composition of the shots, moving the couple into a series of clearly awkward poses. A succession of still photos follows, including clichéd poses of the bride smiling in close-up, the couple looking at each other, the family all smiling (with Simon), and the couple positioned in silhouette against a sunset. The soundtrack of "light," up-tempo, non-diegetic pop accompaniment underscores the artificiality of the photos and encourages an ironic distance from the usual sentiments surrounding the "happy" institution of marriage and weddings. Each cut is accompanied by the sound of an old-fashioned camera shutter and flash bulb, again bringing attention to the constructed, mediated, and artificial nature of the sights captured by the camera. Finally, the bride wilts in one shot, composes herself in an awkward pose, and the last photo becomes the flash of a white screen used as a transition. Wei-wei literally has been bent out of shape to become the blushing bride for the camera's eye.

Throughout the rest of the film, photographs continue to function as visual emblems for the closet. When Wai-tung and Simon attempt to have sex, for example, a cut away to a shot of a framed photo of the bride and groom in their living room bears the visual reminder that they can no longer be themselves in their own home. In the bedroom Wai-tung now shares with Wei-wei, an oversize portrait of the bride and groom dominates the mise-en-scène. The wedding photos on the walls of the closet close in.

The earlier scenes featuring the house cleaning and the studio portraits were presented as comedic, with a welcoming entry for a gay viewer to take an ironic view of the artifice of the closet and the excesses involved in its pictorial construction and legitimization. Later in the film, these same images take on a darker significance, from this perspective, as they overpower the characters within the mise-en-scène.

Still later, after Wai-tung comes out to his mother, photographs take on a sentimental and manipulative function. Mrs Gao takes out a photo album with pictures of Wai-tung as a baby to show to the pregnant Wei-wei. Her tears liberally rain down as she tells her daughter-in-law of the trauma of Wai-tung's cesarean birth, the pain of learning that she could not have other children, and the terror involved in raising a premature, sickly son when her husband was constantly away from home because of his military occupation. The black-and-white photos appear only briefly to punctuate a scene that focuses primarily on

Mrs Gao's face, gestures, and voice. The photos function as physical evidence of her sentiment used to manipulate Wei-wei into sympathizing with her, identifying with her as an enduring mother, and finally capitulating to her wish for Wei-wei not to have an abortion. Although the effect is not immediate, the photos seem to do the trick. Sentiment and melodrama win out over camp irony. The photos exclude a gay way of seeing.

The final, parting scene at the airport also features photographs. Wai-tung, Wei-wei, Simon, and Mr and Mrs Gao all look at the wedding photos together. The camera frames them all, like a family portrait, looking at the photo album. Sentiment turns back around to laughter as they look and laugh at a photo from the wedding banquet in which Wei-wei mistakes a kiss from a toddler for a kiss from Wai-tung. Focusing in on that photo of that moment underscores what brings this "family" together and legitimizes it – that is, the assurance of its continuation through Wei-wei's "son."

If all pictures imply a way of seeing,[17] and ways of seeing imply a perspective on what is viewed and an invitation for the spectator to identify with the perspective constructed by the artist–photographer, then that identification implies an identity – that is, an identification with an identity marked by ethnicity, nation, gender, sexual orientation, and so on. In *The Wedding Banquet*, these photographs show the shifting nature of identity and identification and the contradictions inherent in those shifts. Photos documenting gay life give way to an ironic picture of an artificial closet that becomes a constructed heterosexual desire that metamorphoses into a trap and finally dissolves into sentiment and an improbable nostalgia (that points to a bright and utopian future).

Myths of the Rice Queen and the Asian Gay

If the photographs that punctuate *The Wedding Banquet* underscore any single point, it is that the camera both creates and excludes. As the closet emerges, gay life recedes. Because of this, it becomes important to look at what is not shown in *The Wedding Banquet* and the implications of these exclusions.

When the structure of the film is examined closely, a polarization of characteristics becomes apparent. All of the gay characters in the film are Caucasian men – with the crucial exception of Wai-tung. All of the Asian characters in the film are presented as heterosexual – again with the exception of Wai-tung. In other words, the film posits a not-so-subtle division in which a figure such as Wai-tung, who is both Chinese and gay, becomes an anomaly. Gay Asian Americans, gay Chinese, and all gays of color have a single representative in the figure of Wai-tung. Or, to put it another way, gay Asians disappear into the character of Wai-tung. More than any other character in the film, Wai-tung stands as a symbol of a postmodern merger and erasure of identity. Avowedly homosexual, he falls for a woman and impregnates her. He upholds a Chinese tradition of filial piety and duty and still manages to keep his male lover. Is he gay? Is he heterosexual?[18] Is he traditionally Chinese? Is he modern and "American"? All of these remain impossible to answer completely as an entire community drops out of the picture. Singular and atomistic, Wai-tung can have no identity, because he has no fellows in the film. As a community of gay Chinese (Americans) drops out of the picture, so, too, does a key political element of the film.

In this case, the interracial nature of Wai-tung's relationship with Simon is crucial for the maintenance of the closet and for the preservation of a sense of Chinese ethnicity cleansed of any history of homosexuality. Although Wai-tung denies being "led" into a homosexual life by Simon when he comes out to his mother, the film does little to support any notion of a history of gay life in Asia and Asian America. Wai-tung must go outside of China, Taiwan, and Chinatown to find "someone compatible." Because of this, a polarization of the terms "Chinese" and "homosexual" can be maintained, along with a feeling that Wai-tung is a "unique" case (and a case fairly easily persuaded to be "Chinese," and therefore "heterosexual," at least on occasion).

From this perspective, the montage scene in which the closet is constructed for Mr and Mrs Gao's benefit can be looked at in another way. As the calligraphic scrolls unfurl, Wai-tung steps out of his ethnic closet and comes out as "Chinese." When he plays at being "straight," it is for the benefit of his Chinese acquaintances and family. When placed within the gay world, Wai-tung eats pizza, drinks wine, and has only Caucasian acquaintances. His ethnic identity is swept under the rug.

The consequences of this erasure of gay Asians branch off in many different directions. As the single gay Asian in the film, the figure of Wai-tung can counter extra-textual stereotypes without spelling out the multitude of negative qualities associated with racist and homophobic depictions in the mass media. However, as the film works to counter stereotypes, it also moves away from addressing points of genuine concern. One of these areas involves racism within the gay community and a more general perception of gay Asians as "effeminate."

The Wedding Banquet moves away from this entire issue by feminizing the Caucasian partner in the gay relationship. In contrast to Wai-tung, Simon plays a more effeminate role. He cooks; wears an apron, clingy black tank tops, and jeans; and his earring is prominently displayed. He has the "nurturing" job of physical therapist and takes it upon himself to organize Wai-tung's emotional and familial life (e.g., through suggesting his marriage to Wei-wei and filling her in on all the intimate details of the household's domestic routines for the immigration interview, giving presents to Wai-tung's parents, and helping to cook and care for the aging couple). Simon is "out" to his own family and has no problems with public displays of his sexual orientation (e.g., a peck on the cheek from another gay friend, distributing gay-pride literature, etc.). Wai-tung, on the other hand, sticks to business suits and invites Simon to dinner at a restaurant rather than cooking himself.

Wai-tung's enactment of the "masculine" role in his relationship with Simon goes against stereotypical assumptions about gay Caucasian–Asian relationships. Indeed, gay Asians have complained about racism in the gay community by generally citing the presumption on the part of some Caucasian gays that Asian gays will play a more "subservient" role.[19] According to an anonymous white, gay viewer of the film involved in a relationship with an Asian man: "I think the filmmaker was at most trying to neutralize the Rice Queen motif. And I think he was trying to get beyond stereotypes. In a way, it would almost be more interesting to see a film dive into those issues head on, because it is certainly a relevant issue, both for rice queens and queer Asians" (Anonymous 1997).

The "rice queen," then, may be looking for someone more like Simon than Wai-tung. Erasing the "type" from the film allows the closet to function within the narrative. If Simon were Asian, the closet would collapse, because his "queerness" could not be attributed to cultural differences (e.g., all white Americans must be a little "odd") by the Gao family.

If Wai-tung were more like Simon and Simon more like common perceptions of the "rice queen," the narrative would strain under a different burden. Simon flatters a certain segment of the audience. Given a cinematic history dominated globally by images of Asian men as (generally heterosexual and) rapacious or impotent and effeminate,[20] this presentation of a character like Wai-tung as heterosexually potent and characteristically not "masculine" has a certain appeal.

However, when placed within that same cinematic history of the representation of Asian men in the cinema, *The Wedding Banquet* really does not step radically away from the currently popular depictions. Is Wai-tung the homosexual that different, for example, from the homosexual (and bisexual or otherwise feminized) characters in *The Last Emperor* (Bertolucci 1987), *Farewell My Concubine* (Chen 1993), *Double Happiness* (Shum 1994), and *M. Butterfly* (Cronenberg 1993)? Within a popular history of Asian men depicted as eunuchs, domestic servants, and, more recently, transvestites, Wai-tung has company as he occupies what Rey Chow has called a "feminized space" within world culture: "China exists as an 'other,' feminized space to the West, a space where utopianism and eroticism come into play for various purposes of 'critique'" (Chow 1991, 32).

When the West looks at itself through China (a position certainly available in this film, which may or may not be "from Taiwan" or may or may not be "from America"), opportunities for critical understanding sometimes emerge. Although Wai-tung may well play the "good Chinese son" gone bad in the corrupt West for a Taiwan and overseas Chinese audience, he occupies a different role and "space" for the non-Asian viewer. As a double "other" (homosexual and Asian), Wai-tung becomes, in his marginalization within the dominant American mainstream, surprisingly free to embody a utopian dream of erotic liberty coupled with a cultural critique of homophobia, racism, and ethnocentrism. He becomes a liberal call for tolerance within the American "melting pot" without any dramatic political consequences. Indeed, in his false marriage to Wei-wei, he domesticates and "feminizes" a potentially more potent source of social chaos.

Constructing the Heterosexual – Who's "Queer" Here?

Films such as *The Wedding Banquet* have a certain "art house" following in Europe and America; it must not be forgotten that *Ju Dou* (1990), *Red Sorghum* (1987), and *Raise the Red Lantern* (1991), all three by Zhang Yimou and starring Gong Li, have also been hits in this same international art-film circuit. When China's feminized space is not occupied by a homosexual man, women emerge as victims of Chinese tradition.[21] From this perspective, Wei-wei can be looked at as fulfilling another part of this fantasy. However, as with the case of the contradictory and ultimately indeterminate presentation of Wai-tung's sexuality, Wei-wei's sexuality also ambivalently critiques and upholds very conservative, patriarchal notions.

From the outset, Wei-wei is not a "victim" of traditional patriarchy but a "victim" of its dissolution. Going back a step to the political dimensions of the film as a national allegory, Wei-wei represents a "feminist" mainland, liberated from the "feudal" and Confucian principles embodied by Mr and Mrs Gao. Alcoholic, illegal, fired from a series of low-paying jobs, an unsuccessful artist, Wei-wei needs rescuing. Her "liberation" has led her away from home, hearth, and the stability of marriage. The "green-card" marriage offers her the hope of legal status and freedom from the constant fear of deportation. Also, as she moves into Simon and Wai-tung's basement to establish cohabitation for the immigration office, the film presents her as settling in very comfortably, away from the heat and dreariness of her warehouse loft–slum home. Her salvation rests in her embourgeoisement. Fired because of a misunderstanding with Wai-tung at the outdoor cafe where she worked as a waitress, Wai-tung has freed her, inadvertently, from the presumed dreariness of her working-class job. She can now concentrate on her unappreciated work as an abstract painter, a suitable "hobby" for the "housewife" she plays for immigration and the Gao parents. Wai-tung, the slum lord–husband, delivers on a promise of material comfort and "freedom" not for, but from, the working classes. Prosperous and aloof, Taiwan holds out the same promise for the mainland – that is, the promise of a bourgeois China.

Just as the wedding constructs Wai-tung as a heterosexual groom, it constructs Wei-wei as a bourgeois bride. She must be as completely transformed as Wai-tung in the process, leaving behind her feminism and her working-class roots. For example, the scenes preceding the wedding banquet comically construct Wei-wei to enable her to play the role of the bride. A montage, accompanied by up-tempo accordion music, shows the bride's hair shampooed, facial mask peeled off, hair curlers in place, eyelashes and lip gloss applied. A full-face close-up of the completed bride ends the scene.

In the next scene, her mainland friends surround Wei-wei, in full bridal-party regalia. One remarks in English, "Man, they really piled on the rocks" – referring to the Gao's elaborate and extensive bridal gifts – as she helps organize the bride's jewelry. The dialogue switches to Mandarin, and Mrs Gao says Wei-wei is "beautiful." When Wai-tung and the rest of the groom's party enter, a medium long shot shows the completed bride as she stands up to display her gown. A traditional Chinese "double happiness" decoration on the wall doubles up with the voluminous skirt and veil of Wei-wei's Western gown to underscore the cross-cultural power of the spectacle. As mentioned earlier, Wai-tung fits into the space created for him as viewer of this spectacle, an overdetermined locus of Chinese and Western visions of heterosexuality and bourgeois patriarchy.

Throughout the banquet scenes, Wei-wei continues to evolve into the type of woman that all wedding banquets are supposed to create – a bride desirable enough to overcome the groom's inhibitions. In this case, her desires need only be slightly redirected. Earlier, after going though a litany of her recent affairs and their unhappy outcomes, she laments that she always seems to be attracted to "cute," gay men. With this comment, the script opens another can of worms. Is Wei-wei unhappy with straight men because she is a feminist and unhappy with their chauvinism? Are gay men somehow more "sympathetic" because they don't have all the privileges associated with heterosexuals? Is she not quite "straight" herself and, thus, looking for something "feminine" in (wo)men?

The film, like Freud, closes off all these questions by redirecting Wei-wei's libido into motherhood. The wedding prepares all for this redirection of energy with a series of games and rituals. A young boy jumps on the wedding bed for good luck, and, later, the blindfolded bride mistakenly picks him as her groom when he kisses her cheek. The couple tries to nibble at the same bobbing chicken head as an excuse to kiss. The wedding guests noisily clamor for lengthy, public kisses. Garters fly, and liquor flows. All of the sex games designed to "humiliate" the bride and groom, and bind them together with lots of liquor and loosened inhibitions, serve to soften up the couple for the marriage bed. In the final send-off, the last guests agree to leave only after the couple is naked under the bed covers and all their clothes are on the floor beside them.

At one point, a Caucasian man tells his Caucasian girlfriend that he thought the Chinese were meek and quiet. A Chinese male guest overhears and says: "You're witnessing the results of thousands of years of sexual repression." Actually, they are witnessing the results of a centuries-old collection of practices that traditionally deliver the same result – the consummation of the marriage. Although this may be taken for granted under the mystification of romantic love and marital bliss, it is an event that proves to be none too easy in cases of arranged marriage. In this case, Western and Chinese nuptial traditions come together to create a bride and groom who can consummate the marriage. Although Wei-wei and Wai-tung appear to be a very modern "odd couple," are they really that different from others, such as Mr Gao, who went into battle to avoid an arranged marriage? Would the same tricks of the trade have worked on him if he had not been able to escape into the KMT army? If *The Wedding Banquet* were set in the Qing Dynasty or earlier, could a similar outcome be imagined? With a patriarchal emphasis on sons and the continuation of the family line, who could deny the head of the household his lover (male or female, courtesan or concubine) if he otherwise did his "duty" for the family? Here, the radical multiculturalism of the interracial, transnational ménage à trois falls back into a very conservative sense of Chinese ethnic tradition and values.

Madame Butterfly in New York City

In this case, the modern rebuilding of Chinese patriarchal relations rests on the self-sacrifice of women. Wei-wei provides a modern twist on old "Madame Butterfly" themes.[22] The appearance of Wu Ren Ren/Little Sister Mao (Vanessa Yang) makes this association explicit. A computer date sent to Wai-tung from Taiwan, Ren Ren fits the impossible bill of speaking five languages, being a professional opera singer, and having a PhD. (Her only short-coming is that she has only one doctorate; Wai-tung had demanded two.) After accidentally running into Wei-wei, who is working in a cafe where the two have come for a drink, Wai-tung is "outed" by Wei-wei. Ren Ren then tells her secret. She has a Caucasian boyfriend, and her family does not approve. In this sense, she is like Wai-tung, involved in an illicit interracial affair. At the end of the sequence, Ren Ren sings Cio-Cio San's famous aria from Puccini's *Madama Butterfly*.[23] As she fades out of the plot, a new parallel develops – not between Ren Ren and Wai-tung, but between Cio-Cio San and Wei-wei. Like Cio-Cio San, Wei-wei sacrifices herself to bear a child for a man who does not love her.

Wei-wei suppresses her libido in the continuation of the Gao family line. Although materially better off, she has sacrificed her freedom for this exclusively maternal role. The feminist, "liberated" by Mao and the communists, falls back into the feudal role of a woman in a loveless, arranged marriage, whose only comfort is her son (or sons). In this respect, the film's construction of an accepting multicultural environment, in which heterosexual and homosexual, the ROC and the PRC, China and America come together in harmonious intercourse, is constructed on the ruins of feminism. Wei-wei must accept her mother-in-law's tearful statement that men and children still must "count for something" in a woman's life.

The melodrama of women's sacrifice, glossed over by a comedic tone, underlies *The Wedding Banquet*'s narrative structure. As in other postmodern texts, the blurring of genres underscores a blurring of identity and politics. Feminism, gay rights, and Chinese ethnic identity cannot exist simultaneously within *The Wedding Banquet*. Something must "give" for the narrative to work. In this case, feminism collapses. However, the choice seems somehow arbitrary – part of a postmodern sensibility rather than any genuine misogyny or anti-feminist sentiment. In other postmodern, nostalgic reconstitutions of an imaginary past within a contemporary environment, entire histories of colonialism, racism, and capitalism are conjured up, ground up, and reconfigured in similar ways. Within postmodern culture, radical and reactionary postures coexist within fictions that make it impossible to discern unequivocally a moral high ground for any political position.

Is There an Asian American in the Text?

When watching *The Wedding Banquet*, another comedy–melodrama set within the Chinese American community may come to mind: *Flower Drum Song* (Koster 1961), which has many of the same themes that appear in *The Wedding Banquet*. For example, both movies contain an aging son reluctant to marry, generational conflicts, and a "happy ending" in an arranged marriage. Lee, then, is not working in an arena alien to commercial Hollywood. On the contrary, some of *The Wedding Banquet*'s appeal to more general audiences most likely comes from a familiarity with films that provide a voyeuristic entry into sequestered ethnic American ghettoes. The non-Chinese viewer can remark, along with the Caucasian guests at the wedding, about an ignorance of Chinese customs and practices while enjoying the exotic spectacle of the banquet.

In this case, that vision is limited in some interesting ways. Just as Hokkien speakers, upwardly mobile mainlanders. "out" Asians and others have no place in *The Wedding Banquet*, the Asian American experience presented also has some blind spots. No one goes to New York's Chinatowns in lower Manhattan (primarily Cantonese-speaking from Hong Kong and Guangdong Province) and Queens (primarily Mandarin- and Hokkien-speaking from Taiwan). Immigration problems occur off-screen. No INS raids are depicted. No deportation proceedings are shown. Immigration tests are prepared for but never shown being taken. Wei-wei goes from job to job off-screen, for the most part. Searching for a job without a green card is not shown; employer–employee relations within the illegal labor force move to the fringes of the text. No mainland artists are mugged in Times Square doing portraits for tourists. No sweatshops or massage parlors appear. No racists threaten any of the characters with violence. The edginess of Wei-wei's existence at the fringes of the Asian American community is not a principal part of the events depicted in the plot. Much the same thing happens to Wei-wei's environment as happens to Wai-tung's. The illegal, working-class immigrant and the gay Asian become isolated as oddities rather than being embraced as members of a community.

Asian America is out of the allegorical picture, too. Wei-wei's fetus unifies China; it does not represent a new generation of Asian Americans. Wai-tung and Wei-wei continue to be Chinese, part of a greater China rather than part of a Chinese American community (let alone an Asian American body politic). Ang Lee describes his own experience of being Chinese in New York as follows:

> Of course, I identify with Chinese culture because that was my upbringing, but that becomes very abstract; it's the idea of China. My generation of Chinese has always felt that way. And the sentiment of being Chinese is different in New York than it is

in Taiwan or in China. Wherever you come from, whether it's China or Hong Kong or Taiwan, in New York, you're just Chinese; it's sort of generalized and merged, and people are drawn to each other by that abstract idea of being Chinese. In that way, it was natural to me to include all the different Chinese in New York City in the film, because that's a reflection of my life, a mixture of language and characters, it's kind of natural to me. [Quoted in Berry 1993, 54]

The Wedding Banquet is not unique in its playing out of fantasies about the overseas Chinese for a mixed Asian and Western audience. In fact, there has been a boom in recent years in films set in American or European Chinatowns, usually produced by Hong Kong or Taiwanese concerns.[24] Like *The Wedding Banquet*, most of these films deal less with the development of an Asian American identity among Chinese immigrants than with the creation of a transnational sense of Chinese identity. With the exception of Wayne Wang's feature films on the Chinese American community (e.g., *Chan Is Missing*, 1982; *Dim Sum*, 1985; *Eat a Bowl of Tea*, 1989; and *The Joy Luck Club*, 1993), few of these films have received critical attention as Asian American films. In this respect, as indebted as the film is to its Taiwanese roots and despite its apparent inattention to many critical issues facing Asian Americans, *The Wedding Banquet* did receive attention as more than a Chinese film about the overseas community. Indeed, as daring as its treatment of homosexuality is from the standpoint of a traditionally conservative Taiwanese film culture, *The Wedding Banquet* may be even more daring in its ability to bridge the gap between Chinese film and Asian American film culture. Clearly, it is a film filled with surprises.

The final narrative "surprise" of the film occurs toward the end. Simon and Mr Gao are outside, on the waterfront, doing Mr Gao's physical therapy. Mr Gao says "Happy Birthday" in English to Simon and gives him a *hong bao* filled with cash. Simon has a triple surprise: Mr Gao speaks English; Mr Gao knows that he and Wai-tung are gay lovers; and Mr Gao accepts the homosexual relationship. With Simon, the viewer is also "surprised" by Mr Gao's modernity. The old KMT officer has always been part of a modern, hybridized, transnational, transcultural world. He just never let "us" (the viewer – both East and West) know. According to Chow (1991, 28):

> What is missing from the preoccupation with tradition and authentic originariness as such is the experience of modern Chinese people who have had to live their lives with the knowledge that it is precisely the notion of a still-intact tradition to which they cannot cling – the experience precisely of being impure, "Westernized" Chinese and the bearing of *that* experience on their ways of "seeing" China.

Finally, Mr Gao is as "modern" as Wai-tung is "traditional." Categories collapse, and identity becomes problematized. Old Gao has a "modern" face with a "Western" voice.

Produced, distributed, and marketed within a transnational matrix of economic, political, cultural, ethnic, and linguistic relationships, *The Wedding Banquet* does not posit a singular position for an abstract, "ideal" viewer. Non–Chinese-speaking viewers miss untranslated dialogue as well as plays on the Chinese language and customs. References to "Act Up" are most likely lost on a mainstream audience outside America or unfamiliar with the gay community. Rather than attempting to create a homogenized audience that could conceivably understand everything, *The Wedding Banquet* simply hopes for enough overlap not to lose anyone along the way.

This overlap has certain ideological ramifications. Types need to be broad enough to be recognizable, but not offensive. Political issues need to be broached, but kept safely within the realm of a utopian (and thus, fantastical) fiction. Behind the lively multicultural mix, an organizing principle emerges that builds its liberal vision on the erasure of the experiences of feminists, gay Asians, and other voices of the Asian American community. Within a transnational cinema with a multicultural, cosmopolitan vision of diversity, hierarchies of power and structures of silence still exercise a heavy burden on the emergent desire for social change, harmony, and understanding.

Notes

1 For a definition of Asian American filmmaking and its relationship to Asia and Asian film, see Feng (1995) and Francia (1990).
2 The film's title is *Hsi Yen* in the Wade-Giles system, and *Xi Yan* in pinyin. Given that the film is a Taiwanese production, the Wade-Giles system will be used for the transliteration of proper names (unless they are more commonly rendered in another system of romanization). Individuals differ in their preferences for the rendering of their names; Lee Ang is sometimes Ang Lee, for example, inverting surname and given name. The most commonly seen rendering will be used in this chapter.
3 Fine articles on *The Wedding Banquet* have appeared since I wrote this chapter. Some cover some of the same ground explored here. For more information on the film in relation to the filmmaker's other works, see Dariotis and Fung (1997). For more on *The Wedding Banquet* as a queer text, see Chiang (1998).
4 The most striking illustration of this is in the scene in which Mr Gao blesses Wai-tung and Wei-wei's union as a coming together of Taiwan and the mainland. The English subtitles do not translate the political dimension of the speech.
5 This implication is stated directly in the program booklet.
6 In film, 1989 marked the first major feature to broach any critique of the KMT and its policies: *A City of Sadness* (directed by Hou Hsiao-hsien). Since then, a number of films have variously criticized the KMT version of Chinese–Taiwanese relations. See Chiao (1996).
7 In contrast to the Gaos' fevered attempt to keep the extended family going under any circumstances, Simon represents a common Chinese view that one of the principal ways in which America proves itself inferior to China is in its failure to take the institution of the family seriously. Hence, Mrs Gao is fascinated by Simon's estranged biological father, stepfather, and various types of siblings. Wei-wei, in exasperation, finally stops translating when Simon gets to a half-brother killed in Vietnam.

8 A lot of scholarship has been generated on "Greater China" and an evolving sense of being ethnically Chinese in the modern world. See Tu (1994).

9 Indeed, critics of Jameson have pointed out many of the shortcomings of his conjecture that all Third World texts are "necessarily' national allegories. See Ahmad (1995). In this case, I would say that *The Wedding Banquet* can be taken as a national allegory and as a "postmodern" commercial product, while Jameson tends to see this as an either–or proposition in the article mentioned earlier. Jameson takes a different tack in his look at the Taiwanese film *The Terrorizer* (Yang 1986); see Jameson (1992).

10 What I would term the "ethnic" family melodrama involves those films which deal with domestic tensions within an American family marked as "Other" due to ethnic difference. This has been a staple of the Hollywood sound film since *The Jazz Singer* (Crosland 1927) and usually involves multigenerational conflicts, unassimilated parents (usually mothers), economic difficulties linked to ethnic associations, romantic tensions involving cross-cultural misunderstandings, and so on. The Asian American ethnic family melodrama has been quite evident recently in films such as *The Joy Luck Club* (Wang 1993), among other features.

11 Wang (1993). My thanks to Yang Ming-yu for providing this review and its translation. The term "gay mentality" appears in English in the review, pointing to a tendency to look at "gay life" as "Western" or "foreign."

12 Noted in Berry (1993). For more on Lee and his work, see Ma (1996) and Rayns (1993).

13 The classic article on the operation of the gaze and the representation of the body is Mulvey (1995). While the spectacle of the woman's body has been assumed as a staple of classical cinema, several genres gaze at the male body as spectacle, including Hollywood action adventure and gay porn.

14 For a complete explication of the closet and its meaning in film, see Babuscio (1977), Russo (1981), and Dyer (1990). For a theoretical examination, see Sedgwick (1990).

15 Wei-wei also has a long-distance telephone relationship with her family in Shanghai. The only glimpse given of this relationship and of conditions on the mainland comes in a brief conversation in Shanghaiese. The family has moved into a new flat (with the rapid modernization of the city, many families have moved into new housing in satellite areas in the past few years), and only a few words that nothing is new or wrong are exchanged before the conversation is interrupted by wedding preparations. Just as Wai-tung's family has no idea about his sex life, Wei-wei's family knows nothing about her green-card marriage to a homosexual. The telephone really does little to further communication, while it functions as a means to add to the sense of irony and miscommunication cultivated by the film.

16 All men in Taiwan are required to do a stint in the armed forces. The image conjures up both this masculine rite of passage and the family's military connections.

17 Berger (1972) might note something similar.

18 I am reluctant even to broach the idea of "bisexuality," because it is so foreign to *The Wedding Banquet*. The implication, at the end of the film, is that Wai-tung is not bisexual and will not consider continuing a sexual relationship with both Wei-wei and Simon. Rather, Wei-wei has implicitly given up sex to become the mother of Wai-tung's baby – a point underscored in her conversation with Mrs Gao about the possibility of Wai-tung's getting in touch with his "straight" side after the birth of the

baby. Wei-wei says she's certain that that will not happen. In other words, she accepts that Wai-tung's sexual orientation will always be toward men.

19 This has been brought up by filmmakers and video makers – for example, Nguyen Tan Hoang's *Seven Steps to Sticky Heaven* (n.d.) and Richard Fung's work on Asians in gay pornography. See also Fung (1991). For a listing of films and videos on Asian gay–lesbian themes, see http://www.tufts.edu/%7Estai/QAPA/films.html.

20 See Wong (1978) and Kashiwabara (n.d.).

21 There have been many wonderful critiques of the reception of these films outside China. See Lu (1996) and Chow (1995).

22 See Heung (1997) on the modern Madame Butterfly and Marchetti (1993).

23 For a useful synopsis of the opera, see http://classicalmus.com/bmgclassics/opera/operabutterfly.html. It is important to remember that Puccini's version was not unprecedented, but based on the play by Belasco which had been based on the short story by John Luther Long, himself inspired by the work of French author Pierre Loti. However, it is Puccini's version that still seems to resonate most deeply in current references and retellings.

24 It is impossible to list all the films that have taken advantage of American and European locations to tell stories about the overseas Chinese. See Law (1992) for an excellent collection of essays on the topic.

Works Cited

Ahmad, Aijaz. 1995. "Jameson's Rhetoric of Otherness and the 'National Allegory.'" Pp. 77–82 in *The Post-Colonial Studies Reader*, ed. Bill Ashcroft, Gareth Griffiths and Helen Tiffin. London: Routledge.

Anonymous. 1997. Electronic interview with the author. July.

Babuscio, Jack. 1977. "Camp and the Gay Sensibility." Pp. 40–57 in *Gays and Film*, ed. Richard Dyer. London: British Film Institute.

Berger, John. 1972. *Ways of Seeing*. London: BBC and Penguin.

Berry, Chris. 1993. "Taiwanese Melodrama Returns with a Twist in *The Wedding Banquet*." *Cinemaya* 21 (Fall): 52–54.

Central Motion Picture Corporation. 1993. Publicity book: *The Wedding Banquet* by Ang Lee. Taipei, n.p.

Chiang, Mark. 1998. "Coming Out into the Global System: Postmodern Patriarchies and Transnational Sexualities in *The Wedding Banquet*." Pp. 374–96 in *Q and A: Queer in Asian America*, ed. David L. Eng and Alice Y. Hom. Philadelphia: Temple University Press.

Chiao, Peggy. 1996. "White Terror and the Formosa Incident: Introspections on Recent Political Film from Taiwan." *Cinemaya* 32 (spring): 22–24.

Chow, Rey. 1991. *Woman and Chinese Modernity: The Politics of Reading Between West and East*. Minneapolis: University of Minnesota Press.

——. 1995. *Primitive Passions: Visuality, Sexuality, Ethnography, and Contemporary Chinese Cinema*. NY: Columbia University Press.

Dariotis, Wei-ming, and Eileen Fung. 1997. "Breaking the Soy Sauce Jar: Diaspora and Displacement in the Films of Ang Lee." Pp. 187–220 in *Transnational Chinese Cinemas: Identity, Nationhood, Gender*, ed. Sheldon Hsiao-peng Lu. Honolulu: University of Hawaii Press.

DarkWhite. n.d. "Review of *The Wedding Banquet*, dir. Ang Lee," http://www.users. on.net/darkwhite/movies.htm.

Dyer, Richard. 1990. *Now You See It: Studies on Lesbian and Gay Film*. New York: Routledge.

Feng, Peter. 1995. "In Search of Asian American Cinema." *Cineaste* 21, nos. 1–2 (Winter–Spring): 32–35. (Also http://www.lib.berkeley.edu/MRC/InSearchofAsian.html.)

Francia, Luis. 1990. "Asian Cinema and Asia American Cinema: Separated by a Common Language." *Cinemaya* 9 (Fall): 36–39.

Fung, Richard. 1991. "Center the Margins." Pp. 62–67 in *Moving the Image: Independent Asian Pacific American Media Arts*, ed. Russell Leong. Los Angeles: UCLA Asian American Studies Center and Visual Communications, Southern California Asian American Studies Central.

Heung, Marina. 1997. "The Family Romance of Orientalism: From *Madame Butterfly* to *Indochine*." Pp. 158–83 in *Visions of the East: Orientalism in Film*, ed. Matthew Bernstein and Gaylyn Studlar. New Brunswick, NJ: Rutgers University Press.

Jameson, Fredric. 1986. "Third World Literature in the Era of Multinational Capitalism." *Social Text* 15 (Fall): 65–88.

——. 1992. *The Geopolitical Aesthetic: Cinema and Space in the World System*. Bloomington: Indiana University Press.

Kashiwabara, Amy. n.d. "Vanishing Son: The Appearance, Disappearance, and Assimilation of the Asian-American Man in American Mainstream Media," http://www.lib.berkeley.edu/ MRC/Amydoc.htmd.

Klady, Leonard. 1994. "Pix' Profit Picture Present Surprises." *Variety*, January 10–16, 13.

Law, Kar, ed. 1992. *Overseas Chinese Figures in Cinema*. Hong Kong: The 16th Hong Kong International Film Festival.

Lent, John A. 1990. *The Asian Film Industry*. Austin: University of Texas Press.

Lu, Sheldon. 1996. "Postmodernity, Popular Culture, and the Intellectual: A Report on Post-Tiananmen Cinema." *boundary* 2 23, no. 2 (Summer): 139–69.

Ma, Sheng-mei. 1996. "Ang Lee's Domestic Tragicomedy: Immigrant Nostalgia, Exotic/ Ethnic Tour, Global Market." *Journal of Popular Culture* 30, no. 1 (summer): 191–201.

Marchetti, Gina. 1993. *Romance and the "Yellow Peril": Race, Sex, and Discursive Strategies in Hollywood Fiction*. Berkeley: University of California Press.

Mulvey, Laura. 1975. "Visual Pleasure and Narrative Cinema." *Screen* 16, no. 3 (Fall): 6–18.

Nygaard, Gary. 1995. "Review of *The Wedding Banquet*, dir. Ang Lee" January, http:// www.athena.net/~lavsalon/book_reviews-95.html.

Rayns, Tony. 1993. "*Xiyan* (*The Wedding Banquet*)." *Sight and Sound* 3, no. 10 (October): 56.

Russo, Vito. 1981. *The Celluloid Closet: Homosexuality in the Movies*. NY: Harper and Row.

Sedgwick, Eve K. 1990. *Epistemology of the Closet*. Berkeley: University of California Press.

Tu, Wei-ming, ed. 1994. *The Living Tree: The Changing Meaning of Being Chinese Today*. Stanford, Calif.: Stanford University Press.

Wang, Chi Cheng. 1993. "Review of *The Wedding Banquet*, dir. Ang Lee." *Min Sheng Daily* (Taiwan), 4 March, 31.

Wong, Eugene Franklin. 1978. *On Visual Media Racism: Asians in the American Motion Pictures*. New York: Arno Press.

Films and Videos Cited

Bertolucci, Bernardo. 1987. *The Last Emperor*. Columbia Pictures Corporation, Artisan Entertainment.

Chen, Kaige. 1993. *Farewell My Concubine*. Buena Vista/Miramax Films.

Cronenberg, David. 1993. M. *Butterfly*. Warner Bros.

Crosland, Alan. 1927. *The Jazz Singer*. Warner Bros.

Haynes, Todd. 1991. *Poison*. Bronze Eye Productions.

Hou, Hsiao-hsien. 1989. *City of Sadness*. Artificial eye/3-H Films/Era International.

Koster, Henry. 1961. *Flower Drum Song*. Universal International.

Lee, Ang. 1992. *Pushing Hands*.

——. 1993. *The Wedding Banquet*. Central Motion Picture Corporation/Good Machine.

——. 1994. *Eat Drink Man Woman*. Central Motion Picture Corporation.

——. 1995. *Sense and Sensibility*. Mirage/Columbia.

——. 1997. *The Ice Storm*. Good Machine/Fox Searchlight Pictures.

Molinaro, Edouard. 1978. *La Cage aux Folles*. United Artists.

Nguyen, Tan Hoang. *Seven Steps to Sticky Heaven*. No distributor.

Shum, Mina. 1994. *Double Happiness*. Fine Line Features.

Spielberg, Steven. 1993. *Jurassic Park*. Universal Pictures.

Wang, Wayne. 1982. *Chan Is Missing*. New Yorker Films.

——. 1985. *Dim Sum: A Little Bit of Heart*. CIM/Orion Classics.

——. 1989. *Eat a Bowl of Tea*. American Playhouse/Columbia.

——. 1993. *The Joy Luck Club*. Hollywood Pictures/Buena Vista.

Yang, Edward. 1986. *The Terrorizer*. Central Motion Picture Corporation.

Zhang, Yimou. 1987. *Red Sorghum*. Xi'an Film Studio.

——. 1990. *Ju Dou*. Tokuma Communications/Chinan Film.

——. 1991. *Raise the Red Lantern*. Orion Classics.

17

Another Fine Example of the Oral Tradition? Identification and Subversion in Sherman Alexie's *Smoke Signals*

Jhon Warren Gilroy

My heroes have always killed cowboys.

> Slogan on T-shirt worn by Neil Young.

Say, didn't I kill you twelve movies ago?

> John Wayne to an Indian actor.

Sometimes, it's a good day to die. Sometimes, it's a good day to have breakfast.

> Thomas Builds-the-Fire

59 ◆ INT. BUS (PRESENT DAY) – DAY . . .

THOMAS: Hey, what do you remember about your dad?

Victor ignores Thomas.

THOMAS: I remember one time we had a fry bread eating contest and he ate fifteen pieces of fry bread. It was cool.

Victor sits up in his seat and looks at Thomas.

VICTOR: You know, Thomas? I don't know what you're talking about half the time. Why is that?

Jhon Warren Gilroy, "Another Fine Example of the Oral Tradition? Identification and Subversion in Sherman Alexie's *Smoke Signals*," pp. 23–42 from *Studies in American Indian Literatures* 13:1 (Lincoln: University of Nebraska Press, Spring 2001). © 2001 by Jhon Warren Gilroy. Reprinted by permission of the author.

THOMAS: I don't know.

VICTOR: I mean, you just go on and on talking about nothing. Why can't you have a normal conversation? You're always trying to sound like some damn medicine man or something. I mean, how many times have you seen *Dances With Wolves*? A hundred, two hundred times?

Embarrassed, Thomas ducks his head.

VICTOR: (*con't*)

Oh, jeez, you have seen it that many times, haven't you? Man. Do you think that shit is real? God. Don't you even know how to be a real Indian?

THOMAS: (*whispering*)

I guess not.

Victor is disgusted.

VICTOR: Well, shit, no wonder. Jeez, I guess I'll have to teach you then, enit?

Thomas nods eagerly.

VICTOR: First of all, quit grinning like an idiot. Indians ain't supposed to smile like that. Get stoic.

Thomas tries to look serious. He fails.

VICTOR: No, like this.

Victor gets a very cool look on his face, serious, determined, warriorlike.

VICTOR: You got to look mean or people won't respect you. White people will run all over you if you don't look mean. You got to look like you just got back from killing a buffalo.

THOMAS: But our tribe never hunted buffalo. We were fishermen.

VICTOR: What? You want to look like you just came back from catching a fish? It ain't Dances With Salmon, you know? Man, you think a fisherman is tough? Thomas, you got to look like a warrior.

Thomas gets stoic. He's better this time . . .

On the Road: Re-paving the Powwow Highway

The above scene from *Smoke Signals* exemplifies the major thematic concerns and formal approaches that the film explores. In this scene, Sherman Alexie's personal favorite, we see evidenced the humor, social commentary, and the powerful relationship between filmic representation and American Indian identity. Heavily promoted as the first feature film conceived, written, directed and co-produced by American Indians, the film subverts mainstream viewers' generic expectations through the use of classical film narrative techniques and humor. By creating a film steeped in classical Hollywood norms, yet rooted in an American Indian epistemology, the filmmakers have created a space that invites Euramerican viewers in and then uses humor as a tool for incisive political commentary. The palliative effect of humor works to dissolve racist stereotypes even as it softens the blow of social commentary.

At its heart *Smoke Signals* is a typical road/buddy movie. Thomas Builds-the-Fire and Victor Joseph, the film's main characters, set out to recover the cremated remains of Victor's estranged, alcoholic father who had abandoned Victor and his mother ten years previously. Their trip from the Coeur d'Alene Indian Reservation to Phoenix, Arizona serves as the vehicle for a large number of inset narratives that are presented as both "recounted" and "enacted" flashbacks and stories (Bordwell 78).[1] The film plays off a viewer's familiarity with a form in which the ostensible goal of the journey drives the action of the plot; here, the retrieval of the father's remains, metaphorically the reclaiming of the estranged Father, is not necessarily read as the most important story. It is at the subtextual or philosophical narrative level there exists the potential for subversion of stereotypes, and mainstream viewers' implication in the fabula-making based upon them, becomes more noticeable. Here, the viewer finds herself not in the comfortable, well mapped-out confines of territory, but rather in a frontier space informed by the culture of an Other.

The simultaneous push/pull of a mainstream Euramerican audience's identification with the film's genre, juxtaposed against the alienation of a story and characters that arise from distinctly "Other" cultural backgrounds, creates what American Indian author/critic Louis Owens refers to in *Mixedblood Messages as* a "frontier" space. The creation of this frontier space is necessary if the film is to subvert successfully pejorative stereotypes of contemporary American Indians, Owens re-conceives "frontier" as a space that "is always unstable, multidirectional, hybridized, characterized by heteroglossia, and indeterminate" (26–27). This space where different cultures meet and collide stands in direct opposition to the "static and containable" territory: a space which merely waits to be emptied of its indigenous character and replaced with that which will be called "American." By replacing the film's underlying philosophical message with an American Indian cosmology, *Smoke Signals* creates a frontier environment – particularly for a mainstream Euramerican viewer – to build a bridge from which viewers can examine stereotypical assumptions about American Indians.

The postcolonial implications of Alexie's screenplay's appropriation of the discourse of the privileged center lie in the film's re-possession of a format which Euramerican viewers read easily: that of the road/buddy movie. Our familiarity with the perceptual schemata – the "organized clusters of knowledge [that] guide our hypothesis making" – that we bring to films rooted in classical Hollywood narrative modes, allows mainstream viewers access into the narrative (Bordwell 31). The film's indigenous epistemological origins then re-configure the meanings of classical Hollywood tropes, altering the outcomes of a viewer's attempts at fabula construction.[2] In her explication of the codes and conventions of mainstream American cinema, Susan Hayward proposes that, by its very nature, the "road movie implies discovery, obtaining some self-knowledge," and that "the roadster is male and it is his point of view that we see" (49). By inviting the viewer into a narrative that on a surface level adheres to these classical norms, the film is then able to subvert a mainstream viewer's expectations in three ways: (1) by having that "roadster" male be American Indian; (2) by creating levels of narration that do not adhere to "his point of view"; and (3) by having the mainstream viewer "obtain some self-knowledge" through a character that is decidedly Other.

Cigar Store Indians: Subverting the Stereotypes

Perhaps the most easily recognized subversive effect of *Smoke Signals* is the film's success at countering racist, stereotypical images of American Indians – many of which have been engendered and perpetuated by the very medium in which this narrative appears. Instead of the "usual" tragic, two-dimensional, drunk and vanishing Indian, the narrative depicts fully developed characters living out a unique aspect of contemporary American existence: life on the Coeur d'Alene Indian Reservation. It is here that Alexie's efforts to subvert what he sees as the two most pernicious stereotypes – those of the warrior and the shaman – come most clearly into focus.[3] At key moments, the film's narrative plays off these stereotypes by misdirecting the mainstream viewers' attempts to construct fabula that are based on their pre-conceptions of "Indians." Through this misdirection, mainstream viewers, along with the protagonists, can "obtain some self-knowledge" regarding the stereotypical assumptions that guide their construction of the fabula.

The narrative creates this possibility by generating a recognizable gap between the viewer's prediction of what will occur and what actually happens in the syuzhet. As these predictions are based on cultural misinformation (read: racist stereotypes), the pejorative nature of the schemata upon which viewers create their fabulas is highlighted along with the very act of fabula construction. The most poignant examples of this action occur at points in the narrative where the characters themselves fall victim to this same process: manifested here as internalized racism. Through this simultaneous action, both viewer and character implicated in erroneous fabula construction, the film creates identification and subversion for both an Indian and Euramerican audience.

This identification and subversion are most effectively demonstrated during a crucial scene that occurs near the end of the film. Having been accused of drunkenly assaulting a white man after an automobile accident that they happened upon, Victor and Thomas are questioned by an Arizona Police Chief. The scene is charged with animosity as Victor – in stoic "warrior" mode – responds in a hostile manner to the officer's questions. Both the viewer and the characters no doubt expect the worst. Upon being accused of the drunken assault Victor informs the Chief that he has never had a drink in his life. The officer is shocked by the response and asks them, "Just what kind of Indians are you exactly?"[4]

Victor replies that he is a Coeur d'Alene Indian and that Thomas is as well. Thomas chimes in "exactly." The officer's surprise at an Indian who doesn't drink reflects the stereotypical trope of the drunken Indian. In this scene not only is this stereotype subverted, but the word play on "exactly" takes a colloquial form of speech – the "Chief" slurs Indian just enough to sound like "Injun" – and turns it into an opportunity for Victor and Thomas to define themselves through tribal affiliation. In addition to drawing attention to the communication gap between the two cultures, the tribal specificity further undercuts the two-dimensional conception of American Indians as one homogenous mass rather than a multitude of distinct cultures.

Tellingly, this is the only scene in the film where the loquacious Thomas appears speechless. When the Chief asks him if he has "anything to say about all these charges?" Thomas meekly mutters, "We was framed" (130). Despite the comic relief provided by his response – humor that draws upon the hackneyed cliché response of filmic hoods – Thomas' inability to speak portrays the depth of fear he feels in a situation that he knows must end badly. After all, in the movies, strangers – especially minorities – never fare well in dealings with small-town law enforcement officials. One need not look much farther than the archetypal road movie, *Easy Rider* (Dir. Dennis Hopper, 1969), to see the tragic results of the wrong people in the wrong place at the wrong time.

The scene, however, does not end as the characters and viewers would expect. Instead of being unjustly incarcerated, or worse, Thomas and Victor are freed by the written testimony of the wife of the man who accused Victor of assault.[5] Walking through the police impound yard to retrieve Victor's father's truck, Victor expresses his disbelief that they "got out of that hospital alive." Thomas ironically replies, "Yeah, I guess your warrior look does work sometimes" (130). Thomas' good-natured ribbing of Victor provides both social commentary on the stoic warrior stereotype and comic relief from the previous scene's heavy tone. The meta-narrative nature of Thomas and Victor's incredulous reaction to their release from custody poignantly demonstrates the internalized racist assumptions of the two indigenous protagonists. Ultimately, Thomas and Victor seem to be unaware of the source of their preconceived notions of interactions between minorities and authorities, despite the fact that in an earlier scene Thomas informs Victor and Suzy, "the only thing more pathetic than Indians on TV is Indians watching Indians on TV." Victor evidences this internalized racist self-image most fully in his adoption of the antagonistic warrior role. Goaded on by the assumption that all must end poorly for him as the doomed, tragic figure, he is prepared to fight, even in a situation where resistance is futile.

By mirroring and commenting on the fabula construction process, and its dependence on stereotypical tropes and assumptions, this scene demonstrates the simultaneous push/pull relationship that is created by mainstream Euramerican viewers' identification with the narrative. The viewers, along with the characters, are not only implicated by predicting an outcome based on pre-conceptions, but their subject position is also mirrored in the experience of the Other, who is the victim of the same schemata. The empathetic relationship created by the realization that the characters have fallen victim to the same misguided conceptions – albeit in a much more insidious fashion – is essential to viewers' recognition of the power of stereotypes. From the position of the viewers, this leads to the possibility of an awareness of their own preconceptions, ideas based largely on previous filmic representations of Indians; for the characters, it displays the depth of the medium's potential for enculturation and the internalization of racist self-images.

Stealthy Structures: Classical Territories and the Filmic Frontier

The success of the identification and subversion in the previous scene lies in its accessibility to an audience steeped in the norms of classical Hollywood film. These norms in turn rely on a narrative style that attempts to be as transparent as possible. Through the palliative effect of humor, and by cloaking the subtextual political commentary of the scene in a familiar filmic situation (such as the afore-mentioned scene of the outsider meets the small-town cop), the film presents an approachable and deceptively simple surface narrative. Alas, the apparent surface simplicity of *Smoke Signals* belies its complexity and depth. The collision of this simple surface with the complicated subtextual information drives the divergent mainstream reviewers' commentaries on the film. Running from flat-out racist to shallow, yet culturally sensitive, both the range and volume of mainstream reviewers' reactions are no doubt a testament to the film's groundbreaking accessibility as an American Indian cinematic endeavor.

As mentioned above, the film's appeal to a mainstream Euramerican audience rests largely on the use of easily recognized narrative techniques that include Bordwell's classical narration norms such as the use of psychologically defined characters as causal agencies, clear-cut problems or goals, continuity editing, and arguably a structurally decisive ending. The choice to make a buddy/road movie was no doubt a shrewd move on behalf of Alexie and Eyre, particularly for the level of accessibility this type of film offers to both mainstream Euramerican and Indian audiences. It could be argued that the estrangement created by the use of a more radically divergent narrative technique, coupled with cultural Otherness of an American Indian epistemology, would most likely defeat any substantial potential for large-scale appeal.[6]

Developing large-scale appeal has pragmatic as well as political import. First, as a freshman effort for both the screenwriter and director, the financial and critical success of the film is crucial to insure hope for future projects. The importance of "success" for two individual careers is magnified by the fact that they are ultimately bound up in the role of spokesperson for their cultures whether they accept the mantle or not; simply promoting the film as a "first" for American

Indians would seem to validate this assumption. Alexie is very open about his self-conception as a "populist" artist. Speaking about the success of the film, he has publicly adopted some of the responsibility of an American Indian role model, albeit begrudgingly. Aware of the much wider audience appeal – particularly in the American Indian community – of film over books, Alexie has commented on the film as a text that gives permission to young American Indian artists to take these ideas even further. This film represents a radical departure for indigenous actors, screenwriters, and filmmakers through its appropriation and manipulation of the very medium that has done so much to create our false impressions of American Indian cultures. We can begin to imagine the further import of Alexie's desire to subvert stereotypes by approaching the film with sensitivity to the pervasive nature of these false impressions. Accessibility to both the Euramerican and American Indian audiences is essential if these stereotypes are to be undermined. A viewer need look no further than Victor in order to see the effects of internalized racism. For a Euramerican viewer this is consciousness-raising; to a young Indian viewer, it is fundamental commentary on the process of identity building in a hostile culture. In this light, the author sees the film as truly groundbreaking and feels a sense of responsibility to use his clout as a writer to advance the cause of self-representation.[7]

Secondly, touted as the "first feature film conceived, written, directed and co-produced by American Indians," the film shoulders the burden of demonstrating the economic feasibility of American-Indian produced mainstream cinema.[8] While some of Hollywood's portrayals of American Indians have become more empathetic, there is indeed a dearth of films actually made by Indians about Indians.[9] In a recent conversation, Alexie bemoaned the difficulty of having "white men tell [him] how to write about Indians." One need look no further than the nearly dozen rejected re-writes of the screenplay for his novel *Reservation Blues* to see this in action.[10] While previous films such as *Powwow Highway* – a wildly successful picture on the rez according to Alexie – have gone some ways towards creating less stereotypical Indian characters, their limited success in Hollywood's terms has kept them relegated to the status of novelties. Other more subversive "underground" productions such as Victor Masayesva Jr's *Imagining Indians* (1992) and Gerald Vizenor's *Harold of Orange* (1984) simply do not have the marketability necessary to perform much cultural work outside an academic setting.[11]

Although the issues of the means of production may seem secondary to an analysis of the film, the influence of these economic/practical concerns of accessibility, given the film's position within the discourse of mainstream Hollywood cinema, should not be ignored. Suffice it to say that for the terms of this essay, the success of *Smoke Signals* has indeed cracked open a door. It remains to be fully examined as to how well the film negotiates the difficult spaces between entertaining and educating, and breaking ground and selling out. In addition, time alone will tell if the film is another curiosity or the beginning of a new era of self-representation for American Indians in mainstream Hollywood cinema.

While the choice of the buddy/road film arose partly out of practical concerns, there are other aspects of the genre that lend themselves particularly well to the subversive nature of *Smoke Signals*. Perhaps the most important of these is the dialogue-driven nature of the buddy/road movie. The focus on dialogue underscores the fact that this genre does not rely on the usual suspense regarding the ostensible goal of the narrative. Put simply, much like a "talking heads" film, the buddy/road movie is not plot driven by the viewer's need to solve a mystery or project the outcome of the film. Instead, since we know the most probable outcome of the film – an outcome that is not subverted as the "goal" is achieved, the father's ashes are reclaimed – the viewers' and characters' attention is focused on the way in which the story is told. This refocusing of attention highlights the subtle underlying messages that are being conveyed.[12] In this way, for a mainstream Euramerican viewer, the traditional tension as the narrative unfolds is replaced by awareness of the Otherness of the philosophical underpinnings of the film. In a very clever appropriation of the dominant discourse, the film creates a system of schemata that alerts the viewer to look beyond the surface level of the narrative for deeper philosophical meanings. It is at this subtextual level – a level the viewer is expected to recognize as a feature of the genre itself – that the film functions most subversively.

By simultaneously creating identification for both a Native and Euramerican audience through the common ground of classical film narration, *Smoke Signals* creates a frontier space wherein lies the potential to further interrogate stereotypical depictions of American Indians. To understand more fully just how this space is created, it is necessary to detail how the film departs from the classical Hollywood buddy/road movie tropes in its efforts to subvert these stereotypes.

The first, and most obvious, departure is the use of American Indians as subjects and stars. Simply replacing the white male protagonist is a subversive act. Late in the film, when Thomas is told by one of the accident victims that he and Victor are heroes like the Lone Ranger and Tonto, he replies, "No we're more like Tonto and Tonto." The subversive undercurrent of this scene's humorous content is further punctuated by the fact that this anecdote was used to conclude the film's theatrical trailer. The use of non-traditional characters in stereotypically white male roles has the effect of holding a mirror up to the form itself; the viewer is made aware of the film as an act of representation through the incongruous nature of another subject occupying the space traditionally filled by white males.[13] The traditional subject position of the buddy movie protagonist is further undermined by the lack of attention to a strong heterosexual theme. It is typical of the genre to include a female love interest – which is absent here – which leaves no question as to the relationship between the "buddies." While it can, and should, be argued that women play minor roles in this film – a criticism to which Alexie both bows and contests – they do not serve the usual role of alleviating any ambiguity as to the heterosexual status of the male leads.[14] While the female characters in *Smoke Signals* no doubt contribute important aspects to the narrative, their role is ultimately subordinated to the simultaneously overarching and underlying theme of the relationships between fathers and sons.

Beyond simply replacing white characters with American Indians, the film gives us a wide array of fully developed, non-stereotypical characters. As Alexie states repeatedly in the scene notes at the end of the screenplay: "NOTE TO ALL OTHER FILMMAKERS: Cast Indians as Indians, because you'll get better performances" (158). The characters portrayed defy the stereotypical roles we have come to expect through our inculcation by traditional Hollywood portrayals of American Indians. Instead of pounding on drums and wailing, they listen to contemporary rock and roll music. Drinking the "real thing," Coca-Cola, replaces the firewater-swilling drunken Indian. And lest we forget this is a work by Sherman Alexie, they play basketball. The apparent quirkiness of the residents of the Coeur d'Alene Indian Reservation – e.g. Lester's traffic reports, or Velma and Lucy's backwards driving car – lies in the Otherness of reservation life to a Euramerican viewer. In fact, in my conversation with him, Alexie described the scenes with Velma and Lucy as the "rez-iest" performance ever captured on film. The characters' portrayal as unique individuals, as opposed to static stereotypes, challenges mainstream notions of "Indianness." Life on the Coeur d'Alene Reservation is depicted as dynamic and life affirming: an impression that is further supported by the cinematography's sweeping depiction of the beautiful landscape that the characters inhabit. The narrative simultaneously insists not only the differences inherent in the cultures, but also the radical differences between the actuality of contemporary American Indian life and the stereotypical pictures a non-Native viewer might hold in their minds.[15]

This insistence on difference leads to the final subversion of classical buddy movie narrational norms. In both form and content, the mainstream viewer enters the narrative in a confused place. We are in an Indian space, Owens' frontier. The mainstream viewer's status as outsider is quickly affirmed by the opening voiceover narration that uncovers the central event of the story: the death of Thomas' parents. The viewer's confusion at the beginning of the film is further highlighted by an awareness that while Thomas is providing the voiceover narration, the visual imagery is not necessarily from his point of view. The film subtly switches from a "recounted" narrative level that we may perceive as a psychologically motivated imaginative flashback, to a narrative level that "enacts" this imagined flashback (Bordwell 78). The blurry boundary of the scene's origin of focalization contributes to the viewer's curiosity regarding the nature of Thomas and his knowledge of the stories of the fire.[16] Thomas' voiceover narration serves not only an expository function – giving crucial background information surrounding the death of his parents – but also articulates the cultural necessity of "knowing the stories." As we see throughout the film, it is Thomas' knowledge of the stories – even in the absence of his parents – that keeps him centered. This opening confusion and disorientation sets the pattern for flashback narratives throughout the film that will become increasingly sophisticated, and they are the necessary keys to understanding the deeper narrative subtexts of the film.

Dances with Salmon: Comic Relief and Social Commentary

Throughout the narrative, Thomas' well-grounded nature – based on his knowledge of and relationship to "the stories" that he discusses at the very beginning of the film – aligns him closely with the frontier space represented by the film's culturally informed subtexts. Though not immune to the dominant culture's influence on his self-image as an American Indian, Thomas exists much more easily in the "unstable, multidirectional, hybridized . . . and indeterminate" than Victor. The complexity of Thomas' character shows through in his simultaneously naive yet wise personality. In my interview with actor Evan Adams, he refers to Thomas as "an old Indian woman trapped in a young man's body." Thomas is represented throughout the film as a peaceful, centered individual who, though lacking a father and mother, fulfills his role in the community rather than being spiteful and jaded like Victor. This is most strongly demonstrated by the caretaker role he plays for his grandmother. His self-awareness of his value to the community is made clear in a scene where he finally stands up to Victor for the first time:

THOMAS: . . . You've been moping around the reservation for ten years. Ten years, Victor! Doing what? Playing basketball all day. Telling jokes. You ain't got no job. You ain't got no money. You ain't got nothing.

VICTOR: And what do you got, you goddamn geek? You ain't got no friends. You ain't got nothing either. What do you do all day long? Huh, Thomas huh?

THOMAS: I take care of my grandma.

VICTOR: And I take care of my mom.

THOMAS: You make your mom cry.

VICTOR: Shut up, Thomas!

THOMAS: You make your mom cry. You make her cry her eyes out, Victor. I mean, your dad left her, sure. Yeah, he ran away. But you left her, too. And you're worse because you've lived in the same house with her for ten years, but you ain't really lived there. When your dad left, he took part of you with him. And you let him, too. You let him. (109–10)

By finally standing up to Victor, Thomas is able to clearly articulate his understanding of the difference between himself and his antagonistic friend. Unlike Victor, Thomas finds solace in the stories that he tells and is not overly concerned with the "Truth" as it relates to the facts. Rather, he seeks to preserve and create a meaningful existence through his stories as a way to deal with the hardships of reservation life in general and his tragic past in particular. While Thomas does very much appear to be in touch with a mystical, quasi-mythic understanding of his life and the lives of those around him, he stops far short of being the stereotypical "shaman" figure. He does not have visions or burn sage or recite any Indian wisdom based on knowledge of the old ways or ancient ones. Instead, he is a storyteller: a young man with a unique and creative perspective on the difficult world in which he lives.

Throughout the narrative, the viewers listen to Thomas' stories and for the most part find they occupy a similar position to that of Victor. Victor has "heard the stories a thousand times" and still doesn't know "what the hell Thomas is saying most of the time," repeatedly telling Thomas that "he is so full of shit." From a modernist perspective Victor might easily be seen as the alienated, questing protagonist separated from his self, family, and culture. However, this generalized characterization is complicated by the cultural specificity of his internalized racist assumptions of what it means to be a "real Indian." In one of the film's most humorous and poignantly revealing scenes – the scene with which this essay opens – Victor instructs Thomas on just what it means to be a "real Indian." Chastising Thomas for his dorky three-piece suit and glasses, and belittling him for watching *Dances with Wolves* too many times, Victor tells Thomas that he must "get stoic" because "White people will run all over you if you don't look mean" (62). Victor is blind to his own hypocrisy as he condemns Thomas for participating in the process of self-identification through film, despite the fact that Thomas clearly displays his understanding of his own cultural heritage as a tribe of fisherpeople rather than the stoic buffalo-hunting warriors Victor seeks to emulate. Victor fails to recognize his own conception of the "real Indian" as the stoic warrior: a stereotype heavily informed by the movies and literature that Victor has no doubt been exposed to growing up in eighties America. Ironically, Victor clings to a stereotype that seems to be a mirror image of the John Wayne school of machismo: the emotionless, strong-willed outsider, the perfect protagonist of the buddy/road movie genre.

The lighthearted mood of Victor's sermon on being a "real Indian" – punctuated by the use of humor – is quickly followed by the film's most blatantly racist scene. Having lost their seats on the bus to a couple of stereotypical rednecks, Victor is compelled to take a stand. When he insists that the cowboys are sitting in their seats the "huge" man replies:

> Cowboy #1: (*quietly and threatening*)
> These are our seats now. And there's not a damn thing you can do about it. So why don't you and Super Indian there find yourself someplace else to have a powwow, okay? (65)

After losing a stare-down with the cowboy, Victor grabs Thomas and they find a place in the very back row of the bus, on the bench seat near the bathroom. A perceptive viewer cannot overlook the historical significance of the "back of the bus." In a heavily ironic line Thomas remarks "Jeez, Victor, I guess your warrior look doesn't work every time" (65). Thomas utters this line in a surprised manner; there is no sense that he is taunting Victor. He appears genuinely surprised by the result of the altercation and the lack of effect of Victor's warrior look. But his innocence is complicated when he turns the conversation to point out that the

Indians never win in these situations. At this point in the scene the heavy tone is once again broken with humor:

THOMAS: Man, the cowboys always win, enit?

VICTOR: The cowboys don't always win.

THOMAS: The cowboys *always* win. Look at Tom Mix. Look at Roy Rogers. Look at Clint Eastwood. And what about John Wayne? Man, he was about the toughest cowboy of them all, enit?

VICTOR: You know, in all those movies, you never saw John Wayne's teeth. Not once. I think there's something wrong when you don't see a guy's teeth.

(*breaks into song while pounding a powwow rhythm on the seat*)

Oh, John Wayne's teeth, John Wayne's teeth, hey, hey, hey, hey, ye! Oh, John Wayne's teeth, John Wayne's teeth, hey, hey, hey, hey, hey, ye! Are they false, are they real? Are they plastic, are they steel? Hey, hey, hey, hey, yeeeee!

(*Thomas joins in the song*) (66)

While the song obviously provides some comic relief to lighten the tone at the end of such a powerful scene, it is equally apparent that all of the white people on the bus are unnerved by Victor and Thomas's culture-blurring behavior. Victor and Thomas do, in a sense, get the last word. They may have lost their seats, but not their dignity. This scene is an excellent example of the interplay and balance created by Alexie's use of humor to provide comic relief at the same time it bears the burden of social and historical comment. One need only scratch the surface of these jokes lightly to reveal the heavy political commentary that lies beneath.

The Whole Truth: and Nothing but the Truth

When we dig beneath the surface narratives of the buddy/road movie and the philosophical subtext of a young man attempting to recover the memory of his estranged father, we begin to see *Smoke Signals* as a meditation on the nature of "truth" and "lies." While this topic is by no means unique to American Indian literatures, it takes on a particular significance when placed in this specific cultural context. Understanding Thomas' conception of the truth of stories is essential if we are to recognize his ability to find peace in his life despite being tragically orphaned as an infant. Throughout the film characters constantly interrogate the truth of Thomas' stories. After relating the Vietnam protest story where Victor's father supposedly pummels a National Guard Soldier, Velma and Lucy are duly impressed and ask Victor if his father really did that. Victor's response is that Thomas is "full of shit." Suzy Song, as well, repeatedly asks, "Is that true?" when Thomas relates stories about Victor's mother and her incredible fry bread. It is after relating the story of Arlene Joseph's "Jesus fry bread" that Thomas tellingly demands that Suzy now owes him a story. When she asks him do "You want me to tell the truth? Or do you want lies?" Thomas responds that he wants both (77).

This scene is the most self-conscious point in the narrative regarding the question of "truth" and "lies." Perhaps, if the mainstream viewer is able to recognize the radical, from a Western view, perception of the relationship between truth and lies that Thomas' epistemology represents, this might be seen as the most subversive element of the entire film. By challenging the traditional Western binary of truth and fiction, this may well be the closest approximation of the Other view – to borrow again from Owens – that the viewer receives from the narrative. Arguably, this is the point at which the viewer moves beyond Victor's limited perception of events and his father, and begins to understand the larger philosophical messages of the film that are yet to be revealed to our "alienated protagonist."

In stark contrast to Thomas, Victor never tells anyone his stories, even though Thomas constantly assails him to tell him about his dad. He is reluctant to speak of his past, yet is trapped by his memories of the tumultuous years he spent with his father. The viewer, unlike any of the intra-diegetic narratees, is privileged to Victor's stories as they are all related through psychologically-motivated interior flashbacks. This inside knowledge has a double-edged effect on the viewer. While it enhances our identification with Victor as a main character and gives us crucial back-story information on his relationship with his father, it further distances the viewer from the subtext of the movie, or Thomas's version of the Truth, until the crucial scene described above. Although the lion's share of the narrative is not related from Victor's subjectivity, viewers most closely occupy a parallel position to him with respect to their understanding of the stories as they unfold through Thomas. For example, when mainstream viewers first witness the scene on the bus in which Victor instructs Thomas on how to be a "real Indian," they laugh along with Victor at Thomas' expense. Victor models the internalized version of the stereotypes that mainstream American culture tells itself about what a "real Indian" is. A "real Indian" is certainly not like Thomas Builds-the-Fire, but is instead much more like Victor's conception of himself as the stoic warrior – ultimately just as erroneous a stereotype as the "damn medicine man" that Victor thinks Thomas is trying to be. It is not until later, when Suzy Song reveals Victor's father's guilt over causing the fire that killed Thomas' parents, that viewers realize the full extent to which Victor is a victim at the hands of the stories he has chosen to believe about himself. Victor's inability to see beyond his own internalized stereotypical perceptions of Thomas, himself, and his father keeps him from seeing the greater truths in Thomas' stories. Through the viewers' identification with Victor, the movie holds a mirror up to a mainstream audience that might harbor similarly jaundiced views of American Indian cultures.

It is not until the climatic scene of the movie – in which Victor experiences a "vision" of sorts – that he is able to recognize the importance of Thomas' stories.

In an effort to get help for the victims of an automobile accident, Victor sets off running in the rural Arizona desert night. As he runs, we are assailed with a montage of images and voiceovers that would appear to be psychologically motivated yet include information to which Victor could never have actually been privy. The voices of Suzy Song and Victor's father are juxtaposed with images of the house fire that killed Thomas' parents. Exhausted from running, and spiritually tormented, Victor finally collapses. He literally "sees" his father through Thomas' eyes when he awakes on the side of the road. A point of view shot as Victor reaches for the hand that offers him assistance reveals the smiling face of his father. This is *exactly* the same shot from a previous flashback focalized by Thomas in which he recalls the day he went to Spokane "waiting for a sign" and ran into Victor's father. While this particular scene is lighthearted and quite humorous when it first appears in the narrative, in hindsight it takes on greater significance. When Thomas relates this story, Victor tells him "I've heard this story a thousand times" (52), but he obviously never truly listened. His obsession with the "Truth" as he conceived of it always blinded him to the other possible truths contained within Thomas' stories.

The moment at which Victor has the vision of his father on the side of the road is very brief, but it signals his movement into Thomas' level of understanding of the stories. The fact that the image/vision Victor sees is literally the same image that Thomas "sees" earlier cements the connection between Victor and Thomas. Victor has now internalized Thomas' stories and has made them his own. He literally sees his father through Thomas' eyes: the eyes of a character who venerates Arnold Joseph throughout the film. Victor's crucial moment of identification with Thomas' stories echoes metonymically the film's place in the larger culture. The current focus on issues of self-representation within the scholarly debates surrounding American Indian literatures situates *Smoke Signals* at and as a historically crucial moment. This moment perhaps defines the kernel of an American Indian canon of film, perhaps the next logical step to proceed from the arguably "established" American Indian literary canon. This type of self-representation is essential if audiences – both Indian and Euramerican – are to be exposed to depictions of contemporary American Indian life that do not re-inscribe pejorative stereotypical images. In this way *Smoke Signals* indeed signals the paradigm shift that Alexie sees as necessary for opening a new era of filmic self-representation.

150 ◆ EXT. BUILDS-THE-FIRES' HOUSE – MORNING

*Grandma Builds-the-Fire sitting on the porch of the house. She is happy to see her
  grandson.*
She stands from her chair, walks up to him, and takes him in her arms.
She holds him at arm's length.
GRANDMA: Tell me what happened, Thomas. Tell me what's going to happen . . .

Notes

1 The film is based on Alexie's collection of short stories *The Lone Ranger and Tonto Fistfight in Heaven*. While the bulk of the story line comes directly from a piece entitled "This Is What It Means to Say Phoenix, Arizona," the film incorporates elements from a number of stories in the collection, contributing to its pastiche origin.

2 Bordwell discusses at length a constructivist approach "for a Psychology of Filmic Perception and Cognition" (30–33). Bordwell's discussion of the viewer's use of perceptual schemata echoes the work of Umberto Eco. Eco explicates how the viewer constantly re-evaluates the fabula that s/he constructs in light of the new information we are given by the syuzhet. My argument is that the subversive effects of this film rest on balancing a mainstream viewer's identification with the film through classical cinematic form, with humorous political commentary and an Other worldview.

3 The author has been quoted in numerous interviews regarding his intentions with this film (see: Clark, Peary, Webster, West, Winton). While typically discussions about authorial intention are sticky at best, for the purposes of this discussion Alexie's very public persona serves as a viable benchmark for an analysis of the film and its effects on an audience.

4 All citations from the movie that vary from the screenplay will be cited without page numbers, thus identifying this variance. Where the dialogue from the film matches the written screenplay page numbers will be given.

5 This scene can be read as a response to the more conspiracy-laden theme of *Powwow Highway*. In that film the predictable always happens, but we have a conspiracy of BIA and local law enforcement officials to blame. This justifies the outlaw behavior of the protagonist. In fact, it would be quite interesting to do a side-by-side analysis of the two films to examine how *Smoke Signals* responds to the issues raised by *Powwow Highway*.

6 It is interesting to note that Alexie intends to film *Reservation Blues* as a very jumbled, postmodern film. One could speculate that this might have something to do with his difficulty getting the movie produced. (Personal conversation with Alexie 30 May 2000).

7 In May of 2000, Alexie discussed his deeply-felt responsibilities to younger American Indians in a talk given on his *The Toughest Indian in the World* book tour stop in Bellingham, Washington.

8 In a 1997 interview for *SAIL* with John Purdy, Alexie discusses what he then saw as a three-year window for Indian filmmakers to make a statement. In my recent discussion with the author, he said it has, unfortunately, come and gone.

9 For a close examination of the danger of the feel-good, empathetic Hollywood film – quintessentially represented by *Dances With Wolves* – see Louis Owens' *Mixedblood Messages*, particularly the chapter entitled "Apocalypse at the Two Socks Hop."

10 In my conversations with both Alexie and Adams the difficulty of getting the "green light" for future projects was a sore subject indeed.

11 I would certainly not argue that either of these films was made with mass marketability in mind, but merely mention them to demonstrate the limited exposure that films by American Indian filmmakers have received. For an in-depth discussion of American

Indian representation in film, as well as a more exhaustive look at American Indian-produced films, see Jacquelyn Kilpatrick, *Celluloid Indians: Native Americans and Film*.

12 It would be interesting to compare this notion of "knowing the story" to Louis Owens' treatment of N. Scott Momaday's *House Made of Dawn*. In his book *Other Destinies*, Owens discusses how the novel is formally couched in the terms of an oral discourse. One of the fundamental features of that oral discourse is that we know the whole story before we begin. Just as in all mythic or parabolic stories we know the eventual end of the tale, so we become more attentive to the way in which the story is being told.

13 Part of Alexie's controversial defense of the lack of strong female roles in the film is evidenced by his statements that the American Indian women have not had their roles displaced in the same manner in which the men have. Both *Thelma and Louise* (Dir. Ridley Scott, 1991) and *Priscilla, Queen of the Desert* (Dir. Stephan Elliott, 1994) are excellent examples of other subversions of these particular generic expectations.

14 Alexie's statement, that the American Indian women have not had their roles displaced in the same manner in which the men have, reveals his controversial defense of the lack of strong female roles in the film. This is a fruitful area for exploration, but not for this essay. In terms of the film these notions are complicated by Alexie's desire to have Suzy Song be a "magical" character, although her magical nature does not come through in the film due to the large share of her scenes that ended up on the cutting room floor. While Alexie admits that Suzy's tribal affiliation is elided, in the screen-play he makes it clear that this was a result of editing. This elision is further downplayed in the scene where she says she misses home, and that home is New York. This is another strong example of our mistaken fabula-creation based on stereotypical notions. The pregnant pause that comes before she reveals that home is New York leads the viewer to think she will mention some reservation.

15 Again, it is interesting to compare the depiction of the reservation in *Smoke Signals* to the abject poverty depicted in *Powwow Highway*.

16 See Rimmon-Kenan for a full discussion of the concept of focalization and narration.

Works Cited

Adams, Evan. Personal interview. 1 June 2000.

Alexie, Sherman. Personal interview. 30 May 2000.

——. *Smoke Signals: A Screenplay*. New York: Hyperion, 1998.

Bordwell, David. *Narration in the Fiction Film*. Madison: U of Wisconsin P, 1985.

Brannigan, Edward. *Point of View in the Cinema: A Theory of Narration and Subjectivity in Classical Film*. Berlin: Mouton, 1984.

Clark, John. "No Reservations: With 'Smoke Signals,' Native American Filmmakers Sherman Alexie and Chris Eyre Boldly Turn Stereotypes Upside Down as They Create Singular Indian Characters." *Los Angeles Times* 28 June 1998. Online. Proquest. 16 May 2000.

Hayward, Susan. *Key Concepts in Cinema Studies*. London: Routledge, 1996.

Owens, Louis. *Mixedblood Messages: Literature, Film, Family, Place*. Norman: U of Oklahoma P, 1998.

——. *Other Destinies: Understanding the American Indian Novel*. Norman and London: U of Oklahoma P, 1992.

Peary, Gerald. Rev. of *Smoke Signals*, Screenplay by Sherman Alexie. Dir. Chris Eyre. *Boston Phoenix*. 6 July 1998. http://weeklywire.com/filmvault/boston/s/smokesignals1.html (9 May 2000).

Purdy, John. "Crossroads: A Conversation with Sherman Alexie." *SAIL* 9:4 (Winter 1997): 1–18.

Rimmon-Kenan, Shlomith. *Narrative Fiction: Contemporary Poetics*. London: Methuen, 1983.

Smoke Signals. Screenplay by Sherman Alexie. Dir. Chris Eyre. Perf. Adam Beach, Evan Adams, Irene Bedard, and Gary Farmer. Miramax, 1998.

Vizenor, Gerald, ed. *Narrative Chance: Postmodern Discourse on Native American Indian Literatures*. Albuquerque: U of New Mexico P, 1989.

Webster, Dan. "Mixed 'Signals': Film Version of Alexie Book has Touching Moments and Rough Patches." *Spokesman Review* [Spokane] 3 July 1998. Online. Proquest. 16 May 2000.

West, Dennis, and Joan M. West. "Sending Cinematic 'Smoke Signals': an Interview with Sherman Alexie." *Cineaste* 23:4 (1998): 28–31, 37.

Winton, Ben. "Where There's Smoke . . ." *Native Peoples* 11:4 (1998): 56–58.

Playing Indian in the Nineties: *Pocahontas* and *The Indian in the Cupboard*

Pauline Turner Strong

Hollywood has long taken a leading role in shaping the American tradition of "playing Indian." This chapter considers how this tradition is mobilized in two family films released in 1995: Disney's heavily marketed *Pocahontas* and the Columbia/Paramount adaptation of Lynne Reid Banks's popular children's novel *The Indian in the Cupboard*. Borrowing a concept from Donna Haraway, I would place my "situated knowledge" of these films and their associated playthings at the intersection of, first, my scholarly interest in the production and significance of imagined Indians in Anglo-American culture; second, my memories of "playing Indian" at school, at summer camp, and in Camp Fire Girls during my childhood; and, finally, my experiences rearing two daughters (ages seven and ten when the films were released). In other words, this is what Kathleen Stewart would call a "contaminated" critique, one that is complexly influenced by my participation in the cultural phenomena that it analyzes. I write as a pianist who has played "Colors of the Wind" (the theme song from *Pocahontas*) so often for my daughters' school choir that it runs unbidden through my mind; as a parent who has spent much of a weekend "playing Indian" on CD-ROM, helping seven-year-old Tina "earn symbols" for a computer-generated wampum belt so that we could be inducted as "Friends of the Iroquois"; and, above all, as a cultural critic whose views are influenced both by the insights of my daughters and by my hopes for their generation.

As I sit at my computer composing this essay, a three-inch plastic Indian stands beside the monitor. He wears a scalp lock, yellow leggings and breechcloth, a

Pauline Turner Strong, "Playing Indian in the Nineties: *Pocahontas* and *The Indian in the Cupboard*," pp. 187–205 from Peter C. Rollins and John E. O'Connor (eds), *Hollywood's Indian: The Portrayal of the Native American in Film* (Lexington: The University Press of Kentucky, 1998). © 1998 by The University Press of Kentucky.

yellow knife sheath, and a yellow pouch. Next to him is the case for our video-cassette of *The Indian in the Cupboard*, with the cover reversed, as directed, so that the case simulates a weathered wooden cabinet. Beside the cabinet is a plastic skeleton key, almost as large as the miniature Indian, that can be used to open the cabinet. Although it is possible to purchase the Indian figurine and the key independently, as well as figurines of other characters in the film, ours were packaged with the video, just as a locket was packaged with *The Little Princess.*

Equipped with the miniature Indian, the cabinet, and the key, I can, if I wish, imitate Omri, the nine-year-old American boy whose coming-of-age story is told in the film. Omri, like his English namesake in the novel, is given an Indian figurine that comes to life when locked inside a magical cabinet. My figurine does not come to life, but it nevertheless mocks me as it stands by my computer, underscoring my embeddedness in several traditions – European and Anglo-American, popular and scholarly – that have locked miniature Indians in cabinets, be they late-Renaissance wonder cabinets, children's toy collections, tourists' and collectors' displays, or museum dioramas.

If I wish to simulate Omri's mastery over life I must turn to the CD-ROM version of *The Indian in the Cupboard*, where with my cursor I can animate an Indian figurine – one that, like the miniatures that open the film, appears to be "antique," made of painted porcelain or wood rather than plastic. The figurine reminds me of a miniature cigar-store Indian or a ship's figurehead, as do the seven other Indian figurines on Omri's toy shelf. When I move the cursor in order to place the figurine in the cabinet and turn the key, it "comes to life" and begins to talk to me. Like Omri's miniature friend in the film, this animated Indian is named Little Bear. He identifies himself as an Onondaga of the Wolf clan and introduces me to his Ungachis, his "friends" on the toy shelf. He gives me the name of Henuyeha, or "player."[1] I accompany Little Bear to a promontory overlooking his palisaded village, where his people live in three longhouses.

Descending to the village I meet the Ungachis, whom I will later bring to life as my guides. I recall the many American Indians who have made their living as guides for hunters or anthropologists, as well as the YMCA organization Indian Guides, to which my brother and father once belonged (an organization parodied to good effect in the Disney film *Man of the House*). Foremost among my Onondaga "friends" is a clan mother, Gentle Breeze, who will introduce me to Onondaga words, stories, and symbols referring to the ancestors of the clans – Turtle, Bear, Wolf, Snipe, Beaver, Hawk, Deer, and Eel – as well as to the underwater Panther, the Keeper of the Winds and his Spirit Animals, the Peacemaker, and the Tree of Peace. Another Ungachi, a "chief" named He Knows the Sky, will point out and tell me stories about Grandmother Moon, the Path of the Dead, the Bear, the Seven Children, and Star Girl. ("What I like about the Onondaga," says ten-year-old Katie upon hearing the story of how Star Girl guided the starving people home, "is that it's not only boys and men who do important things.")

An Ungachi named Shares the Songs will teach me to play water drums, a flute, and a variety of rattles, challenging me to remember ever more complex rhythms.

Swift Hunter will teach me to recognize and follow animal tracks, while Keeper of the Words will show me how to make a headdress in the style of each of the Six Nations of the League of the Onondaga. Two children will teach me their games: from Blooming Flower I will learn how to decorate carved templates with beads; from Runs with the Wind, how to play a challenging memory game with seeds of corn, squash, and several varieties of beans.

Succeeding in these various activities requires patience, attentiveness, and a well-developed memory. Each time I succeed I am rewarded with a symbol for my "wampum belt" and the kind of effusive praise Anglo-American children expect. Upon its completion a ceremony is held to present me with the wampum belt and to name me an Ungachi, a "Friend of the Iroquois." I am feasted with a meal of corn, pumpkin, potatoes, squash, deer, roasted turkey, and cornbread. This concludes the ceremony, which I have experienced as a disconcerting example of what Michael Taussig calls "mimetic excess." The resonances are many and diverse: Camp Fire Girl "council fires" at which, proudly wearing my deerskin "ceremonial gown" and the beads I had "earned," I paid homage to Wohelo ("Work, Health, Love"); campfires under the stars at Camp Wilaha and Camp Kotami; classroom lessons and plays about the first Thanksgiving; the councils of "The Grand Order of the Iroquois," a fraternal organization founded by anthropologist Louis Henry Morgan (Bieder); the assimilationist group of reformers known as the "Friends of the Indian" (Prucha); and Vine Deloria's caustic dismissal of "anthropologists and other friends" in *Custer Died for Your Sins.*

Despite my initial discomfort with the power of bringing miniature Onondagas to life – and especially with the power to turn them back into mute "plastic" – I find myself intrigued and charmed by this simulated world. So is Tina, whose favorite game is one in which we bring an English trader to life and barter with him for trade goods. In the process we learn a fair amount about Iroquois hunting, farming, manufactures, and desires for trade goods. (The other Anglo-American figurine – and the only character drawn from the film besides Little Bear – is the cowardly cowboy Boone, with whom we experience the terrors of Omri's room from the perspective of a person three inches in height.) By the time Tina and I are presented with our wampum belts, we have been introduced to many aspects of Onondaga life in the early eighteenth century: the forest, the river, and the clearing; the architecture and layout of the village; corn, beans, and squash, the Three Sisters; the powers of various animals; the Onondaga names and legends of the moon, Milky Way, and several constellations; the manufacture of goods and the practice of reciprocity; the importance of clans and clan matrons. We have heard many Onondaga words and learned to recognize a few. With the exception of the trader and his goods, however, we have encountered no evidence of Iroquois relations with European colonists or with other indigenous peoples.

Little Bear's world is one of order, beauty, and tranquility, free of disruptions from warfare, disease, displacement, or Christian evangelism. It serves simultaneously to arouse powerful feelings of nostalgia and nostalgic feelings of power.

This is a world under control; a world in which people treat each other with respect; a world pervaded by the soothing, rhythmic music of flutes, rattles, and vocables. It is a world in which human relationships tend to be free of conflict, a world in which – as both the textual and celluloid Omri teaches his friend Patrick – "you can't use people" (Banks, *Indian* 129). That we enter this world through the conceit of controlling the lives of miniature Indians and "mastering" the knowledge they have to teach us; that in this world the stereotypical Iroquois warrior is replaced by people living outside of history; that we feel we can be "Friends of the Iroquois" without confronting the political and economic claims that very friendship would make upon us, whether in 1720 – the era in which the CD-ROM is set – or today: such ironies pervade *The Indian in the Cupboard* in all its incarnations.

Destabilizing stereotypes is tricky, as others easily rush in to fill a void. In L. R. Banks's original series of four novels, the figure of Little Bear explicitly replaces the stereotypical Plains Indian with a more localized and complexly rendered representation. When Little Bear comes to life, he does not live up to Omri's expectations of an Indian: he lives in a longhouse rather than a tipi, walks rather than rides a horse, and is unaware of the custom of becoming "blood brothers." In other ways, however, Little Bear more than meets stereotypical expectations: he is a fierce "Iroquois brave" who has taken some thirty scalps; he is volatile, demanding, and interested in "firewater"; he becomes "restive" while watching a Western on television; his English is broken and, early on, mixed with grunts and snarls; he initially thinks of Omri as the "Great White Spirit," only to be disillusioned when the boy fails to live up to his expectations of a deity (20–23, 148). Even so, the most racist typifications are voiced not by the narrator but by "Boohoo" Boone – who, when brought to life, denigrates "Injuns" and "redskins" as "ornery" "savage," and "dirty" only to be convinced otherwise by Omri and Little Bear (99–101). These passages and cover illustrations reminiscent of nineteenth-century dime novels have attracted some criticism (Slapin and Seale 121–22), but the moral of the tale is clear: although Omri at first cherishes his power over Little Bear, calling him "my Indian," he comes to respect Little Bear as an autonomous human being with his own life, times, country, language, and desires (Banks, *Indian* 70, 82).

Lynne Reid Banks is an Englishwoman who spent the war years in Saskatchewan, and the friendship between Omri and Little Bear plays on the alliance between the English and Iroquois during the French and Indian War (1754–63). The historical context of the books, however, is almost completely absent in both the film and the CD-ROM, which transpose Omri from England to New York City. In contrast to the CD-ROM, the film takes place completely in Omri's world, except for a brief visionlike sequence in Little Bear's world. For this reason the film has far less Onondaga content than the CD-ROM, though what there is has been carefully rendered, following the advice of Onondaga consultants Jeanne Shenandoah[2] and Oren Lyons (Yankowitz 31). Nevertheless, the film is just as nostalgic as the CD-ROM. When Little Bear, preparing to return to his own time, asks whether the Onondaga are always a great people, Omri sadly answers in the affirmative, then reluctantly reveals that "it isn't always so good" for them. This is indisputable, but the scene misses a valuable opportunity to show something of the resiliency and the contemporary life of Iroquois people. Portrayed in the past or in miniature, and without visible descendants, Little Bear is out of place, out of time, and an object of intense longing (as Susan Stewart has suggested for miniatures more generally). The film does nothing to help viewers imagine Little Bear's descendants as persons who share a world with Omri even as they share a tradition with Little Bear.

Nevertheless, the film is more successful than the book or CD-ROM in presenting Little Bear as far more than a typification. As played by the Cherokee rap artist Litefoot (Yankowitz), Little Bear dominates the film, even at three inches tall. This Little Bear is not to be patronized. He earns Omri's respect and teaches him to appreciate the awesome responsibility that comes with power over other human beings. Given their relationship, it is particularly jarring to have power over Little Bear, voiced by Litefoot, when playing Omri's role on the CD-ROM. The CD-ROM encourages the Henuyeha, in the spirit of playful learning, to mimic just what Omri learned *not* to do – albeit in the spirit of understanding Little Bear's world. It is doubly disconcerting to possess a plastic figurine of Little Bear. Omri's rejection of objectifying human beings was, predictably, lost on the marketing department – and doubtless on many of its young targets, who may well have added Little Bear to their collection of *Pocahontas*-related figurines from Burger King.

Although the marketing of *The Indian in the Cupboard* and its translation onto CD-ROM undercuts the narrative's critique of objectifying and manipulating human beings, the tensions and contradictions among the message, the medium, and the marketing of Disney's *Pocahontas* are far more blatant. On one level *Pocahontas* can be dismissed as a commercial product through which Disney's powerful marketing machine has revived and exploited the public's perennial fascination with playing Indian – "bringing an American legend to life" in order to hawk beads, baubles, and trinkets to would-be Indian princesses and to those who would seek to please them.[3] On another level, however, Disney's interpretation of the Pocahontas legend – which, following Sommer, we might call the United States' "foundational romance" – makes a serious statement about ethnocentrism, androcentrism, commodification, and exploitation as barriers to the dream of interethnic harmony that Smith and Pocahontas represent. Disney's *Pocahontas* purports to offer a far broader and more devastating cultural critique than *The Indian in the Cupboard*: a critique of the commodity form itself, albeit a consummately commodified critique.

To consider *Pocahontas* in terms of how it meets the challenges posed by its own message takes us beyond the usual attempts to measure the film solely against an uncertain and elusive historical reality Pocahontas may be the first "real-life figure" to be featured in a Disney film, but the pre-Disney Pocahontas was already a highly mythologized heroine known only through colonial and nationalist representations – from the beginning, a product of Anglo-American desire. Disney has drawn on various versions of what Rayna Green calls "the Pocahontas perplex," giving new life and ubiquitous circulation to those versions deemed resonant with contemporary preoccupations. That is to say, the animated Pocahontas is located within the colonial and neocolonial tradition of noble savagism that Berkhofer analyzes in *The White Man's Indian*: the natural virtues she embodies and self-sacrifice she offers are those found in Montaigne and Rousseau, Thoreau and Cooper, Helen Hunt Jackson and *Dances with Wolves*. This is not to imply, to be sure, that Pocahontas is entirely a product of Western colonialism, but that we "know" her only within that arena – which, after all, is tantamount to not knowing her very well at all.

Outside of promotional material, the film's message is articulated most fully in "Colors Of The Wind," the Academy Award–winning song advertised as summing up "the entire spirit and essence of the film." Responding to Smith's recitation of all that the English can teach the "savages," Pocahontas chides him for thinking "the only people who are people" are those who "look and think" like him. Adapting a famous saying of Will Rogers, she urges Smith to "walk the footsteps of a stranger," promising that he will learn things he "never knew" he "never knew."[4] This Pocahontas is, above all, a teacher. Not, as one might expect, a teacher of the Powhatan language, culture, and standards of diplomacy, for the time-consuming process of learning to translate across cultural and linguistic borders is finessed through her mystical ability, as another song puts it, to "Listen with Your Heart." Rather, Pocahontas, a veritable child of nature, is a teacher of tolerance and respect for all life.

This unfortunate impoverishment of Pocahontas's teachings produces a truly awkward moment in the film, when Pocahontas magically switches from English to her native language on first encountering Smith. ("She was just speaking English a moment ago!" observed my daughters when they first saw this scene.) Although a few Algonquian words are sprinkled through the film, and Smith learns how to say "hello" and "goodbye," Disney's *Pocahontas* gives no sense of the intelligence, dedication, patience, and humility needed to "learn things you never knew you never knew." In being figured within the series of recent Disney heroines that includes Ariel, Beauty, and Jasmine (of *The Little Mermaid*, *Beauty and the Beast*, and *Aladdin*, respectively), this most famous of North American cultural mediators is removed from the series that also includes Malinche, Sacajawea, and Sarah Winnemucca. The ability to "listen with your heart" conquers all cultural distance for Pocahontas and John Smith.

This is not to say that it is entirely implausible that Pocahontas teaches Smith tolerance and respect for all life. One of the subtly effective moments in the film is the animated sequence corresponding to the passage in "Colors of the Wind" about walking in the footsteps of a stranger. The footsteps shown are the tracks of a Bear Person, a concept as unfamiliar to most film viewers as it is to John Smith. "Colors Of The Wind" challenges not only ethnocentrism but also androcentrism, and the bear scene goes beyond Disney's ordinary anthropomorphizing to open a window onto an animistic view of the world. More often, however, Pocahontas's relationship to animals (for example, to Meeko the raccoon and Flit the hummingbird) is trivialized,[5] appearing not unlike Cinderella's relationship with her friends, the mice and birds, in the classic Disney film.

In another verse of "Colors of the Wind" Pocahontas contrasts Smith's utilitarian and possessive thinking with her own intimate knowledge of nature. She scolds Smith for seeing the earth as "just a dead thing you can claim," for she knows that each rock, tree, and creature "has a life, has a spirit, has a name." Then, in the most sensual sequence of the film – or indeed of any previous Disney animation – Pocahontas entices Smith to run through the forest's hidden trails, to taste the earth's sun-ripened berries, to roll in the grasses of the meadow, enjoying all these riches "for once" without wondering "what they're worth." The seductive and precocious Pocahontas, who stalks Smith like a wildcat and then rolls with him in the grass, is a "free spirit" who embodies the joys of belonging to an enchanted and uncommodified world. This is not the first time the young Pocahontas has been sexualized – precedents include Smith's own writings as well as John Barth's *The Sot-Weed Factor* – but it is a startling departure for a Disney children's film. Pocahontas's overt sexuality no doubt has multiple motivations, but at one level it marks her as an intrinsic part of the natural world (as a "tribal Eve," according to Supervising Animator Glen Keane) (Hochswender 156).

It is the clear contrast between utilitarian possessiveness and sensual spirituality in scenes and lyrics like these that Russell Means pointed to in calling *Pocahontas* "the single finest work ever done on American Indians by Hollywood" by virtue of being "willing to tell the truth." But the film's critique of capitalist appropriation is enunciated by the same Pocahontas whose licensed image saturates the marketplace – along with that of her father, Powhatan, who, even more ironically, is modeled after and voiced by the same Russell Means who has demonstrated against the use of Indian images as mascots for sports teams. One can only wonder: what is the exotic, sensual, copyrighted Pocahontas if not the mascot for a feminine, earthy, New Age spirituality?

An eager and willing student of Pocahontas, John Smith learns to see maize as the true "riches" of Powhatan's land and presents the gold-hungry Governor Ratcliffe with a golden ear of corn. The play on "golden" makes for an effective scene, but totally excluded from the film is that other sacred American plant, tobacco, which became the salvation of the Virginia economy thanks to John Rolfe, the husband of a mature, Christian, and anglicized Pocahontas never seen in the film. Is this story – told in Barbour's biography and elsewhere – reserved for *Pocahontas II*? Probably not, for the historical Pocahontas's capture by the English as a hostage, transformation into Lady Rebecca Rolfe, and fatal illness during a trip to London does not resonate as well with an Anglo-American audience's expectations as the legend of Smith's capture and salvation by an innocent, loving, and self-sacrificing child of nature.[6]

Resonating with expectations, of course, is what creating a "timeless, universal, and uniquely satisfying motion picture experience" is all about. In imagining Pocahontas the filmmakers relied to some extent on consultation with Native people and scholars, but more on what resonated with their own experiences, desires, and sense of "authenticity" (so central to the Anglo-American tradition of "playing Indian," as Jay Mechling has pointed out). Lyricist Stephen Schwartz said of the composition of "Colors of the Wind" that "we were able to find the parts of ourselves that beat in synchronicity with Pocahontas," while animator Keane declared, "I'm cast as Pocahontas in the film" (Hochswender 156). I suppose this is something like listening with one's heart, but there is a significant tension between such identification and "walk[ing] the footsteps of a stranger." This is not the Pocahontas we never knew we never knew, but the Pocahontas we knew all along, the Pocahontas whose story is "universal" – that is, familiar, rather than strange and shocking and particular. This is a Pocahontas whose tale, like that of Simba in *The Lion King* or Omri in *The Indian in the Cupboard*, fits into the mold of the Western coming-of-age story: Pocahontas, yearning to see (as the song goes) "Just around the Riverbend," grows from youthful irresponsibility to mature self-knowledge through courage and love. It is a Pocahontas who speaks what is known in anthologies (for example, Suzuki and Knudtson) as "the wisdom of the elders," and communes with a Grandmother Willow who appears to be a kindly descendant of the animated trees in *Babes in Toyland*. It is a Pocahontas who, despite a tattoo and over-the-shoulder dress loosely consistent with John White's watercolors of sixteenth-century coastal Algonquians (Hulton, Josephy 183–93), has a Barbie-doll figure, an Asian model's glamour (Hochswender), and an instant attraction to a distinctly Nordic John Smith. In short, Disney has created a New Age Pocahontas embodying Americans' millennial dreams for wholeness and harmony while banishing our nightmares of savagery without and emptiness within.

Just as the dream of tolerance and respect for all life is voiced in song, so too is the nightmare of savagery and emptiness. While the dream is figured as feminine and Indian in the lyrical "Colors of the Wind," the nightmare is presented as masculine and – at least initially – English in the driving and brutal "Savages." Mobilizing stereotypes akin to Boohoo Boone's, but considerably more vicious, this song describes Pocahontas's people as worse than vermin, as "filthy little heathens" whose "skin's a hellish red," as a cursed and disgusting race, as evil, "barely human," and "only good when dead."

"Savages" presents, at its dehumanizing extreme, the ideology of ignoble savagism – less typical, as Bernard Sheehan has shown, of the earliest years of the Jamestown colony than of the years after 1622, when Powhatan's kinsman Opechancanough launched a war of resistance against the English. In the context of the film, however, appearing as the English prepare to attack the Powhatan people, it is extremely effective, serving ironically to underscore the savagery of the English colonists rather than that of the "heathen." Earlier, in the opening to "Colors of the Wind" Pocahontas had gently challenged the ideology of ignoble savagism by asking Smith why, if it was she who was the "ignorant savage," there was so very much he did not know. Characterized as wise and gentle, if mischievous and spirited, Pocahontas is clearly not an ignorant savage. With this already established, the colonists' rhetoric of savagery turns back upon them – at least until Powhatan, advised by a diviner, leads his people in a similar chorus, calling the "paleface" a soulless, bloodless demon distinguished only by his greed. It is the English who are "different from us," who are untrustworthy killers, who are "savages."

Powhatan's portion of "Savages" purports to offer a portrait of the English colonists from the point of view of the colonized. Given what has gone on thus far in the film, and what we know of subsequent history, the accusation rings true. But this passage, too, ultimately rebounds against those who utter it. John Smith is captured and laid out, the executioner's tomahawk is raised, Smith is about to be mercilessly executed . . . and Pocahontas throws her body upon his, successfully pleading with her father for his life. The savagery of fear and intolerance is vanquished through the power of "listen[ing] with your heart."

So the story goes, in Smith's telling, at least. It may be, as Gleach suggests, that this was all an elaborate adoption ceremony in which Smith became a vassal of Powhatan, who ruled over an expanding group of villages. It may be, as I have proposed (in "Captivity in White and Red"), that Pocahontas was playing a traditional female role in choosing between life and death for a sacrificial victim. It may be that the incident is best understood as part of Smith's imaginative and self-serving fabrication of himself – what Greenblatt calls "Renaissance self-fashioning." I would not fault Disney for repeating the rescue as it is commonly known in a film advertised as "an American legend," but the litany "Savages! Savages!" is quite another matter. Its ideological work, in the end, is to level the English and the Powhatan people to the same state of ethnocentric brutishness, portraying ignoble savagism as natural and universal rather than as having particular cultural and historical roots. When these lyrics are disseminated outside the context of the film, in songbooks and on the soundtrack, they may have a particularly harmful impact upon a young and impressionable audience. We don't play the soundtrack in our house, but friends with younger children tell me that, to their horror, they have caught their children singing "Savages, Savages" among themselves, having internalized a racist epithet that remains potent and degrading.[7]

The filmmakers are quite aware that they are in risky territory here and characterize the episode as dealing with "one of the most adult themes ever in a Disney film." The theme is "the ugliness and stupidity that results when people give in to racism and intolerance," and it is refreshing to have it aired, particularly by a studio with a history, even recently, of racist animation. But a more responsible treatment of the theme would be considerably more nuanced, distinguishing between English colonialism and Powhatan resistance, and between the English ideology of savagism and coastal Algonquian attitudes toward their own enemies – whom, as Helen Rountree shows, they generally aimed to politically subordinate and socially incorporate, rather than exterminate and dispossess. This could be done by telling more of Pocahontas's and Powhatan's subsequent dealings with Smith, whom they treated, respectively, as "brother" and *weroance* (a ruler subordinate to Powhatan, the *manamatowick* or supreme ruler).

That *Pocahontas* raises a number of difficult and timely issues is a tribute to its ambition and seriousness of purpose. Indeed, the film begs to be taken as a plea for tolerant, respectful, and harmonious living in a world torn by prejudice, exploitation, ethnic strife, and environmental degradation. So, too, does *The Indian in the Cupboard*, albeit in a more limited fashion. That both films and their associated products and promotions are rife with tensions and ironies exemplifies the limitations of serious cultural critique in an artistic environment devoted to the marketing of dreams. That our children are bombarded with plastic consumables and impoverished caricatures while being admonished to treat other cultures, other creatures, and the land with respect should prompt us to find ways to teach them – and learn from them – the difference between producing and consuming objectified difference, on the one hand, and sustaining respectful relationships across difference, on the other.

In a society founded on objectification, differentiation, and commodification the lesson is a hard one, and one that has characteristically been expressed in an oppositional "Indian" voice. If *Pocahontas* and *The Indian in the Cupboard* can be viewed only with ambivalence because of their own participation in processes of objectification and commodification, the forms of "playing Indian" to which each gives rise may offer genuine possibilities for unlearning these processes and imagining new ones, that is, for learning things we never knew we never knew.[8]

"I love that part of the song," Katie has told me, and Tina and I agree. We often find ourselves singing Pocahontas's lines, and sometimes we stop to wonder at the paradoxical form of learning they suggest. As a first step on a transformative journey, we locked the plastic Indian in his videocase cupboard once and for all and stepped outside to find Star Girl in the night sky.

Notes

1   Onondaga words are treated more or less as proper names on the CD-ROM, and I have anglicized them in this essay. Consulting the sparse published documentation on the Onondaga language, I am delighted to find that Little Bear's term for "player," Henuyeha, is a nominalization of the form used for playing the indigenous game of lacrosse (Hewitt 625). The term for "friend" that I anglicize as Ungachi is transcribed as *onguiatsi, mon ami* in Shea's French–Onondaga dictionary.

2   Jeanne Shenandoah was also a consultant for the CD-ROM, as were Rick Hill and Huron Miller.

3   This and subsequent unattributed quotations are taken from Disney press releases.

4   Paraphrasing the lyrics to "Colors of the Wind" (because of copyright restrictions) does an injustice to Stephen Schwartz's fine poetry, which may be found in song books and on the notes to the soundtrack.

5   The trivialization of Pocahontas's relationship to animals was brought to my attention by a chastening response to the review of *Pocahontas* I posted on H-Net on June 30, 1995. On the electronic list devoted to "teaching social studies in secondary schools," Paul Dennis Gower Sr replied, "PUHLEASE!!!!!! It is, after all, a cartoon. It has a talking raccoon, for crying out loud."

6   The rest of Pocahontas's story would make for an intriguing drama indeed if treated something like Disney's underpublicized *Squanto: A Warrior's Tale*, which does not hesitate to portray the brutality of Squanto's English kidnappers as well as a likely course of events leading to Squanto's allegiance to the English settlers at Plymouth. *Pocahontas: Her True Story*, a televised biography from the Arts & Entertainment network, provides a useful counterpoint to the Disney film but does not do justice to Pocahontas's tale or to the historical context of visual imagery (which is treated transparently as illustrative material, unlike the more historicized treatments of Josephy and Strong's "Search for Otherness").

7   This was a key objection of an open letter regarding *Pocahontas* posted by more than a hundred members of the NatChat listserv on July 18, 1995.

8   This outcome – utopian, perhaps, but consistent with Omri's own course of development – requires that commodified images be taken as "teachable moments" pointing toward more complex, less objectified, understandings.

Works Cited

Banks, Lynne Reid. *The Indian and the Cupboard*. New York: Doubleday, 1981.

——. *The Mystery of the Cupboard*. New York: William Morrow, 1993.

——. *The Return of the Indian*. New York: Doubleday, 1986.

——. *The Secret of the Indian*. New York: Doubleday, 1989.

Barbour, Philip. *Pocahontas and Her World*. Boston: Houghton Mifflin, 1969.

Barth, John. *The Sot-Weed Factor*. Toronto: Bantam Books, 1980.

Berkhofer, Robert F. *The White Man's Indian: Images of the American Indian from Columbus to the Present*. New York: Random House, 1977.

Bieder, Robert E. "The Grand Order of the Iroquois: Influences on Lewis Henry Morgan's Ethnology." *Ethnohistory* 27 (1980): 349–61.

Deloria, Vine. *Custer Died for Your Sins: An Indian Manifesto*. New York: Macmillan, 1969.

Gleach, Frederick W. "Interpreting the Saga of Pocahontas and Captain John Smith." In *Reading Beyond Words: Contexts for Native History*, 21–42. Ed. Jennifer S. H. Brown and Elizabeth Vibert, eds. Peterborough, Ontario: Broadview Press, 1996.

Green, Rayna. "The Pocahontas Perplex: The Image of Indian Women in American Culture." *Massachusetts Review* 16, 4 (1975): 698–714.

Greenblatt, Stephen. *Renaissance Self-Fashioning: From More to Shakespeare*. Chicago: University of Chicago Press, 1980.

Haraway, Donna J. *Simians, Cyborgs, and Women: The Reinvention of Nature*. New York: Routledge, 1991.

Hewitt, J. N. B. "Iroquoian Cosmology, Second Part." *43rd Annual Report of the Bureau of American Ethnology, 1925–26*. Washington, DC: US Government Printing Office, 1928.

Hochswender, Woody. "Pocahontas: A Babe in the Woods." *Harper's Bazaar* (June 1995): 154–57.

Hulton, Paul. *America 1585: The Complete Drawings of John White.* Chapel Hill: University of North Carolina Press and British Musuem Press, 1984.

Jennings, Francis. *The Invasion of America: Colonialism and the Cant of Conquest.* New York: W. W. Norton, 1975.

Josephy, Alvin M., Jr. *Five Hundred Nations: An Illustrated History of North American Indians.* New York: Alfred A. Knopf, 1994.

Mechling, Jay. "'Playing Indian' and the Search for Authenticity in Modern White America." *Prospects* 5 (1980): 17–33.

Prucha, Francis Paul. *Americanizing the American Indians: Writings by the "Friends of the Indian," 1880–1900.* Cambridge: Harvard University Press, 1973.

Rountree, Helen. *The Powhatan Indians of Virginia: Their Traditional Culture.* Norman: University of Oklahoma Press, 1989.

Sharpes, Donald K. "Princess Pocahontas, Rebecca Rolfe (1595–1617)." *American Indian Culture and Research Journal* 19, 4 (1995): 231–39.

Shea, John Gilmary. *A French-Onondaga Dictionary, from a Manuscript of the Seventeenth Century.* 1860. New York: AMS Press, 1970.

Sheehan, Bernard W. *Savagism and Civility: Indians and Englishmen in Colonial Virginia.* Cambridge: Cambridge University Press, 1980.

Slapin, Beverly, and Doris Seale. *Through Indian Eyes: The Native Experience in Books for Children.* Philadelphia: New Society Publishers, 1992.

Smith, John. "A True Relation of Such Occurrences and Accidents of Noate as Hath Hapned in Virginia." In *The Complete Works of Captain John Smith (1580–1631),* 1: 3–117. Philip L. Barbour, ed. Chapel Hill: University of North Carolina Press, 1986.

———. "The Generall Historie of Virginia, New England, and the Summer Isles." In *The Complete Works of Captain John Smith (1580–1631),* 2. Philip L. Barbour, ed. Chapel Hill: University of North Carolina Press, 1986.

Sommer, Doris. *Foundational Fictions: The National Romances of Latin America.* Berkeley and Los Angeles: University of California Press, 1991.

Stewart, Kathleen. "On the Politics of Cultural Theory: A Case for 'Contaminated' Cultural Critique." *Social Research* 58, 2 (1991): 395–412.

Stewart, Susan. *On Longing: Narratives of the Miniature, the Gigantic, the Souvenir, the Collection.* Durham, N.C.: Duke University Press, 1993.

Strong, Pauline Turner. "Captivity in White and Red." In *Crossing Cultures: Essays in the Displacement of Western Civilization,* 33–104. Daniel Segal, ed. Tueson: University of Arizona Press, 1992.

———. "The Search for Otherness." In *Invisible America: Unearthing Our Hidden History,* 24–25. Mark P. Leone and Neil Asher Silberman, eds. New York: Henry Holt, 1995.

Suzuki, David, and Peter Knudtsen. *Wisdom of the Elders: Sacred Native Stories of Nature.* New York: Bantam, 1992.

Taussig, Michael. *Mimesis and Alterity: A Particular History of the Senses.* New York: Routledge, 1993.

Yankowitz, Joan. *Behind the Scenes of "The Indian in the Cupboard."* New York: Scholastic, 1995.

19

"You Are Alright, But . . .": Individual and Collective Representations of Mexicans, Latinos, Anglo-Americans and African-Americans in Steven Soderbergh's *Traffic*

Deborah Shaw

US cinema has a long history of representing Latin Americans and Latinos, a history that has been chronicled in a number of studies (Woll, 1980; Ramírez Berg, 1990, 2002; de Orellana, 1993; Berumen, 1995; Keller, 1994; Richard 1993, 1994).[1] The dominant argument to emerge from these studies is that Latino and Latin American filmic characters throughout much of the 20th century are the products of racist and neo-colonialist discourses and are predominantly stereotypical and negative.[2] Masculine Latino types have been identified as greasers or bandits, Latin lovers, gang members, simple-minded buffoons, violent guerrillas, and, from the 1970s onwards, drug dealers and traffickers.[3] Women's roles have often been limited to that of the "beautiful *señorita*" or "dark lady," the harlot, *cantinera*, the loose bar maid, and the Female Clown (Ramírez Berg, 2002, 70–77). Even when the Hispanic characters have been represented as "good," their screen personas are often naive, and in need of Euro-American heroes to save them, as is the case with common representations of Mexicans in Westerns. In these cases, Mexican villagers are cast as "ideological or political disciples to Anglo character mentors" (Berumen, 1995, 72, 104), who protect them from

Deborah Shaw, "'You Are Alright, But . . .': Individual and Collective Representations of Mexicans, Latinos, Anglo-Americans and African-Americans in Steven Soderbergh's *Traffic*," pp. 211–223 from *Quarterly Review of Film and Video* 22:3 (Philadelphia and London: Taylor & Francis and Routledge, 2005). © 2005. Reprinted by permission of Taylor & Francis Group, LLC, http://www.taylorandfrancis.com

the Mexican villains who are terrorizing them.[4] Other positive stereotypes fall into the categories of exotic others, who bring romance and excitement, such as those seen in the Latin Lover, or the beautiful *señorita*.

Writers on Hispanic representations in Hollywood have attempted to provide social and political explanations for the above. De Orellana argues, for example, that the association of Mexico with anarchy, banditry and confusion, and the association of the United States with order, stability and democracy were used historically to justify expansionism into Mexican territory (de Orellana, 1993, 9). Likewise, Berumen claims that the negative stereotypes of Latin Americans in films of the 1920s were used as "rationale for the frequent US armed interventions in Latin America" (Berumen, 1995, 12). He also argues that the representation of the politically ignorant Latin Americas was used to justify US interference in Latin American domestic politics from the 1950s (Berumen, 1995, 73).

Traffic (Steven Soderbergh, 2000) presents an interesting example of screen representations of Latinos and Mexicans at the start of the 21st century and allows us to consider whether the above-mentioned stereotypes are disappearing in a period when North American cinema is becoming more aware of national and ethnic sensibilities. The representations of the Latino and Mexican characters are, in general terms, less simplistic that those seen in the majority of the previous films written about by the authors mentioned, yet there are still negative representations, which I argue can be related to US foreign policy. While some character portrayals follow the well-established negative conventions referred to, others escape stereotypical treatment. In this article I aim to explore the degree to which the representations in the film succeed in challenging traditional Hollywood visions of Mexico and of US Latinos, and ask how representations of Mexicans and Latinos shed light on contemporary discourses of Mexico and ethnic groups in the United States. I also consider the images of African-Americans and Anglo-Americans and their relationship with the Mexicans and Latinos in an exploration of the film's vision of individual and collective ethnic and national groups.

Traffic, as a multiple Oscar winning feature that achieved high box office takings, is among the highest profile films to feature representations of Mexicans and Hispanics, and to tackle the drug situation in the United States.[5] While it can be located within the policier genre, it is also an issue-based film that succeeded in contributing to the debate on drug trafficking and drug abuse in the United States at the time that George W. Bush was establishing his new administration.[6] Unlike most previous films about drugs which are principally concerned with catching criminals who are frequently Latin American, *Traffic* attempts to provide the "full picture" in terms of drug trafficking, dealing, use and law enforcement.[7] It is a film that provides more sophisticated images of the US and Mexico and produces representations of characters from each respective country that challenge a number of filmic stereotypes. Nevertheless, despite this, there is an unacknowledged neo-colonialist and racist discourse in *Traffic*, which follows in a Hollywood tradition of representing Mexico and Mexicans as a country and a people who are in need of moral, political and institutional guidance from the United States, and which portrays Latinos and African-Americans en masse as dangerous criminals.

In her analysis of race and gender in contemporary Hollywood film, Sharon Willis claims the following:

> At one extreme, we find popular representations that strain to manage differences figured as pure threat in images and stories which mobilize social anxiety, only to reassure mainstream audiences by restoring the privilege of white heterosexuality, white masculinity and the white middle class family. At the other end of the spectrum, we find other representations that strive to accommodate diversity through scripts organized around specific identities and intended to capture new identity-based market segments. (Willis, 1997, 3)

I aim to demonstrate that the film uses elements of both strategies, with *Traffic* challenging racial and ethnic hierarchical categories that have traditionally characterized many mainstream Hollywood films. Nevertheless, the film simultaneously reinforces a number of national and ethnic stereotypes. These representations can be analyzed through a focus on the approach to filmmaking seen in the direction and the cinematic techniques used.[8] My analysis of the film does not focus on the representation of gender in the film as my concern is with ethnic and national representations, nevertheless, it should be acknowledged that *Traffic* is an example of masculinist cinema in that the positions of power are principally held by men, with female parts principally limited to those of wife and mother (Barbara Wakefield, Amy Irving), addict (Caroline Wakefield, Erika Christensen) and lover (an uncredited Salma Hayek as the lover of a Mexican drug kingpin). The exception is Helena Ayala (Catherine Zeta Jones), who takes over her husband's role as a major cocaine importer when he is imprisoned. Nevertheless, the other main players (the traffickers, dealers, police and DEA officers) are men.[9]

It can be argued, then, that *Traffic* both contests and reinforces previous filmic stereotypes. One principal technique used to achieve this is the displaced narrative center. The sites of identification are dispersed throughout the film with the focus on a range of characters and their stories. There are several story lines, all connected by a focus on different stages of the drugs' trail. The main effect of this is that characters are all subordinate to the plot and the problem of drugs. This leads to the destabilizing of the traditional figure of the hero, with a number of "good" characters, from a range of national and ethnic backgrounds, engaged in the "war on drugs" in their separate spheres, all with varying degrees of success.

The editing creates connections between these characters, the law enforcers of the film. These are: Javier Rodríguez Rodríguez (Benicio del Toro), an honest Mexican cop working in Tijuana; the two DEA (Drug Enforcement Administration) agents, the African-American, Montel Gordon (Don Cheadle) and the Latino, Ray Castro (Luis Guzmán); and Bob Wakefield (Michael Douglas), the Anglo-American drug Czar appointed by the President. The first three scenes of

Traffic establish the structural pattern used: audiences are shown Javier and his partner Manolo attempting, but failing to stop the trafficking of drugs into the US from Tijuana; there is then a cut to Wakefield in a law court in his last (drug related) case before he takes up his new role, followed by a cut to Gordon and Castro on the trail of a cocaine distributor in the United States.

This structure has a bearing on the depiction of nationalities and ethnic groups and gender, central to which are questions of point-of-view. In their analysis of the classical Hollywood film, Shohat and Stam explain through their application of Genette's theories of focalization that, "all the ideological points-of-view are integrated into the authoritative liberal perspective of the narrator-focalizer, who, godlike, oversees and evaluates all the positions" (Shohat and Stam, 1994, 206). Here there is no single narrator-focalizer among the characters and Wakefield is the only bourgeois Anglo-American among those who are on the side of "good". The white middle-class family is, then, featured, but it is not in a privileged position in relation to the other characters, and is represented as a dysfunctional unit (that is none-the-less worth fighting to save, as the denouement of their story line suggests). The Mexican, Javier Rodríguez Rodríguez, and the African-American and Latino DEA agents share prominence with Wakefield and are all afforded points-of-view.[10]

All of the good characters are working for, or will work for in Javier's case, the US state in its attempts to prevent drugs from coming into the United States. The film thus represents a positive multicultural, masculine power structure. In the case of these four key characters, traditional ethnic hierarchies are reversed in terms of their effectiveness in the fight against the drug trade. Wakefield, the high-ranking official, appears to stand at the head of the power hierarchy; yet, he is shown to initially be powerless to deal with his own daughter's problems of drug addiction. He stands down from his public role, unable to reconcile his public and private roles, before joining his wife to fully support his daughter.[11] The narration of his story represents the interlinking of the personal and the political, and presents the case that no one man can solve such a complex social issue; a further weakening of the traditional hero-centered narrative.

The two DEA agents are also seen to fail on one level, with Ray Castro killed in their operations. Nevertheless, this section of the film ends with Montel Gordon managing to bug the office of Carl Ayala, an important drug distributor, suggesting that he will secure his arrest. He, thus, achieves more in the fight against drugs than Wakefield. The closest character *Traffic* has to a hero is Javier Rodríguez Rodríguez, shown to be an incorruptible cop in a corrupt system, motivated by a desire to do his job, to protect his weak partner Manolo (Jacob Vargas) and Manolo's wife, and by a desire to do the best for Tijuana. When asked what he wants in exchange for information he gives the DEA about key Mexican drug traffickers he explains that all he wants is for children to be able to play baseball in a safe environment. What is significant is that the lowest character in terms of social hierarchy is the highest in terms of moral integrity and is the most successful in taking on the drug traffickers. Javier is a character who is given agency and is an example of a Latin American character who is not reduced to being the object of an Anglo-American gaze, as has so often been the case with representations of Latino characters (Ramírez Berg, 1990, 293).

Also significant is the fact that Javier's dialogue when in Mexico, along with that of the other Mexican characters, is in Spanish. Non-native English speakers have frequently been given no language of their own in Hollywood films and are seen to be stupid through their inability to "master civilized language" (Shohat and Stam, 1994, 192).[12] Soderbergh has shown an awareness of this problematic form of representation, and a desire to correct past socio-linguistic insensitivities. When asked whether he encountered any resistance to shooting the Mexican part of the film in Spanish with English subtitles, he replied:

> Not much. I had about a five-minute conversation with USA, the production company, about it, sort of explaining why it was important. I said, "If these people don't speak Spanish, the film has no integrity. You just can't expect anyone to take it seriously." (Lemons, 2000)

There are, then, a number of attempts in *Traffic* to confront a traditional Anglo-American focus, seen in the ways in which traditional ethnic identities of the "good" characters are resignified, and in the use of Spanish in the Mexican story line. In addition, the film in its analysis of the drug situation does not identify the problem exclusively in terms of supply, as has been the case in many other filmic representations of drug related crime thrillers, but also explores the issue of demand and addiction in the United States. Nevertheless, many strategies of dominant cinema are adopted, particularly in terms of how "others" are seen.

Commercial Hollywood films have often relied on interplay between familiar and unfamiliar images (Ellis, 1982, 74).[13] While some of the representations in *Traffic* seek to destabilize traditional categories, these are in relation to individual characters, and the film's social coding ultimately rests on familiar/stereotypical depictions of ethnic and national groups (African-Americans, Anglo-Americans, Mexicans and Latinos). The positive Mexican seen in the characterization of Javier is an exception, as are the positive representations of the African-American (Montel) and the Latino (Ray) in contrast with negative group representations. It could be argued that *Traffic* self-consciously inserts these "good" individual characters to detract from criticisms towards negative stereotyping that, without their presence, would be much more evident.[14]

As a film that is, in large part, concerned with drug trafficking, it might appear inevitable that *Traffic* rely on mainly negative representations of Mexico and Mexicans, as it principally features the key players in the drug trade. Yet, what is of concern is the way in which the film nationalizes and racializes the drug issue. In the filmic world of *Traffic* all of the traffickers are Mexican, the distributors are primarily Latino and the dealers are all African-American.[15] It is, for example, significant that the three principal crooks in the United States, Carl Ayala, Eduardo Ruiz and Frankie Flowers/Francisco Flores, appear to be of Mexican origin.

While their national origins are not specified, their names and the fact that they are involved with the Juarez cartel in Tijuana suggest this. There is an additional problematic form of representation in the fact that the odious Flowers/Flores, a hired assassin working for the Obregón brothers, is also gay. Any analysis concerned with questions of sexuality as well as ethnicity has to ask why this psychopathic and cowardly character is gay and promiscuous. It would seem that this is a cheap device used to encourage audience antipathy towards him. A charge of homophobia can, then, also be leveled at *Traffic*, as the only gay character in the film is represented in such a one-dimensional negative way. He is a border character as the Spanish/English versions of his name suggest working on both sides of the Mexican/American border, and in the context of this film comes to stand for the negative effect of Mexican infiltration into the United States.[16]

Another area in which questions can be raised in *Traffic* is the relationship between casting and national identities. The desire for integrity Soderbergh claims in the use of Spanish language for the Mexican scenes is not seen in terms of casting. While Latino actors are used to play the Mexican and Latino parts, no Mexican actors were used in the central roles for the Mexican parts. To give some examples: Benicio del Toro (Javier) is from Puerto Rico, Tomas Milian (Salazar) is a Cuban American, and Benjamin Bratt (Juan Obregón) is an American with a Peruvian mother; only Jacob Vargas (Manolo) is Mexican American. I do not intend to equate the nationality of the actors with the quality of the acting; nevertheless, there are ethical issues involved in the casting choices made, as Shohat and Stam have argued.[17] To gain a sense of a non-US perspective, it is worth considering the acceptability of a hypothetical Mexican film that used only European actors to play North Americans.

In contrast to the representations of individual leading characters, collective depictions of national and racial groups often reinforce stereotypes. Anglo-Americans are primarily cast as honest law enforcers, or as users. This is seen in the focus on the Wakefield family, with Bob the well-meaning drug Czar, and his daughter Caroline and her friends cast as young middle class victims of a drug culture. The film does not show any corruption among the US law enforcers (border controllers, police, members of the DEA, or members of Wakefield's team).[18] The film also shows no users among the African-American, Mexican or Latino communities, which ensures that they are not seen as victims of drug cultures in the way that Anglo-American young people are. In all of these areas there is clearly a "distortion of referentiality," to use Willis's term (Willis, 1997, 5); certain truths are repressed, while others are exposed. Corruption in official circles in Mexico has been well documented, as has corruption in official circles in the US, yet only Mexican corruption is part of this narrative.[19] European Americans are also part of drug crime organizations, and Latinos, African Americans and Mexicans have members of their communities who are victims of drug abuse, as well as suppliers. This seems too obvious to state; nevertheless, these are representations that are absent from *Traffic*.

In one of the most disturbing scenes, the film explicitly illustrates images of racially organized drug cultures. The scene begins with an out of place Wakefield driving in a predominantly African-American part of town, looking for his daughter. The camera ingeniously switches its focus to Caroline when he passes her without seeing her on the other side of the street. There is a rapid cut to a black man, in extreme close-up to the right of the frame, fucking someone; in the next shot it is revealed that the previous shot was seen from Caroline's point-of-view; she is out of focus and expressionless, and is clearly already high. They are interrupted by a client and on his return she has found heroin in his bag; he injects her before he resumes fucking her, obviously his payment. The young, beautiful white girl (Erika Christensen was cast, no doubt, partly due to her innocent looks) is thus reduced to prostitute and heroin user by the black dealer. His face is rarely seen; he is either shot in extreme close up or naked from behind, glistening with sweat, as he goes to answer the knock at his door. He is thus criminalized, dehumanized and sexualized, and can be seen to belong to a Hollywood tradition of negative representations of African-Americans.[20] Caroline, in contrast, is seen in close up with the focus on her face highlighting her status as drug victim.

Interestingly, the film does show some sensitivity towards issues of racial typecasting, and attempts to counter accusations of racist representations within its own discourses. In a scene that follows shortly after Caroline's initiation into heroin use, Seth, Caroline's boyfriend, attempts to explain to Wakefield the economics of drug dealing. He counters Wakefield's shock at the place in which she is living with the following speech:

> All over this great nation of ours a hundred thousand white people from the suburbs are cruising around downtown asking every black person they see. "You got any drugs? You know where I can score some drugs?" Think about the effect that has on the psyche of a black person.

He goes on to argue that white people would behave in exactly the same way if the situation were reversed. These two scenes are another example of the film's dual approach to racial representations. African-Americans are identified en masse as criminals in a way common to so much popular culture, as Michael Moore has demonstrated in *Bowling for Columbine* (2002), while attempts are made to explain why this is the case. This is fiction presenting itself as fact, with fictional techniques expertly used to generate audience sympathy (for the white girl) and antipathy (for the black man). What is most likely to remain in audiences' memories are not Seth's socio-economic arguments, but the graphic image of the black dealer's body covering that of the white girl.

Familiar images of a modern advanced US society and an underdeveloped, corrupt Mexican society are consolidated through the use of sophisticated filming techniques. Different tones are used to signal the many shifts in narrative and their locations, and while Soderbergh's use of color coding is artistically interesting, it is also a central part of the creation of the film's rather limited vision of the

US/Mexican divide. An image of Anglo-America as industrial, wealthy, and cold-hearted is given in the blue metallic tones used whenever Wakefield, wife and daughter are seen. A backward feel is given to the Mexican scenes through the use of a sepia tone; other colors are drained to heighten the sense of a sun drenched, parched geography characterized by lack and poverty.[21] The sunny locations of California are shot and produced using a more conventional Hollywood approach reminiscent of 1970s television shows; the bright sun-filled wealthy suburban settings provide a further contrast to Tijuana's poverty.[22] This, once again, reinforces cultural geographical tropes of "first" and "third" world; none of Mexico's modernity is seen, while poor North America is not visible.

In one scene Wakefield looks through binoculars at Porfirio Madrigal's old house on the other side of the border. Sepia tones are used as the viewer shares Wakefield's point of view, and conventional lighting returns to indicate the US side of the border. This could be radical filmmaking if it were used to show Wakefield's limited vision, but it becomes just another example of distorted images of Mexico when one considers that this is the view of the country shared by the filmmakers. The US side is a stone's throw from Mexico so the lighting has no basis in geographical conditions, but is rather an image of Mexican underdevelopment as seen in the North American imaginary. What is perhaps most significant in this scene and others is the fact that that corrupt Mexicans are implicitly held to be responsible for the underdevelopment. Tijuana is equated with the violent world of rival drug cartels, which are characterized by brutality, greed and megalomania; no mention is made of the many *maquiladora* factories in Tijuana, the assembly plants that resemble sweat shops in which Mexican workers work long hours for minimum wages to produce US goods.[23] The North American state and economic organizations are thus seen to play no part in the poverty of the region.[24]

It is worth noting that the film in addition to avoiding any criticism of US foreign economic policy is overtly apolitical in terms of political affiliation. The precise make up of the administration (Republican or Democrat) is never specified. This ensures that the film is politically safe and does not take any commercial risks through alienating audiences. While the problems in tackling drug crime are exposed, *Traffic* does not attack the policies of any particular government.

North American officials are, then, seen to be honest, while Mexico is seen to be corrupt on all levels, with the honest official as the exception. Javier is, then, the only positive character in a whole cast of villainous Mexican characters. Almost all of the other Mexicans are depicted as corrupt and extremely violent.[25] The villains of the piece are the corrupt General Arturo Salazar, the ruthless traffickers, the Obregón brothers, in charge of the Tijuana cartel, and Porfirio Madrigal, the leader of the rival Juarez cartel.[26] The character who best embodies Mexico's institutional corruption is General Salazar, a military man and the Head of the Federal Drug Forces, whose job it is to fight against trafficking to the United States. In fact, he does wage a war against the Tijuana cartel, but only as he is in the pay of Madrigal.

Salazar fits the caricatured villain familiar in Hollywood screen history, and has many characteristics of the Mexican bandit, such as his violence, his psychopathic tendencies and his involvement in illegal exploits (Berumen, 1995, 25; de Orellana, 1993, 10). Like the Hollywood bandit he is also sadistic and power hungry, and will use any tactics to achieve his ends. He is, however, more sinister as he wears the respectable face of his official role. His light complexion and well groomed appearance mean that the typecasting takes place on a national rather than a racial level: the implicit message seems to be that Mexicans may be white, but they are devious and not to be trusted. The fact that his North American counterpart, Bob Wakefield, is a character of integrity, as are all officials fighting drugs, highlights the film's view of a fundamentally honest US system undermined by Mexican corruption. The contrast between the two is emphasized in their only face to face meeting: Wakefield, concerned about his daughter, asks Salazar about Mexico's procedures for dealing with addicts; Salazar replies that addicts treat themselves by overdosing, leaving one less to worry about.[27] In addition, this erroneously suggests that Mexico has no drug rehabilitation centers for its addicts. Salazar is only caught when Javier provides the DEA with information relating to his dealings, suggesting that the good Mexican cop can only get results if he works for the US agency.

Critics have noted, as has been seen, that Mexicans have traditionally been represented as in need of guidance and rescuing by superior North American heroes (Berumen, 1995, 72, 104; de Orellana, 1993, 6). *Traffic* presents an interesting variation on this theme. Javier, unlike the Mexican villagers of films such as those of *The Magnificent Seven* series, is not a naive simpleton; he is a streetwise cop, who has an intimate understanding of the world of drug trafficking and of the main players, and knows how to protect himself. Nevertheless, he has to turn to the United States to ensure that justice is done. The film argues that only the DEA can have corrupt men like Salazar arrested and implicitly suggests that Mexico has no functioning justice system. Javier becomes one of the film's main heroes when he chooses to work for the US drugs department. Javier's dream of a Tijuana where it is safe for local children to play only becomes possible, within the meaning system of the film, when the United States justice bodies step in. Significantly, DEA officers, not Mexican law enforcement agents, are seen arresting Salazar.[28] The final scene of the film shows Javier watching children playing in a floodlit baseball park; thanks to the fact that he has turned to the United States for help, his dream has come true. Once again, we have an image of Mexico dependent on its northern neighbor for help.

Traffic is a complex film with a number of divergent discourses. In the character of Javier, it creates a well-rounded heroic character who stands in contrast to generations of stereotypical Mexicans invented by Hollywood movies. Ethnic stereotypes are further challenged through the positive central characters of Montel Gordon and Ray Castro, who are witty and sympathetic characters engaged in the fight against trafficking and dealing. In addition, the film deconstructs the apparently privileged world of the Anglo-American drug Czar, by displacing the traditional white male's central point of view and by limiting his powers to resolve drug related problems both nationally and in his own family. Nevertheless, traditional ethnic representations are established in the film's vision of group identities. Familiar Hollywood Mexican villains are seen in the characters of Salazar and his henchmen, in the shadowy figures of Madrigal and the Obregón brothers, and in the psychopathic and cowardly Frankie Flowers/Francisco Flores. In the United States, African-Americans and Latinos are seen to control the drug trade, while Anglo-Americans are cast primarily as the victims of drugs.

The film attempts to present a complete picture of the relationship between the supply of drugs and its use by focusing on interconnecting stories of trafficking and addiction. The film does acknowledge, then, that the scale of criminal activities in Mexican drug trade is due to the market demand in the United States; yet in its representation of Mexico *Traffic* portrays a country that is endemically corrupt, has no functioning justice system, and needs the United States to save it from crime and violence. Evil is still seen to be generated on the Mexican side of the border and a neo-colonialist discourse is seen in the way that North America casts itself as Mexico's savior. Mexico is, once again, the negative other of the United States, which is seen to have a system supported by good men, who are on all levels engaged in the fight against drugs. Margarita de Orellana's concept of the Mexico represented in Hollywood films from between 1911 and 1917 as a negative mirror reflection of the United States, still holds true in a number of areas in *Traffic*.[29] Perhaps the main point to be made is that Mexicans, through films such as *Traffic* (and television programs such as *Kingpin*), are equated with drug trafficking and violent criminal activities in the North American imaginary.[30]

As has been seen, academics have connected traditional filmic representations of Hispanics with US government policies, and these connections can also be made in *Traffic*. The film can be seen both as an attempt to influence government policy and as a reflection of current foreign policy. It argues for treatment over imprisonment for addicts, for a holistic approach to the drug problem, but it also, implicitly, advocates intervention by the DEA in Mexico itself. Mexico's perceived inability and unwillingness to address the issue of drug trafficking could certainly be used to justify the DEA taking over many of drug enforcement roles as part of a "war on drugs," as in currently the case in Mexico, as well as in a number of Latin American countries, such as Colombia, Peru and Bolivia.[31] In fact, the United States has extended its jurisdiction to drug offences committed in Mexico, and has given itself legislative powers to arrest Mexican citizens in their territory, to put them on trial in the United States, to engage in undercover operations, and to pay Mexican police for information (Toro, 1998), powers which are represented and defended in *Traffic*.[32]

The dual approach to national and ethnic representations in this highly regarded film of the early 21st century reflects the state of serious cinema in the United States in an age of both political correctness and global power. The superiority of the United States is asserted, and it perceives that it can only solve its own problems by solving those of other nations. *Traffic* presents an image of a benevolent neo-colonial power that relies on a good multi-ethnic state body to carry out its civilizing mission and to administer justice in its neighboring territory. To return to Willis's categories of representations of diverse identities, images of difference are seen to represent a threat to civilized society, through the film's depictions of entire communities (African-Americans, Latinos, and Mexicans), while ethnic diversity is accommodated through its sensitive and heroic representations of individuals from these same communities (see Willis, 1997, 3). "Good" members of ethnic minorities and "good" foreign individuals are incorporated into the body politic to work within state structures in the fight against "bad" communities and "bad" nations. *Traffic* shows that serious Hollywood cinema is making progress towards addressing the racism of stereotyping, yet reveals that deeply ingrained notions of moral identity still underpin collective representations of Anglo-Americans, ethnic minorities in the US and Mexicans.

Notes

1   I am not referring here to Chicano cinema, or films made by Latinos themselves.

2   There has been some debate about the terminology to use when referring to people of Latin American descent living in the United States. José Cuello has argued that "Hispanic" has more conservative connotations, and, despite its neutral aspirations, it has been criticized for the way that it homogenizes disparate communities through its broad application to those of Latin American descent living in the US and to peoples of Spain and Latin America. "Latino" is a more culturally specific and politically engaged term used to refer to "people of Latin American descent living in the US, particularly those who are born (t)here" (Cuello, 1998). For this reason, in this article I use the term "Latino" when referring to US citizens of Latin American origin, and Hispanic when referring to Latinos and Latin Americans. I use more specific terms, such as "Mexican" and "Mexican American" where appropriate. See Ramírez Berg (2002, 5–6) for an explanation of his use of the term "Latino".

3   Ramírez Berg sees in the drug runner a modern version of the bandit (1990, 294; 2002, 68).

4   Examples of such films include *Crisis* (1950), *Tropical Zone* (1953), *Vera Cruz* (1954), *The Professionals*, 1966, *The Magnificent Seven* (1960), *Guns of the Magnificent Seven* (1969), and *The Magnificent Seven Ride* (1972). For more examples, see Berumen, 1995, 72 and 104.

5   *Traffic* was adapted from a British mini-series, *Traffik*, shown on Channel 4 in 1990. The program focused on interconnecting stories based around drug dealing, policing and use from Pakistan to Europe, and has many common plot ingredients with the film, despite the change in locations. The adaptation won many national and international awards in 2001, including the following Academy Award Oscars: Stephen Soderbergh for Best Director; Stephen Gaghan for Best Writing for a Screenplay Based on Material Previously Produced or Published, Stephen Mirrione for Best Editing and Benicio del Toro for Best Actor in a Supporting Role. For more information see *<http://www.imdb.com/title/tt0181865/awards>*. It also did extremely well commercially: its budget was $48,000,000, low by Hollywood standards and considering its

all star cast, and by July 2001 (6 months after its release) it had grossed $124,107,476 in the US alone, see <*http://www.imdb.com/title/tt0181865/business*>.

6 The film did generate much debate in political circles about the efficacy of national prevention policies, and the need to focus more on treatment for users; for discussions of the political impact of the film, see Leigh Cowan and Wren, 2001; Davies, 2001; Lancaster, 2001.

7 Both Berumen and Keller criticize Hollywood movies for focusing purely on the trafficking side of the drugs issue when represented in Hollywood film (Berumen, 1995, 194; Keller, 1994, 169). Villains were often Hispanics seeking to undermine the fabric of society; see for instance *Scarface* (1983), *High Risk* (1981), *Romancing the Stone* (1984), *Code of Silence* (1985), *Cocaine Wars* (1985), and *Crocodile Dundee* (1988) (Berumen, 194).

8 The director and cinematographer of the film was Stephen Soderbergh; Stephen Gaghan produced the screenplay, based on the screenplay for the television miniseries, written by Simon Moore; the editor was Stephen Mirione.

9 Audiences have a glimpse of female politicians, including real life Senator, Barbara Boxer, at a political party attended by Michael Douglas's character, Wakefeld, but this is no more than a glimpse.

10 Ray Castro's family background is unspecified; Luis Guzmán is a Puerto Rican American. He has played many Latino roles including *The Bone Collector* (1999), *The Limey* (1999), *Boogie Nights* (1997), *Carlito's Way* (1993) among many other roles.

11 Wakefield and his wife are seen at a Narcotics Anonymous meeting, in which Wakefield states that he is there to support Caroline and to listen; he is, thus, presented as a repentant model parent who has learnt from his mistakes.

12 In their words, "by ventriloquizing the world, Hollywood indirectly diminished the possibilities of linguistic self-representation for other nations" (ibid.).

13 John Ellis argues with regard to classic Hollywood narration, that, "filmic narration is an economic system: balancing familiar elements of meaning against the unfamiliar" (ibid.).

14 Sharon Willis has made a similar point in her commentary on the phenomenon in recent Hollywood films of the many representations of black police chiefs. She argues that this seems "designed to counterbalance, in some fantasmatic symmetry, any depictions of African Americans as criminals" (Willis, 1997, 5).

15 The ethnic identities of Carlos Ayala and Eduardo Ruiz are never specified, but their names are clearly Latino. Exceptions are Helena Ayala, who becomes involved in the business through her husband, and Arnie Metzger (Dennis Quaid), Ayala's crooked associate. It is interesting that Catherine Zeta Jones (Helena) is allowed to claim her Welsh identity in the film, through her accent, which makes Metzer the only Anglo-American crook in the film.

16 This is in contrast with the positive subversive meanings given to gay border identities in a range of Chicana writings; see for example, Moraga and Anzaldúa (1981) and Anzaldúa (1987).

17 In their words: "the casting of a non-member of the 'minority' group is a triple insult, implying, a) you are unworthy of self-representation; b) no one from your community is capable of representing you; and c) we, the producers of the film, care little about your offended sensibilities for we have the power and there is nothing you can do about it" (Shohat and Stam, 1994, 190).

18 It is worth noting that Wakefield is a personal friend of the President, yet the issue of cronyism is not addressed, and it is suggested that he attained the job on merit alone.

19 See Levine, 1990, for an exposé of DEA corruption and incompetence; for articles in the Mexican national newspaper, *La Jornada* documenting instances of drug related corruption in the United States, see McNamara, 2001a, McNamara, 2001b, Afp y Reuter, 1996. For an examination of drug related corruption in the Mexican military, see <*http://www.globalexchange.org/countries/mexico/slope/section2.html#corruption*>.

20 For more on traditional representations of African-Americans in Hollywood cinema, including representations of the buck, see Bogle (1989).

21 The scenes involving Wakefield were shot on special film without the use of a filter that eliminates the blue tones (see Silberg, 2001). Soderbergh achieved the sun filled bleached look for the Mexican storyline through significant overexposure, the footage was then digitized and partially desaturated (ibid.). Silberg adds, "then, to boost the contrast and the grain, the facility duped the positive print from the film-out to Ektachrome, from which it struck a negative." For more information on the technical approaches used see ibid. I am grateful to John Caro for this source.

22 To achieve a softer look for the scenes involving Helena, Soderbergh shot with a Pro Mist filter and Kodak's low-contrast 5277 stock (ibid.). Of the scenes, he says, "I wanted to have a sort of idyllic, '70's television-commercial style [. . .] I thought it contrasted nicely with the rot that was going on underneath."

23 For more on maquiladora factories see Iglesias Prieto (1997) and Kamel and Hoffman (1999).

24 In the popular television show *Kingpin* (2003), Mexicans also feature as violent and amoral drug traffickers looking to infiltrate the North American market; for more on *Kingpin*, see <*http://www.nbc.com/Kingpin/index.html*>.

25 Manolo, Javier's partner, can also be seen as an exception, however, while he is not violent he is weak and greedy, and he is caught and shot for trying to sell information about Salazar and Madrigal to the DEA. Money is his motive, in contrast to Javier.

26 Salazar appears to be based on Jesús Gutiérrez Rebollo, the Obregon brothers are based on the Arellano Félix brothers, while Madrigal is based on Amado Carrillo Fuentes; see Cason and Brooks (2001). Rebollo, director of the Instituto Nacional de Combate a las Drogas, Mexico's anti drug unit, was charged 1997 with involvement with drug traffickers (Toro, 1998).

27 In interviews Soderbergh has spoken of the need to put resources into rehabilitation; he has said that people need to "[find] a way to look at this as a healthcare issue, not a criminal issue; something other than filling up prisons with nonviolent users. There are little things we can do to make a big impact. Everyone in law enforcement will tell you, education and treatment work. Money and resources put into them have a concrete effect. That would be a good thing. It's not a very sexy approach, but it works" (Lemons, 2000).

28 This policy is in line with the 1986 Anti-Drug Abuse Act, "which outlawed the manufacture and distribution of drugs outside the United States if they were intended for export to American territory. This law provided the basis for United States federal grand jury indictments of foreign nationals, a practice that has increased over the last ten years" (Toro, 1998).

29   Her conclusion could have been written for *Traffic*: "[Mexico is] a mirror on whose imperfect [. . .] surface the North Americans may glimpse the image of themselves they need to see" (de Orellana, 1993, 14).

30   It is worth noting that images Mexicans create of themselves in Mexican cinema rarely conform to those invented by Hollywood. González Inarritu, on being interviewed about his successful film *Amores perros*, shows an awareness of this in the following comments: "I am not a Mexican with a moustache and a sombrero and a bottle of tequila [. . .] Nor am I a corrupt cop or a drug trafficker. There are millions like me. And this is the world I live in and the one I want to show" (Patterson, 2001).

31   For sources relating to drug trafficking in the Americas, see Bagley (1997) and Nadelmann (1993); for details relating to the Bush administration's policies on drugs, see *<http://www.state.gov/g/inl/rls/fs/8452.htm>*.

32   These are policies which have inevitably led to diplomatic tensions between the two countries (ibid.); tensions which are not represented in *Traffic*.

Works Cited

Anzaldúa, Gloria. *Borderlands/La Frontera: The New Mestiza*. San Francisco: Spinsters, 1987.

Bagley, Bruce M. (ed.). *Drug Trafficking Research in the Americas: An Annotated Bibliography*. Miami: North-South Center, 1997.

Berumen, Frank Javier Garcia. *The Chicano/Hispanic Image in American Film*. New York: Vantage Press, 1995.

Bogle, Donald. *Toms, Coons, Mulattos, Mammies and Bucks*. New York: Continuum, 1989.

De Orellana, Margarita. "The Incursion of North American Fictional Cinema 1911–1917 into the Mexican Revolution," in King, López, Alvarado (eds) *Mediating Two Worlds: Cinematic Encounters in the Americas*. London: BFI Publishing, 1993, 3–14.

Ellis, John. *Visible Fictions: Cinema, Television, Video*. London: Routledge, 1982.

Iglesias Prieto, Norma. *Beautiful Flowers of the Maquiladora Life Histories of Women Workers in Tijuana*. Austin: University of Texas Press, 1997.

Kamel Rachael and Hoffman, Anya (eds). *The Maquiladora Reader*. Pennsylvania: American Friends Service Committee, 1999.

Keller, Gary. *Latinos and United States Film: An Overview and Handbook*. Tempe, AZ: Bilingual Press, 1994.

Levine, Michael. *Deep Cover: The Inside Story of How DEA Infighting, Incompetence, and Subterfuge Lost Us the Biggest Battle of the Drug War*. New York: Delacorte Press, 1990.

Moraga, Cherrie and Anzaldúa, Gloria (eds). *This Bridge Called My Back: Writings by Radical Women of Color*. New York: Kitchen Table, 1981.

Nadelmann, Ethan A. *Cops across Borders: The Internationalization of US Criminal Law*. Pennsylvania: Pennsylvania State UP, 1993.

Ramírez Berg, Charles. "Stereotyping in Films in General and of the Hispanic in Particular," *Howard Journal of Communications* (Summer 1990): 286–300.

Ramírez Berg, Charles. *Latino Images in Film: Stereotypes, Subversion, Resistance*. Austin: University of Texas Press, 2002.

Richard, Alfred Charles. *Censorship and Hollywood's Hispanic Image: An Interpretative Filmography, 1936–1955*. Westport, Connecticut, London: Greenwood Press, 1993.

Richard, Alfred Charles. *Contemporary Hollywood's Negative Hispanic Image: An Interpretative Filmography, 1956–93*. Westport, Connecticut, London: Greenwood Press, 1994.

Shohat, Ella and Stam, Robert. *Unthinking Eurocentrism: Multiculturalism and the Media*. London and New York: Routledge, 1994.

Willis, Sharon. *Race and Gender in Contemporary Hollywood Film*. Durham, NC: Duke UP, 1997.

Woll, Allen. *The Latin Image in American Film*. Los Angeles: UCLA Latin American Center Publications, 1980.

Website Sources

"Awards for *Traffic* (2000)," *The International Movie Database*, <http://www.imdb.com/title/tt0181865/awards>. Accessed January 20, 2004.

"Business Data for *Traffic* (2000)," *The International Movie Database*, <http://www.imdb.com/title/tt0181865/business>. Accessed January 20, 2004.

Afp y Reuter, "Un jurado de San Diego investiga sobornos, revela *The Washington Post*, 21.2.1996," *La Jornada*, February 21, 1996. <http://www.jornada.unam.mx/1996/feb96/96022/eu.html>. Accessed January 20, 2004.

Cason, Jim and Brooks, David, "*Traffic*, película que podría ser la crítica más severa a la lucha antidrogas de EU. *La Jornada*, January 9, 2001, <http://www.jornada.unam.mx/2001/jun01/010616/029n1mun.html>. Accessed January 20, 2004.

Cuello, José, "A Primer on Terminology," <www.detroitpublictv.org/americanfamily/cuello.htm>. Accessed January 20, 2004.

Davies, Frank, "Popular *Traffic* Driving Country's Drug Debate," Media Database Project, *Milwaukee Journal Sentinel*, March 20, 2001, <http://www.mapinc.org/drugnews/v01/n493/a09.html>. Accessed January 20, 2004.

Global Exchange, "Corruption Within the Mexican Military Within the Drug War," <http://www.globalexchange.org/countries/mexico/slope/section2.html#corruption>. Accessed January 20, 2004.

Lancaster, John, "In Senate Debate on Drugs, *Traffic* Moves Minds," Common Dreams News Center, Published in *The Washington Post*, March 15, 2001, <http://www.commondreams.org/headlines01/0315-02.htm>. Accessed January 20, 2004.

Leigh Cowan, Alison and Wren, Christopher S., "'*Traffic* Captures Much of Drug World,' People from the Battle Front Say," Media Database Project, <http://www.mapinc.org/drugnews/v01/n101/a10.html>. Accessed January 20, 2004.

Lemons, Stephen, "A Conversation with Stephen Soderbergh, December 20, 2000." <http://stevensoderbergh.tripod.com/print/salon1200.html>. Accessed January 20, 2004.

McNamara, Joseph (a) "Las políticas antinarcos han creado corrupción policiaca *endémica* en EU, acusa ex jefe policial," *La Jornada*, June 16, 2001, <http://www.jornada.unam.mx/2001/jun01/010617/033n1mun.html>. Accessed January 20, 2004.

McNamara, Joseph (b) "Muchos policías derivan en *gangsters* en EU; la corrupción carcome a agents," *La Jornada*, June 17, 2001, <http://www.jornada.unam.mx/2001/jun01/010617/033n1mun.html>. Accessed January 20, 2004.

Patterson, John, "Aztec cameras," *The Guardian*, May 18, 2001, <*http://millimeter.com/ar/video_fade_black_10/index.htm*>. Accessed January 20, 2004.

Silberg, John, "Fade to Black" *Millimeter*, January 1, 2001, <*http://millimeter.com/ar/video_fade_black_10/index.htm*>. Accessed January 20, 2004.

Toro, María Celia, "The Internationalization of Police: The DEA in Mexico," 1998, <*http://www.indiana.edu/~jah/mexico/mtoro.html#up7*>. Accessed January 20, 2004.

US Department of State, "Fact Sheet: The President's National Drug Control Strategy, February 12, 2002," <*http://www.state.gov/g/inl/rls/fs/8452.htm*>. Accessed January 20, 2004.

Part IV
World Cinema:
Joining Local and Global

Introduction

World cinema is a complex term that embraces films made by people living outside Europe and America and those who have emigrated to Europe and America. The modern period is characterized by emigration in large numbers, first from Europe to America in the nineteenth century, and then in the twentieth century from Asia to America and Europe and later from Africa, Latin America, and the Caribbean to Europe and America. Émigrés may live within diasporic communities formed by large emigrant populations, often established for decades or even centuries. Individual emigrants may also be exiles without a community. Many European filmmakers came to Hollywood beginning in the silent era and continuing into the 1930s and 1940s (Sergei Eisenstein, Ernst Lubitsch, Alexander Korda, Alfred Hitchcock) to escape totalitarianism, or just to make films that would be financially successful in a global market, as Hollywood films were. Films made outside Hollywood's system began with emigrants to the USA making ethnic films (e.g. Yiddish films) and African Americans' separate film production companies in the early twentieth century. European films, especially "art" films, marketed in the USA starting in the 1960s (e.g. by Italian Frederico Fellini, Swedish Ingmar Bergmann, Spanish Luis Buñuel, British New Wave Cinema films of working-class subjects (by directors Tony Richardson, Karel Reisz, Lindsay Anderson), French New Wave directors François Truffaut and Jean-Luc Godard), continue to be vigorous and globally marketed (e.g. Spanish Pedro Almodóvar, Japanese Akira Kurosawa, German Wim Wenders,

Italian Lina Wertmueller). Films from China, for example, are among the many new national cinemas in the 1990s that played to mainstream audiences around the globe.

World cinema generally focuses on non-European films, but not exclusively. Some scholars would include filmmakers Spike Lee, Gregory Nava, and Wayne Wang, whose identities and subjects were outside of and challenging "mainstream" subjects, styles, financing, marketing, and production but still widely popular. Many world films are popular and widely marketed, just as American "indies" have become mainstream in their availability and wide audience reception. World cinema categories must be broad, as the topic embraces diverse and heterogeneous films, mixing folklore, literature, high and popular art forms, and all variations of narrative content and format. Part III of this volume deals with minority films, and this part focuses on films made in countries outside America or Europe. These films will certainly raise issues of gender and race and genre, but they have been selected in order to present challenges to the kinds of styles, storytelling, and spatial and temporal orders that dominate most US and European films.

The first overt challenge to Hollywood and to European film production was the manifesto of the "Third Cinema" by Argentines Fernando Solanas and Octavio Getino in 1976, drawing on the Cuban revolution (1959), earlier resistance movements in Vietnam and North Africa against French colonialism, and other political sources to create a cinema of liberation. The Third Cinema manifesto called for a new kind of film, distinct from, and even in opposition to, the First Cinema of Hollywood and mainstream European films, and Second Cinema films made by avant-garde directors who were "auteurs," authors with complete control. Third Cinema has its own roots in French New Wave (voice-overs and collage styles of Godard and Truffaut), political satires by Buñuel from Spain, other movements like Brazil's Cinema Novo (with its own manifesto, *Esthetic of Hunger*, 1965, by Glauber Rocha), and filmmakers who focused on the downtrodden, like Hector Babenco's *Pixote, Law of the Strongest* (1980). Third Cinema was later supported and reaffirmed in the 1986 Edinburgh Manifesto. Other manifestoes appeared in Cuba, North Africa, and the Middle East. Third Cinema is a cinema with an engaged political conscience and consciousness, and its principles might also apply to many Eastern European (Czech, Hungarian, Polish) films, which resisted Soviet and local dictatorships during the Cold War.

Third Cinema films often share subjects of class conflict and of social and political upheaval and production styles of collaboration rather than the director as heroic "auteur." They appeal to a broad public to avoid the elitism of Second Cinema, hoping to make the audience recognize their social and political situations to avoid the entertainment-numbing mode of

First Cinema. Many Third Cinema filmmakers borrowed ideas from the great Brazilian educator and thinker Paolo Freire (*The Pedagogy of the Oppressed*, 1970) and the writings of Franz Fanon on colonial oppression. The goal of Third Cinema was to activate spectators to become agents of their own political destiny through a democratized cinema. Many of these films focus not on the narrative's goal but on its process. They leave problems and dilemmas unresolved and complex in order to make spectators think, an idea borrowed from Bertoldt Brecht's theater of alienation.

Third Cinema has been used as an umbrella term to embrace geographically diverse films (Roy Armes, 1987) or as a category for shared ideological purposes across films' cultural differences (Jim Pines and Paul Willemen, 1989). Teshome Gabriel's *Third Cinema in the Third World* (1982) summarizes the main characteristics of Third Cinema. While Hollywood and European films focus on the individual's point of view of the protagonist or hero, Third Cinema emphasizes collective history and a communal point of view to explain current political and social circumstances and to promote solutions to circumstances of oppression. Third Cinema productions are less concerned with a character's psychology than with political collective action. The main theme of these films is oppression, and subthemes include class antagonism, the preservation of folk and indigenous cultures (for example, oral storytelling) against European cultural domination, the hypocrisy of religion (especially Christianity), sexism and the emancipation of women, and a call to action that may include advocacy of armed resistance. Films of native people in countries overtaken by Europeans or Americans fit this category, too, such as Australian films about Aborigine life (*The Chant of Jimmy Blacksmith*, 1978; *Rabbit-Proof Fence*, 2002; *The Tracker*, 2004), or New Zealand films about the Maori (*Once Were Warriors*, 1994). Third Cinema filmmakers in many countries created new systems of production and distribution to make their films accessible, especially to rural communities, and to produce as many films as possible in the belief that a steady stream of these films would promote social change, unlike the production of a few "great" films, as in Second Cinema. Their production and distribution were as collective as their narrative focus.

Stylistically, these films used a wide range of anti-Hollywood devices. For example, the close-up that emphasizes and heroizes the individual is avoided in many of these films; music comes from folk culture and silence is used to insist on the visual content and not dilute it with the sometimes false emotion or sentimentality that Hollywood music may impose on a scene. Aesthetic intentions in Third Cinema are subordinate to political and social purposes in determining a film's style using cultural forms, stories, and local circumstances with which ordinary people can identify and for whom revolutionary film offers ideas for political action. Any entertainment value serves to enhance these political intentions. As Gabriel (1982, p. 96) notes, "culture in its mass character moves unevenly in relation to the political and economic factors that shape history," so these films intend to transform local/national contents into international/universal voices for the oppressed. Many films by indigenous peoples in the USA, for example, might be Third Cinema, and some scholars include these films, putting Third Cinema inside the West, at the heart of the imperial beast.

Solanas and Getino describe these films as the means to decolonize cinema (and culture in general), to destroy old modes of production and consumption identified as Hollywood's images of humans, history, and society, and to create instead a cinema that reflects and affects the daily lives of colonized and oppressed people. Documentary techniques were crucial in making such films, even in fictional narrative films (as in Trinh T. Minh-Ha's presentation of pluralism and use of documentary framing in her *Surname Viet, Given Name Nam*, 1989). Gillo Pontecorvo's *The Battle of Algiers* (1966) is exemplary of the mix of documentary, fictional narrative, and historical framework. For Solanas and Getino (2000), a documentary-like style had the potential for revolutionary change and for awakening its audience. Innovation served to interrupt audience expectations and, by so doing, intervene in the audience's experiences to awaken their dormant understanding of their own circumstances. These expectations and functions of Third Cinema were as idealist as they were documentary. While Third Cinema is no longer a powerful force uniting world cinema, its legacy continues to inspire much world cinema.

Another concept is what Hamid Naficy (2001) terms "accented films," made for a combined audience of populations around the globe and embracing exiled and diasporic filmmakers. Their films are "accented," inflected by their displacement, which affects not only their content, characters, styles, and themes, but also their modes of production. These films are often "interstitial," as Naficy (ibid., p. 4) notes, occurring between cultures and across cultures. These films, then, comment on the native homelands in which the directors and intended audience previously lived, as well as on the host countries in which they now live. Among the common features in many of these films, Naficy notes the epistolary narrative (using letters or telephones within the diegesis), giving a sense of presence in absence and offering multiple voices and layers of time that challenge the linear narrative of realist films (ibid., p. 5). These films emphasize territory, roots, and uprootedness, often representing homelands as infinite, timeless, and ideal, and host countries as claustrophobic and hostile (ibid.). These films often focus on journeys and travel sites (ports, airports, borders), and characters' identities are fluid and in process. As for the reception of these films, this may vary with the dual audiences: the diasporic community may prefer certain representations of home and host, while host audiences have other expectations of films and no identity with the homelands represented.

Recently a plethora of world cinema has come from the "Third World" and countries that once struggled under colonialism and then under national or civil strife, including Eastern Europe. Often filmmakers from these countries had been inundated with European and Hollywood films, beginning in the silent era, before making films themselves: for example, Dadasaheb Phalke's first film *Raja Harishchandra* (1913), about the great Indian literary epic *Ramayana*, was influenced by the American film *The Life of Christ* (1906), which he saw in Bombay in 1910 (Dissanayake, 2000, p. 143). The Indian director Satyajit Ray was influenced by silent films and Tarzan movies when he was a child and later by the films of the French director Jean Renoir and the Italian Realist Vittorio De Sica. Many Third World filmmakers balance the influence of Hollywood and European films with the contents of indigenous stories, music, dance, visual art, and local cultures. Countries grouped as Third World are vastly different from each other in every cultural, linguistic, social, historical, and political way imaginable.

Naficy differentiates between exilic, diasporic, and ethnic categories of films and filmmakers, though the categories are not discrete or mutually exclusive (Naficy, 2001, p. 11). Exile may be internal or external, and due to censorship or political repression. External exiles often long to return "home" and retain a primary relationship with that home country, while becoming affected by their host countries as hybridized and multicultural individuals (ibid., p. 13). Exilic films focus on there and then (ibid., p. 15). Diasporic filmmakers are likely to be permanently exiled and may even be hostile to their home countries. People may consider themselves diasporic for generations, making their knowledge of their homelands increasingly "past," unaware at times of changes in the homeland. Their diasporic communities are another version of homeland and demand allegiance and ethnic identity, apart from the homeland culture. Diasporic films convey disjunctions between homeland and host country identities. Some diasporic communities live in their former colonizers (North Africans in France and "beur" films, South Asians and West Indians in Britain). Postcolonial ethnic filmmakers may even have been born in the West to emigrants and may identify with the West, as well as with their ethnic parents and communities. Clearly, some of the films in part III of this volume might fit here, such as *East Is East* or *Mississippi Masala*. Ethnic filmmakers often focus on host country identities, often in conflict with the diasporic or ethnic identities, a conflict between family (ethnic) and cohorts (host country peers). As Naficy notes, diasporic and exilic films are both global and local (ibid., p. 19).

World cinema is often dialogic between the diaspora and the host and sometimes between the diaspora and the homeland (e.g. Ethiopian-born,

American-educated, Haile Gerima's *Sankofa*, 1993, which led to his formation of his own distribution company). Its production is frequently collective, but also marked by single directors who double as writers, actors,
and producers, what Naficy calls the "artisanal" production mode, as
distinct from, even oppositional to, the Hollywood studio venue or the
European or indie "auteur" mode of production. These films are characterized by the use of voices, sounds, local music or dance, or ceremonies, and
languages, relying less on visuals in their narrative trajectories, while tending
to be more ideologically overt than films primarily intended for entertainment (ibid., pp. 24–6). Personal feelings and social bonds are explored,
sometimes at the expense of action or closure. Characters' identities are
fragmented and fluid, rather than "whole" or consistent. The theme of
borders – crossing and recrossing – shapes characters' identities.

The geographical range of filmmakers addressing political and cultural
issues and eschewing film as merely entertainment began to grow in the
1960s, a period of the birth of cinema in the decolonizing world on a grand
scale, including Yilmaz Güney from Turkey, Glauber Rocha and Nelson
Pereira dos Santos from Brazil, Ousmane Sembène from Senegal, Med
Hondo from Mauritania, Satyajit Ray from India (especially his *Apu* trilogy),
Octavio Getino from Argentina, Miguel Littin from Chile, Humberto Solas
and Tomás Gutiérrez Alea and Manuel Octavio Gómez from Cuba, and
Shadi Abdes-Salam from Egypt. This period was followed by a diversity of
styles and subjects and increasing geographical spread in the 1970s and
1980s. Some filmmakers used native languages (Wolof in Sembene's *The
Money Order*, 1968, several languages in *Moolaadé*, 2004, and Quechua
and Amayara Indian languages in Bolivian Jorge Sanjines's films). Many of
these countries share the problems of postcolonial economic fragility, with
industrialization and banking still controlled by European and American
multinational corporations. Dependence on Western support often requires
political conformity and even Western-backed despotism.

More recently films from places hitherto ignored in film history have
emerged to present sophisticated cultural representations that make the
local global. Films from Iran, Egypt, Senegal, Burkina Faso, South Africa,
Algeria, Turkey, China, Cuba, and India's "Bollywood" reflect not only
national talent and interest in films, but also their national identities,
some recently defined and often mixed with ethnic and religious identities
(Hinduism in India, Islam in the Middle East and Central Asia). Following Benedict Anderson's famous description of nationhood as imagined
community born out of experience and projection (since we cannot know
everyone in our own nation), it is clear that to impose a national identity
or difference that defines a nation, film can be a powerful tool, as dictators
have noted since the early twentieth century. Films can impose a national

identity defined by ethnic, religious, gender, or racial traits, making some of the people in the nation outsiders, no matter how long they have lived there (Jews in Europe, Armenians in Turkey, Kurds in Iraq, Blacks and Native Americans in the USA, indigenous peoples throughout the world, Blacks and South Asians in Britain, Muslims in India, etc.). Film can become a vital focus of debate and discussion in the public sphere in which political and social issues are open to public discourse and opposition. Cinema offers a site to suture or contest identities of nation, as well as of gender, class, race, and ethnicity. A recent example of this is the Fifth Generation of filmmakers in China, who, since the 1980s, address in their films such potent topics as the Cultural Revolution through new styles and techniques, such as "minimal narration, striking camera movements, a stress on spatiality, and disruptive montage" (Dissanayake, 2000, p. 147) in such films as Zhang Yimou's *Red Sorghum* (1988) and *To Live* (1994), and Chen Kaige's *Farewell, My Concubine* (1993).

In addition to expressing nationalism with which citizens can identify and through which citizens can be shaped and made to conform, films can attract global audiences and make their country and their cultures accessible and sympathetic to a global audience. Films from the Third World have become increasingly diversified in their purposes, contents, and styles, and are now co-produced by US or European producers, as the world economic globalization affects filmmaking, as it affects all production and consumption through which the Third World still too often serves the economic needs of the USA and Europe, rather than the needs of its own citizens. As Robert Stam (1991, p. 222) notes, the "cultural permeability between dominant and dependent cultures" must not be underestimated. The European and American presumption of universality for their own films may tempt Third World filmmakers seeking international recognition, and erase the politically important representation of local life that acknowledges difference and multiple identities. Concepts attached to Third Cinema, such as "the people," "nation," "culture," are highly problematic and not easily defined or limited, making world cinema increasingly uncategorizable. The failures of revolutionary politics in many parts of the world and the emergence of dictatorships and wars against colonial peoples have inspired more complex, nuanced, and problematic approaches to the earlier idealistic content and themes of Third Cinema. One area of study, for example, is the awareness that changes in aesthetics (postmodernism) and economics (globalization) have not altered the uneven power between the West and the rest of the world, still exploited to satisfy Western consumerism and the consumerism of the upper classes in Third World countries, replicating the colonialism of the past (as criticized in Alejandro González Iñárritu, *Amores Perros*, 2000, and Alfonso Cuarón, *Y Tu Mamá También*, 2001).

Readings in this part emphasize alternative voices, films from countries less familiar to Western audiences, and the complexities of spectatorship in many countries for films that appeal to multiple audiences abroad and at "home." Chaudhuri and Finn examine Iranian films that combine generically separate categories of realism and poetic or fantasy content. Chow's essay explores concepts of home and place, concepts often as unstable and permeable in one's homeland as in diasporic communities, the subjects of Stringer's essay. Ganti explores how Bollywood has influenced American films. Naficy talks about the actual practices of film viewing in Iran, an extraordinary and too little analyzed set of practices that profoundly affect how we view and interpret films. Naficy offers the context of actual viewing by those for whom absolute silence is not part of their film-viewing practice. This kind of content is rare in film studies, and Naficy offers evidence for Altman's interest in the "use factor" of films, beyond the attendance and sales, to explore how people act and see while they are viewing film. Thackway examines the cultural contents of Francophone West African film, which incorporates orality, a form of storytelling, into modern film as a marker of African culture and a resistance, like Naficy's viewing practices, to meanings imposed by films from Europe or the USA. Orality and viewing practices can open up multiple meanings for a film, a process often closed down for Westerners who view films silently, in great quantities and more passively. Essays in this part explore the topic of reception that runs through other parts of this book. Perhaps most clearly in this section, the readings make obvious that, as Altman declares in his study of genre, we must recognize "the ability of audiences to generate their own texts and thus to become intenders, mappers and owners in their own right" (Altman, 1999, p. 212), remaking the films they see according to their own needs, cultures, moments in history, and their mix of chosen and socially dictated subjectivities.

Further Reading

For a long list of African and African diasporic films, see

ArtMattan Productions site: www.africanfilm.com
SPIA Media Productions site: www.spiamedia.com
Stanford's African film site: http://library.stanford.edu/depts/ssrg/africa/film.html

Altman, Rick (1999) *Film/Genre*. London: British Film Institute.
Armes, Roy (1987) *Third World Film Making and the West*. Berkeley: University of California Press.
Barlet, Olivier (2001) *African Cinemas: Decolonizing the Gaze*. London: Zed Books.

Chanan, Michael (2004) *Cuban Cinema*. Minneapolis: University of Minnesota Press.

Chow, Rey (1995) *Primitive Passions: Visuality, Sexuality, Ethnography, and Contemporary Chinese Cinema*. New York: Columbia University Press.

Cowie, Peter (2004) *Revolution! The Explosion of World Cinema in the Sixties*. London: Faber and Faber.

Dissanayake, Wimal (2000) "Issues in World Cinema." In John Hill and Patricia Gibson Church (eds), *World Cinema: Critical Approaches*. New York: Oxford University Press, pp. 143–50.

Freire, Paulo (1970) *The Pedagogy of the Oppressed*. New York: Seabury.

Gabriel, Teshome (1982) *Third Cinema in the Third World: The Aesthetics of Liberation*. Ann Arbor, MI: UMI Research Press.

Gugler, Josef (2004) *African Film: Imaging a Continent*. Bloomington: Indiana University Press.

Harrow, Kenneth W. (1999) *African Cinema. Postcolonial and Feminist Readings*. Trenton, NJ: Africa World Press.

Hill, John and Church Gibson, Pamela (eds) (2000) *World Cinema: Critical Approaches*. New York: Oxford University Press.

MacDougall, David (1998) *Transcultural Cinema*, intro. Lucien Taylor. Princeton, NJ: Princeton University Press.

Martin, Michael T. (ed.) (1997) *New Latin American Cinema*, two volumes. Detroit: Wayne State University Press.

Michel, Manuel (1999) "Toward a Fourth Cinema." *Wide Angle*, 21(3), 70–81.

Nadel, Alan (1997) "A whole New (Disney) World Order: *Aladdin*, Atomic Power and the Muslim Middle East." In Matthew Bernstein and Gaylyn Studlar (eds), *Visions of the East: Orientalism in Film*. New Brunswick, NJ: Rutgers University Press, pp. 184–203.

Naficy, Hamid (2001) *An Accented Cinema: Exilic and Diasporic Filmmaking*. Princeton, NJ: Princeton University Press.

Nowell-Smith, Geoffrey (1999) *The Oxford History of World Cinema*. Oxford: Oxford University Press.

Pines, Jim and Willemen, Paul (eds) (1989) *Questions of Third Cinema*. London: British Film Institute.

Pfaff, Françoise (2004) *African Films*. Bloomington: Indiana University Press.

Quiros, Oscar (1996) "Critical Mass of Cuban Cinema: Art as the Vanguard of Society." *Screen*, 37, 279–93.

Robin, Diana and Jaffe, Ira (eds) (1999) *Redirecting the Gaze: Gender, Theory, and Cinema in the Third World*. Albany: State University of New York Press.

Solanas, Fernando and Getino, Octavio (2000) "Towards a Third Cinema." In Robert Stam and Toby Miller (eds), *Film and Theory: An Anthology*. Oxford: Blackwell, pp. 265–86.

Stam, Robert (1991) "Eurocentrism, Afrocentrism, Polycentrism: Theories of Third Cinema." *Quarterly Review of Film and Video*, 13, 217–37.

Tapper, Richard (ed.) (2002) *The New Iranian Cinema: Politics, Representation and Identity*. London and New York: I. B. Tauris.

367

Thackway, Melissa (2003) *Africa Shoots Back: Alternative Perspectives in Sub-Saharan Francophone African Film.* Bloomington: Indiana University Press.

Ukadike, Nwachukwu Frank (1994) *Black African Cinema.* Berkeley: University of California Press.

Williams, Alan (ed.) (2002) *Film and Nationalism.* New Brunswick, NJ: Rutgers University Press.

Williams, Tony (1997) "Space, Place, and Spectacle: The Crisis Cinema of John Woo," *Cinema Journal,* 36(2), 67–84.

20

Theorizing "Third-World" Film Spectatorship: The Case of Iran and Iranian Cinema

Hamid Naficy

At home, I had lived most intensely in the cinema. . . . In those dark halls,
I had dreamed of a life elsewhere. Now, in the place that for all those years
had been the "elsewhere," no further dream was possible.[1]

This chapter is about cinematic spectatorship in the Third World, specifically in Iran, and more generally about transnational spectatorship of films by Third World populations in film festivals.[2] It seeks to problematize the master narratives of crosscultural cinematic discourses through self-narrativization. I use autobiography in order to avoid the problems which occur in most ethnographic encounters, that is, the effacement of the anthropologist, filmmaker, and film theorist from the text, which can result in denying the essential dynamics of the encounter and in producing a static picture of the people described. "It is this *picture* frozen within the ethnographic text, that becomes the 'culture' of the people" (Crapanzano 1980, p. ix). Indeed, crosscultural cinematic contacts have a polysemy and a dynamics which are rarely revealed in the neutral "invisible writing" of theoreticians and historians of crosscultural and global cinema (invisible, therefore, as in the non self-reflexive Classic Hollywood cinema style). I am not using autobiography nostalgically here, as a return to childhood and to a prelapsarian universe. Rather, I am using it as a searchlight to illuminate not only the essential interiority and multiple subjectivities of film spectatorship but also its undeniable

Hamid Naficy, "Theorizing 'Third-World' Film Spectatorship: The Case of Iran and Iranian Cinema," pp. 183–201 from Anthony R. Guneratne and Wimal Dissanayake (eds), *Rethinking Third Cinema* (London: Routledge, 2003). © 2003 by Hamid Naficy. Reprinted by permission of the author and Routledge, a member of the Taylor & Francis Group.

but undertheorized social and collective dimensions, especially when films cross national and cultural boundaries. To accomplish this task, I rely not only on personal accounts of film viewing but also on audience ethnography, social history, and film theory. I speculate and theorize about the interpellative (hailing) effects of the film texts at the same time that I challenge these effects by invoking historical and cultural practices that seem counterinterpellative (haggling). If, as Teshome Gabriel states, Third Cinema highlights contexts and not individual heroes (1989, p. 60), then this essay is an example of an extension of Third Cinema theory in its emphasis on the social contexts of reception, albeit in directions which the originators of Third Cinema may not have envisaged.

There is, of course, the issue of the physical and discursive "location" of the author. Over forty years have elapsed between my first experience with cinema in Iran and this writing about it from a position in exile in the United States. Discursively, too, much film making and film theory separates my writing here from my early naive film viewing there. To problematize, even dramatize, these issues of (dis)location, and to express the splitting effect of both cinema and of exile on the subjectivities of the so-called Third World spectators, in writing this essay I consciously alternate between using first person and third person pronouns. Many Third World filmmakers – at least the first generation – were wooed to cinema by Western films and a large percentage of them received their filmmaking training in Europe, the United States, and the Soviet Union. However, because of their awareness of unequal and unjust colonial and neocolonial relationships, many of them upon returning to their homelands made films critical of the West and attempted to create their national and individual cinema identities in contradistinction to Western cinema. This essay attempts to theorize, through my own experience, this alienating identification that cinema, along with other institutions of modernization, set into motion – a form of identification that problematizes the received notions of direct and hermetic cultural imperialism. Finally, since my project is to examine Third World film spectatorship, I will emphasize the primary site of this activity, the moviehouse.

Reading Novels, Watching Films

My relation to the West and to Western movies was convoluted and multilayered. It began early and it remained private, familial, social, national, and political all at once. I grew up avidly reading Persian and Western literature and I tried to see as many film adaptations as possible. Indeed, I was perhaps first drawn to cinema through its connection with literature, a connection which resonated reciprocally: it seemed to validate both the original novel and the experience of the cinema. At the same time, both literature and cinema vividly embodied the Western Other with whom I would have to come to terms.

I remember the young man, as I then was, spending the summer of 1960 (Persian year 1339) reading all the great novels that he could get his hands on. He read over 30 of them and saw many film adaptations. One warm spring night in April 1959, he took his Agfa 35mm still camera to the open air theater, *Sinema Mayak*, which was showing Leo Tolstoi's *War and Peace* (1956). He wanted to take color snapshots of the film as it was being shown. Unsure of how the ushers would react to the camera (it was unusual to carry cameras to theaters), he hid it under his jacket. When large close-ups of Pierre and Natasha (played by Henry Fonda and Audrey Hepburn) appeared, he discreetly took timed pictures, holding his breath to reduce the shaking of his hands. Captivated by the great novel, I had spent weeks reading, nurturing, and annotating it – noting in my diary, with a combination of awe and arrogance: "the breadth and the style of the book is utterly amazing. I am trying to understand it as fully as possible because it is worth it" (2/22/1339). He recalled years later that holding color slides of that movie, especially of Audrey Hepburn, had felt like holding a piece of a dream – a condensed image – consisting of Russia (site of the story) and of America (site of the film's production).

At nights, sometimes, I would put myself to sleep by going over scenes of the movies I had just seen. Narrative recall comforted me. One time, as he was falling asleep he remembered scenes from Victor Hugo's *Les Misérables* (1956), starring Jean Gabin. What a moving story! Two years earlier I had spent a part of my summer vacation with my parents in Khunsar, a cool, mountainous region, reading *Les Misérables* during the long afternoon siesta. Everyone would take a one or two hour nap. All was quiet but for the murmuring of the brook nearby rolling and falling over and around rocks. Lying down on my back on the floor, I voraciously consumed the Hugo tale, often crying at the trials of Cozette, Marius, and Jean Valjean. I was so taken with Hugo's style that I filled half a notebook with quotations from the book and wrote in my journal: "This is an amazing and compelling novel. It contains a world of emotions: love, kindness, humanity, conscience, justice, self-sacrifice. . . . It is really a great masterpiece." The memories of reading the novel and watching the movie commingled with the oncoming dreams. These cinematic memories and dreams also enlivened his otherwise drab and lonely waking hours, as he noted in his diary: "In my life these memories and dreams are all that satisfy me" (2/22/1339). Yes, it seems I was buying into the world foreign dream factories were offering.

The Soviet film affecting me the most was the romantic war movie directed by Mikhail Kalatozov, *The Cranes are Flying* (1957). The heroism of the Russian people and the lost romance of the protagonists so moved him that he wrote an unprecedented four page plot summary in his diary (10/15/1337). The film's war scenes and the haunting face of the lead actress, Tatyana Samoilova, were forever etched into his mind. Now, over four decades later, when I read over the plot summary, I am struck by that image of the cranes flying in the sky, the cranes Tatyana looked at in the end in order to remember her lost love, Boris, killed in the war. Now, when I remember that image, I am reminded of my own loss – my country, lost to exile. Such is the power of symmetry, memory!

Hailing the Spectators, Haggling with the Movie

While as a boy I loved Western literature and thrived on it, as I grew my history of involvement with the West became more complex and ambivalent. My first "tangible" impression of North America was provided by my father who in 1953 had gone to the United States to attend Harvard University's medical school. In one of his letters home, he had inserted a two inch patch of his skin, which had peeled off after a long day's stay at the beach in Boston.

This piece of skin, this thin, transparent parchment, became a charismatic talisman: it captured me and my imagination and transported me to Boston harbor, a place I would visit years later. Holding the skin in my hand I felt close to him. In retrospect, I see that this skin was symbolically significant in another sense that only Iranians can fully appreciate. There is a Persian saying about a task or a person being so difficult as to skin you alive. In one sense, that skin-message was my father's way of symbolically communicating to us both the hardship and the pleasure of his first stay in the US. In another sense, that peeled piece of skin could be taken as a metaphor for what American foreign policy was doing to Iran at the time, that is, skinning Iran alive by supporting a coup against Mohammad Mosaddeq, a popularly elected prime minister.[3]

Then, within six months, my father returned bringing with him one of those slide viewers which displays a series of 3-D slides mounted on a round disk. Here was America, not mediated by means of the 35mm movie frames I used to buy as a child from street vendors or by my father's skin, but by means of crisp color slides in stereo – showing the United States' magnificent landscapes. Viewing those clean paved roads gracefully winding through snow-clad Yellowstone national park or Niagara Falls with visitors wearing yellow raincoats to protect them against the mist of the enormous cataract, he felt a deep yearning to be there, to feel and touch them. These images which stimulated synaesthetic pleasure, were more than any other factor responsible not only for planting in my mind the idea of traveling to the United States, but also for influencing my views of that country. While politically I abhorred the American foreign policy for violating my country's sovereignty, he was being wooed to America in the privacy of my own home, by my own father, in a most unconscious manner, and by the most seemingly innocuous agents – color pictures of natural beauty.

Until recently, many structuralist and poststructuralist theorists of cinema borrowing ideas from Louis Althusser, Antonio Gramsci, and Jacques Lacan, among others, postulated that cinema is an ideological state apparatus (ISA) that works to recruit subjects from among individual spectators by means of interpellation (Althusser), the hegemonic work of ideology (Gramsci), and the psychoanalytic process of the mirror-phase (Lacan). Althusser's simple example most clearly crystallizes what is meant: in the street a policeman calls, "hey, you there!" By turning to respond, in that very moment that we swivel on our heels, we have become his subject. Cinema is purported to operate in a similar fashion: ideologically inscribed in hegemony, it acquires the free consent of the spectators as its subjects. Such a formulation posits interpellation as a monolithic, universal, and unilinear process, discouraging escape and resistance. But, if the Althusserian street scene is viewed from the point of view of the subjects, especially in their varying social contexts, we find that the authority–subject relation is often subverted. Similarly, on a social scale, there are cracks, ruptures, inconsistencies, and contradictions, not only among the various ISAs but also within individual ISAs, which make resistance to and subversion of unilinear interpellation possible. Acting like a mirror during the mirror-phase, film creates split subjectivity, not a homogeneous subject at ease but one in dis-ease (dare I say, a diseased subject). As a result, in addition to "hailing" there is much "haggling" in cinematic spectatorship. Yes! Those glorious fictional films and innocent pictures of natural beauty were addressing me personally, and I turned and faced them. I became their subject, I was hailed. I became he. But, the I and the he haggled with each other, for they did not form a unitary subject at ease. There are many ways in which both hailing and haggling between self and other, real and fictional, and indigenous and foreign take place in the moviehouse.

I will examine these by turning to the context of the movies, the sociology and ethnography of their reception, the oral culture's spectatorial routines, and the margins of film history to create a composite narrative about the evolution of film spectatorship in Iran. While my first recollection of film watching is one of intense and anxious emotional reaction caused by narrative suspense, my identification with the diegesis was not total due to the social context of the reception. The moviehouse was a long, narrow, tunnel-like hall with a high ceiling that was filled with people, smoke, and noise. This was a modest theater, located near our house, on Southern Chahar Bagh Street. Before a film began and during obligatory intermissions, amidst the clamor of the young male audience (I don't remember any women), a voice could be heard barely audible above the general hubbub, calling: "Coca Cola, Fanta, cigarettes, seeds, mixed nuts, snacks." It came from a young, disheveled boy carrying a wooden tray full of goods. In the early days of cinema, spectators not only sat in front of the screen but also in the back and, in the open-air theaters, on rooftops. Those who could not afford the price of a regular seat in front of the screen would be given an empty oil can behind the screen to sit on. Women were separated from the men by a curtain or by a divider erected in the middle of the theater. Even without these, women usually sat on one side and men on the other. When the lights finally dimmed, the national anthem was played over a scratchy loudspeaker. Everyone had to rise. The film, typically black and white, flickered on, the shaft of light coming from the projection booth, dancing amidst the smoke and the stench of the hall. In earlier days, some Tehran theaters sold hot food, especially steamy sheep tripe, lamb meat, and bread, which the audience ate while watching the movie (an early version of odorama!). Food was not apparently the sole source of smell since, at times, moviegoers, or their impatient children, who did not want to miss the movie, urinated on the floor instead of leaving the hall for the restroom. Shusha Guppy relates a story about this practice and the way the theater managers and spectators haggled over it:

> In desperation, the management projected a plea on the screen before each show-ing: "Gentlemen are requested to kindly refrain from relieving themselves inside this cinema," or simply, "Please do not urinate here but use lavatories outside." When polite language failed to produce the expected result, harsher words were used: "God's curse on the son-of-a-whore who pisses in this cinema!" or, "Whoever pisses in this place is the son and brother and husband of whores! He himself is a bugger!" No good. Finally, it was thought that the image would succeed where words had proved ineffectual – a drawing of a huge equine penis was projected with the caption: "This will bugger any son of a whore who dares to piss here, and will then take care of his wife, mother and sister as well?" The audience just laughed, and turned the insult back on to the management by drawing similar niceties on the walls of the cinema. Eventually a solution was found: a little ditch was dug all around the auditorium which carried away any liquid from the floor to the sewer. (Guppy 1988, p. 167)

No sooner had the movie started than someone, who in all likelihood had previously seen it, would begin to tell the story out loud moments ahead of the action: "Now *artisteh* (the artist, meaning, the male hero) is going to knock down *dozdeh* (the thief, metaphorically, the bad guy)." Another would intone, "Look, his car is going to go off the cliff," and so on. Some people in the audience objected loudly to the foretelling of the story, as it ruined the drama for them. Others, however, found it helpful since sound movies were not dubbed into the Persian at first and few people could understand the original language anyway. To help comprehension, local distributors began inserting at ten-minute intervals fall-screen captions in Persian, which explained the action.

But these summarizing intertitles did not solve the problem for the majority who were illiterate. That is why students were in demand as intermediaries be-tween the native population and the Western text, a role which they were to fulfill on a more significant scale in years to come. Outside the theaters, men who could not read would solicit young student-types to read the intertitles for them in exchange for a free ticket.[4] The students proved doubly useful once inside: other non-literate people would try to situate themselves within earshot distance of them to benefit from their service. The asynchronous chorus of young boys reading the titles aloud, however, aroused the ire of those who could read. As a result, there was always a vocal conflict and sometimes fist fights between the two groups. You could hear the protesters shouting, "Quiet Mr! Shut up! Shut up!"

There was at the time a performance art of "reciting" or "reading" the curtain that was ingeniously adapted to film exhibitions. Curtain reciters or readers (*pardeh khan*) would hang a curtain in an outdoor plaza on which was painted massive scenes of Shii or Persian mythological and historical tales and great battles. Standing in front of the painting, the reciter would point with a stick to the various scenes, explaining and dramatizing with great showmanship the depicted stories, highlighting the moral or religious lessons to be drawn. During the silent era, a group of enterprising interpreters (called *dilmaj*) syncretically adapted this traditional practice to cinema as did their Japanese counterparts (called *benshis*) in an even longer-lasting tradition. Usually, they would pace in the aisles in the dark, reading out the intertitles. At times, however, they would stand next to the film screen (called "curtain" in Persian) and as the film was projected, they would point with a long stick to the figures on the screen – often warning the spectators of the coming action. At first, their power to foretell the plot was chalked off to their prescience!

When Western language talkies were first introduced to Iran in the early 1930s, naive audiences unaccustomed to speech in cinema conjectured that sound films involved trickery and ventriloquism by skilled actors who were hiding behind the screen (Naficy 1981a, p. 42). Perhaps they thought so because they distrusted cinema (because of its illusionism), Western entertainment (because of its immoral influences), and the entrepreneurial local exhibitors (because of their shady practices).

The intervention of screen readers and student translators in the reception of the movies was in a sense subversive to the original intention of the filmmakers. Since these intermediaries had to translate the intertitles, the subtitles, or the foreign language dialogue in real time, they often resorted to colorful Persian stock expressions, which indigenized and enriched the film experience. This subversive potentiality carried over into the sound era as well, especially when film dubbing became a big business. Since Iranian movies were usually not filmed in sync during production, skillful and versatile voice-over artists dubbed the actors' voices in postproduction. It can be safely said that approximately two dozen voice actors dubbed the majority of Iranian *and* foreign films shown in the country. Audiences drew special pleasure from hearing John Wayne and Jerry Lewis use expressions that Iranian tough guys or comedians used. Such intertextuality hybridized the diegeses and the characters who inhabited them. Also, because each voice-over artist often dubbed the voices of a number of different characters, strange cross-over resonances and dissonances would be set up between voices and characters, which could serve to confuse the mirror-phase identification with individual characters. The dubbing process involved narrative and structural changes as well. The names of characters, lines of dialog, elements of plot, characters' relationships, and even the order of sequences would sometimes undergo changes to make the films both palatable to local tastes and agreeable to the state's political and religious censors. Through drastic manipulation during dubbing, sometimes, a Western tragedy would be turned into an Iranian comedy (Mehrabi 1984, p. 439).[5]

Adding to the disruptive atmosphere of moviehouses and their counterhailing potential was the loud cracking of watermelon, pumpkin, and sunflower seeds, which constantly interrupted the quiet moments of the film.[6] Moreover, in the early days, if the town notables and neighborhood tough guys (*lutis*) arrived late, often the projectionist would stop the film in mid-stream in their honor and resume the screening only after they were seated (Mehrabi 1984, p. 420). Audiences' oral interaction with the diegesis, too, heightened the contentiousness of the viewing experience. People would not hesitate to tell the actors on the screen what they should do next: "Oh, watch out, he is behind you;" "Yeah, punch him hard in the stomach, hit him, hit him." I remember watching *Samson and Delilah* (1949) from the balcony of a theater. When Victor Mature as Samson stood in the doorway to push the pillars apart, eventually destroying the temple, everyone urged him on and applauded wildly. I still remember the spectators' outstretched arms waving above their heads in the eerie, blue light of the projector in the smoke-filled hall.

The West has often fetishized its non-Western other, at first as a Noble Savage (White 1978). But, we struck back! As teenagers we counterhailed the West by fetishizing its movie stars, their names, and the world they stood for, not as icons of savagery but as emblems of civilization and modernity. Some of us took pride in our ability simply to pronounce the stars' names. In fact, the more difficult, the better. Naming them was to identify them, identify with them, and make them part of oneself – competencies to be flaunted. For example, my high school friend Hosain Kalbasi took special pride and pleasure in his ability to pronounce the names of foreign stars out loud during our favorite pastime, strolling in the streets. In a style reminiscent of the "how, now, brown cow" school of pronunciation, he would move with great relish all those facial muscles unused when speaking Persian, in order to reproduce the stars' names accurately, such as Eddy Duchin, Silvana Mangano, Dorothy Lamour, Sophia Loren, Gina Lollobrigida, Edward G. Robinson, Victor Mature, and Montgomery Clift. Passersby would throw looks of surprise and indignation at this group of young *flâneurs*, causing us to laugh heartily at upsetting them.

Other youngsters appropriated various identity markers of the stars, leading to such trends as "Douglasi mustache" (patterned after Douglas Fairbanks Jr's mustache), "Corneli hair style" (emulating Cornel Wilde's bouffant hair style), Charles Boyer's romantic glances, and Dorothy Lamour's posing.[7] This sort of fetishism was highly complex, for it was not only a form of idealization of American culture and the West but also of resisting them through their objectification. Idealizing them was also a way of undermining the traditional patriarchal and Islamic order at home, resulting in much criticism from cultural conservatives (Naficy 1981b, p. 351). As teenagers, we idealized the modern world that the West offered us. Cinemas were seen as signs of "progress" and "civilization" and as sites for secular worship rivaling that of the mosque. The metonymic association of cinema with secular worship was well understood and vehemently objected to by the clerical establishment. For example, Mojtaba Navab-Safavi, a leader of Feda'iyan-e Eslam, a fundamentalist group operating in the 1940s, chose a powerful and graphic metaphor to condemn the cinema's interpellative powers. He called cinema, along with other Western imports (romantic novels and music), a "smelting furnace," which could melt away all the wholesome values and virtues of a Muslim society (Navab-Safavi 1978, p. 4).

The strategies recounted so far, by which Iranian audiences interrupted, talked back to, translated, dubbed, fetishized, objectified, and haggled with the movies and the movie stars, transformed the cinema's "work" from one of hailing to haggling. By thus engaging with the movies, the spectators were no longer just their *consumers* but also the *producers* of their meanings. Making and watching the movies joined together in a "single signifying practice" (Barthes 1977, p. 162). However, these strategies emerged largely spontaneously, often unconsciously, and sometimes as part of the natural process of development and experimentation which accompanies any new invention or discovery. To be sure, there were overt forms of resistance as well. The majority of the moviegoers were of the lower classes. The upper classes disparaged and shunned cinema, particularly locally made films, probably because they attracted the lower classes. The religious lay and elite as well as the secular elite also opposed cinema on religious and moral grounds. The penalty for intransigence was great. For example, my then teenage uncles (Reza and Hosain), who were under the guardianship of their older, religiously inclined brother Karim, received severe beatings for sneaking in to the movies.[8]

Despite the fragmentation of audiences along class lines during my teens (the lower classes usually went to see Egyptian, Indian, and Persian song and dance melodramas, while the educated and the upper classes frequented foreign "art" films), moviehouses became a site for resisting the state's repressive apparatus. Resisting and accommodating the state went beyond tampering with the film during dubbing; it extended into the sites of exhibition. Soon after Reza Shah came to power in the mid-1920s, for example, the government began requiring theater managers to play the national anthem before each film, in honor of which spectators had to rise to their feet. Although enforced during his rule, from the mid-1940s, audiences began to resist this state interjection into their entertainment by remaining seated. The government wavered on enforcing its policy. For a long time it tolerated this sort of passive resistance, then tried to enforce the policy by punishing the non-conformists and finally abandoned it altogether in the late 1960s after it was found to be a political liability.

Despite such interjections moviehouses acted as safe meeting places for political activists. In order to escape the gaze of Reza Shah's police and secret service, for example, leftists chose theaters as meeting places where, in darkness and anonymity, they could exchange words, notes, books, and packages. Bozorg Alavi's famous novel *Cheshmhayash* (*Her Eyes*), about the lift of an anti-Shah painter, contains several episodes in which its leftist protagonists meet clandestinely in theaters. The notion of safety derived from anonymity turned theaters into sites for resisting cultural and religious conventions as well. Many young couples who could not be seen walking the streets together or meeting openly in cafes and restaurants, found the safe darkness of theaters conducive to experiencing rare and thus deliciously charged moments of privacy and intimacy. I remember watching in rapture Elia Kazan's *Splendor in the Grass* (1961), my girlfriend Zhina's hand in mine at the Moulin Rouge theater in Jolfa, the Armenian district of my home town.

Immediately after the revolution of 1979, which ousted the Shah, audiences used the safety of numbers in theaters to voice their opposition to the Islamist government. For example, during the American "hostage crisis," Ayatollah Khomeini had made a particularly colorful and vainglorious speech, threatening to "slap America across the face and appoint a new government" in Iran. A few days after that speech, in an Isfahan theater the electricity went out halfway through a film. Before the lights were turned back on, a clever spectator's voice was heard above the din of the audience, imitating and mocking that particular remark, by saying with great bravado: "I will slap the projectionist across the face. I will appoint a new projectionist," causing a great deal of audience applause.

Engaging with USIA Films

The Western films exported to the Third World are usually commercial and fictional products that appear to be apolitical – even though as I have demonstrated they perform significant ideological work. However, the American government through the United States Information Agency (USIA) produced a massive number of manifestly political and "pedagogic" works such as non-fiction and instructional films that were distributed to many Third World countries, including Iran, in the early 1950s. It was a tumultuous time for the Cold War rivalry of the United States and the Soviet Union. The fall of Prime Minister Mosaddeq had intensified the Cold War tensions, causing the US government to launch an official policy to win the hearts and minds of the non-Communist world. This task was assigned to USIA, which President Truman created in August 1953, in order to:

> Tell all people throughout the world the truth about the official aims and acts of the US, to expose and counter hostile efforts to distort those aims and acts and to present a broad and accurate *picture* of the life and culture of the American people.
> (Naficy 1984: p. 190, emphasis added)

Taking a cue from Truman's formulation, this policy involved increased marketing of American motion pictures to the Third World and production and distribution of documentaries targeted at specific countries, primarily those in "danger" of conversion to Communism. In the case of Iran, which shared a long border with the Soviet Union, this meant showing American-made films to school children and to rural populations by means of mobile film vans and to the general public in commercial cinemas. All in all USIA showed over 800 films dubbed into

Persian, over half of which were the Persian language newsreel *Akhbar-e Iran* (*Iran News*), created specifically for the Iranian market. These dealt with more topical and political issues such as the Point 4 program, the military and development programs in Iran (often involving the US), the activities of the Shah and the royal family, earthquakes, and a variety of human interest stories from the US, the remainder being principally concerned with improving primitive health, nutrition and agricultural methods.[9]

Like many students of my generation, I was a subject of this experiment in influencing hearts and minds. As an elementary school student in an experimental "model" school, planned and funded by the Point 4 program (administered by USIA), I was exposed to many of these films on a regular basis. Every Thursday afternoon (the day before the Iranian weekend), a green mobile film unit would drive into our school yard. A middle-aged man wearing a suit and a tie, who acted as both driver and projectionist, would emerge to set up his portable screen and 16mm Bell and Howell projector in our small recreation rooms. Powered by the generator inside the mobile unit, the projector opened a new world to us. Films were taken seriously enough in my school for teachers to require students to review them in writing. I still have a book of my reviews written in 1953 (1332), when I was in the fourth grade. It contains reviews of 16 films, most of which were shot in Iran and dealt with improving health and hygiene practices. A fourth of them were documentaries about life in the United States.

At first glance, what comes through my reviews and plot summaries is that the USIA films are closed texts. The world of the village is shown to be disturbed by a disease, such as tuberculosis or dysentery, but soon stability and calm is restored thanks to an external agent. The closedness of these texts, however, is somewhat illusory since on further analysis, their wider political connotations become apparent. It seems to me that at the heart of the US policy of technological transfer and development aid for the Third World since the 1950s, was this notion of homogenization and synchronicity of the world within Western consumerist ideology. This is a shift from the earlier policy of diachronicity, promulgated by colonists, which tended to keep the developed and the underdeveloped worlds apart. The emerging form of post-industrial capitalism sought synchronicity in the interest of creating global markets. Therefore, "underdevelopment," as a non-synchronous category, fell outside that ideology and that circuit of power relations, and was therefore considered a threat. It had to be controlled, countered, and contained.

The USIA films seemed designed to produce such a global synchronicity by isolating the problems and their solutions. For example, in these films the wider health, agricultural, economical, and political problems besetting Iran were generally not discussed. Problems were often fragmented and separated from their socio-political roots and contexts. Thus isolated, both the problems and the solutions were universalized and the threat of non-synchronicity was contained. All problems were knowable and soluble by means of Western technology and know-how.

The diegesis of these films was peopled with a central character (usually a young boy such as Said who suffers from tuberculosis) and a central authority figure (such as Doctor Khoshqadam, who treats him). The chief authorities dispensing well-being and prosperity were Point 4 development agents and physicians. These figures invoked and legitimized by proxy the power, knowledge, competence, authority, and, indeed, the right of both the Iranian government (by whom they were employed) and the entire Western economic and industrial apparatus (which trained and sponsored them) to solve indigenous local problems. The packaging of USIA films underscored their politics, for interspersed with the films shot in Iran were movies filmed in the United States, which offered a rival ideal model.

My reviews of these films, written at age ten, are strictly plot summaries. Why? I do not remember the terms under which we were given the review assignments, but I take the absence of evaluative judgment on my part to be a significant strategy, subconsciously applied, which transcends my own shyness. I take these absences to be a deliberate form of resisting, a refusal to make that 180 degree turn and be hailed as the subject of the West. To confine my interaction with the films to pure plot description was to rob them of their life force and effectivity. This apparent distance was not disengagement, but an active form of engagement. Some may take the absence of evaluative criticism to be an indication of my agreement with the films, but in this I tend to side with Jean Baudrillard (1985, p. 588) who suggests that such responses may in fact be a form of "refusal by over-acceptance," that is, a form of haggling. The same process was at work when as teenagers we objectified and over-exaggerated the looks, poses, and gestures of Western movie stars. By these means we were in a sense returning the interpellating gaze.

These forms of spectator counterhailing constituted a kind of crosscultural haggling with the West and with the Shah's government. Nevertheless, the bargaining tended to favor the West, for Westernization was overdetermined in most social spheres.[10] But as the anti-Shah revolution gained momentum in the late 1970s, the balance shifted in the opposite direction. Theaters became not only a site of resistance to and defiance of the government, but also a metonym for Western values, which were now in disfavor. That is why they became such direct targets of revolutionary ire, resulting in the demolition and torching of nearly a third (i.e. over 180) moviehouses nationwide (Naficy 1992, p. 178).

Making Films in the West

My long-term relationship with the West, mediated at great length and from long-distance by means of cinema, finally became intimate and first-hand. Upon graduating from high school, the young man went to England to continue his studies. While there, films continued to be a major source of his knowledge of the

West and a valuable aid in teaching him English. Watching films also had a healing effect on his profound loneliness. Every Friday evening, I would go to the movies, the most gripping and memorable of which was *The Mind Benders* (1963), starring Dirk Bogarde. In retrospect, I consider this film to be a metaphor of my own life as a foreigner. Here I was, an 18-year-old boy who had never flown in an airplane and had never ventured out of my country alone. Now, in a single stroke he was severed from the warmth of a large, extended family and planted abroad – a single, solitary seedling, adrift in a foreign land and surrounded by a reserved people and an unfamiliar language and culture. He was numbed by the experience of it all like the hero of *The Mind Benders*, a scientist played by Bogarde who underwent experiments to determine the effects of total isolation on his psyche. The absence of input made the scientist vulnerable to indoctrination, leading to psychosis. He considered the film significant enough to write about it in the journal I am reading (dated 5/5/1963). His analysis of why I was taken by the film is expressed in a removed, philosophical tone, which ends with the following question: "is it possible for humans to tolerate total isolation?"

In England, I was overwhelmed by input from the new society. But without realizing it I carried out an experiment similar to the one that Bogarde underwent, whereby I isolated myself as a means of re-programming myself to better adapt to the culture of the other. This took the form of solitary acts: reading, studying, going to the movies, and taking long walks in the countryside. Like the film, however, isolation made me more vulnerable to interpellation by the British culture. My journal of this period is filled with agonized poetry, my own or quoted from others, testifying to the cost of this experiment: depression, low self-esteem, and a sense of total isolation. Soon, I found a way out by moving to the United States to begin my formal studies in film and television production.

Yet, barely a month after arriving in Los Angeles, a sense of desolation and rage overtook him and he found solace in Stephen Crane's horrific poetry and Jean Paul Sartre's depressing existentialist philosophy. He copied many of Crane's poems and many passages from Sartre's *Nausea* in my journal. On 4/26/1964, for example, he filled an entire page with the word "nausea," repeated over and over, in a fashion chillingly reminiscent of Jack's possessed writing in Stanley Kubrick's *The Shining* (1980): "All work and no play makes Jack a dull boy." Last night, reading over these diary pages for the first time in many years, hair rose on the back of my neck. And tonight, while screening the film to my students in my film authorship seminar, I realized the similarity between my exilic panic then and Jack's unhinging in the Overlook Hotel.

Up to this point, I had been a consumer of the movies – with the exception of his childhood experiments with a primitive cartoon-strip projector. Now he began to study and make films professionally as a means of talking back to both here and there, and of ripping through my Iranian teenage angst, my English foreigner's isolation, and my American exilic trauma. The self-othering trajectory, begun long ago with photography and film spectatorship in Iran, was being complicated now from this position of exile. The distance that had once separated me from the diegetic world of America and had made that world all the more alluring, was dissolving with transplantation. The "elsewhere" was now "here." Me, myself, I, he – all of me – were here in the West at once, no distance separated us. But, unity, wholeness and ease were illusive, and, besides, a switch was taking place. Another elsewhere, another other, was now looming large. I am speaking of home, against which he had begun to define me anew.

One of his video projects at UCLA's MFA program in film production, entitled *REM* (*Rapid Eye Movement*, 1969), inscribed some of these anxieties about wholeness, partiality and dis-ease. This surreal video, which was largely conceived during dreamtime, involved a teenage boy and girl on a quest in a mountainous, desolate land. The futility of their external quest was reflected in their limited interpersonal relationship, symbolized by their dialog during the thirty-minute video, which consisted of appropriately inflected repetition of a single word, "toilet." In one scene, they are on all fours in tattered clothing circling each other like two beasts and viciously barking the two-syllable word at each other. At the end, the young man finds in a dry creek-bed a television set, which shows an image of him discovering the set. At that point, the image on the TV cuts to a whole brain that is placed outside a skull on a table. A hand, indeed my own hand, reaches into the frame and proceeds to mash and knead the brain like so much dough. Was he smashing my brains, or was it the foreign culture doing it? Was this a literalization of the self-othering that had begun long ago, with my first exposure to photography, Western literature, cinema, and color slides of American national parks? Whatever the impetus for and interpretation of these dissociative images, cinematic self-othering would become a major academic concern of his (cf. Naficy 2000) in the years to come.

Something else, some new type of othering was also going on, however; one that resulted from being in exile. Both *REM* and my thesis project, a computer-animated video called *Salamander Syncope* (1971), in their choice of titles pointed to, and in their content and form embraced, one of the frequent responses of the exiles to the trauma of deterritorialization: paralysis and fracturing. Only years later in the course of writing books on exile cultures and identities (Naficy 1993, 2001) and of revising this essay would he become fully aware of these early manifestations of my concern with exilic self-othering. It was indeed by making films and writing books that he attempted to understand and express my agonized and agonistic life in exile. These acts of self-definition countered years of spectatorial self-othering and hailing by modernity and by Western films. Now, however, a new reversed form of spectatorship was to begin, with other consequences.

Exilic Film Festivals in the West

This involved watching Iranian films in Europe and the United States instead of viewing Western films in Iran. It also involved organizing and curating film festivals that showcased Iranian, Third World, and exilic and diasporic films. Such forms of spectatorship and exhibition resulted in complex and highly slippery subjectivities that are open to all sorts of intercultural and translational haggling. For example, in June 1995 while conducting research in Paris for a book on Iranian cinema, I attended a private screening of Mohsen Makhmalbaf's *A Time to Love* (*Nowbat-e Asheai*, 1991) at MK2 Productions, which was considering the film for distribution. Made by one of the best-known new directors to emerge from Iran since the revolution of 1979, the film had been banned in Iran for its love theme, bold treatment of a love triangle. My friend Azadeh Kian and I were the only spectators in the comfortably appointed screening room. Makhmalbaf, who lives in Iran, had shot the film in Turkey (perhaps partly to avoid Iranian censors) with all the film's dialogue in Turkish, a language I did not know beyond certain words. The film was subtitled, but in French, which at times passed too fast for my understanding, especially since I was trying to take notes. On these occasions, I would nudge Azadeh who would whisper the Persian translation into my ears. Trying to keep up with her translation and with the ongoing film and its subtitles, I was forced to take notes hurriedly in English and Persian, whichever served the moment best. Thus, watching this single film involved multiple acts of translation across four cultures and languages. This chain of linguistic and cultural signification pointed to the radical shifts that had occurred in the globalization of cinema since my childhood. In those days, cinema screens were monopolized by the West, particularly by American films, and Third World people were more consumers of these films than producers of their own narratives. But now we were making and exhibiting our films, not only in our own countries but also across national boundaries, and we were finding receptive audiences, not only in film festivals but also in commercial venues. Significantly, what occurred in that screening room involved not only watching but also reading, hearing, translating, and writing a film – all of which are part of the spectatorial activities and competencies needed for these new globalized Third World and diasporized cinemas, what I have elsewhere called "accented films" (Naficy 1999).

Film festivals are prime sites for intensified national and transnational translations and mistranslations, as well as hailing and haggling over acts of representation. He understood this to his bones, when in 1990 I organized at UCLA the first major film festival of Iranian films in the United States, featuring a large number of postrevolutionary films and introducing the new works of such veterans as Abbas Kiarostarni, Bahram Baizai, Amir Naderi and Dariush Mehrjui, as well as post-revolutionary works by Mohsen Makhmalbaf, Rakhshan Benetemad, Said Ebrahimifar and Abdolfazil Jalili. For almost a decade, the anti-Iranian politics and policies in the US and the Islamic Republic's hostility towards both the American government and the Iranians abroad had discouraged importation of post-revolutionary films. As a result, this cinema was largely unknown and unavailable here even though Iranian films had begun to receive high praise at international festivals elsewhere. The UCLA event and the ensuing controversy helped change all that.

The planned festival came under vociferous criticism by some exiles, particularly by extreme rightist and leftist media producers and filmmakers, who alleged that it would whitewash the Islamist government's human rights violations. Some exiled opponents of the government, particularly filmmaker and actor Parviz Sayyad, called festival organizers, including myself, members of the pro-government "cultural militia in exile" (Sayyad 1996, p. 55) and "celebrators of fascism" (p. 57). He mobilized sexual metaphors, in the style of the clerics he detested, to accuse festival organizers of "flattery" (p. 77), "flirting with" (p. 36), and "going to bed with" (p. 10) the oppressive Islamist regime. Our aims, according to him, were political: to "purify" the government (p. 54), "conceal" its evil deeds and human rights violations (p. 55), help it "re-gain its lost prestige" (p. 132), "neutralize all opposition movements" against it (p. 31), and, finally, "deceive" the foreigners about those deeds and violations (p. 82). Sayyad and his cohorts called for a total boycott of Iranian film festivals abroad.

The man who took snapshots of films and knew loneliness also knew most of the protesting filmmakers, had worked with some of them before, and had even promoted their films in academic circles, including those of Sayyad. Their protest and what became personal attacks were very painful to him, particularly as I was not at all interested in promoting the Islamist regime and had published criticism of its cultural politics and treatment of artists. Rather, my purpose was to encourage those who were making high quality films under difficult conditions and widespread censorship inside Iran by exposing their films to both Iranian and international audiences. To honor them and to provide a forum for discussing filmmaking under the Islamic Republic, I had invited two well-known auteurs, Abbas Kiarostami and Dariush Mehrjui, to be the festival guests.

Festival spectators were in turn impressed and the Iranians among them were touched by the films from the homeland and they embraced the festival enthusiastically. They flocked to the theater in large numbers, from as far away as New York City, Washington, DC, and Houston, and at times stood in line for over eight hours to obtain tickets. The atmosphere was festive but somewhat tense because of the presence of well-known exiled entertainers holding placards and protest signs. It was there that Kiarostami walked up to Sayyad and sardonically offered to take his place in the protest line to free him to go inside to see the films that he was objecting to, sight unseen. Needless to say he did not accept the invitation, although other protesters later attended some screenings.

What Kiarostami and Mehrjui told the audiences inside imparted an understanding about the intense ideological battle over cinema that was raging inside Iran. It became clear to them that the filmmakers there were no pawns of the government; nor were they collaborators in its ideological projects. What the festival accomplished was to create an image of Iran as a complex living culture and society, not one that was totally silenced, subjugated, or ruined by the backward ruling mullahs, as the festival opponents claimed. Filmmakers and audiences in Iran through various haggling strategies had found ways of expressing themselves despite the clerical domination of the ISAs. Even some government officials connected with film supported this nascent post-revolutionary cinema. So, to the extent that this festival as a site of cultural translation and transaction showed that the Islamist regime was not monolithic, it permitted a more realistic and nuanced representation of the dynamics of culture and society in Iran. These counterhegemonic functions brought to light by the festival more than made up for the pain that the orchestrated misinformation and personal attacks of the politicized exiles had caused.

Their vehemence suggested that the debate was not so much over Iranian politics as it was over exilic politics. Many artists in exile were perhaps envious because while their careers had languished or had been ruined by exile, those of their counterparts such as Kiarostami and Mehrjui were flourishing even under heavy censorship. The exiles also wished to maintain the comforting psychological barriers that they themselves had created by their fetishized and frozen representations of Iran as a ruined land filled with victimized people. The intense audience involvement with the movies, however, indicated that the films had succeeded in breaking through those barriers, unleashing the threat that heretofore had been kept in check – that of the homeland unfettered by repressions and distortions of exilic politics. The result of such a breakthrough was that spectators, many of them tearful upon exiting the theater, began to contemplate the unthinkable: the possibility of reconciliation, even return (Naficy 1993, p. 170). A similar cinematic reconciliation, the opposite of cinematic self-othering, occurred in him as I completed my film studies PhD that same spring and for the first time since the revolution returned home for a brief cathartic visit.

Like other film festivals, the UCLA event not only created awareness and facilitated debate and exchange of ideas about filmmakers, films, and censorship mechanisms, but also served the important function of creating interest for the new films among Western film critics, distributors and exhibitors. Several of the festival films were picked up for US commercial distribution, and festivals of Iranian cinema gradually became a regular, annual event in many cities in the United States and Europe.[11] In 1992, the Toronto International Film Festival called Iranian cinema "one of the pre-eminent national cinemas in the world today" (Festival catalog, p. 8). No filmmaker received more critical and popular acclaim abroad than Kiarostami, whose picture appeared on the cover of the July–August 1995 issue of *Cahiers du cinéma* (no. 493) above the caption which declared simply: "Kiarostami le magnifique." Inside, nearly fifty pages were devoted to his works. In due course the films of the majority of the directors who had contributed to the festival gained international recognition and distribution.

I had been othered by my experience as a film spectator. But it is part of the polysemy of cinema that I was able to use that agent of my othering in my reconstructive project of selfing. Indeed, making films, teaching and writing about films, and organizing film festivals were his strategies for my self-understanding, self-narrativization, and self-fashioning both at home and in exile. These strategies were in the final analysis forms of sublation, which resolved my non-Western and Western contradictions into a newly formed hybridized unity. It involved identifying with the West, idealizing it, fetishizing it, consuming it, becoming subject to and consumed by it, resisting and subverting it, and finally contributing to its remaking. It was a heterologic process by which I, me, myself, and he gradually – but not permanently or unproblematically – came to map onto one another, creating a partial and multiple subject who was simultaneously both here and there.

Notes

1   Naipaul, V. S., "The Enigma of Arrival" (1986), p. 41.
2   This essay is a considerably revised version of Naficy 1996.
3   The political context of the time was this: around the time my father left Iran, the nationalist and popular politician Mohammad Mosaddeq had become prime minister. He launched a series of reforms, chief among them, curbing the power of the royal family and nationalizing the British oil assets in Iran. These and other policies caused a great deal of political havoc both at home and abroad. While the Americans, interested in stemming the British monopoly in Iranian politics and economy, first supported Mosaddeq, they soon turned against him fearing a communist takeover in Iran. The confluence of British and American interests resulted in a coup in the summer of 1953, which led to Mosaddeq's ousting and his arrest and the return of the Shah to power. Intellectuals particularly felt betrayed by the US. The memory of this betrayal was to play a role in the anti-Americanism of the 1979 revolution and the subsequent "hostage crisis."
4   This situation may have attracted homosexuals who were rumored to frequent the moviehouses.
5   After the Islamic revolution of 1979, dubbing became more of a politico-religious instrument, consciously and openly employed to remove or alter offensive Western influences and women's representations. For details, see Naficy 1992, 1994.
6   Iranians' appetite for seeds is so great that a journal estimated that in 1984 alone a total of 200 million tumans worth of seeds had been consumed in Iranian theaters ($25,000,000 then). See "Ja'i Bara-ye Masraf-e Tannaqolat va Tanvir-e Afkar," *Mahnameh-ye Sinema'i-ye Film* 3:31 (Azar 1364/November 1985), p. 4.
7   This is reminiscent of the citizens of Abidjan, Ivory Coast, who in Jean Rouch's film *I, A Black* (*Moi Un Noir*, 1957) frequent a bar named Chicago and adopt the name and identity markers of famous movie stars, such as Edward G. Robinson and Dorothy Lamour. See my interview with Rouch (Naficy 1979).
8   Parental worry about cinema was partially justified in so far as popular forms of entertainment in Iran like in many other countries involved practices some of which were considered by mainstream culture to be immoral and unethical.
9   For a description of the production and distribution of USIA films made in Iran, including *Iran News*, and a full list of the films, see Issari 1989 and Naficy 1984.
10 For theorization of how cinema and Westernization were overdetermined in Iran, see Naficy 2000.
11 Facets Multimedia in Chicago and http://www.IranianMovies.com/ are two mail-order sources of videos of Iranian cinema.

References

Barthes, Roland (1977) *Image/Music/Text* (Stephen Heath, trans.), New York: Hill and Wang.

Baudrillard, Jean (1985) "The Masses: The Implosion of the Social in the Media," *New Literary History* 3 (Spring), pp. 577–89.

Crapanzano, Vincent (1980) *Tuhami: Portrait of a Moroccan*, Chicago: University of Chicago Press.

Gabriel, Teshome H. (1989) "Third Cinema as Guardian of Popular Memory," in Jim Pines and Paul Willemen (eds) *Questions of Third Cinema*, London: BFI.

Guppy, Shusha (1988) *The Blindfold Horse: Memories of a Persian Childhood*, Boston: Beacon Press.

Issari, Mohammad Ali (1989) *Cinema in Iran, 1900–1979*, New York: Scarecrow Press.

Mehrabi, Masud (1984/1363) *Tarikhe- Sinema-ve Iran az Aghaz ta 1357*, Tehran: Entesharat-e Film.

Naficy, Hamid (1979) "Jean Rouch: A Personal Perspective," *Quarterly Review of Film Studies* (Summer), pp. 339–61.

Naficy, Hamid (1981a) "Iranian Documentaries," *Jump Cut* No. 26, pp. 41–4.

Naficy, Hamid (1981b) "Cinema as a Political Instrument," in Michael Bonine and Nikki Keddie (eds) *Modern Iran: The Dialectic of Continuity and Change*, Albany, NY: SUNY Press, pp. 341–59.

Naficy, Hamid (1984) *Iran Media Index*, Westport, CT: Greenwood Press.

Naficy, Hamid (1992) "Islamizing Film Culture," in Samih Farsoun and Mehrdad Mashayekhi (eds) *Iran: Political Culture in the Islamic Republic*, London: Routledge, pp. 173–208.

Naficy, Hamid (1993) *The Making of Exile Cultures: Iranian Television in Los Angeles*, Minneapolis: University of Minnesota Press.

Naficy, Hamid (1994) "Veiled Visions/Powerful Presences: Women in Post-revolutionary Iranian Cinema," in Mahnaz Afkhami and Erika Friedl (eds) *In the Eye of the Storm: Women in Postrevolutionary Iran*, London and New York: I. B. Taurus and Syracuse University Press, pp. 131–50.

Naficy, Hamid (1996) "Theorizing 'Third World' Film Spectatorship," *Wide Angle* 18:4 (October, 1996), pp. 3–26.

Naficy, Hamid (1999) "Between Rocks and Hard Places: the Interstitial Mode of Production in Exilic Cinema," in Hamid Naficy (ed.) *Home, Exile, Homeland: Film, Media, and the Politics of Place*, London and New York: Routledge, pp. 125–47.

Naficy, Hamid (2000) "Self-Othering: A Postcolonial Discourse on Cinematic First Contact," in Fawzia Afzal-Khan and Kalpana Seshadri-Crooks (eds) *The Pre-Occupation of Post-Colonial Studies*, Durham, NC: Duke University Press.

Naficy, Hamid (2001) *An Accented Cinema: Exilic and Diasporic Filmmaking*, Princeton: Princeton University Press.

Naipaul, V. S. (1986) "The Enigma of Arrival," *New Yorker* (August 11), p. 41.

Navab-Safavi, Mojtaba (1978/1357) *Jame'eh va Hokumat-e Eslami*, Qom: Entesharat-e Hejrat.

Sayyad, Parviz (1996) *Rah-e Doshvar-e Sinema-ye dar Tab'id*, Los Angeles: Parsian.

White, Hayden (1978) "The Noble Savage theme as Fetish," in *Topics of Discourse: Essays in Cultural Criticism*, Baltimore: Johns Hopkins University Press, pp. 183–96.

21

The Open Image:
Poetic Realism and the
New Iranian Cinema

Shohini Chaudhuri and Howard Finn

When Mohsen Makhmalbaf's *Safar e Ghandehar/Kandahar* was screened at London's Institute for Contemporary Arts in Autumn 2001 it drew sell-out audiences, as it did in other European and North American cities. The film's success, partly due to its timely release, also reflects an enthusiasm internationally for Iranian films which has been gathering momentum in recent years. This essay focuses on one characteristic of 'New Iranian Cinema' which has evidently intrigued both critics and audiences, namely the foregrounding of a certain type of ambiguous, epiphanic image. We attempt to explore these images, which we have chosen – very simply – to call 'open images'. One might read these images directly in terms of the political and cultural climate of the Islamic Republic which engendered them, as part of the broader ongoing critical debate on the relationship of these films to contemporary Iranian social reality. Our intention, however, is primarily to draw structural and aesthetic comparisons across different national cinemas; to show, among other things, how a repressed political dimension returns within the ostensibly apolitical aesthetic form of the open image.

The term 'image' encompasses shot, frame and scene, and includes sound components – open images may deploy any of these elements. Open images are not necessarily extraordinary images; they often belong to the order of the everyday. While watching a film one may meet them with some resistance – yet they have the property of producing virtual after-images in the mind. Although their

Shohini Chaudhuri and Howard Finn, "The Open Image: Poetic Realism and the New Iranian Cinema," pp. 38–57 from *Screen* 44:1 (Oxford: Oxford University Press, Spring 2003). © 2003 by The John Logie Baird Centre. Reprinted by permission of the author and Oxford University Press.

effects are ambiguous, the images exhibit identifiable signs and techniques, and this essay provides a classification of the open image drawing on concepts from Pier Paolo Pasolini's theory of poetic realism, Paul Schrader's notion of the arrested image – stasis – as a cinematic signifier of transcendence, and Gilles Deleuze's theory of the time-image. We will sketch out the historical emergence of the open image in Italian neorealism and its reflexive turn in the French new wave, and then apply our account of the open image to particular films drawn from the New Iranian Cinema.

Pasolini: Poetic Neorealism

The influence of Italian neorealism and the French new wave on Iranian cinema is commonly asserted – and hotly contested. Within Iran, this trend in critical debate might appear as another 'injection' of cultural imperialism, which the revolutionary regime has sought to resist by curtailing imports of first world cinema and actively promoting appreciation of films from the developing world.[1] However, we will argue that it is with reason that critics invoke Italian and French antecedents, because of the crucial role these cinemas played in the historical formation of the open image.

Those who oppose the 'hackneyed' references to neorealism in discussions on Iranian cinema tend to over-emphasize neorealism's so-called 'realist' aspects.[2] This use of reality as a yardstick to measure neorealism, whether it be in terms of its social content or its aesthetics, has resulted in the dominant framing of the middle and late works of Luchino Visconti, Federico Fellini and Michelangelo Antonioni as 'post' neorealist. We prefer to emphasize a poetic conception of neorealism and, consequently, argue that these directors do not represent a break with neorealism; rather, they bring forward poetic qualities which were inherent in neorealism from the beginning.[3]

This poetic conception is articulated in Pasolini's essay 'The cinema of poetry' (1965). Pasolini claims that filmmakers imbue the 'image-signs' they use with their personal expression as well as giving them general meanings.[4] These signs can eventually acquire conventional meanings (as they have in Hollywood codes), constituting a 'cinema of prose'. At the other extreme is the 'cinema of poetry', made possible by the cinematic counterpart of free indirect discourse in literature: the 'free indirect subjective'. Here, the filmmaker's viewpoint becomes one with the character's; Pasolini refers to instances in *Deserto Rosso/Red Desert* (1964), in which Antonioni's viewpoint merges with that of the neurotic heroine Giuliana. The colours and objects around Giuliana are transformed in accordance with her psychological state – a cart of fruit turns grey to reflect her uncertainty, an industrial workshop dominated by the colour of bright red plastic directly materializes her sense of danger. We no longer have the objective shot (which corresponds to indirect discourse) nor the subjective shot (direct discourse), but *a vision which has liberated itself from the two* – the free indirect subjective.

Pasolini traces the free indirect subjective (and with it the cinema of poetry) from Roberto Rossellini and the founding works of Italian neorealism. Compared to the overdetermined narrative image-sign system of the cinema of prose, the images that constitute the cinema of poetry are infinite in possibility, but can be identified in terms of the cinematic style or means by which they are achieved. Pasolini notes a few of the characteristics of these free indirect subjective images under the heading of 'obsessive framing': the close juxtaposition of shots showing slightly different viewpoints of the same object; the static shot of a scene in which characters enter and leave the frame; the stillness of a shot upon an object. The free indirect subjective image is rooted in the diegesis (the character and narrative perspective) and the obsessive vision (psychology/aesthetic) of the filmmaker, yet such images cannot be straightforwardly deciphered as a revelation of either a character's psychological state or that of the filmmaker.[5] Instead the unresolved tension between the two viewpoints – character and filmmaker – creates an ambiguity, a space in which the image appears to emerge from somewhere other. This 'other' perspective is often, as in Antonioni's films, felt to reside in the camera itself, particularly in those scenes where the camera continues recording empty reality after people and identifiable human consciousness have departed – the camera as the uncanny eye of surveillance. Commenting on Pasolini's theory of the free indirect subjective, Deleuze refers to this emphasis on a 'reflecting consciousness' distinct from that of both character and director as a 'camera consciousness . . . a properly cinematographic *Cogito*'.[6] However, we would prefer to stress not an imagined source of subjective or subjectless viewpoint, but rather the otherness of the images as objects, as intrusions of the real – having taken on a degree of autonomy from all identifiable viewpoints.

Schrader: Images of Stasis

A common characteristic of the open image is stasis. An obvious indication of this in several of the Iranian films to be discussed is the use of the long-held freeze-frame as closing image: *Nun va Goldun/Moment of Innocence* (Mohsen Makhmalbaf, 1996), *Nama-ye Nazdik/Close-Up* (Abbas Kiarostami, 1989) and *Sib/The Apple* (Samira Makhmalbaf, 1998) all end on a freeze-frame and they all freeze characters mid-action – that is, in overt movement. As a cinematic device this can probably be traced back to the influence of the famous closing freeze-frame of Antoine running towards the sea in François Truffaut's *Les Quatre Cents Coups/400 Blows* (1959) – the new wave film closest in sensibility to New Iranian Cinema. One of the few attempts to elaborate an aesthetic of stasis remains Schrader's *Transcendental Style* (1972). Among the key characteristics of what he calls 'transcendental style' are the following:

- The everyday: a meticulous representation of the dull, banal commonplaces of everyday living, involving understated acting and dedramatization.
- Disparity: an actual or potential disunity between man and his environment, which culminates in a decisive action.
- Stasis: a frozen view of life, which does not resolve the preceding disparity but transcends it.[7]

What Schrader calls the 'stasis shot' within his stylistics of the transcendental style is close to our conception of the open image within the stylistics of neorealism, insofar as they both involve the fracturing of the everyday by something 'other.' (Dedramatization and disparity, too, have a bearing on the production of open images, as we shall see.)

An aesthetic of stasis appears paradoxical given that an essential component of cinema is movement. Cinema can be seen as opposed to the photograph: even though it is constituted by still photographs, these are not perceived as such in the act of viewing, although they may be extracted (as distinct frames). As Jean Mitry, among others, has noted, the photographic image has a melancholy relationship to its referent:

> The photograph of a person retains the impression of his presence. It constantly refers back to him. His going away merely reinforces the impression that this image is the only testimony of what his physical appearance was at a particular moment in his existence.[8]

In the cinematic image this 'testimony' is desired yet paradoxical, out of reach (because the moving image is always moving beyond the particular moment). We would argue that the stylistics of 'transcendental' stasis common to the open image is, in part, an attempt to imbue the moving image with the photographic aura. Following Henri Bergson and William James,[9] we can presume that it is inevitable that the moving image of real-time duration will be broken down by memory into discrete images of moments and then synthesized or reconstructed into a privileged static image or a series of quasi-static images. Memory privileges the fleeting motionless image over direct visual representation of duration.

The photographic aura accrues to the cinematic image of stasis as an 'always already' recollected image. The image from a film that impresses itself upon our consciousness constantly refers back to its *presence*. Echoing Mitry, the fact that we are no longer watching the film, the fact that we saw it five hours or five years ago, 'merely reinforces the impression that this image is the only testimony' not only of the 'appearance' of the film, but of *our experience* of watching the film 'at a particular moment' of our existence. The static image thus finds itself embroiled in notions of presence, absence and death, especially when it is experienced in cinema – that is, in relation to moving images, and to duration. It is the aura of the fixed, static image which throws the passing of time, of existence, into relief; and all these existential terms suggest that the religious underpinning of Schrader's 'transcendentalist style' – an anathema to most film theorists – is impossible to repress.

In the examples from Iranian cinema to be discussed, stasis (arrested images, the fixed long-shot, the freeze-frame or images of empty spaces) will be seen as auspicious for open images, but not invariably so. Although Schrader equates stasis, austerity and what he terms the 'sparse' with transcendental style, he points out that the long-take stasis films of avant-garde art, usually depicting objects in real time (the minimalist cinema of Michael Snow or today's video installations), fail to evoke the transcendental effect – such an effect is only produced by stasis as a break within 'realist' narrative: for an image to be 'arrested' it must previously flow.[10]

Likewise, we contend that the open image only has meaning as a deferral of an otherwise implied narrative closure. It is this context that gives rise to viewer resistance to stasis, experienced as boredom, though boredom might be an integral part of the aesthetic experience – for the diachronic arts, especially film, the occasional 'space' of boredom is a way in which real-time duration is defamiliarized and then made retrievable to the reconstructed imaging of memory. It may be the *longueur* that facilitates the 'opening' of image in narrative. The experience of resistance, of boredom, may be transformed into the experience of the transcendental, of ecstasy. In Schrader's words: 'When the image stops, the viewer keeps going, moving deeper and deeper, one might say, into the image. This is the "miracle" of sacred art.'[11]

Deleuze: The Time-Image

Deleuze's writings on cinema, *Cinema 1: The Movement-Image* (1983) and *Cinema 2: The Time-Image* (1985), investigate the opening out of the image in direct images of time; not external, chronological time, but the time of concrete duration. These direct time-images are characterized by a lack of causal links. Movement-images, on the other hand, are defined by causal links. In Deleuze's neurological terminology, movement-images show 'sensory-motor' connections between stimulus and response. Something is seen, for example, and an action, perception or feeling is given as a reaction.[12] The time-image is created when such sensory-motor links in the image are suspended or broken. When the situation no longer extends into action, films give rise to pure optical and sound situations. Something has become 'too strong' in the image, something which cannot be reduced to what happens or what is perceived or felt (by the characters).[13] The break between movement-images and time-images is not clear-cut, but generally time-images belong to cinema's 'postclassical' phase. Time-images are connotative rather than denotative, imbuing objects with a number of associations. Deleuze suggests they might have political implications: 'It is precisely the weakness of the motor linkages, the weak connections', he writes, 'that are capable of releasing huge forces of disintegration', producing images of process, of transformation;

such images are not an obscurantist turning away from the political, but the open-ended politicization of the image.[14] This argument has become relevant again in the light of the controversy surrounding the (a)political trajectory of the New Iranian Cinema.[15]

In Deleuze's account, Italian neorealism is the film movement that most epitomizes the break between the movement-image and the time-image. This break came about, he claims, for reasons both internal and external to cinema. External circumstances were provided by postwar devastation, reconstruction and diaspora. As cities were demolished and rebuilt, wastelands (such as derelict and disused out-of-town sites) proliferated, and people became displaced from their settings, the determinate environments associated with the movement-image became blurred. After World War II, circumstances internal to cinema made it ready to respond to these external conditions, particularly in postfascist Italy. The sensory-motor links between motivation and action gave way to new forms, such as the meandering journey, which accorded more with the transformed landscapes. Cinema gave rise to images of indeterminate settings – 'any-spaces-whatever'[16] which became pure optical and sound situations.

When we turn the emphasis from neorealism's 'realism' to its poeticism and its production of pure optical and sound situations, the ground on which the common view of neorealism stands begins to shift. No longer can we see it simply in terms of its commitment to record 'reality'. All those features which justified that view – its association with nonprofessional actors, contemporary social and political topics dealing with ordinary people, combining fictional drama with documentary, and location shooting – must be put into contact with something else. The settings retain their reality, but they are no longer situations that disclose actions as they would in traditional realism. Instead, they open onto thought, dream, memory and feelings of *déjà-vu*, as the action 'floats' in the situation. Viewers no longer perceive a sensory-motor image to which they respond by identifying with the characters. Instead, they undergo 'a dream-like connection through the intermediary of the liberated sense organs.'[17]

Rather than extending into movement, the pure optical and sound image enters into relation with a virtual image, and 'forms a circuit with it', as if it has linked up with an image we recall from somewhere else.[18] But it is most effective when our memory falters and we cannot remember: as Bergson realized, 'attentive recognition informs us to a much greater degree when it fails than when it succeeds', and the same applies to cinema.[19] When the present optical perception fails to make a link with either a motor-image or a recollection-image, 'it enters into relation with genuinely virtual elements, feelings of *déjà-vu* or the past "in general" (I must have seen that man somewhere . . .), dream images (I have the feeling that I saw him in a dream . . .)'.[20] This opening-out of the image seems to occur regardless of the content – the images may be of 'everyday banality' or 'exceptional limit-circumstances', but their predominant optical and sound situations, Deleuze writes, are 'subjective images, memories of childhood, sound and visual dreams or fantasies'.[21]

Neorealist Location: Disconnected Spaces

The discussion so far is pertinent not only to work that is generally termed 'post' neorealist, but also to the key neorealist films such as Rossellini's war trilogy, Vittorio De Sica's *Ladri di Biciclette/Bicycle Thieves* (1948) and Visconti's *La Terra Trema/The Earth Trembles* (1948). There is a formalism and a penchant for aestheticized stasis in Visconti's vision – and a corresponding deployment of devices that would come to be associated with the poetic postneorealism of Antonioni and Pasolini (such as fixed shots as characters enter and exit the frame). Thus, *La Terra Trema* exploits the effects of documenting social reality and combines this with fictional (re)construction by way of a formalist aesthetic, a combination prefiguring – amongst much else – the most widely-recognized strategy of the New Iranian Cinema, from Kiarostami's *Close-Up* to Samira Makhmalbaf's *The Apple*.

The 'reality effects' in *La Terra Trema* would be nothing without the visual stylization and theatrical staging that characterizes each shot. The film makes striking compositions out of the natural surroundings – with views of the rocks which enclose the harbour and the image of the women, their black shawls billowing in the wind, standing on rocks, straining seaward for the brothers' return. The film keeps returning to the view of the rocks, which might be seen as an attempt to anchor the story in a specific locale – the rocks being signs of a distinctive, recognizable place. However, silhouetted in the dusk they become ambiguous and, in our associations, break free from their geographically-specific moorings and also from their symbolic moorings (where they represent the isolation of the village from the outside world). They are no longer the rocks of a particular harbour in Sicily, but (to adapt the Deleuzian term) 'any-rocks-whatever'.

This brings us to another aspect of neorealism's break with traditional realism. While the latter is characterized by determined spaces, neorealism loses the specific geospatial coordinates of a given locale and rearranges the references. Deleuze contends that one can refer to 'Riemanian spaces' in neorealism, where the 'connecting of parts is not predetermined but can take place in many ways'.[22] Landscapes or cityscapes attain a hallucinatory, crystalline quality that looks forward to later Antonioni (the trilogy, *Red Desert*, *Zabriskie Point* [1969]) or the Zone in Andrei Tarkovsky's *Stalker* (1979). Such spatial indeterminacy is a feature of the New Iranian Cinema, in which a character's quest traverses the labyrinthine pathway of either city streets (*Badkonak-e Sefid/The White Balloon* [Jafar Panahi, 1995], *Dayereh/The Circle* [Jafar Panahi, 2000]), the tracks of villages/ rural areas (*Khaneh-ye Dust Kojast/Where Is My Friend's House?* [Abbas Kiarostami, 1987], *Zir-e Darakhtan-e Zeytun/Through the Olive Trees* [Abbas Kiarostami, 1994], *Bad Ma-ra Khahad Bord/The Wind Will Carry Us* [Abbas Kiarostami, 1999]) or passes over barren mountainous landscapes (*Takhteh Siyah/Blackboards* [Samira Makhmalbaf, 1999], *Zamani Barayé Masti Asbha/A Time for Drunken Horses* [Bahman Ghobadi, 2000]). Alternatively, characters may navigate the labyrinthine topology of the liminal space where equally barren city and rural environments meet (*Ta'm-e Gilas/A Taste of Cherry* [Abbas Kiarostami, 1997]). The circuitous quest makes even the most concrete places fleetingly uncanny – both for the character and for the viewer.

Deleuze refers to the 'dispersive and lacunary reality' in Rossellini's *Paisà* (1946), where locales fragment into unstable configurations.[23] This feature is carried further in Antonioni, where the Deleuzian 'any-space-whatever' is constituted from geometrical blocks of whites, shadows and colours – starting with almost empty urban riverbank shots in *Netteza Urbana* (1948), and the deserted stadium in *Cronaca di un Amore/Chronicle of a Love* (1950), going on to the final scene showing the rendezvous point devoid of protagonists in *L'Eclisse/The Eclipse* (1962) and the industrial landscapes of *Red Desert*. These emptied or disconnected spaces obtain a relative autonomy from the surrounding narrative, enabling them to become open images.

The neorealist locations inspired by the indeterminate environments created by the postwar situation attract a new type of protagonist who – because images no longer obey sensory-motor rules – tends to see rather than act. For this reason, as Deleuze suggests, the role of the child, who mostly looks on in wonder or confusion while unable to intervene, becomes significant.[24] In this development, where the child's gaze and the pure optical and sound image meet, neorealism is clearly the crucial turning point (for example, Rossellini's *Germania Anno Zero/Germany Year Zero* [1947] and De Sica's *Bicycle Thieves*). It is a development which will be vital for some of the most powerful open images in New Iranian Cinema and helps to explain its many child protagonists (*Where Is My Friend's House?*, *The White Balloon*, *The Apple*) in terms other than those of sentimental humanism.[25]

French New Wave: The Reflexive Turn

The French new wave adapted much of the image repertoire created by neorealism, but gave the images a reflexive spin, an effect that can also be seen in New Iranian Cinema. The French directors specialized in images of movements that falsify perspective, taking further a tendency already assumed by neorealism (and which gave rise to its disconnected spaces). With reference to a Deleuzian analysis, two salient characteristics can be briefly noted here: firstly, the 'irrational' cuts (which have disjunctive rather than conjunctive value), typified by Godard; secondly, the 'crystal image', which recurs across the French new wave films, but is best typified by Alain Resnais.[26]

As already mentioned, the pure optical and sound situation, instead of extending into movement, enters into relationship with a virtual image (thought, dream, memory or *déjà-vu*). A crystal image occurs when an actual optical image and a virtual image form a circuit and coalesce or exchange places.[27] The most familiar instance of the crystal image is the mirror. A famous example is in *Citizen Kane* (Orson Welles, 1941) where we see Kane passing between two facing mirrors; as the mirror images recede infinitely, the actual and the virtual become indistinguishable. Alternatively, the crystal image may have what Deleuze calls 'an internal disposition', like 'a seed in relation to the environment'.[28] Here the crystal image has a mise-en-abyme structure, where the seed is the virtual image crystallizing the environment ('environment' denotes both the physical landscape and the diegetic reality of the film). The paperweight that falls from the dying man's hand as he utters the word 'Rosebud' in the opening of *Citizen Kane* is an example of such a crystal image, the paperweight being the 'seed' or mise-en-abyme of the environment, Xanadu (and also the uncertain 'seed' of the story itself).

Deleuze argues that the crystal image is the true 'genetic moment' of pure optical-sound situations, which 'are nothing but slivers of crystal-images'.[29] In Resnais's film *L'Année Dernière à Marienbad/Last Year in Marienbad* (1961), the hotel (indeed the whole film) is a crystal, maze-like, mirroring infinite probabilities. The film-within-a-film (characteristic of so many Godard and new wave films) is a type of crystal-image, including the film which takes its own process of making as its object – but, as Deleuze implies, this work in the mirror must be 'justified from elsewhere' if it is to succeed (that is, the self-reflexivity must not be in and for itself).[30] It is no surprise therefore that the film-within-a-film should so often provide the context for open images in New Iranian Cinema (*Close-Up*, *Through the Olive Trees, Salaam Cinema* [Mohsen Makhmalbaf, 1995], *A Moment of Innocence*). The overt reflexivity of Iranian cinema is not merely a borrowing of Brechtian devices via Godard and the French new wave, but rather something integral to its form and always 'justified from elsewhere' by the neorealist diegesis.

In the following sections, we will show how Iranian cinema has developed for its own purposes elements drawn from the stylistic theories and practices discussed above, resulting in a recognizable aesthetic structured around the privileging of open images. Some of these elements correspond very closely to what we have already seen in (post)neorealism, while others develop the stylistics of the open image to a new degree, bringing into being new distinctive types. By refocusing existing debates in terms of the open image, we ensure that the cinema's 'poetic realism', so often obscured, is kept in view.

Disconnected Spaces

The majority of recent Iranian films are structured by a 'quest' through a realist location. But such classical neorealist locations are stylized – naturalistic specificity of location giving way to poetic universalism. Moreover, as the quest becomes a meandering circular itinerary so location breaks down into disconnected spaces: *A Taste of Cherry, The Wind Will Carry Us, The Circle*, even *The White Balloon* and *The Apple*, display variations of this process. In Kiarostami's *Where Is My Friend's House?*, schoolboy Ahmad mistakenly takes his friend Mohammad's homework book. Knowing that the teacher will expel Mohammad if he does not do his homework in the correct book, Ahmad sets off to return it, although no one can tell him where Mohammad lives. The quest will never be completed; Ahmad running up and down the zigzag path between villages stands for the whole structure of the film, the meandering, or indirect, journey form. The film's cinematography has the effect of erasing the precise co-ordinates (the villages Koker and Poshteh in Northern Iran) and instead gives rise to disconnected spaces in which the various sensory-motor linkages begin to come apart.

The way in which characters become lost in the liminal zone between disconnected spaces takes on an overtly political aspect in Samira Makhmalbaf's *Blackboards* and Ghobadi's *A Time for Drunken Horses*. In these films the narrative is driven by its characters' attempts to cross the border between Iran and Iraq, but the landscape gradually dissolves into disconnected spaces: 'border' ceases to be an identifiable, recognizable place and instead signifies a nightmarish unstable zone of inexplicable military atrocity. The idea for *Blackboards* began with the landscape: when Samira Makhmalbaf was walking in Kurdistan with her father, she was struck by the harsh infertililty of some parts of the landscape, and selected these for her film's location.[31] They give an overwhelming impression of inhospitality, with red, stony, steep ascents; a hint of menace is underscored by the film's use of offscreen sound to indicate helicopter surveillance and border patrols. The treatment of landscape in the film places a neorealist emphasis on the relationship between characters and their lived-in surroundings, where characters are 'moulded' in the image of the environment.[32] The recalcitrance of the landscape rubs off on the characters: the obdurate, weather-beaten old patriarchs and the hardy boy smugglers. The itinerant teachers are out of place in this landscape – and they look it, ungainly with their blackboards, searching for pupils, when nobody wants to be taught. As a result of this 'free indirect' relationship between character and landscape (where the vision of the landscape is filtered through that of the character), poetic open images are possible in every scene. But it is not only the teachers who are displaced; eventually, as they near the border, all the Kurdish characters in the film become 'lost', 'disconnected' from the landscape, and the landscape itself dissolves into disconnected spaces of desolation.

This disconnection is reflected in the editing of *Blackboards* as well as in its mise-en-scène. Whereas Hollywood editing ensures spatial continuity from shot to shot, the editing in this film tends to present a given scene as disconnected fragments of space. This, too, highlights the instability of space, spatial disruption and disorientation. For example, in one conversation scene (between a teacher and an old man who asks him to read a letter), the camera alternates from one character to the other, with each character occupying a separate frame; but unlike the Hollywood shot/reverse-shot structure, there is little common space from shot to shot. This kind of spatial system is characteristic of the House of Makhmalbaf films discussed here. Instead of cutting from a spatial whole to a part, sequences are often entirely constructed from parts, especially in the many scenes taking place before closed (or partially-closed) doorways. Here the doorway functions as an internal frame, marking the barrier to our vision, and emphasizing the selectiveness of what we see. There are closeups of disembodied women's hands giving directions, handing out soup or watering flowers (*Moment of Innocence, The Apple*) from behind doors that are barely ajar. Thus, the disconnected spaces of Iranian cinema also gesture to concerns about the limits of what can be shown (from a non-Iranian perspective, it is tempting to read this allegorically as referring to censorship restrictions).

The Fixed Long-shot/Long-take

Both the fixed long-shot and the long-take are typical components of an aesthetic of 'stasis' as outlined by Schrader and typical vehicles for the open image. The zigzag path on the hill between villages in *Where Is My Friend's House?* is an exemplary open image. We see Ahmad's tiny figure running up and down across the hillside three times in the film, mostly in a static framing and in long shot. The distant view and length of the take in the absence of any conventional action force us to concentrate on the image and absorb the abstraction imposed on the environment. Kiarostami had the path specially built for the film (and planted a tree on the top of the hill), which reflects his concern for not just recording reality, but making it carry certain poetic resonances. Some of these are symbolic (aside from resonances specific to Persian culture, the tree on the top stands for friendship, while Ahmad's zigzagging symbolizes the hurrying-around in modern life, Kiarostami says).[33] However, the static long-shot frame and its duration give the cinematic image an openness in excess of its closed symbolism, allowing it to connect with virtual images in the mind.[34]

Kiarostami's *Through the Olive Trees* concludes with a long-take showing a young peasant, Hossein, following the girl, Tahereh, to whom he has proposed marriage. The two figures wend their way through an olive orchard and along zigzag paths across a valley, finally disappearing into almost invisible dots in the distance. Because of the real-time, fixed point-of-view determination of the scene, making us strain to follow the two speck-figures on a path, we scrutinize the moving image as if it were a photograph containing the sublime object, the veiled secret. This is an important quality of the open image and an aspect of its residual photographic aura.

As discussed earlier in relation to Schrader, in a film where every image is equally open there can be no openness; the term becomes meaningless due to the lack of distinguishing qualities and contrast. This is also true of the individual image: the open image must contain a level of closure, of limitation, which enables the openness to reveal itself and, by the same token, allows the play of universality and particularity to show forth. This seems to be how Kiarostami approached, technically, the universalizing of Hossein and Tahereh in the final scene of *Through the Olive Trees*: by holding the viewer in an extreme way to the image, both temporally (four minutes) and spatially (long- and wide-shot of one scene), the eventual release of interpretative desire is all the more pronounced. Kiarostami comments:

> The film-maker has carried the film up to here, and now it is given up to the audience to think about it and watch these characters from very far away. I like the last shot because of its openness. Until that moment social differences were dividing these two people, but as human beings they were equal. The class system separated them, but in nature and in long shot I felt that these two could get closer to their real selves, that is to their inner needs, without giving any value to the social norms.[35]

In the process of becoming extra-diegetic archetypes, Hossein and Tahereh continue to be inflected with what seem to be, for Kiarostami, the three primary levels of being: the personal level of love; the social level of class difference; the existential level of nature. The universalizing never loses sight of the particular.

Child's Gaze

When Ahmad undertakes his quest in *Where Is My Friend's House?*, many obstacles and detours are put in his path, mostly by interfering or unhelpful adults. The bewilderment of the child in the world of adults is key to the film's emotional power. Kiarostami has said that the actor was chosen because of his gaze, a decision which revives the child's role as a witness in neorealism.[36] One might have expected him, therefore, to exploit this by having many facial closeups expressing precisely this bafflement; but although the image of Ahmad's startled face is one we are likely to take away from the film, there are not many closeups. Instead Kiarostami prefers medium closeups, moving out to extreme long-shots, blocking direct identification with Ahmad's gaze and instead making the viewer work through a 'free indirect subjective'[37] (Pasolini) relation between the gaze of the character and a given image, between the child's gaze and the gaze of the film.

The most bewildering sequence in the film, both for Ahmad and for the viewer, is the wander through the narrow streets of Poshteh. The set is a labyrinth, a crystalline or Riemanian space, but one which creates more anxiety than those in Italian neorealism, for here the meandering structure of the film in general, and this sequence in particular, directly confronts what Deleuze calls the child's motor-helplessness in the adult's world. The anxiety and helplessness of the child lost in the forbidding labyrinth is encapsulated in the film's title, a plea to which nobody has a proper answer. Everyday signs become mysteriously ominous: a man, dwarfed and bent over by the bundle of twigs he is carrying, looks like a walking bush; brown trousers on a washing line are a false sign (Ahmad believes, mistakenly, that they belong to his friend). Ahmad stumbles from one dead-end to another, following the ambiguous and imprecise directions that denizens of the village give him; meanwhile we hear off-camera sounds – the sudden mewing of cats, a dog barking, the distant clacking of a passing train, all the more puzzling and ambiguous for their absence in the scene. When, finally, Ahmad encounters an old carpenter, his quest is suspended: the carpenter takes him on a tour of the doors and windows of the village. Sensory-motor linkages in the image come utterly apart here: not only is there no extension into action *per se*, but the scene itself ceases to make sense. Dream-like sensations descend on the viewer as the narrative enters this extraordinary lull. What takes hold instead is optical play: teasing glimpses of kaleidoscopic projections of light on the walls of the old houses. These, supposedly, are all cast through windows and doors from lit interiors, but the bizarre positioning of some of this shadow-play gives the lie to such a rational explanation. This image of the play of light is not reducible to realism, but is a reflexive motif on the technology that projects the images that we see.

Dedramatization/Unsympathetic Characters

In classical Hollywood narrative the protagonist becomes the moral yardstick against which we measure all the other characters in a film; he is the character with whom we most identify, and we can do this because he is presented as sympathetic, despite his foibles. The presence of unsympathetic characters, central to many Iranian films, marks a divergence from the Hollywood norm but connects with a development out of neorealism represented especially by Antonioni. In an added self-reflexive ambiguity many of these central characters are film directors: seemingly insensitive and aloof manipulators of their casts – Mohsen Makhmalbaf taking this even further by 'playing himself' as the manipulative director in *Salaam Cinema* and *A Moment of Innocence*. This blocking of identification relates to the muted performances Iranian directors draw from their actors, especially from adults, an ambiguity of acting register closer to neorealism and Rossellini than to the uniform flatness of Bresson or Ozu, a dedramatization that creates space for the intensification of images. In Deleuzian terms, when identification with characters does take place, the sensory-motor arc remains intact – there is a connection between what is seen and a motor reaction (our identification with that character in that situation). The failure of identification with characters snaps the sensory-motor chain, and liberates the senses: we become more receptive to other aspects of the film. In particular, it facilitates connections with virtual images which will return in the viewer's memory.

In Kiarostami's *The Wind Will Carry Us*, the unsympathetic central character is the film producer protagonist, Behzad, who is insensitive and irresponsible in his attempts to exploit the rural village he has come to film. In a disturbing scene, Behzad on a hillside kicks over a tortoise – there are some conventional reverse-shots of the character looking down on the back of the tortoise, though it is the tortoise and its movement which is the dominant real-time image (filling the image-frame), beyond any conventional point of view or narrative requirements. Behzad loses interest and walks off but we (to our relief) see the desperate tortoise managing to right itself and continue on its way. As with similar scenes in Antonioni, a reductive explanation is possible: when Behzad kicks over the tortoise he gives expression to the way in which his individual alienation (bourgeois, urban) necessarily alienates him from existence itself (nature). Such alienation (at the three levels of personality, class and the existential) is manifest in the very arbitrariness of his cruelty and the fact that it is unthinking curiosity rather than intentional cruelty – he does not stay to extract sadistic pleasure from the up-turned tortoise's plight. But Behzad is not hero, villain or victim; identification with him and his act remains disconnected, open, as does the image of the tortoise – obsessively framed in excess of the narrative requirement – or to put it in Pasolini's terms, a poetic image infuses a prosaic narrative with its ambiguity.

Open Image/Crystal Image

Open images are a feature of film endings, closing scenes which try not to close down a narrative but rather open it out to the viewer's consideration, to 'live on' after the film itself has finished. A striking example is in Kiarostami's *A Taste of Cherry*, where the central character, Mr Badiei, plans to commit suicide in the evening, but must find someone who will come the following morning to bury him. Towards the end of the film Badiei takes an overdose and lies down in his self-dug grave. The screen goes completely black for a few seconds. Suddenly the film cuts from darkness to light, from film to grainy video stock. Characters that we saw earlier are now seen waiting around, like actors on a film set, while motifs from the film (marching soldiers counting in unison) are repeated verite-style.

This change to grainy video stock to give a verite effect is a common feature of New Iranian Cinema. An early example is Kiarostami's use of video for the real trial scene of the 'fake Makhmalbaf' case in *Close-Up*. In *A Taste of Cherry* the documentary effect is subverted. The verite coda does not assert, in Brechtian fashion, that the foregoing film is just a representation, because the fuzzy imaging of the video reality seems far stranger than the tangible diegetic reality of the preceding narrative; instead, the intrusion of this uncanny real marks a shift to the poetic. The switch from night and death to day and life, far from resolving the narrative, creates an ambiguity, an openness, as if we are now watching images of life after death – whether or not our central character actually died or not. Following the blacked-out image, the temporal relation between the coda and the preceding narrative is thrown into confusion, as is the relation between diegesis and meta-diegetic documentary. The coda – evoking dream or *déjà-vu* – is not a recollection or flashback but a merging or short-circuiting of past and present, forming a crystal image.

While *A Taste of Cherry* ends with 'documentary' in video, Samira Makhmalbaf's *The Apple* uses videocam for its documentary beginning, thus setting up the whole film as a Deleuzian crystal image. The film follows the adventures of two girls who have spent most of their lives locked up at home under their father's watchful eye. The first image shows an outstretched hand watering a plant. This shot documents the everyday, yet makes it abstract – the stationary camera waits for the hand to enter the frame. The shot composition is austere, almost abstract – flat, with the camera axis perpendicular to the background. It is a form of abstraction which does not remove the everyday, but opens it into dimensions other than the everyday. It raises possible symbolic meanings relating to the narrative – the plant is in the open, receiving the sun, unlike the housebound girls. Yet the image resists any one-to-one correspondence between the sign and meaning.

The story for *The Apple* is taken straight from Tehran television news, and uses the family members concerned to act as themselves – but the director introduces significant props, such as the dangling apple and mirror, into her reimagining of the events. Several open images in this film come from scenes which make use of these symbolic props. This is because their intrusion into the reconstruction of events that took place in actuality only a few days before produces an uncanny effect; the irreducible quality alluded to above never vanishes. Makhmalbaf began filming even as the events were happening – her documentary section, using video, shows the girls at the welfare centre while the reconstruction of the girls' release into the outside world started only four days after it happened. As a result, the whole film becomes a crystal image, but one in which the work in the mirror is put in the scene in a peculiarly uncanny fashion, for not only are the symbolic props a constant reminder that this is a fictional reconstruction, but they directly materialize the twins' process of coming to terms with the outside world. They, like the film, examine themselves in the mirror (given to them as a present by the social worker). Even the apple, which is such an overdetermined symbol in the Judaeo-Islamic-Christian cultural inheritance, becomes detached from those particular moorings to configure the twins' curiosity about the world.

Mohsen Makhmalbaf's *A Moment of Innocence*, a film which films itself in the process of its own constitution, contains particularly intricate crystalline open images. Makhmalbaf plays himself as the (unsympathetic) director of a film which looks reflexively at his own past – and might be said to reconstitute that past. For there is a significant disparity between the past as it happened and the past which is recollected in the film. In the former, Makhmalbaf, an Islamic revolutionary, aged seventeen, tried to disarm one of the Shah's policemen, was shot by him, and subsequently imprisoned in a Pahlavi jail. By contrast, the film (made long after Makhmalbaf renounced his revolutionary fervour) represents the policeman as a sensitive man, in love with a mysterious woman who seemed to ask him for the time, or for directions, at every opportunity. It also tells us that this woman was Makhmalbaf's cousin and accomplice (whose flirtation is merely to distract the policeman while Makhmalbaf stabs him with a knife); the two revolutionaries are in love with each other, and together they want to save the world using any means – including violence. In the film's reconstruction of history, the ideal of saving the world through love is contrasted with the means of violence – this is the version that the youngsters are asked to reenact, but their failure to reenact this version introduces yet another alternative (nonviolent) reality, which calls into question Makhmalbaf's attempt to reconstitute – and manipulate – the past. The young actors do not wish to take up arms against each other – the 'Young Makhmalbaf' repeatedly sobs and throws away the knife that he has been directed to thrust into the policeman's side. The 'Young Policeman' refuses to draw his gun. In the climax of the film-within-a-film, the 'Policeman', on impulse, offers the woman the flower which he had been instructed not to give her, and 'Makhmalbaf' in turn donates to the policeman the flatbread under which he was supposed to conceal the knife; the film closes with this image of exchange, the veiled woman caught in between, arrested in a freeze-frame.

The fusion of reality and its poetic remake in *A Moment of Innocence* develops into a very complex crystal image, in which no component is entirely independent from any other – this has the antirealist consequence that characters who have never met before act as if they knew each other intimately. For all the film's intricate design, the components in the film do not just slot neatly inside each other – they open onto each other, overlapping. In this respect the film, like so many Iranian films (*The Circle, The Wind Will Carry Us, A Taste of Cherry*), structurally resembles the musical round – which, according to Deleuze, is an instance of a crystal – with its rhythmically-modulated repetitions. In *A Moment of Innocence*, the first scene of the policeman strand ends when a woman happens to come by and asks him the time. 'It happened just like that!' exclaims the policeman as she walks away. We then cut to the Makhmalbaf strand, where the part of the cousin is allocated to the young actor's own cousin. When, finally alone, she calls into a shop where the clocks have all stopped, then walks towards the rehearsing policemen, the encounter we saw before is repeated. This time we recognize the woman, and realize that the two scenes/strands have not been taking place in sequence (which is how we have experienced them), but simultaneously. The narrative then takes up the policeman strand from exactly where it was left before, but the repetition has underlined the words 'It happened just like that!' with a new ambiguity.

There are political implications in this use of the crystal image as a round, which, Deleuze writes, describes 'the rising and falling back of pasts which are preserved.'[38] As the round progresses, more and more alternative realities are negotiated and put into contact with the past 'as it happened'; the actual images are made to confront virtual images, generating multiple fictional possibilities. As such, *Moment of Innocence* utilizes the properties of the open image (crystalline ambiguity, indeterminacy) in a way that subtly undermines the Islamic regime itself. That regime, which temporarily banned the film, states that there is only one reality; but even in the one, the film points out, there are many.[39] The shop where the clocks are frozen signals the arrest of linear time, the severing of sensory-motor links, and the release of subjective possibilities.

Freeze-frame

The freeze-frame which ends *Moment of Innocence* suspends within its single image the competing determinants of Islamic fundamentalism, revolutionary idealism, terrorism, law and order, adolescent romance, unrequited love, revenge and pacifism. The freeze-frame 'arrests' the precise 'moment' where history and its attempted re-enactment interpenetrate – that is, the past (the original terrorist act of the young Makhmalbaf and accomplice) is transfigured by the present (the actors' refusal to repeat the original violent act). The original terrorists' act, the original lovelorn policeman's naive response, the actors' spontaneous refusal of violence, and the middle-aged protagonists' witnessing of this refusal in the re-enactment, are no longer separate moments in time but all joined to constitute the moment of innocence. Although there is a synthesis of past and present and of the competing ideologies in this moment, this image, there is no resolution, no closure. Instead the viewer is left to read the freeze-frame tableau and the contradictions held within it as an open image.

It might be argued that the tendency towards the allegorical evident in New Iranian Cinema pulls the films' open images towards narrative determinism. *The Apple*, for instance, can be read in terms of feminist allegory. In the concluding scene, the blind, chadored mother wanders out of the house, into the alleyway, and reaches for the dangling apple. The final shot freezes her with the apple firmly in her grasp (an allegory about women seizing opportunities). The imprisonment of the girls may be a code, enabling the film to pass the censor, for the restrictions imposed on women in Iran. Nonetheless, neither the allegorical-symbolic nor the documentary elements/codes have hegemony, and the closing freeze-frame of *The Apple* is an open image in that it 'suspends' interpretation between competing narrative codes.

A groundbreaking Iranian film in terms of popular (commercial) international success was Panahi's *The White Balloon*. This is the story of a seven-year-old girl, Razieh, meandering around a few Tehran streets, on her way to buy a goldfish for New Year, and losing her money. It displays all the characteristics we have come to expect – a play with real-time duration, natural locations, a repetitive, cyclical structure, and a child protagonist on a quest. Because of its popularity in the West, critics – inside and outside Iran – have taken issue with the film, alleging that it does not reflect Iranian political reality (claiming that it provides propaganda for western audiences instead). This often bitter debate has been replayed with almost every subsequent Iranian film (more recently, critics have been charging that the films are too negative.) In terms of our classification of the open image, *The White Balloon* suggests that even in a film that appears to be completely apolitical, there is in fact a political aspect, and this relates to the forms we have been discussing. At the end of the film Razieh and her older brother, Ali, recover their 500-toman banknote with help from an Afghan balloon seller. Razieh and Ali then, without thought, abandon their saviour, buy the goldfish and return home. The film ends with the clock ticking down to the New Year, an ominous offscreen explosion, and a freeze-frame: the Afghan refugee boy with his white balloon.

The Afghan boy is in every sense 'marginal' to the narrative – this is, of course, the point. He has barely figured in the film, neither has the white balloon. And, one might add, neither have the Iranian political situation nor the question of Afghan refugees in Iran. Yet *The White Balloon* is the title of the film and this is the final image – one that, by its very unexpectedness and the fact that it is a long-held freeze-frame, announces itself as the crucial image of the film, a static image we are given the necessary time to 'read'. Identification with (the now unsympathetic) Razieh's quest is called into question; the implication is that the Afghan refugee will not be going home to celebrate the New Year – he has no home. But the image is too ambiguous, too 'strong', to be reduced to one level of interpretation. The freeze-frame of the Afghan boy and his white balloon feeds back into and modifies the whole preceding 'charming' narrative, the entire chain of images. The best open images 'open up' the films in which they appear (turn the films into crystal images) and open films 'out' to the world, rendering the absent political reality present.

We would not argue that ambiguity or indeterminacy are inherently radical – indeterminacy can itself be politically determined in opposing ways – but that Iranian filmmakers have utilized the open image to circumvent a particularly strict form of censorship and point to the plurality of truth and experience in a political context where a repressive notion of one truth is imposed by the state. The dogmatic constructions of reality associated with the Iranian state have, of course, their equivalents elsewhere. The appeal of New Iranian Cinema in the West may have less to do with 'sympathy' for an exoticized 'other' under conditions of repression than with self-recognition. The open images of Iranian film remind us of the loss of such images in most contemporary cinema, the loss of cinema's particular space for creative interpretation and critical reflection.

Notes

1   General department of Cinematographic Research and Relations, *Post-Revolution Iranian Cinema* (Tehran: Ministry of Ershad-e Eslami, 1982), p. 8.
2   See Mir-Ahmad-e Mir-Ehsan, 'Dark light', in Rose Issa and Sheila Whitaker (eds), *Life and Art: the New Iranian Cinema* (London: British Film Institute, 1999), p. 113.

3 Sam Rohdie makes a similar point when, tracing connections between Rossellini and 'post' neorealism, he argues that the 'reality' Italian neorealism reflects is the 'reality' of film language; its experimentation with language implies concerns beyond the merely representational. Sam Rohdie, *The Passion of Pier Paolo Pasolini* (London: British Film Institute, 1995), pp. 15–16.

4 Pier Paolo Pasolini, 'The cinema of poetry', in Bill Nichols (ed.), *Movies and Methods: an Anthology*, Volume 1 (Berkeley: University of California Press, 1976), p. 544.

5 Ibid., pp. 552–3.

6 Gilles Deleuze, *Cinema 1: Movement Image*, trans. Hugh Tomlinson and Barbara Habberjam (London: Athlone Press, 1992), p. 74.

7 Paul Schrader, *Transcendental Style in Film: Ozu, Bresson, Dreyer* (New York: Da Capo, 1972), pp. 39, 42, 49.

8 Jean Mitry, *Semiotics and the Analysis of Film*, trans. Christopher King (London: Athlone Press, 2000), p. 31.

9 Henri Bergson, *Matter and Memory*, trans. N. M. Paul and W. S. Palmer (New York: Zone Books, 1991); William James, *Principles of Psychology*, Volume 1 (London: Macmillan, 1890).

10 Schrader, *Transcendental Style in Film*, p. 160.

11 Ibid., p. 161.

12 Deleuze, *Cinema 1*, p. 70.

13 Gilles Deleuze, *Cinema 2: The Time-Image*, trans. Hugh Tomlinson and Robert Galeta (London: Athlone Press, 1994), p. 18.

14 Ibid., p. 19.

15 Controversy over the politics of internationally successful Iranian films reflects ideological tensions amongst intellectuals in Iran and in Iranian elite circles. For criticism of Kiarostami and the 'festival film' see, for example, Azadeh Farahmand, 'Perspectives on recent (international acclaim for) Iranian cinema', in Richard Tapper (ed.), *The New Iranian Cinema: Politics, Representation and Identity* (London: IB Taurus, 2002), pp. 86–108. This debate has also had some impact amongst non-Iranian critics. The often unenthusiastic reviews of Iranian films in *Sight and Sound* during the 1990s tended to characterize the films as sentimental and apolitical. See, for example, Simon Louvish's review of *The White Balloon*, *Sight and Sound*, vol. 6, no. 3 (1996), p. 64; vol. 6, no. 4 (1996), p. 64.

16 Deleuze, *Cinema 2*, p. 5.

17 Ibid., p. 4.

18 Ibid., p. 48.

19 Ibid., p. 54.

20 Ibid., pp. 54–5.

21 Ibid., p. 6.

22 Ibid., p. 129.

23 Deleuze, *Cinema 1*, p. 212.

24 Deleuze, *Cinema 2*, p. 3.

25 There are, of course, many reasons for the predominance of child protagonists in Iranian film: censorship codes relating to the depiction of women, as has been extensively discussed elsewhere; the long-standing role of the Centre for the Intellectual Development of Children and Young Adults (associated most notably with Kiarostami); the important crosscurrents between Iranian and Indian film – the impact of neorealism

in Iran undoubtedly bears the influence of Satyajit Ray (especially *The Apu Trilogy* [1955–9]).

26 Deleuze, *Cinema 2*, p. 248.

27 Ibid., p. 69.

28 Ibid., p. 71.

29 Ibid., p. 69.

30 Ibid., p. 77.

31 Samira Makhmalbaf, interview with Jahanbakhsh Nouraei, *Iran International*, vol. 8, no. 1 (2000), p. 17.

32 For the neorealist exposition, see Giuseppe De Santis, 'Towards an Italian landscape', in David Overby (ed.), *Springtime in Italy: a Reader on Neorealism* (London: Tantivy Press, 1978), p. 126.

33 Abbas Kiarostami, interview with Robert Richter, *Kinder und Jugendkorrespondenz*, no. 42 (1990), p. 24.

34 David Bordwell sees Kiarostami as ironizing his own practice of using static images in the film-within-the-film of *Through the Olive Trees*, 'gently mocking this minimalism' with shots that activate 'angular depth and offscreen space' and 'throw into relief the static, planimetric images in the film that the characters are shooting'. David Bordwell, *On the History of Film Style* (Cambridge, MA: Harvard University Press, 1997), pp. 262–3.

35 Kiarostami, interview with Nassia Hamid, *Sight and Sound*, vol. 7, no. 2 (February 1997), p. 23.

36 Kiarostami, talking after the screening, National Film Theatre, London, 21 June 1999.

37 Pasolini, 'The cinema of poetry', pp. 551–3.

38 Deleuze, *Cinema 2*, p. 93.

39 The religious underpinning of these images referred to earlier does not, in out view, compromise their dissident potential. That religious underpinning is not synonymous with state religion or any other hegemonic versions of reality.

22

The Seductions of Homecoming: Place, Authenticity and Chen Kaige's *Temptress Moon*

Rey Chow

> *That sentiment accompanying the absence of home – homesickness – can cut two ways: it can be a yearning for the authentic home (situated in the past or in the future) or it can be the recognition of the inauthenticity of all homes.*
>
> Rosemary Marangoly George (75)

Even though it has been an overwhelmingly successful phenomenon worldwide, contemporary Chinese cinema is often greeted by Chinese-speaking audiences with hostility. It is as if the accomplishments of this cinema have an impossible task in returning home. The simple fact that it has traveled abroad and been gazed at with interest by "foreigners" is apparently enough to cause it to lose trustworthiness as wholly and genuinely Chinese. The films of the two most well-known directors, Chen Kaige and Zhang Yimou, for instance, have continued to be attacked for their tendencies to pander to the tastes of Western audiences eager for the orientalized, exotic images of a China whose history they ignore or falsify. This problematic, which is the problematic of authenticity, is familiar to all those engaged in cross-cultural studies.[1] In the late 1990s, when filmmaking and film watching are obviously global events involving ineluctable interaction with the "foreign," how might a film intervene in the tenacious and persistent demands for authenticity? I believe that Chen's 1996 film *Feng yue* (*Temptress*

Rey Chow, "The Seductions of Homecoming: Place, Authenticity and Chen Kaige's *Temptress Moon*," pp. 3–17 from *NARRATIVE* 6:1 (Columbus: The Ohio State University Press, January 1998). © 1998 by the Ohio State University Press. Reprinted by permission of the publisher.

Moon) can in many ways be seen as such an intervention,[2] the director's own cultural complexes notwithstanding. A discussion of this may begin with the significance of place in the film narrative. Place, as we shall see, is not only the setting that shapes characters in action; it is also the locus of specifically filmic significations of "home" and authenticity.

The Flight from Home

Topographically, *Temptress Moon* shifts back and forth between the countryside of Jiangnan (the location of the wealthy Pang clan) and the metropolis of Shanghai, which was among the earliest Chinese cities to be opened to foreign trade in the mid-nineteenth century (as a result of the Opium War of 1839–42). In the film, visual and architectural details combine to convey the sharp differences between the two locations as "tradition" and "modernity" respectively. The Pang family house, situated by a river, is a well-endowed ancient estate with its air of unbreakable heritage and kinship order; the solemnity and reticence typical of tribal bondage find their expression in darkish interiors with their austere, muted décor. Shanghai, by contrast, is a world of bright and gaudy colors, loud and vibrant foreign dance-hall music, fast-moving vehicles, and ruthless, mercenary human relations. Contrary to the mood of languid eternality that shrouds the old books, arcane utensils, and antique furnishings in the Pang household, Shanghai's Westernized domestic spaces are characterized by a much less permanent, because much newer, sense of time. In an apartment rented for the purpose of an illicit relationship, for instance, a vase of roses, a rocking chair, a window pane, a closet mirror, and the occasional music of a piano from afar all suggest the aura of a larger culture in the process of change. For those living in the countryside, meanwhile, everything from the city, including clothes, shoes, and hairstyles, and personal possessions such as pocket watches, slippers, razors, soaps, hats, and photographs alike take on the historic fascination of "modernity," the legend, the sign that separates Shanghai from the rest of China's hinterland.

It is in Shanghai that we meet the adult figure of the leading male character, Yu Zhongliang. Zhongliang is by profession a special kind of gigolo. A key member of a Shanghai mafia in the 1910s, Zhongliang's work involves the seduction and blackmail of rich married women who fall for him. Using the pseudonym "Xiao Xie."* Zhongliang would entice a woman into a secret affair; after the affair has gone on for a while, a typical scene is staged by the mafia: while Zhongliang is making love with the woman during one of their trysts, gangsters of the mafia would burst in on the scene, blindfold the woman, and threaten to report the affair to her husband unless the woman agrees to pay them a large sum of money. In the process, the woman would be told that her lover "Xiao Xie" is dead. After she is thus psychologically destroyed, Zhongliang would leave quietly with his cohorts and move on to the next target.

Zhongliang's professional success is the result of his familiarity with topography of another kind – a particular strategic spot on a woman's body. Typically, as he gains intimacy with a woman, he would kiss her on one ear, nibbling at the ear until the earring comes off. The earring, like Diderot's "bijoux indiscrets," is therefore the site of a female sexual confession.[3] For the mafia, this "memento" of a single earring exists as a repeated symbol of Zhongliang's invincibility. Although every case of extortion is carried out with the announcement that "Xiao Xie" is dead, in the next shot Zhongliang is usually alive and well, speedily departing from the scene of destruction for the next scene of conquest. Zhongliang's ease at the two sub-places that govern his life in Shanghai, married women's earlobes and the boudoirs of clandestine affairs, makes him indispensable to the mafia. Dada (or Boss), the head of the mafia, openly speaks of Zhongliang as someone he cannot do without.

To the audience, however, the smoothness with which Zhongliang moves about in Shanghai carries a different set of connotations. When the film begins, years prior to his Shanghai career, Zhongliang has just arrived at the residence of the Pangs in the countryside of Jiangnan after both his parents died. His only relative is his sister, Xiuyi, who is married to the young master Pang. Despite being officially the brother-in-law of the young master, Zhongliang is in effect treated as a servant. Between the lowly task of serving opium to his decrepit and perverse brother-in-law, and the intimate, incestuous affection of his sister, the young boy is plunged into a confusing encounter with the adult world. The twin experiences of a cruel adult male and a desirous adult female culminate in a scene in which Zhongliang's brother-in-law orders him to kiss his sister, who, sitting alongside the bed, acquiesces smilingly by opening her arms toward the boy. Fearful and reluctant, Zhongliang approaches the older woman while holding the opium-serving tray, his hands shaking violently. Amid the unforgettable noise of the opium utensils tossing against one another, his gaze is arrested on one of Xiuyi's earrings.

The place that is supposed to be a home for the displaced orphan child thus serves, in terms of narrative structure, as the unbearable site of infantile seduction (in the etymological sense of the word *infant* as *in-fans*, the state of speechlessness).[4] Like many first encounters with sexuality, the meaning of his experience with the sadomasochistic relationship of the two adults eludes Zhongliang and leaves him speechless. Architecturally, the traumatic nature of this seduction is mirrored by the circular, labyrinthine structure of the Pang estate, where a seemingly infinite series of doors and chambers, each connected with yet indistinguishable from the others, precludes any clear notion of entry or exit. Unable to comprehend (that is, to fully enter or fully leave behind) this primary encounter with sexuality, Zhongliang retains it through a certain repeated pattern of behavior. Having illicit relationships with married women that begin with the stealing of a single earring becomes his symptom and trademark, which turns a painful remembrance virtually into an industry. Although Zhongliang is a successful seducer, his success is presented from the beginning as a facade – a cover-up and a displacement of the trauma of *his own seduction*.

Meanwhile, there is another incident which makes it impossible for him to remain with the Pang family. Acting from resentment, he uses his opportunity of serving opium to poison his brother-in-law with a dose of arsenic, which causes the man to become brain-dead. In fear that his murderous act would be discovered, Zhongliang escapes. This escape clarifies the teleological tendency of the narrative of *Temptress Moon*. As an adopted home for Zhongliang, the backward, decadent countryside of the Pangs is significant as the site of a sexual primal scene that has shaped his character *negatively*. In order to be, Zhongliang must leave. His existential autonomy, in other words, will have to be established as a flight from the shock that is supposedly "home." But where will he flee from there?

Zhongliang intends to head for Beijing, the site of the historic, student-led May Fourth Movement of 1919, which sought, among other things, to revolutionize and modernize the Chinese written language and culture. To make sure that the audience understands this point, Chen Kaige inserts a scene in which Zhongliang, with other passengers, is hurrying along the railway, shouting: "Is this the train to Beijing?" Crucially, however, this intention is intercepted when Zhongliang, robbed of all his luggage before boarding the train, is picked up by Dada's gangsters and transported to Shanghai instead. Rather than Beijing, the enlightened capital city of modern China, in which he might have been able to receive a proper education, Zhongliang is literally abducted into a new home, the depraved underground world of Shanghai, where he soon emerges as the favorite son. He is so at home in this Westernized, commercial city that Dada, who may be regarded as Zhongliang's adopted father, says to him: "You belong to Shanghai; Shanghai cannot do without you."[5]

The escape from "home" leads not to liberation and enlightenment but rather to another type of entrapment. In the decadence of Shanghai, Zhongliang remains enslaved to an autocratic, violent, and immoral patriarchal community. His two masters, the poisonous Pangs in the countryside and the poisonous mafia in the metropolis, echo each other in the control they exert over him, and his life in Shanghai, despite its glamor and success, becomes a symmetrical double to his life in Jiangnan. We may even go so far as to say that in fact, it is precisely as he becomes existentially autonomous and seemingly acquires agency as an adult human being that the shadow of the past begins to loom the darkest. He may have physically left "home," but psychically "home" has never left him.

This unfinished relationship with home is evident, for instance, in Zhongliang's affair with a nameless woman. In one scene, in which he is waiting for her in her apartment at Tianxiangli (Heavenly Lane) in Shanghai, we as well as he are transported by hallucinatory images from his current surroundings back to his former home: first, the woman's picture, which bears a striking resemblance to Xiuyi; then a flashback to the scene of Zhongliang's childhood seduction; finally, the woman herself appearing, putting her hands over Zhongliang's eyes from behind – a gesture that once again reminds us of the games Xiuyi used to play with her younger brother. This attachment to a figure who visually conjures the past constitutes an obstacle in Zhongliang's job: despite Dada's urging, Zhongliang is unable to bring himself to destroy this woman. He tries to delay her destruction by prolonging their relationship. In this postponement, this reluctance to execute, we recognize the prelude to his ultimate return home.

The Homecoming . . . As You Wish

Dada's new target is Pang Ruyi, Xiuyi's sister-in-law, whom he wants Zhongliang to seduce. After Xiuyi's husband becomes brain-dead and leaves the clan without a male to succeed the old master, the Pang elders decide to appoint Ruyi as the head of the clan. Since Ruyi is female, they also appoint Duanwu, Ruyi's younger cousin from a poor, distant branch of the family, as her male companion.

Upon receiving instructions for his new task, Zhongliang's first reaction is a firm refusal: "As you know," he says to Dada, "I will never go to the town of the Pangs." The next thing we know, he is there against his conscious will.

Strictly speaking, Ruyi is merely the latest in Zhongliang's series of targets, but what distinguishes her from the other women is precisely her topographical location. The fact that this wealthy and powerful woman lives in his former home means that his seduction of her is inevitably commingled with a fateful revisit to the scene of his own seduction. In the course of the film we are made to understand that Ruyi is topographically distinctive in another sense. Unlike the women in Shanghai, Ruyi is a virgin, a "place" yet untouched by the rest of the world because, having been raised in an opium-filled house, she remains unwanted by most families looking for a prospective daughter-in-law. Despite her "poisonous" history, moreover, Ruyi comes across as a beautiful person with a refreshing, untainted sense of personal integrity.

Like her name, which means "as you wish" in Chinese, Ruyi likes to act according to her own wishes, which are, contrary to her conservative upbringing, entirely independent and liberatory. After becoming the head of the clan, for instance, she orders the retirement of her father's concubines, much to the anger of the clan elders. Then, after meeting Zhongliang, she is direct in her expression of interest in him: one day, she even asks him to teach her how to ride a bicycle. This occasion gives Zhongliang the opportunity to become intimate with her, but when he kisses her on the ear and comes away as usual with one of the earrings, Ruyi reacts by taking off the other earring and offering it to him as well. This unusual event, which epitomizes Ruyi's difference from all the other women Zhongliang has conquered, does not escape the notice of his cohort, who asks: "How come there are two earrings this time?"

If the possession of the single earring is Zhongliang's means of surviving the trauma of an illicit sexual experience, which he must nonetheless keep repeating –

through the screening work of fetishization and continual repression – in order to attain a false sense of equilibrium, this equilibrium is now disturbed by the voluntary gift of the other earring by an unsuspecting Ruyi. By giving him the other earring, Ruyi offers Zhongliang something he had never found at home – a love which does not carry with it the connotations of enslavement, illicitness, and humiliation. As such, Ruyi's boldness and spontaneity stand as a force that has the potential of pulling Zhongliang out of the stupor that is his entire existence so far. Through this "virgin territory" that is the independent-minded woman at home, Zhongliang could have found redemption. Yet in spite of this, he remains unmoved. In a scene following the offer of the second earring, we find him displaying disgust at Ruyi, who, being in love, has secretly gone into his room to look at his belongings. Instead of reciprocating her attention, Zhongliang merely feels resentful and loses his temper. Accusing her of a lack of respect for his privacy, he reminds her bitterly of the class hierarchy that used to separate them – that he was, at one time, a servant at her house.

The Seduction of the Seduced

The strong, innocent woman who offers him true love thus remains, topographically, a goal which Zhongliang has the potential of reaching but somehow misses. Instead, he continues to aim consciously at the Ruyi that is his professional target – the rich woman to be cheated, blackmailed, and then abandoned. As in the case of his journey toward Beijing, however, Zhongliang's conscious move toward Ruyi is diverted en route, bringing about an unexpected turn in his plan. This turn occurs when Ruyi asks Zhongliang to meet her in the family boathouse by the riverside one evening. For her, it is a rendezvous with a new found love; for him, it is an opportunity to carry out his duty and finally have sex with her. As they begin to make love, Zhongliang, confident that Ruyi is inexperienced and that he should take control, suddenly hears her confess: in order to please him (who she believes likes women more than girls because of the picture of the nameless woman she has seen in his belongings), she says, she has already had sex with Duanwu. She has deliberately gotten rid of her virginity so that he would love her.

Zhongliang's face at this point has nothing of the look of someone who is happy at discovering that he is being loved. Instead, it is contorted with anguish. Since the film narrative does not offer any explanation, we must use the clues we have to speculate. Ruyi's independent behavior overwhelms Zhongliang, we might say, not because she has casually given her virginity to someone whom she does not really love nor even because she has performed a selfless deed for his sake. Rather, it overwhelms him because she has unwittingly plunged him into the abyss of his own past. For, in sacrificing her virginity, her *integrity*, for him, is Ruyi not exactly like the other women, and ultimately like Xiuyi? And, is Ruyi's incestuous relationship with Duanwu not a frightful mirror image of Xiuyi's incestuous relationship with Zhongliang years ago? With the binding intensity of the unanticipated *déjà vu*, Ruyi's confession strikes Zhongliang as if it were *his own* flashback, his own involuntary memory: though (and perhaps precisely as) a picture performed by *others*, it forces him to recognize himself. Like the character Cheng Dieyi in Chen's *Farewell My Concubine* who is finally tamed by the sight of a performance of the story he has been resisting, Zhongliang is finally tamed and, instead of seducing others, becomes seduced once again into playing the role that is his fate.[6]

If this chance (re)seduction of Zhongliang, which constitutes the major narrative turning point, can be described as the ultimate meaning of his homecoming, what is the relationship between seduction and home? Etymologically, "seduction" refers to a leading astray, the opposite of going home. As the paradigm of Odysseus demonstrates, a man must, in order to return home, be determined to stave off seduction – to refuse to succumb to the sirens. In *Temptress Moon*, importantly, this classic opposition between home and seduction has broken down. Consciously, indeed, home is what Zhongliang resists and rejects, and yet in his negative, flighty mode as a professional seducer, he seems nonetheless to keep turning back, to keep clinging to something he does not fully comprehend. And, as he tries to ignore his own feelings about "home" and ventures forth with the task of seduction in cold-blooded indifference toward everyone at home, including the innocent woman who loves him, what he stumbles upon is none other than the "homely" (intimate), yet also seduced (gone-astray), part of himself.

Seductions of the former home involve the memory of and attachment to the entire scenario of Zhongliang's early encounter, a scenario composed by particular configurations of relationships in their enigmatic violence and intensity. Such violence and intensity have remained unrecognized, we may say, until Zhongliang sees it in the form of an other, an image presented by another person. If this *imaging* of how "others do it" may be described as a visual guide to home, then homecoming itself is, strictly speaking, a seduction of the already seduced. Working by the force of memory, which erupts at the sight/site of that which has already been experienced once before, this homecoming can be extraordinarily powerful. In fact, it is lethal.

What is most interesting about this double seduction – this state of being seduced encountering itself at the sight/site of an other – is that it no longer revolves around one particular character. At the point of Zhongliang's discovery of Ruyi's relationship with Duanwu, the story line of *Temptress Moon* is no longer narratologically reducible to the relationship between the "leading" characters, Zhongliang and Ruyi, but must instead be understood as a series of compound relationships involving differentiations on multiple planes and scales, including the sexual, familial, class, rural, metropolitan, modern, and feudalist. Such differentiations, moreover, exceed any restrictive hierarchical arrangement. A diagram would help clarify their superimposed nature as follows:

Zhongliang and Xiuyi	: Duanwu and Ruyi	: Zhongliang and Ruyi
Zhongliang and Xiuyi	: Zhongliang and women in Shanghai	: Zhongliang and woman at Tianxiangli
Zhongliang and the Pangs	: Zhongliang and the Shanghai mafia	
Zhongliang and the Shanghai mafia	: Duanwu and the Pangs	

In these relationship-series, every character becomes the narrative hinge for the emergence and development of another character, and every relationship becomes the double of another relationship. The subjectivity of a character is, hence, no longer a matter of his/her inner world but is the result of his/her interactions with others. Accordingly, the significance of each character no longer has an independent value but can only be established through his/her entanglement with other characters. While this may be obvious, it is also worth emphasizing in consideration of our persistently essentialist ways of thinking about characterization (as real-life persons). In *Temptress Moon*, since "meaning" cannot stabilize upon such multi-layered relationships, characterization takes on a topographical or even archaeological significance: characters themselves become intersecting places or crossroads, digs or ruins, all with multifaceted messages. In the case of Zhongliang, for instance, "character" is the meeting of a "prehistory," in which lie the remnants of a traumatic experience, which he does not under-stand and cannot express, and a "posthistory," which is a belated, deferred re-imaging, in the form of an other (scene), of that prehistory. If the ineluctab-ility of this meeting is an ineluctable return home, then homecoming itself is always (the repetition of) a going-astray, a departure that has already taken place.

The Man in Flight, the Women Bound, and the Country-Bumpkin-Turned-Nouveau-Riche

As the film approaches its end, Zhongliang is unsettled by his own feelings for Ruyi but must still fulfill his duty to Dada. Dada has meanwhile sensed that Zhongliang has changed. In order to prevent further harm, he decides to stage a scene in which Ruyi will discover for herself Zhongliang's identity as a gigolo. Dada is convinced that, once Ruyi sees this, she will no longer love Zhongliang, and Zhongliang will have to become once again his professionally cool and efficient self. This exposure of Zhongliang happens in Shanghai. By intricate arrangements, Ruyi is indeed forced to witness Zhongliang's act from the window of an apartment opposite his in Shanghai: He is making love to the woman at Tianxiangli for the last time, with the gangsters breaking in in their usual fashion, with threats for the woman, and so forth. Only this time, the woman, who refuses to be blindfolded and insists on confronting Zhongliang, commits suicide upon learning the truth.

Contrary to Dada's expectations, Ruyi remains determined in her love for Zhongliang. Even so, she is unable to hear from Zhongliang what she wants the most – the verbal affirmation that he, too, loves her. Heartbroken, Ruyi returns to the countryside and prepares to marry another man. Upon learning that Ruyi is to get married, Zhongliang hurries back to his former home once more and confesses that he does, in fact, love her. He even proposes that the two of them elope to Beijing "for real this time." Ruyi refuses to change her mind. In despair, Zhongliang replicates the other episode that resides in the "primal scene": just as he used arsenic to poison his brother-in-law, so he now prepares a dose of opium mixed with arsenic for Ruyi, who consumes it unawares and becomes brain-dead as well. This act of poisoning completes the saga of Zhongliang's homecoming. As he tries to escape again from the countryside, he is gunned down by Dada's gangsters. If his initial arrival at the Pangs' family residence – by boat at night, through water – is a kind of birth, then the countryside now serves also as his tomb.

Throughout the film, Zhongliang's character is portrayed with a compelling depth, which is the result, ironically, of his need from the very first to escape. Like many writers of the May Fourth period (the landmark period in which Chinese literature became "modern"), Chen relies for the construction of male subjectivity on what may be called the paradigm of fright-and-flight.[7] Hence, just as in the preceding *Farewell My Concubine*, *Temptress Moon* is full of instances of exaggerated music and sound, body movements, close-ups, and dialogues, which together with the cinematography (by Christopher Doyle) of fast-moving shots and changes of shots amplify the effects of a psychologically persecuted male character who seems always on the run.[8] In narratological terms, Zhongliang is hence constituted – visually and aurally as well as through the plot – by *patterns of departure* that help convey all the questions of his identity: "what is Zhongliang running from?"; "Where is he going?"; "Whom will he meet on the way?"; and so forth. This negative pose of a male character on the run is a kind of "resistance" that, ultimately, delivers him home against his will. At the same time, if such a male "psyche" is the legacy of a mainstream modernism that defines itself in opposition to the *socius*, then what is revealed in the seductions of Zhongliang's homecoming is perhaps the unviability of this dissident masculinity as inscribed in the paradigm of fright-and-flight, a paradigm which is being subverted by the network of characters and relationships that sprawl around Zhongliang like a labyrinth. In the light of this unwilling captivity – and demise – of the Man in Flight, the women characters become very interesting.

Unlike Zhongliang, the women characters are all place-bound, both in terms of their physical and their mental locations: Xiuyi is stuck in the countryside and in her bond to a brain-dead husband; the women of the metropolis are trapped by the Shanghai way of life and by their own illicit sexual desires; even Ruyi, who is the most independent of all, remains a prisoner of her home and her heart. (Even though she is about to get married at the end, she consumes opium one more time simply because it has been prepared by Zhongliang, the man she once loved.) However, if these women are ultimately victimized in various ways by their topographical and bodily confinement (a loveless marriage, psychological destruction, suicide, and brain damage), the bold defiance of patriarchal culture expressed by each of them nevertheless signifies a different concept of flight and departure that may, in due course, not have to lead back to the "home" that is the original place of captivity. As I have commented elsewhere, Chen is typically ambiguous and ambivalent in the manner he handles questions regarding women. Here, as always, he has left the implications of the women characters' fates in the form only of a suggestion, a possibility in all its open-endedness.[9]

Indirectly, Zhongliang's homecoming is what causes the power of the Pang clan to pass to Ruyi's servant-companion Duanwu. Like Zhongliang, Duanwu has been exploited by an older female for sexual purposes, but unlike Zhongliang, he seems to be unperturbed by this "initiation." He remains loyal to Ruyi until they reach Shanghai, where he discovers, he says, the war between the sexes. After Ruyi fails to confirm that Zhongliang loves her, Duanwu rapes her. Later, as they arrive home, he even exposes her relationships with both him and Zhongliang to the man she is about to marry. At the end, when Ruyi becomes permanently brain-damaged by arsenic, Duanwu logically succeeds her as the head of the clan. Like most characters in the film, that of Duanwu is far from being well-developed (his transformation in Shanghai, for instance, lacks persuasiveness), but he is thought-provoking as a type. What Duanwu stands for, in contrast to Zhongliang, is a new type of man – a new class perhaps – who has been abused but who somehow manages not to have repressed and internalized such abuse; instead, when the right moment occurs, this type of man would turn the violence he has experienced to his own advantage by directing it at fresh victims. Lacking the sensitivity and self-doubt, and hence vulnerability, of Zhongliang, Duanwu makes it to the top through petty cunning, hypocrisy, and opportunism. His success is, Chen's film seems to say, the vulgar success of the country-bumpkin-turned-*nouveau riche*.

Filmmaking as Homecoming

For a filmmaker, the paths of seduction lie not only in narrativization or characterization but also in film language itself. Is not the movie screen the ultimate place of irresistible allure? If China and Chinese history are the home to which Chen attempts to return, what might be said about this particular homecoming that is filmmaking?

The story of *Temptress Moon* takes place at a crucial moment in the historical meeting between East and West – the 1911 Revolution, after which China shifted from the imperial to the republican era. Having been documented, described, debated, narrativized, and fantasized countless times, this moment can indeed be rewritten – schematically, of course – as a certain "primal scene" in which violence and progress converge, and in which the traditional, imperial patriarchal society gives way, albeit sluggishly, to a Westernized, feminized, and modernized state, henceforth to be ruled by the will of "the people." A contemporary Chinese director's revisit of this, modern China's critical historical moment, much like Zhongliang's revisit of his former home at the Pangs, cannot be naive or simplistically nativist. This is probably why, besides the convoluted narrative and the superimposed effects of characterization, Chen's film is also remarkably reminiscent of other films about modern China. To that extent, *Temptress Moon* stands as an assemblage of allusions, often calling to mind previous films that one has seen.

To cite a striking example of pure screen resemblance: in the scene in which Duanwu is to receive the honor of being appointed as the companion to Ruyi, who has just been made the head of the clan, the young boy is shown to be running into the ancestral parlor while the entire clan stands in observation of the ceremony. In a great hurry, Duanwu throws his proper clothes on while running. In the context of the story of *Temptress Moon*, this demonstration of haste is rather illogical – there is no reason why Duanwu should need to be rushed in the manner he is – until we realize that the scene is probably an allusion to a scene in the older Chinese director Li Hanxiang's *Huoshao yuanming yuan*.[10] In Li's film, which is set during the reign of the late Qing Emperor Xian Feng, there is a scene featuring Prince Kung, one of the emperor's brothers, who has to rush from Beijing to attend Xian Feng's funeral in Jehol (in 1861). Since, by historical account, clothing for different imperial occasions was greatly ritualized, and since the prince was coming from Beijing in haste, the character in Li's film is shown to be throwing on the proper funereal garb befitting the brother of the emperor as he dashes into the funeral parlor. Chen probably so liked the compelling ambience of that scene that he had to recreate it in his own work, even when it is not contextually necessary.

But the film which has left its marks most vividly on Chen's is, interestingly, not one made by a Chinese director – Bernardo Bertolucci's *The Last Emperor* (a film in which Chen was an extra, playing one of the anonymous guards standing at the entrance to the palace). It is from this film that Chen has made copious imaginative borrowings, from the construction of characters and narrative episodes to the use of architecture, interior décor, lighting, and individual screen images. For instance, just as the bulk of the story of *The Last Emperor* is historically situated in the transition period between the Qing Dynasty and the Republic of China, so the story of *Temptress Moon* begins with the 1911 Revolution, when the Qing Dynasty officially ended, and lasts until around 1920.[11] The poignancy of this epochal moment is in both cases portrayed through the life of a child – Pu Yi, the boy emperor, in one case and Ruyi, the future successor to the "throne" of the Pang clan, in the other. Both children are held captive in a privileged environment that is represented, with fascination, as out of sync with modern times. Like the little Pu Yi, Ruyi is full of mischief. In an early scene, she has to be chased out of the ancestral parlor where girls are not allowed; the doors the elders close in order to shut her inside her quarters are, in terms of cinematographic angles, a clear imitation of the high imperial gates that shut Pu Yi in the Forbidden City.*

Like Pu Yi also, Ruyi ascends to power by accident, when a proper male heir has failed to appear at the necessary moment. When she becomes the head of the Pang clan, Ruyi, once again reminding us of Pu Yi, introduces unprecedented policies that cause great consternation. Her order to retire her father's concubines, an act which is reminiscent of Pu Yi's historic retiring of the eunuchs of the palace, is shown to be a rather futile attempt at household reform. (The scene in which the concubines leave the family estate is visually reminiscent of the one in Bertolucci's film in which the royal family, led by the grown emperor, is forced to leave the forbidden city.) Above all, being cloistered in the prison-like world of her family town, Ruyi is ignorant of and longing for the new, modernized world outside. The arrival of Zhongliang from Shanghai, then, is not unlike the arrival of Reginald Johnston, Pu Yi's Scottish tutor, who brings Western education to the young emperor, including the fashionable item of a bicycle – an important detail which Chen does not neglect to include in his story.

The point of mentioning some of the borrowings Chen has obviously made from other films is not to accuse him of lack of originality. Rather, it is to emphasize that like writing, filmmaking, too, is conditioned by the utterances of others, the references others made in and of the past. In the case of film, of course, the more accurate word to use is "gazes," and what I mentioned as "allusions" a moment ago should be understood not simply as contents of the story but also as *ways of gazing* that have been inscribed in previous films. For a contemporary Chinese director making a film about modern China, the questions are especially complex: if making a film about one's own culture is a certain kind of homecoming, how does one go about mediating between the desire for portraying that "home" exactly as one thinks one knows it and the allure of multiple images that are already made of it by others and seen by millions more? In the light of the thematics of place, then, the older films of Li, Bertolucci, and others must be regarded as so many versions of a *topos* in its dual resonance as geography and as knowledge. Capturing the physical place, modern China, on film, these directors' works have also become sites of learning – visual archives on which directors such as Chen draw for their own work of imaging China. As these others' gazes beckon in their orientalist, exoticizing, or meticulously historical modes, the homecoming that is filmmaking inevitably becomes a process of citation and review, and – even as one produces a new collage of perspectives – of being (re)seduced with the sights/sites of others.

To return to the question of "authenticity" I raised at the beginning, it is virtually impossible for a director such as Chen to be "authentic" – if by "authenticity" we mean the quality of being "bona fide" to the point of containing no

impurities, no traces of others. Once this is understood, we will see that, paradoxically, the impossibility of being authentic is exactly the reason Chen's work
can be so provocative. Not-being-authentic here translates into a remarkable
filmic *self-consciousness*, reflecting and refracting the ways modern China has been
looked at by others, Chinese and non-Chinese, in the past century and a half.

The Final Image of Homesickness

And yet, despite offering a self-conscious statement of what filmmaking amounts
to in the postcolonial age by incorporating into his own film others' gazes and
perspectives, Chen seems unable to overcome a familiar kind of emotion in
relation to home – nostalgia. He expresses this emotion, as he has often done in
his previous works, through children. For his concluding image, Chen inserts an
early scene from the childhood years of Ruyi, Duanwu, and Zhongliang: Ruyi
and Duanwu are playing and running with their backs to the audience; Zhongliang,
slightly older, is coming from the opposite direction facing us. As Ruyi and
Duanwu turn their heads, the three children are looking at us at the same time.
This moment is frozen as the final still. The gazes of the three children are a
reminder of an exclamation made earlier by Zhongliang: "How nice it would
be," he says, "if only we didn't have to grow up!" In terms of theorizations of the
gaze, this *visual* conclusion confirms the ontological-representational relation
that can, according to Slavoj Žižek, be asserted between nostalgia and children.
Žižek argues that in the nostalgic mode, what is fascinating is not so much the
displayed scene as "a certain gaze, the gaze of the 'other,' of the hypothetical,
mythic spectator" who was still able to "take it seriously" (114). "The innocent,
naive gaze of the other that fascinates us in nostalgia," he writes, "is in the last
resort always the gaze of the child" (114).

In terms of place, meanwhile, what the gaze of the child (as explained by
Žižek) signifies is the longing for a *utopia*, a non-place, a place that does not
exist. In the context of *Temptress Moon*, this is borne out by the fact that the
three children were, even as children, never allowed to be innocent, naive, or
happy; childhood for them was not idyllic but filled with abuse and loneliness. In
spite of the knowledge that his film has presented, however, the ending Chen
supplies can only be read as a deliberate erasure of such knowledge. By invoking
(and fetishizing) the gaze of the child, Chen forces certain narrative elements
which have hitherto run quietly parallel to one another to crystallize and converge. The final image makes it possible to articulate these elements for the first
time as *tendencies of idealization* that are present throughout the story from the
beginning. And what is being idealized, whether by way of plot, characterization,
or final screen image, is the non-existent. Like Zhongliang's journey toward
Beijing, and like his designs on Ruyi, the invocation of childhood is a maneuver
that is doomed to fail. The enlightened, revolutionary capital city of modern

China, the pure virgin woman in the countryside, and the still, innocent gazes of children all turn out to be unreachable places. Yet precisely because they are unreachable, they seem all the more "authentic," all the more to be longed for. We thus have the vicious circle of a cultural complex in which idealism leads, as it always does, to homesickness, and vice versa.

Ironically, the implications of Chen's concluding image bring him much closer to the critics who accuse him of forsaking the "authentic" China. In their reluctance to give up what is irretrievably lost, be it a hypothetical childhood or a mythical Chineseness, the director and his critics are finally united as perpetrators of the seductions of a certain kind of homecoming, a well-trodden path familiar to all. As they probably know only too well, such paths lead nowhere. But that, it should be added, is also probably why their homesickness persists.

Notes

This essay is based on the version of the film *Temptress Moon* I saw in Hong Kong in the summer of 1996. Unfortunately, some of the scenes have been edited and cut from the North American version. (Places which contain discrepancies between the Asian and North American versions are marked by asterisks.)

1   This is a problematic the politics of which I have considered in detail in Chow (1995); see in particular Part II, Chapter Four.

2   Story by Chen and Wang Anyi; filmscript by Shu Qi. Please bear in mind that in the Chinese language, *feng yue*, literally "wind, moon," is a euphemism for eroticism or matters of sex.

3   This reference to Diderot has, of course, been made famous by Foucault (77–80).

4   For an authoritative discussion of the problematic of seduction in psychoanalysis, see Laplanche, Chapter 3: "Foundations: Towards a General Theory of Seduction" (89–151).

5   Lee Edelman commented thoughtfully that Zhongliang cannot reach Beijing because he has, literally from the outset, been "shanghaied." Hence, for Zhongliang, Beijing remains nothing more than a fantasy. This is evident in a revealing scene in which he interrogates Ruyi about her ignorance of the outside world. In his pretentious attempt to educate her, he describes Beijing in lyrical, revolutionary, but entirely bookish terms – as a place where the sky is blue, the walls are high, the girl students all have short hair and wear long black skirts, and so forth. While he has thus succeeded in seducing Ruyi with his professed enlightenment, he is painfully aware that he is, in effect, performing his own lack.

6   In *Farewell My Concubine*, Chen takes pains to show the process in which Cheng Dieyi "becomes" the character of the concubine in the opera of the same title. While a boy-apprentice in the Beijing opera troupe with which his mother left him, Dieyi is for a long time unable to accept his role as a woman and unable to speak his lines correctly. Because of this failure, he is severely punished, and he tries to run away. He would have successfully escaped, but on his way he unexpectedly comes across a street performance of none other than the opera *Farewell My Concubine*. Completely absorbed and moved, he changes his mind and returns to the troupe. From then on,

he accepts, performs, and identifies with his assigned role – and fate – of "concubine" to the end.

7   For instance, the typical scenario in some of Lu Xun's short stories is that of a male narrator emotionally shocked by a spectacle of social injustice, regarding which he feels impotent; in spite of his sympathies for the victim(s), such a narrator usually takes flight in one form or another. Likewise, in Ba Jin's *Jia* (*The Family*), the predominant narrative action is placed in the characters who, feeling indignant at the corrupt nature of the feudalist patriarchal family system, attempt to rebel and take leave. Readers acquainted with modern Chinese literature are asked to see a more detailed discussion of this connection with May Fourth writings in Chow (1997), also on *Temptress Moon*, which complements the present discussion. Insofar as Chan associates home and countryside with backwardness, he is modernist in his author-ial perspective, a perspective that is different from the sentimental idealization/romanticization of the countryside as the place of simple and eternal truths that also runs throughout modern and contemporary Chinese literary culture. A recent example of this latter tendency is found in Zhang Yimou's 1995 film *Shanghai Triad*, in which the point-of-view character, a child fascinated by Shanghai, nonetheless sees truth at the end through his experience in the countryside.

8   This can perhaps be described by way of the phrase "motion and emotion" (first used by Wim Wenders); see Tony Rayns's brief discussion, which is based on some of the rushes rather than on the finished film. The North American version of the film, because it has been heavily edited with many abrupt shifts of scenes, comes across as even more discontinuous and discomforting than the version shown in Hong Kong and Taiwan. In "Bulunbulei de youhuo," I offer a related discussion of the effects generated by Chen's use of motion in terms of *melodrama*.

9   For more elaborate discussions of the status of women in Chen's other films, see the relevant sections in Chow (1995).

10 This is one of a series of films made by Li on the late Qing during the 1970s and 1980s. Others include *Chuilian tingzheng, Xi tai hou, Qing guo qing cheng, ying tai xi xue*, and *Huo long*. Li, a director who left mainland China in the 1950s, worked both in Taiwan and Hong Kong. He died in 1996 in the midst of making a film in Beijing. Li first became well-known in the 1960s with films he made for Shaw Brothers Ltd (in Hong Kong) and for his own company Guo Lian (in Taiwan). When box office trends no longer favored the styles of his early works, he made a series of pornographic films in order to stay in the business, and it was due to the success of these pornographic films that he received funding for his major historical films about the late Qing. One of his pornographic films was entitled *Feng yue bao jian* [Precious lessons in matters of sex], which plays on the Chinese term "feng yue," which, as I pointed out, is a euphemism for "matters of sex." Since Li's film, I believe, pornographic films have often been referred to as "Feng yue pian" in Chinese. Is it a coincidence that Chen adopted "Feng yue" as the title of his film?

11 Rayns offers the following account: "In Beijing in 1993, while he was still searching for a scriptwriter for *Temptress Moon* and trying to deal with the Film Bureau's demands for cuts in *Farewell My Concubine*, Chen joked to me that he would defin-itely set his next film in 1920 – a year before the Chinese Communist Party held its first (underground) congress in Shanghai. That way, he implied, his scenario couldn't possibly be accused of misrepresenting the Party's role. So much for jokes in present-day China: the film is indeed set in 1920 . . ." (13).

Works Cited

Ba Jin (1931) *Jia*. Hong Kong: Tiandi tushu [1985].

Chow, Rey (1995) *Primitive Passions: Visuality, Sexuality, Ethnicity, and Contemporary Chinese Cinema*. New York: Columbia University Press.

Chow, Rey (1997) "Bulunbulei de youhou." *Comparative Literature and Cultural Studies* (Fu Jen University, Taipei) 1.

Edelman, Lee (1997) Comment [on Rey Chow's paper], delivered at the Annual Conference of *Narrative*, University of Florida, April.

Foucault, Michel (1980) *The History of Sexuality, Volume 1*, trans. Robert Hurley. New York: Vintage.

George, Rosemary Marangoly (1992) "Traveling Light: Of Immigration, Invisible Suitcases, and Gunny Sacks." *Differences: A Journal of Feminist Cultural Studies* 4:2 (Summer), 72–99.

Laplanche, Jean (1989) *New Foundations for Psychoanalysis*, trans. David Macey. Oxford: Blackwell.

Rayns, Tony (1996) "Motion and Emotion." *Sight and Sound* (March), 11–13.

Žižek, Slavoj (1991) *Looking Awry: An Introduction to Jacques Lacan through Popular Culture*. Cambridge, MA: MIT Press.

23

Cultural Identity and Diaspora in Contemporary Hong Kong Cinema

Julian Stringer

The reader will be forgiven for questioning whether this chapter really belongs in a collection of articles on Asian American screen cultures. After all, my title clearly states that I intend to write about Hong Kong cinema, and Hong Kong cinema is not the same thing as US cinema. If I am not going to focus on the work of Asian Americans, what business does this chapter have being here? My response takes the form of two arguments. First, the Hong Kong films I want to look at are intimately related to the screen life of Asian Americans. Second, these same films are significant because they represent Asian American screen identities that are in the process of formation.

To illustrate these two points, it may be enough simply to observe how the Hong Kong and US film industries already interrelate across a number of levels of influence. Consider the crossover of production personnel. While Chinese and Western filmmakers have long been in the habit of traveling to each other's shores (especially after the Asian American star Bruce Lee achieved international prominence in the early 1970s), the traffic has intensified markedly in recent years. More specifically, as the July 1, 1997, deadline for China's resumption of sovereign control over Hong Kong crept ever nearer, more and more Hong Kong filmmakers made the United. States their home. The case of director John Woo is well known (*Hard Target* [1993]; *Broken Arrow* [1994]; *Face/Off* [1997]), but there is more to the US–Hong Kong film connection than just him. These days, going to the mall just wouldn't be going to the mall without the promise of a new Jackie Chan movie (*Rumble in the Bronx* [Tong 1996b]; *Police Story 3: Supercop* [Tong 1996a]; *Police Story 4: First Strike* [Tong 1997]), and in addition to working with Woo on *Hard Target*, the action star Jean-Claude Van Damme has made films with the Hong Kong directors Ringo Lam (*Maximum Risk* [1996]), and Tsui Hark (*Double Team* [1997]). Actress Maggie Cheung auditioned for a part in *Heat* (Mann and Smithee 1995) but didn't get it; her colleague Sylvia Chang was offered the same role but didn't want it. And as I was writing this chapter, one of Hong Kong's greatest stars, Chow Yun-Fat, was making his Hollywood debut in *The Replacement Killers* (Fuqua 1998), and another top name, Michelle Yeoh, had just appeared in the James Bond film *Tomorrow Never Dies* (Spottiswoode 1997).

Within the bustle of such activity lie the seeds of an emergent Asian American cinema. Although this cinema may still be limited to the action-movie genre, the links that connect Hong Kong to Hollywood have already been recognized and welcomed by both mainstream industry personnel and Asian American media workers. For example, while the former honored Jackie Chan with an MTV lifetime award in 1995, the members of the Asian American Arts Foundation (a fund-raising organization in the San Francisco Bay Area) extended their own welcome to Chow Yun-Fat by presenting him with a Transpacific Award during their annual ceremony in 1994. During his special appearance at the Center for the Arts Theater in San Francisco's Yerba Buena Gardens, Chow rubbed shoulders with such celebrated Asian Americans as the author Maxine Hong Kingston and the artist Ruth Asawa.

In addition to this crossover of talent, recent Hong Kong titles as generically and stylistically diverse as *Alan and Eric – Between Hello and Goodbye* (Chan 1991), *A Better Tomorrow II* (Woo 1987), *Comrades, Almost a Love Story* (Chan 1998), *Eight Taels of Cold* (Cheung 1989), *Farewell China* (Law 1990), *The Master* (Tsui 1991a), *My American Grandson* (Hui 1991), *Once Upon a Time in China and America* (Kam-Bo 1997), *Siao Yu* (Chang 1995), and *Twin Dragons* (Lam and Tsui 1992) have made the experiences of Asian Americans part of their very subject matter. Such films explore related questions. What are the constituent features of Hong Kong's new postcolonial identity? How has mass migration and displacement affected this sense of identity? What can the United States offer traveling Chinese?

These works do not resemble the kind of Asian American cinema that some people have already begun to identify and celebrate, but they do anticipate the formation of new Asian American screen cultures. Each of these titles can be read as a map, a guidebook offering advice to prospective overseas Chinese about the skills they need to possess in order to get on in the new world. In other words, they anticipate what a future cinema may look like. (And as Mandarin becomes Hong Kong's next official language, the Cantonese vernacular may yet live on in the cinematic diaspora.) If nothing else, the exploration of such thematic material presents filmmakers with a practical link to Asian Americans working inside the US film industry, and hence with the possibility of securing work through the manipulation of new channels of cooperation and funding.[1] The phenomenon also exhibits a marked circularity. Many of the filmmakers who established or benefited from Hong Kong's post-1979 "New Wave" were themselves educated in the United States (Allen Fong, Tsui Hark, Mabel Cheung). Their successors are now well placed to lead Hong Kong's productive infiltration into the American film industry.

The historical fact of mass migration has, crucially, also set the seal on the consolidation of an active Hong Kong fan culture across the United States. Fueled by the obsessions and resources of those who have brought their city's movie madness with them, these subcultural consumers are transforming the marketplace. Main Street video shops now stock the odd kung-fu title and Chinese ghost movie, and in addition to articles in specialist magazines, mass-market publications such as *The New Yorker* and *Time* carry features on key films and stars.[2] Put these various clusters of activity together and it is not hard to see how the Hong Kong film diaspora will play a key role in determining the direction some Asian American screen cultures are likely to move in over the next few years.

At the same time, however, it should also be recognized that the migration of Hong Kong residents alone does not fully account for the increasing popularity of Hong Kong films in the mainstream US marketplace. The distribution of titles to other Asian societies with large migrant streams to the United States, such as China and Taiwan, should also be acknowledged, as should the popularity of Hong Kong action stars among African American audiences.[3] Most significantly, interest in Hong Kong movies is growing among many Asian Americans who grew up in the United States. Spurred by the work of Asian American programmers, Hong Kong film festivals are springing up on more and more college campuses, and Asian Media Access, an Asian American nonprofit organization operating out of Minneapolis, is striking new prints of contemporary classics to meet the demand. This phenomenon is explored in *Beyond Asiaphilia* (1997), a short video by the Asian American director Valerie Soe. Juxtaposing Soe's own autobiographical experiences with interviews with a number of Asian American men about their avid interest in Hong Kong movies, the video makes explicit connections between the reception of Hong Kong cinema in the United States and the recognition and formation of Asian American identities.

The significance of such cultural practices, then, cannot be established solely through a consideration of the changes brought about by the spread of the Hong Kong diaspora. The reception of Hong Kong cinema in the United States should not be separated from larger questions of Asian American history. As recent work on immigration trends makes clear, any discussion of Asian American identity needs to take into account a range of economic, political, and cultural factors that are linked to the global restructuring and integration taking place across the Pacific Rim as well as within the United States (Ong, Bonacich, and Cheng 1994; Hamamoto and Torres 997). These factors have contributed to the conditions necessary for the mass acceptance of Hong Kong movies in the United States.

Although this is not the place to go into great detail about what these extremely broad and complex factors are, three in particular should be mentioned. First, the end of the Cold War in 1989, and the Tiananmen Square massacre in June of the same year, generated new and unforeseen relationships among Hong Kong, China, and the United States. Second, the spread of transnational capitalism and the proliferation of global media and instant electronic technology have eroded established cultural boundaries, allowing Hong Kong's popular culture to make deep inroads into American society. Third, the construction of pan-ethnic Asian American alliances in the United States offers an environment that is supportive of cultural artifacts that express the diversity of the Asian American experience (Espiritu 1992).

These reconfigurations have focused attention on the dynamics of Asian American identity. According to L. Ling-Chi Wang, much previous social-science research on the subject worked within a dual paradigm that conceptualized Asian Americans as subject to both racial exclusion and oppression through strict assimilation to Anglo-American norms, and through residual loyalty to an imagined homeland (Wang 1995, 159). Against this reductive schema, Wang advances the proposition that Asian American identity should be represented through an alternative paradigm – one that fully recognizes the legitimacy of the cultural assets and values that immigrants bring to the United States and the integral part they play in its vision. This paradigm must also recognize that Asian Americans are entitled to all the rights and privileges promised in the Declaration of Independence and in the US constitution. In addition, changing global conditions need to be understood as a continuous influence on the formation of Asian American identities: "*Under the new paradigm, racial exclusion or oppression and extraterritorial domination converge and interact in the Chinese American community, establishing a permanent structure of dual domination and creating its own internal dynamics and unique institutions*" (ibid.; italics in original).

In another recent article, Wang further problematizes the dual structure of assimilation and loyalty by probing the importance of the concept of "roots" for diasporic Chinese societies. He offers a typology of how the term has been signified within Asian American and Anglo-American locations. To summarize these briefly, the concept of the *sojourner mentality* refers to the image of Chinese as aliens, strangers, pariahs, and outcasts; *total assimilation* assumes that Chinese Americans come to regard the need to be accepted by white society as their primary obsession; *accommodation* means the forced settling down in a foreign land and public adoption of its lifestyle (e.g., the situation that some Chinese students faced in the United States after Tiananmen) and differs from *assimilation* in that its terms are worked out by Chinese themselves; *ethnic pride and consciousness* seek to liberate Chinese Americans from the dual domination of racial oppression and extraterritorial domination through the development of a distinct Chinese American identity, one rooted in experience and a belief in a community with shared interests and a common destiny in the United States; and, finally, *the uprooted* refers primarily to those elite overseas students who decide, for a variety of reasons, not to return to their countries of origin. Many of these elites then opt for *accommodation* in the new environment (Wang 1991).

The mapping of such a typology suggests the complexity of images of migration to the United States in Hong Kong cinema, as well as the diversity of issues that are potentially opened for Asian American audiences in the act of reception. Indeed, when considering the increasing popularity of Hong Kong movies in the United States, one might start by asking how the terms of Wang's paradigm are reflected in the ways that individual titles explore questions of migration and arrival.

Three recent films from Hong Kong introduce the subject of migration to the United States in order to suggest how they signify Asian American identities in the process of formation. The films are *An Autumn Tale* (Cheung 1988), *Full Moon in New York* (Kwan 1990), and *Rumble in the Bronx* (Tong 1996b). After noting these films' engagement with issues of cultural identity and displacement, I will offer a short critique of what some critics consider their aesthetic and political limitations.

In each of these three titles, the United States is imagined as what Stuart Hall (1994, 401) calls "the third term" – namely, a cultural space, neither Chinese nor European, where East meets West and new identities are negotiated. This "third term" encompasses two different ways of thinking about "cultural identity." On the one hand, it gestures toward a shared culture, "a sort of collective 'one true self,' hiding inside the many other, more superficial or artificially imposed 'selves,' which people with a shared history and ancestry hold in common" (ibid., 393). On the other hand, there is a "second, related but different view of cultural identity. This second position recognizes that, as well as the many points of similarity, there are also critical points of deep and significant *difference* which constitute 'what we really are.' . . . Cultural identity, in this second sense, is a matter of 'becoming' as well as of 'being.' It belongs to the future as much as to the past" (ibid., 394).

These three films open "the third term" as a space for the formation of Asian American identities by exploring two interrelated themes – namely, the specific nature of Hong Kong's postcolonial situation and the diverse aspirations and experiences of Chinese immigrants to the United States. Clearly, new identities are being negotiated here within a different cultural space because of Hong Kong's own stature as a global city. When local citizens are already participants in the international economy, old structures of domination no longer apply. *An Autumn Tale*, *Full Moon*, and *Rumble* work to establish common ground between the old and new worlds by putting questions of travel and arrival into dialogical engagement with each other. This is not a case of "culture clash" or the assimilation–loyalty binary so much as it is the exploration of a variety of in-between social positions. In other words, the films concern themselves with the subtle teasing out of similarities and differences among Chinese, Chinese American, and Asian American subjectivities.

A quick plot summary of each title should help illustrate the appropriate dramatic situations. *An Autumn Tale* concerns Jennifer (Cherie Cheung), a Hong Kong student enrolled in acting classes at New York University and the problems she faces in the United States. Living in a poor neighborhood, she receives help from her cousin, a former sailor and Chinatown community leader named Sam Pan (Chow Yun-Fat). The two become more intimate with each other after Jennifer discovers that her "Westernized" boyfriend from Hong Kong, Vincent (Danny Chan), has discovered "free choice" and begun to date an Asian American woman. However, Jennifer and Sam Pan do not consummate their relationship. When Jennifer finally takes a job on Long Island – with the implication that she will hook up once more with the economically mobile Vincent – Sam Pan is left to face a bleak future alone in Chinatown. A final scene reunites Jennifer and Sam Pan, but the meeting is revealed as nothing more than a fantasy projection (hers? his?).

In *Full Moon*, three Chinese women meet and strike up a friendship. Lee Jieu (Maggie Cheung) is a lesbian real estate speculator and restaurant owner from Hong Kong; Wang Hsiung Ping (Sylvia Chang) is a politically savvy actress from Taiwan; and Zhao Hong (Siqin Gaowa) is a newlywed from Shanghai with a boorish Chinese American husband and a desire to bring her mother to the States. The three women endure numerous confrontations and misunderstandings, but they soon come to respect and share the strategies each has chosen for survival within the Big Apple's inhospitable terrain.

Rumble opens with the arrival of Keung (Jackie Chan) from Hong Kong for a three-month visit to his Chinese American relatives in New York. Keung soon befriends the new owner of his uncle's former supermarket, Helena (Anita Mui), as well as a member of the local street gang, a young Asian American woman named Nancy (Francoise Yip). While helping out at the supermarket and looking after his family, Keung gets in trouble with the hoodlums and ends up in a number of fights. Later, though, Keung and the gang cooperate with each other to defeat a bunch of murderous diamond thieves.

These three films, in different ways and with different degrees of success, represent Hall's two conceptions of cultural identity as the struggle between "being" Chinese and "becoming" Asian American (Feng 1996). In *An Autumn Tale*, for example, the fact that Jennifer and Sam Pan occupy different class positions affects the formation of their Asian American identities. Although both live in Brooklyn and mix with whites, Latinos, and African Americans, Jennifer's command of English and deployment of middle-class social skills enables her to move to the suburbs of Long Island by securing a job as a babysitter for the daughter of a rich Asian American woman, while Sam Pan is left to mingle and fight with the neighborhood Chinese gangs. His experiences frustrate him: "You talk all yes talk, I talk all no talk," he complains to one white policeman. Jennifer is able to establish a new identity with her university friends without assimilating to white norms. Despite his aspiration to "get the green card, then the gold card," Sam Pan has no means to move out of Chinatown. When he picks Jennifer up from the airport in the opening scene, Sam Pan amuses himself by speaking in Japanese, precisely because the African American cop who moves him along cannot distinguish among different Asian people. Indeed, by the time Jennifer leaves him, Sam Pan appears to have lost all hope of individuality – he will shout "I AIN'T NO YELLOW COW!" at cops for the rest of his days. (In an iconic moment, familiar from so many other Hong Kong movies, the smile has been wiped off Chow Yun-Fat's face.) It is significant, however, that while Jennifer opts for accommodation in her new environment, Sam Pan's situation is all the more poignant for being left unresolved. By the end of the film, his cultural identity cannot be defined easily within the parameters of Wang's typology. Sam Pan's experiences could form the basis of a new ethnic pride and consciousness, or they could lead to his stigmatization via the terms of the sojourner mentality. The very openness of these different possibilities suggests the presence of "the third term."

Jackie Chan dramatizes the process of "becoming" Asian American through the development of his transnational star image, which has now taken on a global orientation. In *Rumble*, as in all of his recent work, Chan functions first as a repository of Chinese cultural values overseas, and his position as a charming intermediary between warring factions ("Don't you know," he implores a gang of toughs, "you are the scum of Society?") provides a perfect metaphor for this transnational success. Yet Chan is a highly ambiguous figure. His image appeals differently to different audiences, whose responses again suggest the opening up of "the third term" for his Asian American fans.

Consider four aspects of *Rumble*. First, part of the film's interest lies in the fact that, although the codes of decency and loyalty trotted out in the script suggest traces of the logic of Chinese extraterritorial domination, the narrative (unusual for a crossover US hit) nowhere suggests its binary opposite – assimilation to white norms. Second, the fact that music by a variety of African American artists was added to the soundtrack for US release suggests a conscious attempt to appeal to black audiences.[4] Third, although Chan's image combines not just the moral conviction that comes from a perfect coordination of mind and body but also a raging sexuality, it is telling that the love interest in this and other Jackie Chan films distributed in the United States is rather tentatively, and con-fusingly, split. In *Rumble*, he is set up with Helena, then with Nancy, but neither romance is developed conclusively. Although this narrative strategy – the hero is allowed to fight but not fuck – is certainly common in the martial-arts genre, it also plays very neatly into the US mainstream media's stereotyping of Asian American men as asexual beings. Finally, however – and most importantly – the interviews in *Beyond Asiaphilia* testify to how some Asian American spectators resist such stereotypes by relishing the physical display and sexual power of Chan's body.

Themes of sexual power and performance, and of the adoption of a new identity as necessary for the process of survival in the United States, are also picked up in *Full Moon*. During one memorable scene, Hsiung Ping auditions for the role of Lady Macbeth, but she is turned down by a white male casting director, who bleats, "What makes a Chinese woman, or a Japanese woman, think that she can play Lady Macbeth?" (Even with Hsiung Ping's excellent command of English, she significantly is not referred to here as an Asian American; it is also significant that, like the black cop in *An Autumn Tale*, the man patronizingly conflates two completely different Asian cultures.) After describing the singularly vicious brutalities that a certain Chinese empress inflicted on her enemies, Hsiung Ping, a hint of disgust around her mouth, retorts, "With an ancestor like the empress, don't tell me I cannot play Lady Macbeth!"[5]

Part of the negotiation of issues of cultural identity and displacement in these films involves an exploration of the gap between the imaginative potential offered by travel to the new world and the humdrum fact of arrival. In *An Autumn Tale*, Sam Pan paints a picture of the Brooklyn Bridge for Jennifer because she cannot afford a room with a real view. Later, as she drives across the bridge with Vincent, the painting is framed next to its original referent, suggesting the distance between fantasy and reality. This sense that a potential space exists between the articulation of existing and emergent identities is further emphasized in *Full Moon*. For example, there is the moment when Zhao Hong, after talking with Ah Jieu about geomancy, attempts to bring the good *chi* of New York City into her high-rise apartment by opening all of its windows. After she has done so, a reverse shot takes us outside, and a slow zoom pulls back to reveal her living space as just one small box among many others. How many stories lie untold behind so many closed curtains? Kwan punctuates the narrative with brief shots of city exteriors, which, in addition to offering viewers the visual memory of another dazzling skyline (Hong Kong's), generate an uncanny feeling of complete stasis. Even when camera movement is used, it produces an unusual effect. When a crane shot traverses an empty street, the movement is executed in slow motion, approximating how an unfamiliar space may appear ominous and strange to the newcomer.

As a number of historians have noted, since the mid-1960s real-estate investment has promised to allow urbanized Chinese societies in the United States the chance to grow and, hence, to allow Asian American identities to flourish within the sanctuary of "ethnic enclaves" (Kwong 1987). *Full Moon* exhibits a significant thematic focus on real-estate investment among Chinatown denizens. However, as Sam Pan's experiences in *An Autumn Tale* testify, the reality is that overseas Chinese more often than not end up trapped and exploited within economically depressed ghettos. The main characters in Kwan's film struggle to move out of their own "ethnic enclaves," but this is not presented as a simple case of assimilation to mainstream values. From "little Hong Kong" to Manhattan, *Full Moon* opens a potential space where a new paradigm of identity can be formulated. The film recognizes that Asian Americans occupy all parts of the social- and economic-class spectrum and so cannot be typed in any casual manner.[6]

Rumble occupies an in-between social status by the very fact that it is itself something of a hybrid. Distributed state to state by New Line Pictures, but rush-released to meet a Chinese New Year deadline, the film does more than just exhibit a duality of languages (English and Cantonese) on its soundtrack.

The movie works as a synthesis of the Hong Kong action film and the US juvenile-delinquency picture. The Chinese family and business obligations that so often make their way into Jackie Chan star narratives are placed back to back with a wild assortment of marginalized and multiracial characters, making the whole package play like an updated version of *Rebel Without a Cause* (Ray 1955). The new Chinese kid on the block is taunted until he fights back, a younger man idolizes his friend, and there is even a nighttime chicken run (performed this time not by two car-driving buddies on a desolate hillside but by two young urban women on motorbikes). Such scenes illustrate the range of social alliances that open in the process of negotiating different Asian American identities.

To return to Hall's other definition of cultural identity, however, it is also possible to see how each of the three films tries to construct a shared identity among people of Chinese descent. That is to say, there is a simultaneous attempt to locate a spiritual core of "Chineseness," a collective "one true self" that remains apart from mainstream US culture. The narratives describe various ways in which overseas Chinese are interpellated into the United States at the same time that they construct representations of "true Chineseness." And yet, because these titles locate examples of what the subaltern studies scholar Partha Chatterjee calls an "inner domain of national culture" in different places, the fact that such notions of extraterritorial domination coexist simultaneously with global cultural dynamics is highlighted.

For Chatterjee, the "inner domain" of a postcolonial national culture is the colonial subject's "essential" spiritual and cultural identity, the "outer domain" the Western-style material culture that is resisted:

> The material is the domain of the "outside," of the economy and of statecraft, of science and technology, a domain where the West had proved its superiority and the East had succumbed. . . . The spiritual, on the other hand, is an "inner" domain bearing the "essential" marks of cultural identity. The greater one's success in imitating Western skills in the material domain, therefore, the greater the need to preserve the distinctiveness of one's spiritual culture. . . . Nationalism declares the domain of the spiritual its sovereign territory and refuses to allow the colonial power to intervene in that domain. . . . The colonial state, in other words, is kept out of the "inner" domain of national culture, but it is not as though this so-called spiritual domain is left unchanged. In fact, here nationalism launches its most powerful, creative and historically significant project: to fashion a "modern" national culture that is nevertheless not Western. [Chatterjee 1993, 6]

It may come as no surprise that, as a metaphor for the uniqueness of being Chinese, a sensitivity to the delights of food surfaces in each film, and that this sensitivity is then contrasted with the blandness of "American" cuisine. Sam Pan teaches Jennifer how to cook proper ginger soup; Ah Jieu owns a Hunan restaurant (but one that specializes in Peking Duck!); and Keung helps out at the local Chinese grocery store. However, it is worth drawing attention to two other subjects explicitly tied into this "inner" culture.

In *An Autumn Tale*, the Chinatown gambling den provides Sam Pan with his retreat from trouble and strife. A spate of gambling films dominated the Hong Kong box office during the late 1980s, and these scenes of Chow Yun-Fat trying his luck with the arbitrary fates dealt out at card games – flaunting his wad before losing the lot – foreshadow the same actor's later incarnation as the "God of Gamblers" (*God of Gamblers* [Wong 1989] and *God of Gamblers Returns* [Wong 1995]). As linked to economic and class mobility, the aesthetics of gambling are based on chance and luck rather than on work and achievement. Mabel Cheung's decision to include such a location in a movie about Asian Americans in the Big Apple raises a number of issues – about the restructuring of economic relations between Hong Kong and New York, about the hopes and disappointments that accompany overseas migration, and about how gambling in Chinatown can itself provide the cause of nothing but trouble and strife.

In *Full Moon*, the emphasis is more on the body as the site of core identities. The focus in Kwan's film is on the politics of sex and romance. The three protagonists first meet at Lee Jieu's restaurant, where, after taking one look at the menu, Hsiung Ping accuses Jieu of adapting Chinese dishes to Western tastes. Jieu, who has been trying to evict Hsiung Ping's white boyfriend from one of her apartments, spits back that, no, Hsiung Ping herself is the Chinese dish offered up for American tastes. This concern with the racial and ethnic politics of sexuality later finds its boldest statement in Kwan's visualization and celebration of Chinese gayness. Hsiung Ping tells Zhao Hong about the mainland's long tradition of homosexuality, a tradition that the film insists has been suppressed and needs representing. Such rhetoric encourages sympathetic subcultural reception practices, just as the film as a whole encourages people from distinct Chinese societies to learn to live with their own differences. What is being validated is the very diversity of a community with shared values and a common destiny in the United States.

Now, a short critique of what might be considered the aesthetic limitations of these films. In his work on the postcolonial dynamics of modern Hong Kong cinema, Ackbar Abbas notes that the exploration of spatial and temporal issues has been a central and impressive concern – witness the use of time travel and reincarnation narratives, the balancing of multiple diegetic spaces in titles such as *Rouge* (Kwan 1987), *Iceman Cometh* (Fok 1989), *Center Stage* (Kwan 1991), *The Reincarnation of Golden Lotus* (Law 1989), and *Song of the Exile* (Hui 1990). These films distinguish themselves through brilliant use of multiple temporal frameworks (Abbas 1997; Stringer 1997). Such manipulation of space and time allows these films to travel internationally by galvanizing art cinema and film festival audiences. In addition, these films have drawn attention to the importance of issues of social mobility and fantasy to Hong Kong's own historical situation.

By contrast, Hong Kong films that imagine the United States and Asian American identities are noticeably less likely to take on board such spatial and temporal issues. The ability to imagine another time and another place presupposes the ability to be socially mobile, to be able to move on to someplace else. *An Autumn Tale*, *Full Moon*, and *Rumble* exhibit a lack of mobility across space and time, a diegetic stasis that indicates a fundamental inability to imagine the coexistence of other times and other places. Abbas implied this when he made the observation that, next to films such as *Rouge* and *Center Stage*, some of the Hong Kong film industry's "attempts to be 'international' – by using a foreign city as background, for example, as in Clara Law's [*sic*] well-regarded *Autumn Story*, a film about Hong Kong Chinese in New York made in the late eighties – may strike us as awkward and provincial" (Abbas 1997, 28).[7]

This criticism cuts two ways. Abbas has elsewhere suggested that Hong Kong cinema's recent love affair with high-tech special effects and spectacle enables the formation of its unique postcolonial identity ("a postcoloniality that precedes decolonization" [ibid., 6]). "This interest in special effects suggests not only that the Hong Kong cinema has caught up with the new technologies; more importantly, it now places the filmic action in a new technological, and by implication, transnational space" (Abbas 1996, 298). Innovative and fantastic special effects please diverse international audiences and promote Hong Kong's film industry as technologically more advanced than that of the People's Republic of China. More than that, the effects help open up what Abbas (echoing Hall) calls "the third space" – "where East and West are overcome and discredited as separate notions, and another space or a space of otherness is introduced" (ibid., 300). Against these standards, the three films I have been looking at must be branded aesthetically impoverished and found wanting. By the time he made *Rumble*, not even Jackie Chan could push his body to perform the stunts he was able to do as a younger man; *An Autumn Tale*'s final fantasy scene is noticeably lackluster, a matter of a simple, "impossible" change from day to night in the space of one shot; and *Full Moon* has none of the subtlety of some of Kwan's earlier and later work.

Yet it seems to me that Abbas misses an important point here: Hong Kong films about the United States and Asian Americans are working with a set of concerns that resonate in the act of *reception* as much as they resonate textually. The "third space" they aim to introduce may be another space, or a space of Otherness, but is also a very specific geographical location – in this case, New York. This space is not just presented as a site for the allegorical disappearance of Hong Kong cultural identity. It also functions as a location for the mapping out of potential Asian American identities. For this reason, it is somewhat unfair to compare the promise of a new space imagined in Hong Kong with the reality found by filmmakers who have traveled on location to the United States. When Sam Pan beats up the owner of a Chinese restaurant in *An Autumn Tale*, for example, the scene undoubtedly appears "awkward and provincial" when compared with the sensational kung-fu dramas that Abbas writes about, such as *Once Upon a Time in China* (Tsui 1991b) and *Ashes of Time* (Wong 1994). But because the stunning visual compositions conjured up in these two movies would be out of place in Brooklyn, Cheung suggestively stages her fight scene for what it is – namely, a low-budget parody of a similar interethnic fight scene from *The Godfather* (Coppola 1972).

Or, to give another illustration, when Jennifer first reaches New York, she is advised by Vincent to take advantage of all that the new world has to offer. "Now you're here," he tells her, "you should experience different lifestyles and broaden your horizons." Later, as Jennifer and Sam Pan discuss their lives while strolling along the shore of Long Island, Jennifer repeats this advice in the form of an assertion that she wants to travel and see the world. For Sam Pan, however, the search is over. "I've been everywhere," he says, smiling. "I want to stay here and open a restaurant facing the Atlantic Ocean." The point this exchange is trying to make is clear: Sam Pan may not get to fulfill his dream because, unlike Jennifer, he can't speak English, he is structurally excluded from New York's capitalist miracle, and he has no white friends. Yet by offering a highly tentative fantasy in its very last moments, the film suggests that Sam Pan may yet come to embody an alternative paradigm of Asian American identity.

The creative exploration of such themes should not be confused with a failure of nerve or lack of experimentation on the part of traveling Hong Kong filmmakers. Compared with other recent titles from the settlement, these three films do not strike the viewer as particularly eye-popping or gut-wrenching because they use a very down-to-earth style to locate very down-to-earth material. While concerned with the diasporic consciousness of Chinese people who have made it to the new world, they do not imagine the United States as itself a place of mobility. This contradiction can be read as anxiety over the threat of assimilation and over the loss of an "essential" "inner domain" – a "one true self" – within the dynamics of migration and postcolonialism. The attractions of *An Autumn Tale*, *Full Moon*, and *Rumble* pull in different directions. On the one hand, their narratives dramatize how the immigrant may lose social mobility and monetary power once she or he arrives in Uncle Sam's backyard. On the other hand, they do this productively by exploring some of the forms that Asian American identities may take.

The most successful recent films from Hong Kong construct a new localized subjectivity through an imaginative manipulation of formal questions, opening a space where transcultural identities may flourish after 1997. Films that imagine the United States sacrifice this in favor of a flattening out of imaginative potential. Aspiring to explore similarities and differences within and between Chinese, Chinese American, and Asian American identities, they expose audiences to the migrant's own experiences and to her or his own vulnerability and lack of opportunity, as well as to the ethnic pride and consciousness that bonds Asian American communities. Some critics might conclude from this that traveling Hong Kong filmmakers have yet to find ways to integrate themselves into the United States in the manner that Hong Kong star culture has managed to transform US film culture and retain its own "inner" self-identity. However, I would not want to put the blame on unimaginative filmmakers. Rather than perceiving this strategy as a symptom of a short-term artistic retreat, it can be viewed instead as the difficult, but necessary, first step in the long-term project of moving beyond outdated paradigms. Comparing these few titles about Asian American identities with other contemporary movies from Hong Kong, one finds that, although the Chinese diaspora is presented far more imaginatively and fluidly than the realities of Asian American life itself, Asian American cultural identity is still being explored in all of its diversity.

Finally, even if it is true that some titles distributed in the United States do not offer the fascinations and pleasures of effects and spectacle, does this really matter? The indications are that Asian American audiences are using Hong Kong cinema for their own purposes. Fantasies and meanings are being created in the act of reception. As Alvin Lu explains in *Beyond Asiaphilia*, "For a while it was, like, 'Oh, there's no Asians in Hollywood,' but now it doesn't matter. You can just watch Hong Kong movies!" The possibilities opened by such moments of pan-ethnic appropriation are worth support and further consideration.

Notes

Acknowledgments: Thanks to Sandra Liu and Darrell Hamamoto for their extremely detailed and generous advice on an earlier draft of this chapter.

1   Wayne Wang, for example, worked with the Hong Kong director Allen Fong on *Life Is Cheap . . . But Toilet Paper Is Expensive* (1990) and with the actress Maggie Cheung on *Chinese Box* (1997).

2   See Ansen (1996), Corliss (1996), Dannen (1995), and Wolf (1996).

3   Yvonne Tasker (1993, 21–23) has noted the influence of Hong Kong cinema on such "blaxploitation" movies as *Black Belt Jones* (Clouse 1974) and the Warner Bros./Shaw Brothers *Cleopatra Jones* series. More recently, my friend Tobias Nagl pointed to the sampling of Hong Kong movies by contemporary rap crews (e.g., Wu-Tang Clan, Ol' Dirty Bastard's "Return to the 36th Chamber: The Dirty Version"). Nagl also reports that Hong Kong productions have blockbuster status in Kingston, Jamaica, where Jet Li is a superstar.

4   This observation is based on viewing the Hong Kong and US versions of the film. Mark Gallagher ignores this aspect of Chan's star appeal in his article "Masculinity in Translation: Jackie Chan's Transcultural Star Text" (1997).

5   In a similar fashion, Jennifer's personal development in *An Autumn Tale* is charted through her progress as an actress. Her adoption of a "successful" identity of accommodation is tied to the creative transformation of her professional life.

6   It is worth drawing attention to the interconnectedness of Kwan's vision. As a Chinese director, he recognizes the existence of Asian American identities as they cut across class and national boundaries. As a gay man, he perceives the existence of similarly expansive homosexual communities.

7   See also Lynn Pan (1992, 63): "On the whole, Hong Kong filmmakers have portrayed the world of the Chinese abroad as little more than a kind of transplanted Hong Kong, with the adopted country acting merely as a backdrop."

Works Cited

Abbas, Ackbar. 1996. "Cultural Studies in a Postculture." Pp. 289–312 in *Disciplinarity and Dissent in Cultural Studies*, ed. Cary Nelson and Dilip Parameshwar Gaonkar. London and New York: Routledge.

——. 1997. *Hong Kong: Culture and the Politics of Disappearance*. Minneapolis: University of Minnesota Press.

Ansen, David. 1996. "Chinese Takeout." *Newsweek* (February 19), 66–69.

Chatterjee, Partha. 1993. *The Nation and Its Fragments: Colonial and Postcolonial Histories*. Princeton, NJ: Princeton University Press.

Corliss, Richard. 1996. "Go West, Hong Kong." *Time* (February 26), 67.

Dannen, Fredric. 1995. "Hong Kong Babylon." *New Yorker* (August 7), 30–39.

Espiritu, Yen Le. 1992. *Asian American Panethnicity: Bridging Institutions and Identities*. Philadelphia: Temple University Press.

Feng, Peter. 1996. "Being Chinese American, Becoming Asian American: *Chan Is Missing*." *Cinema Journal* 35, no. 4 (Summer), 88–118.

Gallagher, Mark. 1997. "Masculinity in Translation: Jackie Chan's Transcultural Star Text." *Velvet Light Trap*, vol. 39 (Spring), 23–41.

Hall, Stuart. 1994. "Cultural Identity and Diaspora." Pp. 392–403 in *Colonial Discourse and Post-Colonial Theory: A Reader*, ed. Patrick Williams and Laura Chrisman. London: Harvester Wheatsheaf.

Hamamoto, Darrell Y., and Rodolfo D. Torres, ed. 1997. *New American Destinies: A Reader in Contemporary Asian and Latino Immigration*. London and New York: Routledge.

Kwong, Peter. 1987. *The New Chinatown*. New York: Hill and Wang.

Ong, Paul, Edna Bonacich, and Lucie Cheng, ed. 1994. *The New Asian Immigration in Los Angeles and Global Restructuring*. Philadelphia: Temple University Press.

Pan, Lynn. "Chinese Emigres on Screen." 1992. *The 16th Hong Kong International Film Festival: Overseas Figures in Chinese Cinema*. Hong Kong: Urban Council, 59–64.

Stringer, Julian. 1997. "Centre Stage: Reconstructing the Bio-Pic." *Cineaction* 42 (February), 28–39.

Tasker, Yvonne. 1993. *Spectacular Bodies: Gender, Genre, and the Action Cinema*. London and New York: Routledge.

Wang, L. Ling-Chi. 1991. "Roots and Changing Identity of the Chinese in the United States." *Daedalus* 120, no. 2 (Spring), 181–206.

——. 1995. "The Structure of Dual Domination: Toward a Paradigm for the Study of the Chinese Diaspora in the United States." *Amerasia Journal* 21, no. 1–2 (Winter-Spring), 149–69.

Wolf, Jaime. 1996. "Jackie Chan, American Action Hero?" *New York Times Magazine* (January 21), 22.

Films and Videos Cited

Chan, Peter. 1991. *Alan and Erie – Between Hello and Goodbye*. No distributor (US).

——. 1998. *Comrades: Almost a Love Story*. Rim (US).

Chang, Sylvia. 1995. *Siao Yu*. Central Motion Pictures.

Cheung, Mabel. 1988. *An Autumn Tale*. No distributor (US).

——. 1989. *Eight Tales of Gold*. No distributor (US).

Clouse, Robert. 1974. *Black Belt Jones*. Warner Bros.

Coppola, Francis Ford. 1972. *The Godfather*. Paramount.

Fok, Clarence Yiu Leung. 1989. *Iceman Cometh*. Golden Harvest.

Fuqua, Antoine. 1998. *The Replacement Killers*. Columbia Pictures.

Hui, Ann. 1990. *Song of the Exile*. No distributor (US).

——. 1991. *My American Grandson*. No distributor (US).

Kam-Bo, Sammo Hung. 1997. *Once Upon a Time in China and America*. Film Workshop/Oliver Stone Production.

Kwan, Stanley. 1987. *Rouge*. No distributor (US).

——. 1990. *Full Moon in New York*. No distributor (US).

——. 1991. *Center Stage*. *Swift* Distribution (France). No distributor (US).

Lam, Ringo. 1996. *Maximum Risk*. Columbia Pictures.

——. and Tsui Hark. 1992. *Twin Dragons*. Miramax.

Law, Clara. 1989. *The Reincarnation of Golden Lotus*. No distributor (US).

——. 1990. *Farewell China*. No distributor (US).

Mann, Michael, and Alan Smithee. 1995. *Heat*. Warner Bros.

Ray, Nicholas. 1955. *Rebel Without a Cause*. Warner Bros.

Soe, Valerie. 1997. *Beyond Asiaphilia*. Oxygen Productions (US).

Spottiswoode, Roger. 1997. *Tomorrow Never Dies*. MGM/UA.

Tong, Stanley. 1996a. *Police Story 3: Supercop*. Dimension Films (US).

——. 1996b. *Rumble in the Bronx*. Buena Vista Pictures (US).

——. 1997. *Police Story 4: First Strike*. New Line Cinema (US).

Tsui, Hark. 1991a. *The Master*. Paragon Films.

——. 1991b. *Once Upon a Time in China*. Film Workshop.

——. 1997. *Double Team*. Columbia Pictures.

Wang, Wayne. 1990. *Life Is Cheap . . . But Toilet Paper Is Expensive*. No distributor (US).

——. 1997. *Chinese Box*. Trimark.

Wong, Jing. 1989. *God of Gamblers*. No distributor (US).

——. 1995. *God of Gamblers Returns*. No distributor (US).

Wong, Kar-wai. 1994. *Ashes of Time*. Scholar Productions.

Woo, John. 1987. *A Better Tomorrow II*. Cinema City.

——. 1993. *Hard Target*. Universal.

——. 1996. *Broken Arrow*. Twentieth Century Fox.

——. 1997. *Face/Off*. Buena Vista.

24

"And Yet My Heart Is Still Indian": The Bombay Film Industry and the (H)Indianization of Hollywood

Tejaswini Ganti

"Failed Attraction"

I got to Radhika's place around 7 o'clock. Everyone else had already arrived and assembled in her bedroom in front of the TV, some on the bed, some on the floor, and some on the treadmill. There were nine of us, two women and seven men, ranging in age from early twenties to early thirties. We had gathered to watch Fatal Attraction on laser disc because Radhika, who was an actress, and her friends – a director, a cinematographer, a screenwriter, an assistant director, and a few actors – were thinking about remaking it into a Hindi film. Although most of them had seen the film before, they were watching it that night to decide whether to remake it.

During a particularly passionate sex scene, Radhika asked Tarun, who would be directing the potential remake, "What will you do? Will you show a song here? How are you going to show them having great sex?"[1]

Tarun said, "I can do it."

"How can you?" pressed Radhika.

"I'll do it," assured Tarun.

"No, not like how you did in your last film, not with shadows and silhouettes and close shots. That's not going to do it."

Tejaswini Ganti, "'And Yet My Heart Is Still Indian': The Bombay Film Industry and the (H)Indianization of Hollywood," pp. 281–300 from Faye D. Ginsburg, Lila Abu-Lughod and Brian Larkin (eds), *Media Worlds: Anthropology on New Terrain* (Berkeley: University of California Press, 2002). © 2002 by the Regents of the University of California. Reprinted by permission of the University of California Press.

When Tarun asserted, "Don't worry, I can do it," Radhika objected: "But wait, if you do it, I can't be seen doing that with someone I just met for the very first time! I can't do that!"

Tarun pointed out, "But you're not stable" [referring to the character, not to Radhika].

Radhika protested, "I don't want to be mentally unstable! It's quite unfashionable now; that's just not what's done!"

After the film was over, Tarun declared, "We can't make this film." Imran, who was a writer, concurred, "You're right. It doesn't work. It's really boring."[2]

In this essay, I examine why Tarun and his colleagues think *Fatal Attraction* cannot be remade into a Hindi film, to reveal how commercial film production is a practice imbued with a "difference-producing set of relations" (Gupta and Ferguson 1997: 46) between filmmakers and audiences. The Bombay film industry, one of the world's largest commercial film industries, which is increasingly referred to as "Bollywood" within and outside India, is a notoriously appropriative industry constantly on the lookout for new talent, faces, and stories. Although the driving force within the Bombay industry is commercial success, it is a difficult goal pursued by many and achieved by few. One of the strategies employed by Hindi filmmakers to reduce the chances of box-office failure is to remake or adapt Hollywood, Telugu, Tamil, and older Hindi films.[3] Bombay filmmakers regard box-office successes or "hits" in other Indian languages as attractive remake material because, having already succeeded with a set of audiences, such films are perceived as having a higher probability of succeeding with Hindi film audiences as well. Hollywood films, however, are not selected only on the basis of box-office outcome but are chosen for plots that seem novel and amenable to adaptation. Although remakes from other Indian languages resemble the original screenplay, adaptations of Hollywood films barely do because they have been transformed – or "Indianized," in industry parlance – to conform with the conventions of Hindi cinema.

I examine the process of "Indianization," drawing on first-hand observations of filmmakers watching Hollywood films, participation during the production of *Ghulam* – a film inspired by *On the Waterfront*, and conversations and interviews with members of the Bombay film industry.[4] Instead of comparing a Hindi film with the Hollywood "original" (Nayar 1997), I focus on the decisions, evaluations, and negotiations around Indianization in order to "turn from a project of juxtaposing pre-existing differences to one of exploring the construction of differences in historical process" (Gupta and Ferguson 1997: 46). Although Bombay filmmakers have been adapting Hollywood films for decades, the media landscape in which they operate has changed considerably since the entry of satellite and cable television in 1991, with the resulting increase in the number of television channels available locally, regionally, and nationally.[5] Filmmakers explain that because they are competing with television for audiences they must create a cinematic experience extraordinary enough to seduce audiences away from their television sets at home and into theaters, and Hindi film production since the mid-1990s has been marked by vastly improved production values, increased spectacle, foreign locales, slick marketing, and subsequently higher costs. The presence of satellite channels such as Star Movies and TNT that broadcast feature films also means that some portion of the audience has access to the Hollywood films that are the sources for adaptations.

Unlike recent work on cinematic remakes (Horton and McDougal 1998) and cross-cultural adaptations (Horton 1998; Aufderheide 1998; Nayar 1997), which are primarily concerned with questions of narrative, genre, and intertextuality, I examine Indianization, not as a relationship between texts but as a relationship between filmmakers and audiences. Much of the ethnographic research about the mass media has centered on television audiences and the moment of reception. However, as Ien Ang (1991) and Barry Dornfeld (1998) have argued, the idea of the audience must also be located in the production process. Whereas other scholars have examined Indianization with the purpose of delimiting what is uniquely "Indian" about the codes and conventions of mainstream Hindi cinema (Thomas 1985, 1995; Nayar (1997), I outline Indianization as a practice that allows one to see how Hindi filmmakers think about and construct their audiences.

Not every Hollywood film is capable of being "Indianized," however, and as the opening anecdote indicates, sometimes after watching a particular film closely the director decides that the film is unsuitable for adaptation. Unlike other methods, an ethnographic focus on media production provides access to these "negative" instances or episodes in which films get rejected in the conceptualization stage. Such moments of inchoate production reveal how Hindi filmmakers operate as cultural mediators, evaluating the appropriateness for their audiences of stories, characterizations, and themes from certain Hollywood films. I detail how Hindi filmmakers frequently elaborate the difference between their films and Hollywood films in a language of constraints and compulsions as mediated through the figure of "the audience." What becomes apparent during the processes of selection and adaptation is filmmakers' ambivalence toward their audiences, and I argue that rather than "indigenizing" or domesticating difference (Tobin 1992), Indianization is a practice of constituting difference – between India and the West, and more important, between filmmakers and audiences.

In thinking about the process of film production in terms of social relations, specifically the "relation of knowing" (Ohmann 1996) that producers exhibit toward their audiences, my goal is to bypass the dichotomies that have characterized the study of Hindi cinema and represent producers as an interpretive community. In much of this scholarship, depending on whether the focus is on films as texts or on the popularity of certain genres, producers are represented as isomorphic either with their films or with their audiences.[6] Rather than viewing the relationship between filmmakers and audiences according to an effects model or a reflectionist model, I see it as a "hermeneutic circle" in which there are multiple sites during the production, transmission, and reception of a media-text at which meaning can be constructed (Michaels 1990). By examining Indianization

I reveal some of the "audience fictions" (Traube 1996) operating within the Hindi film industry and how such assumptions about reception affect filmmaking, thus illustrating the highly mediated nature of commercial film production.

Screening Culture: Selecting a Film for Adaptation

Tarun's statement that *Fatal Attraction* "can't be made" refers to the perceived lack of audience interest rather than any technical inability on the part of himself and his crew. Throughout the filmmaking process, Hindi filmmakers justify their narrative, dramatic, and aesthetic choices according to what they believe audiences will accept and reject. In the process of trying to produce a "hit," filmmakers theorize about audiences' motivations for seeing a film and how they derive pleasure from it. Rather than relying on any formal market research, their claims about audience tastes and preferences are based on a mix of intuition, observation of box-office successes and failures, and first-hand viewing of films in theaters with audiences. In this section, I examine how deciding which film is suitable for adaptation involves a complex amalgam of factors such as filmmakers' interpretations of films, their own film-viewing experiences, their assessment of a film's novelty, loyalty to the narrative conventions of Hindi cinema, and filmmakers' assumptions about their audiences.

After we had finished watching *Fatal Attraction*, Tarun, Imran, and Radhika engaged in a long discussion about the film. Tarun and Imran dissected the plot and screenplay, explaining to the rest of the room why the film was not appropriate for an Indian context. Their discussion centered on the audience. Because the goal of box-office success is articulated completely in terms of audience desire, taste, and satisfaction, their overwhelming concern was what would draw audiences to see this film. Since there had been a spate of Hindi films recently about obsession, the group was trying to figure out the "USP" (unique selling point) for this film that would make it stand out from the others. While Tarun and Radhika kept stating that they wanted to do something different from what had been done before, during their discussion it became apparent that they felt constrained by the issue of adultery and the characterizations of the male protagonist and the other woman.

What was particularly vexing to the group was the adaptation of Glenn Close's character of a lustful, obsessive other woman into an Indian context. The discussion kept trying to answer the question: Why would this woman have an affair with this man if she knew he were married? It is not that such a character could not exist in a Hindi film, but Tarun and Radhika's concern was to represent the other woman differently from a classic Hindi film "vamp." They hashed out a few scenarios in which the woman initially did not know that the man was married, but these were rejected because they felt that would render the man as extremely unsympathetic, which was also deemed undesirable. The question that kept arising in the discussion was whether audiences could "identify" with this film.

The term "identification" kept popping up in my conversations with filmmakers as the basic tenet of the relationship between viewers and a film in order for it to elicit pleasure and thus succeed commercially. As a concept, "identification" encompasses a range of meanings from literal similarities between audiences and the characters on screen to a familiarity with the circumstances, scenarios, and conflicts depicted in the film. Javed Akhtar, a highly successful screenwriter, lyricist, and poet, describes it: "Whatever is happening on the screen should make him laugh, should make him cry, he should be able to identify with it. He should be able to fantasize and at the same time, if it is too real, then he won't like it. If it has nothing to do with reality, then too he won't like it" (interview, 1996). From a Hindi filmmaker's point of view, identification is not dependent upon an aesthetic of social realism or even a realistic mise-en-scène (which could even impede pleasure according to Akhtar), but more dependent on whether the portrayal of the joys, sorrows, and dilemmas faced by the characters are able to resonate with – rather than replicate – audiences' own experiences.

Thus, according to filmmakers, the inability of viewers to "identify" with a film would lead to its failure at the box office – the most common explanation offered for the poor fate of Hollywood films in India. Since 1994, when *Jurassic Park* was released in India in its original and dubbed Hindi versions and was a huge box-office success, a small number of Hollywood films have been dubbed into Hindi and released annually.[7] However, none have been able to repeat *Jurassic Park's* success, and in fact most do so poorly at the box office that the *Jurassic Park* experience is dismissed as an anomaly. As Rajat Barjatya, the marketing director for Rajshri Productions, asserts, "*Jurassic Park* is a very different film. People came for the curiosity: you know, what is a dinosaur? And how has a Hollywood film been dubbed first time in Hindi? There was a curiosity value attached to it – that's no longer the case" (interview, 1996).[8]

Hindi filmmakers do not perceive Hollywood as a threat to their business, citing the failure of most films as proof that audiences in India cannot relate to Hollywood films. Taran Adarsh, editor of *Trade Guide*, a trade weekly, asserts that audiences derive pleasure only from familiar stars and narratives:

I have asked a lot many people who have seen dubbed versions of English films and they say *ki*, "*bhai, yeh sab theek hai*" [This is all fine and good], they have the gloss, they have the glitter, everything, but "*yeh gore chamdi-waale, Hindi kaise bol sakte hain?*" [How can these white-skinned people speak Hindi?] It's like that. So the fact [is] that that identification is absolutely missing. . . . When I say Nana Patekar [an actor] is more popular, *kyon?* [Why?] *Kyon ki woh gaali deta hai.* [Because he curses.] *Pakad leta hai gale se, aur bolta hai,* "*Tu ne, tum log is* country *ko barbaad kar rahe ho!*" [He grabs you by the throat and says, "You, you people are destroying this country!"] *Phalana jo bhi ho* [Whatever it is], whatever he wants to say, and the guy sitting there, he somehow, feels as a person I am an impotent person, because there are certain things I cannot do. I cannot achieve in life, and when I see that guy doing it, he's doing the right thing. He's bashing up a criminal, which I can't. So that's where hero worship comes in, and that's where foreign films cannot be accepted because we just cannot, the identification is missing, the chemistry is missing absolutely. (Interview, 1996)

In Adarsh's view, the alien bodies, histories, and modes of address of Hollywood films are not capable of evoking in Indian audiences the psychological or emotional responses necessary for viewing pleasure. Identification can be understood as a type of cultural empathy, and in contemplating the adaptation of *Fatal Attraction* Tarun and Radhika were searching for ways to represent the characters so that they might evoke some form of empathy.

Although Hollywood films are characterized as unpleasurable for Hindi film audiences, they are not so for filmmakers who have access to them through laser discs and satellite television as well as trips abroad.[9] It is usually through such leisure viewing that a filmmaker stumbles across a film that he or she finds appealing and a potential candidate for adaptation. For example, *Ghulam*'s writer, Anjum Rajabali, explained that when he was approached by the director and producer to write a script with the only requirement that it be about two brothers, he happened to have just seen *On the Waterfront* at home and was very impressed by it. When Rajabali wrote out the screenplay exactly as it was, with merely the settings and characters changed for India, he realized, "It obviously didn't work! I said, *yeh to kya hai*? [What is this?] What am I doing? This doesn't work. *On the Waterfront* doesn't work in India" (interview, 1996). Because he liked the film immensely, he searched for what he had found so compelling about the film, which then helped him to construct the basic premise of *Ghulam*.

> *Chalo* [okay], but what did I like? I liked the relationship between the two brothers because it reminded me of my relationship with my brother at some stage and my relationship with my father. . . . That sentence, "You're my brother you should have looked after me," which Marlon Brando says to Rod Steiger, that for me became the starting point. Okay, that is my experience, and there I felt I had found the rib – Eve was made of the rib, no? I felt I had found the rib on which I could construct a human being, an entire story. I began with that and worked around. (Interview, 1996)

Rajabali's statements reveal how filmmakers themselves must be able to "identify" with a Hollywood film in order for it to be a candidate for adaptation. Later, when he reflected upon the experience, Rajabali remarked, "Perhaps unconsciously I realized that there was a universality in the story of *Waterfront* and that is why I am so impressed with it. I could interpret it in my own way, my own Indian way" (E-mail, April 9, 1998).

"Universality" is a very salient concept within the Bombay film industry as Hindi film makers aim for mass rather than niche audiences. "From 6 to 60" was a phrase I heard uttered frequently, describing how filmmakers strive to make films that appeal to everyone, regardless of age. A Hindi film is deemed an unqualified success only if it is a nationwide or an "all-India" hit, communicating to filmmakers that linguistically, regionally, and religiously diverse audiences have been able to "identify" with the film. Hollywood films that are perceived as having the potential to be adapted for an Indian context are described as having elements of "universal appeal"; those that are not are labeled "regional." Such a classification parallels the common discursive division of cinema in India into Hindi cinema or regional cinema by Bombay filmmakers: films in languages other than Hindi are referred to as "regional" films whose appeal is regarded as limited to specific geographic and linguistic constituencies. Vikram Bhatt, *Ghulam*'s director, explains how he judges whether a film is capable of being Indianized and what constitutes universal appeal:

> A Hollywood film has to have its relevance with our audiences. For me the film has to be that of a universal appeal, by which I mean that a film needs to be centered around a human emotion more then a set of circumstances. When I remade *Unlawful Entry*, it was because the film was about a villain's lust for a married woman. Lust is a universal emotion. People from all over the world regardless of the language understand it. *Ghulam*, though not a remake, was definitely inspired from *On the Waterfront*, which again is a story of two brothers against an oppressor, again, making it an understandable emotion. Every film need not he based on a universal emotion, but then it might have the portrayal of a very regional problem, making it difficult to adapt. Take, for example, films like *Mississippi Burning* or *Missing*. These are films that can't be made because their problems are relevant only to their regions. (E-mail, November 13, 1998)

Bhatt's comments illustrate how "emotion" refers to interpersonal relationships rather than an individual's internal state of being, a point that is elaborated later. Films that have been adapted in the recent past – *Sabrina*, *Kramer vs. Kramer*, *Mrs Doubtfire*, *The Hard Way*, *Sleeping with the Enemy*, *French Kiss*, and *An Affair to Remember* – are all centered on relationships – romantic, marital, parental, filial, or friendship – allowing Hindi filmmakers to add new twists to narratives that are predominantly about romantic love, kinship, or the myriad levels of duty.

Although films that are centered on human relationships are thought to have wide appeal, *Fatal Attraction* was regarded as unsuitable by Tarun and his colleagues because they felt the manner in which marital infidelity was handled in the film would not be acceptable to audiences. In addition to the concept of identification, Hindi filmmakers exercise their discretionary judgment through the idea of "acceptance," by which they mean audience approval of a film's plot, theme, or characterizations, as signified by its fate at the box office. Filmmakers portray audiences in India as very sensitive, particularly about sexual mores, when discussing what they would and would not like to see, and represent audience sensibilities as a constraint upon the kind of narratives and characterizations available to them. Tarun explains why he was having such difficulty with the characterization of the male protagonist in *Fatal Attraction*:

The audience does not understand protagonists with loose moral values. I don't mean drinking or anti-establishment or any thing like that. What I mean is more like a man willing to sell his wife for a night or a man who is willing to swap his wife with his neighbor for a night.[10] We have always placed our heroes on pedestals and sometimes it becomes very difficult. If you want to make films about normal people with their normal needs and normal drawbacks, then you have to really be very innovative so as not to hurt the audiences. The term used in story sittings is *yeh to accept nahin hoga* [This will not be accepted]. Loose moral values are only for the antagonist. (E-mail, March 7, 1999)

By explaining narrative and generic conventions as a consequence of audience sensibilities and desires, Tarun's statements reveal how filmmakers perceive their audiences as placing definite limits upon their filmmaking practices, which they may not follow otherwise. The paternalism expressed toward audiences also sets up a clear separation between filmmakers and audiences.

Filmmakers operate with a distinct sense of moral boundaries, usually pertaining to ideal kinship behavior, that cannot be transgressed when determining whether a Hollywood film is suitable for adaptation. Tarun abandoned the idea of adapting *Fatal Attraction* because he felt that audiences would not tolerate a protagonist who committed adultery simply out of boredom. He stated, "The audience will see him as a villain if he left a happy marriage just to go out and have a nice time. The concept of monotony in a marriage does not work here because most marriages are monotonous – the hero must have a bitch of a wife or something should be wrong in his marriage" (Internet chat, May 4, 1999). In addition to the generic convention in Hindi cinema in which a "hero" is someone who upholds the moral order, Tarun's decision is based on an assessment of social norms that to him renders the primary motivation for the plot incomprehensible to audiences. Tarun determines that marital monotony is not a meaningful concept to audiences – that is, they would be unable to identify with it and therefore would find it unacceptable – demonstrating how filmmakers' notions of identification and acceptance can operate to exclude certain themes. But Hollywood is characterized as free from all such compulsions. Screenwriter Sutanu Gupta states bluntly:

There a widower can just meet a divorcee in a pub and they go to bed and then the story starts. We can't have that. We just can't have that. Though in a song you can suggest that, I think these days that is what is being suggested, but we still have not reached that permission where you can just, the two characters come and meet and get along in life and then the story starts about something. (Interview, 1996)

Gupta uses a series of what may be regarded as social taboos and symbols of deviance to contrast what he sees as the lack of a moral universe in a Hollywood film with the implicitly moral one of the Hindi film, as well as to posit a metonymic association between cinema and society. "There" refers to both Hollywood and the West, and "permission" refers to the sexual freedom that is not allowed by either Indian audiences or Indian society. Gupta's comment about songs, however, points to a space within the Hindi film form that may be able to accommodate a blurring of boundaries and indicates that acceptable representations may have more to do with *how* something is represented than with *what* is represented. Hindi films do not shy away from representing moral or social transgressions, an obvious example being the predominance of romantic love that frequently crosses boundaries of class, and sometimes caste, region, and religion. In fact, much of the dramatic and narrative tension in a Hindi film arises from threats to the moral or social order.

What must be stressed is that filmmakers' ideas about what constitutes acceptable representations are not fixed but fluid, and they are highly dependent upon commercial success or failure. Filmmakers' assessments of audiences are continually revised or reinforced based on how films perform at the box office. For every "rule" about narrative, plot, or characterization that filmmakers assert cannot be broken there are examples of mainstream Hindi films – based on original screenplays rather than adaptations – that have done so and enjoyed commercial success. The process of adapting a Hollywood film, however, generates a self-consciousness about social norms and moral codes that can make filmmakers more cautious than when they produce films from an original screenplay.[11] Because the practice of adaptation is motivated by a conscious desire to manage risk, Indianization tends to be a conservative process that precludes innovation in narrative and generic practices.

Although in Indianization the selection and encoding process of Hindi filmmaking is structured mainly through filmmakers' assumptions about their audiences, it also demonstrates how filmmakers themselves constitute an audience when they watch Hollywood films with an eye to adapting them in Hindi. With Rajabali's personal narrative about the inspiration for *Ghulam*, we can see how filmmakers react to films in ways that resonate with their own lives. The act of picking a Hollywood film to adapt is often based on personal cinematic preferences. Tarun and Radhika had initially been very enthusiastic about the possibility of remaking *Fatal Attraction* because they thought it was an interesting film, and Radhika was excited about the histrionic opportunities available in the character of the obsessive other woman.

Although the initial interest in a particular film may be based on personal tastes and preferences, once filmmakers embark upon the task of adaptation, they justify their choices according to what they believe audiences will accept and reject. Determinations of which Hollywood films can or cannot be made demonstrate how Hindi filmmakers operate as cultural mediators with respect to their audiences' tastes and preferences. Through the concepts of identification and acceptance, we can see how filmmakers implicitly delineate a difference between their viewing habits and those of their audiences. This is especially clear in both Tarun's and Gupta's statements about how audiences cannot understand or cannot accept certain moral transgressions in films; the implication is that they have no such difficulties and can derive viewing pleasure from a greater diversity of plots, themes, and characterizations than their audiences.

447

Casting Culture: Three Methods of "Indianizing" a Film

In the previous section, I discussed what sorts of plots, characterizations, and themes Bombay filmmakers feel they *cannot* use when aiming for wide-scale commercial success. This section focuses on what filmmakers feel they *must* do in order to adapt a Hollywood film appropriately so that it has the potential for box-office success. These include the addition of "emotions," the expansion of the narrative, and the inclusion of songs, which are explained by filmmakers in terms of audience expectations as well as cultural antecedents.

"Emotion"

At one point in the screening of *Fatal Attraction*, Imran declared, "We can't have the woman getting pregnant. That's so syrupy, but the Americans liked it be cause they're so starved of emotion," and everybody murmured assent. Along with identification and acceptance, "emotion" is another concept used in the Bombay film industry to underscore the alien nature of Hollywood. Hindi filmmakers frequently describe Hollywood films as "dry" or "lacking in emotion" and claim that in order to Indianize a film, one has to "add emotions." Anjum Rajabali explains:

> When you Indianize a subject, you add emotions. Lots of them. Feelings like love, hate, sacrifice, of revenge, pangs of separation. But, in a Hollywood film if a hero and heroine were to separate and you had five scenes underlining how they are suffering because they miss each other, people might find that soppy and corny too. Not here. Our mythology, our poetry, our literature is full of situations where lovers pine for each other. (E-mail, April 9, 1998)

Rajabali's statements illustrate the rich repository of meaning attributed to the word "emotion." He uses words that are transactional – love, hate, sacrifice – to define emotion, rather than those that denote states of being such as happiness, anger, or sadness. Revenge and pangs of separation may seem unusual in a list of emotions, but their inclusion demonstrates that for Hindi filmmakers emotions are not about an individual but about his or her relationship with others. Rather than referring to internal states, filmmakers are referring to social life in their discussions about emotion (Abu-Lughod and Lutz 1990), which has been described as a general feature of the discourse of emotion in India (Lynch 1990). Therefore, adding emotions to a film involves placing a character in a web of social relations of which kin are the most significant and common in Hindi films. The absence of kinship-related conflicts and dilemmas in Hollywood films, articulated as a lack of emotion, is offered as a reason for audiences' inability to identify with such films. Rajabali asserts: "That is why I think subjects like James Bond, detective stories, westerns and the like don't work as they are here. Who were James Bond's parents? Does Clint Eastwood of *Good, Bad, Ugly* love anyone? What about his brothers or sisters?" (Ibid.)

Rajabali illustrates the primacy of kinship relations in Hindi films by describing his impressions of a Hollywood film, *Murder in the First*, and how it would have been made in India.

> One brief flashback showed Kevin Bacon stealing bread for his sister and getting jailed, thus starting the whole story. In an Indian film, we'd have dwelt on that hugely, hugely. Really exploited that to underline the tragedy of the guy. Then, later [Christian] Slater brings Bacon's long-lost sister along to convince Bacon to testify or something. Bacon is very uncomfortable with her, behaves very awkwardly with her, turns away finally, and goes inside. After that scene, the sister doesn't feature in the film at all. It works, in the context of this film. But, Jesus, here the first thing that Bacon would've asked of Slater was "Bring my sister to me," and she'd have been the moving force of the film. (Ibid.)

Adding emotions is also about making narratives more moral because being connected to others means that one's actions have consequences greater than oneself. Rajabali speculates that the greater concern with morality in Hindi films has to do with the continuing presence and relevance of older narrative traditions:

> Our myths are full of them [emotions]. Take the *Mahabharat* and you'll see what I mean. Every situation has feelings – dilemmas, other kinds of conflicts, confrontations, sacrifices, moral issues coming up all the time. In a Hollywood film, James Bond kills on the job; here we need to justify it, because morality plays a more important part in our lives, because of our mythology, I suppose. (Ibid.)

While mythology is offered as an underlying reason for the moral universe of a Hindi film, when speaking about a specific film Rajabali invokes the need for audiences to feel sympathy for the protagonist, akin to the ideas of identification and acceptance:

> *Kiss before Dying* was effectively remade as *Baazigar* [Gambler]. In the original, the hero's motive was to get rich by any means since he used to see the big company's train pass his house every day and that made him envious and ambitious enough to end up killing all those girls. That was enough – his plain ambition. But, in *Baazigar*, that wouldn't have worked. Guy killing for ambition? No sympathy for him at all. But, if the guy had a back-story, wherein his father was cheated by this company *wallah* [guy] and now the guy wants the company back as revenge and retribution for that. Okay, now he's my man. I can consider forgiving him all those killings. Not entirely of course, killing is killing, so he has to die himself in the end, but he will carry my sympathy with him. (Ibid.)

449

Narrative

During a scripting session for *Ghulam*, its director, Vikram Bhatt, quipped, "In *On The Waterfront*, they start right away. They have no pre-story. Everything in a Hollywood film just happens boom, boom, boom; here all the way up to the interval, there's all kinds of other things happening."[12] What Bhatt was referring to was how the incident at the very beginning of *Waterfront* – the heroine's brother being killed – takes place halfway through *Ghulam*. Sutanu Gupta compares the difficulty of writing a Hindi film with the straightforward narrative of a Hollywood film:

> You see our films, it is more difficult to make, twenty times more difficult than the Hollywood film. A Hollywood film can interest their audiences with one track – you can have a bomb in a bus, a girl is driving the bus, and a man has to save the bus driver and the bus passengers.[13] This is the whole film! We can't do a film like that. It could be our climax, only one scene in the film. (Interview, 1996)

Hollywood films are frequently described as "single-track," and filmmakers express their amazement and envy at how films can be made on "one line" – a phrase conveying that a story's simple plot can be related in a sentence. However, such films are considered inadequate for audiences in India, as Gupta explains:

> When the audience comes to the theater, they have a very set belief, that the kind of entertainment, which is given in cinema, should be containing everything – they should see part of family life; they should see romance; they should have songs; everything they want! Which becomes very difficult. At the same time, they hate hodge-podge films. They want to know what is the emphasis – whether it's an action film or it's a thriller or it's a revenge or it's a ghost story or it's a love story. This is difficult to maintain. It's a massive kind of a balance to perform . . . so that's why we find it damn difficult to achieve very successful films always. (Ibid.)

Gupta's statements illustrate that filmmakers perceive their audiences as demanding and set in their ideas about the kinds of films they want to see. He presents audiences as providing him boundaries with which he has to juggle their demands. Yet at the same time the desire for complicated narrative and the fact that an entire Hollywood film could be a mere scene in a Hindi film bestows a sophistication and mastery to the audience usually not attributed to them in public discourses about cinema in India, which overwhelmingly characterizes audiences as the illiterate and unrefined "masses."

Thus adapting a Hollywood film involves enhancing the narrative in a variety of ways. Subplots or parallel "tracks" – romantic, comedic, dramatic – are seen as necessary additions. According to writers, the inclusion of "emotions" leads to greater narrative complexity because close family relationships provide moving stories of their own. In *Ghulam* a whole prehistory to the main narrative emerges through a flashback about the hero's childhood relationship with his father. The trauma of his father's suicide is presented as an underlying reason for the hero's petty hoodlum-like behavior. The first half of *Ghulam* is also taken up with situating the principal characters socially, developingthe romance between the hero and heroine, establishing how the neighborhood is under the control of a crime boss, and portraying the interactions between the hero and the heroine's idealistic brother. Javed Akhtar likens a Hollywood screenplay to a short story and a Hindi film's to a saga and states that Indian audiences "want a story that will engulf generations and eras, a larger period of time, and incidents, big influences on a larger spectrum. . . . You see a short story will have a beginning and the end, but these sagas have to have a beginning, a middle, and the end" (interview, 1996).

Songs

The sheer ubiquity of diegetic music in Indian cinema is probably its most distinctive feature.[14] To those unfamiliar with popular Indian cinema, song sequences appear as ruptures in continuity and verisimilitude. However, rather than being an extraneous feature, music and song in popular cinema define and propel plot development, and many films would lose their narrative coherence if their songs were removed. Hindi filmmakers spend a great deal of time and energy crafting the song sequences, which play a variety of functions within a film's narrative and provide the main element of cinematic spectacle. One of the main functions according to screenwriters, who with the director determine the "song situations" within a screenplay, is to display emotion. Rajabali explains that every time he comes to a point of intense feelings in the screenplay he sees if a song will convey it better: "Where an emotion becomes intense, usually a song helps to underline it. It also cuts away the need for verbalization through dialogue and creates a mood that cues the viewer in to the state of mind of the characters or the narrator" (e-mail, April 9, 1998).

The most common emotion expressed musically in Hindi films is love, and in films like *Ghulam* where a love story is not the main focus of the plot, a "romantic track" is developed primarily through songs between the hero and the heroine. Even a love story focuses on the overcoming of obstacles to marriage rather than the process of falling in love, so songs provide a more efficient way to depict the romance developing between the hero and heroine than many scenes of dialogue. For example, the entire process of falling in love, from the initial attraction to the realization of being soulmates, can be established over the course of four or five songs, or about thirty minutes of screen time. Rajabali elaborates:

> When the first "thunderbolt" strikes either [the hero or the heroine], they express it through a song. When their love intensifies, usually the standard rain sequence,

another song.[15] If there is a breach or a tragedy in the relationship because of which they separate, we deal with it musically. So, extreme happiness, extreme love, extreme sadness, all of these qualify as song situations. (Ibid.)

Songs are part of an elaborate system of allusions to, rather than explicit portrayals of, sexuality and physical intimacy in Hindi films as filmmakers navigate the perceived moral conservatism of their audiences, as well as the representational boundaries set by the Indian state through its censorship codes. Songs are the primary vehicles for representing fantasy, desire, and passion, so any form of sexual activity in a Hollywood film would most likely be transformed into a song sequence in a Hindi film, a point made explicit while watching *Fatal Attraction* when Radhika asked Tarun, "What will you do? Will you show a song here?" In addition to expressing intense emotion and signifying physical intimacy, songs are frequently used to facilitate the passage of time, evoke memories, aid in characterization, and operate as a mode of indirect address. Rajabali states, "See if you accept the dictum that songs are required almost invariably – all screenplays don't need them – then you keep that in mind while writing the screenplay. If you don't have enough situations for songs, then you have to create them" (ibid.).

However, some writers and directors, especially those who prefer to make genres other than love stories, view having to create song situations as burdensome, with the burden compounded when attempting to adapt a Hollywood film. I recall one director who was trying to adapt *Judgment Night* – a film that takes place in one night about an all-male group of friends who accidentally witness a murder and then have to flee – being utterly confounded about what kind of song situations would be plausible in such a film.[16] Most writers acknowledge that songs are not necessary to every film and can be awkward in certain genres, but come to terms with them in various ways. Rajabali rationalizes music in terms of tradition: "Once you really treat your own storytelling objectives and methods as part of a larger continuity of the storytelling traditions in India, integrating songs becomes more easy. In myths, legends, and their rendering in folk theater, etc., one finds lots of music" (ibid.).

Whereas Rajabali offers a culturalist justification, others point to the significant economic role played by music within the film industry. Tarun asserts, "Of course one would love to make a movie without songs, but the only really hampering factor is the economic and marketing aspect of songs" (Internet chat, May 4, 1999). Gupta resigns himself to their presence, citing the pressure of music companies: "My kind of film, the kind of stories that I write, the song situations are difficult to find. I guess the songs have to be there and there have to be enough gaps between the songs, at least five to six songs you require, because forty minutes recorded tape, the music companies want, that is the contract" (interview, 1996).

Music is absolutely essential to the marketing and financing of popular Hindi films. The sale of music rights has become a source of finance for filmmaking:

audio companies vying for the top production companies in the industry are willing to pay sums that may amount to as much as 25 percent of a film's budget. There have only been a few examples of popular Hindi films without songs – so few that their most memorable feature is the absence of songs. Not having songs signifies that the film is outside the mainstream of the Bombay film industry, possibly even an "art film," which to most people in the industry means death at the box office. Songs are usually recorded before a film commences shooting, and a few of the song sequences are shot early in the production phase so that they can be used to sell a film to distributors. Songs have also become the most significant form of a film's publicity; Indian television has been packed with film-based programming, mostly around film music, since the onset of cable and satellite television in 1991. Even before a film has completed production, some-times months in advance, its song sequences start airing on the numerous film-based programs on television or appear as commercials between other programs. There are plenty of rumors and stories in the industry about distributors and financiers pressuring filmmakers to add songs to films to increase their prospects at the box office.

Exhibitors and others in the film trade assert that songs give Hindi films a competitive edge over Hollywood films. In an article about Hollywood's presence in India in the English-language film magazine *Filmfare*, the publicity manager of 20th Century Fox in India states, "Though 20th Century Fox is linked with the STAR network (satellite channels), Hindi films still have an advantage. They have songs to draw the audience. We don't!" (Kumar 1995: 170). In the same article the joint manager of two movie theaters in Bombay, one devoted to foreign films and the other to Hindi, explains his significantly lower box-office collections at the former theater: "It's just that Hindi films have songs, dances . . . emotions. Indians want everything and they get the works only in Indian cinema" (ibid.). The overwhelming commercial significance of music can be frustrating according to Tarun: "You see it should be a choice for the director to use songs or not, it is the compulsion that really wears us down" (Internet chat, May 4, 1999).

Tarun's frustration arises partly from the altered media landscape since the late 1990s in which Hindi filmmakers not only have had to compete with cable and satellite television for audiences but also to contend with the presence of dubbed Hollywood films. The increased emphasis on songs, spectacle, and kinship-related conflicts in Hindi films made in the 1990s could be seen as a response to these changes in the media landscape. In Indianizing Hollywood films for Indian audiences, Bombay filmmakers feel more compelled to consciously heighten and intensify the differences between their films and the "originals." Tarun's frustra-tion is the most explicit, but one can detect traces of frustration in some of the other filmmakers' statements presented in this section. Gupta's statements about Hindi films' narrative complexity and even Rajabali's thoughtful comments about songs belie a certain ambivalence toward these conventions.

Conclusion

The framework of commercial cinema production constructs a totalizing and tautological universe in which Bombay filmmakers' relationship to the abstract collectivity known as "Indian society" is mediated by box-office outcome. Through the concepts of identification and acceptance we can see how commercial success or failure is interpreted by filmmakers as a barometer of social attitudes and moral sensibilities, providing the basis for their knowledge about audiences. The practice of Indianization illustrates the ambivalent nature of filmmakers' relationship to their audiences. Although audiences in India are characterized as having very specific tastes that cannot be satisfied through Hollywood films, the same sensibilities that reject Hollywood and thus protect Hindi filmmakers from competition can also constrain them in their own filmmaking practices. They perceive their audiences as limiting the types of themes, plots, and characterizations available and therefore also limiting the kinds of films they can make.

While nearly all categories of social difference are elided in favor of presenting a monolithic Indian audience,[17] Indianization is also a site for Hindi filmmakers to elaborate differences between themselves and their audiences. When filmmakers describe audiences in India as unable to empathize with Hollywood films because of their alien themes and alien morality, the assumption running through such descriptions is that they, the filmmakers, have no such problems. Both film production and consumption become sites to imagine difference. The fact that Bombay filmmakers are able to enjoy and accept Hollywood films while their audiences cannot produces an opposition between traditional, conservative, and prudish audiences and modern, sophisticated, and worldly filmmakers. Whereas the process of Indianization operates as a commentary about the character and psyche of the vast filmgoing public in India, it also illustrates that "the 'distance' between the rich in Bombay and those in London may be much shorter than that between different classes in 'the same' city" (Gupta and Ferguson 1997: 50).

Rather than reflecting the essence of "Indian culture," I have tried to show how the highly reflexive and objectifying process of Indianization generates "culture effects" (Kondo 1992), signifying practices that produce the essence of "Indianness." Whether it is the generic convention of diegetic music, the thematic focus on kinship, or the imagining of audience response via concepts such as identification and acceptance, Hindi filmmakers are continuously elaborating the differences between their films and Hollywood films. The process of filmmaking predicated upon perceived cultural constraints leads to an image of shared collective norms. Whatever their ambivalence toward it, the process of Indianization becomes an arena for Hindi filmmakers to construct difference at the level of the nation – between an undifferentiated "Indianness" and its other, the West as represented by Hollywood.

Notes

The phrase in the title, "And Yet My Heart Is Still Indian" (*Phir bhi dil hai Hindustani*), will be recognized by all Hindi film viewers. It is from the well-known song "Mera Jootha Hai Japani" (My Shoes Are Japanese), which was heard in the 1955 movie *Sri 420* (Mr. 420). The phrase is also the title of a Hindi film released in January 2000.

1   The presence of English as a language of production, apparent from the interviews and informal communication, may surprise some readers, but it is a testament to the cosmopolitan nature of the Bombay film industry, where people hail from nearly every linguistic region in India and are not necessarily native Hindi speakers. As a consequence, although the language of the films may be Hindi, the language of production is multilingual, encompassing all of the major Indian languages, of which English has become one. Some screenwriters even write their scripts in English and then have them translated into Hindi by others more proficient in the language – a practice that obviously warrants further attention but is beyond the scope of this essay.

2   I observed this incident on May 9, 1996, during fieldwork in Bombay funded by an American Institute of Indian Studies Junior Fellowship for dissertation research. Although many of my informants were celebrities and thus public figures, because the episodes and conversations occurred in private, informal settings and did not result in anything as public as a film, I have followed the standard anthropological practice of using pseudonyms and have avoided last names because they are markers of caste, religion, and/or region in India. When quoting from formal interviews, I have kept the original names of informants.

3   Telugu and Tamil are languages spoken in the southern Indian states of Andhra Pradesh and Tamil Nadu, both home to film industries equally and sometimes more prolific than Bombay's.

4   *Ghulam* literally means "vassal" but in the film's context refers to a person both psychologically and physically under someone's control. *Ghulam* started production in November 1996 and was released in June 1998, quickly becoming a commercial success. As an assistant to the director, I was involved with preproduction such as scripting, location hunting, and casting.

5   These changes are a consequence of the new regime in state economic policy – mandated by IMF structural adjustment policies in 1991 – characterized as "liberalization," which has allowed multinational corporations greater access to various sectors of the Indian economy.

6   For the most recent example of the former see Prasad 1998, and for the latter see Nandy 1998.

7   In 1999, a total of 154 Hindi films were released, out of which sixteen were dubbed Hollywood films.

8   Rajshri produced *Hum Aapke Hain Koun!* in 1994, the same year as *Jurassic Park*, which is reputed to be the most successful film in India to date, netting over 2 billion rupees according to trade experts (ticket prices at the time of its release ranged from 5 to 50 rupees).

9   Many Hindi films have song sequences shot in Europe, North America, or Australia. Stars frequently go abroad to perform in elaborate stage shows. Many filmmakers also vacation abroad.

10   This is an allusion to *Indecent Proposal.*

11   Readers familiar with Indian cinema may wonder why I have not discussed the Indian Censor Board. Though filmmaking in India is a private enterprise, all films for theatrical release have to be cleared and rated by the government's Central Board of Film Censors, a practice initiated by the British colonial authorities, who heavily censored any allusion to self-governance, the Indian nationalist movement, or Indian independence. During discussions of how to Indianize a film, the censors were rarely mentioned except as an obstacle to be overcome rather than as a constraint. Censors are viewed as capricious and nit-picking, and filmmakers have employed a variety of strategies to deal with them, such as leaving scenes longer than desired, knowing that the censors will ask for cuts. Film censorship in India is a very complex issue that is beyond the scope of this article.

12   All mainstream Indian films are presented in two halves, with an intermission referred to as the "interval" placed at a point of suspense or at a dramatic turn in the narrative.

13   This is an allusion to *Speed.*

14   In a narrative film, diegesis refers to the world of the film's story, and diegetic music is music presented as originating from a source within the film's world.

15   Rain, associated with fertility and rebirth, has always been invested with erotic, sensual significance in Hindu mythology, classical literature, and music. Indian classical music has many songs in which the anticipation of the monsoon rains is likened to a person's anticipation of his or her lover.

16   The film was abandoned for various reasons.

17   Audiences are portrayed as monolithic only in the case of Indianization; otherwise Hindi filmmakers classify audiences according to class, region, language, ethnicity, gender, and generation. See Ganti 2000 for a more detailed discussion of how Hindi filmmakers categorize and imagine their audiences.

References

Abu-Lughod, Lila, and Catherine A. Lutz, eds. 1990. *Language and the Politics of Emotion.* Cambridge, England: Cambridge University Press.

Adarsh, Taran. 1996. Interview with author, September 29, Bombay.

Akhtar, Javed. 1996. Interview with author, November 25, Bombay.

Ang, Ien. 1991. *Desperately Seeking the Audience.* London: Routledge.

Aufderheide, Patricia. 1998. Made in Hong Kong: Translation and Transmutation. In *Play It Again Sam: Retakes on Remakes,* edited by Andrew Horton and Stuart Y. McDougal, pp. 191–99. Berkeley: University of California Press.

Barjatya, Rajat. 1996. Interview with author, April 29, Bombay.

Dornfeld, Barry. 1998. *Producing Public Television, Producing Public Culture.* Princeton, NJ: Princeton University Press.

Ganti, Tejaswini. 2000. Casting Culture: The Social Life of Hindi Film Production in Contemporary India. PhD diss., Department of Anthropology, New York University.

Gupta, Akhil, and James Ferguson. 1997. Beyond "Culture": Space, Identity, and the Politics of Difference. In *Culture, Power, Place: Explorations in Critical Anthropology,* edited by Akhil Gupta and James Ferguson, pp. 33–51. Durham, NC: Duke University Press.

Gupta, Sutanu. 1996. Interview with author, November 2, 18, Bombay.

Horton, Andrew. 1998. Cinematic Makeovers and Cultural Border Crossings: Kusturica's *Time of the Gypsies* and *Coppola's Godfather and Godfather II*. In *Play It Again Sam: Retakes on Remakes*, edited by Andrew Horton and Stuart Y. McDougal, pp. 172–90. Berkeley: University of California Press.

Horton, Andrew, and Stuart Y. McDougal, eds. 1998. *Play It Again Sam: Retakes on Remakes*. Berkeley: University of California Press.

Kondo, Dorinne. 1992. The Aesthetics and Politics of Japanese Identity in the Fashion Industry. In *Re-made in Japan: Everyday Life and Consumer Taste in a Changing Society*, edited by Joseph J. Tobin, pp. 176–203. New Haven, Conn.: Yale University Press.

Kumar, N. 1995. Born in the USA. *Filmfare* (November): 170–73.

Lynch, Owen M., ed. 1990. *Divine Passions: The Social Construction of Emotion in India*. Berkeley: University of California Press.

Michaels, Eric. 1990. A Model of Teleported Texts (with Reference to Aboriginal Television). *Continuum* 3 (2): 8–31.

Nandy, Ashis. 1998. Indian Popular Cinema as a Slum's Eye View of Politics. In *The Secret Politics of Our Desires: Innocence, Culpability and Indian Popular Cinema*, edited by Ashis Nandy, pp. 1–18. Delhi: Oxford University Press.

Nayar, Sheila J. 1997. The Values of Fantasy: Indian Popular Cinema through Western Scripts. *Journal of Popular Culture* 31 (1): 73–90.

Ohmann, Richard. 1996. Knowing/Creating Wants. In *Making and Selling Culture*, edited by Richard Ohmann, pp. 224–38. Hanover, NH: University Press of New England.

Prasad, Madhav. 1998. *Ideology of the Hindi Film: A Historical Construction*. Delhi: Oxford University Press.

Rajabali, Anjum. 1996. Interview with author, September 14, Bombay.

Thomas, Rosie. 1985. Indian Cinema, Pleasures and Popularity. *Screen* 26 (3–4): 116–31.

——. 1995. Melodrama and the Negotiation of Morality in Mainstream Hindi Film. In *Consuming Modernity: Public Culture in a South Asian World*, edited by Carol A. Breckenridge, pp. 157–82. Minneapolis: University of Minnesota Press.

Tobin Joseph J., ed. 1992. *Re-made in Japan: Everyday Life and Consumer Taste in a Changing Society*. New Haven, Conn.: Yale University Press.

Traube, Elizabeth. 1996. Introduction. In *Making and Selling Culture*, edited by Richard Ohmann, pp. xi–xxiii. Hanover, NH: University Press of New England.

25

Future Past: Integrating Orality into Francophone West African Film

Melissa Thackway

This essay proposes to look at ways in which film, an art form originally imported to West Africa, both draws on and re-articulates the region's traditional oral narrative codes. Taking Adama Drabo's *Taafe Fanga* (Mali, 1997) and Jean-Marie Teno's *Clando* (Cameroon, 1996) as its main examples, I aim to highlight the stylistic and thematic influences of the oral traditions on francophone West African film, and the way in which film perpetuates orality's referencing of the past to reflect upon the present and the future.[1] This analysis will help clarify some of these films' agendas and styles, as it illustrates the ways in which this reworking of oral narrative techniques has conferred what can, tentatively and without wanting to be too essentialist, be referred to as a certain specificity of francophone West African film.

Before looking at these specific filmic examples, however, I will first of all consider the sociopolitical context in which West African filmmaking was born in order to shed light on this significant cinematic embracing of orality. Secondly, some of the local characteristics of the arts and the role of the artist which have influenced West Africa's filmmakers will be outlined.[2]

When discussing francophone West African film, it is important to remember that filmmaking developed in the region in the aftermath of the highly influential Independence era. Early West African film was thus inevitably marked by the liberation era and its political agendas. Filmmakers 'coming to voice' at that time were faced with the legacy of misrepresentative images of Africa and its peoples

Melissa Thackway, "Future Past: Integrating Orality into Francophone West African Film," pp. 229–42 from *Matatu: Journal for African Culture and Society* 25:1 (Amsterdam: Editions Rodopi, September 2002). © 2002 by Matatu. Reprinted by permission of Editions Rodopi B.V.

made in the West. These images both reflected and reinforced the racialist, white supremacist theories of the nineteenth century and helped to justify Western imperialism in Africa. African characters in film were thus predominantly absent and/or voiceless, and reduced to a range of stereotypes that frequently depicted Africans as devious or as subservient and childlike.

The existence of what was ultimately little other than the projection of the West's exotic and/or hegemonic fantasies inevitably prompted many West African directors to counter such images with alternative representations of their own. For many filmmakers, film thus became, and often remains, a means of challenging Western hegemony. Film, indeed, offered filmmakers a medium in which to restore African dignity by establishing a plurality of perspectives and voices that portray African realities from an African point of view. Such political desires clearly reflected the intellectual climate of the liberation era in which theorists such as Frantz Fanon and Amilcar Cabral posited culture as a powerful tool for mental decolonization.[3] This concept was no doubt particularly resonant in the West African cultural context, in which the arts 'traditionally' play a socio-educational role.[4]

In the postcolonial context, therefore, the first generation of filmmakers, and to a large degree a number of contemporary filmmakers, inevitably faced the issue of representation, especially as film is a visual medium. This frequently led to the embracing of both a politically committed vein of filmmaking and a traditional, community-based understanding of the artist as being at the service of his or her people. It also resulted in the widespread desire to explore West Africa's diverse and multiple identities in film. Filmmakers thus appropriated the medium, using it to define themselves and to position Africa and its people as the subjects rather than the objects of representation. In the process, they often consciously or unconsciously identified with existing West African conceptions of the role of the artist and the arts, embracing local narrative traditions and codes, the better to reflect these identities and realities. This tendency has become all the more marked in recent years with the development and diversification of West African cinema, which has led to a greater desire to explore and experiment with film language and styles.

Just like all West African cultural forms, francophone West African film has thus been influenced by, and tends to reflect, West African views of humans, of their environment and their communal organization. Not only are the arts here generally destined for the whole community, but the different art forms are commonly interrelated and juxtaposed and often totally integrated into people's daily lives and activities. Audiences thus customarily play a key participatory role in performances, responding to the narrator in codified call-and-response refrains, as can be seen in the filmed storytelling sessions in Drabo's *Taafe Fanga*. Interestingly, such participatory practices are often transposed to the popular movie theatre in West Africa, the audience frequently interacting with a film by interjecting remarks, clapping along to songs, or providing running commentaries of the popular Indian and karate films screened without subtitles.

The spatial organization of a number of francophone West African films similarly reflects a symbiosis between humans and their environment. Spectators will, for example, notice the importance accorded to landscapes, skies, trees and other natural elements in the composition of shots. Shots are often held once the characters have left the frame, the camera focusing on the environment. Slow, sweeping pans across landscapes often situate characters in relation to their surroundings and reinforce a sense of their identification with the environment. Unlike mainstream Western film, spatial considerations thus frequently take precedence over temporal concerns. Many films, such as Jean-Marie Teno's *Clando*, thus include extended journey sequences rather than ellipses, the landscape or the journey itself taking on symbolic significance in the narrative. Long- and medium-shot compositions, frontal frames, and group shots are also predominant, placing emphasis on the group. This accentuates the community-based spatial organization, and/or relates the characters to their environment. While such framing may seem stylized or theatrical to Western viewers used to shot/counter-shot type framing, it re-creates the kind of communal performance space characteristic of traditional outdoor theatre in West Africa. The ties between traditional Malian Koteba theatre and film are particularly clear in *Taafe Fanga*, which Adama Drabo originally wrote as a play, and account for the film's theatrical group and/or character movements, and acting styles.

Coming specifically to orality: the oral tale remains the main form of narrative expression throughout West Africa. Not only are tales a form of entertainment, but also traditionally play a fundamental socio-educational role. Stories are used to pass on a community's moral codes, values, belief-systems and collective memory, thereby reinforcing social cohesion and providing a forum for addressing social issues and conflicts.

The language of the tales is often highly metaphoric and will be read on different levels by different audiences. To the youngest member of the audience, the tales are essentially a form of entertainment; to initiates they are a source of wisdom. Not only are the tales educational, therefore, but they also frequently employ allegory and/or satire to articulate protest and criticism. In the postcolonial context referred to above, filmmakers have often openly embraced this politically committed stance. This is clear from the Pan-African Federation of Filmmakers' (FEPACI) 1975 Algiers Charter, which states:

> The cinema has a vital part to play because it is a means of education, information and consciousness raising, as well as a stimulus to creativity. . . . The stereotyped image of the solitary and marginal creator which is widespread in Western capitalist society must be rejected by African film-makers, who must, on the contrary, see themselves as creative artisans at the service of their people.

It is important to stress that the tales regularly evolve, their messages being up-dated and adapted to suit their period. This helps to account for the fact that oral tales are still present and alive today. Indeed, as Christopher Miller claims, "the lessons of the past are . . . constantly translated into the terms of the present," as will later be seen to be the case in both *Taafe Fanga* and *Clando*.[5]

The centrality and key social role of oral traditions accounts for their influence on all the contemporary art forms of West Africa, including cinema. This centrality reflects the reverence accorded to speech itself in many West African societies. Many West African creation myths confer a sacred origin on the word, which is described as a divine force breathed into humans. Words are thus thought to have the power to harmonize or to upset the natural balance between the forces of the earth. This explains both the importance of ritualized speech in the ceremonies aimed at modifying this balance, and the preference in many societies for controlled, enigmatic, ritualized speech. This is again clear from the predilection for proverbs, described by Isidore Okpewho as having "a philosophical depth which is the result of a careful and sensitive observation of human conduct and experience of the surrounding nature," and as being "treated with authority and respect because they are regarded as truth tested by time."[6]

Such attitudes to speech are reflected in many films, including *Taafe Fanga* and *Clando*. Long, often static moments of speech form a part of the internal logic and rhythm of many films, and characters often resort to proverbs. There is also a pronounced tendency to include ritualized moments of speech, such as greetings and discussions, in the central diegesis of the film. While highly uncharacteristic of Western film, where the traditions of logical, linear development mean that dialogue is generally used to advance the narrative, dialogue in francophone West African film is rarely just a narrative tool; it is there to be listened to. This ritualized speech is often distinguished by its staged settings, the centrality of speaker in frame, and its static, unobtrusive camera work, which, by not controlling or directing the viewer's gaze, leaves him or her free to listen.

In a culture in which the word takes on such importance, it is unsurprising that there are people who 'specialize' in the word. While commonly referred to under the generic term *griot*, this non-indigenous term masks a multitude of roles and statuses that vary from one ethnic group or region to another. A griot's functions may range from that of scholar, mediator or advisor to that of musician and storyteller or parasitic scandal-monger; hence the fact that the griot is sometimes revered, sometimes despised. Irrespective of status, however, the griot is always considered capable of manipulating the sacred force of the word.

What is of interest to us here is the fact that griots, whatever their status, are central figures in West African societies and their arts, and have become a point of reference also for the filmmakers. Directors appear particularly to identify with the griot's freedom to broach taboo topics or to criticize abuses of power. Once again, this also corresponds to the conception of the artist as a committed player in his or her community. The most striking example of this influence is the fact that a number of filmmakers liken their role to that of the griot. The veteran Senegalese filmmaker Ousmane Sembène, for example, has often described the filmmakers' role as that of the modern griot, insisting that, "the artist must in many ways be the mouth and ears of his people . . . this corresponds to the role of the griot in traditional African culture," and has called for film to emulate the traditional night-time storytelling sessions.[7]

Like the griot in *Taafe Fanga*, director Adama Drabo similarly describes his role as being "to interrogate the past to reflect upon and to forge the present and the future."[8] This understanding of the past as a point of reference is again frequently articulated in the works of liberation theorists and reiterates the importance of history and collective memory in both the oral traditions and other West African cultural forms. This is particularly clear in a series of films including Jean-Marie Teno's *Afrique, je te plumerai* (Cameroon, 1991), David Achkar's *Allah Tantou* (Guinea, 1990), François Woukoache's *Asientos* (Cameroon, 1995), and Safi Faye's *Fad'jal* (Senegal, 1979), which interrogate and re-create history and memory from a highly personal point of view firmly rooted in the present. These films thereby offer a powerful reflection on the relation between past and present that also challenges Western readings of history by articulating readings from an African point of view.

Other filmmakers who do not actually liken themselves to the griot nonetheless acknowledge that oral tales and their narrative techniques have influenced their work, whether consciously or not. This is hardly surprising in cultures where the oral tale remains the predominant narrative form. The filmmaker Jean-Marie Teno confirms, for example, that "tales are part of my childhood, of the dramatic art in a given area where I grew up and therefore subconsciously influence my work."[9] However, it is important to stress that, just as in all contemporary art forms, the techniques and codes of orature have been updated and blended with other artistic and/or filmic influences, whether local or imported. They thus form a new, hybrid version of orality – or "secondary orality," as Keyan Tomaselli and Maureen Eke aptly describe it – which should not be confused with orality itself.[10]

This brings us to some of the specific stylistic and structural influences of orature on film, taking *Taafe Fanga* and *Clando* as two very different but representative examples. *Taafe Fanga* is one of a number of recent films that have overtly adapted the tale format and its codes to the screen, using a griot character to introduce and narrate the main diegesis.[11] Other films, such as *Clando*, weave narrated tales into the main filmic narrative in order to illustrate or elaborate a theme developed in the film.[12] Other films, again, are marked by the narrative codes and/or key preoccupations of the oral traditions without necessarily adopting the tale format.

In Adama Drabo's *Taafe Fanga*, the opening sequence, in which the griot Sidiki Diabaté arrives in a crowded urban compound, nonchalantly switching off the black-and-white Hollywood musical running on the television before proceeding to narrate a tale, serves to introduce the griot/narrator figure. Drabo thereby immediately establishes the film's tale structure and positions the spectator in relation to the tale. At the same time, the entry of the griot emphasizes the fact that 'traditional' storytelling is still very much alive as part of West African society. However, although Diabaté affirms the predominance of local forms of entertainment by turning off the television, the television sequence at same time acknowledges the presence and popularity of these imported forms.

The ensuing sequence, in which the griot asks his audience to select the topic of the tale, goes on to stress the collective nature of the storytelling session. The audience's participatory role is further highlighted by the way in which people accompany the griot's playing of the kora (a 21-string harp-lute) by clicking their fingers to the music. The circular panning movement of the camera, which further highlights the harmony of the group, accentuates this. When a mysterious woman enters the compound, however, provoking a scuffle as she goes to sit with the men, the griot takes inspiration from the incident to narrate the legend of the Dogon women's takeover of power, the legend becoming the main narrative of the film. This demonstrates the way in which griots draw lessons from the events around them and, as becomes apparent as the film unravels, the way in which present events recall those from the past, which are in turn used to reflect upon the present. Indeed, by going to sit with the men the stranger deliberately defies the order of the compound, which reproduces the divisions between men and women in society at large. This challenge to male order and to the stereotype of the subservient African woman is echoed in both the past and present tenses of the film, which, as the title meaning 'skirt power' suggests, explores the question of patriarchal domination.[13]

As the first establishing shots of the Dogon village in which the story of the women's revolt and quest for power is set take us into the past tense of the film, Sidiki Diabaté's kora is heard off-screen. This links the film's contemporary present tense to the main body of the film set in the past, thereby reminding the spectator that the issues of the past are to be taken as a lesson for the present. Throughout the rest of the film, the griot's presence, hence the fact that this is a tale, is recalled each time the kora punctuates the film narrative and whenever this instrument serves as a musical interlude between scenes, linking time and place, as is often the case in the oral tales.

A similar technique is found in Teno's *Clando*, in which the allegorical hunter tale, intermittently narrated in voice-over by the main character Sobgui when he travels to Germany after being imprisoned and tortured in Cameroon for political reasons, is always accompanied by African bush sounds. This creates both an imaginary realm for the tale and an aural leitmotif evocative of the African space in the sequences set in Europe, adding an extra dimension to one of the film's central themes – the immigrant condition in Europe and relations with the homeland.

The orature-inspired technique of using music or leitmotifs as a structuring device lends overall coherence to the narrative, especially when the griot/narrator introduces parallel stories and digressions to illustrate the main narrative, as is again common in tales. Examples of this narrative layering are found in *Taafe Fanga* when Yandju, one of the characters in the past tense of the film, narrates her own story to the children one night, or when elements of Dogon cosmogony are explained. Narrative layering is also found in *Clando* when Sobgui narrates the hunter tale, or in the quasi-documentary sequences in which the traditional *tontine* meetings are filmed and explained. While Western audiences more used to narrative causality might find such digressions disconcerting or take them as a sign of poor narrative construction, West African audiences are used to such digressions in the tales.

This characteristic layering of narrative threads and registers in both tales and films and the lack of division between the different art forms and/or their aesthetic and functional character give rise to a mixing of Western film genres in a number of francophone West African films, whether or not they adopt the tale format. It is interesting to note that *Afrique, je te plumerai, Allah Tantou, Asientos* and *Fad'jal*, which actively interrogate and examine the ties between history and memory, are characterized by this unconstrained juxtaposition of documentary and fiction. This ultimately gives rise to a new, hybrid genre that goes beyond traditional generic classifications. The non-linear presentation of these films' different histories is also closer to the narrative discontinuity of tales than to Western historiographic traditions that favour the chronological, linear mode and is further accentuated by the way in which their histories are also fragmented and interspersed with other related elements in the films. In *Afrique, je te plumerai*, for example, Teno's personal memories and his filmed investigation of the Cameroonian publishing sector are repeatedly woven into the film's presentation of disparate episodes of Cameroonian colonial history. Fictional scenes and real footage from the Rwandan genocide punctuate the description of the African slave trade in *Asientos*, and, in *Fad'jal*, scenes of village life punctuate the chronicle of the founding of a Serer village.

Each of these films draws similarly on, and shifts freely through, a wide variety of styles and modes of address, ranging from unobtrusive *cinéma-vérité* styles to self-conscious and/or subjective camera work. They also mix a variety of formats, archive footage, newsreels, photos, newspaper articles and drawings as they build up layers of images meanings and texts. Their generic blending and diversity of registers and formats appear, then, to be inspired by the narrative traditions of orature, and contribute to creating a new, dynamic hybrid genre.

As is common in oral tales, *Taafe Fanga* contains a number of songs that also play a structuring role. Their words provide a commentary or a reflection on the events depicted, thereby adding another narrative voice to the film, as is again often the case in the tales. This is clear in the (female) griotte's song, when the women take over control in the film –

Have you ever seen a goat bite a dog? O night of power! The extraordinary has taken place. Being a woman is not a weakness: it's believing so that is. Women have been given power. They will keep it. If you attack the Mande women, they will sell your hide for a cola nut. Come and take a look! The skirt has floored the trouser

– the final words of the song echoing those of the man who wrestles with the mysterious woman at the start of the film, thereby stressing once more the link between the film's two narrative tenses.[14]

Taafe Fanga is not simply structured as a tale, but, as already mentioned, also contains its own tale and narrative digressions, which create a narrative layering often found in tales. Yandju's storytelling sequence, for example, not only provides a pause in the narrative, offering a moment of entertainment unto itself, but also serves as an allegory for what will happen to the stolen mask if the women refuse to give it back. The sequence again stresses the social importance of the act of storytelling, the tale serving here as a moment of reconciliation between the warring girls and boys. This reinforcing of the cohesion of the group is again emphasized by the way the camera focuses on the whole group, highlighting the collective. The children and Yandju also answer one another in traditional call-and-response patterns, thereby setting up an echo with storytelling session at the beginning of the film, which once again links past and present.

It is also interesting to note here that the same woman plays Yandju and the stranger in the compound. Their bright red clothes and the Dogon cross motif on the stranger's *boubou* at the outset of the film visually accentuate this link. This suggests that the griot is inspired by both the incident and the actual person, which further blurs the boundary between the film's reality and fiction, past and present, and adds a magical dimension that is also common in the tales.

The repetition of such musical and visual leitmotifs and of narrative incidents and the way in which they are filmed is another common structuring device found in the oral tales. Several narrative incidents and their shot sequences are repeated in *Taafe Fanga*. The confrontation between Yayémè and her husband Agro in the Dogon village echoes the opening confrontation between the stranger and the angry man in the compound, for example, both women standing up to the men's violent domination. This again sets up echoes within the film, giving it cohesion and linking the film's various narrative tenses. In *Clando*, the periodic recounting of the hunter tale and its accompanying bush sounds similarly form a thematic and aural leitmotif that again gives the film narrative continuity, as does the circular repetition of the film's opening and closing shots.

Both *Taafe Fanga* and *Clando*'s hunter tale offer examples of the allegorical register and metaphoric language of orature, which West African audiences will quickly recognize and read as such. In *Taafe Fanga*, the story of the Dogon women's take-over of power and the subsequent male–female role-reversal allegorizes both male–female relations in the present and power relations in general. Timbé's argument that the women need an economic base to consolidate their power can be read, for example, as a veiled reference to Africa and the economic hegemony of the Western powers. In *Clando*, the tale of the hunter who goes to find food for his starving village, only to get lost before returning to find that his village's lot has improved in his absence, evokes the question of African emigration to Europe and whether or not it is better to sacrifice oneself, suffering hardship abroad, or to return home. The allegoric register encourages audiences to interpret and analyse the meaning of a tale or film, just as the static camera work leaves viewers free to direct their own gaze.

Satire is also common in both tales and traditional theatre forms, such as the Koteba in Mali, which directors including Drabo often cite as an influence. In the Koteba, satire is used to mock figures of authority and to attack abuses of power, thereby encouraging reflection through laughter. Numerous West African directors have embraced the political potential of satire. *Taafe Fanga*, like other satiric works, thus addresses the question of power on a humorous note, and power struggles are again a common theme in the tales. Accusations from some quarters that films from the 1980s and 1990s like *Taafe Fanga*, which have been dubbed somewhat disparagingly as 'return to the source' films, have sold out to Western exoticism seem to ignore the politically committed nature of their allegorical and/or satiric messages, however, and to ignore the fact that such works are generally very popular in West Africa.

The structure of both *Taafe Fanga* and *Clando* is characteristic of a number of recurrencies identified and described by Denise Paulme in her extensive study of African tales.[15] *Clando*, for example, recalls both the 'mirror' and the 'quest' tale. In the popular quest tales, the protagonist is faced with a challenge or task (here of finding a friend's long-lost son, Rigobert Chamba, in Germany), which usually takes him or her on an initiatory journey of some kind that in turn brings about some form of self-knowledge (here Sobgui's journey to Germany and his meeting with Irène, which helps to awaken his political commitment and gives him the resolve to act). Such tales and films usually adopt a circular structure, the protagonist finding him- or herself back at the point of departure, but changed by what has been learned on the journey. *Clando* thus ends as it starts with shots of Douala filmed from a moving taxi, but, as the final words of Sobgui's voice-over conversation with Irène indicate, his experience and encounters in Germany have given him the necessary self-knowledge to evolve. As in the 'mirror' tales, in which two protagonists react in opposite ways to the same situation, providing examples of how or how not to behave, *Clando* also proposes contrasting attitudes to life in Europe through Sobgui and Rigobert Chamba's diametrically opposed experiences, one of which is positive, the other disastrous.

Taafe Fanga is typical of the 'descendant' tales in which the status quo (here of male–female relationships) is upset due to the intrusion of an outsider (in this case the mask, which enables the women to take over power), before order is established again. This upsetting and re-establishing of the status quo may also be seen to reflect the Dogon conception of the spiral of order and disorder, which is explained in one mystical sequence of the film and which reflects a traditionally cyclical conception of time. What is particularly significant here, however, is that while the restitution of the status quo is traditionally seen as positive in tales, *Taafe Fanga* provides a characteristic example of the way in which orature is updated by inversing the traditional message. Not only is the upsetting of the status quo seen as timely and beneficial, the film having negatively portrayed male order, but, even though male order is re-established, the final words of the film lie with the girl-child Kouni who, as a child, traditionally symbolizes hope for the future, and with the griotte, both of whom effectively promise that women will one day be free. The restoration of male power is not seen as good, therefore, but offers a warning about what will happen if the patterns of domination and sub-ordination are simply reversed rather than being fundamentally modified, the film thus offering a more progressive message. Drabo himself says of the film's ending, "This story is a warning to women. Women took control of power in the past, but they lost it. We must stop history from repeating itself. The defeat can be turned into a victory, if we correct the errors of the past," which also once again highlights the way in which the lessons of the past can be used to inform the present.[16] Similarly, the hunter tale in *Clando* demonstrates how the traditional tale format can be adopted to address contemporary issues such as the pressure felt by African emigrants to succeed in Europe and to ensure their families well-being back home.

Numerous archetypal characters and/or themes of the oral tales have similarly found their way into francophone West African film. Once again, they are often up-dated or adapted, as is also the case in the tales. West African audiences will again quickly recognize and interpret standard character traits and their symbolic significance. In *Taafe Fanga*, for example, Kouni is typical of what Denise Paulme describes as the oral tales' archetypally precocious child-character who habitually defies and outwits figures of authority. As mentioned above, children are also commonly the symbol of hope. Kouni thus plays a pivotal role in the film's plot and it is significant that she is the one to pronounce the final words of reconciliation. The precociously clever child is a positive character in West Africa, and so, by putting these words in Kouni's mouth, Drabo reinforces the positive reception of the film's message.

The didactic message of both films and their overt addressing of sociopolitical issues, notably the abuse of power, is also characteristic of the tales, which, as mentioned earlier, are often a vector for exploring sociocultural issues.

Finally, the magical realism of the tale universe has been carried over into film. This supernatural realm is present in society at large, where there are generally considered to be no concrete divisions between the lands of the living and dead, the natural and supernatural. It is unsurprising, therefore, that tales and film should glide unaffectedly from one realm to another. As Drabo puts it, "We evolve in this atmosphere all our lives, so it seems normal to me that my films, which are an emanation of my whole culture, obviously be infused with this knowledge that people call magic."[17]

Such representations of the supernatural herald a reclaiming of traditional beliefs and the way in which they are represented. It is indeed interesting to note that, since the 1980s and 1990s, these representations have been a far cry both from the exotic mystifications of Western representations and from earlier African representations that often condemned such beliefs in the name of modernity. Today's representations tend to be less inhibited, less judgemental, and less con-cerned with the Western gaze, hence showing these beliefs to be an integral part of the cultural environment in which the films are set. A number of films like *Taafe Fanga* thus convey and/or rehabilitate other understandings of human existence, in this case the Dogon conception of the spiral of order and disorder.

This far from exhaustive appraisal has aimed at providing just a few instances of the many ways in which filmmakers in West Africa have adopted and above all adapted the narrative techniques and fundamental preoccupations of orature to film, thereby helping to forge rich and syncretic forms that can be described as "secondary orality." This process has brought new aesthetic and thematic dimensions to an originally imported medium, both conferring a certain specificity on francophone West African film and broadening its expressive possibilities. Thanks to such cinematic reworkings of orality, film has thus been fully integrated into the cultural environment it portrays, successfully reflecting West African cultural and artistic sensibilities.

Notes

1 If I use the somewhat contentious term 'francophone' West African film, which masks linguistic diversity by misleadingly implying that all the films in question are in French, it is primarily to narrow down the scope of this study. At the same time, it also highlights the fact that, despite their diversity, film cultures in 'francophone' West Africa share not only specific socio-cultural and political heritages, but also modes of production that are marked by their continuing ties with the former colonial power, France.

2 When discussing cultural forms and the place and role of the arts and artists in West Africa, it is important to remember that while there are cultural convergences that arise from shared periods of history, ethnic alliances, trade links, migrations, and other factors which, for the sake of this discussion, will be focused on here, we must not lose sight of the fact that West Africa is a vast, heterogeneous geographical zone inhabited by a multitude of ethnic groups, each with its own cultural specificities.

3 See Frantz Fanon, *The Wretched of the Earth*, tr. Constance Farrington (*Les damnés de la terre*, 1961; Harmondsworth: Penguin, 1983), and Amilcar Cabral, *Unity and Struggle: Speeches and Writings*, texts selected by the PAIGC, tr. Michael Wolfers (*Unité et lutte I: l'arme de la théorie*, 1975; London: Heinemann Educational, 1980).

4 It is important to clarify my use of the term 'traditional' here, as it has often been used in the West to describe precolonial Africa as a homogeneous and monolithic entity fundamentally opposed to the 'modern' (by which we can read 'Western'). In reality, of course, the cultures that existed in West Africa prior to European colonization were syncretic, changing and plural. Furthermore, many elements of 'traditional' culture are still very much alive today, rather than being relics of an unchanging, static past; hence the need to understand 'traditional' in an essentially flexible manner.

5 Christopher Miller, *Theories of Africans: Francophone Literature and Anthropology in Africa* (Chicago: U of Chicago P, 1990): 98.

6 Isidore Okpewho, *African Oral Literature: Backgrounds, Character, and Continuity* (Bloomington & Indianapolis: Indiana UP, 1992): 235.

7 Ousmane Sembène, "Filmmakers and African Culture," *Africa* 71 (1977): 80.

8 "Comme dit le griot au début de mon film, mon devoir est d'emprisonner le passé pour préparer le présent et l'avenir"; unpublished interview with the author, Ouagadougou, February 1997 (my tr.).

9 "Les contes font partie de mon enfance, d'une dramaturgie dans un espace donné où j'ai grandi, et donc ils influencent mon travail d'une manière inconsciente"; unpublished interview with the author, Paris, August 1997 (my tr.).

10 Keyan Tomaselli & Maureen Eke, "Secondary Orality in South African Film," *Iris* 18 (Spring 1995): 61–71.

11 Other recent examples include Dani Kouyaté's *Keita! L'Héritage du Griot* (Burkina Faso, 1995) and Cheick Oumar Sissoko's *Guimba* (Mali, 1995).

12 Other notable examples include Teno's *Afrique, je te plumerai* (Cameroon, 1991), Souleymane Cissé's *Waati* (Mali, 1995), Safi Faye's *Fad'jal* (Senegal, 1979), or Fadika Kramo Lancine's *Djeli* (Ivory Coast, 1980) and *Wariko* (1993).

13 The same past–present relationship is found in Safi Faye's *Fad'jal*, in which the episodes of village history narrated by the elders are related to events and issues affecting the village in the present. In this film, the whole process of oral transmission is celebrated, as is clear from the film's opening citation of Amadou Hampaté Bâ's famous phrase, "In Africa when an old man dies, a library burns."

14 "Qui a vu la chèvre mordre le chien? O nuit de pouvoir. L'extraordinaire s'est produit. Etre femme n'est pas faiblesse. C'est le croire qui l'est. Le pouvoir a été donné aux femmes. Elles le garderont. Si tu t'en prends aux femmes du Mande, elles te vendront pour une noix de cola. Portez vos yeux ici! Le pagne a terrassé le pantalon" (my tr.).

15 Denise Paulme, *La Mère dévorante: Essai sur la morphologie des contes africains* (Paris: Gallimard, 1976).

16 "Cette histoire est un avertissement aux femmes. Les femmes ont eu à prendre le pouvoir autrefois et elles l'ont perdu. Il faut faire en sorte que l'histoire ne se répète pas. La défaite peut être transformée en victoire si l'on corrige les erreurs du passé"; unpublished interview with the author, Ouagadougou, February 1997 (my tr.).

17 "Nous baignons dans cette ambiance toute notre vie, donc il me semble normal que mes films, qui me sortent de toute ma culture, soient forcément teintés de ces connaissances que l'on appelle magie"; unpublished interview with the author (my tr.).

Works Cited

Cabral, Amilcar. *Unity and Struggle: Speeches and Writings*, texts selected by the PAIGC, tr. Michael Wolfers (*Unité et lutte I: l'arme de la théorie*, 1975; London: Heinemann Educational, 1980).

Fanon, Frantz. *The Wretched of the Earth*, tr. Constance Farrington (*Les damnés de la terre*, 1961; Harmondsworth: Penguin, 1983).

Miller, Christopher. *Theories of Africans: Francophone Literature and Anthropology in Africa* (Chicago: U of Chicago P, 1990).

Okpewho, Isidore. *African Oral Literature: Backgrounds, Character, and Continuity* (Bloomington & Indianapolis: Indiana UP, 1992).

Paulme, Denise. *La Mère dévorante: Essai sur la morphologie des contes africains* (Paris: Gallimard, 1976).

Sembène, Ousmane. "Filmmakers and African Culture," *Africa* 71 (1977): 39–41.

Tomaselli, Keyan, & Maureen Eke. "Secondary Orality in South African Film," *Iris* 18 (1995): 61–71.

Filmography

Achkar, David. *Allah Tantou* (16 mm, colour, documentary, 52 min, Archibald Films: France, 1990).

Drabo, Adama. *Taafe Fanga* (35 mm, colour, fiction, 100 min, TaareFilms/CNCP/ZDF: Mali/Germany, 1997).

Faye, Safi. *Fad'jal* (16 mm, colour, docu-fiction, 108 min, SafiFilms/Ministère des Rélations Extérieurs/INA: Senegal/France, 1979).

Teno, Jean-Marie. *Afrique, je te plumerai* (16 mm, colour, docu-fiction, 92 min, Films du Raphia: France, 1991).

——. *Clando* (35 mm, colour, fiction, 98 min, Films du Raphia/ARTE/ZDF: France/Germany, 1996).

Woukoache, François. *Asientos* (35 mm, colour, docu-fiction, 52 min, PCB Pictures: Belgium, 1995).

Acknowledgments

The editor and publisher gratefully acknowledge the permission granted to reproduce the copyright material in this book:

Chapter 1: Rick Altman, "Conclusion: A Semantic/Syntactic/Pragmatic Approach to Genre," pp. 207–15, plus relevant bibliography from *Film/Genre*. London: BFI Publishing, 1999. © 1999 by Rick Altman. Reprinted by permission of the author.

Epigraph to Chapter 1: Rick Altman, "A Semantic/Syntactic Approach to Film Genre," pp. 13–15 from *Cinema Journal* 23:3 (Spring 1984). © 1984 by the University of Texas Press. Reprinted by permission of the author and University of Texas Press.

Chapter 2: Linda Williams, "Film Bodies: Gender, Genre, and Excess," pp. 2–13 from *Film Quarterly* 44:4 (Summer 1991). © 1991 by The Regents of the University of California. Reprinted by permission of the author and The University of California Press.

Chapter 3: Ernesto R. Acevedo-Muñoz, "The Body and Spain: Pedro Almodóvar's *All About My Mother*," pp. 25–38 from *Quarterly Review of Film and Video* 21:1 (2004) (Philadelphia and London: Taylor & Francis and Routledge). © 2004. Reprinted by permission of Taylor & Francis Group, LLC, http://www.taylorandfrancis.com

Chapter 4: Bülent Diken and Carsten Bagge Laustsen, "Enjoy Your Fight! – 'Fight Club' as a Symptom of the Network Society," pp. 349–67 from *Cultural Values* 6:4 (2002) (London: Taylor & Francis and Routledge). © 2002 by Cultural Values. Reprinted by permission of Taylor & Francis.

Epigraph to Chapter 4: G. Deleuze and C. Parnet, p. 140 from *Dialogues* (New York: Columbia University Press, 1987). © 1987 by G. Deleuze and C. Parnet. Reprinted by permission of Columbia University Press.

Chapter 5: Laura Kipnis, "Film and Changing Technologies," pp. 211–20 from John Hill and Pamela Church Gibson (eds), *World Cinema: Critical Approaches* (Oxford: Oxford

University Press, 2000). © 2000 John Hill and Pamela Church Gibson. Reprinted by permission of Oxford University Press.

Chapter 6: Carl Boggs and Tom Pollard, "Postmodern Cinema and Hollywood Culture in an Age of Corporate Colonization," pp. 159–81 from *Democracy and Nature* 7:1 (March 2001) © 2001 by *Democracy and Nature*. Reprinted by permission of the Editorial Board of the *International Journal of Inclusive Democracy*.

Chapter 7: Mary Flanagan, "Mobile Identities, Digital Stars, and Post Cinematic Selves," pp. 77–93 from *Wide Angle* 21:1 (1999) (Baltimore: The Johns Hopkins University Press). © 1999 by Wide Angle. Reprinted by permission of The Ohio University School of Film.

Chapter 8: Lola Young, "'Nothing Is as It Seems': Re-viewing *The Crying Game*," pp. 273–85 from Pat Kirkham and Janet Thumin (eds), *Me Jane: Masculinity, Movies and Women* (London: Lawrence and Wishart, 1995). © 1995 by Lola Young. Reprinted by permission of Lawrence and Wishart.

Epigraph to Chapter 8: Michel Foucault, p. 110 from Lawrence D. Kritzman (ed.), *Michel Foucault: Politics, Philosophy, Culture: Interviews and Other Writings, 1977–1984* (London: Routledge, 1998). © 1988 by Routledge, Chapman & Hall, Inc. Reprinted by permission of Routledge/Taylor & Francis Group, LLC.

Chapter 9: Peter Lehman, "Crying over the Melodramatic Penis: Melodrama and Male Nudity in Films of the 90s," pp. 25–41 from Peter Lehman (ed.), *Masculinity: Bodies, Movies, Culture* (London: Routledge, 2001). © 2001 by Routledge. Reprinted by permission of Routledge/Taylor & Francis Group, LLC.

Chapter 10: Julianne Pidduck, "Travels with Sally Potter's Orlando: Gender, Narrative, Movement," pp. 172–89 from *Screen* 38:2 (Summer 1997) (Oxford: Oxford University Press). © 1997 by The John Logie Baird Centre. Reprinted by permission of the author and Oxford University Press.

Chapter 11: Alpana Sharma, "Body Matters: the Politics of Provocation in Mira Nair's Films," pp. 91–103 from *Quarterly Review of Film and Video* 18:1 (Philadelphia and London: Taylor & Francis and Routledge, 2001). © 2001. Reprinted by permission of Taylor & Francis Group, LLC, http://www.taylorandfrancis.com

Chapter 12: Yvonne Tasker, "Cowgirl Tales," pp. 51–64 from *Working Girls: Gender and Sexuality in Popular Cinema* (London and New York: Routledge, 1998). © 1998 by Yvonne Tasker. Reprinted by permission of the author and Routledge, a member of the Taylor & Francis Group.

Chapter 13: Nicola Evans, "The Family Changes Colour: Interracial Families in Contemporary Hollywood Cinema," pp. 271–92 from *Screen* 43:3 (Oxford: Oxford University Press, Autumn 2002). © 2002 by The John Logie Baird Centre. Reprinted by permission of the author and Oxford University Press.

Epigraph to Chapter 13: Patricia J. Williams, p. 189 from *The Alchemy of Race and Rights* (Cambridge, MA: Harvard University Press 1991). © 1991 by the President and Fellows of Harvard College. Reprinted by permission of Harvard University Press.

Chapter 14: Dan Flory, "Black on White: *Film Noir* and the Epistemology of Race in Recent African American Cinema," pp. 82–90; 96–108 plus 110–14, 15–16 (notes) from *Journal of Social Philosophy* 31:1. © 2000 by Blackwell Publishing Ltd.

Chapter 15: Peter X Feng, "Being Chinese American, Becoming Asian American: Chan Is Missing," pp. 88–118 from *Cinema Journal* 35:4 (Austin: University of Texas Press, Summer 1996). © 1996 by the University of Texas Press, PO Box 7819, Austin, TX 78713-7819. This revised version was published as "Becoming Asian American" in *Identities in Motion: Asian American Film and Video* (Durham, NC: Duke University Press, 2002). Reprinted by permission of the author and University of Texas Press.

Chapter 16: Gina Marchetti, "*The Wedding Banquet*: Global Chinese Cinema and the Asian American Experience," pp. 275–97 from Darrell Y. Hamamoto and Sandra Liu (eds), *Countervisions: Asian American Film Criticism* (Philadelphia: Temple University Press, 2000). © 2000 by Temple University. Reprinted by permission of Temple University Press. All rights reserved.

Chapter 17: Jhon Warren Gilroy, "Another Fine Example of the Oral Tradition? Identification and Subversion in Sherman Alexie's *Smoke Signals*," pp. 23–42 from *Studies in American Indian Literatures* 13:1 (Lincoln: University of Nebraska Press, Spring 2001). © 2001 by Jhon Warren Gilroy. Reprinted by permission of the author.

Chapter 18: Pauline Turner Strong, "Playing Indian in the Nineties: *Pocahontas* and *The Indian in the Cupboard*," pp. 187–205 from Peter C. Rollins and John E. O'Connor (eds), *Hollywood's Indian: The Portrayal of the Native American in Film* (Lexington: The University Press of Kentucky, 1998). © 1998 by The University Press of Kentucky.

Chapter 19: Deborah Shaw, "'You Are Alright, But . . .': Individual and Collective Representations of Mexicans, Latinos, Anglo-Americans and African-Americans in Steven Soderbergh's *Traffic*," pp. 211–223 from *Quarterly Review of Film and Video* 22:3 (Philadelphia and London: Taylor & Francis and Routledge, 2005). © 2005. Reprinted by permission of Taylor & Francis Group, LLC, http://www.taylorandfrancis.com

Chapter 20: Hamid Naficy, "Theorizing 'Third-World' Film Spectatorship: The Case of Iran and Iranian Cinema," pp. 183–201 from Anthony R. Guneratne and Wimal Dissanayake (eds), *Rethinking Third Cinema* (London: Routledge, 2003). © 2003 by Hamid Naficy. Reprinted by permission of the author and Routledge, a member of the Taylor & Francis Group.

Epigraph to Chapter 20: V. S. Naipaul, p. 41 from *The Enigma of Arrival* (New York: Knopf, 1986). © 1986 by V. S. Naipaul. Reprinted by permission of Random House, Inc.

Chapter 21: Shohini Chaudhuri and Howard Finn, "The Open Image: Poetic Realism and the New Iranian Cinema," pp. 38–57 from *Screen* 44:1 (Oxford: Oxford University Press, Spring 2003). © 2003 by The John Logie Baird Centre. Reprinted by permission of the author and Oxford University Press.

Chapter 22: Rey Chow, "The Seductions of Homecoming: Place, Authenticity and Chen Kaige's *Temptress Moon*," pp. 3–17 from *NARRATIVE* 6:1 (Columbus: The Ohio State University Press, January 1998). © 1998 by the Ohio State University Press. Reprinted by permission of the publisher.

Chapter 23: Julian Stringer, "Cultural Identity and Diaspora in Contemporary Hong Kong Cinema," pp. 298–312 from Darrell Y. Hamamoto and Sandra Liu (eds), *Countervisions: Asian American Film Criticism* (Philadelphia: Temple University Press, 2000). © 2000 by Temple University. Reprinted by permission of Temple University Press. All rights reserved.

Chapter 24: Tejaswini Ganti, "'And Yet My Heart Is Still Indian': The Bombay Film Industry and the (H)Indianization of Hollywood," pp. 281–300 from Faye D. Ginsburg, Lila Abu-Lughod and Brian Larkin (eds), *Media Worlds: Anthropology on New Terrain* (Berkeley: University of California Press, 2002). © 2002 by the Regents of the University of California. Reprinted by permission of the University of California Press.

Chapter 25: Melissa Thackway, "Future Past: Integrating Orality into Francophone West African Film," pp. 229–42 from *Matatu: Journal for African Culture and Society* 25:1 (Amsterdam: Editions Rodopi, September 2002). © 2002 by Matatu. Reprinted by permission of Editions Rodopi B.V.

Every effort has been made to trace copyright holders and to obtain their permission for the use of copyright material. The publisher apologizes for any errors or omissions in the above list and would be grateful if notified of any corrections that should be incorporated in future reprints or editions of this book.